Evolutionary Psychology in the Business Sciences

Gad Saad
Editor

Evolutionary Psychology in the Business Sciences

Editor
Dr. Gad Saad
Concordia University
John Molson School of Business
De Maisonneuve Blvd. W. 1455
H3G 1M8 Montreal Québec
Canada
gadsaad@jmsb.concordia.ca

ISBN 978-3-540-92783-9   e-ISBN 978-3-540-92784-6
DOI 10.1007/978-3-540-92784-6
Springer Heidelberg Dordrecht London New York

© Springer-Verlag Berlin Heidelberg 2011
This work is subject to copyright. All rights are reserved, whether the whole or part of the material is concerned, specifically the rights of translation, reprinting, reuse of illustrations, recitation, broadcasting, reproduction on microfilm or in any other way, and storage in data banks. Duplication of this publication or parts thereof is permitted only under the provisions of the German Copyright Law of September 9, 1965, in its current version, and permission for use must always be obtained from Springer. Violations are liable to prosecution under the German Copyright Law.
The use of general descriptive names, registered names, trademarks, etc. in this publication does not imply, even in the absence of a specific statement, that such names are exempt from the relevant protective laws and regulations and therefore free for general use.

Cover design: eStudio Calamar S.L.

Printed on acid-free paper

Springer is part of Springer Science+Business Media (www.springer.com)

To Amar and Samra, my perfect and eternal companions.

Foreword

The Third Chimpanzee in the Ordinary Business of Life

Occasionally a synthesis transforms a discipline so profoundly that later generations will not remember it as synthetic. They will know just the elements that endure in textbook passages. Two examples come to mind: *On the Origins of Species* (Darwin 1859) and *The General Theory of Employment, Money and Interest* (Keynes 1936). Charles Darwin (1859:63) credits Thomas Malthus' *An Essay on the Principle of Population* (1798) for having inspired natural selection. In contrast to Darwin's transdisciplinary synthesis, that of *The General Theory* is only disciplinary (Leijonhufvud 1968). John Maynard Keynes writes "The ideas which are here expressed so laboriously are extremely simple and should be obvious. The difficulty lies, not in the new ideas, but in escaping from the old ones, which ramify, for those brought up as most of us have been, into every corner of our minds" (1936: viii). For non-rational behavior that lay beyond the domain of economics, Keynes invoked "animal spirits" and left it at that (1936:161–162). He dismissed evolution in an earlier essay as "the doctrine which seemed to draw all things out of Chance, Chaos, and Old Time...The Principle of Survival of the Fittest could be regarded as a vast generalization of Ricardian economics" (1926:14).

"Animal spirits" is Keynes' recognition that non-rational behavior must be addressed. But merely recognizing something is not very satisfying, intellectually speaking. Scientists relish puzzle-solving and some will suggest that natural selection can explain the origins of behavior and even discern patterns hitherto missed. Darwin was the first to do so, but not yet in those terms. "He who understands [the] baboon would do more for metaphysics than Locke" (1838:84). The allusion to our primate cousins is hardly rhetorical either then or now. Polymath Jared Diamond (1992) re-classifies *Homo sapiens sapiens* as "the third chimpanzee" in an award-winning book by the same title and primatologist Frans de Waal enjoys similar success exposing *Our Inner Ape* (2005). Diamond and de Waal notwithstanding, most puzzle-solvers of behavior write solely for technical journals. They hail from diverse disciplines and are now doing what Thomas Kuhn (1962) famously termed "normal science". Under the banner of "evolutionary psychology", the cumulative scholarship is immense.

Gad Saad is at the forefront. He has breathtakingly synthesized the literature in an engaging prose while suggesting new research streams. The transdisciplinary agenda of *The Evolutionary Bases of Consumption* (2007) and *The Consuming Instinct* (2011) has been expanded in *Evolutionary Psychology in the Business Sciences* (Saad ed. 2011). It is the third installment of what will surely become a landmark trilogy. The focus is ostensibly business but I would respectfully disagree; business is too narrow a reading of the broad subject matter covered. A popular nineteenth-century definition of economics was the "the study of mankind in the ordinary business of life" (Marshall 1890:1). In the twenty-first century, Saad and his colleagues are explaining the evolution of us—the third chimpanzee—in the ordinary business of life. Transformation is underway.

Joseph Henry Vogel
Professor of Economics
University of Puerto Rico-Rio Piedras
www.josephhenryvogel.com

References

Darwin C (1838) Notebook M. The complete works of Charles Darwin online. Available at: http://darwin-online.org.uk
Darwin C (1859) On the origin of species by means of natural selection. Murray, London
de Waal F (2005) Our inner ape: a leading primatologist explains why we are who we are. Penguin, New York
Diamond J (1992) The third chimpanzee: the evolution and future of the human animal. HarperCollins, New York
Keynes J (1926) The end of laissez-faire. Hogarth Press, London
Keynes J (1936) The general theory of employment, interest and money. Macmillan, London
Kuhn T (1962) The structure of scientific revolutions. University of Chicago Press, Chicago
Leijonhufvud A (1968) On Keynesian economics and the economics of Keynes. Oxford University Press, New York
Malthus T (1798) An essay on the principle of population. Library of Economics and Liberty. Available at: http://www.econlib.org/library/Malthus/malPlong.html
Marshall A (1890) Principles of economics. Macmillan, London
Saad G (2007) The evolutionary bases of consumption. Psychology Press, Mahwah
Saad G (2011) The consuming instinct: what juicy burgers, Ferraris, pornography, and gift giving reveal about human nature. Prometheus Books, New York
Saad G (ed) (2011) Evolutionary psychology in the business sciences. Springer, Heidelberg

Preface

Two important "Darwinian" anniversaries were celebrated in 2009: (1) the 150-year anniversary of the publication of Charles Darwin's *On the Origin of Species*; and (2) the 200-year anniversary of Charles Darwin's birth. If he were alive today, the great scientist would be astonished to see the extent to which his work has influenced countless academic disciplines. In my introductory article of a special issue that I guest edited on the future of evolutionary psychology in the journal *Futures*, I provided a long list of disciplines that have been infused with evolutionary theorizing (see Saad 2011, Table 1 for representative references for each of the listed areas). These cover all university faculties including the fine arts and the humanities (aesthetics/art, architecture, dance, epistemology, ethics, history, interior design, law, literary studies, morality, musicology, religious studies, and urban design); the social sciences (anthropology, archaeology, consumer behavior, criminology, economics, education, family studies, international relations, linguistics, political science, psychology, public administration, public policy, and sociology); and the natural and applied sciences (agriculture, animal husbandry, biology, biomimetics, computer science, dietetics/nutrition, ecology, engineering, immunology, medicine, neurosciences, nursing, pharmacology, physics, physiology, and psychiatry). This should dispel the notion that evolutionary theorizing is largely restricted to the field of biology. The reality is that any phenomenon that involves biological organisms is within the purview of evolutionary theory.

Over the past 12 years, a growing number of special issues in academic journals have been devoted to the applications of evolutionary psychology (or related evolutionary formalisms) in business-related disciplines. These include in decreasing chronological order:

Leadership Quarterly: forthcoming special issue on the biology of leadership; guest edited by Carl Senior, Nick Lee, and Michael Butler

Organizational Behavior and Human Decision Processes: 2009 special issue on the biological basis of business; guest edited by Colin Camerer, Drazen Prelec, and Scott Shane

IEEE Transactions on Professional Communication: 2008 special issue on Darwinian perspectives on electronic communication; guest edited by Ned Kock

Group Dynamics: Theory, Research, and Practice: 2008 special issue on evolutionary approaches to group dynamics; guest edited by Mark Van Vugt and Mark Schaller

Managerial and Decision Economics: 2006 special issue on evolutionary psychology in management; guest edited by Satoshi Kanazawa

Journal of Organizational Behavior: 2006 special issue on evolutionary psychology in organizational behavior; guest edited by Rod White and Nigel Nicholson

Ruffin Series in Business Ethics: 2004 special issue on business, science, and ethics; applying evolutionary theory in understanding business ethics; guest edited by R. Edward Freeman and Patricia H. Werhane

Journal of Business Venturing: 2004 special issue on evolutionary approaches in entrepreneurship albeit these were not necessarily based on principles from evolutionary psychology; guest edited by Scott Shane

Psychology & Marketing: 2003 special issue on evolution and consumption; guest edited by Donald Hantula

Managerial and Decision Economics: 1998 special issue on management, organization, and human nature; guest edited by Lívia Markóczy and Jeff Goldberg

Notwithstanding these rare special issues, and despite a pronounced increase in the applications of evolutionary psychology (EP) and related biological formalisms in much of the social sciences, the great majority of business scholars are, unaware of, and at times are hostile to, the relevance of EP to their fields. It should be self-evident that all business phenomena, whether those relevant to consumers, employees, or employers, do not exist outside of our common biological heritage. Ultimately, to fully understand *Homo economics*, *Homo corporaticus*, or *Homo consumericus*, requires that one recognize the biological forces that have shaped the evolution of *Homo sapiens*.

The Adapted Mind, the classic edited book by Barkow, Cosmides, and Tooby (1992) contains some of the early seminal EP papers. Its influence is in part due to the fact that it demonstrated the relevance of EP across numerous disciplines and topics of interest including culture, social exchange, food sharing, mate preference, pregnancy sickness, maternal behaviors, language, color perception, spatial abilities, landscape preferences, psychodynamic processes, and gossip. More recently, Somit and Peterson (2001) edited a less known book albeit equal in its ability to highlight the transdisciplinarity and interdisciplinarity afforded by the evolutionary behavioral sciences. It is comprised of an exhaustive set of chapters covering evolutionary approaches across a wide range of disciplines including anthropology, economics, history, international relations, law, philosophy, political philosophy, political science, psychology, and psychiatry. Notwithstanding these important edited tomes, there currently does not exist a single book that serves as the central repository of works operating at the intersection of EP and the business disciplines. This edited book serves this important function by pulling together a collection of chapters wherein scholars demonstrate the applications of EP across several business settings. Given its interdisciplinary nature, it should be of interest to several distinct camps of scholars including evolutionary behavioral scientists housed outside of the business school, as well as business scholars wishing to explore ways by which to "Darwinize" their research streams.

References

Barkow JH, Cosmides L, Tooby J (eds) (1992) The adapted mind: evolutionary psychology and the generation of culture. Oxford University Press, New York

Saad G (2011) The future of evolutionary psychology is bright. Futures forthcoming

Somit A, Peterson SA (eds) (2001) Evolutionary approaches in the behavioral sciences: toward a better understanding of human nature. Elsevier, New York

Acknowledgements

I thank Dr. Birgit Leick, the acquisitions editor with whom I had originally communicated, for having contacted me to gauge my interest in publishing this edited book with Springer. Seldom does an author receive such an unsolicited query, so this was a definitive sign of Springer's strong support and enthusiasm for this project. Birgit ended up leaving Springer, and was aptly replaced by Christian Rauscher who has been equally supportive throughout the process. I thank them both for their laudable professionalism.

I am indebted to all of the scholars who expressed an interest in submitting or who did submit their manuscripts, but whose works were not included in this edited book. In many instances, this was due to a poor fit between the works in question and the objectives of this book. I seldom rejected a chapter because of poor quality. Hence, I am optimistic that many of the non-included works will find their appropriate outlets. To serve as an editor on such a project is at times a challenging and daunting task. However, I was fortunate to interact with authors who not only submitted engaging manuscripts of high quality, but also were a pleasure to interact with.

Knowing that I could rely on the love and support of my family at the end of a long workday made the arduous journey that much more enjoyable. A happy home allows an author and/or editor to pursue his professional endeavors with clarity and determined focus. Thank you for providing me with such unconditional affection and solace.

Endorsements

"There are different versions of evolutionary psychology, but all of them ask us to take the fact of human evolution seriously. Culture is hugely important in economic development but that does not mean that biological influences can be ignored. This collection of essays presents a number of interesting views on the extent of their possible influence in business contexts."

Geoffrey Hodgson, Research Professor in Business Studies (University of Hertfordshire, UK), and co-author of *Darwin's Conjecture: The Search for General Principles of Social and Economic Evolution (2010)*.

This book covers many pieces of the puzzle related to how the evolution of the human species underpins our approaches to the business sciences. Humans have engaged in business, as an important everyday activity within all societies and cultures, for millennia. However, Saad argues that we still have little understanding of the evolutionary psychology basis for the business sciences. He discusses the biological roots of *Homo sapiens* and modern-day *Homo consumericus*. With this and other books by Gad Saad we are seeing important questions about the evolutionary psychology underpinnings of the business sciences being addressed in a comprehensive and scientific manner. Starting with an exploration from a broad range of evolutionary, cognitive, biological, and behavioral scientific fields, this book provides an evolutionary theoretical framework for building the business sciences. As with any good research book, it raises more questions than it answers. It is essential reading for all those interested in the broad business sciences, management, economics, and the behavioral sciences.

Amanda Spink, Professor and Chair of Information Science (Loughborough University, UK), and author of *Information Behavior: An Evolutionary Instinct* (2010).

Evolutionary theory has provided critical insights into our understanding of human behavior. And guess what? Businesses are made of humans for humans. Gad Saad is a pioneer in bringing evolutionary ideas into a business context, and in this impressive volume, he has gathered a collection of essays from the world's top researchers in this field – synthesizing cutting-edge knowledge about evolutionary biology, psychology, and business behavior. From marketing to management to finance, understanding the ancestral roots of modern business behavior provides powerful new insights for both researchers and practitioners. It is impossible to understand decision making without understanding human nature, and this book lends insight into seemingly baffling questions like "why do young men tend to choose riskier portfolios than young women?" and "why do most organizations have rules against nepotism even though people are more likely to trust, and less likely to cheat, family members?" This is a must-have volume for anyone interested in how to harness human nature for effective advertising, leadership, decision making, and organizational behavior.

Douglas T. Kenrick, Professor of Psychology (Arizona State University), and author of *Sex, Murder, and the Meaning of Life: A Psychologist Investigates How Evolution, Cognition, and Complexity Are Revolutionizing Our View of Human Nature* (2011).

Contents

The Missing Link: The Biological Roots of the Business Sciences 1
Gad Saad

Fundamental Motives and Business Decisions 17
Vladas Griskevicius, Joshua M. Ackerman,
Bram Van den Bergh, and Yexin Jessica Li

Intrasexual Competition Within Organizations 41
Abraham P. Buunk, Thomas V. Pollet, Pieternel Dijkstra,
and Karlijn Massar

**Evolutionary Psychology and Sex Differences
in Workplace Patterns** 71
Kingsley R. Browne

**The Adaptationist Theory of Cooperation in Groups:
Evolutionary Predictions for Organizational Cooperation** 95
Michael E. Price and Dominic D.P. Johnson

**Caveman Executive Leadership: Evolved Leadership
Preferences and Biological Sex** 135
Gregg R. Murray and Susan M. Murray

Leadership in Organizations: An Evolutionary Perspective 165
Brian R. Spisak, Nigel Nicholson, and Mark van Vugt

**Hardwired to Monitor: An Empirical Investigation
of Agency-Type Social Contracts in Business Organizations** 191
David M. Wasieleski

The Role for Signaling Theory and Receiver Psychology in Marketing 225
Bria Dunham

Cue Management: Using Fitness Cues to Enhance Advertising Effectiveness 257
Patrick Vyncke

"Evolutionary Store Atmospherics" – Designing with Evolution in Mind 289
Yannick Joye, Karolien Poels, and Kim Willems

Rationality and Utility: Economics and Evolutionary Psychology 319
C. Monica Capra and Paul H. Rubin

Media Compensation Theory: A Darwinian Perspective on Adaptation to Electronic Communication and Collaboration 339
Donald A. Hantula, Ned Kock, John P. D'Arcy, and Darleen M. DeRosa

Index 365

Author Bios

Joshua M. Ackerman is Assistant Professor of Management Science at the Sloan School of Management, Massachusetts Institute of Technology. His research focuses on evolutionary and nonconscious influences on social coordination processes, including the ways in which our perceptions, evaluations, and decisions are subtly shaped by the people around us. His research has been published in top journals in marketing, psychology, and biology.

Kingsley R. Browne is a Professor of Law at Wayne State University Law School in Detroit, Michigan. He specializes in employment discrimination law and the impact of biological/psychological sex differences in the workplace (including the military). His publications include *Co-ed Combat: The New Evidence That Women Shouldn't Fight the Nation's Wars* (2007), Sentinel (Penguin, USA); *Biology at Work: Rethinking Sexual Equality* (2002), Rutgers University Press, in the *Rutgers Series in Human Evolution* (Robert L. Trivers, series editor); and *Divided Labours: An Evolutionary View of Women at Work* (1998), Weidenfeld & Nicolson, London (U.S. edition, Yale University Press, 1999), in the *Darwinism Today* series (Helena Cronin & Oliver Curry, series editors).

Abraham P. (Bram) Buunk obtained his Ph.D. at the University of Utrecht, The Netherlands, in 1980. He was an Associate Professor in Organizational Psychology at Radboud University, The Netherlands, a Fulbright Scholar at the University of California, Los Angeles, and a Professor of Social Psychology at the University of Groningen, The Netherlands. Since 2005 he is Academy Professor on behalf of the Royal Netherlands Academy of Arts and Sciences (KNAW). He is affiliated with the University of Groningen and with various universities in Spain and South America. He has published widely on close relationships, organizational behavior and evolutionary psychology, supervised over 40 doctoral dissertations, and served on many scientific boards and committees.

C. Monica Capra is an Associate Professor of Economics at Emory University in Atlanta. Dr. Capra specializes in experimental and behavioral economics. She has published many articles in her field, some in the most prestigious economic journals. When she joined Emory in 2003, Capra began collaboration with neuroscientists.

Since then, she has published several articles on the new and promising field of Neuroeconomics. Dr. Capra is an adjunct professor in the Center for Neuropolicy and the Institute of Human Rights at Emory. Previously, she taught at WLU and at CalTech. She consulted with the Central Bank of Bolivia and the Bolivian Ministry of Hydrocarbons. More recently, she visited Groupe d'Analyse et de Theorie Economicque (GATE) in Lyon, France and the Human Neuroimaging Lab at the Baylor College of Medicine in Houston. She has addressed many business, professional, and academic audiences in the US and abroad. Dr. Capra received her Ph.D. from the University of Virginia in 1999.

John D'Arcy is an Assistant Professor in the Department of Management, Mendoza College of Business, at the University of Notre Dame. He holds a B.S. in Finance and Business Logistics from The Pennsylvania State University, an M.B.A. in Management Information Systems from LaSalle University, and a Ph.D. in Management Information Systems from Temple University. Dr. D'Arcy's research interests include information assurance and security, virtual teams, and human-computer interaction. His work has been published in a number of journals including *Computers & Security, Communications of the ACM, Risk Management and Insurance Review, Human Resource Management, Information Systems Research,* and *Decision Support Systems.*

Darleen DeRosa is a managing partner at OnPoint Consulting. Darleen brings ten years of consulting experience, with expertise in talent management, executive assessment, virtual teams, and organizational assessment. Darleen previously was an Executive Director in the Assessment practice at Russell Reynolds Associates. Darleen conducted assessments of senior executives and worked closely with CEOs and Boards. Darleen previously served as Assessment Practice Leader for Right Management, where she grew the assessment practice. Darleen provided assessment solutions to help organizations facilitate selection, succession, and leadership development initiatives. Darleen received her B.A. from the College of the Holy Cross and her M.A. and Ph.D. in social/organizational psychology from Temple University. Darleen is a member of The Society for Industrial and Organizational Psychology (SIOP) and other professional organizations. She has published book chapters and articles in journals, and recently co-authored *Virtual Team Success: A Practical Guide to Working and Leading From a Distance.*

Pieternel Dijkstra obtained her Ph.D. at the University of Groningen, The Netherlands, in 2001, and is since a freelance researcher, writer and teacher. She contributes regularly to various media, including newspapers, radio and television on psychological topics. Together with researchers of the University of Groningen, she studies topics such as social comparison, jealousy and intimate relationships. She has published many scientific articles in various domains, written hundreds of popular articles on topics such as marital conflict and body image, and has written 11 popular psychology books, on topics such as jealousy and love.

Bria Dunham completed her Ph.D. in Anthropology at Rutgers University in 2010, where she studied signaling theory as applied to contemporary human courtship.

She is currently pursuing a Master of Public Health degree at New York University, where she brings an evolutionary perspective into global public health research and practice. Dr. Dunham's current research interests include evolutionary medicine, parent-offspring conflict, and decision-making in maternity care.

Vladas Griskevicius is Assistant Professor of Marketing at the Carlson School of Management at the University of Minnesota. His research examines the ancestral roots of modern consumer behavior. Using theoretical principles from evolutionary biology, he investigates how modern behavior is driven by ancestral motives, which often steer conscious decisions in unconscious ways. His research has been published in top journals in marketing and psychology.

Donald A. Hantula is an organizational psychologist, Associate Professor of Psychology, and director of the Decision Making Laboratory at Temple University. He is the past Executive Editor of the *Journal of Social Psychology*, current Associate Editor of the *Journal of Organizational Behavior Management,* and has edited special issues of other journals on topics such as: experiments in e-commerce, evolutionary perspectives on consumption, Darwinian Perspectives on Electronic Communication, and Consumer Behavior Analysis. He served on the National Science Foundation's Decision Risk and Management Sciences review panel and remains an ad hoc reviewer for government and private research funding agencies. Don has published in many high impact journals including the *Journal of the American Medical Association, Journal of Applied Psychology, Journal of Economic Psychology, Organizational Behavior and Human Decision Processes* and *Behavior Research Methods*. His research in evolutionary behavioral economics combines behavior analytic and Darwinian theory to focus on questions in financial and consumer decision making, escalation of commitment, performance improvement, and human/technology interactions. He has published over 80 articles and book chapters; has authored or edited 10 books, manuals, and technical reports, made over 150 presentations at national and international scientific meetings, and is a busy researcher, consultant and speaker.

Dominic D.P. Johnson received a D.Phil. from Oxford University in evolutionary biology, and a Ph.D. from Geneva University in political science. Drawing on both disciplines, he is interested in how new research on evolution, biology and human nature is challenging theories of international relations, conflict, and cooperation. He has published two books: "Overconfidence and War: The Havoc and Glory of Positive Illusions" (Harvard University Press, 2004) argues that common psychological biases to maintain overly positive images of our capabilities, our control over events, and the future, play a key role in the causes of war; *Failing to Win: Perceptions of Victory and Defeat in International Politics* (Harvard University Press, 2006), with Dominic Tierney, examines how and why popular misperceptions commonly create undeserved victories or defeats in international wars and crises. His current work focuses on the role of evolutionary dynamics, evolutionary psychology, and religion in human conflict and cooperation.

Yannick Joye holds an MA in philosophy and obtained his Ph.D. at the University of Ghent (Belgium) in 2007 and he now works at the University of Leuven

(Belgium) as a postdoctoral research fellow of the Research Foundation Flanders (FWO). He is currently involved in research on the evolutionary origins of architecture (i.e., building behavior) and also inquires the psychological mechanisms underlying human attitudes towards natural environments. Yannick has published, among others, in *Environmental Values*, *Environment and Planning B* and *Review of General Psychology*.

Yexin Jessica Li has a B.S. degree in Biology and Society from Cornell University. She is currently a Ph.D. student in psychology at Arizona State University. Her research interests center on the ultimate causes of consumer behavior, focusing on how they can help us better understand the synergistic effects of gender, ecology, and motivation on the choices that people make.

Ned Kock is Professor of Information Systems and Director of the Collaborative for International Technology Studies at Texas A&M International University. He is an active member of the Human Behavior and Evolution Society and the Association for Information Systems, and has recently guest-edited the Special Issue on Darwinian Perspectives on Electronic Communication published in the IEEE Transactions on Professional Communication. Ned has published his research in a number of high-impact journals including *Communications of the ACM*, *Decision Support Systems*, *European Journal of Information Systems*, *European Journal of Operational Research*, *IEEE Transactions (various)*, *Information & Management*, *Information Systems Journal*, *Journal of the Association for Information Systems*, *MIS Quarterly*, and *Organization Science*. He is the Founding Editor-in-Chief of the *International Journal of e-Collaboration*, Associate Editor of the *Journal of Systems and Information Technology*, and Associate Editor for Information Systems of the journal *IEEE Transactions on Professional Communication*. His research interests include evolution and human behavior toward technology, action research, ethical and legal issues in technology research and management, e-collaboration, and business process improvement.

Karlijn Massar obtained her Ph.D. at the University of Groningen, The Netherlands, in 2009. Her dissertation research focused on the unconscious evaluation of rivals in jealousy evoking situations, using methods from social cognition, in particular subliminal priming. Her research was published in several international journals. She was a postdoctoral researcher with Professor Buunk, studying especially intrasexual competition, and teaching a course on applying social psychological theories. She is currently an Assistant Professor of Social Psychology at Maastricht University, the Netherlands.

Gregg R. Murray is an Assistant Professor of Political Science in the College of Arts and Sciences at Texas Tech University. His primary research focuses on the application of evolutionary theory to issues in political behavior and attitudes. In particular, Murray's research has looked at questions regarding the potential for effects of evolutionary forces on citizens' and other followers' preferences for leaders and on individuals' emergence as leaders. His interest in political leadership and followership is stimulated in part by his previous work as a political campaign manager and consultant. He received his Ph.D. from the University of Houston in 2003.

Susan M. Murray is a doctoral candidate in Accounting at the Rawls College of Business at Texas Tech University. She expects to attain her doctorate in 2011. Her interest in leadership issues began while serving as an officer in the United States Navy and continued throughout her career in corporate accounting, which she pursued after attaining her Masters in Business Administration in 1995. She became Certified in Management Accounting (CMA) and Financial Management (CFM) while also passing the Certified Public Accounting (CPA) exam in 1996. Employing both experimental and archival methods, her primary research interests are accounting disclosures and corporate social responsibility. In particular, she is focused on the link between environmental performance and disclosures and the impact of affect on perceptions of environmental performance and risk.

Nigel Nicholson is Professor of Organizational Behavior and a former Research Dean at London Business School, where since 1996 in his teaching and research he has been introducing and applying the ideas of evolutionary psychology to business. He has published extensively on this, and in many other areas of OB: work performance; the psychology of labor relations; managerial role transitions; risk behavior in financial markets; leadership and personality; and family business. His current work focuses on self regulation, leadership, and related topics in personal development. He directs both open enrolment and custom executive programs for senior executives at London Business School.

Karolien Poels is an Assistant Professor of Strategic Communication at the University of Antwerp (Belgium), specialising in advertising, consumer psychology and digital gaming research. She has an M.A. in Communication Studies and a Ph.D. in Social Sciences (both from Ghent University). She previously worked as a post doc researcher at the Human Technology Interaction Group of Eindhoven University of Technology (The Netherlands), where she was involved in a European project on the experience of digital gaming. Her current research mainly focuses on the experience and consumption of digital media (e.g. digital games, virtual worlds) and strategic communication in digital worlds (e.g., In-game advertising). She published in international peer reviewed journals such as *Journal of Advertising Research*, *Journal of Advertising*, and *Journal of Business Research*.

Thomas V. Pollet obtained his Ph.D. at Newcastle University (UK) in 2008. He has since worked as an Assistant Professor of Evolutionary Social Psychology at the University of Groningen, The Netherlands, where he teaches several courses on evolution and human behavior and carries out research using an evolutionary framework. He has published on a wide variety of topics such as sexual selection for male wealth, sibling relationships, grand parenting, childlessness, parental investment and the evolution of social networks. He is currently working on sexual selection for grip strength as well as other human traits under sexual selection.

Michael E. Price is Lecturer in Psychology at Brunel University, West London, and co-Director of the Brunel Centre for Culture and Evolutionary Psychology. Before arriving at Brunel, he was a postdoc jointly sponsored by the Santa Fe Institute and the Indiana University Workshop in Political Theory and Policy Analysis, and a Visiting Lecturer in Organizational Behavior at the Olin School of Business, Washington University in St. Louis. He received his Ph.D. in biosocial anthropology from the University of California, Santa Barbara, where he conducted fieldwork among Amazonian Yanomamö and Shuar groups in affiliation with the UCSB Center for Evolutionary Psychology. Most of Michael's research has focused on evolutionary psychological aspects of cooperation in groups, and he is currently investigating how individual physical characteristics (e.g. muscularity, attractiveness, bodily symmetry) influence one's preference for egalitarianism (social equality).

Paul H. Rubin is Samuel Candler Dobbs Professor of Economics at Emory University in Atlanta and editor in chief of Managerial and Decision Economics. He is a Fellow of the Public Choice Society and former Vice President of the Southern Economics Association, and is associated with several think tanks. Dr. Rubin has been Senior Staff Economist at President Reagan's Council of Economic Advisers, Chief Economist at the U.S. Consumer Product Safety Commission, Director of Advertising Economics at the FTC and vice-president of Glassman-Oliver Economic Consultants, Inc. He has taught economics at the University of Georgia, City University of New York, VPI, and GWU Law School. Dr. Rubin has written or edited eleven books (including *Darwinian Politics*, Rutgers Press, 2002) and published over one hundred and fifty articles and chapters in reputed journals. Dr. Rubin contributes to the *Wall Street Journal* and other leading newspapers. He has consulted and advised widely on litigation related matters. He has addressed numerous business, professional, government and academic audiences. Dr. Rubin received his Ph.D. from Purdue University in 1970.

Gad Saad is Professor of Marketing at Concordia University (Montreal, Canada) and the holder of the Concordia University Research Chair in Evolutionary Behavioral Sciences and Darwinian Consumption. He has held Visiting Associate Professorships at Cornell University, Dartmouth College, and the University of California – Irvine. He is the author of *The Evolutionary Bases of Consumption* (Lawrence Erlbaum, 2007), and *The Consuming Instinct: What Juicy Burgers, Ferraris, Pornography, and Gift Giving Reveal About Human Nature* (Prometheus Books, 2011). He has published 55+ scientific papers many of which lie at the intersection of evolutionary psychology and a broad range of disciplines including consumer behavior, marketing, advertising, medicine, and economics. Dr. Saad is a highly popular blogger for *Psychology Today*. Since November 2008, his posts have amassed 1,144,000+ total views. He received a B.Sc. in mathematics and computer science (1988) and an M.B.A. (1990) both from McGill University, and his M.S. (1993) and Ph.D. (1994) from Cornell University.

Brian R. Spisak currently holds a research position in the Department of Social and Organizational Psychology at the VU University Amsterdam, the Netherlands. The core of his research centers on the origins of leadership and followership and what that can tell us about group behavior. Using this evolutionary framework, he is currently developing a perception-based application for reducing intergroup group conflict in collaboration with the United States Office of Naval Research. His work, particularly on voting behavior, has been featured in a variety of media outlets including the New Scientist and BBC World Service. In addition to the evolution of group processes, he has emerging interests in network science, artificial intelligence, and capacity building in developing regions. He has extensive experience working with both public and private sector organizations.

Bram Van den Bergh is Assistant Professor at the Rotterdam School of Management, Erasmus University, the Netherlands. His research interests are in the field of intertemporal preferences, probabilistic choice, social dilemmas, prosocial behavior, embodied cognition, and mate preferences. His research has been published in top journals in marketing, psychology, and biology.

Mark van Vugt is Professor of Social and Organizational Psychology at the VU University Amsterdam, the Netherlands, where he leads a research group on Leadership. His research interests include the application of evolutionary theories to group dynamics and organizational processes. He has published extensively on themes such as leadership, cooperation, gender differences, and intergroup relations. His current work focuses on the biology and neuroscience of leadership. He is the author of several textbooks and a popular science book on leadership, titled *Selected,* which will come out in 2010 with Profile and Harper Collins. In addition, Mark van Vugt currently serves as an Associate Editor of the *Journal of Personality and Social Psychology.*

Patrick Vyncke works at the Department of Communication Sciences of Ghent University in Belgium. After graduating in Communication Sciences he worked for 4 years at the Belgian National Fund For Scientific Research on a research project regarding advertising processing and planning. Through this research project he obtained his Ph.D. degree in Communication Sciences. After ending the project, he returned to the Department of Communication Sciences of Ghent University, soon becoming a full-time professor involved in teaching and researching the underlying dynamics of advertising processing and consumer behavior. In the end, this brought him to the field of evolutionary psychology. Now, he holds a strong conviction that this perspective will turn out to be the most fruitful perspective on both advertising processing and consumer behavior ever to have been developed.

David M. Wasieleski is an Associate Professor in Management in the Palumbo-Donahue School of Business at Duquesne University. David completed his doctorate in Business Environment and Public Policy in the Katz Graduate School of Business at the University of Pittsburgh. He received a B.A. in Economics and a Certificate Degree in Accounting from Pitt, and an M.B.A. from Duquesne University. For eight years, he worked as a marketing representative in the home-building industry. His academic research focuses on natural science approaches to understanding ethical decision-making and the formation of social contracts within organizational contexts. He also studies cognitive biases on decision-making and behavior in workplace environments. At Duquesne, he teaches business ethics, organizational behavior, and public policy.

Kim Willems is a Ph.D. student affiliated with both the University of Hasselt (UHasselt) and the Vrije Universiteit Brussel (VUB). Her research focuses on retail differentiation strategies, such as, for example, store atmospherics. Kim is furthermore interested in the roles of customer value and self-congruity theory in retailing. She has published in the *Journal of Product & Brand Management* and *Urban Forestry & Urban Greening*.

The Missing Link: The Biological Roots of the Business Sciences

Gad Saad

Abstract Despite a growing infusion of the evolutionary behavioral sciences in general, and evolutionary psychology in particular, across a wide range of disciplines, the business sciences have been slow in recognizing the relevance and explanatory power afforded by this consilient meta-framework. Humans possess minds and bodies that have been forged by a long evolutionary history. Hence, to fully comprehend all of the human cognitions, emotions, preferences, choices, and behaviors that shape marketplace realities, be it those of consumers, employees, or employers, business scholars must incorporate biology and evolutionary theory within their theoretical toolkits. Scientists typically operate at the *proximate* realm, namely they seek to explain the mechanistic details of phenomena whereas ultimate explanations tackle the Darwinian forces that would have led to their evolution. Both levels of analyses are needed when investigating biological organisms including *Homo consumericus* and *Homo corporaticus*.

Keywords Proximate and ultimate explanations · Consilience · Biology · Business · Interdisciplinary · Evolutionary psychology

1 Introduction

A scientist who studies any animal, short of humans, would never dream of doing so while ignoring the biological and evolutionary forces that have shaped its phylogenetic history. Yet several generations of social scientists, be it sociologists, cultural anthropologists, economists, or social psychologists, to name a few, have considered it perfectly natural to disregard the biological roots of *Homo sapiens*. Nowhere

G. Saad
Concordia University, John Molson School of Business, De Maisonneuve Blvd. W. 1455, H3G 1M8 Montreal, QC, Canada
e-mail: gadsaad@jmsb.concordia.ca

is the disconnection between the study of human behavior and its biological bases as evident as in the business sciences. This seems quite peculiar given the endless evident ways by which our biology shapes our actions be it as consumers, employees, and/or employers. Our innate preferences for highly caloric foods, pornographic films, and products that improve our stock in the mating market (e.g., plastic surgery and cosmetics for women; luxury cars for men) are manifestations of our biological heritage. The dynamics of the subordinate-supervisor (or employee-employer) relationship is a vestige of the dominance pecking order inherent to many social and hierarchical species. That an interviewer might succumb to the allure of a physically attractive prospective employee is an instinctual penchant for beauty that is difficult to overcome. That a financial trader's fluctuating hormones (e.g., testosterone) or situational hunger (blood sugar levels) might affect his tolerance for risk is obviously due to physiological realities. In 1973, Theodosius Dobzhansky, the famed evolutionary geneticist wrote an influential article titled: "Nothing in biology makes sense except in the light of evolution". His insight is equally true when applied to business, namely I propose that nothing in business makes sense except in the light of evolution (more specifically, evolutionary psychology).

2 Key Principles of Evolutionary Psychology

A foundational tenet of evolutionary psychology (EP) is that in the same way that our various organs have each evolved to solved specific problems of evolutionary import, our minds are comprised of domain-specific algorithms, each of which has evolved as a solution to a particular evolutionary challenge (e.g., choosing a mate, investing in kin, avoiding environmental threats, establishing coalitions with non-kin). Accordingly, EP rejects the premise that the human mind is a blank slate that is otherwise infinitely malleable. Furthermore, EP proclaims that it is insufficient to attribute the genesis of a phenomenon to learning, culture, and/or socialization (see Tooby and Cosmides 1992 for a critique of the Standard Social Science Model, which overly relies on such explanatory accounts). To the extent that many forms of learning occur in exactly the same way irrespective of time or place, it becomes incumbent to provide an ultimate explanation for such environmental agents. In other words, in most instances, nurture exists in its particular forms because of nature.

EP is the latest of a long list of disciplines that seeks to understand the Darwinian roots of human cognition, behaviors, emotions, and preferences. Its predecessors include ethology, sociobiology, behavioral ecology, Darwinian anthropology, and gene-culture coevolution modeling (see Laland and Brown 2002 for an overview of these approaches). Whereas each of these evolutionary disciplines makes unique epistemological claims, they are all concerned with ultimate causation, namely investigating the evolutionary forces that have led to our biological-based human nature. Most scientists including business scholars operate within the proximate realm, namely they investigate the mechanistic details of a given phenomenon without caring about its Darwinian genesis (if any). A concrete example, an investigation of conspicuous consumption, might illuminate the epistemological distinction between proximate and ultimate explanations. Proximate explorations might include developing a scale to measure one's proclivity to engage in acts of conspicuous consumption; establishing a relationship between conspicuous consumption and materialism; and ascertaining a link between conspicuous consumption and macroeconomic conditions. An ultimate investigation of conspicuous consumption would ask the Darwinian *why* question, namely why have we evolved the universal need to engage in various forms of sexual signaling, of which conspicuous consumption is an instantiation (cf. Griskevicius et al. 2007; Lycett and Dunbar 2000; Saad and Vongas 2009; Sundie et al. 2010). Note that an ultimate explanation does not invalidate proximate ones. Rather, both levels of analyses work in tandem in achieving a complete understanding of a given biological-based phenomenon. It is self-evident then that the behaviors of all human agents involved in business transactions, be it consumers, employees, or employers, cannot be fully understood if we restrict our analyses to the proximate realm.

3 Evolutionary Theory and Biology in the Business Sciences

Whereas the application of EP in the business sciences is a nascent endeavor, works at the nexus of evolutionary theory and business have a more established history. An example of an evolutionary approach that precedes the EP paradigm is game theoretic modeling, which utilizes countless principles from evolutionary theory across a wide range of business disciplines (e.g., evolutionarily stable strategies). Other non-EP-based works that utilize evolutionary notions such as variation, selection, inheritance, replication, adaptation, and retention, include those in entrepreneurship (Aldrich and Martinez 2001), and in organizational ecology (Hanna and Freeman 1989). These approaches are at times grouped under the heading of *Generalized Darwinism*, as a means of explaining how social, economic, and cultural entities can evolve in ways fully congruent with evolutionary theory (Hodgson and Knudsen 2010). Memetic theory is yet another evolutionary framework that seeks to explain how memes (the cultural analogues of genes) can diffuse in a population. For example, catchy advertising slogans that spread via a viral process can be modeled using memetic theory (see Frank 1999; Marsden 1998, 2002; and Pech 2003, for applications of memetic theory in various business settings). Each of the latter approaches is founded on evolutionary principles albeit none seeks to explain the Darwinian forces that have shaped individuals' minds and subsequent behaviors in the marketplace. The latter objective is within the purview of EP.

Neuroeconomics is perhaps one of the most popular contemporary research streams at the nexus of biology and business albeit it is seldom evolutionarily informed (see Glimcher et al. 2009 for a recent overview of neuroeconomics, and Ariely and Berns 2010 for a synopsis of the related field of neuromarketing).

Specifically, neuroeconomists investigate the unique neuronal firings implicit to specific economic-related tasks (e.g., choosing between two competing gambles). Clearly, neuroeconomists recognize the import of our biology when making decisions, albeit they rarely if ever ask the ultimate *why* question, namely why our brains might have evolved the particular computational systems that are elucidated via the brain imaging paradigm. As such, most neuroeconomists restrict their explorations to the proximate realm albeit a growing number of scientists are calling for greater infusion of evolutionary theorizing within the neurosciences (cf. Garcia and Saad 2008; Platek et al. 2007).

The *status syndrome* is another example of a documented non-evolutionary-based phenomenon that is otherwise at the nexus of biology and business (Marmot 2004). Specifically, this social epidemiological approach has established a negative relationship between one's occupational status and health outcomes. The argument is that employees who operate in lower status positions have lesser job control and lesser daily autonomy. This serves to elevate their cortisol levels, akin to the manner in which subordinates in many social species possess higher cortisol levels by virtue of their lower social rank. Elevated levels of cortisol have been associated with numerous deleterious health outcomes including a greater likelihood of heart disease. Hence, it is literally the case that your job could be killing you. Needless to say, the status syndrome could not have been uncovered void of an understanding of various biological and physiological realities, which in this case manifest themselves in work settings.

Are leaders born or made? What about consumers, entrepreneurs, financial traders, and numerous other agents within the marketplace? To what extent do our unique environments and life experiences versus our genetic makeup influence our behaviors in the marketplace? Twin registries are often used to determine the extent to which the variance in a given trait or proclivity is due to genetic versus environmental influences. A growing number of scholars are utilizing this paradigm within business contexts including in consumer behavior (Simonson and Sela 2011), behavioral economics (Cesarini et al. 2008), financial decision-making (Cesarini et al. 2010), entrepreneurship (Nicolaou et al. 2008), job and occupational switching (McCall et al. 1997), and leadership styles (Johnson et al. 1998). Not surprisingly, the totality of such studies suggests that our genes play an important role in shaping our behaviors and preferences across a wide range of business settings.

To summarize, biologically informed research streams exist within the business sciences albeit they constitute a minuscule proportion of all published works. In many instances, such studies are not explicitly rooted within an evolutionary framework, and rarely are they grounded on EP-based principles. The remainder of this section serves as a repository of references that operate at the nexus of EP (and related evolutionary frameworks) and the business sciences. It would be impossible to provide a detailed discussion of each of the cited references. Rather, my goal is to provide the proverbial "one-stop" source for scholars wishing to gauge the breadth of business-related areas wherein EP along with related biological formalisms have been applied. Many of the cited references were not written with an explicit business lens. For example, whereas many product categories have been investigated from an evolutionary perspective, the great majority of such studies were neither published in business journals nor authored by business scholars. Given that consumers utilize products as sexual signals in the mating market, it is perhaps not surprising that many of the investigated products are mating-related including perfume (Milinski and Wedekind 2001; Roberts et al. 2009; Wedekind et al. 2007), engagement/wedding rings (Cronk and Dunham 2007; Uller and Johansson 2003), cars (Dunn and Searle 2010; Shuler and McCord 2010), hair (Hinsz et al. 2001; Mesko and Bereczkei 2004), plastic surgery (Singh and Randall 2007), sun tanning (Saad and Peng 2006), clothes (Barber 1999; Hill et al. 2005; Townsend and Levy 1990), high heels (Smith 1999), and cosmetics/skin quality (Russell 2009; Samson et al. 2010).

Other consumer-related phenomena that have been tackled via an evolutionary lens include food-related issues (Katz 1990; Nabhan 2004; New et al. 2007; Ohtsubo 2009; Saad 2006a; Sherman and Billing 1999; Sherman and Hash 2001; Wrangham 2009; Wrangham and Conklin-Brittain 2003); gambling (Gray 2004; Spinella 2003; Steiner et al. 2010); pornography (Malamuth 1996; Pound 2002); online advertisements of female escorts (Saad 2008a); song lyrics (Saad 2011a); flowers (Haviland-Jones et al. 2005); toys (Alexander 2003; Alexander and Hines 2002; Berenbaum and Hines 1992; Hassett et al. 2008); the news (Davis and McLeod 2003; Shoemaker 1996); video games (Mendenhall et al. 2010a; Mendenhall et al. 2010b); gift giving (Jonason et al. 2009; Mysterud et al. 2006; Saad and Gill 2003); the role of birth order in consumer settings (Saad et al. 2005); offline shopping (Dennis and McCall 2005) and online behaviors/shopping (DiClemente and Hantula 2003; Piazza and Bering 2009; Saad 2010a; Stenstrom et al. 2008; Stenstrom and Saad 2010); various types of design issues (Whyte 2007) including landscape design (Falk and Balling 2010), architectural design (Kellert et al. 2008; Tsui 1999), interior design (Scott 1993), product design (Moss et al. 2007; Windhager et al. 2008), and the use of biomimicry for product design (Bar-Cohen 2006; Benyus 2002); branding (Hirschman 2010); green/sustainable consumption (Griskevicius et al. 2010; Jackson 2005), as well as the use of green principles in advertising (Hartmann and Apaolaza-Ibáñez 2010) and in retailing (Joye et al. 2010); pets (Archer 1997; Payne and Jaffe 2005; Roy and Christenfeld 2004); money (Briers et al. 2006; Lea and Webley 2006); sex differences in the acceptance of a new service, namely hospital DNA paternity testing (Hayward and Rohwer 2004); service encounters between nightclub patrons and bouncers (Salter et al. 2005); and pleasurable consumption (Wallenstein 2008). Despite the incontrovertible relevance of EP in elucidating the biological roots of our consumer instinct, the great majority of consumer scholars remain perfectly oblivious to the evolutionary forces that have shaped *Homo consumericus*.

Next, I provide a list of biologically and/or evolutionary-informed works spanning the gamut of business disciplines beginning with those disciplines most closely aligned to my research interests: consumer behavior/marketing (Colarelli and Dettman 2003; Miller 2009; Saad 2006b, 2007, 2010b, 2011b; Saad and Gill 2000); advertising (Ambler and Hollier 2004; Cary 2000; Griskevicius et al. 2009; Saad 2004); political marketing (Saad 2003); product evolution (Massey 1999);

relationship marketing (Eyuboglu and Buja 2007; Palmer 2000); decision making/ rationality (Chen et al. 2006; Gigerenzer 2000; Haselton et al. 2009; Kenrick et al. 2009; McDermott et al. 2008; Saad et al. 2009; Waksberg et al. 2009); intertemporal choice (Daly and Wilson 2005; Van den Bergh et al. 2008; Wang and Dvorak 2010; Wilson and Daly 2004); economics (Ben-Ner and Putterman 2000; Burd 2010; Cordes 2006; Dopfer 2005; Gandolfi et al. 2000; Hagen and Hammerstein 2006; Henrich et al. 2004; Hodgson and Knudsen 2010; Koppl 2005; Saad and Gill 2001); executive decision making (Nicholson 2000); family business (Nicholson 2008); human resource management (Colarelli 2003); personnel psychology (Luxen and Van De Vijver 2006); organizational politics (Braithwaite 2005; Vredenburgh and Shea-VanFossen 2010); workplace gossip (Kniffin and Wilson 2010); salary distribution within organizations (Kniffin 2009); facial features and career success (Mueller and Mazur 1996; Rule and Ambady 2008, 2009); organizational citizenship behavior (Salamon and Deutsch 2006); leadership (Van Vugt 2006); sexual harassment in organizations (Browne 2006); technological change (Devezas 2005; Ziman 2000); total quality management (Coelho et al. 2004); accounting (Basu and Waymire 2006; Dickhaut et al. 2010); finance (Lo 2005); management information systems and information science (Kock 2009; Spink 2010); public administration (Meyer-Emerick 2007); public relations (Greenwood 2010); business ethics (Wasieleski and Hayibor 2009); legal matters including justice and equal employment law (Jones and Goldsmith 2005; Spitz 1998; Walsh 2000); and lekking behavior in organizational settings (Braithwaite 2008). This list of references should serve as a testament to the relevance and explanatory power of EP and related biological principles in tackling endless domains of business import.

4 Benefits of Darwinizing the Business Sciences

The incorporation of EP within the business sciences yields at the very least three key epistemological benefits (see Saad 2007, chapter 7 for a detailed discussion of such benefits in Darwinizing the study of consumption). First, it permits for much greater consilience (Wilson 1998) both within any particular business discipline as well as across disciplines. Consilience refers to the unification of knowledge under a common, parsimonious, and coherent theoretical umbrella. Historically, whereas the natural sciences have been defined by their ability to generate consilient core knowledge, the social sciences are infamous for their inability to achieve any semblance of consilience. Take my own discipline of consumer behavior as an example. Feminist consumer scholars balk at the idea that innate biological forces might drive sex differences in consumption. Postmodernist consumer researchers reject the possibility that human universals manifest themselves in the consumption arena, as they subscribe to the tenet that no universals could exist ("all knowledge is relative and subjective"). Consumer scholars who adhere to social constructivism minimize if not outright reject the role of biology in explaining consumption, as they presume that cultural learning shapes much of our consummatory nature. Clearly, such positions are antithetical to the creation of a consilient body of knowledge, as they each espouse worldviews that immediately destroy the interdisciplinary bridges afforded by various biological-based disciplines (see Saad 2008b for a discussion of the reasons that most marketing scholars reject the relevance of biology in explaining consumer behavior).

A second benefit of incorporating EP within the business sciences lies in its vast ability to promote and facilitate interdisciplinary works. Interdisciplinarity is an inherent feature of many of the greatest scientific advances (see Garcia et al. 2011 for relevant references). However, the manner in which business disciplines are organized leaves little room for deep interdisciplinary explorations. Business fields certainly make use of advances in various cognate disciplines (e.g., marketing and finance modelers utilize econometric techniques developed by economists and statisticians; consumer scholars borrow theories developed by social psychologists); however this is not what I mean by interdisciplinary work. Maximally interdisciplinary endeavors are those wherein a common problem is tackled from radically different perspectives, ultimately yielding a completed jigsaw puzzle. In other words, each discipline contributes its unique pieces to the unfolding jigsaw puzzle. For example, a full understanding of eating disorders might involve the contributions of consumer psychologists, food psychologists, clinical psychologists, and evolutionary psychologists. To reiterate, EP serves as a universal key to unlock the rigid disciplinary doors that are otherwise erected to protect one's paradigmatic turf.

A third benefit of infusing biology and evolutionary thinking into the business sciences is that it opens up novel research questions and corresponding hypotheses that would have otherwise been invisible to the scholar who solely operates in the non-biological realm. Take for example the role that testosterone plays in our daily lives. Of relevance to business scholars, its effects have been explored in areas as varied as financial trading (Coates et al. 2009; Coates and Herbert 2008; Sapienza et al. 2009), conspicuous consumption (Saad and Vongas 2009), entrepreneurship (White et al. 2006), and sports viewing (Bernhardt et al. 1998). Hormones also affect women's behaviors in profound ways, perhaps none as clearly as those implicit to a woman's menstrual cycle. A growing number of researchers have recognized the role of the menstrual cycle across several business settings including food consumption (Fessler 2001, 2003; Saad and Stenstrom 2010), beautification practices including choice of clothing (Durante et al. 2011; Durante et al. 2008; Grammer et al. 2004; Haselton et al. 2007; Saad and Stenstrom 2010), in organizational settings (Durante and Saad 2010), and in service encounters (Miller et al. 2007). Clearly, the effects of the menstrual cycle on women's behaviors, choices, and preferences could never be fully investigated void of an understanding of EP and related physiological realities.

Whereas some hormones manifest themselves in largely sex-specific manners, oxytocin augments affiliational behaviors for both sexes across several evolutionarily relevant contexts. For example, oxytocin is released subsequent to a sexual encounter, thus earning it the moniker of the cuddling hormone. It is also released when a mother is breastfeeding, and as such it augments maternal nurturance. Finally, it is operative when individuals, who are otherwise not biologically related, interact with one another, in so doing it promotes greater non-kin trust. Paul Zak has been at the forefront of researching the relationship between oxytocin and economic interactions (cf. Zak 2008; Zak et al. 2007). To reiterate, whether studying the effects of testosterone, menstrual-related hormones, or oxytocin on our behaviors, emotions, or cognitions, in various business settings, it is clear that none of these topics could have been broached void of recognizing the evolutionary-based biological forces that have shaped our endocrinological system.

5 Broad Set of Issues Covered in This Edited Book

The ability of EP to permeate across business disciplines is well captured by the breadth of issues tackled by the contributing authors. Griskevicius et al. explore how an understanding of the evolutionary roots of our motivational system can elucidate business decisions in areas as varied as persuasion and advertising; innovation and creativity; intertemporal choice, self-control, and risk; negotiation; and helping, generosity, and cooperation. Buunk et al. discuss the evolutionary roots of intrasexual competition as manifested within organizational settings. Browne tackles sex differences in workplace patterns including the glass ceiling effect, the gender gap in compensation, and occupational segregation. Price and Johnson offer the Adaptationist Theory of Cooperation in Groups as a meta-framework for understanding cooperation within organizational settings. Murray and Murray provide evidence stemming from three separate studies to explain the greater preponderance of, and preference for, male leaders. Spisak, Nicholson, and van Vugt also explore leadership with an emphasis on the evolutionary roots of leader-follower dynamics. Across two studies, Wasieleski investigates how evolved cheater-detection algorithms manifest themselves in business settings. Dunham applies biological-based signaling theory as a meta-framework for understanding various forms of business communication (e.g., advertising). On a related note, Vyncke demonstrates how fitness-related cues (e.g., facial symmetry or waist-to-hip ratio) can ameliorate the perceived efficacy of an ad. Joye, Poels, and Willems argue that optimal store designs are those congruent with evolved aesthetic preferences. Capra and Rubin highlight the evolutionary roots of a wide range of violations of rational choice, which behavioral decision theorists have been so adept at uncovering. Finally, Hantula et al. offer Media Compensation Theory as a meta-framework for understanding the Darwinian genesis of electronic communications and collaboration. Incidentally, the interdisciplinarity that is afforded by EP is evident in the departmental affiliations and/or academic training of the contributing authors. These include marketing, psychology (social, organizational, and evolutionary), law, economics, management information systems, anthropology, evolutionary biology, politics, philosophy, organizational behavior, strategic communication, communication sciences, and business environment and public policy.

6 Conclusion

One of the metrics of prestige of any scientific discipline is whether it has the epistemological clout to generate accurate foundational knowledge that is unified under parsimonious and coherent theoretical frameworks. Physics, chemistry, and biology constitute such fields whereas sociology, political science, and economics do not. To the extent that the business sciences have largely imported their theoretical frameworks from cognate disciplines in the social sciences, they have historically lacked the requisite consilience implicit to high-ranking scientific disciplines. The evolutionary behavioral sciences offer such a unifying framework. Ultimately, the biological revolution that has swept the twentieth century will continue unabated in its forward march. Accordingly, there is no reason for business scholars to remain isolated from the natural sciences in general, and biology and EP in particular. The same evolutionary forces that have shaped the minds and bodies of *Homo sapiens* drive *Homo businessicus*.

It is important to reiterate that ultimate-level explorations, such as those implicit to EP, are not mutually exclusive of the myriad of proximate-level research streams. Both levels of scientific inquiry are typically needed when studying a phenomenon involving a biological organism, be it an orchid, an amoeba, a lion, or a human. The preponderance of academic research, whether business-related or not, will continue to take place at the proximate level. However, by infusing an understanding of our biological heritage into the relevant theoretical toolboxes, business scholars can build a more accurate, complete, and organized core base of knowledge, of the forces that drive us in the marketplace.

References

Aldrich HE, Martinez MA (2001) Many are called, but few are chosen: an evolutionary perspective of the study of entrepreneurship. Entrepreneurship Theor Pract 25:41–56

Alexander GM (2003) An evolutionary perspective of sex-typed toy preferences: pink, blue, and the brain. Arch Sex Behav 32:7–14

Alexander GM, Hines M (2002) Sex differences in response to children's toys in nonhuman primates (*Cercopithecus aethiops sabaeus*). Evol Hum Behav 23:467–479

Ambler T, Hollier EA (2004) The waste in advertising is the part that works. J Advert Res 44:375–389

Archer J (1997) Why do people love their pets? Evol Hum Behav 18:237–259

Ariely D, Berns GS (2010) Neuromarketing: the hope and hype of neuroimaging in business. Nat Rev Neurosci 11:284–292

Barber N (1999) Women's dress fashions as a function of reproductive strategy. Sex Roles 40:459–471

Bar-Cohen Y (2006) Biomimetics—using nature to inspire human innovation. Bioinspir Biomim 1:P1–P12

Basu S, Waymire GB (2006) Recordkeeping and human evolution. Account Horiz 20:201–229

Ben-Ner A, Putterman L (2000) On some implications of evolutionary psychology for the study of preferences and institutions. J Econ Behav Organ 43:91–99

Benyus JM (2002) Biomimicry: innovation inspired by nature. Harper Perennial, New York

Berenbaum SA, Hines M (1992) Early androgens are related to childhood sex-typed toy preferences. Psychol Sci 3:203–206

Bernhardt PC, Dabbs JM Jr, Fielden JA, Lutter CD (1998) Testosterone changes during vicarious experiences of winning and losing among fans at sporting events. Physiol Behav 65:59–62

Braithwaite J (2005) Hunter-gatherer human nature and health system safety: an evolutionary cleft stick? Int J Qual Health Care 17:541–545

Braithwaite J (2008) Lekking displays in contemporary organizations: ethologically oriented, evolutionary and cross-species accounts of male dominance. J Health Organ Manage 22:529–559

Briers B, Pandelaere M, Dewitte S, Warlop L (2006) Hungry for money: The desire for caloric resources increases the desire for financial resources and vice versa. Psychol Sci 17:939–943

Browne KR (2006) Sex, power, and dominance: the evolutionary psychology of sexual harassment. Manage Decis Econ 27:145–158

Burd M (2010) Hunting, gathering, investing, globalizing: the biological roots of economic behaviour. Syst Res Behav Sci 27:510–522

Cary MS (2000) Ad strategy and the stone age brain. J Advertising Res 40:103–106

Cesarini D, Dawes CT, Fowler JH, Johannesson M, Lichtenstein P, Wallace B (2008) Heritability of cooperative behavior in the trust game. Proc Natl Acad Sci USA 105:3721–3726

Cesarini D, Johannesson M, Lichtenstein P, Sandewall Ö, Wallace B (2010) Genetic variation in financial decision-making. J Finance 65:1725–1754

Chen MK, Lakshminarayanan V, Santos LR (2006) How basic are behavioral biases? Evidence from capuchin monkey trading behavior. J Polit Econ 114:517–537

Coates JM, Gurnell M, Rustichini A (2009) Second-to-fourth digit ratio predicts success among high-frequency financial traders. Proc Natl Acad Sci USA 106:623–628

Coates JM, Herbert J (2008) Endogenous steroids and financial risk taking on a London trading floor. Proc Natl Acad Sci USA 105:6167–6172

Coelho PRP, McClure JE, Tunc E (2004) Managing *Homo sapiens*. Total Qual Manage 15:191–204

Colarelli SM (2003) No best way: an evolutionary perspective on human resource management. Praeger, Westport

Colarelli SM, Dettman JR (2003) Intuitive evolutionary perspectives in marketing practices. Psychol Market 20:837–865

Cordes C (2006) Darwinism in economics: from analogy to continuity. J Evol Econ 16:529–541

Cronk L, Dunham B (2007) Amounts spent on engagement rings reflect aspects of male and female mate quality. Hum Nat 18:329–333

Daly M, Wilson M (2005) Carpe diem: adaptation and devaluing the future. Q Rev Biol 80:55–60

Davis H, McLeod SL (2003) Why humans value sensational news: an evolutionary perspective. Evol Hum Behav 24:208–216

Dennis C, McCall A (2005) The savannah hypothesis of shopping. Bus Strat Rev 16:12–16

Devezas TC (2005) Evolutionary theory of technological change: state-of-the-art and new approaches. Technol Forecast Soc Change 72:1137–1152

Dickhaut J, Basu S, McCabe K, Waymire G (2010) Neuroaccounting: consilience between the biologically evolved brain and culturally evolved accounting principles. Acc Horiz 24:221–255

DiClemente DF, Hantula DA (2003) Optimal foraging online: increasing sensitivity to delay. Psychol Mark 20:785–809

Dopfer K (2005) (Ed) The evolutionary foundations of economics. Cambridge University Press, Cambridge

Dunn MJ, Searle R (2010) Effect of manipulated prestige-car ownership on both sex attractiveness ratings. Br J Psychol 101:69–80

Durante KM, Griskevicius V, Hill SE, Perilloux C, Li NP (2011) Ovulation, female competition, and product choice: hormonal influences on consumer behavior. J Cons Res 37:921–934

Durante KM, Li NP, Haselton MG (2008) Changes in women's choice of dress across the ovulatory cycle: naturalistic and laboratory task-based evidence. Pers Soc Psychol Bull 34:1451–1460

Durante KM, Saad G (2010) Ovulatory shifts in women's social motives and behaviors: implications for corporate organizations. In: Stanton A, Day M, Welpe I (eds) Neuroeconomics and the firm. Edward Elgar, Northampton, pp 116–130

Eyuboglu N, Buja A (2007) Quasi-Darwinian selection in marketing relationships. J Mark 71:48–62

Falk JH, Balling JD (2010) Evolutionary influence on human landscape preference. Environ Behav 42:479–493

Fessler DMT (2001) Luteal phase immunosuppression and meat eating. Riv Biol Biol Forum 94:403–426

Fessler DMT (2003) No time to eat: an adaptationist account of periovulatory behavioral changes. Q Rev Biol 78:3–21

Frank J (1999) Applying memetics to financial markets: do markets evolve towards efficiency. J Memet 3. Available at http://cfpm.org/jom-emit/1999/vol3/frank_j.html

Gandolfi AE, Gandolfi AS, Barash DP (2000) Economics as an evolutionary science: from utility to fitness. Transaction Publishers, Piscataway

Garcia JR, Geher G, Crosier B, Saad G, Gambacorta D, Johnsen L, Pranckitas E (2011) The interdisciplinarity of evolutionary approaches to human behavior: a key to survival in the ivory archipelago. Futures, forthcoming

Garcia JR, Saad G (2008) Evolutionary neuromarketing: Darwinizing the neuroimaging paradigm for consumer behavior. J Consum Behav 7:397–414

Gigerenzer G (2000) Adaptive thinking: rationality in the real world. Oxford University Press, New York

Glimcher PW, Camerer CF, Fehr E, Poldrack RA (eds) (2009) Neuroeconomics: decision making and the brain. Academic Press, London

Grammer K, Renninger L, Fischer B (2004) Disco clothing, female sexual motivation, and relationship status: is she dressed to impress? J Sex Res 41:66–74

Gray PB (2004) Evolutionary and cross-cultural perspectives on gambling. J Gambl Stud 20:347–371

Greenwood CA (2010) Evolutionary theory: the missing link for conceptualizing public relations. J Public Relat Res 22:456–476

Griskevicius V, Goldstein NJ, Mortensen CR, Sundie JM, Cialdini RB, Kenrick DT (2009) Fear and loving in Las Vegas: evolution, emotion, and persuasion. J Mark Res XLVI:384–395

Griskevicius V, Tybur JM, Sundie JM, Cialdini RB, Miller GF, Kenrick DT (2007) Blatant benevolence and conspicuous consumption: when romantic motives elicit strategic costly signals. J Pers Soc Psychol 93:85–102

Griskevicius V, Tybur JM, Van den Bergh B (2010) Going green to be seen: status, reputation, and conspicuous conservation. J Pers Soc Psychol 98:392–404

Hagen EH, Hammerstein P (2006) Game theory and human evolution: a critique of some recent interpretations of experimental games. Theor Popul Biol 69:339–348

Hanna MT, Freeman J (1989) Organizational ecology. Harvard University Press, Cambridge

Hartmann P, Apaolaza-Ibáñez V (2010) Beyond savanna: an evolutionary and environmental psychology approach to behavioral effects of nature scenery in green advertising. J Environ Psychol 30:119–128

Haselton MG, Bryant GA, Wilke A, Frederick DA, Galperin A, Frankenhuis WE, Moore T (2009) Adaptive rationality: an evolutionary perspective on cognitive bias. Soc Cognition 27:732–762

Haselton MG, Mortezaie M, Pillsworth EG, Bleske-Rechek A, Frederick DA (2007) Ovulatory shifts in human female ornamentation: near ovulation, women dress to impress. Horm Behav 51:40–45

Hassett JM, Siebert ER, Wallen K (2008) Sex differences in rhesus monkey toy preferences parallel those of children. Horm Behav 54:359–364

Haviland-Jones J, Rosario HH, Wilson P, McGuire TR (2005) An environmental approach to positive emotion: flowers. Evol Psychol 3:104–132

Hayward LS, Rohwer S (2004) Sex differences in attitudes toward paternity testing. Evol Hum Behav 25:242–248

Henrich J, Boyd R, Bowles S, Camerer C, Fehr E, Gintis H (eds) (2004) Foundations of human sociality: economic experiments and ethnographic evidence from fifteen small-scale societies. Oxford University Press, New York

Hill RA, Donovan S, Koyama NF (2005) Female sexual advertisement reflects resource availability in twentieth-century UK society. Hum Nat 16:266–277

Hinsz VB, Matz DC, Patience RA (2001) Does women's hair signal reproductive potential? J Exp Soc Psychol 37:166–172

Hirschman EC (2010) Evolutionary branding. Psychol Mark 27:568–583

Hodgson GM, Knudsen T (2010) Darwin's conjecture: the search for general principles of social and economic evolution. University of Chicago Press, Chicago

Jackson T (2005) Live better by consuming less? Is there a "double dividend" in sustainable consumption? J Ind Ecol 9:19–36

Johnson AM, Vernon PA, McCarthy JM, Molson M, Harris JA, Jang KL (1998) Nature vs nurture: are leaders born or made? A behavior genetic investigation of leadership style. Twin Res 1:216–223

Jonason PK, Cetrulo JF, Madrid JM, Morrison C (2009) Gift-giving as a courtship or mate-retention tactic?: Insights from non-human models. Evol Psychol 7:89–103

Jones OD, Goldsmith TH (2005) Law and behavioral biology. Columbia Law Rev 105:405–502

Joye Y, Willems K, Brengman M, Wolf K (2010) The effects of urban retail greenery on consumer experience: reviewing the evidence from a restorative perspective. Urban Forestry & Urban Greening 9:57–64

Katz SH (1990) An evolutionary theory of cuisine. Hum Nat 1:233–259

Kellert SR, Heerwagen J, Mador M (eds) (2008) Biophilic design: the theory, science and practice of bringing buildings to life. Wiley, New York

Kenrick DT, Griskevicius V, Sundie JM, Li NP, Li YJ, Neuberg SL (2009) Deep rationality: the evolutionary economics of decision making. Soc Cogn 27:764–785

Kniffin KM (2009) Evolutionary perspectives on salary dispersion within firms. J Bioecon 11:23–42

Kniffin KM, Wilson DS (2010) Evolutionary perspectives on workplace gossip: why and how gossip can serve groups. Group Organ Manage 35:150–176

Kock N (2009) Information systems theorizing based on evolutionary psychology: an interdisciplinary review and theory integration framework. MIS Q 33:395–418

Koppl R (ed) (2005) Evolutionary psychology and economic theory. Elsevier, Amsterdam

Laland KN, Brown GR (2002) Sense and nonsense: evolutionary perspectives on human behaviour. Oxford University Press, Oxford

Lea SEG, Webley P (2006) Money as a tool, money as drug: the biological psychology of a strong incentive. Behav Brain Sci 29:161–176

Lo AW (2005) Reconciling efficient markets with behavioral finance: the adaptive markets hypothesis. J Invest Consult 7:21–44

Luxen MF, Van De Vijver FJR (2006) Facial attractiveness, sexual selection, and personnel selection: when evolved preferences matter. J Organ Behav 27:241–255

Lycett JE, Dunbar RIM (2000) Mobile phones as lekking devices among human males. Hum Nat 11:93–104

Malamuth NM (1996) Sexually explicit media, gender differences, and evolutionary theory. J Commun 46:8–31

Marmot M (2004) The status syndrome: how social standing affects our health and longevity. Times Books, New York

Marsden P (2002) Brand positioning: meme's the word. Mark Intell Plann 20:307–312

Marsden PS (1998) Memetics: a new paradigm for understanding customer behaviour and influence. Mark Intell Plann 16:363–368

Massey GR (1999) Product evolution: a Darwinian or Lamarckian phenomenon? J Prod Brand Manage 8:301–318

McCall BP, Cavanaugh MA, Arvey RD, Taubman P (1997) Genetic influences on job and occupational switching. J Vocat Behav 50:60–77

McDermott R, Fowler JH, Smirnov O (2008) On the evolutionary origin of prospect theory preferences. J Polit 70:335–350

Mendenhall Z, Nepomuceno M, Saad G (2010a) Exploring video games from an evolutionary psychological perspective. In: Lee I (ed) Encyclopedia of e-business development and management in the global economy. IGI Global, Hershey, pp 734–742

Mendenhall Z, Saad G, Nepomuceno MV (2010b) *Homo virtualensis*: evolutionary psychology as a tool for studying videogames. In: Kock N (ed) Evolutionary psychology and information systems research: a new approach to studying the effects of modern technologies on human behavior. Springer, Heidelberg, pp 305–328

Mesko N, Bereczkei T (2004) Hairstyle as an adaptive means of displaying phenotypic quality. Hum Nat 15:251–270

Meyer-Emerick N (2007) Public administration and the life sciences. Adm Soc 38:689–708

Milinski M, Wedekind C (2001) Evidence for MHC-correlated perfume preferences in humans. Behav Ecol 12:140–149

Miller G (2009) Spent: sex, evolution, and consumer behavior. Viking Adult, New York

Miller G, Tybur JM, Jordan BD (2007) Ovulatory cycle effects on tip earnings by lap dancers: economic evidence for human estrus? Evol Hum Behav 28:375–381

Moss G, Hamilton C, Neave N (2007) Evolutionary factors in design preferences. J Brand Manage 14:313–323

Mueller U, Mazur A (1996) Facial dominance of West Point cadets as a predictor of later military rank. Soc Forces 74:823–850

Mysterud I, Drevon T, Slagsvold T (2006) An evolutionary interpretation of gift-giving behavior in modern Norwegian society. Evol Psychol 4:406–425

Nabhan GP (2004) Why some like it hot: food, genes and cultural diversity. Island Press, Washington, DC

New J, Krasnow MM, Truxaw D, Gaulin SJC (2007) Spatial adaptations for plant foraging: women excel and calories count. Proc R Soc B Biol Sci 274:2679–2684

Nicholson N (2000) Executive instinct: managing the human animal in the information age. Crown Business, New York

Nicholson N (2008) Evolutionary psychology and family business: a new synthesis for theory, research, and practice. Fam Bus Rev XXI:103–118

Nicolaou N, Shane S, Cherkas L, Hunkin J, Spector TD (2008) Is the tendency to engage in entrepreneurship genetic? Manage Sci 54:167–179

Ohtsubo Y (2009) Adaptive ingredients against food spoilage in Japanese cuisine. Int J Food Sci Nutr 60:677–687

Palmer A (2000) Co-operation and competition: a Darwinian synthesis of relationship marketing. Eur J Mark 34:687–704

Payne C, Jaffe K (2005) Self seeks like: many humans choose their dog pets following rules used for assortative mating. J Ethol 23:15–18

Pech RJ (2003) Memetics and innovation: profit through balanced meme management. Eur J Innov Manage 6:111–117

Piazza J, Bering JM (2009) Evolutionary cyber-psychology: applying an evolutionary framework to Internet behavior. Comput Hum Behav 25:1258–1269

Platek SM, Keenan JP, Shackelford TK (eds) (2007) Evolutionary cognitive neuroscience. MIT Press, Cambridge

Pound N (2002) Male interest in visual cues of sperm competition risk. Evol Hum Behav 23:443–466

Roberts SC, Little AC, Lyndon A, Roberts J, Havlicek J, Wright RL (2009) Manipulation of body odour alters men's self-confidence and judgements of their visual attractiveness by women. Int J Cosmet Sci 31:47–54

Roy MM, Christenfeld NJS (2004) Do dogs resemble their owners? Psychol Sci 15:361–363
Rule NO, Ambady N (2008) The face of success: inferences from chief executive officers' appearance predict company profits. Psychol Sci 19:109–111
Rule NO, Ambady N (2009) She's got the look: inferences from female chief executive officers' faces predict their success. Sex Roles 61:644–652
Russell R (2009) A sex difference in facial contrast and its exaggeration by cosmetics. Perception 38:1211–1219
Saad G (2003) Evolution and political marketing. In: Peterson SA, Somit A (eds) Human nature and public policy: an evolutionary approach. Palgrave Macmillan, New York, pp 121–138
Saad G (2004) Applying evolutionary psychology in understanding the representation of women in advertisements. Psychol Mark 21:593–612
Saad G (2006a) Blame our evolved gustatory preferences. Young Consum 7:72–75
Saad G (2006b) Applying evolutionary psychology in understanding the Darwinian roots of consumption phenomena. Manage Decis Econ 27:189–201
Saad G (2007) The evolutionary bases of consumption. Lawrence Erlbaum, Mahwah
Saad G (2008a) Advertised waist-to-hip ratios of online female escorts: an evolutionary perspective. Int J e-Collaboration 4:40–50
Saad G (2008b) The collective amnesia of marketing scholars regarding consumers' biological and evolutionary roots. Market Theory 8:425–448
Saad G (2010a) Using the Internet to study human universals. In: Lee I (ed) Encyclopedia of e-business development and management in the global economy. IGI Global, Hershey, pp 719–724
Saad G (2010b) The Darwinian underpinnings of consumption. In: Maclaran P, Saren M, Stern B, Tadajewski M (eds) The handbook of marketing theory. Sage, London, pp 457–475
Saad G (2011a) Songs lyrics as windows to our evolved human nature. In: Andrews A, Carroll J (eds) The evolutionary review: art, science, culture, vol 2. SUNY Press, Albany, pp 127–133
Saad G (2011b) The consuming instinct: what juicy burgers, Ferraris, pornography, and gift giving reveal about human nature. Prometheus Books, Amherst
Saad G, Eba A, Sejean R (2009) Sex differences when searching for a mate: a process-tracing approach. J Behav Decis Mak 22:171–190
Saad G, Gill T (2000) Applications of evolutionary psychology in marketing. Psychol Market 17:1005–1034
Saad G, Gill T (2001) Sex differences in the ultimatum game: an evolutionary psychology perspective. J Bioecon 3:171–193
Saad G, Gill T (2003) An evolutionary psychology perspective on gift giving among young adults. Psychol Market 20:765–784
Saad G, Gill T, Nataraajan R (2005) Are laterborns more innovative and non-conforming consumers than firstborns? A Darwinian perspective. J Bus Res 58:902–909
Saad G, Peng A (2006) Applying Darwinian principles in designing effective intervention strategies: the case of sun tanning. Psychol Market 23:617–638
Saad G, Stenstrom E (2010) Calories, beauty, and ovulation: the effects of the menstrual cycle on food and appearance-related consumption. Working paper, Concordia University, Canada
Saad G, Vongas JG (2009) The effect of conspicuous consumption on men's testosterone levels. Organ Behav Hum Decis Process 110:80–92
Salamon SD, Deutsch Y (2006) OCB as a handicap: an evolutionary psychological perspective. J Organ Behav 27:185–199
Salter F, Grammer K, Rikowski A (2005) Sex differences in negotiating with powerful males: an ethological analysis of approaches to nightclub doormen. Hum Nat 16:306–321
Samson N, Fink B, Matts PJ (2010) Visible skin condition and perception of human facial appearance. Int J Cosmet Sci 32:167–184
Sapienza P, Zingales L, Maestripieri D (2009) Gender differences in financial risk aversion and career choices are affected by testosterone. Proc Natl Acad Sci USA 106:15268–15273

Scott SC (1993) Visual attributes related to preference in interior environments. J Inter Des 18:7–16

Sherman PW, Billing J (1999) Darwinian gastronomy: why we use spices. BioScience 49:453–463

Sherman PW, Hash GA (2001) Why vegetable recipes are not very spicy. Evol Hum Behav 22:147–163

Shoemaker PJ (1996) Hardwired for news: using biological and cultural evolution to explain the surveillance function. J Commun 46:32–47

Shuler GA, McCord DM (2010) Determinants of male attractiveness: "Hotness" ratings as a function of perceived resources. Am J Psychol Res 6: 10–23. Accessed at http://www.mcneese.edu/ajpr/issues.html on 2 Feb 2010

Simonson I, Sela A (2011) On the heritability of consumer decision making: an exploratory approach for studying genetic effects on judgment and choice. J Cons Res 37:951–966

Singh D, Randall PK (2007) Beauty is in the eye of the plastic surgeon: waist-hip ratio (WHR) and women's attractiveness. Pers Individ Differ 43:329–340

Smith EO (1999) High heels and evolution: natural selection, sexual selection and high heels. Psychol Evol Gend 1:245–277

Spinella M (2003) Evolutionary mismatch, neural reward circuits, and pathological gambling. Int J Neurosci 113:503–512

Spink A (2010) Information behavior: an evolutionary instinct. Springer, Heidelberg

Spitz J (1998) Human nature and judicial interpretation of equal employment law. Manage Decis Econ 19:521–535

Steiner ET, Barchard KA, Meana M, Hadi F, Gray PB (2010) The deal on testosterone responses to poker competition. Curr Psychol 29:45–51

Stenstrom E, Saad G (2010) The neurocognitive and evolutionary bases of sex differences in website design preferences: recommendations for e-business managers. In: Lee I (ed) Encyclopedia of e-business development and management in the global economy. IGI Global, Hershey, pp 725–733

Stenstrom E, Stenstrom P, Saad G, Cheikhrouhou S (2008) Online hunting and gathering: an evolutionary perspective on sex differences in website preferences and navigation. IEEE Trans Prof Commun 51:155–168

Sundie JM, Kenrick DT, Griskevicius V, Tybur JM, Vohs KD, Beal DJ (2010) Peacocks, Porsches, and Thorstein Veblen: conspicuous consumption as a sexual signaling system. J Pers Soc Psychol doi: 10.1037/a0021669

Tooby J, Cosmides L (1992) Psychological foundations of culture. In: Barkow JH, Cosmides L, Tooby J (eds) The adapted mind: evolutionary psychology and the generation of culture. Oxford University Press, New York, pp 19–136

Townsend JM, Levy GD (1990) Effects of potential partners' costume and physical attractiveness on sexuality and partner selection. J Psychol 124:371–389

Tsui E (1999) Evolutionary architecture: nature as a basis for design. Wiley, New York

Uller T, Johansson LC (2003) Human mate choice and the wedding ring effect: are married men more attractive? Hum Nat 14:267–276

Van den Bergh B, Dewitte S, Warlop L (2008) Bikinis instigate generalized impatience in intertemporal choice. J Consum Res 35:85–97

Van Vugt M (2006) Evolutionary origins of leadership and followership. Pers Soc Psychol Rev 10:354–371

Vredenburgh D, Shea-VanFossen R (2010) Human nature, organizational politics, and human resource development. Hum Res Dev Rev 9:26–47

Waksberg AJ, Smith AB, Burd M (2009) Can irrational behaviour maximise fitness? Behav Ecol Sociobiol 63:461–471

Wallenstein G (2008) The pleasure instinct: why we crave adventure, chocolate, pheromones, and music. Wiley, New York

Walsh A (2000) Evolutionary psychology and the origins of justice. Justice Q 17:841–864

Wang XT, Dvorak RD (2010) Sweet future: fluctuating blood glucose levels affect future discounting. Psychol Sci 21:183–188
Wasieleski DM, Hayibor S (2009) Evolutionary psychology and business ethics research. Bus Ethics Q 19:587–616
Wedekind C, Escher S, Van de Waal M, Frei E (2007) The major histocompatibility complex and perfumers' descriptions of human body odors. Evol Psychol 5:330–343
White RE, Thornhill S, Hampson E (2006) Entrepreneurs and evolutionary biology: the relationship between testosterone and new venture creation. Organ Behav Hum Decis Process 100:21–34
Whyte J (2007) Evolutionary theories and design practices. Des Issues 23:46–54
Wilson EO (1998) Consilience: the unity of knowledge. Abacus, London
Wilson M, Daly M (2004) Do pretty women inspire men to discount the future? Proc R Soc Lond B Suppl 271:S177–S179
Windhager S, Slice DE, Schaefer K, Oberzaucher E, Thorstensen T, Grammer K (2008) Face to face: the perception of automotive designs. Hum Nat 19:331–346
Wrangham R (2009) Catching fire: how cooking made us human. Basic Books, New York
Wrangham R, Conklin-Brittain NL (2003) Cooking as a biological trait. Comp Biochem Physiol A 136:35–46
Zak PJ (2008) The neurobiology of trust. Sci Am June:88–95
Zak PJ, Stanton AA, Ahmadi S (2007) Oxytocin increases generosity in humans. PLoS ONE 2 (11):e1128. doi:10.1371/journal.pone.0001128
Ziman J (ed) (2000) Technological innovation as an evolutionary process. Cambridge University Press, Cambridge

Fundamental Motives and Business Decisions

Vladas Griskevicius, Joshua M. Ackerman, Bram Van den Bergh, and Yexin Jessica Li

Abstract You walk into a crowded negotiation room. Who do you notice? Who do you later remember? Do you try to fit in, or attempt to stand out from others? Do you accept the first reasonable offer, or do you balk at that offer? The answers likely depend critically on your current motivational state. Emerging evidence shows that a person's behavior differs—sometimes dramatically—depending on whether that person is concerned with personal safety, romance, status-seeking, affiliation, or is motivated to attain some other evolutionary important goal. A growing body of research suggests that certain motivational states are considered "fundamental" in a biological sense because of their implications for evolutionary fitness. In this chapter, we overview the fundamental motives framework, highlighting its applications for business decision-making in marketing, management, entrepreneurship, and finance. We then review recent research that has used this approach to study specific business-relevant topics such as risky financial decision-making, negotiation, advertising, and innovation. Bridging evolutionary biology and business, the fundamental motives framework not only provides novel insights into workplace decisions, but also holds promise as a powerful approach for understanding how behavior in business contexts connects to other aspects of human and animal behavior.

Keywords Motivation · Marketing · Decision-making · Decision biases · Advertising

V. Griskevicius (✉)
Carlson School of Management, University of Minnesota, 321 Nineteenth Avenue South, Suite 3-150 Minneapolis, MN 55455-0438, USA

J.M. Ackerman
Massachusetts Institute of Technology, Cambridge, MA, USA

B. Van den Bergh
Erasmus University, Rotterdam, Netherlands

Y.J. Li
Arizona State University, Tempe, AZ, USA

1 Fundamental Motives and Business Decisions

Consider the following questions. Why is it that:

- The rules of rational economic choice cannot explain most everyday resource exchanges (Kenrick et al. 2008)?
- People are exceptionally good at solving normally difficult logical problems if such problems are framed in terms of catching a cheater on a social contract (Cosmides and Tooby 1992)?
- Young men choose riskier retirement portfolios than women (Sundén and Surette 1998)?
- Many organizations have rules against nepotism, even though people are more likely to trust, and less likely to cheat, family members (Ackerman et al. 2007)?

In what follows, we will argue that each of these questions, as well the whole range of questions about risky decisions, innovation, negotiation, cooperation, and advertising, can be better answered by an understanding of an emerging set of ideas at the intersection of evolutionary biology, economics, physical and cultural anthropology, and cognitive science.

Consider the following situation. You walk into a crowded negotiation room. Who do you notice? Who do you later remember? Do you try to fit in, or attempt to stand out from others? Do you accept the first reasonable offer, or do you balk at that offer? The answers likely depend critically on your current motivational state. Emerging evidence shows that behavioral responses toward other people differ—sometimes dramatically—depending on whether individual decision-makers are concerned with personal safety, are interested in romance, or are motivated to attain some other evolutionary important goal. Indeed, a growing body of research suggests that certain motivational states, considered "fundamental" in a biological sense, produce adaptively functional effects relevant to information processing and decision-making.

In the first part of this chapter, we overview the fundamental motives framework and highlight its applications for a number of business decision-making arenas, including marketing, management, entrepreneurship, and finance. We then review recent research that has used this approach to study specific business-relevant topics such as risky decision-making, negotiation, advertising, and innovation. Bridging evolutionary biology and business, the fundamental motives framework not only provides novel insights into workplace decisions, but also holds promise as a powerful approach for understanding how behavior in business contexts connects to other aspects of human and animal behavior.

2 The Fundamental Motives Framework

From an evolutionary perspective, motivational systems have been shaped by natural and sexual selection to produce behaviors that increase reproductive fitness. For any social animal, including *Homo sapiens*, reproduction involves much more than sex. To reproduce successfully—to produce viable offspring and raise them to reproductive age—human beings must achieve many subsidiary goals, including affiliation, self-protection, status attainment, mate-attraction, mate-retention, and child-rearing. Some of these goals may at first glance appear similar (e.g., finding mates, making friends, and caring for children are all associated with rewards and concomitant "positive" feelings), but these goals are qualitatively distinct: Successful attainment of each goal requires different—and sometimes opposing—cognitive and behavioral responses. An emerging literature at the intersection of evolutionary biology and cognitive science suggests that these goals are managed by distinct motivational systems (Kenrick et al. 2010; Schaller et al. 2007). This research suggests that achieving goals within different evolutionarily recurring goal "domains," such as self-protection and mate-attraction, are facilitated by distinct motivational systems. Given the important implications that these goals have had for reproductive fitness and human evolution, the underlying motives can be considered "fundamental."

This domain-specific approach to human motivation is consistent with a wealth of research on both human and non-human animals, showing that conceptually distinct adaptive problems often invoke psychologically distinct cognitive systems (e.g., Cosmides and Tooby 1992; Kenrick and Luce 2000). For example, birds use distinct, domain-specific neuropsychological systems for learning and remembering information about species song, poisonous foods, and spatial position of food caches. Similarly, humans use distinct, domain-specific systems and neural architectures for learning and remembering words, faces, and nausea-inducing foods (e.g., Klein et al. 2002; Öhman and Mineka 2001; Sherry and Schacter 1987).

The key implication of the fundamental motives framework for business decisions is that solving problems in different motivational domains often requires qualitatively different solutions. That is, the different fundamental domains are associated with different domain-specific decision-biases. For example, there are important documented distinctions between the exchange rules and decision-making biases involving the domains of affiliation, self-protection, status, mate attraction, mate retention, and kin care (e.g., Ackerman and Kenrick 2008; Schaller et al. 2007). This means that people use somewhat different exchange rules when interacting with workplace friends and allies (*affiliation*), dangerous and threatening others (*self-protection*), competitors and superiors (*status*), opposite-sex co-workers (*mate-search*), a spouse (*mate-retention*), or relatives (*kin care*). In Table 1 we present an overview of this framework, outlining the domains of social life and their associated fundamental goals, as well as the evolutionary biological theories associated with each domain.

Because different social domains involve somewhat different exchange rules, each domain—and each fundamental motive system—is associated with specific types of adaptive biases and motives (e.g., Ackerman and Kenrick 2008; Sundie et al. 2006). We highlight some of these documented biases in Table 1. For example, self-protection concerns lead people to be more conforming; status concerns lead men to take more risks; and mate-attraction concerns lead women to become more agreeable (Ermer et al. 2007; Griskevicius et al. 2006b). A key

Table 1 Different fundamental social domains and motives, associated evolutionary theories, documented domain-specific decision biases, and examples of business applications

Social domain & Associated goal	Relevant evolutionary theories & Social exchange rules	Typical decision biases	Business applications
Affiliation Form and maintain cooperative alliances	*Reciprocal Altruism & Social Contract Theory*: Equality between close associates	Sensitivity to reciprocity and fairness violations Propensity to conform when feeling isolated Sensitivity to others' trustworthiness Women more likely to treat close others communally	New employees should highly value social capital Productive teams of friends should be kept together and not encouraged to compete within group, though between-team competition may be beneficial Equality violations should be addressed immediately Group membership certainty (e.g., job security) important for stimulating creative thinking
Status Gain and maintain social status	*Intra-Sexual Selection & Dominance Hierarchy*: Superiors provide resources & protection in exchange for assistance & support	Risk-taking more attractive for young unmated men and less attractive for women Reputational concerns of male dominance & female cooperativeness Power stability concerns	Create rules for promotion that account for males' relatively stronger tendency to seek status, even when females are well-qualified Modify stability of leadership roles to influence degree of risk-taking behavior Increase awareness about the presence of potential mates on male status-seeking
Self-Protection Protect oneself and valued others from threats	*Coalitional Psychology & Universal Fear Mechanisms*: Strict tit-for-tat with outgroup members	Overestimation of anger in males Enhanced attention to threat cues and increased memory for angry out-group faces Increased ingroup cooperation (in males) and conformity under threat	Presence of outgroup threat can elevate ingroup allegiance and acquiescence Reduce perception of external threats to increase ingroup's outside-the-box thinking Manage all threat and outgroup cues prior to interactions

Motive	Theory	Effects	Business implications
Mate Attraction Attract desirable mates	*Inter-Sexual Selection & Parental Investment*: Females exchange youth, health and fertility for male resources and/or long-term commitment	Propensity to become more creative Males become impatient and resist conformity Females become more agreeable and outwardly altruistic Competition between similar, unfamiliar others; cooperation with close others	Cues to potential mates can be used to increase creativity, problem-solving abilities, and public help-giving During negotiations, mating cues may promote evaluation and barrier-building in women, and active barrier-breaking in men
Mate Retention Retain and foster long-term mating bonds	*Attachment Theory & Strategic Interference Theory*: Communal sharing with relationship partner, diminished attention to equity	Attention by women to other physically attractive women Attention by men to other socially dominant men Inattention to attractive opposite-sex individuals Stronger focus on resource preservation than resource display	The same mating cues may focus single and romantically committed people on different target attributes In negotiations and advertising and product development, using a mix of single and committed team members may prevent "tunnel vision"
Kin Care Invest in and care for offspring and genetic relatives	*Kin Selection & Inclusive Fitness*: Intrinsically lopsided exchange from parents to offspring	Relative insensitivity to inequity between relatives (discounted by degree of relatedness) Grandparental investment highest by grandmother in daughter's offspring Allowable violations of many social norms (e.g., reactance more common)	Nepotism useful for increasing cooperation and preventing selfish cheating Nepotism may impede creativity and innovation Family members make good team members, but bad objective evaluators Fictive kinship can be used in situations lacking actual relatedness

implication of this framework is that the same information from the environment may be interpreted and acted upon very differently depending on which motivational system has been primed to process this information (Griskevicius et al. 2009a; Kenrick et al. 2010; Maner et al. 2005). Because ecological cues related to a specific domain are known to trigger a specific fundamental motivational system, people interpret and act upon incoming information differently depending on whether they have been primed with self-protection cues (e.g., they recently read a news story about a murder), mate-search cues (e.g., they recently saw an attractive opposite-sex individual), status cues (e.g., they recently heard about a promotion), affiliation cues (e.g., they were recently socially rejected), or kin care cues (e.g., they recently saw a photos of their child). The mere exposure to these types of cues is known to trigger a cascade of goal-directed perceptions, cognitions, and behavioral strategies, leading individuals to interpret and act upon the same information in different ways (e.g., Bargh 2006; Maner et al. 2007; Griskevicius et al. 2009a, b).

A theoretical framework focusing on fundamental motives provides texture and predictive specificity to supplement traditional ways of conceptualizing motivational systems. For instance, compare the fundamental motives framework with conceptualizations that characterize motives according to approach versus avoidance behavior, or according to an association with positive versus negative affect (Kenrick and Shiota 2008). Although useful, these dichotomous classification schemes often fail to capture the psychologically distinct nature of specific motivational states, limiting their ability to successfully predict the specific ways in which fitness-relevant motivational states orchestrate social cognition and behavior.

For example, being insulted to your face or seeing a scorpion on the ground might trigger either approach behaviors or avoidance behaviors, depending on currently active motivations in concert with functionally relevant environmental cues. A person might respond very differently to the insult if he's feeling fear versus anger, and respond differently to the scorpion on the rug near one's child versus on a rock in the desert. As these examples suggest, positive and negative affect are not always directly correlated with approach and avoidance behaviors, and the same stimulus may be regarded as positive or negative depending on motivation and functional context. The fundamental motives framework has generated numerous lines of research drawing directly on theories from evolutionary biology and psychology to predict *a priori* a highly-textured set of cognitive and behavioral responses to functionally relevant events (e.g., Ackerman and Kenrick 2008; Maner et al. 2005; Ackerman et al. 2009; Kenrick et al. 2010).

3 Fundamental Motives and Different Areas of Business Behavior

In Table 1 we provide examples of how the adaptive decision-biases associated with each fundamental motive can manifest themselves in business decisions. Because consumers, managers, suppliers, and employees are likely to behave differently depending on which fundamental motive system has been primed, this framework has vast implications for marketing, management, entrepreneurship, and finance. Indeed, evolution-inspired research has begun to reveal a number of interesting findings on negotiation, group performance, innovation, advertising, and other business-relevant behaviors (e.g., Griskevicius et al. 2009a, b; Colarelli 2003; Saad 2007; Van den Bergh et al. 2008). Although the implications of evolutionary thinking for business remain largely unexplored, in the remainder of the chapter we review some of the emerging research from these areas. After highlighting how an evolutionary approach can add insight into each area, we review recent findings in each area consistent with the fundamental motives framework. These findings suggest that the fundamental motives framework can be applied to improve worker performance, steer consumer decisions, and improve management strategies.

3.1 Persuasion and Advertising

Getting people to adopt a new product or idea can be difficult. Seventy-five to ninety percent of new products fail to catch on, and more than half of new businesses fail within the first 4 years (Ogawa and Piller 2006). To compete for a limited number of consumer dollars, companies use a variety of advertising tactics. Although there may initially appear to be a plethora of different tactics, many effective advertising tactics are rooted in a small number of persuasion principles (Cialdini 2008), including the principle of *Scarcity* (people value things that are rare or scarce) and the principle of *Social Proof* (people look to the behavior of similar others when they are unsure how to behave). Both of these persuasion principles are known to increase the effectiveness of ads and sales pitches, which leads them to be widely used in marketing strategies and consistently appear on a short list of proven persuasion tactics (e.g., Hoyer and MacInnis 2006; Myers 2004; Pratkanis and Aronson 2000; Solomon 2004).

Persuasion tactics based on these principles generally work as heuristic cues. Although scholars have been investigating decision heuristics for several decades, few researchers have considered their implications from an evolutionary perspective. The study of decision heuristics has typically been conducted with primary focus on heuristics as built-in biases in judgment, which can regularly produce decision errors or irrational choices (e.g., Nisbett and Ross 1980; Kahneman et al. 1982). From an evolutionary perspective, however, heuristics are seen as efficient and accurate solutions to recurring adaptive problems; the use of such heuristics results in solutions that are, on average, quick and effective (e.g., Gigerenzer and Selten 2001; Gigerenzer et al. 1999). For instance, while the heuristic tendency to follow an expert might periodically lead to a bad decision, following this heuristic will usually lead to much better choices than choosing at random. Relying on these heuristics helps individuals not only make fast and effective decisions, but also enables people to negotiate adaptive problems of social living. For example, the sense of obligation to reciprocate a gift, the tendency to value scarce items, and the desire to say "yes" to people we like, all have highly plausible evolutionary underpinnings (Sundie et al. 2006).

A consideration of fundamental motives leads to novel predictions regarding when such heuristics should be especially effective in persuasion, and when they might backfire. Recall that different types of affectively arousing stimuli, such as an attractive opposite-sex individual or a threatening out-group male, can prime different fundamental motive systems. This consideration raises the question of how affective arousal might influence the persuasiveness of heuristics. Several well-established domain-general theoretical models make predictions about how arousal and affect might influence the effectiveness of persuasion heuristics. Arousal-based models predict that arousal should generally inhibit deep processing, meaning that any state of arousal would increase the effectiveness of heuristics (Pham 1996; Sonbonmatsu and Kardes 1988). Affective valence-based models, on the other hand, differentiate between positive and negative feelings, predicting a different pattern for each of these two types of affect (e.g., Schwarz and Bless 1991). According to such dual-process models, positive feelings should lead to shallower processing and increased effectiveness of heuristics. In contrast, negative feelings should lead to more careful processing and decreased effectiveness of persuasion heuristics.

The fundamental motives framework predicts yet a different pattern, suggesting that different affective states should lead people to be persuaded by some types of heuristic cues but not by others. For example, this framework suggests that the same affective state might lead one heuristic to be more effective, while leading another heuristic to be less effective. These competing predictions were tested across a series of experiments in which people watched a video clip that activated self-protection motives (an arousing negative affect state) or mate-attraction motives (an arousing positive affect state) (Griskevicius et al. 2009a, b). People then viewed ads for various products, whereby the ads contained heuristic appeals either to social proof (e.g., "over a million sold") or to scarcity (e.g., "limited edition").

The findings across studies were consistent with predictions made from by the fundamental motives framework, but were not consistent with predictions made either by arousal models (which predict that both arousing states of fear and romantic desire should lead all heuristics to be more effective) or by affect-based dual-process models (which predict that the positive affect state of romantic desire should make heuristics more effective, whereas the negative affect state of fear should lead them to be less effective). Instead, consistent with predictions from the fundamental motives framework, self-protection motives led social proof heuristics to be *more* effective, while leading scarcity heuristics to be *less* effective (Griskevicius et al. 2009a, b). Consistent with the evolutionary self-protection strategy of safety in numbers (Alcock 2005), when people were scared, they were especially eager to blend in with the crowd and especially unwilling to be unique. In contrast, mate-attraction motives led scarcity appeals to be *more* persuasive, while leading social proof appeals to be significantly *less* persuasive (Griskevicius et al. 2009a, b). Consistent with the evolutionary mate-attraction strategy of salient positive differentiation (Miller 2000), people in a romantic state were especially eager to stand out and especially unwilling to purchase the same product that is already owned by over a million others.

These findings have important theoretical and practical implications. First, the predictions that were derived from an evolutionary model were different from those of two other theoretical models, demonstrating clearly how an evolutionary approach can generate novel and testable business-relevant hypotheses. Second, these findings have implications for advertisers. For instance, although television advertisers have traditionally relied on viewer demographic information to determine where and when to purchase airtime, a fundamental motives approach suggests that they might more carefully consider the content of the specific program during which their ads will air. For example, while touting the uniqueness of a product might be effective during a program that elicits romantic desire, the same ad aired during a fear-eliciting program such as a police drama might actually make the same product unappealing. Conversely, explicitly stating that a product is a best-seller should be especially effective during a fear-eliciting program, but it likely to be counter-effective if used during a romantic show (for more on how evolutionary approaches can inform advertising see Ambler and Hollier 2004; Colarelli and Dettman 2003; Saad 2004, 2007).

3.2 Innovation and Creativity

Innovation and creativity drive the development of new products and ideas. Not surprisingly, organizational departments such as marketing and R&D generally want their employees to be maximally creative, often providing sizable financial incentives for innovative ideas and products. Evolutionary considerations of the origins and function of creativity (e.g., Simonton 1999), however, suggests that people are more responsive to some types of incentives than others. That is, research we discuss below suggests that activating fundamental motives related to mating may naturally spur people to be more creative. To understand why, it is important to consider first how human creativity may have evolved.

It was initially presumed that our creative abilities evolved because they somehow enhanced the likelihood of our ancestors' survival. But this presumption failed to explain several key features of creativity: Not only have other large-brained animals not evolved similar creativity capacities (suggesting that creativity, per se, is not necessarily pertinent to survival), but many human displays of creativity are highly valued socially, yet are difficult to explain in terms of survival value. For example, a farmer produces more tangible survival benefits in a week than a team of musicians, poets, and sculptors will likely produce in a lifetime. Yet a provocative melody, poem, or sculpture is likely to elicit greater appreciation than an absolutely perfect melon, potato, or zucchini.

Instead of providing direct survival benefits, theorists have proposed that creativity and our abilities to innovate may have evolved via sexual selection (Miller 2000). Unlike natural selection, whereby traits evolve solely because they enhance the probability of an individual's survival, Darwin (1871) suggested that some traits, such as the elaborate plumage of peacocks, evolve via sexual selection— they evolve because they enhance an individual's ability to attract a mate (Gould and Gould 1989). Supporting this viewpoint, human creativity has multiple features in common with sexually selected traits across species. Just as members of various species prefer partners with prominent sexually selected traits such as brilliant tails, humans—especially when women are choosing men—show a desire for creativity in a romantic partner (Buss and Barnes 1986; Li et al. 2002). Sexually selected traits across species also tend to function as markers of genetic quality (Møller and Petrie 2002; Zahavi and Zahavi 1997). The peacock with the most impressive tail, for example, by definition possesses high genetic quality: Not only has he survived despite having such a burdensome and costly ornament, but also the brightness and symmetry of his tail indicate his ability to find food and resist infection. Creativity may provide a similar function in humans.

Consistent with the premise that creativity has in part evolved via sexual selection, research shows that mating motives can produce boosts in creativity. For example, men who have just seen photos of attractive women—activating a mate-attraction motive—are more creative (Griskevicius et al. 2006a). Presenting men with cues of attractive and sexy women led these men to solve more problems that required creative thinking and to write stories that were judged as more creative. Moreover, men primed with mating cues were more innovative in solving problems even when compared to a group of men who had a monetary incentive to be creative (Griskevicius et al. 2006a). Thus, in the same way that the presence of peahens leads peacocks to instinctively display their ornate tails, the presence of cues suggesting a mating opportunity appears to lead men to instinctively display their creativity.

It is noteworthy that mate-attraction goals led men but not women to become more creative. This sex-specific effect is consistent with the fact that ornate sexually selected traits are much more likely to occur in mammalian males than females. This sex difference stems from the fact that most males in the animal kingdom provide little to no care for offspring, meaning that females are much choosier when it comes to selecting a mate (Trivers 1972; also see Buss and Schmitt 1993). Unlike most mammals, however, human males in long-term relationships do provide significant care for offspring. This difference suggests that while women should not necessarily be motivated to display creativity to attract men for brief romantic relationships, women should be motivated to display creativity when trying to maintain a relationship with a romantic partner (i.e., when women have an active motive for mate retention). Indeed, when women were primed with thoughts of wanting to stay with an ideal romantic partner, they also became more creative (Griskevicius et al. 2006a).

In sum, evolutionary research suggests that the desire to impress and to retain the opposite sex is a powerful motivator in human ingenuity. These findings have intriguing implications for fostering innovation in the workplace. For example, brain storming sessions may benefit from a mixed-gender composition, R&D and other creative departments may put extra emphasis on achieving gender balance within ideation groups, and exposure to opposite-sex individuals might be encouraged in office seating styles (e.g., cubicles vs. an open-bullpen office) when creative thinking is needed. It is important to note that these suggestions are not designed to foster office romance, but having these romantic cues in the environment—even subtle strategies such as imagining potential romantic partners before beginning work on a project—may provide better results than typical monetary incentives alone.

3.3 Intertemporal Choice, Self-Control, and Risk

Organizational leaders need to balance the trade-off between short-term results and long-term strategic planning. Consumers need to balance similar types of trade-offs, as when considering the short-term benefits and long-term consequences of eating chocolate cake. An evolutionary perspective suggests that these types of intertemporal trade-offs may be resolved differently depending on the fundamental motive system that has been primed to process the information. Before examining how different motives influence desire for immediate rewards, consider how humans have evolved to respond to rewards.

For most of human evolutionary history, it has been adaptive for our ancestors to value immediate rewards. A bird in the hand has always been better than two birds in the bush. The evolutionarily-recent transition from being hunters-gatherers to farmers had important consequences for these time-preferences (Tucker 2006). Whereas hunter-gatherers focus on short-term returns because their labor is often rewarded the same day, farmers need to adopt a more farsighted perspective because they need to wait several months to begin to see the fruits of their labor. These changes in resource acquisition and lifestyle decisions were made possible by an enhanced ability to exert self-control, delay gratification in the service of more beneficial long-term outcomes. However, when our ancestors shifted from foraging to food production, our evolved short-term preferences were not eradicated. People in present-day societies often still weigh immediate outcomes more heavily than more distant ones.

Consistent with our evolutionary history, neuroscientific evidence shows that immediate and delayed rewards appear to be governed by different neural systems (McClure et al. 2004). For example, evolutionarily-older brain systems, such as the limbic system, are activated when choosing between immediate rewards (e.g., $1 right now or $2 tomorrow); but such older systems are less active when choosing between delayed rewards (e.g., $1 in 365 days or $2 in 366 days). In the latter case, the evolutionarily-recent pre-frontal cortex is more involved.

Although researchers have often considered one's ability to delay gratification as an individual difference, the ability to delay gratification is highly sensitive to evolutionarily-relevant contexts. Recent findings show that activation of ancient brain systems related to mating uncovers our myopic, hunter-gatherer-like preferences. The priming of mating cues leads men to place greater value on current rewards. For example, men who fondle lingerie become more impatient when choosing between smaller and earlier versus larger and later rewards (Van den Bergh et al. 2008). Similarly, men who viewed photos of attractive women chose to take less money now than a significantly larger amount of money in the future (Wilson and Daly 2004). These studies suggest that upon the priming of mating cues, men become impatient (i.e., prefer less money now over more money in the future).

Similar to the way in which humans have evolved to prefer immediate rewards, evidence from modern groups living in hunter-gatherer and horticultural societies suggests that people (and many other animals) are generally risk-averse, preferring to invest in activities with relatively low risks as opposed to those with potentially higher, but riskier, outcomes (Winterhalder 2007). Such risk aversion is also consistent with standard observation in market economics (Png and Lehman 2007) and helps to explain, at an evolutionary level, the ubiquitous gain-loss framing effects predicted by prospect theory (Kahneman and Tversky 1979).

Evolutionary approaches suggest that people's willingness to take risks should be highly sensitive to the fundamental motive system that is currently active. For example, given that self-protection is associated with vigilance and caution, self-protection cues are known to lead people to become risk-averse (Lerner and Keltner 2001). Other domain-specific cues, however, have been shown to increase risk-taking. Men's risky decision-making can be strongly influenced by whether their peers are watching their decisions: The presence of other men generally facilitates willingness to choose high-risk/high-gain gambles in young men (Daly and Wilson 2001). In fact, when men are primed with cues for competition and status, they take significantly more risks with their money (Ermer et al. 2008). In contrast, women's financial risk-taking appears to be unaffected by cues of vigilance or competition with other women. Research has yet to examine how activating the fundamental motives of kin care or mate-retention might influence risk-taking, but such domains are likely to have specific effects on risk-taking behavior (Kenrick et al. 2010).

The tendency for young males to be more risky than young females is clearly understandable through the evolutionary lens (Saad 2007). But these sex-specific tendencies can also have long-term economic consequences. For instance, young single men are generally more likely to adopt riskier investment strategies in their retirement packages than are women, and at retirement time those men tend to have earned, on average, substantially higher yields on their investments (Sundén and Surette 1998). The findings that activation of different fundamental motives can make people risk-takers or risk-avoiders have powerful implications for business decision-making. Many companies implicitly prime such motivations already (e.g., insurance companies highlight self-protective concerns when selling policies), and other companies may find it useful to employ motivational strategies with an understanding of their evolutionary implications. For example, investment brokers might activate specific fundamental motives when attempting to influence the level of risk their clients are willing to take in their investments.

3.4 Negotiation

When two or more parties, such as consumers and sellers, have a conflict of interest, they often will attempt to resolve this conflict through a process of negotiation and bargaining (Raffia 1982; Rubin and Brown 1975). This process can be tremendously complex, but typically involves a series of sequential proposals and decisions as one party attempts to maximize an element of the interaction (e.g., how much to charge for a product) and the other party attempts to minimize the same element (e.g., how much to pay for the product). From an evolutionary viewpoint, negotiation can be viewed as a social coordination problem that entails trade-offs between costs and benefits relevant to fundamental motivations (Ackerman and Kenrick 2008). These trade-offs are commonly studied in light of contextual and party-specific influences within negotiation games such as the Prisoner's Dilemma or Ultimatum Game (e.g., Axelrod 1984; Rubin and Brown 1975; Saad and Gill 2001a, b). Perceptions about these trade-offs can fluctuate depending on what fundamental motive is currently active (Ackerman and Kenrick 2008), changing people's behavior throughout the interaction. For example, status-relevant cues such as the presence of a briefcase and expensive pen lying innocuously in a negotiation room can reduce the amount proposed for opening offers (Kay et al. 2004), and exposure to attractive opposite-sex individuals increases the likelihood of accepting an unfair deal in bargaining situations (Van den Bergh and Dewitte 2006).

There are several basic difficulties involved in negotiations, all of which are candidates for evolutionary analysis. Perhaps the most important concern is the uncertainty inherent in such situations. Where should discussions take place? What is a given good worth? What opening proposal should I make? Is that company's representative telling the truth? Uncertainty represents a central problem from an evolutionary perspective. Individuals must detect interpersonal and environmental signals in ways that benefit the perceivers, understand which action to take in novel situations and make decisions that minimize costs. Unfortunately, the limits of cognitive capacity constrain these abilities, leading people to employ a range of fallible processing heuristics (e.g., Kahneman et al. 1982). Fortunately, these heuristics have been shaped by evolution to produce positive outcomes on average, at least when these outcomes are considered in terms of their functional relevance.

Consider the problem of detecting whether another party is being deceptive. A number of mental mechanisms can be brought to bear on this question. First, a person will likely use evolved "mind-reading" abilities (*theory of mind*) to intuit the other's knowledge and goals in that situation (Premack and Woodruff 1978). People also (unconsciously) perform complex signal detection analyses to identify and interpret the meaning of interpersonal cues (e.g., Ackerman et al. 2006; Ackerman et al. 2009; Becker et al. 2011). These analyses are shaped by both active motives and cognitive biases that tend to overweigh functionally costly errors, producing evolutionarily cautious responses (Haselton and Nettle 2006). This process tends to be positive for one's fundamental goal pursuit, but may impair current bargaining outcomes. For instance, if one party is a member of a group stereotypically associated with deceptiveness and lack of trust (e.g., lawyers), a self-protection motive may be activated (see Cottrell and Neuberg 2005; Cottrell et al. 2007). Because deception has been a recurrent problem over evolutionary time, people have evolved an inherent ability to detect and manage cheaters, especially within social exchange contexts (Cosmides and Tooby 1992). When a lawyer accompanies one party to a negotiation, activated motivations are liable to decrease trust and cause skeptical and intransigent responses from the other party. Unfortunately, the same is true when individuals are members of any groups associated with a lack of trust (e.g., in the U.S., Mexican-Americans; Cottrell and Neuberg 2005).

Cognitive mechanisms shaped by their functional utility for addressing ancestral problems also play a role in other aspects of negotiation, such as evaluation (e.g., determining the market value of an item), decision making (e.g., settling on a reservation price), time management (e.g., coping with impatience), and forecasting (e.g., judging how the recipient of an offer will respond). For instance, it is difficult to determine the real, experiential value of many goods and services (e.g., Ariely et al. 2006), but other, fitness-relevant goods are often inherently evaluable (Hsee et al. 2009). That is, people seemingly do not have a good sense of the absolute value of unique or abstract items (e.g., interest rates, listening to poetry readings, carats in a diamond), but they are innately able to make more accurate evaluations about functionally-relevant consumption experiences (e.g., drinking milk, feeling temperature, undergoing social isolation) (Hsee et al. 2009).

Evaluation, decision-making, and forecasting effects are influenced by interactions between personal and environmental factors. Consider the example of gender differences in negotiation outcomes. Past findings have indicated that men tend to outperform women when bargaining for themselves over salary and sale prices (see Bowles et al. 2005; Stuhlmacher and Walters 1999). Why would this be? One possibility is that these bargaining contexts take the form of competitive environments, whereas evolutionary theorizing and evidence suggests that women's interpersonal orientation tends to be more communally-focused (Ackerman et al. 2007; Cross and Madson 1997). In fact, research demonstrates that when women are asked to negotiate *for someone else*, they perform better both compared to men and compared to women negotiating for themselves (Bowles et al. 2005). We might expect that another method of producing communal feelings, activating the fundamental motive for kin care motive (e.g., by highlighting the family-run nature of a business), would help people achieve more profitable outcomes when acting as negotiators for their company or a third party. This motive may even lead to better outcomes for men than for women, as men would have more room to move in terms of their communal orientation. Although negotiation researchers have amassed a detailed understanding of negotiation dynamics, they may still place too little weight on functionally-important variables such as fundamental motives.

Given these types of findings, what techniques should an evolutionarily-minded negotiator be aware of or use to bargain more effectively? An understanding of fundamental motives implies that framing the interaction is of utmost importance. Placement of motive-relevant cues can powerfully influence decisions to accept or reject offers, even when those cues are incidental to the overall goal of the interaction (Ackerman and Kenrick 2008). For example, cues to self-protective threat (e.g., darkness, angry expressions, germs) are liable to negatively bias decisions and offers made by out-group members (e.g., companies that share an antagonistic relationship). Negotiators may thus want to pay special attention to the time of day and the state of health of the negotiating team. Interestingly, cues that prime self-protective threat may actually have a positive effect on perceptions of in-group members (e.g., employees of the same company) (Becker et al. 2011). People negotiating salaries or positions within a company may find better outcomes under these conditions. Similar outcomes should follow if a sense of affiliation can be established between parties (as underlies relationship marketing; Berry 1983). While motivated by affiliation, having others present may be a positive situation, but this is unlikely to be the case when status motives are active. Instead, the presence of an audience is likely to be aversive during negotiations over status changes (e.g., promotions, mergers) because status hierarchies tend to be primarily relevant to intragroup interactions (Ackerman and Kenrick 2008). One solution is to cast the audience as a status-irrelevant mediator of the negotiation (e.g., Pruitt and Johnson 1970).

Cues to yet another fundamental motive, mate search, may also produce complex outcomes within business deliberations (e.g., Griskevicius et al. 2006b). Consider a natural form of negotiation—courtship. Romantic courtship can be framed as a coordination problem in which one party plays the role of seller (in heterosexual interactions, often the man will attempt to "sell" his own suitability as a romantic partner), and another party plays the role of buyer (the woman will make the decision). In fact, women are especially likely to help each other construct romantic barriers and thresholds, whereas men are especially likely to help each other break down those barriers and overcome those thresholds (Ackerman and Kenrick 2009). If these patterns are representative of more general strategies, it may be that, during platonic bargaining, women perform better as cost-minimizing negotiators (i.e., buyers) and men as benefit-maximizing negotiators (i.e., sellers). Of course, the particular costs and benefits being negotiated are likely relevant; more so than men, women may sacrifice economic outcomes in favor of interpersonal capital such as the maintenance of social relationships (Curhan et al. 2008). Studies like the ones reviewed above highlight the importance of properly structuring cohesive negotiation teams (e.g., tailoring the gender and group makeup of teams) as well as negotiation environments (e.g., providing cues to affiliation, family, and even self-protective threat where appropriate).

3.5 *Helping, Generosity, and Cooperation*

Family businesses have always made up a substantial portion of the corporate world, with estimates as high as 90 % for all businesses in the United States, including 37 % of the Fortune 500 companies (The University of Tulsa College of

Business Administration 2000). Yet there is an intriguing difference between firms that are family-run versus those that are led by individuals who are unrelated to their employees: Family-run firms tend to perform better and operate more efficiently (McConaughy et al. 2001; Anderson and Reeb 2003), yet the nepotism they engender can lead to free-riding and worsening performance in subsequent generations (Perez-Gonzalez 2006; Villalonga and Amit 2006). This telling difference can be traced to the different motivational systems regulating our interactions with close kin versus those regulating interactions with friends and with strangers (see Nicholson 2008; Nicholson and Björnberg 2005). An understanding of these fundamental motive systems not only sheds light on why humans have not evolved to be perfectly selfish, but also on the circumstances that engender the most cooperation.

From an evolutionary perspective, the fact that people are quite helpful rather than completely selfish has always been puzzling. On the surface, natural selection would not appear to favor individuals who give away their own resources to benefit others. Some such helping, however, can be understood in light of the biological principle of kin selection (Hamilton 1964). *Kin selection* holds that individuals' actions are designed not so much to ensure the survival of the individual, but to ensure the survival of the genes making up that individual—genes that are shared with one's kin. Consistent with this principle, nepotistic biases are found across species, and individuals behave more benevolently towards others the more closely the givers are related to the recipients of the aid (e.g., Burnstein et al. 1994). For example, the value of gifts given to family members tracks the genetic relatedness those kin share (Saad and Gill 2003). After death, not only do people bequeath more than 92% of their assets to relatives, but descendants receive more money in relative proportion to the genetic overlap they share with the deceased individual (Smith et al. 1987).

Consideration of kin selection has important ramifications for decision-making. Consider the case of someone confronting a prisoner's dilemma-type decision involving either a brother or an unrelated group member. Because a brother shares roughly 50% of the decision-maker's genes, the decision-maker can be expected to devalue outcomes in which his brother does poorly at a small gain to himself (Kenrick et al. 2008). This has tremendous implications for business decisions: Competition for a bonus between strangers in the workplace may manifest itself as cooperation between relatives in a family-controlled firm. Successful joint tasks between strangers might lead to individual credit-taking, whereas the same situation might lead to credit-giving between kin (Ackerman et al. 2007). Essentially, conflicts that are zero-sum games for unrelated strangers might well be transformed into cooperative games for kin. Of course, this is true across cultures as well: "Chinese companies are almost always family firms. A Chinese proverb says— with less whimsy and more hard-nosed sense than most—'You can only trust close relatives'" (Fritz 1997:51).

The theory of kin selection, however, fails to explain helping toward non-relatives. Evolutionary theorists have explained such non-kin helping in light of the theory of *reciprocal altruism* (Trivers 1971), whereby individuals help non-relatives because the helpers benefit by being helped in return. For instance, people and many species of animals are much more likely to help someone who can reciprocate the favor in the future (e.g., Fehr et al. 1997). Even without a strong reliance on reciprocity, certain non-kin can also receive the interpersonal benefits that accompany familial relationships. For instance, people who share similar attitudes to us are implicitly associated with kinship concepts (Park and Schaller 2005), and people with whom we share a superficial facial resemblance tend to inspire increased trust (DeBruine 2002). Such cues, along with repeated positive interactions, can lead to the formation of friendship and even "psychological kinship" (Bailey 1988). Interestingly, the nature of interactions among ancestral humans may have predisposed women, more than men, to treat their friends like kin. Thus, under everyday conditions, women show more cooperative and less self-serving tendencies with their friends than do men (Ackerman et al. 2007). The evolved mechanisms that produce psychological kinship can be leveraged to increase altruistic tendencies in the kin-free business world. By priming a kin care motive through the use of fictive kinship terminology and (especially) behavior, intra-office altruism may increase, and less time may be spent on needless competitive pursuits.

Yet kin selection, reciprocal altruism, and psychological kinship all cannot fully explain helping such as large philanthropic gifts to non-kin or even handouts to beggars who will never reciprocate these favors. For instance, it is difficult to understand from these perspectives why 70% of U.S. households give money to charity or why nearly 10 million Americans each year give blood to strangers whom they will never meet. The key to understanding such behaviors from an evolutionary perspective lies in the importance of building and maintaining reputations (Griskevicius et al. 2010; Semmann et al. 2005). Earning a reputation as a cooperative and helpful group member is extremely valuable: Individuals with such reputations are not only seen as more trustworthy (Barclay 2004), but they are also more desirable as friends, allies, leaders, and romantic partners (Cottrell et al. 2007; Griskevicius et al. 2007; Jensen-Campbell et al. 1995; Milinski et al. 2000). Indeed, research suggests that helping others is neurologically similar to helping oneself: Helping others stimulates the same evolutionarily ancient areas of the brain that process rewards (Harbaugh et al. 2007), which can lead people to experience even greater happiness than helping themselves (Dunn et al. 2008).

The functional importance of these reputational concerns for solving the adaptive problems of affiliation, status, and attracting mates also makes reputation a valuable tool within business contexts. Consider that when public goods games are played while the players are being watched, the players are more generous (Hardy and Van Vugt 2006). Observers and other players perceive such generous individuals as having higher status. Consistent with the reputational benefits of helping, recent research shows that activating status motives can lead people to be more altruistic, especially when it comes to self-sacrificing to benefit the environment (Griskevicius et al. 2010). Activating status motives, for example, led people to choose pro-environmental green products over more self-indulgent non-green products, meaning that status motives led people to forgo luxury when given the opportunity to choose green products that could signal one's prosocial nature (and thus boost social status). Companies interested in promoting environmental awareness, responsibility or donation might provide a means of ensuring that an individual's green reputation is advertised among a status-relevant audience. Being helpful also enhances attractiveness to potential romantic partners. For example, after being primed with mating cues, men and women become more generous with charitable donations (Griskevicius et al. 2007). As is the case with helping in public goods games, these status and mating-related helping boosts are driven by reputational concerns. Neither status nor mating motives actually lead people to be more altruistic in private settings (e.g., taking shorter showers to conserve energy or picking up trash by oneself). Instead, status and mating goals only increase helping that is public and that can clearly influence one's reputation (Griskevicius et al. 2007; Griskevicius et al. 2010). Thus, businesses interested in leveraging reputational concerns (e.g., by activating relevant fundamental motives) should take into account the necessity of doing so within a social context.

Considering the evolutionary importance of a cooperative reputation, people are not only sensitive to being watched, but they are also sensitive to mere cues of being watched. Consider the following situation that commonly occurs in the public coffee room at work: When a person gets coffee, he or she is supposed to pay a specified amount. But given that individuals are not under constant surveillance, many employees take advantage of this public good by paying less than they are supposed to or by not paying at all. In a clever field experiment, researchers tested whether coffee payments would be influenced by the presence of a picture of a pair of eyes in the coffee room. Compared to a control condition in which flowers appeared in the same place, people voluntarily paid nearly three times as much for their coffee when a pair of eyes was in the room (Bateson et al. 2006). Similar types of effects are also obtained even when the picture of eyes is highly stylized, suggesting that people are attuned specifically to eye-like objects (Haley and Fessler 2005).

These findings have tremendous implications for both organizational cooperation and productivity. For example, many companies are concerned that employees spend too much time at work dallying on the Internet, thereby decreasing productivity. This concern often leads companies to place surveillance on computers, which can erode trust in management and diminish employee happiness. The coffee study, however, suggests that simply placing cues of being watched, such as a monitor background that contains a pair of eyes, might significantly decrease unwanted work activity and foster (at least superficial) cooperation. Many companies currently attempt to establish more substantial cooperation by increasing the camaraderie felt among employees, thus making it more likely that kin- and friend-relevant behaviors will prevail. This may indeed be a successful strategy, though these companies need to weigh the benefits of closer relationships with the potential downsides of these relationships, including an increased tolerance of social loafing, complacency and sentiment-based decision-making (Nicholson 2008; Schulze et al. 2001; Villalonga and Amit 2006).

4 Conclusion

Evolutionary approaches have successfully led to large numbers of theoretical advancements in the fields of biology, ecology, anthropology, and psychology. But evolutionary models are only now beginning to make inroads into our understanding of economics, marketing, management, and other types of business sciences. In this chapter we presented the fundamental motives framework as a way to view business decisions from an evolutionary perspective. This framework holds that human beings confront modern business issues—including negotiation, investment, product choice, employee management—with brains that have evolved to deal with fundamental recurring social problems that needed to be solved by our ancestors. These social problems include affiliation, self-protection, status attainment, mate-attraction, mate-retention, and child-rearing (see Table 1). Building on accumulating empirical and theoretical work, the fundamental motives framework posits that solving problems in each of these domains is associated with distinct motivational systems. Although the modern world appears to be very different that our ancestral environment, in some ways ancestral groups were very similar to modern human groups; both groups involve status hierarchies, kin members, sex differences in motivational biases, and reciprocal alliances (Hagen 2005; Hill and Hurtado 1996). In other ways, underlying human adaptive biases are mismatched to modern business settings. For example, most of our business interactions today involve unrelated strangers with whom we might interact only once or perhaps never meet.

Just as the understanding of social behavior in general has been enhanced by applying evolutionary models (e.g., Schaller et al. 2007), the fundamental motives framework provides fertile ground for a wide range of insights into business behavior. While in the current chapter we discussed how this approach can provide insight into several business-relevant topics, many others remain to be explored, including employee violence, job stress, workplace discrimination, gender conflict, employee turnover, and workplace romantic relationships. It is important to note that evolutionary models do not aim to replace other theoretical approaches. Rather, evolutionary approaches can be fruitfully integrated into almost any area of research as a means of complementing the existing theoretical models and existing explanations at different levels of analysis. Both evolutionary and other explanations (e.g., proximate explanations) are needed for a complete understanding of business behavior and the various realms of economic decision-making. A consideration of how evolution has shaped our brains is likely to lead to a broader scientific understanding of how and why people behave and think as they do.

References

Ackerman J, Kenrick DT (2008) The costs of benefits: help-refusals highlight key trade-offs of social life. Pers Soc Psychol Rev 12(2):118–140

Ackerman JM, Shapiro JR, Neuberg SL, Kenrick DT, Becker DV, Griskevicius V, Maner JK, Schaller M (2006) From out-group homogeneity to out-group heterogeneity. Psychological Science 17:836–840

Ackerman JM, Kenrick DT (2009) Cooperative courtship: helping friends raise and raze relationship barriers. Pers Soc Psychol Bull 35(10):1285–1300

Ackerman J, Kenrick DT, Schaller M (2007) Is friendship akin to kinship? Evol Hum Behav 28:365–374

Ackerman JM, Becker DV, Mortensen CR, Sasaki T, Neuberg SL, Kenrick DT (2009) A pox on the mind: disjunction of attention and memory in the processing of physical disfigurement. J Exp Soc Psychol 45:478–485

Alcock J (2005) Animal behavior: an evolutionary approach, 8th edn. Sinauer Associates, Sunderland

Ambler T, Hollier EA (2004) The waste in advertising is the part that works. J Advertising Res 44:375–389

Anderson RC, Reeb DM (2003) Founding family ownership and firm performance: evidence from the S&P 500. J Finance 58:1301–1326

Ariely D, Loewenstein G, Prelec D (2006) Tom Sawyer and the construction of value. J Econ Behav Organ 60:1–10

Axelrod R (1984) The evolution of cooperation. Basic Books, New York

Bailey KG (1988) Psychological kinship: implications for the helping professions. Psychother Theor Res Pract Train 25:132–141

Barclay P (2004) Trustworthiness and competitive altruism can also solve the "tragedy of the commons". Evol Hum Behav 25:209–220

Bargh JA (2006) What have we been priming all these years? On the development, mechanisms, and ecology of nonconscious social behavior. Eur J Soc Psychol 36:147–168

Bateson M, Nettle D, Roberts G (2006) Cues of being watched enhance cooperation in a real-world setting. Biol Lett 2(3):412–414

Becker DV, Mortensen CR, Ackerman JM, Shapiro JR, Anderson US, Sasaki T et al (2011) Self-protection and revenge-mindedness modulate detection of enemy insignia. Manuscript submitted for publication

Berry LL (1983) Relationship marketing. In: Berry LL, Shostack GL, Upah GD (eds) Emerging perspectives on service marketing. American Marketing Association, Chicago, pp 25–28

Bowles HR, Babcock L, MacGinn KL (2005) Constraints and triggers: situational mechanics of gender in negotiation. J Pers Soc Psychol 89:951–965

Burnstein E, Crandall C, Kitayama S (1994) Some neo-Darwin decision rules for altruism: weighing cues for inclusive fitness as a function of the biological importance of the decision. J Pers Soc Psychol 67:773–789

Buss DM, Barnes M (1986) Preferences in human mate selection. J Pers Soc Psychol 50:559–570

Buss DM, Schmitt DP (1993) Sexual strategies theory: an evolutionary perspective on human mating. Psychol Rev 100:204–232

Cialdini RB (2008) Influence: science and practice, 5th edn. Allyn & Bacon, New York

Colarelli SM (2003) No best way: an evolutionary perspective on human resource management. Praeger, Greenwich

Colarelli SM, Dettman JR (2003) Intuitive evolutionary perspectives in marketing. Psychol Market 20:837–865

Cosmides L, Tooby J (1992) Cognitive adaptations for social exchange. In: Barkow JH, Cosmides L, Tooby J (eds) The adapted mind. Oxford University Press, Oxford, pp 163–228

Cottrell CA, Neuberg SL (2005) Different emotional reactions to different groups: A sociofunctional threat-based approach to 'prejudice'. Journal of Personality and Social Psychology 88:770–789

Cottrell C, Neuberg S, Li N (2007) What do people desire in others? A sociofunctional perspective on the importance of different valued characteristics. J Pers Soc Psychol 92:208–231

Cross SE, Madson L (1997) Models of the self: self-construals and gender. Psychol Bull 122:5–37

Curhan JR, Neale MA, Ross L, Rosencranz-Engelmann J (2008) Relational accommodation in negotiation: effects of egalitarianism and gender on economic efficiency and relational capital. Organ Behav Hum Decis Process 107:192–205

Daly M, Wilson M (2001) Risk-taking, intrasexual competition, and homicide. In: French JA, Kamil AC, Leger DW (eds) Evolutionary psychology and motivation, vol 7, Nebraska Symposium on Motivation. University of Nebraska Press, Lincoln, pp 1–36

Darwin C (1871) The descent of man, and sexual selection in relation to sex (2 vols). John Murray, London (reprinted in 1981 by Princeton University Press)
DeBruine LM (2002) Facial resemblance enhances trust. Proc R Soc Lond B 269:1307–1312
Dunn EW, Aknin LB, Norton MI (2008) Spending money on others promotes happiness. Science 319:1687–1688
Ermer E, Cosmides L, Tooby J (2007) Functional specialization and the adaptationist program. In: Gangestad SW, Simpson JA (eds) The evolution of mind: fundamental questions and controversies. The Guilford Press, New York
Ermer E, Cosmides L, Tooby J (2008) Relative status regulates risky decision-making about resources in men: evidence for the co-evolution of motivation and cognition. Evol Hum Behav 29:106–118
Fehr E, Gachter S, Kirchsteiger G (1997) Reciprocity as a contract enforcement device. Econometrica 65:833–860
Fritz R (1997) Wars of succession: the blessings, curses and lessons that family owned firms offer anyone in business. Merritt Publishing, Santa Monica
Gigerenzer G, Selten R (2001) Rethinking rationality. In: Gigerenzer G, Selten R (eds) Bounded rationality: the adaptive toolbox. MIT Press, Cambridge, pp 1–12
Gigerenzer G, Todd PM, ABC Research Group (1999) Simple heuristics that make us smart. Oxford University Press, New York
Gould JL, Gould CG (1989) Sexual selection. Scientific American Library; 2nd edition
Griskevicius V, Cialdini RB, Kenrick DT (2006a) Peacocks, Picasso, and parental investment: the effects of romantic motives on creativity. J Pers Soc Psychol 91:63–76
Griskevicius V, Goldstein NJ, Mortensen CR, Cialdini RB, Kenrick DT (2006b) Going along versus going alone: when fundamental motives facilitate strategic (non)conformity. J Pers Soc Psychol 91:281–294
Griskevicius V, Tybur JM, Sundie JM, Cialdini RB, Miller GF, Kenrick DT (2007) Blatant benevolence and conspicuous consumption: when romantic motives elicit costly displays. J Pers Soc Psychol 93:85–102
Griskevicius V, Goldstein NJ, Mortensen CR, Sundie JM, Cialdini RB, Kenrick DT (2009a) Fear and loving in Las Vegas: evolution, emotion, and persuasion. J Marketing Res 46:385–395
Griskevicius V, Tybur JM, Gangestad SW, Perea EF, Shapiro JR, Kenrick DT (2009b) Aggress to impress: hostility as an evolved context-dependent strategy. J Pers Soc Psychol 96:980–994
Griskevicius V, Tybur JM, Van den Bergh B (2010) Going green to be seen: status, reputation, and conspicuous conservation. J Pers Soc Psychol 98(3):392–404
Hagen E (2005) Controversial issues in evolutionary psychology. In: Buss D (ed) The handbook of evolutionary psychology. John Wiley & Sons, Hoboken, NJ, pp 145–176
Haley KJ, Fessler DMT (2005) Nobody's watching? Subtle cues affect generosity in an anonymous economic game. Evol Hum Behav 26:245–256
Hamilton WD (1964) The genetical evolution of social behavior: I and II. J Theor Biol 7:1–52
Harbaugh WT, Mayr U, Burghart DR (2007) Neural responses to taxation and voluntary giving reveal motives for charitable donations. Science 316:1622–1625
Hardy CL, Van Vugt M (2006) Nice guys finish first: the competitive altruism hypothesis. Pers Soc Psychol Bull 32:1402
Haselton MG, Nettle D (2006) The paranoid optimist: an integrative evolutionary model of cognitive biases. Pers Soc Psychol Rev 10:47–66
Hill K, Hurtado AM (1996) Ache life history. Aldine De Gruyter, New York
Hoyer WD, MacInnis DJ (2006) Consumer behavior, 4th edn. Houghton Mifflin Company, New York
Hsee CK, Yang Y, Li N, Shen L (2009) Wealth, warmth and wellbeing: whether happiness is relative or absolute depends on whether it is about money, acquisition, or consumption. J Marketing Res 46(3):396–409
Jensen-Campbell LA, Graziano WC, West SG (1995) Dominance, prosocial orientation, and female preferences: do nice guys really finish last. J Pers Soc Psychol 68:427–440
Kahneman D, Tversky A (1979) Prospect theory: an analysis of decision under risk. Econometrica 47:263–291

Kahneman D, Slovic P, Tversky A (1982) Judgment under uncertainty: heuristics and biases. Cambridge University Press, New York

Kay AC, Wheeler SC, Bargh JA, Ross L (2004) Material priming: the influence of mundane physical objects on situational construal and competitive behavioral choice. Organ Behav Hum Decis Process 95:83–96

Kenrick DT, Luce CL (2000) An evolutionary life-history model of gender differences and similarities. In: Eckes T, Trautner HM (eds) The developmental social psychology of gender. Erlbaum, Hillsdale, pp 35–64

Kenrick DT, Shiota MN (2008) Approach and avoidance motivation(s): an evolutionary perspective. In: Elliot AJ (ed) Handbook of approach and avoidance motivation. Erlbaum, Mahwah

Kenrick DT, Sundie JM, Kurzban R (2008) Cooperation and conflict between kith, kin, and strangers: game theory by domains. In: Crawford C, Krebs D (eds) Foundations of evolutionary psychology. Erlbaum, Mahwah

Kenrick DT, Griskevicius V, Neuberg SL, Schaller M (2010) Renovating the pyramid of needs: contemporary extensions built upon ancient foundations. Perspect Psychol Sci 5:292–314

Klein SB, Cosmides L, Tooby J, Chance S (2002) Decisions and the evolution of memory: multiple systems, multiple functions. Psychol Rev 109:306–329

Lerner JS, Keltner D (2001) Fear, anger, and risk. J Pers Soc Psychol 81:146–159

Li NP, Bailey JM, Kenrick DT, Linsenmeier JA (2002) The necessities and luxuries of mate preferences: ting the trade-offs. J Pers Soc Psychol 82:947–955

Maner JK, Kenrick DT, Becker DV, Robertson TE, Hofer B, Neuberg SL, Delton AW, Butner J, Schaller M (2005) Functional projection: how fundamental social motives can bias interpersonal perception. J Pers Soc Psychol 88:63–78

Maner JK, Nathan DeWall C, Baumeister RF, Schaller M (2007) Does social exclusion motivate interpersonal reconnection? Resolving the "Porcupine Problem". J Pers Soc Psychol 92:42–55

McClure EB, Monk CS, Nelson EE, Zarahn E, Leibenluft E, Bilder RM, Charney DS (2004) A developmental examination of gender differences in brain engagement during evaluation of threat. Biol Psychiatry 55:1047–1055

McConaughy DL, Matthews CH, Fialko AS (2001) Founding family controlled firms: performance, risk and value. J Small Bus Manage 39:31–49

Milinski D, Semmann D, Krambeck H (2000) Donors to charity gain in both indirect reciprocity and political reputation. Proc R Soc 269:881–883

Miller GF (2000) The mating mind. Doubleday, New York

Møller AP, Petrie M (2002) Condition -dependence, multiple sexual signals, and immunocompetence in peacocks. Behav Ecol 13:248–253

Myers D (2004) Social psychology, 8th edn. McGraw-Hill, New York

Nicholson N (2008) Evolutionary psychology and family business: a new synthesis for theory, research, and practice. Fam Bus Rev 21:103–118

Nicholson N, Björnberg A (2005) Evolutionary psychology and the family firm: structure, culture and performance. In: Tomaselli S, Melin L (eds) Family firms in the wind of change. Research Forum Proceedings, IFERA, Lausanne

Nisbett RE, Ross L (1980) Human interferences: strategies and shortcomings of social judgment. Prentice-Hall, Englewood Cliffs

Ogawa S, Piller FT (2006) Reducing the risk of new product development. MIT?Sloan Manage Rev 47:65–71

Öhman A, Mineka S (2001) Fears, phobias, and preparedness: toward an evolved module of fear and fear learning. Psychol Rev 108:483–522

Park JH, Schaller M (2005) Does attitude similarity serve as a heuristic cue for kinship? Evidence of an implicit cognitive association. Evol Hum Behav 26:158–170

Perez-Gonzalez F (2006) Inherited control and firm performance. Am Econ Rev 96:1559–1588

Pham MT (1996) Cue representation and selection effects of arousal on persuasion. J Consum Res 22(4):144–159

Png I, Lehman D (2007) Managerial economics. Blackwell, Malden

Pratkanis AR, Aronson E (2000) Age of propaganda: the everyday use and abuse of persuasion, 2nd edn. W. H. Freeman, New York

Premack DG, Woodruff G (1978) Does the chimpanzee have a theory of mind? Behav Brain Sci 1:515–526

Pruitt DG, Johnson DF (1970) Mediation as an aid to face saving in negotiation. J Pers Soc Psychol 14:239–246

Raffia H (1982) The art and science of negotiation. Harvard University Press, Cambridge

Rubin JZ, Brown BR (1975) The social psychology of bargaining and negotiation. Academic, New York

Saad G (2004) Applying evolutionary psychology in understanding the representation of women in advertisements. Psychol Market 21(8):593–612

Saad G (2007) The evolutionary bases of consumption. Lawrence Erlbaum Associates Publishers, Mahwah

Saad G, Gill T (2001a) The effects of a recipient's gender in the modified dictator game. Appl Econ Lett 8:463–466

Saad G, Gill T (2001b) Sex differences in the ultimatum game: an evolutionary psychology perspective. J Bioecon 3:171–193

Saad G, Gill T (2003) An evolutionary psychology perspective on gift giving among young adults. Psychol Market 20:765–784

Schaller M, Park JH, Kenrick DT (2007) Human evolution and social cognition. In: Dunbar RIM, Barrett L (eds) Oxford handbook of evolutionary psychology. Oxford University Press, Oxford, pp 491–504

Schulze WS, Lubatkin MH, Dino RN, Buchholtz AK (2001) Agency relationships in family firms: theory and evidence. Organ Sci 12:99–116

Schwarz N, Bless H (1991) Happy and mindless, but sad and smart? The impact of affective states on analytic reasoning. In: Forgas JP (ed) Emotion and social judgment. Pergamon, Oxford, pp 55–71

Semmann D, Krambeck H, Milinski M (2005) Reputation is valuable within and outside one's social group. Behav Ecol Sociobiol 57:611–616

Sherry DF, Schacter DL (1987) The evolution of multiple memory systems. Psychol Rev 94:439–454

Simonton DK (1999) Origins of genius: Darwinian perspectives on creativity. Oxford University Press, Oxford

Smith MS, Kish BJ, Crawford CB (1987) Inheritance of wealth as human kin investment. Ethol Sociobiol 8:171–182

Solomon MR (2004) Consumer behavior, 6th edn. Pearson Prentice Hall, Upper Saddle River, New Jersey. Prentice Hall is a subsidiary of Pearson education

Sonbonmatsu DM, Kardes FR (1988) The effects of physiological arousal on information processing and persuasion. J Consum Res 15:379–385

Stuhlmacher AF, Walters AE (1999) Gender differences in negotiation outcome: a meta-analysis. Pers Psychol 52:653–677

Sundén AE, Surette BJ (1998) Gender differences in the allocation of assets in retirement savings plans. Am Econ Rev 88:207–211

Sundie JM, Cialdini RB, Griskevicius V, Kenrick DT (2006) Evolutionary social influence. In: Schaller M, Simpson JA, Kenrick DT (eds) Evolution and social psychology. Psychology Press, New York, pp 287–316

The University of Tulsa College of Business Administration (2000) The Family-Owned Business Institute. [On-line] Available: http://www.galstar.com/~persson/fobi2/

Trivers RL (1971) The evolution of reciprocal altruism. Q Rev Biol 46:35–57

Trivers RL (1972) Parental investment and sexual selection. In: Campbell B (ed) Sexual selection and the descent of man: 1871–1971. Aldine, Chicago, pp 136–179

Tucker B (2006) A future discounting explanation for the persistence of a mixed foraging-horticulture strategy among the Mikea of Madagascar. In: Kennett DJ, Winterhalder B (eds) Behavioral ecology and the transition to agriculture. University of California Press, Berkeley

Van den Bergh B, Dewitte S (2006) Digit ratio (2D:4D) moderates the impact of sexual cues on men's decisions in ultimatum games. Proc R Soc B-Bio 273:2091–2095

Van den Bergh B, Dewitte S, Warlop L (2008) Bikinis instigate generalized impatience in intertemporal choice. J Consum Res 35:85–97

Villalonga B, Amit R (2006) How do family ownership, control and management affect firm value? J Financ Econ 80:385–417

Wilson M, Daly M (2004) Do pretty women inspire men to discount the future? Proc R Soc B 271 Suppl 4:177–179

Winterhalder B (2007) Risk and decision-making. In: Dunbar R, Barrett L (eds) Oxford handbook of evolutionary psychology. Oxford University Press, Oxford

Zahavi A, Zahavi A (1997) The handicap principle: a missing piece of Darwin's puzzle. Oxford University Press, New-York, Oxford

Intrasexual Competition Within Organizations

Abraham P. Buunk, Thomas V. Pollet, Pieternel Dijkstra, and Karlijn Massar

Abstract Intrasexual competition refers to rivalry with same-sex others that is, ultimately, driven by the motive to obtain and maintain access to mates. In the present chapter we provide evidence that intrasexual competition also plays an important role in workers' behaviours, emotions and preferences in the relationship with other workers, and, as a result, may have far reaching consequences for organizations. More specifically, we discuss the types of intrasexual competition that exist, the way these types of intrasexual competition translate into employees' emotions and behaviours, and the extent to which men and women adopt different intrasexual competitive strategies. Problems in the workplace may occur because intrasexual competition has taken on a dynamic of its own, and influences behaviours and preferences of employees even when this may be maladaptive for the individual or the organization.

Keywords Sex differences · Intrasexual competition · Sexual selection · Social comparison · Jealousy · Envy · Status

1 Introduction

Intrasexual competition refers to rivalry with same-sex others that is, ultimately, driven by the motive to obtain and maintain access to mates. Darwin (1871) already recognized the importance of intrasexual competition for sexual selection, and suggested that it led to important behavioural adaptations for attracting mates and for gathering the necessary resources for reproduction and offspring care. It is

A.P. Buunk (✉)
Royal Netherlands Academy of Arts and Sciences and University of Groningen, Groningen, The Netherlands

T.V. Pollet and P. Dijkstra,
Department Psychology, University of Groningen, The Netherlands

K. Massar
Department of Social Psychology, University Maastricht, Maastricht, The Netherlands

important to realize that males can sire offspring with a single sexual act, whereas in most species females have to invest much more than males in producing offspring (Trivers 1972). Females are therefore, as it were, generally a scarce resource over which males compete (Andersson 1994). Indeed, in species in which males invest little in their offspring, they usually engage in quite fierce competition with other males over the access to females, whereas females show few signs of intrasexual competition. Overall, men compete with other men for access to reproductive resources, including resources such as political influence and social status that can be converted into reproductive opportunity, either because these are directly attractive to females or because these help conquer rival males (Tooby and Cosmides 1988; Sidanius and Pratto 1999).

For most of our evolutionary history, humans have lived in small-scale societies where women could usually determine quite easily the status of men. However, until a few decades ago, most organizations were male dominated, and many organizations still are. Even though there are often no women around to observe the position of males viz. others, it seems that the tendency to engage in intrasexual competition is sufficiently hard wired, that it may even surface in organizations where the direct benefits of engaging in such competition may not be immediately obvious. Male intrasexual competition often takes the form of a somewhat ritualized competition over the acquisition of those skills and resources that define status within a given culture (Sidanius and Pratto 1999). In preindustrial societies in which male-male competition has been studied, it has consistently been found that a man's status is directly related to his reproductive success (Betzig 1982, 1986). Even in contemporary Western society high-income men have more biological children than low-income men, whereas among women the opposite is true (Hopcroft 2005; Nettle and Pollet 2008). Overall, organizations are traditionally an important domain for intrasexual competition among males, i.e., for fights over status, prestige, and resources, and eventually the outcomes of such competition may have important consequences for the opportunities of attracting and keeping mates. With the increasing influx of women in organizations, intrasexual competition among males may have become more salient and prevalent, as the presence of women tend to make men more aware of their status, and more eager to demonstrate that they can beat other men. For example, an experiment showed that men increased their cooperation in an economic game when observed by women (Iredale et al. 2008). That is, men exhibit competitive altruism: they compete by being generous and forego individual benefits (Van Vugt et al. 2007). Behaving altruistically may improve one's reputation and status: others often attribute charisma to those who sacrifice their own needs to those of others or the group (De Cremer and Van Knippenberg 2004).

Although men may choose not to, many men, as women do, invest resources and parental care in their offspring. As a result, both sexes are discriminating in the choice of mates, and therefore both sexes will engage in competition with same-sex conspecifics. In this chapter, we first present evidence that competition within organizations is usually intrasexual rather than intersexual. We then discuss the role of envy in the evocation of competition, individual differences in competition and the different strategies males and females may adopt in competing with each other. Throughout this chapter, we will discuss the implications of these topics for organizations and suggest ways to deal with the problems that evolutionary-driven strategies of competition may create in an organizational context.

2 Competition Within Organizations Is Generally Intrasexual

Dominance hierarchies revolve around relative rather than absolute positions and individuals are more concerned about getting ahead of another rather than about achieving an absolute position (see e.g., Buunk and Ybema 1997). Hill and Buss (2006) report studies which show that indeed, men and women possess a positional bias, making them attend to the positional rather than to the absolute value of resources that are known to affect survival or reproduction, and to personal attributes that affect others' abilities to acquire such resources. These authors showed that when choosing between having an absolutely larger income or an income that was absolutely less but larger than one's rivals' incomes, both men and women chose the greater positional income. Moreover, the positional bias seems to be sex-differentiated illustrated by the finding that women, more than men, preferred to be less attractive in an absolute sense, but more attractive than their rivals (e.g., scoring a 5 when rivals score a 3), over being more attractive in an absolute sense but less attractive than their rivals (e.g., scoring a 7 when rivals score a 9).

Although in contemporary organizational settings, women are often in direct competition with males, it is our contention that, as a result of a long evolutionary history of male-male competition, on an emotional and unconscious level, males will still perceive other males, and not females, as their primary rivals. Similarly, as women have in our evolutionary past rarely competed with males, they are more likely to see other females as competitors. A few decades ago, various studies were conducted in the field of social comparison, to determine with *whom* men and women compare themselves – do women compare mostly with women, and men with men? While in laboratory experiments many participants compared themselves with both genders in order to evaluate their performance and their pay, in general in such experiments a pronounced preference for comparisons with others of the same gender over others of the other gender was found (Feldman and Ruble 1981; Miller 1984; Suls et al. 1979). Studies employing an interview methodology have also shown that men and women tend to compare themselves with respect to their jobs more with same-sex others than with opposite-sex others, although women tend to compare themselves more with men than vice versa (Crosby 1982; Saad and Gill 2001a). Buunk and Van der Laan (2002) presented women with a successful target that was either male or female. Their results showed that women preferred to compare themselves more with the same-sex target than with the opposite-sex target and saw the situation of the female target as a more likely potential future for themselves. Buunk and Van der Laan (2002) concluded that women see other women as more relevant standards than men for how they may fare in their professional careers. Of course, a similar line of reasoning applies to men, for whom other men are more relevant comparison targets. A clear indication that also men much more strongly compete with men than with women, was found by Saad and Gill (2001b). In their study participants took part in a two-person ultimatum game, in which one was the allocator and the other the recipient and the allocator had to split a given sum of money with the recipient. The recipient could either accept or reject the offer. If accepted, both players received their respective splits, if rejected neither of them got anything. The results showed that men made more generous offers when pitted against a woman as opposed to a man. Women, on the other hand, made equal offers independently of the sex of the recipient. The finding that, in this case, women did not compete more with women than with men, may be attributed to the *dimension* of competition, i.e. money. In general, money is a much more important arena of competition for men than for women, who compete, much more than men, with each other on attributes such as physical attractiveness (Dijkstra and Buunk 1998).

A study by Steil and Hay (1997), using a sample of men and women with prestigious, male-dominated careers, showed that the choice of the comparison target is not only determined by one's own sex, but also by one's income. In this study it was found that women were significantly more likely to make opposite-sex comparisons than men, and that the higher a woman's income became, the more likely she was to compare her accomplishments regarding promotion, compensation, responsibility, and influence in decision making predominantly with men. For men, the opposite effect was found: the lower their income, the more likely they were to also compare with women. Apparently, men with low incomes identify more easily with women, who, in general have lower incomes than men. Steil and Hay's study is interesting for organizations. It has been argued that women in organizations, because of the lack of female leaders, may suffer from the lack of female role models (e.g., Linehan and Scullion 2008). Steil and Hay's study, however, suggests that this concern is not entirely founded. Ambitious women seem to select their comparison targets not, or not solely on the basis of sex, but on the basis of the status or income level they aspire. Therefore, even if there were more female leaders, women may not perceive these women as suitable role models. Jandeska and Kraimer (2005), for instance, found that female leaders in male-dominated organizations were less inclined to engage in role modeling behaviors, such as mentoring junior colleagues.

In sum, we have described several lines of evidence that point to the fact that competition within organizations typically occurs within a sex. It appears that such a view is consistent with our human evolutionary past, which exhibits a long history of intrasexual competition.

3 Envy in the Workplace

The emotion of envy is assumed to link social comparisons to competition. Envy stems from social comparison with others who are doing better or who possess more favorable attributes (Fischer et al. 2009). Envy stimulates individuals to narrow the gap between themselves and the superior other. Although envy is often seen as a negative or destructive emotion, two types of envy can be distinguished that are very different from each other: *malicious* envy and *benign* envy. Both appear to motivate individuals to decrease the status gap between themselves and others. Yet they do so in different ways. Benign envy leads individuals to close the gap by moving themselves up to the level of the other (Van de Ven et al. 2009). In contrast, malicious envy leads individuals to do so by pulling the other down to one's own position. Whereas benign envy stimulates individuals to self-promote and improve the self, for instance, by observational learning and affiliation with a superior other, malicious envy encourages individuals to derogate or even damage rivals. From an evolutionary psychological point of view, benign envy may seem the more adaptive form of the two types of envy: it alerts individuals to fitness-relevant advantages enjoyed by rivals, motivating them to acquire those same advantages (Hill and Buss 2006, 2008). Nonetheless, malicious envy may help reduce differences in status as well as helping preserve equal relations (Keltner et al. 2006). It may also help workers maintain high levels of self-esteem (Buunk and Ybema 1997; Salovey and Rodin 1991).

In organizations, both types of envy may occur. Illustrating the potentially negative effect of benign envy, Gino and Pierce (2009) found that, in the visible proximity of monetary abundant wealth or wealthy others, individuals are more likely to cheat due to feelings of envy. Employees who feel their company or employer is extremely rich may therefore more easily engage in unethical behaviors, such as those related to financial fraud, enriching themselves in an attempt to close the monetary gap between themselves and their CEO. Malicious jealousy often leads to the derogation of rivals, which in the work place often takes the form of bullying, harassment and negative gossip. Research in a male dominated work setting, i.e. the Norwegian marine industry, showed that, on a weekly basis, 7% of the workers reported being subjected to at least one of the following behaviors from coworkers or supervisors: ridicule and insulting teasing, verbal abuse, rumors and gossip spread about themselves, offending remarks, recurring reminders on blunders, hostility or silence when entering a conversation, or the devaluing of one's effort and work. As many as 22% of workers reported being subjected to one or more of these acts at least monthly (Einarsen and Raknes 1997). In line with the fact that competition within organizations is mainly intrasexual, a review by Schuster (1996) showed that male bullies most often victimize males whereas females victimize females more often. Moreover, the type of attacks differs. Women seem to be more spiteful, and talk behind others' backs, ridicule others, spread rumors, or make indirect allusions. Typical male tactics are to permanently assign others to new tasks, to stop talking to someone, and to assign tasks that violate others' self-esteem. Envy is also sex-specific in another way: whereas women feel most envious of same-sex rivals who are physically attractive, men feel more envious of same-sex rivals who are able to attract an attractive romantic partner, and of rivals who have more sexual experience than they have (Hill and Buss 2008).

Benign envy and malicious envy may also occur together. This is illustrated in is a phenomenon that Försterling et al. (2007) call the 'sexual attribution bias' (SAB). In a study on attributions, these authors found that the success of attractive same-sex others was consistently ascribed to luck and less to ability, whereas the success of attractive opposite-sex others was attributed more to ability and less to luck. Thus, both men and women apparently see only same-sex others as rivals, feel threatened by the success of attractive same-sex others, and feel a need to 'downplay' this success. The SAB fosters a favorable assessment of the self in relation to the same-sex rival that ensures persistence of competition, reducing the rival's chances of succeeding. To remain believable, individuals usually do not derogate their rivals on all attributes. They give them credit for success in domains they regard as unimportant. Only in domains that are perceived to be important, individuals devalue their rival (Buunk and Gibbons 2007; Schmitt 1988).

As envy is likely an evolved, and thus difficult to avoid, emotion and therefore difficult to avoid, it may lead, in the workplace it to a host of negative outcomes at the individual and group level. In a review of studies on envy in organizations, Duffy et al. (2008) showed that workplace envy is related to poorer leader-member exchange, lower job satisfaction, less liking for coworkers, lower organization-based self-esteem, lower group performance, higher turnover, higher absence rates, and higher social loafing. For example, Geurts et al. (1994) found that bus drivers who perceived others as better off than themselves did engage more in absenteeism. In a study among Spanish teachers, Buunk et al. (2007) found that a feeling of being defeated in the sense of being passed by others predicted burnout among men, but not among women. Fischer et al. (2009) found a possible explanation for the negative effect of envy on performance. In three experiments these authors showed that envious individuals were less willing to share high-quality information with envied colleagues. Since information exchange is crucial for successful cooperation, group performance may suffer as a consequence. In a similar vein, being bullied has been found to be related to burnout, stress and decreased job satisfaction in several segments of the job market, ranging from construction to educational and medical settings (Meliá and Becerril 2007; Van Dick and Wagner 2001).

Fortunately, there are indications that organizations can control, at least some of, the negative consequences of envy. In his study, Vecchio (2000) found envy to be related to several work unit variables. More specifically, he showed that, as the reward system in a unit was more competitive, employees experienced more envy. In contrast, as workers experienced more autonomy in their jobs and had more considerate supervisors, they experienced less envy towards co-workers. Although this study was only correlational in nature, its findings do provide organizations with at least some avenues to control workplace envy and its negative consequences. That is, by uncoupling individual rewards from those of others, enhancing job autonomy and recruiting kind and empathic managers, organizations may reduce levels of workplace envy to acceptable levels.

4 Individual Differences in Intrasexual Competition

While it seems clear that both sexes tend to compete largely with same-sex others, there are important individual differences in the extent to which both males and females engage in intrasexual competition. Some individuals seem to have as their major goal to 'beat' others, and to attain and maintain their high status position in the organization, whereas others seem to have as their major goal to be a good team member and to contribute to the benefits of the organization. In other words, whereas some aim to achieve status by pursuing personal goals and by dominating their colleagues, others aim to do so by helping their group attain success, even if group goals conflict with their personal goals. Studies on leadership show that both strategies may be effective ways of achieving status. Brunell et al. (2008), for instance, showed that, especially in leaderless groups, narcissistic individuals, i.e. relatively self-centred individuals who are low in empathy, emerge as leaders. On the other hand, relatively altruistic individuals who are willing to sacrifice their own needs to the group are usually highly respected and admired by group members and often nominated as leaders (Choi and Mai-Dalton 1998). These individual differences have been captured by various social psychological theories, including the theory of social value orientations (Van Lange et al. 1997), theories of achievement motivation (Atkinson 1957), and the need for power (McClelland et al. 1985). There is evidence that such differences are partially heritable (Bouchard and McGue 1990; Tellegen et al. 1988). Evolutionary psychology may help explain the existence of individual, genetically based, differences in intrasexual competition and the strategies individuals use to compete with same-sex members.

From an evolutionary-psychological point of view, individual differences such as these, may exist for several reasons. First, combinations of specific individual differences may result in equally viable behavioural strategies (Penke et al. 2007). Although each behavioral strategy has its specific costs and benefits, the net effect may be the same (Nettle 2006). For instance, as stated above, both narcissism and altruism may help individuals gain higher group status and can, as such, both be considered adaptive strategies. Figueredo et al. (2005) argued that personality differences may be adaptive in social competition because of the operation of frequency dependent selection. Frequency dependent selection implies that there does not exist a single optimal strategy, and that various distinct strategies may all be heritable. Different strategies may have developed because, under different conditions, different strategies may be adaptive. For example, in a population with predominantly cooperative individuals, there would be a niche for competitive individuals, and vice versa. Translated to modern organizations, in an organization or unit with predominantly cooperative individuals, the competitive and narcissistic individual may be highly effective at achieving status. The opposite may be true as well: in an organization or unit with predominantly competitive and narcissistic individuals, there may be a niche for altruism. Finally, it has been argued that individuals are genetically predisposed to have personality characteristics that, to a certain extent, are malleable. As a result, situational demands may push individuals to develop certain strategies and traits over other ones (Penke et al. 2007; Saad 2007), a phenomenon Gangestad and Simpson (2000) refer to as strategic pluralism.

Drawing on a blossoming animal literature, Nettle (2006) suggested that different levels of the same trait might be adaptive under different conditions. Indeed, it seems probable that being strongly intrasexually competitive and selfish may be adaptive under certain conditions, when, for instance, life expectancy is low, others are low in altruism as well, and when the level of social organization is low. Yet the same competitive behaviour may be maladaptive under other conditions, for instance, when others are high in altruism or in complex social groups (Rushton 1985). Findings from studies on species as diverse as great tits (*Parus Major*) to big horn sheep (*Ovis canadensis*) demonstrate that traits such as aggressiveness towards conspecifics, boldness, and risk taking have different fitness payoffs in different environments (Dingemanse and Réale 2005). The same applies to humans. It has, for instance, been found that a high level of sibling rivalry may reflect an uncertain environment in which the individual learns that one has to compete over access to resources (Salmon 2005). In a similar vein, it has been found that Machiavellianism, i.e. the ability to manipulate others, is especially encouraged in leaders who are responsible for conduct toward other groups or organizations (Wilson et al. 1996).

To assess individual differences in intrasexual competition, especially within organizations, Buunk and Fisher (2009) developed the Intrasexual Competition Scale. The scale does not assess the strategies that individuals might use in intrasexual competition, which have been investigated by Buss (1991) and others, but rather intrasexual competition as an attitude. This attitudinal focus concerns the degree to which individuals view the confrontation with same-sex individuals in competitive terms, and implicates a number of phenomena that have been well-described in the psychological literature, albeit not in a mating context. These phenomena include the desire to outperform others rather than to perform well (Van Yperen 2003); the desire to view oneself as better than others (cf. self-enhancement, Zuckerman and O'Loughlin 2006); envy and frustration when others are better off and negative feelings towards such others (Smith and Kim 2007); and malicious pleasure or schadenfreude when high achievers ("tall poppies") lose face (Feather 1994). The latter may be seen as the result of the derogation of a rival, a frequently used strategy during intrasexual competition. The Intrasexual Competition Scale (ICS) operationalized these phenomena, particularly on dimensions relevant to mating, and included only items formulated with respect to same-sex others. In addition, following up on a study by Luxen and Van de Vijver (2006) who showed that women often reject attractive women as candidates for a position in their department, the scale included questions on the resistance to having others with higher mate value as close colleagues. The 12-item scale was constructed simultaneously in The Netherlands and Canada, and proved to be sex neutral, to possess high reliability, to have a high degree of cross-national equivalence, and to be related to self-reports of sibling rivalry in one's childhood (Buunk and Fisher 2009). The ICS may help reveal workers' level of intrasexual competition and help explain why some workers adopt certain strategies of intrasexual competition, while others do not. The ICS may also help researchers map the costs and benefits of these strategies, in terms of, for instance, employees' wellbeing and productivity and the organization's culture and output. Finally, determining workers' degree of competitiveness may help recruiters select the best candidate for the job. For instance, in some occupational fields, such as sales, high levels of competitiveness are required or, at least, thought of as desirable. Likewise, there are indications that, when units are characterized by strong intra-unit competition, there is a need for a relatively egalitarian, personalized, and communal leader, instead of a leader who ads to the unit's competitive culture (Van Vugt and Spisak 2008). In these cases, the ICS may help select the right leader.

5 Intrasexual Competition and Signaling

One way in which intrasexual competition can take place is via ritualized displays. As Veblen noted in 1899, conspicuous consumption and conspicuous leisure might be ways of engaging in status competition. Saad and Vongas (2009) found that men's testosterone levels are responsive to fluctuations in their status as triggered by acts of conspicuous consumption. That is, male testosterone levels increased after driving an expensive sports car while they decreased after driving an old family sedan. In addition, this study showed that, when men's social status was threatened by the wealth displays of a male rival in the presence of a female, male testosterone levels increased. The Saad and Vorgas study suggests that showing off by means of conspicuous consumption is an evolved mechanism for responding to intra-sexual challenges. Building on Veblen (1899), Miller (2000) suggested that conspicuous consumption could be seen as a handicap signal. Handicap signaling refers to the evolution of an honest signal, which cannot be copied because it is very costly to produce (Zahavi and Zahavi 1997). In this way, for example, human males could show off and signal to other men and potential mates: 'I can afford all this'. Indeed there is abundant evidence that this type of male costly signaling via conspicuous consumption is common in traditional societies (Hawkes and Bliege Bird 2002; Bird et al. 2001). Some have even argued that men's hunting has evolved, in part, as a signaling strategy (Hawkes and Bliege Bird 2002). Hunting is not always necessarily an effective activity. While it may result in obtaining food and warding off starvation, often the time spent hunting could in many cases be better allocated to gathering food in other ways. Hunting does however, appear to provide some cues about an individual's quality to relevant audiences: good hunters are subsequently preferred as mates or allies. Also in modern society in general, and in organizations specifically, men use conspicuous consumption as a strategy of intrasexual competition (Miller 2009). Lycett and Dunbar (2000) demonstrated this by showing that mobile phones could be construed as lekking devices, i.e. as in grouse (e.g. Gibson and Bradbury 1985), human males aggregate and conspicuously display their features in order to attract females. In this study, males were more inclined to conspicuously display their mobile phones as the composition of their group became more male-biased. Men appear to aggregate in groups and compete via ritualized displays, such as by showing off their mobile phones.

In line with the present argument, individuals within an organization, especially men, compete for higher wages, better fringe benefits, more prestigious job titles, and larger offices. They show off with expensive mobile phones and clothing and by giving generous diner parties to subordinates and clients. The same may apply to organizations as a whole: they may build unique and expensive offices and attract distinguished CEO's by means of high salaries and bonuses to impress clients and competitors. However, in so doing organizations may overshoot the mark. Both organizations and workers may become trapped in a never ending cycle: to intimidate others who show off by means of conspicuous consumption, they have to come up with even more expensive or unique goods ('Keeping up with the Jones's'). Their rivals, in response will do the same, which triggers again the tendency to engage in conspicuous consumption, etc. In times of financial crisis, workers and their organizations may not be able to continue this 'rat race' and, when they do, end up in financial problems. Recently, in the Netherlands, a middle-sized bank, i.e. the DSB Bank, came into serious financial trouble for this exact same reason. Only a couple of month's before, the bank had bought art for tens of millions of euro's, and received a loan from another bank in order to build a museum that was to be named after the DSB bank's CEO. These prestigious undertakings were one of the reasons that the bank had no financial reserves left when business slowed down due to the financial crisis. As a result, in September 2009 the DSB Bank was declared bankrupt. Thus, organizations and their workers may become so caught up in the strategy of conspicuous consumption that it backfires. Due to the ubiquitous drive for conspicuous consumption, organizations are often faced with job applicants – especially men – that are less interested in the content of the job, than in the salary and the lease-car that come with it. Workers may become easily dissatisfied when they learn that colleagues make more money, and they may even leave the organization when they find out that other employers pay a higher salary for the same job. In other words, conspicuous consumption may undermine workers' intrinsic motivation by making material wealth an important criterion of success. Moreover, in our society, conspicuous consumption itself seems to have lost a large part of its function. According to Miller (2009), because of the high standard of living, in our society the display of wealth no longer reflects the deeper mental traits that, in our evolutionary past, were related to conspicuous consumption, such as endurance, ambition, intelligence, and creativity: in our society practically everyone can buy and display luxurious goods due to credit loans. However, this reasoning seems to ignore the evolved tendency to engage in a continuing arms race, which would result in the acquisition of luxury goods that few others can afford, like a BMW of over $100,000, or a watch of over $25,000.

Intrasexual competition may also take place in a covert way, via nonverbal behaviour, rather than as overt competition. Sometimes there is minimal visible intrasexual competition albeit relatively stable dominance hierarchies are established. There is evidence that even adolescents and young children form relatively stable dominance hierarchies (Savin-Williams 1976, 1979; Sluckin and Smith 1977). Likewise, dominance hierarchies are established within organizations. As discussed later in greater detail, non-verbal cues, such as body build or posture, provide information about someone's rank or dominance, a form of impression management within organizations (see Gardner and Martinko 1988; Wayne and Liden 1995). Impression management refers to strategies employed by individuals to maintain a positive image of themselves by presenting themselves in a favorable light to others (Schlenker 1980; Elsbach and Sutton 1992). Direct intrasexual conflicts within an organization are often avoided by non-verbal interactions in which dominance and submission are negotiated, a topic we will discuss in more detail later in this chapter'.

6 Different Forms of Intrasexual Competition

Among humans, particularly male-male intrasexual competition is quite a complex and multifaceted phenomenon. Earlier in this chapter, we discussed two strategies of gaining status, i.e. a relatively selfish and narcissistic strategy and a relatively altruistic strategy. In addition, on a different level, two other types of intrasexual competitive strategies may be distinguished. First, there exists in many species *direct*, physical competition. That is, males may engage in fierce threats and fights to attain a high status in the group, and to prevent other males from access to females, and as such maintain exclusive sexual access to females (Andersson 1994). Among primates, for example, baboons, such conflicts are common (Walters and Seyfarth 1987; Wrangham and Peterson 1996). The second type of intrasexual competition is more *indirect*, and consists of showing off to females those characteristics that may signal good genetic quality. This type of intrasexual competition is driven by *intersexual* selection, i.e., the selection by females for male traits that are indicators of good genes or would lead to 'sexy sons'. For instance, in birds of paradise, females' preference for male ornamentation has lead to intrasexual competition between males for the most attractive plumage (Andersson 1994). According to Gilbert et al. (1995), in humans, the ability to engage in both types of intrasexual competition is represented in the self-concept. Consequently, Gilbert et al. (1995) have suggested that humans may have developed two major types of self-concepts. The first is based on perceptions regarding one's ability to display intimidation and dominance in order to get control over desirable social outcomes and status, and is called 'resource holding potential' (RHP). Gilbert et al. hypothesized that human self-esteem has evolved out of the perception of how one is doing in comparison with others, and that self-esteem may be lower with the loss of reproductively useful resources (e.g., loss of mates to rivals, or the loss or inability to gain a higher position in the status hierarchy). However, the same authors noted that status and prestige not only have to be fought over, but also are often bestowed on others, especially those who display attractive attributes. The second type of self-concept therefore reflects the more indirect type of intrasexual competition, consisting of perceptions regarding one's ability to attract favorable attention from both members of the opposite and the same sex and is referred to as 'social attention-holding power' (SAHP). Gilbert et al. (1995) suggest that by comparing oneself with others on RHP and SAHP, one is able to determine one's standing relative to both rivals and potential mates and obtain information about the best strategy to follow to maximize reproductive opportunities.

Both types of self-concepts are highly likely to affect worker' behaviors and attitudes towards the organization and colleagues. Research on worker's RHP and SHP is, however, lacking. According to Gilbert et al. (1995) RHP is closely reflected by the traditional concept of self-esteem. Whereas the traditional concept of self-esteem views self-esteem as a one-dimensional concept, Tafarodi and Swann (1995, 2001) argued self-esteem to consist of two different, underlying factors, i.e. self-liking (the subjective evaluation of oneself as a social being) and self-competence (internal conceptions of success and failure in performing tasks). Whereas the first factor closely resembles SHP, the second seems to reflect RHP and thus the traditional conceptualization of self-esteem. Research has confirmed the importance of making a distinction between these two factors of self-esteem with regard to workplace behaviors. Tafarodi and Vu (1997), for instance, showed that failure on a task only led those who suffered from low self-liking (SHP) to become unmotivated and inclined to give up. In contrast, those with low self-competence did not suffer a greater decrement in persistence relative to those high in self-competence. In fact, those low in self-competence were inclined to persist more when tasks became difficult than those high in self-competence. This is an important finding for understanding organizational behavior. It is often thought that workers who experience a lack in motivation due to task failure or difficulty should be helped by regaining confidence in their ability to do the job. Tafarodi and Vu's study, however, suggests something else. Motivating workers to persist at a difficult task or after failure may be best done by strengthening their SHP, for instance, by expressing liking for them and by making them feel nurtured, accepted and appreciated for who they are. In addition, it has been found that self-competence, but not self-liking, is related to increased cognitive ability and to both academic and creative achievements (Mar et al. 2006). This latter finding may, of course, be due to the fact that intelligent and creative workers have more reason to feel self-competent than other workers. Nonetheless, it is possible that workers may become more inventive and creative when their self-competence is boosted, for instance, by providing them with positive feedback when they succeed in a task. Evidence indeed points in this direction (e.g., Zhou 1998). Although providing workers with positive feedback seems a very simple intervention, many organizations only rarely provide their workers with feedback at all or provide mainly negative feedback (Ilgen and Davis 2000).

7 Physical Dominance as a Male Intrasexual Competition Strategy

Especially among young males with few resources, intrasexual competition is to a large extent driven by direct physical competition, i.e., by what Gilbert and colleagues (1995) refer to as competition for RHP. Physical dominance refers to the elevated social rank that is achieved by male physical competition and physical power (Barber 1995; Kemper 1990; Hill and Hurtado 1996; Rushton 1995). It requires individuals to be healthy, physically strong, and aggressive, i.e. exactly those characteristics that are signaled by an athletic body (Frederick and Haselton 2007). The strategy of physical dominance seems to be effective in particular for younger men: whereas they do not possess a high status yet in a larger social context, they are at their peak with regard to health and fitness (Kemper 1990). The degree to which men are able to engage in the strategy of physical dominance is related to their physical appearance. Men with an athletic body build have been found to be relatively competitive (Quinn and Wilson 1989) and to like physical adventure, exercise, risk, and car speed relatively more (Child 1950; Quinn and Wilson 1989; Sheldon and Stevens 1942). Compared to men with a less athletic body build, men with an athletic build show lower anxiety and may therefore be high in sensation seeking, and tend to engage often in impulsive, aggressive, antisocial, and disorderly behavior (for a review until 1964 see Domey et al. 1964; see also Verdonck and Walker 1976). Not only the body, also the male face signals physical dominance. For instance, men who are high in testosterone – an important hormone regulating aggressive behavior – have larger jaws and a more prominent brow ridge than other men, and as a result are perceived as more masculine and dominant (Penton-Voak and Chen 2004). Thus, both body and face convey information about an individual's level of dominance (Zuckerman 1986) and may communicate threat (Bailey et al. 1976; Massar and Buunk 2009).

As a result of male intrasexual competition, humans seem to have developed specific mental mechanisms to detect body-related cues indicative of a rival's level of threat, the ability to infer rivalry-related traits from those cues and to estimate the degree of threat a rival poses (Buunk et al. 2007a; Thornhill and Grammer 1999). According to Frederick and Haselton (2007) a man's body morphology signals his fitness and the presence of genes that could potentially increase his reproductive success (see also Geary 2005). An athletic build characterized by a high degree of muscularity and broad shoulders, for instance, could demonstrate that a male is in a good condition. Especially when men are confronted with unknown or threatening rivals, quick first impressions of rivals may be of essential importance to survival and fitness (Massar and Buunk 2009). Indeed, Bar et al. (2006) showed that first impressions of males, especially those that are perceived as a threat, are usually made within the first 39 ms, solely on the basis of visual information. Research using the zero-acquaintance-paradigm, in which participants are asked to judge personality attributes of people based on short, silent video clips of often no more than 30 s, shows that people are often quite accurate when making judgments about, for instance, someone's self-esteem, status, and level of altruism (e.g., Yeagley et al. 2007). Quick first impressions, such as these, are enabled by stereotypes, i.e. ideas or beliefs about what another person is like, based on what group that person belongs to. The stereotypes we refer to here are body-related stereotypes, i.e. stereotypes that make assumptions on the basis of a person's body or face. Although stereotypes are overgeneralizations in the sense that they attribute the same characteristics to all members of a group, they often do have a kernel of truth in them. In broad lines, body-related related stereotypes match the actual relations between body and attributes. For instance, the perception that men with an athletic body build are stronger, more sportive, more competitive, more dominant, healthier and more energetic (Butler et al. 1993; Lerner and Korn 1972; Ryckman et al. 1989), is relatively accurate.

As a result, during intrasexual competition, body related stereotypes may facilitate men to form fast and relatively accurate impressions of their rivals and, in so doing, may enhance competitive success and prevent a possible loss of status (Fiske 1992). More specifically, like in many other species, by assessing the physical features of other males and deriving conclusions from these features, men may challenge those who can be beaten so as not to miss out on opportunities to raise their status (or their reproductive success in other ways) that could be available, while it may prevent them from competing with superior males, as that would be a waste of energy and would bring substantial costs. In support of this line of reasoning, Tiedens and Fragale (2003) found that men changed their behaviour when being in the same room as a male who, due to his bodily posture, was perceived as dominant: confronted with such a male, men behaved relatively submissively.

Although one might expect that in organizations such as the army, the police, and the fire brigade, physical features may contribute to status, one might argue that in most modern organizations physical dominance will play a relatively unimportant role. Why would men bother about a rival who has qualities that hardly matter for occupational success? However, there are various strands of evidence that do suggest that such qualities matter more than one might expect. The first piece of evidence comes from a study on work-related jealousy in Argentina (Buunk et al. 2010). Jealousy may not only exist within romantic relationships, but also within relationships in a work context. It must be noted that also in the workplace, jealousy and envy are two distinct emotions. Workplace jealousy refers to the pattern of thoughts, emotions, and behaviors that results from an employee's loss of self-esteem or the loss of outcomes associated with a working relationship, due to a rival. Jealousy may, for instance, be evoked when a worker perceives his or her superior to pay attention to a new colleague at the expense of time spent with him or her. In essence, workplace jealousy is triadic in that it involves three principals: the focal employee, the rival, and the valued target person. In contrast, employee envy, although also a stress response, is defined in essentially dyadic terms: it refers to a pattern of thoughts, emotions, and behaviors that results from an employee's loss of self-esteem in response to a referent other's obtainment of outcomes that one strongly desires (Vecchio 2000). A common feature of both employee jealousy and envy, however, is the diminution of self-worth that occurs as a result of social comparison.

In the Argentinean study by Buunk et al. (2010), adult participants were presented with a scenario describing how one's satisfying and close relationship with one's supervisor was threatened because a new employee seemed to develop a close relationship with the same supervisor. For each of 24 presented characteristics, participants were asked how jealous they would be if the rival possessed this characteristic. Among males, physical dominance of the rival evoked more jealousy than among females. Especially among males high in intra-sexual competition (as measured with the scale described earlier, Buunk and Fisher 2009), physical dominance of a rival evoked jealousy, but only when the supervisor was also a male. It seems as if a same-sex group makes competition along sex-specific characteristics especially salient; in any case, it does not seem to be the presence of an opposite sex supervisor that triggers competition on these characteristics. These findings suggest that intra-sexual competition has a dynamic of its own, and is induced more by the presence of same-sex others than by the presence of opposite sex others (cf. Buunk and Fisher 2009; Campbell 2002; Geary 1998).

The second, albeit more indirect, evidence for the fact that physical qualities matter more than one might expect, comes from studies showing that height has more effect on attaining status in organizations than is often assumed. Taller men tend to attain higher positions in organizations. In humans, height is one of the first features that others notice and is associated with status. For instance, one study found that full professors were .47 in. taller than associate professors, who were .26 in. taller than assistant professors, who were 1.24 in. taller than the average nonacademic (Hensley 1993). The relationship between height and status also leads individuals to distort their perceptions of men's height, and, as a result, to hold – relatively accurate – stereotypes about height (Wilson 1968; Jackson and Ervin 1992). Research, for instance, shows that, the same male is perceived to be taller as his status increases: when, for instance, a man is described as a student, he is estimated to be about 2.5 in. shorter than when he is described as a professor (Wilson 1968). The reproductive advantages of height for males are apparent in the female preference for taller males (Kurzban and Weeden 2005; Pawlowski 2003; Shepperd and Strathman 1989). Indeed, taller men receive more replies to dating announcements (Pawlowski and Koziel 2002), have more physically attractive girlfriends (Feingold 1982), are less jealous (Buunk et al. 2008), and have more reproductive success (Mueller and Mazur 2001; Nettle 2002; Pawlowski et al. 2000). Given that height is highly heritable (one recent estimate – in a study using the Danish Twin Registry – found heritability coefficients of .69 for men and .81 for women; Schousboe et al. 2004), females choosing tall males are more likely to have tall male offspring, who in turn would be preferred by females. Male height has been found to be correlated with physical health, as well as with morphological symmetry (Manning 1995; Silventoinen et al. 1999). There is some evidence that shorter people may live longer than taller people if environmental factors are compatible with a small body size (Samaras et al. 2003; Weeden and Sabini 2005). However, this does not contradict the evidence that height is related to good genes in men, as height could contribute to fitness at reproductive ages while imposing costs at later ages.

8 Eminence as a Male Intrasexual Competition Strategy

However, height does not necessarily signal physical strength. There is some evidence that a lean and relatively weak body in terms of muscularity is characteristic of intelligent men. In fact, in many modern organizations, what Sheldon and

Stevens (1942) referred to as an *ectomorph* body build may be more advantageous, i.e., a body build based upon a high level of development of the nervous system, characterized by a linear, long and fragile body build with thin muscles and bones. Such a body type seems to best reflect the strategy of eminence. Eminence refers to the elevated rank that is achieved, more gradually, through socially approved accomplishments, such as education and political career making, reflecting the more indirect form of intrasexual competition. It requires individuals to be intelligent and to invest in intellectual activities, and as a consequence, to have, at least to some extent, an inward and reflective orientation. With age, as men's physical dominance declines, the strategy of eminence will have greater success (Kemper 1990; Hill and Hurtado 1996; Rushton 1995). That is, men relying upon the strategy of eminence, although they may not be very successful early in life, often reach their peak later in life (Buss 1994). Therefore, a trade-off with age seems to take place between the strategies of physical dominance and eminence. Note that, in contrast to the strategy of physical dominance, the strategy of eminence requires individuals to delay the gratification of needs. This can be placed within a broader life history framework (Roff 1992; Stearns 1992). In life history theory, a distinction is made between two strategies, an r versus.K strategy. The r-strategy is characterized by a 'fast development': short growth, early sexual maturation, having many offspring of low quality and an overall short lifespan. The K-strategy, in contrast, is characterized by 'slow development': a long growth span, late sexual maturation, few offspring of high quality and an overall long lifespan. While these concepts are typically applied to species, they can also be applied to individual differences. Physical dominance as a strategy is akin to an r-strategy, as it is characterized by a fast development and a short term strategy. Eminence, in contrast, is closer related to a K-strategy, characterized by slow development and a long term strategy.

There is indeed evidence from older studies that an ectomorph body build is associated with higher levels of intelligence and academic success (Kagan 1966; Sanford et al. 1943), and more recent evidence suggests that height, which may in part reflect and ectomorph build, is correlated with cognitive abilities (Case and Paxon 2006) which translates into higher wages (Judge and Cable 2004; Loh 1993). In addition, ectomorphism in men has been found to correlate positively with interest in high status and intellectually challenging vocations such as school superintendent, physician, minister, lawyer, and researcher (Cupcea 1939; Deabler et al. 1975; Garn and Gertler 1950; Tanner 1954), and negatively with lower status and intellectually less challenging occupations, such as bus driver (Deabler et al. 1975). Again, stereotypes about ectomorph men, seem, at least partially, to parallel actual relationships between the ectomorph body build and personality traits. For instance, ectomorph men are usually perceived as more intelligent and scholarly than men with different body builds (Butler et al. 1993; Ryckman et al. 1989), perceptions that are relatively accurate.

To conclude, competition between men within organizations often revolves around physical dominance, even in work contexts where physical strength and effort is not required to adequately execute tasks. Although, in these cases, men may not engage in physical threats or fights with rivals, they do compete with each other on those traits that reflect physical dominance and a high RHP, such as height and a muscular body build. In contrast, men in organizations may compete with each other by means of displaying characteristics that reflect high levels of eminence, such as having a degree, being intelligent, and possessing an ectomorph body build.

The fact that physical features, such as length and body build, as well as body-related stereotypes, are related to status, dominance and eminence pose an interesting challenge for organizations. For instance, it may cause recruiters to show a selection bias, unconsciously favoring those candidates who show the 'right' physical features, but who do not necessarily possess the right competencies for the job. While stereotypes may hold a kernel of truth, they overgeneralize attributes to all members of a group. Although, in general, for instance, ectomorph men may be intellectually more gifted than mesomorph men, of course not every ectomorph man is more intelligent than every mesomorph men. The risk is that body-related stereotypes affect recruitment decisions disproportionally in favor of men with a specific appearance. In itself, this does not always pose a problem. In vocations that include manual labor and that require physical strength, such as construction worker or gardener, having a relatively athletic body build often forms a necessity to perform well on the job. In these cases, preferring an athletic body build makes perfect sense.

However, this is not the case in higher level jobs that require intellectual and social competencies that can be less accurately derived from someone's appearance. In this case reliance on body-related stereotypes may backfire. Recruiters may, for instance, unconsciously feel intimidated by a tall candidate or a candidate with an athletic body build and attribute positive characteristics to him he does not necessarily possess. For example, tall men are, in general, seen as more desirable individuals: they are thought of as socially and physically more attractive (Jackson and Ervin 1992). Moreover, they are thought of as more competent (Cann 1991). The overly positive view of athletic and tall men may cause recruiters to prefer those men over others, even if those others are potentially more competent. Body-related stereotypes may have similar effects in other work-related situations were first impressions are relevant, for instance, in situations where workers deal with customers, clients or co-workers they hardly know. In all these cases, first impressions, preferences, behaviors and judgments are likely to be colored by evolutionary driven, body-related stereotypes. As a result, body-related stereotyping may result in negative discrimination. In Western societies, negative discrimination is seen as an unacceptable phenomenon, which should be eliminated. However, because of the long evolutionary history of body-related stereotypes, these are highly resistant to change and freeing our minds from those stereotypes may require a lot of cognitive effort. In fact, it may not be a realistic goal to adopt. However, rather than rejecting body-related stereotypes, it seems wiser to accept that they are part of our nature, and that, under specific conditions, stereotypes have served and serve adaptive functions. This is not to say that negative discrimination in the work place is to be allowed. Knowledge of the influence of body-related stereotypes is probably one of the most powerful tools to prevent stereotyping from evolving into discriminative action. That is, by becoming aware of the way our impressions and decisions are guided by body-related stereotypes, we may become more objective judges and recruiters. It must be noted that body-related stereotypes usually lose at least part of their power once individuals get to know each other. As more individuating information about someone becomes available, individuals create a more personalized image of the other person (Eagly et al. 1991). Thus, body-related stereotypes especially affect our behaviors and preferences in situations, that, from an evolutionary point of view, were crucial to survival, i.e. in those instances were one was to meet a new individual and it was of essential importance to make fast and decisive judgments about competitive threats and opportunities.

9 Physical Attractiveness as Female Intrasexual Competition Strategy

While it has often been assumed that men are more intrasexually competitive and physically aggressive than women (Archer 2006; Cashdan 1998), in the past decades it has been become increasingly clear that women can be intrasexually quite competitive if not aggressive (Bettencourt and Miller 1996; Frodi et al. 1977; Campbell 2004 for a review). For example, in a cross-cultural examination, Burbank (1987) found that in polygynous societies, co-wives may intrasexually compete for food and money, paternal care for their offspring, and for their offspring's inheritance. In 61% of the 137 cultures analysed by Burbank, women engaged in physical aggression, typically fighting other women over men. It has, for instance, been found that, among women visiting a bar, many cases of physical aggression involve female opponents who are fighting over an actual or potential romantic partner (Collins et al. 2007).

While throughout human history, men have competed primarily in the domains of status, resources, and dominance, women have tended to compete primarily in the domain of physical attractiveness (Campbell 2002; Cashdan 1998; Merten 1997). For example, when confronted with highly attractive rivals, women tend to "dislike" such a rival, particular when she makes intrasexual competition salient, such as when she is conversing with a male (Baenninger et al. 1993). Women most often rate the tactic of attracting attention to their appearance as most effective in competition with others, regardless of what the competition is about (Walters and Crawford 1994; Cashdan 1998). Dijkstra and Buunk (1998) presented data from a series of studies with different methods documenting that romantic jealousy in males is more likely to be evoked by the dominance of the rival, and in females by the physical attractiveness of the rival. Joseph (1985) also found that females were critical of other women, particularly attractive ones, and were concerned about their own appearance in relation to other women, and that ambiguous cues depicting attractive individuals looking at their same sex counterparts evoked responses of jealousy, fear, envy, insecurity, and mistrust in women, but not men. Thus, women tend to compete with each another to an important extent by attempting to look more attractive than other women (Buss 1994; Saad 2007; Saad and Peng 2006). In addition, women also stigmatize or exclude other women as a form of competition (Björkqvist et al. 1992), and often use gossip to derogate other women's appearance and reputation (Campbell 2004). Hess and Hagen (2009) argued that women use gossip as a strategy for intrasexual competition. Women form coalitions with other women in order to gossip about rivals. Rucas and colleagues (2006) found evidence that women use gossip as a strategic tool in a study of the Tsimane of Bolivia. By derogating, for instance, other women's ability as a housekeeper, wife and mother, these other women were seen as less desirable by men. Because women compete with each other over physical attractiveness, gossip often functions to derogate other women's appearance. According to Campbell (2004), the fact that women care more about other women's opinion rather than that of men, suggests that, also among women, intrasexual competition has developed a dynamic of its own, even when it does not lead to being preferred more by the opposite sex. As suggested by Durante and Saad (2010), competitive behaviors such as gossiping and enhancing one's attractiveness, are elevated when women are nearest to ovulation. That is, the motivation to compete intrasexually is especially high at the time when conception is most likely. Several studies point in this direction. For instance, photographs of women near ovulation are consistently rated by both men and women as "trying to look more attractive or fashionable" compared to photographs of women at low-fertility points in the cycle (Haselton et al. 2007). This suggests that women are enhancing their own attractiveness more near ovulation, possibly to increase their ability to compete with other women for a male attention. In addition, women have been found to select outfits that are more revealing and sexy near ovulation, particularly when preparing for a social event (Durante et al. 2008). On a related note, when women are most fertile, they rate photographs of other women as lower in attractiveness, suggesting that women are derogating their competitors when fertility within their cycle is highest (Fisher 2004).

The role of physical attractiveness in work-related intrasexual competition is nicely illustrated by a series of studies by Luxen and Van de Vijver (2006), among both HRM professionals and students, that examined the effect of facial attractiveness on hiring decisions. They first found evidence for a mate-selection motive when the frequency of interaction between the job applicant and the participant was expected to be high. Under this condition, both men and women showed a preference to hire a highly attractive opposite-sex member over an unattractive opposite-sex other, with males showing this tendency more than women. However, with respect to same-sex candidates, a quite different pattern was found, clearly pointing to intrasexual competition: women were less likely to hire a highly attractive female applicant than an unattractive female applicant. The male participants did not show this bias.

This is not at all to imply that for males physical attractiveness is irrelevant in intrasexual competition. In fact, for both sexes, physical attractiveness is a desirable attribute s reflected by the physical attractiveness stereotype. According to this stereotype, attractive individuals – both men and women – are more socially competent, self-confident, intelligent, competent and healthier (Eagly et al. 1991). To what extent this stereotype reflects the truth is not quite clear. According to Feingold (1992) good-looking people are not as good as we think. That is, Feingold found attractive people only to be more socially skilled, and probably as a consequence, to feel less lonely and to be more popular than less attractive people. Other studies, however, indicate that the kernel of truth in the physical attractiveness stereotype is much stronger than Feingold's review suggests. For instance, there is evidence that men high in physical attractiveness tend to have more occupational success (Collins and Zebrowitz 1995; Frieze et al. 1991; Judge and Cable 2004; Roszell et al. 1989). Likewise, Shackelford and Larsen (1999) found that people with symmetric – i.e. relatively attractive – faces were more extraverted, less neurotic, more optimistic, more self-confident, less envious and jealous, and suffered less from physical health complaints, such as headaches and an upset stomach. In a similar vein, women with an hour-glass shaped body – a characteristic that is perceived as highly attractive by both men and women – have been found to be healthier and more fertile than women with a more linear body shape (Singh 1993).

As other body-related stereotypes, the physical attractiveness stereotype may, unknowingly, affect behaviours and preferences of workers, for instance during recruitment and hiring decisions. For instance, Desrumaux (2005) had forty recruiting agents rate applicants and rank them in terms of suitability for different types of jobs: irrespective of job type, attractive applicants were preferred to unattractive ones. However, this seems to apply primarily to female applicants (Heilman and Stopeck 1985a). In addition, a study by Marlowe, Schneider and Nelson (1996) showed that experienced managers are less susceptible to attractiveness biases than their less experienced counterparts, but only when the applicant is a male, suggesting that the physical attractiveness stereotype concerning females is more resistant to change than the physical attractiveness stereotype concerning males. When the applicant is female, less attractive female applicants seem routinely at a disadvantage regardless of the managerial experience of the recruiting manager. Nevertheless, physical attractiveness seems to favor women only when the position is a non-managerial one (Heilman and Stopeck 1985a). When seeking a managerial position, attractive women were thought to be less qualified for the job than unattractive women, and were offered a lower starting salary. When women do reach the executive level, physical attractiveness often remains a disadvantage for them. Heilman and Stopeck (1985b), for instance, showed that workers attributed the corporate success of unattractive female managers more often to their ability than the corporate success of attractive female managers whose success was more often attributed to good luck. The finding that attractive women are at a disadvantage at the managerial level, is usually explained by the stereotype of attractive women as more feminine and nurturing, and as less assertive and self-confident. From an evolutionary psychological point of view this femininity stereotype makes perfect sense: as we discussed earlier, attractive women are indeed more fertile and able to bear children than less attractive women.

Although, in general, attractive people may be more socially skilled, of course not every attractive individual is more socially skilled than every unattractive individual. Thus, at the individual level, body-related stereotypes may negatively affect recruitment decisions, for instance by favoring unattractive women over attractive ones for managerial jobs. Managerial experiences seem not enough to counter this influence. Knowledge about the influence of body-related stereotypes may be the best tool to protect organizations from hiring individuals on the basis of attractiveness, rather than on the basis of actual competencies. In addition, Luxen and Van de Vijver's study suggests that, when one or more applicants are female, it seems wise to make sure that the recruitment team is not exclusively female

As a result of their long evolutionary history, males seem to have more cognitive and behavioral mechanisms to deal with intrasexual competition, and to keep their bonding with members of the same sex intact despite the omnipresent competition (Daly and Wilson 1988; Sidanius and Pratto 1999; Tooby and Cosmides 1988). In contrast, women seem to have more problems with accepting that another female is occupationally more successful than they are. More so than men, women often put pressure on other women not to be too ambitious, and women may refrain from pursuing a career out of fear of alienating other women. This could be, partially, due to their stronger communal orientation (Campbell 2002; Hrdy 1999; Yee et al. 1998). Successful women also have a tendency to hinder the careers of other women. For example, there is evidence that female leaders are often harsher in judging their female than their male subordinates, whereas men do not make a difference in this respect between subordinates of different genders. In a survey of over 600 Australian women in senior positions, Rindfleish and Sheridan (2003) found that less than 40% actively supported programmes for bringing in more women in executive boards. In a second study of 250 women who sat on executive boards, more than four out of ten of these managers, said that women on executive boards should not address or take action to improve women's representation on those boards. Of course, we do not know how many men had the same opinion, but these findings do suggest that many women do not favor policies of positive discrimination of women. Even more so, women may actively hinder other women's careers, as illustrated by two studies by Ellemers et al. (2004) on female and male faculty's evaluations of doctoral students' commitment to their career. In these studies, female faculty members, but not male faculty members, tended to assume that female doctoral students are less committed to a scientific career than their male counterparts. Male and female doctoral students did not reliably differ in their self-reported commitment to different work aspects. The finding that women, typically in senior positions, actively hinder other women's career progression has been coined the 'Queen bee syndrome' (Mavin 2008; Staines et al. 1973). The queen bee can be defined as 'a bitch who stings other women if her power is threatened' (Mavin 2008, p. 75).

Again, these findings suggest that organizations should carefully compose their recruitment teams, including men and women of different ages. Including men in the recruitment team may prevent an unnecessarily harsh judgment of attractive, young applicants when hiring for managerial positions. In addition, older women, for instance female experts over 60, may be included in the team to make sure the perspective of both sexes is included . Because of their age and different life stage, these women may not feel the need to compete with young women and hinder their careers.

10 Conclusion

Although there have been few studies directly examining intrasexual competition at work, the evidence thus far suggests that it exists and plays a pivotal role within organizations. The similarities between romantic and work relationships suggest the existence of an evolved mechanism underlying intrasexual competition, including social comparisons, envy, and the activation of body-related stereotypes, which not only functions within romantic relationships, but also within the evolutionarily novel work contexts. The fact that the intrasexual competition that has evolved over mates and resources, extrapolates to the work place probably occurs because our Stone Age ancestors lived in societies that did not make a clear distinction between private life and workplace life. It is thus noteworthy that these 'old' mechanisms still influence our private and workplace behaviours, especially since intrasexual competition evolved in societies that were quite different from those found in present organizations. In contrast to the small groups (up to 150 people; Dunbar 1998) our evolutionary ancestors lived and worked in, modern organizations are often characterized by interdependence and competitiveness between hundreds of people (people that are all working for the same big organization), by interdependence and competitiveness between smaller groups of people (different departments within the same organization), and by the presence of women in charge of groups (female managers). Thus, it seems that in this evolutionarily novel context of the work place, the same mechanisms tend to affect people's behaviours and preferences, and similar sex differences in, for instance, envy, bullying and social comparison, seem to arise as did thousands of years ago even though, in the novel context, these may be perceived as irrational as they and cause problems for the organization or its members. As discussed in the current chapter, intrasexual competition may, for instance, cause workers to bully each other and recruiters to select candidates based on biased perceptions of abilities. In addition, we presented evidence that shows that the intrasexual competition mechanisms that evolved during human evolution serve men better than women when it comes to obtaining occupational success. While for men the features that characterize their intrasexual competition still tend to be associated with occupational success and status, intrasexual competition among human females is based more so on physical attractiveness. The present evidence suggests that even in professional domains in which attractiveness is assumed to be irrelevant, women still compete heavily in this domain. Women often reject attractive women as candidates for a position in their department, and are particularly jealous of same-sex colleagues who are physically more attractive.

Applying evolutionary psychology to organizational issues, such as workplace envy and the effect of body-related stereotypes on hiring decisions, may be a fruitful approach. The concept of intrasexual competition elucidates why, for instance, female managers may hinder other women's careers, why some people work so hard that they get burned out and why workers ruin their relationships with co-workers by gossiping about them. Evolutionary psychology may also help explain why certain policy measures may not be effective or backfire. The government may, for instance, take measures that intend to enhance the participation of ethnic minorities or handicapped people in the work force, or, that require organizations to hire women for managerial positions. However, policy measures such as these do not take into account humans' inner drive to compete with members of the same sex. Although from a societal or rational point of view, for instance, positive discrimination of women or ethnic minorities may be desirable, it may clash with workers' feelings of fairness in the competitive game, and result in envy or bullying. Policy measures that demand people to resist or oppose their evolutionary based inner drives may have a low chance of success. A policy based on understanding of our human nature and at preventing its pitfalls (rather than changing the basics of who we are) seems more effective.

References

Andersson MB (1994) Sexual selection. Princeton University Press, Princeton
Archer J (2006) The importance of theory for evaluating evidence on sex differences. Am Psychol 61:638–639
Atkinson JW (1957) Motivational determinants of risk-taking behavior. Psychol Rev 64:359–372
Baenninger MA, Baenninger R, Houle D (1993) Attractiveness, attentiveness, and perceived male shortage: their influence on perceptions of other females. Ethol Sociobiol 14:293–304
Bailey KG, Caffrey JV, Hartnett JJ (1976) Body size as implied threat: effects on personal space and person perception. Percept Mot Skills 43:223–230
Bar M, Neta M, Linz H (2006) Very first impressions. Emotion 6:269–278
Barber N (1995) The evolutionary psychology of physical attractiveness: sexual selection and human morphology. Ethol Sociobiol 16:395–424
Bettencourt BA, Miller N (1996) Gender differences in aggression as a function of provocation: a meta-analysis. Psychol Bull 119:422–447
Betzig L (1982) Despotism and differential reproduction. Ethol Sociobiol 3:209–221
Betzig L (1986) Despotism and differential reproduction: a Darwinian view of history. Aldine, New York
Bird RB, Smith EA, Bird DW (2001) The hunting handicap: costly signaling in human foraging strategies. Behav Ecol Sociobiol 50:9–19
Björkqvist K, Lagerspetz KM, Kaukiainen A (1992) Do girls manipulate and boys fight? Developmental trends in regard to direct and indirect aggression. Aggress Behav 18:117–127
Bouchard TJ, McGue M (1990) Genetic and rearing environmental influences on adult personality: an analysis of adopted twins reared apart. J Pers 58:263–292
Brunell AB, Gentry WA, Campbell WK, Hoffman BJ, Kuhnert KW, DeMarree KG (2008) Leader emergence: the case of the narcissistic leader. Pers Soc Psychol Bull 34:1663–1676
Burbank VK (1987) Female aggression in cross-cultural perspective. Behav Sci Res 21:70–100
Buss DM (1991) Evolutionary personality psychology. Annu Rev Psychol 42:459–491
Buss DM (1994) The evolution of desire: strategies of human mating. Basic Books, New York
Butler VJ, Ryckman RM, Thornton B, Bouchard RL (1993) Assessment of the full content of physique stereotypes with a free-response format. J Soc Psychol 133:147–162
Buunk AP, Castro Solano A, Zurriaga R, González P (2011) Gender differences in the jealousy-evoking effect of rival characteristics: a study in Spain and Argentina. J Cross Cult Psychol 42:323–439
Buunk AP, Park JH, Zurriaga R, Klavina L, Massar K (2008) Height predicts jealousy differently for men and women. Evol Hum Beh 29:133–139

Buunk AP, Fisher M (2009) Individual differences in intrasexual competition. J Evol Psychol 7:37–48
Buunk AP, Gibbons FX (2007) Social comparison: the end of a theory and the emergence of a field. Organ Behav Hum Dec 102:3–21
Buunk AP, aan 't Goor J, Castro Solano A (2010) Intra-sexual competition at work: sex differences in the jealousy-evoking effect of rival characteristics in work settings. J Soc Pers Relat 27:671–684
Buunk AP, Massar K, Dijkstra P (2007a) A social cognitive evolutionary approach to jealousy: the automatic evaluation of one's romantic rivals. In: Forgas J, Haselton M, Von Hippel W (eds) Evolution and the social mind: evolutionary psychology and social cognition. Psychology Press, New York, pp 213–228
Buunk AP, Peiró JM, Rodríguez I, Bravo JM (2007b) A loss of status and a sense of defeat: an evolutionary perspective on professional burnout. Eur J Pers 21:471–485
Buunk AP, Van der Laan V (2002) Do women need female role models? Subjective social status and the effects of same-sex and opposite sex comparisons. Rev Int Psychol Soc 15:129–155
Buunk AP, Ybema JF (1997) Social comparisons and occupational stress: the identification-contrast model. In: Buunk BP, Gibbons FX (eds) Health, coping and well being: perspectives from social comparison theory. Erlbaum, Hillsdale, pp 359–388
Campbell A (2002) A mind of her own: the evolutionary psychology of women. University Press, Oxford
Campbell A (2004) Female competition: causes, constraints, content, and contexts. J Sex Res 41:16–26
Cann A (1991) Stereotypes about physical and social characteristics based on social and professional competence information. J Soc Psychol 131:225–231
Case A, Paxon C (2006) Height, health, and cognitive function at older ages. Am Econ Rev Pap Proc 98:463–467
Cashdan E (1998) Are men more competitive than women? Br J Soc Psychol 37:213–229
Child IL (1950) The relation of somatotype to self-ratings on Sheldon's temperamental traits. J Pers 18:440–453
Choi Y, Mai-Dalton RR (1998) On the leadership function of self-sacrifice. Leadersh Quart 9:475–501
Collins LR, Quickley B, Leonard KE (2007) Women's physical aggression in bars: an event-based examination of precipitants and predictors of severity. Aggress Behav 33:304–313
Collins MA, Zebrowitz LA (1995) The contributions of appearance to occupational outcomes in civilian and military settings. J Appl Soc Psychol 25:129–163
Crosby F (1982) Relative deprivation among working women. Oxford University Press, New York
Cupcea S (1939) Constitutie morfologica si intelligenta. Revista de Psihologie 2:169–176
Daly M, Wilson M (1988) Homicide. Aldine De Gruyter, New York
Darwin C (1871) The descent of man and selection in relation to sex. John Murray, London
Deabler HL, Hartl EM, Willis CA (1975) Physique and personality: somatotype and vocational interest. Percept Mot Skills 41:382
De Cremer D, Van Knippenberg D (2004) Leader self-sacrifice and leadership effectiveness: the moderating role of leader self-confidence. Organ Behav Hum Decis Process 95:140–155
Desrumaux P (2005) Informations normatives et stéréotypiques: Effets de l'internalité/externalité, du genre, de l'apparence physique et du type hiérarchique et sexuel du poste sur les décisions de recrutement/Normative and stereotypic information: Effects of internality/externality, gender, physical appearance, and position level and sex type of the job on hiring decisions. Rev Int Psychol Soc 18:165–199
Dijkstra P, Buunk BP (1998) Jealousy as a function of rival characteristics: an evolutionary perspective. Pers Soc Psychol Bull 24:1158–1166
Dingemanse NJ, Réale D (2005) Natural selection and animal personality. Behaviour 142:1165–1190

Domey RG, Duckworth JE, Morandi AJ (1964) Taxonomies and correlates of physique. Psychol Bull 62:411–426

Duffy MK, Shaw JD, Schaubroeck JM (2008) Envy in organizational life. In: Smith RH (ed) Envy: theory and research. Oxford University Press, New York, pp 167–189

Dunbar RIM (1998) The social brain hypothesis. Evol Anthropol 6:178–190

Durante KM, Li NP, Haselton MG (2008) Changes in women's choice of dress across the ovulatory cycle: naturalistic and laboratory task-based evidence. Pers Soc Psychol Bull 34:1451–1460

Durante KM, Saad G (2010) Ovulatory shifts in women's social motives and behaviors: implications for corporate organizations. To appear In: Day M, Stanton A, Welpe I (eds) Neuroeconomics and the Firm. Edward Elgar, Northhampton

Eagly AH, Ashmore RD, Makhijani MG, Longo LC (1991) What is beautiful is good, but...: a meta-analytic review of research on the physical attractiveness stereotype. Psychol Bull 110:109–128

Einarsen S, Raknes BI (1997) Harassment in the workplace and the victimization of men. Violence Vict 12:247–263

Ellemers N, Van den Heuvel H, De Gilder D, Maass A, Bonvini A (2004) The underrepresentation of women in science: differential commitment or the queen bee syndrome? Br J Soc Psychol 43:315–338

Elsbach K, Sutton RI (1992) Acquiring organizational legitimacy through illegitimate actions: a marriage of institutional and impression management theories'. Acad Manage J 35: 699–738

Feather NT (1994) Attitudes towards high achievers and reactions to their fall: theory and research concerning tall poppies. Adv Exp Soc Psychol 26:1–73

Feingold A (1982) Do taller men have prettier girlfriends? Psychol Rep 50:810

Feingold A (1992) Good-looking people are not what we think. Psychol Bull 111:304–341

Feldman NS, Ruble DN (1981) Social comparison strategies: dimensions offered and options taken. Pers Soc Psychol Bull 7:11–16

Figueredo AJ, Sefcek JA, Vasquez G, Brumbach BH, King JE, Jacobs WJ (2005) Evolutionary personality psychology. In: Buss DM (ed) The handbook of evolutionary psychology. Wiley, Hoboken, pp 851–877

Fischer P, Kastenmüller A, Frey D, Peus C (2009) Social comparison and information transmission in the work context. J Appl Soc Psychol 39:42–61

Fisher ML (2004) Female intrasexual competition decreases female facial attractiveness. Proc R Soc Lond Biol Lett 271:283–285

Fiske ST (1992) Stereotypes work... but only sometimes: Comment on how to motivate the 'unfinished mind.'. Psychol Inq 3:161–162

Försterling F, Preikschas S, Agthe M (2007) Ability, luck, and looks: an evolutionary look at achievement ascriptions and the sexual attribution bias. J Pers Soc Psychol 92:775–788

Frederick D, Haselton MG (2007) Why is muscularity sexy? Tests of the fitness indicator hypothesis. Pers Soc Psychol Bull 33:1167–1183

Frodi A, Macaulay J, Thome P (1977) Are women always less aggressive than men? A review of the experimental literature. Psychol Bull 84:634–660

Frieze IH, Olson JE, Russell J (1991) Attractiveness and income for men and women in management. J Appl Soc Psychol 21:1039–1057

Gangestad SW, Simpson JA (2000) The evolution of human mating: trade-offs and strategic pluralism. Behav Brain Sci 23:573–587

Gardner WL, Martinko MJ (1988) Impression management in organizations. J Manage 14: 321–338

Garn SM, Gertler MM (1950) An association between type of work and physique in an industrial group. Am J Phys Anthropol 8:387–397

Geary DC (1998) Male, female: the evolution of human sex differences. American Psychological Association, Washington

Geary DC (2005) Evolution of paternal investment. In: Buss DM (ed) The handbook of evolutionary psychology. John Wiley and Sons, Hoboken, pp 483–505

Geurts SA, Buunk BP, Schaufeli WB (1994) Health complaints, social comparisons and absenteeism. Work Stress 8:220–234

Gibson RM, Bradbury JW (1985) Sexual selection in lekking sage grouse: phenotypic correlates of male mating success. Behav Ecol Sociobiol 18:117–123

Gilbert P, Price J, Allan S (1995) Social comparison, social attractiveness and evolution: how might they be related? New Ideas Psychol 13:149–165

Gino F, Pierce L (2009) The abundance effect: unethical behavior in the presence of wealth. Organ Behav Hum Decis Process 109:142–155

Haselton MG, Mortezaie M, Pillsworth EG, Bleske-Rechek A, Frederick DA (2007) Ovulatory shifts in human female ornamentation: near ovulation, women dress to impress. Horm Behav 51:41–45

Hawkes K, Bliege Bird R (2002) Showing off, handicap signaling, and the evolution of men's work. Evol Anthropol 11:58–67

Heilman ME, Stopeck MH (1985a) Being attractive, advantage or disadvantage? Performance-based evaluations and recommended personnel actions as a function of appearance, sex, and job type. Organ Behav Hum Decis Process 35:202–215

Heilman ME, Stopeck MH (1985b) Attractiveness and corporate success: different causal attributions for males and females. J Appl Psychol 70:379–388

Hensley WE (1993) Height as a measure of success in academe. J Hum Behav 30:40–46

Hess NH, Hagen EH (2009) Informational warfare: coalitional gossiping as a strategy for within-group aggression. Preprint available on http://anthro.vancouver.wsu.edu/publications/

Hill SE, Buss DM (2006) Envy and positional bias in the evolutionary psychology of management. Managerial Decis Econ 27:131–143

Hill SE, Buss DM (2008) The evolutionary psychology of envy. In: Smith RH (ed) Envy: theory and research. Oxford University Press, New York, pp 60–70

Hill K, Hurtado AM (1996) Ache life history. Walter de Gruyter, New York

Hopcroft RL (2005) Parental status and differential investment in sons and daughters: Trivers-Willard revisited. Soc Forces 83:1111–1136

Hrdy SB (1999) Mother nature: natural selection and the female of the species. Chatto & Windus, London

Ilgen DR, Davis CA (2000) Bearing bad news: reactions to negative performance feedback. Appl Psychol-Int Rev 49(3):550–565

Iredale W, Van Vugt M, Dunbar RIM (2008) Showing off in humans: male generosity as mate signal. Evol Psychol 6:386–392

Jackson LA, Ervin KS (1992) Height stereotypes of women and men: the liabilities of shortness for both sexes. J Soc Psychol 132:433–445

Jandeska KE, Kraimer ML (2005) Women's perceptions of organizational culture, work attitudes, and role-modeling behaviors. J Managerial Issues 17:461–478

Joseph R (1985) Competition between women. Psychol J Hum Behav 22:1–12

Judge TA, Cable DM (2004) The effect of physical height on workplace success and income: preliminary test of a theoretical model. J Appl Psychol 89:428–441

Kagan J (1966) Body build and conceptual impulsivity in children. J Pers 34:118–128

Kemper TD (1990) Social structure and testosterone: explorations of the socio-bio-social chain. Rutgers University Press, New Brunswick

Keltner D, Haift J, Shiota MN (2006) Social functions and the evolution of emotions. In: Schaller MA, Simpson JA, Kenrick DT (eds) Evolution and social psychology. Psychology Press, New York, pp 115–142

Kurzban R, Weeden J (2005) HurryDate: mate preferences in action. Evol Hum Behav 26:227–244

Lerner RM, Korn SJ (1972) The development of body-build stereotypes in males. Child Dev 3:908–920

Linehan M, Scullion H (2008) The development of female global managers: the role of mentoring and networking. J Bus Ethics 83:29–40
Loh ES (1993) The economic effects of physical appearance. Soc Sci Quart 74:420–438
Luxen MF, Van de Vijver FJR (2006) Facial attractiveness, sexual selection, and personnel selection: when evolved preferences matter. J Organ Behav 27:241–255
Lycett J, Dunbar RIM (2000) Mobile phones as lekking devices among human males. Hum Nat 11:93–104
Manning JT (1995) Fluctuating asymmetry and body weight in men and women: implications for sexual selection. Ethol Sociobiol 16:145–153
Mar RA, DeYoung CG, Higgins DM, Peterson JB (2006) Self-liking and self-competence separate self-evaluation from self-deception: associations with personality, ability, and achievement. J Pers 74:1047–1078
Marlowe CM, Schneider SL, Nelson CE (1996) Gender and attractiveness biases in hiring decisions: are more experienced managers less biased? J Appl Psychol 81:11–21
Massar K, Buunk AP (2009) Rivals in the mind's eye: jealous responses after subliminal exposure to body shapes. Pers Individ Differ 46:129–134
Mavin S (2008) Queen Bees, wannabees, and afraid to bees: no more 'best enemies' for women in management? Br J Manage 19:75–s84
Meliá JL, Becerril M (2007) Psychosocial sources of stress and burnout in the construction sector: a structural equation model. Psicothema 19:679–686
McClelland DC, Maddocks JA, McAdams DP (1985) The need for power, brain norepinephrine turnover, and memory. Motiv Emotion 9:1–10
Merten DE (1997) The Meaning of meanness: popularity, competition, and conflict among junior high school girls. Sociol Educ 70:175–191
Miller CT (1984) Self-schemas, gender, and social comparison: a clarification of the related attributes hypothesis. J Pers Soc Psychol 46:1222–1229
Miller GF (2000) The mating mind. Heinemann, London
Miller GF (2009) Spent: sex, evolution, and consumer behavior. Viking Adult, New York
Mueller U, Mazur A (2001) Evidence of unconstrained directional selection for male tallness. Behav Ecol Sociobiol 50:302–311
Nettle D (2002) Height and reproductive success in a cohort of British men. Hum Nat 13:473–491
Nettle D (2006) The evolution of personality variation in humans and other animals. Am Psychol 61:622–631
Nettle D, Pollet TV (2008) Natural selection on male wealth in humans. Am Nat 172:658–666
Pawlowski B (2003) Variable preferences for sexual dimorphism in height as a strategy for increasing the pool of potential partners in humans. Proc R Soc Lond B 270:709–712
Pawlowski B, Dunbar RIM, Lipowicz A (2000) Tall men have more reproductive success. Nature 403:156
Pawlowski B, Koziel S (2002) The impact of traits offered in personal advertisements. Evol Hum Behav 23:139–149
Penke L, Denissen JJA, Miller GF (2007) The evolutionary genetics of personality. Eur J Pers 21:549–587
Penton-Voak IS, Chen JY (2004) High salivary testosterone is linked to masculine male facial appearance in humans. Evol Hum Behav 25:229–241
Quinn TJ, Wilson BR (1989) Somatotype and Type A behavior in college-age adults. Psychol Rep 65:15–18
Rindfleish J, Sheridan A (2003) No change from within: senior women managers' response to gendered organizational structures. Women Manage Rev 18:299–310
Roff DA (1992) The evolution of life histories. Springer, New York
Roszell P, Kennedy D, Grabb E (1989) Physical attractiveness and income attainment among Canadians. J Psychol 123:547–559

Rucas SL, Gurven M, Kaplan H, Winking J, Gangestad S, Crespo M (2006) Female intrasexual competition and reputational effects on attractiveness among the Tsimane of Bolivia. Evol Hum Behav 27:40–52

Rushton PJ (1985) Differential K theory: the sociobiology of individual and group differences. Pers Individ Differ 6:441–452

Rushton PJ (1995) Race, evolution, and behavior: a life history perspective. Transaction Publishers, New Brunswick

Ryckman RM, Robbins MA, Kaczor LM, Gold JA (1989) Male and female raters ' stereotyping of male and female physiques. Pers Soc Psychol Bull 15:244–251

Saad G (2007) A multitude of environments for a consilient Darwinian meta-theory of personality: the environment of evolutionary adaptedness, local niches, the ontogenetic environment and situational contexts. Eur J Pers 21:624–626

Saad G, Gill T (2001a) Gender differences when choosing between salary allocation options. Appl Econ Lett 8:531–533

Saad G, Gill T (2001b) Sex differences in the ultimatum game: an evolutionary psychology perspective. J Bioecon 3:171–193

Saad G, Peng A (2006) Applying Darwinian principles in designing effective intervention strategies: the case of sun tanning. Psychol Market 23:617–638

Saad G, Vongas JG (2009) The effect of conspicuous consumption on men's testosterone levels. Organ Behav Hum Decis Process 110:80–92

Salmon C (2005) Parenting and kinship. In: Buss DM (ed) The handbook of evolutionary psychology. Wiley, Hoboken, pp 506–527

Salovey P, Rodin J (1991) Provoking jealousy and envy: domain relevance and self-esteem threat. J Soc Clin Psychol 10:395–413

Samaras TT, Harold E, Storms LH (2003) Is height related to longevity? Life Sci 72:1781–1802

Sanford RN, Adkins MM, Miller RB, Cobb EA (1943) Physique, personality and scholarship: a cooperative study of school children. Monogr Soc Res Child Dev 8:705

Savin-Williams RC (1976) An ethological study of dominance formation and maintenance in a group of human adolescents. Child Dev 47:972–979

Savin-Williams RC (1979) Dominance hierarchies in groups of early adolescents. Child Dev 50:923–935

Shackelford TK, Larsen RJ (1999) Facial attractiveness and physical health. Evol Hum Behav 20:71–76

Schlenker BR (1980) Impression management: the self-concept, social identity, and interpersonal relations. Brooks/Cole, Monterey

Schmitt BD (1988) Social comparison in romantic jealousy. Pers Soc Psychol Bull 14:374–387

Schousboe K, Visscher PM, Erbas B, Kyvik KO, Hopper JL, Henriksen JE et al (2004) Twin study of genetic and environmental influences on adult body size, shape, and composition. Int J Obes 28:39–48

Schuster B (1996) Rejection, exclusion, and harassment at work and in schools. An integration of results from research on mobbing, bullying, and peer rejection. Eur Psychol 1:293–317

Sheldon WH, Stevens SS (1942) The varieties of temperament: a psychology of constitutional differences. Harper, Oxford

Shepperd JA, Strathman AJ (1989) Attractiveness and height: the role of stature in dating preference, frequency of dating, and perceptions of attractiveness. Pers Soc Psychol Bull 15:617–627

Sidanius J, Pratto F (1999) Social dominance. Cambridge University Press, Cambridge

Silventoinen K, Lahelma E, Rahkonen O (1999) Social background, adult body-height and health. Int J Epidemiol 28:911–918

Singh D (1993) Adaptive significance of female physical attractiveness: role of waist-to-hip ratio. J Pers Soc Psychol 65:293–307

Smith RH, Kim SH (2007) Comprehending envy. Psychol Bull 133:46–64

Sluckin AM, Smith PK (1977) Two approaches to the concept of dominance in preschool children. Child Dev 48:917–923

Staines G, Travis C, Jayerante E (1973) The queen bee syndrome. Psychol Today 7:55–60

Steil JM, Hay JL (1997) Social comparison in the workplace: a study of 60 dual-career couples. Pers Soc Psychol Bull 23:427–438

Stearns SC (1992) The evolution of life histories. Oxford University Press, Oxford

Suls J, Gaes G, Gastorf JW (1979) Evaluating a sex-related ability: comparison with same-, opposite-, and combined-sex norms. J Res Pers 13:294–304

Tafarodi RW, Swann WB (1995) Self-liking and self-competence as dimensions of global self-esteem: initial validation of a measure. J Pers Assess 65:322–342

Tafarodi RW, Swann WB (2001) Two-dimensional self-esteem: theory and measurement. Pers Individ Differ 31:653–673

Tafarodi RW, Vu C (1997) Two-dimensional self-esteem and reactions to success and failure. Pers Soc Psychol Bull 23:626–635

Tanner JM (1954) Physique and choice of a career. Eugen Rev 46:149–157

Tellegen A, Lykken DT, Bouchard J, Wilcox KJ, Segal NL, Rich S (1988) Personality similarity in twins reared apart and together. J Pers Soc Psychol 54:1031–1039

Tiedens LZ, Fragale AR (2003) Power moves: complementarity in dominant and submissive nonverbal behavior. J Pers Soc Psychol 84:558–568

Thornhill R, Grammer K (1999) The body and face of woman: one ornament that signals quality? Evol Hum Behav 20:105–120

Tooby J, Cosmides L (1988) The evolution of war and its cognitive foundations. Institute for Evolutionary Studies technical report 88-1

Trivers RL (1972) Parental investment and sexual selection. In: Campbell B (ed) Sexual selection and the descent of man, 1871–1971. Aldine, Chicago, pp 136–179

Van de Ven N, Zeelenberg M, Pieters R (2009) Leveling up and down: the experiences of benign and malicious envy. Emotion 9:419–429

Van Dick R, Wagner U (2001) Stress and strain in teaching: a structural equation approach. Br J Educ Psychol 71:243–259

Van Lange PAM, Otten W, de Bruin EMN, Joireman JA (1997) Development of prosocial, individualistic, and competitive orientations: theory and preliminary evidence. J Pers Soc Psychol 73:733–746

Van Vugt M, Roberts G, Hardy C (2007) Competitive altruism: development of reputation-based cooperation in groups. In: Dunbar RIM, Barrett L (eds) Handbook of evolutionary psychology. Oxford University Press, Oxford, pp 531–540

Van Vugt M, Spisak BR (2008) Sex differences in the emergence of leadership during competitions within and between groups. Psychol Sci 19:854–858

Van Yperen NW (2003) Task interest and actual performance: the moderating effects of assigned and adopted purpose goals. J Pers Soc Psychol 85:1006–1015

Veblen (1899 [1934]) The theory of the leisure class. New York, Modern Library

Vecchio RP (2000) Negative emotion in the workplace: employee jealousy and envy. Int J Stress Manage 7:161–179

Verdonck PF, Walker RN (1976) Body build and behavior in emotionally disturbed Dutch children. Genet Psychol Monogr 94:149–173

Walters S, Crawford CB (1994) The importance of mate attraction for intrasexual competition in men and women. Ethol Sociobiol 15:5–30

Walters JR, Seyfarth RM (1987) Conflict and cooperation. In: Smuts BB, Cheney DL, Seyfarth RM, Wrangham RW, Struhsaker TT (eds) Primate societies. University of Chicago Press, Chicago, pp 306–318

Wayne SJ, Liden RC (1995) Effects of impression management on performance ratings: a longitudinal study. Acad Manage J 18:232–260

Weeden J, Sabini J (2005) Physical attractiveness and health in Western societies: a review. Psychol Bull 131:635–653

Wilson PR (1968) Perceptual distortions of height as a function of ascribed academic status. J Soc Psychol 74:97–102

Wilson DS, Near D, Miller RR (1996) Machiavellianism: a synthesis of the evolutionary and psychological literatures. Psychol Bull 119:285–299

Wrangham RW, Peterson G (1996) Demonic males: apes and the origins of human violence. Houghton, Mifflin and Company, Boston

Yeagley E, Morling B, Nelson M (2007) Nonverbal zero-acquaintance accuracy of self-esteem, social dominance orientation, and satisfaction with life. J Res Pers 41:1099–1106

Yee JL, Greenberg MS, Beach SR (1998) Attitudes toward various modes of coping with criminal victimizations: the effects of gender and type of crime. J Soc Clin Psychol 17:273–294

Zahavi A, Zahavi A (1997) The handicap principle: a missing piece of Darwin's puzzle. Oxford University Press, Oxford

Zhou J (1998) Feedback valence, feedback style, task autonomy, and achievement orientation: interactive effects on creative performance. J Appl Psychol 83:261–276

Zuckerman M (1986) On the meaning and implications of facial prominence. J Nonverbal Behav 10:215–229

Zuckerman M, O'Loughlin RE (2006) Self-enhancement by social comparison: a prospective analysis. Pers Soc Psychol Bull 32:751–760

Evolutionary Psychology and Sex Differences in Workplace Patterns

Kingsley R. Browne

Abstract Differences in workplace outcomes – such as the "glass ceiling", the "gender gap in compensation", and "occupational segregation" – are often attributed primarily to social forces. However, biological sex differences with roots in our evolutionary history and mediated by sex hormones also play an important role.

The sexes differ, on average, along a number of temperamental and cognitive dimensions. Males are higher in competitiveness, dominance-seeking, and risk-taking, while females are higher in nurturance. Males have an advantage in mechanical ability and on some spatial and mathematical tasks, while females outperform males on other spatial and computational tasks, as well as on many verbal tasks. Females tend to be more "person-oriented" and males more "thing-oriented".

Talents and tastes have major workplace effects, as they influence how high in organizations people progress, how much money they make, and what jobs they hold. Men are more likely to subordinate other things – often including families – to maintain a single-minded focus on success and to take the risks necessary to become top executives. Men earn more money than women because, among other reasons, they tend to work more hours, occupy riskier jobs, and work in less-pleasant environments. Many jobs continue to be highly segregated by sex not just because of cognitive and physical sex differences, but probably even more strongly because of differences in occupational interests.

Keywords Sex differences · Temperament · Workplace · Testosterone · Glass ceiling · Gender gap · Occupational segregation

K.R. Browne
Wayne State University Law School, Detroit, MI 48202, USA
e-mail: kingsley.browne@wayne.edu

1 Introduction

Discussions about sex differences in occupational outcomes typically rest, at least implicitly, upon the "Standard Social Science Model" (SSSM) (Tooby and Cosmides 1992). This model assumes that psychological sex differences are purely products of socialization rather than of a sexually dimorphic mind produced by natural selection. Differences in workplace outcomes – whether the "glass ceiling", the "gender gap in compensation", or "occupational segregation" – are assumed to result from discriminatory action, whether overt discrimination by employers, sex-based socialization that nudges women away from high-paying positions and "male occupations", or institutions based upon "male norms".

Reflexive assumptions of purely social causes ignore the wealth of information about sex differences revealed over recent decades. Even a decade and a half ago, Alice Eagly (1995:154) could write about the literature on sex differences as follows: "Those who have immersed themselves in this area of science have begun to realize that it is not cultural stereotypes that have been shattered by contemporary psychological research but the scientific consensus forged in the feminist movement of the 1970s". Since that writing, the literature documenting sex differences has ballooned, and evolutionary psychologists have provided explanations of their origins (Geary 2009; Buss 2007; Mealey 2000). Sex differences in temperament, interest, and ability play out in a particularly visible way in the workplace, where the relationship between talents and tastes, on the one hand, and occupational outcomes, on the other, leads to different workplace outcomes for the two sexes (Browne 2006, 2002).

Explanations based on broad social causes provide little insight into the complexity of workplace patterns. Although it is true that women are not proportionately represented in the executive suite, for example, they have reached near-parity among new lawyers and doctors. Similarly, women do not earn, on average, as much as men do, but women who perform the same work and display the same workplace attachment as men earn approximately the same as comparable men. Women have also not made proportionate inroads in some occupations, with some, such as mechanics, firefighting, and theoretical physics having relatively few women. On the other hand, women are rapidly taking over other occupations, such as psychology, pharmacy, and veterinary medicine (Browne 2002). Evolutionary psychology provides a more nuanced explanation for these patterns than the entirely sociological account can.

The first section of this chapter will describe sex differences in temperament, vocational interest, and cognitive abilities, and show how these differences influence occupational patterns. In the second section, the focus will shift to causes: why do the sexes exhibit these differences and what are the proximate mechanisms by which they develop? Finally, we will turn to an examination of the weaknesses of the view, so prevalent during the past half-century, that observed sex differences can be explained solely as products of socialization.

2 Temperamental and Cognitive Sex Differences and Their Workplace Consequences

2.1 Temperamental Sex Differences and the "Glass Ceiling" and the "Gender Gap" in Compensation

The sexes display average differences on a variety of temperamental measures. Males, for example, exhibit greater motivations to achieve certain kinds of extra-domestic success. They display greater direct competitiveness, and competition tends to be a more positive experience for males than it is for females (Benenson et al. 2002). Adding a competitive component to a task increases both the performance and the intrinsic motivation of males but not of females (Van Vugt et al. 2007; Conti et al. 2001). Relatedly, males engage in more dominance behaviors, that is, behaviors designed to obtain power, influence, prerogatives, or resources (Mazur and Booth 1998).

The sexes also differ in their propensity for risk (Byrnes et al. 1999). Men predominate in such risky recreational activities as car racing, skydiving, and hang-gliding (Schrader and Wann 1999), and they are disproportionately represented in risky employment. From 1992 through 2007, men made up between 91% and 93% of all U.S. deaths in the workplace (U.S. Department of Labor 2008a:2, 2009a), a pattern observed in other countries as well (Grazier and Sloane 2008; Lin et al. 2008). Females are more averse not just to physical risk but also to social risk (Larkin and Pines 2003), including financial risk (Fehr-Duda et al. 2006), and this sex difference may in part be responsible for sex differences in achievement-orientation (Arch 1993).

The sexes also differ in nurturance and interest in children, traits that are negatively correlated with such traits as dominance. Females in all societies exhibit more nurturing behavior than males, both inside and outside the family. Throughout the world, women are the primary caretakers of the young, the sick, and the old (Maccoby and Jacklin 1974). This difference, along with those mentioned previously, has substantial workplace effects.

2.1.1 Temperament and the "Glass Ceiling"

These sex differences seem to be at least in part responsible for the tendency of women to be under-represented at the highest levels of organizations. It should be emphasized that although the term "glass ceiling" implies an external barrier to advancement, the term itself is merely a description of statistical outcomes not an identification of causes.

Successful executives of both sexes possess a constellation of male-like traits. They tend to be competitive, assertive, ambitious, strongly career-oriented risk-takers (Morrison et al. 1992:28–32). They also are usually willing to subordinate other things in their lives – often including families – to maintain a single-minded focus on success.

Risk preferences also play an important role in career outcomes, as they can affect both the attainment of, and performance in, a given position. Risk preferences influence occupational choices (Halaby 2003), and some jobs carry more career risk than others. One of the hallmarks of the successful executive is a taste for risk (Grey and Gordon 1978). A study of over 500 top executives found that willingness to take risks was the primary determinant of success, as measured by wealth, income, position, and authority (MacCrimmon and Wehrung 1990). Because achievement opportunities are often coupled with uncertainty and the potential for loss, they may appear threatening to the risk-averse. Hennig and Jardim (1977:23) noted that "men see risk as loss or gain; winning or losing; danger or opportunity", while "women see risk as entirely negative. It is loss, danger, injury, ruin, hurt". Because of the visibility of their impact on the bottom line, "line" positions, such as running a plant or division, carry more career risk than "staff" jobs, such as human resources or public relations. In most organizations, line positions are a critical part of the executive career path, and women's lack of line experience is a key contributor to their pattern of advancement (Townsend 1996).

Attainment of the highest corporate positions requires more than just the right personality. It frequently requires decades of devotion to career, long hours, and frequent travel and relocations. Women are less willing than men to make these sacrifices, both because of family issues and because the payoff–being "top dog" – is not valued by women as much as it is by men (Schwartz 1992). Women are also less willing to uproot themselves from networks of friends and relatives to move off to a new city (Baldridge et al. 2006), even though relocation may be a de facto prerequisite for advancement.

Marriage and children have different impacts on men and women. When women marry, and especially after they have children, they tend to reduce their work involvement, whereas men tend to increase theirs (Harrell 1993). Many women remain out of the work force for an extended time after childbirth, and if they do return to work, many cut back substantially on their work commitment (Schwartz 1992). To an observer with an evolutionary perspective, it is unsurprising to learn that mammalian mothers find it emotionally difficult to separate from their young. That reluctance, however, can be an impediment to reaching the executive suite.

2.1.2 Temperament and Income: The "Gender Gap" in Compensation

The same factors that contribute to women's under-representation in the executive ranks also affect their compensation. The term "gender gap in compensation" refers to the fact that full-time female employees, on average, earn less than full-time male employees. In 2007, the female-to-male annual earnings ratio in the United States was .778 (U.S. Census Bureau 2008), indicating that the average full-time female worker earned 77.8 cents for every dollar earned by a male. The *weekly* earnings disparity was smaller (a ratio of .802) (U.S. Department of Labor 2008b:252, Table 37), reflecting the fact that women work slightly fewer weeks per year. This ratio still overstates the earnings disparity, however, because, as we will see below, men also work substantially more hours per week than women.

Although the gender gap is often simplistically invoked as proof of wage discrimination, the fact that most of the pay gap occurs across, rather than within, occupations, is powerful evidence that ordinary wage discrimination – employers paying women less than men for the same job – is not the primary cause (Groshen 1991). But if discrimination is not the primary contributor, what is? The answer is that there is a broad array of factors, many of which, like contributors to the glass ceiling, reflect sex differences in psychological proclivities. In general, men tend to invest more of themselves in the workplace to attain both status and resources; women tend to invest relatively more of themselves in their families and less in the workplace. Men earn more in large part because they tend to work more hours and have lower absenteeism, occupy riskier jobs, work in less-pleasant environments, obtain greater job-related education and training, and have fewer extended withdrawals from the work force (Browne 2002).

Studies uniformly find substantial sex differences in hours worked. In 2006, for example, full-time male employees worked approximately 15% more hours than full-time female employees (41.8 h versus 36.2 h) (U.S. Department of Labor 2007:63, Table 21). A study of managers found that six times as many female managers as male managers had spouses who worked more hours than they did (Burke 1998).

Attitudes toward risk also affect compensation, since, all else being equal, risky jobs pay more than non-risky jobs (Filer 1985). Men predominate in the riskiest jobs; indeed, a list of the most dangerous occupations consists of overwhelmingly male-dominated jobs, such as fisherman, logger, airplane pilot, iron and steel worker, and roofer (U.S. Department of Labor 2009b:16). As previously mentioned, men constitute over 90% of workplace deaths. The higher the proportion of women in an occupation, the less likely it is that the occupation involves hazardous (or otherwise onerous) working conditions (Kilbourne and England 1996).

The relationship between attitudes toward risk and compensation is not limited to physical risk. Some jobs entail substantial "career risk", such as the line jobs referred to previously. Men have a substantially higher preference for "tournament" situations in which there are winners and losers (Niederle and Vesterlund 2008), such as the "partnership tournament" prevalent in large law firms, under which many associates compete for a limited number of partnerships (Galanter and Palay 1991). Moreover, men are more comfortable than women with compensation systems having a greater component of contingent pay, such as commissions and bonuses, which cause employees to bear more of the risk of short-run variations in performance (Chauvin and Ash 1994).

A wide variety of other factors contribute to the gender gap. Women attach greater importance than men to non-wage aspects of jobs such as relations with coworkers and supervisors, flexible hours, shorter commute time, part-time opportunities, and pleasant surroundings (Konrad et al. 2000). Many of the low-paid jobs occupied by women are low-paid in part because they have these desirable characteristics and are therefore in higher demand. Filer (1985) attributes a substantial portion of the wage gap to the fact that men tend to take jobs that are less attractive in some way than those filled by women. That is, women give up some amount of wages in exchange for other attractive job attributes, so that, in Adam Smith's (1776:65) terminology, the "whole of the advantages and disadvantages of the different employments of labour and stock [are] either perfectly equal, or continually tending toward equality".

Sex differences in productivity also contribute to the wage gap. Although productivity is often difficult to measure, a series of studies in Israel and the United States found female employees to be less productive than male employees (Hellerstein and Neumark 1998; Hellerstein et al. 1996). Studies of piecework workers have demonstrated similar productivity differences (Rhoads 1993), and numerous studies of academics have shown that male faculty typically produce about 50% more articles than their female counterparts (Xie and Shauman 1998; Zuckerman 1991). Cole and Fiorentine (1991:223) suggest that male scientists outproduce female scientists "because it is more important to men to be occupationally successful than it is to women" – that is, to be recognized as being at the top of the hierarchy.

Much of the wage gap, like the glass ceiling, is related to marital and family status. One study found that single women without children earned over 95% of single men's pay, while married mothers earned only 60% of married men's pay (Blau and Kahn 1992). Among individuals between the ages of 27 and 33 without children, women's earnings are approximately equal to men's (Furchtgott-Roth and Stolba 1999). Women with children work fewer hours than women without children and are more likely to work intermittently, both factors that reduce earnings (Korenman and Neumark 1992).

The "gender gap" in compensation is largely an illusion. It mostly disappears when variables that legitimately affect compensation – many of which are related to evolutionarily derived sex differences – are included in the analysis. As will be seen below, many of these same factors, along with average differences in cognitive abilities, influence the occupations that individuals choose to pursue.

2.2 Sex Differences in Vocational Interest and Cognitive Abilities and Their Impact on Occupational Segregation

2.2.1 Sex Differences in Vocational Interest

In addition to basic elements of temperament and personality such as risk preference and dominance, the sexes also differ in "vocational personality" (Holland 1997), as revealed by such instruments as the Strong Interest Inventory and the Self-Directed Search. Reliable sex differences are exhibited on at least five of the six Holland General Occupational Themes. Males score substantially higher on the Realistic (building/working outdoors and with things), *Investigative* (abstract problems/science/math), and *Enterprising* (persuasion/selling/business) themes.

Females, in contrast, score higher on *Artistic* (art/drama/language) and *Social* (helping/teaching). The sixth theme – *Conventional* (organizing/clerical/processing data) – shows little difference (Aros et al. 1998). Kaufman and McLean (1998) found effect sizes (absolute values) on the General Occupational Themes ranging from a very large 1.28 to a trivial .06: Realistic (1.28), Investigative (.56), Artistic (−.29), Social (−.29), Enterprising (.19), and Conventional (.06).

Underlying the Holland Occupational Themes are two dimensions: "People-Things" and "Ideas-Data" (Prediger 1982). Although sex differences on the "Ideas-Data" dimension are not consistently found, large differences are found on the "People-Things" dimension, with women tending to cluster toward the "People" end and men toward the "Things" end (Lippa 1998), mirroring the more people-oriented tendency of females. A recent meta-analysis of studies spanning four decades concluded that "[t]hese sex differences are remarkably consistent across age and over time" (Su et al. 2009:880).

The Risk Taking/Adventure style of the Strong Interest Inventory also reveals substantial sex differences. This style largely replicates the Adventure Basic Interest Scale (BIS) from earlier versions of the test (Kaufman and McLean 1998). The sex difference on the Adventure scale was reliably one of the two largest on the Basic Interest Scales ($d = 1.21$ in the Kaufman and McLean study), the other being mechanical activity ($d = 1.29$). The highest scorers on the Adventure Personal Style are police officers, whereas the lowest are dental assistants. Women with high Adventure scores tend not only to gravitate to stereotypically male occupations, but also to marry later and desire fewer children (Douce and Hansen 1990).

Vocational-interest tests measure the kinds of jobs that people would find congenial, but they are distinct from tests of ability. According to the "Theory of Work Adjustment" (Dawis and Lofquist 1984), two dimensions of correspondence between the individual and the job are required for a successful job match: "satisfactoriness" and "satisfaction" The latter refers to correspondence of the occupational rewards (e.g., type of work, working conditions, compensation) and the individual's values and interests; the former refers to correspondence between the individual's abilities and the demands of the occupation. That is, it is not enough to be interested in a job; one must also have the talent to perform it competently. So, both differences in vocational interest and differences in abilities are potentially relevant to job choice.

2.2.2 Sex Differences in Cognitive Abilities

The sexes differ on a variety of cognitive measures. Any difference in general intelligence is small, although there may be a slight advantage favoring males (Geary 2009). What seems better established is that because of greater male variability in IQ, a disproportionate number of males are found in both the very high and very low ends of the IQ distribution. For purposes of our inquiry, however, the specific patterns of cognitive strengths may be more important than differences in the distribution of general intelligence.

Males outperform females on a number of spatial tasks, especially mental rotation, spatial perception, and targeting tasks, such as guiding and intercepting projectiles (Kimura 1999). A meta-analysis of mental-rotation studies found an average effect size of .66 for adults, and the effect size in many studies exceeds 1.0 (Voyer et al. 1995). Spatial rotation is correlated with a variety of other abilities, such as mechanical ability, map reading, way-finding, mathematical reasoning, and success as a pilot (Hegarty and Waller 2005). Robust sex differences in targeting, again with effect sizes usually exceeding 1.0 and sometimes approaching 2.0 have also been found (Watson and Kimura 1991; Hines et al. 2003). Females, on the other hand, outperform males on the spatial task of "object location", that is, remembering where an object is located and identifying which objects in an array have been moved from their prior location (Silverman and Eals 1992). In navigating the environment, men are more attuned to compass directions, while women are more attentive to landmarks (Galea and Kimura 1993). These differences persist even in evolutionarily novel contexts, such as navigating shopping malls (Kruger and Byker 2009) and the internet (Stenstrom et al. 2008).

The sexes also differ in mathematical performance. Males excel in mathematical reasoning, especially reasoning involving abstract thinking, and females excel in computation (Kimura 1999). The sex difference is relatively small ($d \approx 0.10$–0.25) in nationally representative samples, though in more select samples, differences tend to be larger (Jensen 1998). On the mathematics portion of the SAT, for example, the effect size is about 0.3 (College Board 2009:1, Table 2). Because males are more variable in performance, they outnumber females by almost two-to-one in the top 10% of math ability.

The sexes also differ in mechanical ability. Males outperform females in mechanical comprehension on the Differential Aptitude Test ($d \approx 0.9$) (Lubinski and Benbow 1992) and on the Air Force Officer Qualification Test ($d \approx 0.95$) (Carretta 1997). Males outnumber females by approximately eight to one in the top 10% of mechanical reasoning ability (Hedges and Nowell 1995).

Females outperform males on a number of verbal tasks, including spelling, grammar, verbal fluency, and verbal memory. In fact, the female advantage in verbal abilities exceeds the male advantage in mathematical ability in broadly representative samples (Freeman 2004). In more select samples, however, the female advantage often declines or disappears. On the Critical Reading portion of the SAT, males regularly outperform females, although the effect size is very small (ranging from $d \approx .02$ to $d \approx 0.08$ in recent years), and on the new Writing portion, females outperform males by a small amount ($d \approx .10$) (College Board 2009:1, Table 2).

2.2.3 Occupational Distributions and Sex Differences in Vocational Interest and Ability

Not surprisingly, there is a relationship between vocational interests and abilities, on the one hand, and occupational distributions on the others. Despite changing social views, a substantial amount of occupational segregation persists. Over 90%

of bank tellers, receptionists, registered nurses, and pre-school teachers are female, for example, and over 90% of electrical engineers, firefighters, mechanics, and pest exterminators are male (Browne 2002). Women are still relatively under-represented in some scientific fields, such as mathematics, physics, and engineering. Notwithstanding the seemingly entrenched segregation in some occupations, however, women have made breathtaking advances in others that would have been unimaginable a half-century ago. Professions such as law and medicine are reaching parity among new entrants (American Bar Association n.d; Association of American Medical Colleges 2008), and almost two-thirds of new pharmacists and three-quarters of new veterinarians are women (American Association of Colleges of Pharmacy 2010; McPheron 2007). This pattern – "progress" in some occupations but not in others – is what must be explained by any comprehensive account of the workplace.

Concern about under-representation of women has focused primarily on scientific, technical, and blue-collar occupations. The occupations of concern are often referred to as "traditionally male" or "nontraditional". These labels are misleading, however, as virtually all occupations not specifically reserved for women were "traditionally" filled mostly by men. What distinguishes these occupations is the *current* representation of women. The U.S. Department of Labor, for example, considers an occupation "nontraditional" if women comprise 25% or less of total employment (U.S. Department of Labor 2009c). It would thus be more precise to label these fields "persistently male", with the important issue being why these occupations have remained predominantly male when so many others have become fully integrated or even predominantly female.

As we will see, occupations in which women remain scarce have some distinctive features. The pattern to these occupational distributions is more explainable by differences between the sexes than it is by such forces as sexist socialization.

Women in Science and Technology

The familiar sociological explanation for the scarcity of women in science is that girls are directed away from science by parents, teachers, and peers and encouraged to take more appropriately feminine classes (Dresselhaus et al. 1994). When girls go off to college, they find a "well fortified bastion of sexism" that is hostile and unwelcoming to them, a hostility so great that one observer has pronounced it "shocking . . . that there are any women in science at all" (Holloway 1993:95).

The reality is quite different, as women's representation in scientific fields varies greatly. In 2005–2006, women earned 20% of the doctorates in engineering, 49% in biological and biomedical sciences, and 73% in psychology (Snyder et al. 2009:433, Table 292). There is also substantial differentiation by sex even within fields. Among Ph.D. recipients in 2006, women were scarce in mining/mineral and petroleum engineering (6% and 8%, respectively), but more heavily represented in bioengineering and environmental health (34.1% and 40.3%, respectively). In biology, women earned 28% of the entomology degrees, but 81% of those in nutritional sciences. In psychology, women earned 55% of the degrees in psychometrics and quantitative psychology but 81% of those in developmental and child psychology. In the social sciences, women were "under-represented" in political science (41%) but "over-represented" in anthropology and sociology (57% and 62%, respectively) (National Science Foundation 2009).

It would be an odd hostility that would produce this variegated pattern. Engineering is hostile to women, although bioengineering is less hostile than mining/mineral engineering; biology is welcoming to women, except for entomology, which is not. A more plausible explanation is differential interest and ability. The fields in which there are relatively few women tend to have a low social dimension – engineering, physics, mathematics, entomology – while those attracting relatively large numbers of women – such as anthropology, sociology, biology, developmental and child psychology, nutritional sciences, environmental health, and bioengineering – have a higher social content. The fields avoided by women also tend to be the most mathematically and spatially demanding, and, although spatial ability is not typically directly screened for in admission to science programs, it is an important predictor of success in scientific fields (Shea et al. 2001). Given the relative positions of males and females on the "people-things" dimension and the disproportion of men at the very highest levels of mathematical and spatial ability, it would be surprising to find sexual parity in each of these widely differing fields.

There is little evidence for the frequent assertion that girls are turned away from science careers. Boys and girls are approximately equally represented in high-school math and science courses (Freeman 2004:72), and girls are actually less likely than boys to believe that they have not received serious attention from teachers about science (Collier et al. 1998). College women are more likely than men to report that they chose science majors because of encouragement from parents or teachers, while more men report that they chose science because of a long-term interest in the subject (Seymour and Hewitt 1997).

Part of the sex difference in mathematics and science participation undoubtedly reflects the increasing sexual disparity in mathematical talent at the extreme high end of ability. Although the "gifted" are often discussed as if they were a homogeneous group, they are highly diverse in ability. The range of the top one percent of scores on a typical IQ test ($\approx$135–200+) is as broad as that of the middle 96% of scores ($\approx$66–134); that is, it accounts for a full one-third of the entire score distribution (Benbow and Lubinski 1993). The combination of a higher male mean and greater variability causes males to especially outnumber females in the top quarter of the top 1% of mathematical ability, a group from which a major portion of scientists in quantitative fields is derived.

A potentially even more significant fact is that even among those with very high math and science ability, the sexes differ in their commitment to math and science. Gifted males gravitate strongly to math and inorganic sciences, and gifted females spread out among math and inorganic sciences, medical and organic sciences, and humanities and arts (Lubinski et al. 2001). Lubinski and Benbow (1992) reported that gifted females at one university enrolled in math and science courses and English and foreign language courses in approximately equal proportions, while males were six times as likely to enroll in math and science courses as in English and foreign language. Women follow this more varied pattern not because they lack ability but because they "are more socially and esthetically oriented and have interests that are more evenly divided among investigative, social, and artistic pursuits" (Lubinski et al. 1993:702). This difference is also reflected in the decision to advance to higher levels of education. Lubinski and Benbow (1992) found that approximately 8% of mathematically gifted males, but only 1% of gifted females, were pursuing doctorates in mathematics, engineering, or the physical sciences. One possible explanation for this pattern is that high-math women tend to have higher verbal ability than high-math men, providing them a greater range of opportunities (Lubinski et al. 2001).

Attitudes toward risk may also influence selection of careers in mathematics and the hard sciences. In these fields, more than in the humanities and social sciences, there are "right answers", and scientific creativity can be judged more objectively. This greater objectivity may account for the fact that the sciences have suffered less from the grade inflation that has plagued the humanities and social sciences (Rosovsky and Hartley 2002). Simply put, studying science is a "risk" – presenting a real possibility of failure – in a way that study in many other fields is not (Osborne et al. 2003).

Attribution of women's relatively slow advancement in some scientific occupations to men's putative resistance to women presents a paradox: women have made the least progress in occupations providing the most concrete measures of successful job performance. Because of science's relatively objective criteria, Doreen Kimura (1999:76) has argued that one might "expect success in science to be, if anything, *more* rather than less related to merit, than in other areas of scholarship". Yet women have thrived in fields with more subjective standards, suggesting that generalized anti-woman bias cannot explain the distribution of men and women in academic fields.

Women's "under-representation" in a given field is not a sufficient basis to brand it hostile to women. As we will see below, women are similarly under-represented in many blue-collar occupations, and there is likewise little evidence that unfair exclusion of women who want to pursue these occupations is primarily to blame. Instead, the general pattern is in accordance with the sex differences that we have already discussed.

Women in Blue-Collar Occupations

Despite integration of women into many white-collar occupations, including prestigious ones such as law and medicine, women's representation in blue-collar occupations has been relatively stable (O'Farrell 1999). Women remain scarce in many such occupations, such as firefighter (4.8% female), construction laborer (3.1%), aircraft pilot and flight engineer (2.6%), auto mechanic (1.6%), carpenter (1.5%), electrician (1%), and mason (0.4%) (U.S. Department of Labor 2009c). The conventional explanation is that women tend not to seek these jobs because they are not considered "appropriate" for women, and that when women do pursue them, they face both discrimination and sexual harassment. These are not altogether false explanations, but they are grossly incomplete.

Women's low participation rate in most blue-collar jobs is consistent with the sex differences previously described. Some of the largest sex differences are on the "Realistic" theme, which measures interest in building, repairing, and working outdoors. Most blue-collar occupations are heavily oriented toward the Realistic dimension (Holland 1997), and, of course, many blue-collar occupations also require a high degree of mechanical ability. Blue-collar occupations may also require substantial physical strength, but women have only one-half to two-thirds the upper-body strength of men (Pheasant 1983). The effect size is often greater than 2.0, so there is even less overlap between the sexes in strength than there is in height (Browne 2007). Although many jobs have changed in ways that diminish the importance of women's relative lack of strength (Weinberg 2000), others have not. Heavy-equipment mechanics, for example, require not just mechanical ability but also substantial physical strength. These job attributes plausibly explain the fact that only about 1% of such positions are filled by women (U.S. Department of Labor 2009c).

Studies of women's job-attribute preferences consistently show a disinclination toward the physically strenuous, dirty, and dangerous work entailed in many blue-collar occupations (Browne 2002). Women, more than men, prefer comfortable and clean working environments, but blue-collar jobs often involve outside work in unpleasant weather or inside work in environments characterized by noise, heat, and disagreeable smells. Moreover, many blue-collar occupations are physically dangerous, and it is the dangerous blue-collar jobs that tend to exhibit the most heavily skewed sex ratio (Browne 2002).

These occupational patterns are all consistent with the well-documented sex differences previously discussed. An important question remains, however: where do these sex differences come from?

3 Origins of Sex Differences

The existence of the above-described differences, though not uncontroversial, kindles less debate than their potential causes. The causal debate is not between those who believe differences are caused solely by biology and those who believe that socialization is exclusively responsible. Instead, the debate is between those who attribute sex differences virtually entirely to social forces and those who believe that biology plays an important, though not exclusive, role. Put another way, it is between those who think the human mind is inherently sexually monomorphic and those who think it is naturally dimorphic. To those who believe the human mind is dimorphic, the ultimate cause is thought to be the selective advantage that the sexually disparate traits conferred on members of the two sexes during our evolutionary history, with sex hormones acting as a major proximate cause.

3.1 Evolution by Natural Selection: The Ultimate Cause of Psychological Sex Differences

Natural selection is often equated with "the survival of the fittest", a term that tends to focus attention on the "hostile forces of nature." Because natural forces have presumably operated in largely the same manner on the two sexes, one might think that the selective forces acting on men and women would have been the same. However, selective pressures relating to mating and reproduction have often been different for the two sexes, and these different selective pressures have left lasting imprints on our minds (and bodies).

Darwin called selection based upon mating success "sexual selection", in contrast to "natural" selection, which he viewed as being based primarily upon survival success (Darwin 1871, Vol. I:256). The key factor driving sexual selection is the "relative parental investment of the sexes in their offspring" (Trivers 1972:141). Trivers showed that the sex with the greater parental investment becomes a resource for which members of the less-investing sex will compete. Individuals of the less-investing sex can increase their reproductive success through numerous partners in a way that members of the other sex cannot, a fact having far-reaching physical and psychological implications. Among mammals, internal gestation ensures that the more-investing sex is female, though among some fish and bird groups, males incubate the eggs and are the more-investing sex and the sex over which primary competition occurs (Trivers 1972).

Centrally important to the origin of sex differences is the fact that male reproductive variance exceeds that of females. Reproductive effort can be channeled to either mating or parenting. Among mammals, males tend to devote relatively more effort toward mating, while females tend to channel more effort into caring for young. In many species, mating season becomes a season of male dominance displays and combat (Alexander et al. 1979). Among humans and some other primates, such as chimpanzees, male dominance is not exclusively tied to physical prowess, but also to skill at coalition formation (de Waal 1982). Because female mammals necessarily invest substantial time and energy in gestating and nursing their offspring, they cannot specialize in mating, as males can. The result of this asymmetry is that many more males than females will not reproduce at all, but the most successful male will have far more offspring than the most successful female (Alexander et al. 1979).

The greater reproductive variance of males raises the stakes of the mating game for them. Most women will receive some reproductive "payoff", although not necessarily an equal one, as their mates will vary in terms of both genetic quality and willingness to invest in offspring. Many men, however, will reap no reproductive payoff at all. Therefore, evolutionary theory predicts that males should exhibit greater dominance- and status-seeking, greater promiscuity, and greater risk-taking behavior (particularly with respect to acquisition of status, resources, and mates). If the male can establish himself as a desirable mate, he may sire many offspring; if not, he may sire none at all.

Empirical data support these predictions. Men worldwide exhibit more risk taking, promiscuity, and dominance behaviors, and those who achieve positions of status have superior access to mates and enhanced reproductive success (Buss 2007). These same behaviors do not translate into increased reproductive success for women, however, as multiple mates do not generally result in an increased number of children for them. Moreover, not only does risk-taking carry smaller reproductive rewards for women, it also imposes greater reproductive costs, as the life prospects of a child in primitive societies were more impaired by loss of its mother than of its father (Campbell 1999).

In addition to shaping sex differences in temperament, natural selection also seems to have left an imprint on cognitive capacities. Hunting and warfare place a premium on dynamic spatial perception and targeting accuracy (Kolakowski and Malina 1974), as well as on a sense of direction allowing hunters to proceed directly home rather than retracing a lengthy route followed in pursuit of prey. The female advantage at object location is also consistent with our hunter-gatherer heritage, as gatherers often return to the same location in search of food (Silverman and Eals 1992). In our ancestral environment, of course, there would have been no direct selective pressure for mathematical ability, but that ability may be a by-product of spatial ability (Geary 1996). Although verbal ability is valuable to both sexes (Miller 2000), men's lesser verbal ability may be a byproduct of selection for higher spatial ability, as there may be a tradeoff between the two kinds of ability (Halpern 2000).

The fact that a plausible evolutionary story can be told about the origins of sex differences does not, of course, mean that the biological explanation is correct. There is more direct evidence for biological roots, however, and that evidence comes from the study of sex hormones.

3.2 Hormones: A Proximate Cause of Many Sex Differences

One advantage that evolutionary psychologists studying sex differences have over those who study other phenomena is that not only is an adaptive account plausible, much is also known about the proximate mechanisms involved. Although the story is complex, and social factors can be important, a major portion of that story comes from sex hormones.

Sexual differentiation of the brain is caused by the same sex hormones that cause sexual differentiation of the body: male sex hormones, or androgens, primarily testosterone; and female sex hormones, primarily the estrogen estradiol. The female form, being the "default" form (Mealey 2000:14), will develop in the absence of androgens. In fetuses, the primary source of androgens is the testes of males, although smaller amounts are produced by the adrenal glands of both sexes.

Androgens affect the brain in two different ways. During a critical period of fetal brain development, they exert an "organizing" effect, causing masculinization of the brain. The "activational" effect, whereby circulating hormones influence behavior more directly, occurs later in life, especially at and after puberty.

3.2.1 Organizing Effects

Some of the earliest evidence for organizing effects of androgens came from girls with congenital adrenal hyperplasia (CAH), a condition in which the adrenal gland produces excessive levels of androgens during fetal brain development. Girls with CAH have a more "masculine" behavioral pattern than normal girls, tending to be tomboys who are more likely to play with boys and with "boy toys" and having less interest in infants and marriage than unaffected girls (Berenbaum and Snyder 1995; Leveroni and Berenbaum 1998). They also score substantially higher on "detachment", a trait inversely correlated with empathy and nurturance, and lower on "indirect aggression", a form of aggression more commonly associated with females (Helleday et al. 1993). They perform better than unaffected girls on targeting tasks (Hines et al. 2003) and have higher levels of spatial ability (Puts et al. 2008). Especially significant for our purposes is the finding that CAH girls also have more male-like occupational preferences (Berenbaum 1999). The relationship between androgen exposure and masculinization seems to be dose sensitive, so that the higher the exposure level, the greater the behavioral masculinization (Servin et al. 2003).

One criticism of the CAH data is that behavioral masculinization of CAH girls might be caused not by androgens but rather by differential parental treatment of the girls because of their masculinized genitals (Wood and Eagly 2002). This facially plausible explanation is not well supported by the evidence, however. Indeed, parents are actually less tolerant of masculine-typed behavior in their CAH daughters (Servin et al. 2003; Pasterski et al. 2005). Thus, if anything, differential treatment of CAH girls would tend to push them toward, rather than away from, more female-typical behavior.

Support for the hormonal explanation also comes from normal populations. Hines et al. (2002) found a linear relationship between maternal testosterone levels during pregnancy and masculine-typed behavior in daughters at age 3-1/2. The mother's testosterone level during pregnancy is also inversely correlated with the daughter's sex-typed behavior as an adult and is actually a stronger predictor of the daughter's adult behavior than is the daughter's own adult testosterone level (Udry et al. 1995). The spatial ability of 7-year-old girls has also been found to correlate positively with prenatal testosterone (Grimshaw et al. 1995b), as has sex-differentiated play in 6–10 year olds (Auyeung et al. 2009). Among normal girls, higher prenatal testosterone levels are associated with a more male-like pattern of lateralization of brain function (Grimshaw et al. 1995a).

3.2.2 Activational Effects

Circulating hormones also have more immediately observable effects. An association between circulating testosterone and dominance behaviors is frequently found, although the direction of causation is not always clear (Tremblay et al. 1998). A much larger body of data supports a relationship between hormones and cognitive performance. For example, the optimal level of testosterone for spatial ability appears to be in the low-normal male range so that, among men, those in the low-normal range have the highest ability, while among women, those with the highest testosterone levels tend to have the highest ability (Gouchie and Kimura 1991). Accordingly, low-testosterone women take longer than high-testosterone women to navigate the Virtual Water Maze, a test of spatial performance (Burkitt et al. 2007).

Female performance on cognitive tasks also varies with hormone changes in the menstrual cycle. Spatial performance tends to be highest in low-estrogen phases (when the testosterone/estrogen ratio is at its highest), and performance on verbal tasks tends to be highest in the high-estrogen portions of the cycle (Hampson 1990; McCormick and Teillon 2001).

Exogenous hormones produce consistent effects. Spatial performance in female-to-male transsexuals, for example, increases after androgen therapy (Slabbekoorn et al. 1999). Cross-sex hormone treatments are also associated with an increase in both aggression-proneness and sexual arousability in females and a decrease in males (Van Goozen et al. 1995). Even a single administration of testosterone to women can enhance mental-rotation performance (Aleman et al. 2004), while administration of testosterone to normal men reduces their spatial performance (O'Connor et al. 2001), consistent with the finding that men in the low-normal range perform best.

Although testosterone gets the bulk of the attention, estrogen is also influential. Women's risk-taking activities vary over the menstrual cycle, with risk-taking decreasing during ovulation, when estrogen levels are high (Bröder and Hohmann 2003). Estrogen also seems to depress spatial ability (Hausmann et al. 2000), which may at least partially explain both the increased sex difference in spatial ability observed after puberty and the tendency of extremely feminine women to have relatively low spatial ability (Nyborg 1994).

It is not suggested here that a particular pattern of hormone exposure is both a necessary and sufficient cause of particular behaviors. Rather, prenatal hormones appear to predispose individuals to developing sex-typed behavior patterns. For example, Udry (2000) has found that responsiveness of females to encouragement of femininity is inversely related to their mothers' testosterone levels during the second trimester of pregnancy, suggesting that prenatal exposure to high levels of testosterone may "immunize" against feminine socialization.

From a biological perspective, explanations incorporating both biological and environmental (social) forces are standard fare. From the sociological perspective, however, explanations invoking biology as even a partial cause are often viewed with deep suspicion. As we will see below, however, the purely social explanation is very difficult to credit.

4 Biology or Society (or Both)?

Appreciation of man's place in nature makes the social-constructionist view difficult to accept, implying as it does that humans have somehow slipped the bonds of connection to the animal kingdom. Although many object to the idea that sex differences in temperament are products of natural selection (e.g., Wood and Eagly 2002), almost no one argues that *physical* sexual dimorphism is a social construct. Yet acceptance of the biological origins of physical differences and denial of such origins for psychological differences presents a puzzle. If greater male strength is an evolved adaptation, it must be an adaptation *for* something. If it is an adaptation for male-male competition, as it is in most species (Plavcan and Van Schaik 1997), it would be surprising if it were not also accompanied by the behavioral dimorphism found in those species.

There are other reasons to be suspicious of purely sociological explanations. Many differences appear early in life, before a child has had an opportunity to absorb social expectations of sex-appropriate behavior. Even newborns display a difference in "thing versus people" orientation, with girls attending more to human faces and boys paying more attention to moving objects (Connellan et al. 2000), and newborn girls are measurably more "cuddly" than boys (Benenson et al. 1999). A sex difference in mental-rotation has also been observed as early as 3 months (Moore and Johnson 2008; Quinn and Liben 2008). Similarly, sex differences in toy choices and playmate preferences appear before children can identify their own sex or the sex of others (Alexander et al. 2009; Servin et al. 1999), and sex differences in competition and risk-taking also appear early in childhood (Weinberger and Stein 2008).

Animal studies paint a picture consistent with the human data. Female mammals in a variety of species are behaviorally masculinized by prenatal androgen exposure, for example, and males who are castrated, either chemically or surgically, prior to the critical period for psychosexual differentiation develop stereotypic female behaviors (Goy et al. 1988). Female monkeys show cognitive changes across the menstrual cycle similar to those found in women (Lacreuse et al. 2001), and young monkeys demonstrate the same sex-typed toy preferences that young children do (Hassett et al. 2008).

It is often correctly noted that society can amplify natural sex differences (Campbell and Eaton 1999), but it can also act to mitigate them, though not necessarily successfully. For example, the tendency of children to segregate by sex persists in the face of contrary pressure, with children in self-organized groups being more likely to be segregated by sex than children in groups organized by adults (Martin and Fabes 2002). Similarly, parents' gifts are more likely to be sex-typed when they purchase toys specifically requested by their children than when they purchase unrequested toys (Fisher-Thompson 1993).

If sex differences were pure social constructs, one might think that changes in social roles and attitudes would have led to a reduction in sex-typing, including sex stereotypes and "gendered" self-concepts. Instead, however, there has been substantial stability – and, in fact, some increase – in sex-typing over recent decades (Lueptow et al. 2001). Similarly, one might have predicted that the sexually egalitarian ethos of western societies would attenuate sex differences in personality. Instead, however, compared to more traditional societies, societies characterized by greater freedom and sexual equality show *larger* sex differences in personality (Costa et al. 2001; McCrae et al. 2005; Schmitt et al. 2008). It may be that the greater freedom in modern societies allows individuals more opportunity to "be themselves", and it so happens that their "selves" are sexually dimorphic.

In sum, there is little support for the argument that commonly observed sex differences are mere social constructs. They have an underlying biological foundation upon which social forces can build, and that foundation will continue to exist whether we acknowledge it or not.

5 Conclusion

Men and women are different. They have – on average – different temperaments, priorities, and even definitions of success in life. These differences flow in part from underlying biological differences that were adaptive in our evolutionary history. A major proximate cause of these differences is the interaction of sex hormones and the brain; they are not simply artifacts of western civilization or industrialism. These differences incline men and women toward different workplace choices, leading ineluctably to different workplace outcomes.

Descriptions of average group differences are often misinterpreted as implying limitations on individuals. When Harvard President Lawrence Summers suggested that there might be biological reasons for the dearth of women in certain scientific fields, many female scientists took offense, as if he were challenging their competence as scientists (Browne 2005). Yet Summers was referring not to women who actually chose careers in the hard sciences, but rather to women who did not. Some of those women who did not pursue such careers probably pursued careers in psychology, which has a larger gender gap in Ph.D.'s awarded (favoring females) than mathematics does (favoring males), or in anthropology, which has a larger gap (favoring females) than geology does (favoring males) (National Science Foundation 2009).

Modern biology and psychology provide greater insight into existing workplace patterns than the purely social explanation provided by the SSSM. The data do not tell us, however, whether we should celebrate or condemn these differences, and they do not by themselves provide answers to many questions facing employers and policymakers. What, if anything, for example, should companies do to achieve sexual parity in areas in which women are under-represented? Should those same companies be as concerned about sexual parity in areas in which men are under-represented? What public policy initiatives are appropriate under the circumstances? These questions are heavily value-laden, and the values are not provided by evolutionary psychology or any other branch of science.

Although it is important that women and men be free to choose their career directions, it makes little sense to assume that their choices will be – or should be – identical. If freedom of choice is the goal, we should respect people's choices even if we think they are not choosing wisely, a judgment that those actually making the choice are in a better position to make than those observing from the outside.

References

Aleman A, Bronk E, Kessels RPC, Koppeschaar HPF, van Honk J (2004) A single administration of testosterone improves visuospatial ability in young women. Psychoneuroendocrinology 29:612–617

Alexander RD, Hoogland JL, Howard RD, Noonan KM, Sherman PW (1979) Sexual dimorphisms and breeding systems in pinnipeds, ungulates, primates, and humans. In: Alexander RD (ed) Evolutionary biology and human social behavior. Duxbury Press, North Scituate, pp 402–435

Alexander GM, Wilcox T, Woods R (2009) Sex differences in infants' visual interest in toys. Arch Sex Behav 3:427–433

American Association of Colleges of Pharmacy (2010). Academic pharmacy's vital statistics. Retrieved from http://www.aacp.org/about/Pages/Vitalstats.aspx

American Bar Association (n.d.) First year and total J.D. enrollment by gender 1947–2008. Retrieved from http://www.abanet.org/legaled/statistics/charts/stats%20-%206.pdf

Arch EC (1993) Risk-taking: A motivational basis for sex differences. Psychol Rep 73:3–11

Aros JR, Henly GA, Curtis NT (1998) Occupational sextype and sex differences in vocational preference-measured interest relationships. J Vocat Behav 53:227–242

Association of American Medical Colleges (2008) U.S. medical school applicants and students 1982–83 to 2007–08. Retrieved from http://www.aamc.org/data/facts/charts1982to2007.pdf

Auyeung B, Baron-Cohen S, Ashwin E, Knickmeyer R, Taylor K, Hackett G, Hines M (2009) Fetal testosterone predicts sexually differentiated childhood behavior in girls and in boys. Psychol Sci 20:144–148

Baldridge DC, Eddleston KA, Veiga JF (2006) Saying "no" to being uprooted: the impact of family and gender on willingness to relocate. J Occup Organ Psychol 79:131–149

Benbow CP, Lubinski D (1993) Psychological profiles of the mathematically talented: some sex differences and evidence supporting their biological basis. In: The origins and development of high ability (Ciba Foundation Symposium). Wiley, Chichester

Benenson JF, Philippoussis M, Leeb R (1999) Sex differences in neonates' cuddliness. J Genet Psychol 160:332–342

Benenson JF, Roy R, Waite A, Goldbaum S, Linders L, Simpson A (2002) Greater discomfort as a proximate cause of sex differences in competition. Merrill Palmer Q 48:225–247

Berenbaum SA (1999) Effects of early androgens on sex-typed activities and interests in adolescents with congenital adrenal hyperplasia. Horm Behav 35:102–110

Berenbaum SA, Snyder E (1995) Early hormonal influences on childhood sex-typed activity and playmate preferences: implications for the development of sexual orientation. Dev Psychol 31:31–42

Blau F, Kahn L (1992) The gender earnings gap: learning from international comparisons. Am Econ Rev 82:533–538

Bröder A, Hohmann N (2003) Variations in risk taking behavior over the menstrual cycle: an improved replication. Evol Hum Behav 24:391–398

Browne KR (2002) Biology at work: Rethinking sexual equality. Rutgers University Press, New Brunswick

Browne KR (2005) Women in science: biological factors should not be ignored. Cardozo Women's Law J 11:509–528

Browne KR (2006) Evolved sex differences and occupational segregation. J Organ Behav 27:143–162

Browne KR (2007) Co-ed combat: the new evidence that women shouldn't fight the nation's wars. Sentinel (Penguin), New York

Burke RJ (1998) Dual career couples: are men still advantaged? Psychol Rep 82:209–210

Burkitt J, Widman D, Saucier DM (2007) Evidence for the influence of testosterone in the performance of spatial navigation in a virtual water maze in women but not in men. Horm Behav 51:649–654

Buss DM (2007) Evolutionary psychology: the new science of the mind, 3rd edn. Allyn & Bacon, New York
Byrnes JP, Miller DC, Schafer WD (1999) Gender differences in risk-taking: a meta-analysis. Psychol Bull 125:367–383
Campbell A (1999) Staying alive: evolution, culture, and women's intrasexual aggression. Behav Brain Sci 22:203–252
Campbell DW, Eaton WO (1999) Sex differences in the activity level of infants. Infant Child Dev 8:1–17
Carretta TR (1997) Group differences on US Air Force pilot selection tests. Int J Sel Assess 5:115–127
Chauvin KW, Ash RA (1994) Gender earnings differentials in total pay, base pay, and contingent pay. Ind Labor Relat Rev 47:634–649
Cole S, Fiorentine R (1991) Discrimination against women in science: the confusion of outcome with process. In: Zuckerman H, Cole JR, Bruer JT (eds) The outer circle: women in the scientific community. W. W. Norton, New York, pp 205–226
College Board (2009) 2009 College-bound seniors: total group profile. Retrieved from http://professionals.collegeboard.com/profdownload/cbs-2009-national-TOTAL-GROUP.pdf
Collier CM, Spokane AR, Bazler JA (1998) Appraising science career interests in adolescent girls and boys. J Career Assess 6:37–48
Connellan J, Baron-Cohen S, Wheelwright S, Batki A, Ahluwalia J (2000) Sex differences in human neonatal social perception. Infant Behav Dev 23:113–118
Conti R, Collins MA, Picariello ML (2001) The impact of competition on intrinsic motivation and creativity: considering gender, gender segregation and gender role orientation. Pers Individ Differ 31:1273–1289
Costa PT, Terracciano A, McCrae RR (2001) Gender differences in personality traits across cultures: robust and surprising findings. J Pers Soc Psychol 81:322–331
Darwin C (1871) The descent of man and selection in relation to sex. Murray, London
Dawis RV, Lofquist LH (1984) A psychological theory of work adjustment. University of Minnesota Press, Minneapolis
de Waal FBM (1982) Chimpanzee politics: power and sex among apes. Jonathon Cape, London
Douce LA, Hansen JC (1990) Willingness to take risks and college women's career choice. J Vocat Behav 36:258–273
Dresselhaus MS, Franz JR, Clark BC (1994) United States: interventions to increase the participation of women in physics. Science 263:1392–1393
Eagly AH (1995) The science and politics of comparing women and men. Am Psychol 50:145–158
Fehr-Duda H, de Gennaro M, Schubert R (2006) Gender, financial risk, and probability weights. Theory Decis 60:283–313
Filer RK (1985) Male-female wage differences: the importance of compensating differentials. Ind Labor Relat Rev 38:426–437
Fisher-Thompson D (1993) Adult toy purchases for children: factors affecting sex-typed toy selection. J Appl Dev Psychol 14:385–406
Freeman CE (2004) Trends in educational equity of girls and women: 2004. U.S. Department of Education, National Center for Education Statistics (NCES 2005–016), U.S. Government Printing Office, Washington, DC
Furchtgott-Roth D, Stolba C (1999) Women's figures: an illustrated guide to the economic progress of women in America. AEI Press, Washington, DC
Galanter M, Palay T (1991) Tournament of lawyers: the transformation of the big law firm. University of Chicago Press, Chicago
Galea LA, Kimura D (1993) Sex differences in route-learning. Pers Individ Differ 14:53–65
Geary DC (1996) Sexual selection and sex differences in mathematical abilities. Behav Brain Sci 19:229–284
Geary DC (2009) Male, female: the evolution of human sex differences, 2nd edn. American Psychological Association, Washington, DC

Gouchie C, Kimura D (1991) The relationship between testosterone levels and cognitive ability patterns. Psychoneuroendocrinology 16:323–334

Goy RF, Bercovitch FB, McBrair MC (1988) Behavior masculinization is independent of genital masculinization in prenatally androgenized female rhesus macaques. Horm Behav 22:552–571

Grazier S, Sloane PJ (2008) Accident risk, gender, family status and occupational choice in the UK. Labour Econ 15:938–957

Grey RJ, Gordon GG (1978) Risk-taking managers: who gets the top jobs? Manage Rev 67:8–13

Grimshaw GM, Bryden MP, Finegan JK (1995a) Relations between prenatal testosterone and cerebral lateralization in children. Neuropsychology 9:68–79

Grimshaw GM, Sitarenios G, Finegan JK (1995b) Mental rotation at 7 years: relation with prenatal testosterone levels and spatial play experiences. Brain Cogn 29:85–100

Groshen EL (1991) The structure of the female/male wage differential. J Hum Resour 26:457–472

Halaby CN (2003) Where job values come from: family and schooling background, cognitive ability, and gender. Am Sociol Rev 68:251–278

Halpern DF (2000) Sex differences in cognitive abilities, 3rd edn. Erlbaum, Mahwah

Hampson E (1990) Variations in sex-related cognitive abilities across the menstrual cycle. Brain Cogn 14:26–43

Harrell TW (1993) The association of marriage and MBA earnings. Psychol Rep 72:955–964

Hassett JM, Siebert ER, Wallen K (2008) Sex differences in rhesus monkey toy preferences parallel those of children. Horm Behav 54:359–364

Hausmann M, Slabbekoorn D, Van Goozen SHM, Cohen-Kettenis PT, Güntürkün O (2000) Sex hormones affect spatial abilities during the menstrual cycle. Behav Neurosci 114:1245–1250

Hedges LV, Nowell A (1995) Sex differences in mental test scores, variability, and numbers of high-scoring individuals. Science 269(5220):41–45

Hegarty M, Waller D (2005) Individual differences in spatial abilities. In: Shah P, Miyake A (eds) The Cambridge handbook of visuospatial thinking. Cambridge University Press, New York, pp 121–169

Helleday J, Edman G, Ritzen EM, Siwers B (1993) Personality characteristics and platelet MAO activity in women with congenital adrenal hyperplasia (CAH). Psychoneuroendocrinology 18:343–354

Hellerstein JK, Neumark D (1998) Wage discrimination, segregation, and sex differences in wages and productivity within and between plants. Ind Relat 37:232–260

Hellerstein JK, Neumark D, and Troske KR (1996) Wages, productivity, and worker characteristics: evidence from plant-level production functions and wage equations. Working paper 5626, National Bureau of Economic Research

Hennig M, Jardim A (1977) The managerial woman. Anchor Press/Doubleday, Garden City

Hines M, Golombok S, Rust J, Johnston KJ, Golding J, Avon Longitudinal Study of Parents and Children Study Team (2002) Testosterone during pregnancy and gender role behavior of preschool children: a longitudinal, population study. Child Dev 73:1678–1687

Hines M, Fane BA, Pasterski VL, Mathews GA, Conway GS, Brook C (2003) Spatial abilities following prenatal androgen abnormality: targeting and mental rotations performance in individuals with congenital adrenal hyperplasia. Psychoneuroendocrinology 28:1010–1026

Holland JL (1997) Making vocational choices: a theory of vocational personalities and work environments, 3rd edn. Psychological Assessment Resources, Odessa

Holloway M (1993) A lab of her own. Sci Am 269:94–103

Jensen AR (1998) The g factor: the science of mental ability. Praeger, Westport

Kaufman AS, McLean JE (1998) An investigation into the relationship between interests and intelligence. J Clin Psychol 54:279–295

Kilbourne BS, England P (1996) Occupational skill, gender, and earnings. In: Dubeck PJ, Borman K (eds) Women and work: a handbook. Garland Publishing, New York, pp 68–70

Kimura D (1999) Sex and cognition. MIT Press, Cambridge

Kolakowski D, Malina RM (1974) Spatial ability, throwing accuracy and man's hunting heritage. Nature 251:410–412

Konrad AM, Ritchie JE Jr, Lieb P, Corrigall E (2000) Sex differences and similarities in job attribute preferences: A meta-analysis. Psychol Bull 126:593–641

Korenman S, Neumark D (1992) Marriage, motherhood, and wages. J Hum Resour 27:233–255

Kruger D, Byker D (2009) Evolved foraging psychology underlies sex differences in shopping experiences and behaviors. J Soc Evol Cult Psychol 3(4):1–15

Lacreuse A, Verreault M, Herndon JG (2001) Fluctuations in spatial recognition memory across the menstrual cycle in female rhesus monkeys. Psychoneuroendocrinology 26:623–639

Larkin JE, Pines HA (2003) Gender and risk in public performance. Sex Roles 49:197–210

Leveroni C, Berenbaum SA (1998) Early androgen effects on interest in infants: evidence from children with congenital adrenal hyperplasia. Dev Neuropsychol 14:321–340

Lin Y-H, Chen C-Y, Luo J-L (2008) Gender and age distribution of occupational fatalities in Taiwan. Accid Anal Prev 40(4):1604–1610

Lippa R (1998) Gender-related individual differences and the structure of vocational interests: the importance of the people-things dimension. J Pers Soc Psychol 74:996–1009

Lubinski D, Benbow CP (1992) Gender differences in abilities and preferences among the gifted: implications for the math-science pipeline. Curr Dir Psychol Sci 1:61–66

Lubinski D, Benbow CP, Sanders CE (1993) Reconceptualizing gender differences in achievement among the gifted. In: Heller KA, Mönks FJ, Passow AH (eds) International handbook of research and development of giftedness and talent. Pergamon Press, Oxford, pp 693–707

Lubinski D, Webb RM, Morelock MJ, Benbow CP (2001) Top 1 in 10, 000: a 10-year follow-up of the profoundly gifted. J Appl Psychol 86:718–729

Lueptow LB, Garovich-Szabo L, Lueptow MB (2001) Social change and the persistence of sex typing: 1974–1997. Soc Forces 80:1–35

Maccoby EE, Jacklin CN (1974) The psychology of sex differences. Stanford University Press, Stanford

MacCrimmon KR, Wehrung DA (1990) Characteristics of risk taking executives. Manage Sci 36:422–435

Martin CL, Fabes RA (2002) The stability and consequences of young children's same-sex peer interactions. Dev Psychol 37:431–446

Mazur A, Booth A (1998) Testosterone and dominance in men. Behav Brain Sci 21:352–397

McCormick CM, Teillon SM (2001) Menstrual cycle variation in spatial ability: relation to salivary cortisol levels. Horm Behav 39:29–38

McCrae RR, Terracciano A, Personality Profiles of Culture Project (2005) Universal features of personality traits from the observer's perspective: Data from 50 cultures. J Pers Soc Psychol 88:547–561

McPheron T (2007) 2007 is DVM year of the woman. JAVMA News. June 15. Retrieved from http://www.avma.org/onlnews/javma/jun07/070615d.asp

Mealey L (2000) Sex differences: developmental and evolutionary strategies. Academic, San Diego

Miller GF (2000) The mating mind: how sexual choice shaped the evolution of human nature. Doubleday, New York

Moore DS, Johnson SP (2008) Mental rotation in human infants. Psychol Sci 19:1063–1066

Morrison AM, White RP, Van Velsor E, Center for Creative Leadership (1992) Breaking the glass ceiling: can women reach the top of America's largest corporations? Updated edn. Addison-Wesley, Reading

National Science Foundation (2009) Science and Engineering Doctorate Awards: 2006. NSF 09-311. Retrieved from http://nsf.gov/statistics/nsf09311/pdf/nsf09311.pdf

Niederle M, Vesterlund L (2008) Gender differences in competition. Negot J 24:447–463

Nyborg H (1994) Hormones, sex, and society: the science of physiology. Praeger, Westport

O'Connor DB, Archer J, Hair WM, Wu FCW (2001) Activational effects of testosterone on cognitive function in men. Neuropsychologia 39:1385–1394

O'Farrell B (1999) Women in blue collar and related occupations at the end of the millennium. Q Rev Econ Finance 39:699–722

Osborne J, Simon S, Collins S (2003) Attitudes towards science: a review of the literature and its implications. Int J Sci Educ 25:1049–1079

Pasterski VL, Geffner ME, Brain C, Hindmarsh P, Brook C, Hines M (2005) Prenatal hormones and postnatal socialization by parents as determinants of male-typical toy play in girls with congenital adrenal hyperplasia. Child Dev 76:264–278

Pheasant ST (1983) Sex differences in strength: some observations on their variability. Appl Ergon 14:205–211

Plavcan JM, Van Schaik CP (1997) Intrasexual competition and body weight dimorphism in anthropoid primates. Am J Phys Anthropol 103:37–68

Prediger DJ (1982) Dimensions underlying Holland's hexagon: missing link between interests and occupations? J Vocat Behav 21:259–287

Puts DA, McDaniel MA, Jordan CL, Breedlove SM (2008) Spatial ability and prenatal androgens: meta-analyses of congenital adrenal hyperplasia and digit ratio (2D:4D) studies. Arch Sex Behav 37:100–111

Quinn PC, Liben LS (2008) A sex difference in mental rotation in young infants. Psychol Sci 19:1067–1070

Rhoads SE (1993) Incomparable worth: pay equity meets the market. Cambridge University Press, New York

Rosovsky H, Hartley M (2002) Evaluation and the academy: are we doing the right thing? Grade inflation and letters of recommendation. American Academy of Arts & Sciences, at 5–6 (2002). Retrieved from http://www.amacad.org/publications/monographs/Evaluation_and_the_Academy.pdf

Schmitt DP, Realo A, Voracek M, Allik J (2008) Why can't a man be more like a woman? Sex differences in Big Five personality traits across 55 cultures. J Pers Soc Psychol 94:168–182

Schrader MP, Wann DL (1999) High-risk recreation: the relationship between participant characteristics and degree of involvement. J Sport Behav 22:426–441

Schwartz FN (1992) Breaking with tradition: women and work, the new facts of life. Warner Books, New York

Servin A, Bohlin G, Berlin L (1999) Sex differences in 1-, 3-, and 5-year-olds' toy choice in a structured play-session. Scand J Psychol 40:43–48

Servin A, Nordenström A, Larsson A, Bohlin G (2003) Prenatal androgens and gender-typed behavior: a study of girls with mild and severe forms of congenital adrenal hyperplasia. Dev Psychol 39:440–450

Seymour E, Hewitt NM (1997) Talking about leaving. Westview Press, Boulder

Shea DL, Lubinski D, Benbow CP (2001) Importance of assessing spatial ability in intellectually talented young adolescents: a 20-year longitudinal study. J Educ Psychol 93:604–614

Silverman I, Eals M (1992) Sex differences in spatial abilities: evolutionary theory and data. In: Barkow JH, Cosmides L, Tooby J (eds) The adapted mind: evolutionary psychology and the generation of culture. Oxford University Press, New York, pp 533–553

Slabbekoorn D, van Goozen SHM, Megens J, Gooren LJG, Cohen-Kettenis P (1999) Activating effects of cross-sex hormones on cognitive functioning: a study of short-term and long-term hormone effects in transsexuals. Psychoneuroendocrinology 24:423–447

Smith A (1776) Wealth of nations. Harriman House, Petersfield

Snyder TD, Dillow SA, Hoffman CM (2009) Digest of Education Statistics 2008. National Center for Education Statistics (NCES 2009-020), Institute of Education Sciences, U.S. Department of Education, Washington, DC

Stenstrom E, Stenstrom P, Saad G, Cheikhrouhou S (2008) Online hunting and gathering: an evolutionary perspective on sex differences in website preferences and navigation. IEEE Trans Prof Commun 51(2):155–168

Su R, Rounds J, Armstrong PI (2009) Men and things, women and people: a meta-analysis of sex differences in interests. Psychol Bull 135:859–884

Tooby J, Cosmides L (1992) The psychological foundations of culture. In: Barkow JH, Cosmides L, Tooby J (eds) The adapted mind: evolutionary psychology and the generation of culture. Oxford University Press, New York, pp 19–136

Townsend B (1996) Room at the top for women. Am Demogr 18(7):28–37

Tremblay RE, Schaal B, Boulerice B, Arseneault L, Soussignan RG, Paquette D et al (1998) Testosterone, physical aggression, dominance, and physical development in early adolescence. Int J Behav Dev 22:753–777

Trivers RL (1972) Parental investment and sexual selection. In: Campbell BG (ed) Sexual selection and the descent of man. Aldine, Chicago, pp 136–179

Udry JR (2000) Biological limits of gender construction. Am Sociol Rev 65:443–457

Udry JR, Morris NM, Kovenock J (1995) Androgen effects on women's gendered behaviour. J Biosoc Sci 27:359–368

U.S. Census Bureau (2008) Income, poverty, and health insurance coverage in the United States: 2007. Current population reports: consumer income. Retrieved from http://www.census.gov/prod/2008pubs/p60-235.pdf

U.S. Department of Labor (2007) Women in the labor force: a databook bureau of labor statistics. Bureau of Labor Statistics. Retrieved from http://www.bls.gov/cps/wlf-databook-2007.pdf

U.S. Department of Labor (2008a) Census of fatal occupational injuries all worker profile, 1992–2002. Bureau of Labor Statistics. Retrieved from http://www.bls.gov/iif/oshwc/cfoi/cftb0186.pdf

U.S. Department of Labor (2008b) Employment and earnings, January 2008, Bureau of Labor Statistics. Retrieved from http://www.bls.gov/opub/ee/empearn200801.pdf

U.S. Department of Labor (2009a) Census of Fatal Occupational Injuries (CFOI) – Current and Revised Data. Bureau of Labor Statistics. Retrieved from http://www.bls.gov/iif/oshcfoi1.htm

U.S. Department of Labor (2009b) Census of fatal occupational injuries charts, 1992–2007 (revised data). Retrieved from http://www.bls.gov/iif/oshwc/cfoi/cfch0006.pdf

U.S. Department of Labor (2009c) Quick facts on nontraditional occupations for women. Women's Bureau. Retrieved from http://www.dol.gov/wb/factsheets/nontra2008.htm

Van Goozen SH, Cohen-Kettenis PT, Gooren LJ, Frijda NH, Van de Poll NE (1995) Gender differences in behaviour: activating effects of cross-gender hormones. Psychoneuroendocrinology 20:343–363

Van Vugt M, De Cremer D, Janssen DP (2007) Gender differences in cooperation and competition: the male-warrior hypothesis. Psychol Sci 18:19–23

Voyer D, Voyer S, Bryden MP (1995) Magnitude of sex differences in spatial abilities: a meta-analysis and consideration of critical variables. Psychol Bull 117:250–270

Watson NV, Kimura D (1991) Nontrivial sex differences in throwing and intercepting: relation to psychometrically-defined spatial functions. Pers Individ Differ 12:375–385

Weinberg BA (2000) Computer use and the demand for female workers. Ind Labor Relat Rev 53:290–305

Weinberger N, Stein K (2008) Early competitive game playing in same- and mixed-gender peer groups. Merrill Palmer Q 54:499–514

Wood W, Eagly AH (2002) A cross-cultural analysis of the behavior of women and men: implications for the origins of sex differences. Psychol Bull 128:699–727

Xie Y, Shauman KA (1998) Sex differences in research productivity: new evidence about an old puzzle. Am Sociol Rev 63:847–870

Zuckerman H (1991) The careers of men and women scientists: a review of current research. In: Zuckerman H, Cole JR, Bruer JT (eds) The outer circle: women in the scientific community. W.W. Norton, New York

The Adaptationist Theory of Cooperation in Groups: Evolutionary Predictions for Organizational Cooperation

Michael E. Price and Dominic D.P. Johnson

Abstract Managers could more effectively promote cooperation within their organizations if they had greater understanding of how evolution designed people to cooperate. Here we present a theory of group cooperation – the Adaptationist Theory of Cooperation in Groups (ATCG) – that is primarily an effort to pull together the scattered findings of a large number of evolution-minded researchers, and to integrate these findings into a single coherent theory. We present ATCG in three main sections: first, we discuss the basic premise that group cooperation evolved because it allowed individuals to acquire personal fitness benefits from acting in synergy with others; second, we examine the cooperative strategy that most often prevails in successful groups, "reciprocal altruism", and the free rider problem that constantly threatens it; and third, we explore how cooperative behavior is affected by differences (a) among individuals, (b) between the sexes, and (c) among different kinds of resources that a group may share. Throughout all of these sections, we suggest ways in which ATCG's predictions could be usefully applied in real organizations. We conclude that while ATCG is consistent in some regards with existing theories from organizational behaviour, its individual-level adaptationist perspective allows it to make a variety of novel predictions.

Keywords Cooperation · Groups · Teams · Reciprocal altruism · Free riders · Organizational behavior · Evolutionary psychology

---

M.E. Price (✉)
Department of Psychology, School of Social Sciences, Brunel University, Uxbridge, UK, UB8 3PH
e-mail: michael.price@brunel.ac.uk

D.D.P. Johnson
Politics and International Relations, School of Social and Political Science, University of Edinburgh, Edinburgh, UK, EH8 9LD
e-mail: dominic.johnson@ed.ac.uk

1 Introduction

Unlike the vast majority of other species, human individuals achieve remarkable levels of cooperation, even among large groups of non-relations or strangers. This ability is a vital characteristic of human nature; without it, human social life would be unrecognizably different: there would be no villages, cities, or nations; no organized religions, armies, or political parties; and no communities, collectives, or companies. Researchers in the biological and social sciences have long been preoccupied with understanding group cooperation, not only because of its importance, but also because achieving this understanding has proven surprisingly challenging. However, significant progress has been made in our understanding of the evolutionarily adaptations humans possess for cooperating in groups. If we are to understand how to improve cooperation today, we need to understand what these adaptations are, how they work, when they align or clash with modern social settings, and how to trigger them to increase efficiency. In this chapter we present a new evolutionary theory of group cooperation—the "Adaptationist Theory of Cooperation in Groups"—that is a product of this progress. We will abbreviate this theory as ATCG, both for the sake of efficiency, and because this acronym recalls the four bases of DNA (adenine, thymine, cytosine, and guanine) and thus conveniently highlights the theory's biological foundations.

We should be clear from the beginning that ATCG is not "our" theory of cooperation in groups. ATCG has been informed by our own research, but it is first and foremost an effort to integrate the scattered findings of a large number of researchers – most of whom have investigated cooperation from an explicitly evolutionary, individual-level adaptationist perspective – into a relatively comprehensive and coherent theory. We think such an integrative effort is needed because despite all of the progress that has been made in evolutionary psychology towards understanding various aspects of group cooperation, these findings have not been presented in any kind of comprehensive theoretical package. This lack of integration makes it harder to draw out the most important insights from the less important ones (especially for a specific context such as organizational behaviour), and also harder to communicate these findings efficiently to other academics and to the people in organizations who would most benefit from applying the findings.

As we discuss ATCG, we provide examples of how this theory can be applied to achieve better understanding, prediction, and promotion of cooperation in modern human organizations, and ways in which it compliments and diverges from the predictions of existing theories from evolutionary and social science. According to the philosopher of science Imre Lakatos (1978), an advance in scientific theory occurs when a new theory is introduced that makes all of the same predictions as the existing theory or theories, but adds additional, novel predictions. We believe that by this standard, ATCG constitutes scientific progress. While ATCG shares some predictions with pre-existing theories from mainstream organizational behavior and social science, it also generates a variety of unique predictions about how people will cooperate in organizations.

The sketch of ATCG that follows is divided up into three main sections. In Sect. 2, we discuss the fundamental issue of how ancestral humans gained individual fitness advantages by engaging in group cooperation. In Sect. 3, we examine the most important cooperative strategy that is engaged in by members of productive groups, "reciprocal altruism", as well as the free rider problem that can derail this strategy and wreck productivity. In Sect. 4, we look at how cooperative behavior changes depending on individual differences, sex differences, and differences in the class of resource being shared. In our conclusion we review how ATCG overlaps with and diverges from existing theories of organizational cooperation.

2 How Cooperation Benefits Individual Fitness

2.1 *Darwin's Focus on Individuals*

Darwin's theory of adaptation by natural selection (1859) focused on individuals: natural selection endows individuals with adaptations that improve their "fitness" (their ability to survive and reproduce). In considering how humans are adapted to cooperate in groups, it is crucial to maintain this individual-level focus, and to ask: how did cooperation benefit the fitness of individual cooperators in ancestral environments (Alexander 1987)? It is this individual-level focus of Darwinian theory that has caused cooperative behavior to often seem profoundly puzzling from an evolutionary perspective. Darwin himself noted that cooperative (or "altruistic") acts, such as a bee's suicidal sting in defense of its hive, posed a major challenge to his theory. If cooperative acts benefit the fitness of others at the expense of the cooperator, then non-cooperators (also known as "cheaters", "defectors" or "free riders") will always achieve higher payoffs, and thus exploit cooperators to extinction. Ever since Darwin, the evolution of cooperation has been considered a central problem – or indeed *the* central problem – of behavioral biology (Wilson 1975).

Over the past several decades, however, biologists have made significant progress towards solving this central problem by producing several theories of cooperation, including two that have become especially well-established. The first is "kin selection" (Hamilton 1964), a theory of gene-level cooperation that explains altruism among close genetic kin. The second is "reciprocal altruism" (Trivers 1971), which explains mutually beneficial exchange between interactants who are not necessarily genetically related. These two theories are now routinely used to solve Darwin's puzzle of cooperation. Kin selection is important to a vast variety of species, including humans, while reciprocal altruism is important to humans (who possess, as discussed below, the social cognitive skills to engage in reciprocity successfully) but relatively unimportant to most other species (Dugatkin 1997; Stevens and Hauser 2004; West et al. 2007). ATCG is designed to explain cooperation in groups of *non*-relatives, and although kin selection theory would not therefore appear to apply, it is relevant to a deep theoretical understanding of such cooperation (because kin altruism and reciprocal altruism probably both evolved via the same fundamental process of genic self-favoritism; see Price 2006a). Nevertheless, ATCG can be described and applied effectively without much reference to kin selection, so for the sake of efficiency we will not discuss this theory further. On the other hand, ATCG is more directly founded on Trivers' (1971) reciprocal altruism, and this theory is discussed in more detail below.

Having pointed out the importance of the individual-level perspective, we should note that there is a history of confusion and controversy surrounding this perspective. Despite the progress that has made in explaining how cooperation benefits individual fitness, some theorists maintain that individual-level theories are insufficient to account for the complexity of cooperation in human groups, and that some kind of group selection theory is required (Boyd and Richerson 1988; Wilson and Sober 1994; Gintis 2000; Gintis et al. 2003; Wilson and Wilson 2007). A purely group selectionist theory would predict that individual cooperative behavior evolved to benefit the average fitness of the group as a whole, as opposed to the cooperator's own individual fitness, and thus is a radically different perspective from that of the individual-level theory. For example, while the individual-level theory predicts that individuals will work in organizations in order to receive compensation and benefit themselves, group selection predicts that they will work for free in order to benefit the organization.

Group selection has long been a controversial topic in behavioral biology. Darwin (1871) himself even considered whether group selection could have played some role in the evolution of human moral sentiments, and throughout much of the twentieth century "naïve" group selectionist theories – focusing on how a behavior evolved to benefit the group or species, without considering how it affected the individual – were common in biology (Wilson and Wilson 2007). This "naïve" period ended when biologist George Williams published his influential critique of group selection, which drew attention to the special conditions that it requires, and emphasized that ordinary individual-level hypotheses should be examined first, before resorting to more exotic, higher-level alternatives (Williams 1966). In more recent years, however, group selection has made something of a comeback, in relatively sophisticated forms such as multilevel selection, which theorizes that selection has important effects simultaneously at multiple levels, including intra-genomic, individual, and group levels (Wilson and Wilson 2007).

We agree with the multilevel selectionists that in studies of any kind of behavior, it is always wise to consider whether multilevel selection theory could enhance one's ability to predict the features of that behavior. However at this stage we do not see any advantages, in terms of improving ATCG's predictive power, in adopting the theoretical view that cooperative behavior in groups of non-relatives evolved to produce benefits at any level other than that of individual fitness. While ATCG makes many predictions that assume selection occurred at the individual level, it makes none which assume selection occurred at the group (or any other) level. Moreover, individual selection is the simplest and least exotic level of selection that one can examine in the course of an adaptationist analysis

(Williams 1966). Therefore, in keeping with Occam's razor and with Williams' (1966, p. v) dictum that "adaptation should be attributed to no higher a level or organization than is demanded by the evidence", our chapter maintains an individual-level focus.

Before leaving the topic of group selection behind, we should emphasize that all of ATCG's predictions that are presented throughout this chapter follow from the individual-level adaptationist perspective, while as far as we can tell, not a single one of them would follow from a purely group selectionist perspective. The irrelevance here of the purely group selectionist perspective should be apparent in the very beginning (i.e. the present section) of this chapter, as we elaborate on ATCG's foundational premise that cooperation evolved because it allowed cooperators to gain individual fitness advantages. Of course, the drastically divergent predictions of these two approaches are offered a litmus test by how things really work in the real world. As we will show, predictions that have been made from the individual-level perspective have so far been widely supported.

2.2 Cooperation Evolved Because It Produced Synergistic Benefits for Cooperative Individuals

ATCG takes account of ethnographic and archaeological evidence suggesting that in the environments in which humans evolved, cooperating in groups (for purposes of hunting, warfare, shelter construction, predator defense, etc.) afforded individuals benefits that they could not have obtained by acting alone (Lee and DeVore 1968; Alexander 1987; Kelly 1995; Keeley 1996). If you could acquire 5 lb of rabbit meat by hunting alone, as opposed to 50 lb of mammoth meat by participating in a group hunt, then cooperation would have offered a ten-fold advantage, holding effort and all other costs constant. Of course, the costs of cooperation cannot be overlooked. Some of these costs would also be present in a solitary activity (e.g. expenditure of time and energy), but others would have been unique to cooperation (e.g. coordination and social interaction costs). A member of a group mammoth hunt, in contrast to a lone rabbit hunter, has to worry about such things as meeting his co-members at a certain time, coordinating his movements with those of his co-members during the hunt, and ensuring that he receives a fair share of the meat – not to mention avoiding getting trampled to death. But as long as the synergistic benefits of cooperation provided the individual with benefits that outweighed these costs, then cooperation would have offered an individual fitness advantage. ATCG assumes that opportunities to engage in individually adaptive cooperation arose regularly in ancestral environments, and therefore that the human mind evolved to become skilled at recognizing and taking advantage of these opportunities.

2.3 Social Status is a Key Second-Order Benefit of Cooperation

ATCG also notes that the benefits of cooperation can involve much more than just a share of the first-order benefit that the interaction produces (e.g., mammoth meat). Even if a hunting party member had no need for mammoth meat, he could still acquire a second-order benefit from cooperation. For example, he might learn about the hunting techniques of skilled co-members, or gain a chance to practice his own techniques. But the second-order benefit he could have acquired that is most relevant to our discussion is social status. By social status, we simply mean the power to bestow benefits, or inflict harm, on other people. By helping the group bring down a mammoth, for example, a skilled hunter could prove his willingness and ability to generate value (meat) for others. Others would benefit from having this hunter in their group in future interactions, and would suffer if he left the group or refused to help them hunt. This dependence of others would make the hunter high-status (i.e., powerful [Emerson 1962]), and in order to remain within his favour, others would be motivated to act to benefit (and to avoid harming) him. His social status could thus serve as a magnet for many kinds of economic resources. Further, this association between status and resources would have made the hunter more sexually attractive to females, which would have increased his access to reproductive resources as well.

The links that are drawn in the above example between hunting and status, and between status and sexual attractiveness, are not just theoretical. Field studies show that hunting skill is associated positively with social status and reproductive success in hunter-gatherer societies (review in Smith 2004). More generally, male social status relates positively to reproductive success in premodern societies (Chagnon 1979, 1988; Betzig 1986), and females in all kinds of societies tend to find higher status men more attractive (Buss 1989; review in Davies and Shackelford 2008). But the main point of the above example is to illustrate a central proposition of ATCG: by cooperating in groups, an individual can make himself valuable to others and thus obtain the crucial resource of social status. Even if that individual has no interest in the first-order resource that the group is producing, the prospect of acquiring status might make him regard participation as worthwhile.

Just as social status was a highly relevant second-order benefit of cooperation in ancestral groups, so it is in modern organizations. These organizations face a basic challenge of motivating employees to contribute to the production of resources that are not for their own consumption. Employees of a biotechnology firm, for example, may need to cooperate to design a new artificial leg, even if most of them are not going to use this product themselves. The method of motivating employees that is used in most organizations is to offer them social status in exchange for their help in producing the first-order resource. And just as in the ancestral past, higher status contributors – those on whom production most depends – attract greater economic compensation, in order to convince them to remain in the organization and to continue to contribute.

2.4 Synergistic Cooperation Is Inherently Advantageous, But There Is Nothing Inherently Synergistic About Cooperation

ATCG proposes that evolution designed people not just for cooperation, but for cooperation that brought individual benefits. As noted above, for cooperation to be individually-adaptive, it must be synergistic. If Person X is a good hunter who can obtain 5 lb of rabbit meat by hunting alone, versus 5 lb of shared deer meat by hunting in a group, then cooperation offers no first-order synergistic benefits for X. There might be second-order benefits to cooperating (e.g. the opportunity to acquire status), but these would need to be high enough to overcome the automatic costs of cooperation (e.g. coordination costs); otherwise, the adaptive choice for X would be to hunt alone. And if cooperation actually caused X's share of the first-order resource to decrease – if X could obtain more meat by hunting alone than he could via cooperation – then cooperation's likelihood of being the adaptive choice for X would go down even further.

Of course, even if cooperation were maladaptive for X, it could be adaptive for some of X's potential interaction partners. If Person Y could obtain no meat by hunting alone, versus some meat by hunting in a group with X, then Y would have an interest in convincing X to join the hunt. The best way for Y to do this would be to offer X a relatively large share of first- or second-order benefits that would compensate X for his relatively large contribution, and thus make cooperation adaptive for X. We'll discuss the importance of these kinds of benefit-to-contribution ratios, and their relevance to modern organizational contexts, later in this chapter. But for now, we want to focus on the idea that while synergistic cooperation is inherently advantageous, there is nothing inherently synergistic about cooperation.

2.5 Synergistic Cooperation (or the Lack Thereof) in Real Organizations

As the result of trends in organizational practices such as the increased popularity of work teams (Douglas and Gardner 2004), many organizations strive to cultivate a culture of cooperation and communication in which group action is seen as being inherently superior to individual action (Hall 2007; for a military example, see Rielly 2000). This enthusiasm for cooperation is to some extent understandable: cooperation can often be genuinely productive, sometimes astoundingly so, and many people reflexively assume cooperation to be a "good thing" wherever it appears. However, cooperation can also be imposed on individuals who would be more productive if permitted to produce alone. For example, many organizations encourage their employees to generate ideas in brainstorming groups of interacting individuals (Rietzschel et al. 2006), despite substantial evidence that "nominal groups" – consisting of individuals who work alone to generate ideas that are then pooled – generate more ideas, and more high-quality ideas, than groups of interacting individuals (Diehl and Stroebe 1987; Rietzschel et al. 2006).

As examples of the kind of non-synergistic cooperation that is routinely encouraged in organizations, consider an employee who by herself could come up with a brilliant marketing strategy, but who must compromise her idea in order to accommodate the inferior and counterproductive contributions of her team members; or consider three employees who must incur significant coordination and communication costs in order to jointly write a report that turns out no better than what any one of them could have written alone. And most members of organizations will, at one time or another, have had to serve on a committee that seemed to reach decisions and take actions much more slowly and ineffectively than an individual could have done. For employees trapped in non-synergistic cooperative interactions, enthusiasm for cooperation may be buoyed by the expectation of some second-order reward ("this committee is a waste of time, but serving on it will look good on my résumé"). But even if this second order justification is forthcoming, these employees' respect for their employer will likely fall due to their perception that management is encouraging employees to engage in pointless and counterproductive cooperation. Employees may also tolerate situations of non-synergistic cooperation in order to avoid appearing as uncooperative or arrogant; they may fear that if they point out that cooperation is counterproductive, they will appear as poor team players – that is, as though they want to shirk their responsibilities, or as though they think they are too talented to have to compromise with team members. Or they may simply be afraid to contradict their manager's judgment that cooperation is the best approach, or just lack the data to conclude that one strategy is better than the other. Whatever reason an employee may have for remaining in non-synergistic interactions, if he could avoid such interactions without fear of negative consequences, then it would increase productivity both for himself and for his organization.

ATCG's recognition that adaptive cooperation must produce individual-level synergistic benefits is an essential first step to untangling the motives for cooperation in the real world. However, it is not yet a solution to the puzzle of cooperation, because it explains only why individuals would be motivated to cooperate in the first place. Even if they are so motivated, how do they ensure that they are receiving an adequate level of compensation, and that they are not being exploited by others in their group? To address these questions, we need to consider the role of reciprocal altruism as the dominant cooperative strategy in groups.

3 Promoting Reciprocity and Avoiding Free Riders

3.1 Can Reciprocal Altruism Explain Cooperation in Groups?

As noted in Sect. 2, Trivers' (1971) theory of reciprocal altruism is the leading evolutionary explanation for the evolution of cooperation among genetic non-relatives. Reciprocal altruism has been applied most commonly to interactions between two individuals. For example, if person X can pay a small cost to provide a big benefit to person Y, and Y can later pay a small cost to provide a big benefit to X, then the exchange interaction will be mutually beneficial; X and Y will have each paid a small cost in exchange for a big benefit. The risk to the individual in such an interaction is that your partner will prove to be a cheater: if your "altruism" is not reciprocated, then you will have maladaptively paid a cost for no benefit. Thus, while reciprocity offers big advantages to those who can find reliable partners, it also involves the risk of getting paired with a cheater (Cosmides and Tooby 2005). In order to engage in reciprocity successfully, an organism must have a high level of cognitive sophistication, in order to recognize and remember cheaters and to avoid interacting with them. Humans definitely do possess the requisite cognitive abilities, but the extent to which other species do is unclear (Cosmides and Tooby 2005; West et al. 2007; Stevens and Hauser 2004; for a review of the mixed evidence regarding primate reciprocity, see Silk 2005).

While the theory of reciprocal altruism has been used relatively uncontroversially to explain the evolution of cooperation in two-person interactions in a wide range of disciplines from biology to anthropology to economics (Trivers 2006), its applicability to n-person (group) interactions has engendered more disagreement. This applicability is important to ATCG and to this chapter, because organizations involve n-person interactions, that is, multiple people working together to fulfil some group goal. The ability of reciprocity to evolve in such groups depends on several factors. One of these factors is the type of reciprocity strategy involved: for example "continuous" reciprocity strategies, which match the mean co-member contribution, evolve more successfully under many conditions than do "discrete", all-or-nothing reciprocity strategies (which contribute fully if a threshold percentage of co-members contribute, but otherwise contribute nothing at all; Johnson et al. 2008; Takezawa and Price 2010). Another factor is the size of the group: reciprocity evolves more easily in small groups (e.g., fewer than ten members) than in large groups (Boyd and Richerson 1988; Takezawa and Price 2010). Reciprocity's disadvantageousness in large groups is due to the fact that as groups get larger, the probability increases that groups will be infiltrated by "free riders" (the term assigned to cheaters in cooperative group contexts).

Some researchers have suggested that because reciprocity does not evolve well in large groups, an explanation besides reciprocity is needed to explain n-person cooperation (Boyd and Richerson 1988; Henrich 2004). However, reciprocity's disadvantageousness in large groups would probably not have been an obstacle to its evolution in ancestral human groups, which tended to be small. According to a comprehensive survey of foraging societies (Kelly 1995), the average hunter-gatherer band consists of about 25 people, of which seven or eight are full-time adult foragers. Given the sexual division of labor, the average n-person interaction will involve half of these adults, that is, 3–4 people – a group size which is well within the range in which reciprocity could evolve. For this reason, ATCG agrees with the perspective of evolutionary psychologists who have suggested that the best evolutionary explanation for organizational cooperation is n-person reciprocity (Price 2006a; Tooby et al. 2006). Although we work in large groups today, we may nevertheless act *as if* we are in small groups, because our cognitive machinery for cooperation evolved in small groups, not large ones.

3.2 Reciprocity in Groups: Striving for "Fair" Compensation

So if ATCG predicts that the average group member will behave as a reciprocal altruist, what does that mean exactly? It means that in exchange for his contribution to fulfilment of the group's goal, he will expect to receive a share of group benefits that is proportional to the relative size of his contribution. For example, if he has contributed the most to bringing down a mammoth, then he will expect to receive the best share of mammoth meat out of anyone in the group, or some second-order reward of equivalent magnitude (for example, the biggest increase in social status out of anyone in the group). ATCG predicts that if the group member perceives his own benefit-to-contribution ratio to be at least as large as those obtained by his co-members, then he should perceive his level of compensation to be "fair", and he should be motivated to continue cooperating; if, on the other hand, he perceives this ratio to be relatively small, then he should experience a sense of unfairness and lose motivation to continue cooperating. A worker who is reliable and hard working but gets no recognition or reward for such behavior will soon slack off. Consistent with this prediction, a standard finding in behavioral economics is that on average, group members are more willing to contribute to public good production when they perceive that their benefit-to-contribution ratios are no less than those of co-members (Ledyard 1995; Croson 2007; Fischbacher et al. 2001; Kurzban and Houser 2005). Behavioral economists often refer to such reciprocal altruism as "conditional cooperation" (Fischbacher et al. 2001).

In pursuing a fair benefit-to-contribution ratio, the cooperator is accomplishing two goals. First, he is ensuring that he is getting as substantial a return as possible on his investment of cooperative effort. Second, he is avoiding being exploited by free riders (i.e., members with relatively high benefit-to-contribution ratios). We will discuss each of these two goals in turn.

3.3 Why Pursue Fairness? Maximizing the Advantage of Being a Cooperator

To the extent that the cooperator's effort is benefitting group co-members, he has power to negotiate the terms of the relationship. If his co-members refuse to grant him benefits that are proportional to the size of his contribution, he may reduce effort, refuse to continue to contribute, or leave the group. ATCG predicts that he will strive for a level of compensation that is at least commensurate with the exchange value of the services he provides to co-members. (He may well strive for more compensation than is fair, but his motivation to do so will depend on the consequences of free riding; see discussion later in this section).

In a well-managed group – one in which rewards are allocated fairly – higher contributors should reap greater benefits and should thus be advantaged over lower contributors. Members may thus engage in "competitive altruism" (Roberts 1998), that is, compete with co-members to be seen as the highest contributors to group goals, and those seen as the most altruistic should receive the greatest rewards. By competing to be the most altruistic member of the group, cooperators behave just as "self-interestedly" as any free rider; the difference is that while the free rider's self-interest benefits himself while harming the group, the competitive altruist's self-interest benefits both himself *and* the group. The predictions of competitive altruism theory, which are shared with ATCG, have been supported in experimental and field studies. For example, among Amazonian Shuar hunter-horticulturalists, villagers who work the hardest in cooperative tasks are allocated the highest social status (Price 2003, 2006a), and a similar link between altruism and status has been found in studies of British students (Hardy and Van Vugt 2006). Barclay and Willer (2007) also found that economic game participants compete to be more generous than others, in order to increase the likelihood that they will be chosen for potentially lucrative cooperative partnerships.

In order to motivate employees to behave in group-beneficial ways, then, managers must allocate rewards fairly, and allow employees to compete for these rewards by contributing in ways that most benefit the organization. If an employee makes a contribution that benefits the organization, for example by introducing a product improvement or new marketing strategy, a manager should never assume that the employee was selflessly motivated or is indifferent about being recognized and rewarded for this contribution, even if that employee modestly plays down the extent of his or her own contribution. If an employee does not receive some individual-level benefit that is commensurate with the value of his or her contribution, the employee will probably feel angry and exploited and lose motivation to cooperate (see below discussion of the exploitation problem). Further, to the extent that this lack of fairness is observed by others in the organization, it will send a message to these others that they have little incentive to act in pro-organization ways.

On the other hand, because a group's cooperative goals may sometimes conflict with the competitive aspirations of its individual members, a delicate balance must be maintained between the "competitive" and "altruistic" aspects of group cooperation, lest the former overwhelm the latter. An inherent risk in groups characterized by competitive altruism is that individual members will so strongly desire to contribute highly to group goals, in order to outcompete co-members for the rewards of contribution, that their contributions will actually have a negative impact on group productivity. A desire for personal glory, for example, may lead a employee (especially, for reasons discussed in Sect. 4 below, a male employee) to engage in group-damaging behaviors such as interrupting his co-members at meetings, denigrating his co-members' contributions to a group project, or pursuing a group leadership position for which he is under-qualified. All of these may invoke the dislike of colleagues and undermine morale and cooperation. In order to dissuade competitive altruists from becoming overly competitive, managers should always ensure that status rewards are based not on individual performance per se, but on the extent to which this performance has helped the group achieve its goals. Moreover, the rules must be transparent so that the incentive is visible to all and does not come as a surprise or appear unique to the recipient.

Interestingly, the fact that excessive status-seeking can threaten group goals is recognized in small-scale societies (Boehm 2001). Among Ju/'hoansi hunter gatherers in Botswana, good hunters achieve high status because they help secure meat for other group members. However, in order to prevent good hunters from becoming too oriented towards self-glorification as opposed to group-provisioning, group members make a practice of "insulting the meat", where they systematically denigrate the game that the hunter brings home (Lee 1993). That is not to suggest that hunters do not see through this ruse, nor that ritual insults would be the best way to curb excessive status-seeking in modern organizations. However, the fact that this problem is recognized by hunter-gatherers does suggest that it is fundamental to human nature: individuals are adapted to compete for status by cooperating in groups, and in order for their cooperative efforts to succeed, their competitive impulses must be continuously kept in check.

3.4 Why Pursue Fairness? Neutralizing Free Riders

The second goal the cooperator accomplishes by striving for a fair benefit-to-contribution ratio is avoiding being exploited by free riders (i.e., members with relatively high benefit-to-contribution ratios, who reap the benefits of others' efforts and contribute little themselves). To understand why this exploitation problem is such a serious concern for cooperators, we will start out by considering why free riders exist in the first place.

Imagine an ancestral hunter who joins a group mammoth hunt because he would gain more meat than he could by chasing rabbits alone. While it would be better for the co-members if the hunter contributed more while taking less mammoth meat in return, it would be better for the hunter to contribute less while taking more meat. The members who would reap the highest net benefits in this interaction – and who would therefore gain the highest fitness advantages – would be the free riders who contributed the least while taking the most. Each member can thus potentially gain a *free rider advantage* (Olson 1965; Hardin 1968). Experimental and field evidence from all types of societies – from hunter-gatherers to Western business organizations – attests to the universality of the free rider problem: when group members have the opportunity to acquire the free rider advantage, many will do so, as long as they do not expect to get caught (Albanese and Van Fleet 1985; Kidwell and Bennett 1993; Ostrom 1990; Andreoni 1988; Fehr and Gächter 2000; Price 2006a).

In addition to having to decide whether to seek the free rider advantage themselves, ancestral group members also had to avoid being exploited by co-members who did free ride or attempted to free ride. Members who failed to solve this *exploitation problem* would have been at an adaptive disadvantage relative to free riders, so genes for nonchalance in the face of this problem tended to disappear from ancestral gene pools. A basic finding of mathematical models of the evolution of cooperation is that when free rider problems are allowed to proliferate, cooperators eventually get exploited to extinction (Hamilton 1964; Henrich 2004). If cooperators perceive that they are facing an exploitation problem, and that the only way that they can reduce their own exploitation is by refusing to contribute further, then that is what they will do. Cross-cultural evidence confirms the prediction that cooperators react to exploitation by reducing their own contributions, and that as a result, unchecked free riding leads to the disintegration of group cooperation (Ostrom 1990). This disintegration process can be clearly observed in laboratory experiments in group cooperation. At first, people start out with high levels of cooperation, but with each round people become less and less cooperative (Ledyard 1995; Fehr and Gächter 2000; Croson 2007). This decay occurs because once some members begin free riding, their co-members respond by ratcheting down their own contributions, in order to mitigate their own exploitation. Free riders, in turn, then lower their own contributions further, in order to maintain their advantage. As this negatively reciprocal process progresses, levels of cooperation dwindle towards zero. It's obvious to an outsider that everyone would have been better off if all had continued to contribute, but from any one participant's perspective, it is disadvantageous to continue to cooperate if others are not.

Social scientists have been aware of free rider problem for decades, due especially to two highly influential publications that flagged the importance and prevalence of the "collective action problem" and the "tragedy of the commons" (Olson 1965; Hardin 1968). Thus, ATCG's focus on this problem is nothing new. However, despite widespread awareness of this problem, many mainstream organizational behavior theories have more or less overlooked it (for example equity theory, as noted below). While it may be easy to preach and promote cooperation, it is hard to sustain it unless you tackle the free rider problem. ATCG's individual-level adaptationist perspective not only affirms the centrality of this problem to organizational cooperation (Tooby et al. 2006), but also, as detailed below, allows ATCG to shed new light on the problem and propose workable solutions for how the free-rider problem can be solved.

3.5 The Consequences Problem: Punishment and Ostracization of Free Riders

If cooperators withhold their contributions in order to solve the exploitation problem, group cooperation decays. They may successfully avoid exploitation, but this only worsens the prospects for cooperation. One way to solve the exploitation problem while avoiding this decay would be to neutralize or reverse the free rider advantage for others, by imposing some kind of punitive or reputational cost on free riders, or by excluding them from the interaction (Price et al. 2002). The gravity of this *consequences problem* will depend on the extent to which free riders' co-members (or other interested parties) are willing and able to impose these consequences.

Cross-cultural evidence from experimental and real-world groups suggests that when given opportunities to impose consequences on free riders, members do so (Ostrom 2000). These consequences frequently take the form of monetary fines (Yamagishi 1986; Fehr and Gächter 2000; Price 2006a; Nikiforakis 2008) and social costs like ostracization (Cinyabuguma et al. 2005; Sheldon et al. 2000; Page et al. 2005; Barclay and Willer 2007). When such consequences are imposed, free riding can be deterred, and groups can avoid the collapse of cooperation that unsanctioned free riding induces. (Note that punishment in groups can itself involve a [second-order] free rider problem; for a discussion of how evolution may solve this problem, see Price 2003). This evidence is consistent with ATCG's prediction that in order for a group to sustain cooperative productivity, members will need some mechanism for imposing negative consequences on free riders. ATCG also predicts that the group's highest contributors will be the most likely to support the imposition of these consequences, because they will be the most vulnerable to the exploitation problem. This is supported by empirical evidence. For example, higher contributors exhibit more punitive sentiment towards free riders (Price et al. 2002; Shinada, Yamagishi and Ohmura 2004; Price 2005) and people who participate more frequently in cooperative interactions are more likely to base their moral judgements of others on the extent to which these others have engaged in free riding (Price 2006b).

The process by which cooperators choose to interact with each other while avoiding free riders is known in biology and evolutionary psychology as positive assortation or partner choice (Hamilton 1964; Price 2006a; Barclay and Willer 2007; Johnson et al. 2008). ATCG predicts that members who are willing to cooperate reciprocally should tend to prefer, seek, and retain co-members who are also willing to cooperate reciprocally. In other words, cooperators should stick together and ostracize free riders. Evidence for positive assortation has been consistently produced by group cooperation experiments: when participants are permitted to choose their interaction partners, based on information about potential partners' contribution levels in previous interactions, then relatively cooperative individuals choose each other and form relatively productive groups (Ehrhart and Keser 1999; Sheldon et al. 2000; Page et al. 2005; Barclay and Willer 2007). The free riders prefer cooperators too (if they did not, they would end up with no one to exploit), but with partnerships being based on mutual choice, they end up getting left out in the cold.

3.6 Solving the Free Rider Problem in Real Organizations

Free riding spreads infectiously and can be hard to stamp out once established. ATCG suggests that managers ought to take free riding seriously, and work to solve any free rider problem that may threaten the health of their organization. It also suggests that the best way for managers to solve the free rider problem, and thus solve the exploitation problem for high contributors, is to make employees plainly aware that there will be a consequences problem for those who pursue a free rider advantage. Efforts can focus on both detection and punishment, both of which are necessary for an effective deterrent. Employees must expect that these consequences will be consistent enough and severe enough to neutralize or reverse the free rider advantage. However that does not mean that the most effective way for managers to solve such problems will usually be through the direct imposition of harsh punishments. The threat of coercion can do more harm than good, if it "crowds out" voluntarily cooperative behavior (Titmuss 1970; Vollan 2008): employees who are motivated to cooperate without any threat of punishment may resent the unnecessary coercion and actually cooperate (or excel) less when threatened than they otherwise would. Direct punishment can also backfire if it is administered unjustly, for example in a manner suggesting that the punisher is motivated by his own overt selfishness as opposed to concern for the common good (Fehr and Rockenbach 2002). Finally, direct punishment can cause anger, resentment, and a desire for retaliation among the punished. In public goods games, for example, a significant proportion of free riders who are punished will retaliate by attempting to punish the person who punished them (Cinyabuguma et al. 2006; Nikiforakis 2008).

Despite the risks and costs associated with administering direct punishment, it may sometimes be the most appropriate and effective way to deal with egregious cases of free riding. However, there are also more low key methods for solving free rider problems or possibly even precluding them entirely. In order to effectively introduce a consequences problem, the key is to think broadly about what will deter would-be free riders. Even in the absence of direct punitive costs, adjustments can be made to organizational environments that will make employees perceive that free riding will not pay. Below are a number of ways to help solve the free rider problem by increasing the salience of free rider detection and/or punishment.

3.6.1 Solution One: Cognitive Cues of Detection

Experiments suggest that free riding can be reduced even through the use of relatively subtle cues that invoke our evolved cognitive mechanisms associated with cooperation. For example, by featuring stylized depictions of eyes as screen wallpaper on the computers used by economic game participants; eye-like representations suggest (not necessarily consciously) a risk of detection and thus apparently make participants more wary of the consequences problem (Haley and Fessler 2005; Bateson et al. 2006; Burnham and Hare 2007). The depictions of eyes used in these studies were crude representations; no rational person would mistake them for real human eyes that could actually see and monitor behavior. Nevertheless, these depictions were sufficient to reduce free riding. While unorthodox, these results suggest that an office décor containing eye-like depictions (e.g., in screen wallpaper or integrated within artwork) might unobtrusively generate cognitive cues that lead to reduced free riding. Recall that human cooperation evolved in small groups that were much more intimate than the sprawling organizations of modern societies. Thus there is a problematic "mismatch" between our evolved cognitive mechanisms and the environments of modern organizations. These organizations demand high levels of cooperation but usually do not adequately simulate the environments to which these cognitive mechanisms are adapted. One way of closing the gap is by reinstating some of the missing features of the environments in which those mechanisms evolved. Compared to existing theories of organizational behavior, ATCG is unique in proposing that organizations can enhance productivity by strategically reconstructing key elements of human ancestral environments. Further, as the eye studies show, these elements do not need to actually function as they did in ancestral environments (i.e., eye depictions do not need to actually monitor behavior), or even be particularly life-like, in order to affect behavior.

3.6.2 Solution Two: Mutual Monitoring and Peer Evaluation

Just as depictions of eyes can increase cooperation by suggesting that one's behavior is being monitored, actual monitoring should also be an effective way to minimize free riding. It is much easier to get away with free riding if your co-members cannot verify the extent of your work effort, and a major (and underappreciated) advantage of open plan offices is that when employees cannot wall themselves off from one another, they can more easily engage in mutual monitoring. Peer evaluations are another way to promote mutual monitoring; if members of a group project are given opportunities to evaluate each other's contributions, for example, it provides a voice for high contributors and thus lessens their vulnerability to exploitation.

3.6.3 Solution Three: Small Groups

Recall that reciprocity is more evolutionary stable in small groups, that is, fewer than about ten members (Boyd and Richerson 1988; Takezawa and Price 2010), and that human adaptations for cooperation probably evolved in groups that were no larger than this. Small groups should enhance cooperativeness by allowing for more effective mutual monitoring, because monitoring becomes more difficult, and eventually becomes impossible, as groups become larger. Thus in smaller groups free riders have a greater risk of being detected, and high contributors have more reason to believe that their contributions are being noticed and appreciated by other group members. The fact that reciprocity is easier to achieve in small groups is probably a major reason why small work teams (again, of no more than about ten members) appear to be most effective (Govindarajan and Gupta 2001).

3.6.4 Solution Four: Positive Assortation (Partner Choice)

Another effective way to regulate free riding in self-directed work teams might be to allow the more cooperative members of these teams to positively assort. Managers, instead of monitoring contributions and penalizing free riders themselves, could try leaving these tasks to team members. If employees are given freedom to select their own cooperative partners, high-contributing team members can follow their instincts to partner with other high contributors and thus avoid free riders. The result will likely be a relatively productive group of members who are free to contribute fully, without fear of the exploitation problem. Of course this process will probably also create some relatively unproductive groups, consisting of less cooperative members who have been shunned. Ideally, however, this unproductivity will be a short-term cost leading to long-term benefits; the ostracization of uncooperative members will raise their awareness of their reputational problem and may convince them to change their ways – or flag them for evaluation, training, or dismissal.

3.6.5 Solution Five: Whistle Blowing

Managers should also take care to not downplay the concerns of employees who voice unhappiness about the extent of others' free riding. As noted above, an organization's highest contributors will have the most to lose from others' free riding, and will thus be more likely to detect, and experience punitive sentiment towards, free riders (Price et al. 2002; Shinada et al. 2004; Price 2005, 2006b). By ignoring and failing to act on employee concerns about free riders, a manager will risk alienating the organization's most valuable employees, and will seem to lend tacit approval to the exploitation of these employees by free riders. Cooperation can collapse quickly and easily if free riders take hold, so early warning systems should be highly valued.

Finally, managers should remember that they themselves are as vulnerable as lower-level employees to being tempted by the free rider advantage. Free riding in organizations is usually seen as a problem that occurs at sub-managerial levels (Albanese and Van Fleet 1985; Kidwell and Bennett 1993), but there is no theoretical reason to expect that free riding should be more prevalent at these levels, as managers are as capable as anyone of acquiring disproportionately high benefit-to-contribution ratios, especially if they have good people below them producing work that can be passed off as their own. The perception of managerial free riding may increase under poor economic conditions, because when organizations fail, managerial contributions will more likely be perceived as low or negative, even as managerial compensation remains high. A good deal of public outrage throughout the recent financial crisis has been targeted specifically at managers who reaped huge rewards for making hugely *negative* contributions to organizational goals. For example, Sir Fred Goodwin received an annual pension of £700,000 after leading RBS to the largest annual corporate loss in UK history (Treanor 2009).

This 'massive reward for massive failure' pattern is a grotesque parody of the reciprocity rule that people use to assess the fairness of compensation, i.e., "reward should be proportional to contribution". Thus bankers like Sir Fred are perceived as supremely exploitative free riders. Since managers cannot be relied upon to police their own free riding, this task must fall to stakeholders whose interests lie in promoting the success of the organization as a whole, and who realize that free riding at any level is a threat to that success.

3.7 Is ATCG More Predictive than Equity Theory?

As noted above, ATCG assumes that in order to cooperate adaptively, group members must ensure that their benefit-to-contribution ratios are no smaller than those of co-members. Readers who are already familiar with equity theory (Adams 1963, 1965) may recognize that this focus on the benefit-to-contribution ratio is essentially similar to Adams' emphasis on the relationship of "outcomes" to "inputs." As suggested by this similarity, ATCG and equity theory do have much in common; however they also have some fundamental differences. Before comparing the two theories explicitly, we will first present a brief review of equity theory.

Equity theory (Adams 1963, 1965) is one of the best-known and most successful theories in the field of organizational behavior: when Miner (2003) asked 71 organizational behavior scholars to rank the importance of 73 organizational behavior theories, equity theory finished in third place overall, and was the top-finishing theory of cooperative behavior. (Equity theory has also been broadened to apply to social relationships in general, e.g. marriages [Walster et al. 1978]). Simply stated, equity theory predicts that a member of an organization (referred to by Adams as "Person") will assess the ratio of the benefit that he receives from his job (his "outcome") to the contribution that he makes to his organization (his "input"), and compare this ratio to some referent individual or group ("Other"). Other will often be Person's organizational co-members (although Other may also be something quite different, for example Person in a former job). Adams considers equity theory to be a special case of cognitive dissonance theory, a widely-studied psychological phenomenon in which people attempt to minimize the perceived discrepancy between their desires and their actual experience (Festinger 1957; Cooper 2007). As such, equity theory's fundamental prediction is that Person will be content if his own ratio is similar to Other's ratio, and distressed if these ratios are different, because the latter situation should produce more perceived dissonance.

If Person does perceive dissonant ratios, then he will attempt to make them less dissonant – that is, more equitable – by adjusting the outcomes/inputs of himself and/or of Other. Person's attempts to increase equity will be motivated by the emotion of anger if Person is disadvantaged by the inequity, and by the emotion of guilt if Person is advantaged by the inequity. Therefore if Person perceives that Other is making the same salary (outcome) in exchange for less work effort (input), then Person will be motivated by anger to rectify this inequity by reducing his own effort or extracting increased effort from Other, or by convincing management to raise his own salary or lower Other's salary. By the same token (and this is equity theory's most extraordinary prediction), if Person perceives that his own salary is higher than Other's, even though their effort levels are equal, then Person will be motivated by guilt to strive to increase his own effort, lower Other's effort, reduce his own salary, or increase Other's salary. Equity theory predicts aversion to self-advantageous inequity because of its roots in cognitive dissonance theory: self-advantageous inequity is just as dissonant as self-disadvantageous inequity, and should therefore be just as distressing.

Despite predicting that Person will seek to avoid self-advantageous inequity, equity theory also predicts that Person will be more tolerant of such unfairness than he will be of self-disadvantageous inequity. In other words, equity theory is somewhat asymmetrical in that while it predicts that Person will object both to being underrewarded and to being overrewarded, it also predicts more vigorous objection to underreward than to overreward. The theory cannot gracefully account for this asymmetry, because its dissonance theory foundations offer little insight about why underreward should cause more distress than overreward. Adams deals with the asymmetry by suggesting that overreward situations may seem more tolerable due to Person's egocentric bias: "Person is motivated to minimize his costs and to maximize his gains" (Adams 1965: 284). However if Person is thus motivated, then why does equity theory predict in the first place that Person should *avoid* rather than *seek* overreward situations? This bolting-on of egocentric bias does not seem to be an internally consistent way of dealing with the asymmetry, and egocentric bias is probably best seen as only an auxiliary or ad hoc hypothesis (Lakatos 1978), rather than a core hypothesis, of equity theory.

3.8 Efforts to Rescue Equity Theory in Situations of Overreward

Equity theory is regarded as a successful theory in large part because its prediction of aversion to underreward has received strong empirical support (Mowday and Colwell 2003; Colquitt et al. 2005). However, a consistent criticism of equity theory is that its prediction of aversion to overreward has received less support (Bolino and Turnley 2008): while people usually object strenuously to self-disadvantageous inequity, they do not reliably do so to self-advantageous inequity. In order to explain this lack of aversion to overreward, many researchers have implicitly or explicitly invoked Adams' ad hoc egocentric bias hypothesis (Greenberg 1983; Thompson and Loewenstein 1992; Diekmann et al. 1997; Leung et al. 2004).

An alternative approach to explain the lack of aversion to overreward is to suggest that individuals vary in term of their "equity sensitivity" (Huseman et al. 1985; 1987; Miles et al. 1989; Akan et al. 2009). Equity sensitivity research suggests that people can be divided up into three classes, based on how they score on a continuous measure of equity sensitivity: a relatively rare class of "benevolent" individuals, who prefer outcome-to-input ratios that are lower than co-members (underreward), coexists with more common classes of "equity sensitive" individuals, who prefer ratios that are equal to co-members, and "entitled" individuals, who prefer ratios that are higher than co-members (overreward). From this perspective, free riders would most likely come from the "entitled" class. This classification scheme is basically similar to those proposed by evolutionary-oriented behavioral economics researchers (Fischbacher et al. 2001; Kurzban and Houser 2005), whose empirical findings suggest that while most people, when playing cooperation games, can be classified as reciprocal altruists (who usually cooperate as long as co-members cooperate, similar to equity sensitives), a minority behave as free riders (who usually do not cooperate, similar to entitleds), and an even smaller minority behave as unconditional cooperators (who usually cooperate even when co-members do not, similar to benevolents).

3.9 Predictions of ATCG That Differ from Those of Equity Theory

The refinements to equity theory mentioned above make some progress towards helping equity theory explain the lack of aversion to overreward. By proposing that in addition to seeking equity, many people exhibit egocentric bias, and some people behave as entitleds who prefer overreward, equity theory is better able to explain why free riding is such a universal problem in groups. Still, these refinements do not put equity theory on a par with ATCG, in terms of being able to make predictions and provide solutions to the free rider problem. ATCG's advantages in this regard are of three kinds.

3.9.1 Prediction One: The Free Rider Problem Can Be Solved Via Social Consequences

First, ATCG correctly predicts how people will change their cooperative behavior in response to external social influences. The only mechanisms proposed by equity theory for what motivates individual responses to inequity are the emotions of guilt and anger. For example, while benevolents are predicted to experience relatively low anger upon being underrewarded, entitleds are predicted to experience relatively low guilt upon being overrewarded (Miles et al. 1989). Individuals are portrayed as having fixed equity sensitivity orientations that are regulated internally by emotions, and little attention is given to the idea that people are capable of changing their behavior (let alone switching orientations) in response to external social influences. Thus, if you are the manager of an organization that is bedeviled with too many entitleds, there isn't much you can do except either expect the organization to fail, or else try to replace the entitleds with benevolents or equity sensitives. ATCG, on the other hand, predicts that group members will become interested in changing their behavior depending on social influences, especially those that deter free riding.

3.9.2 Prediction Two: The Emergence of a Particular Cooperative Strategy Will Depend on the Frequencies of Other Strategies

ATCG's second advantage over equity theory is that it predicts the circumstances under which a particular kind of cooperative strategy will emerge in an organization. Equity sensitivity theory simply assigns people to different equity sensitivity categories, without considering the dynamics of how these categories should interact with one another, or the conditions under which any particular category should emerge as dominant in an organization. ATCG, in contrast, is capable of making some principled predictions along these lines. These predictions, which specify how any cooperative strategy (i.e. reciprocity, free riding, or unconditional cooperation) can emerge as a frequency-dependent adaptive response to the presence of other strategies, will be discussed in Sect. 4.

3.9.3 Prediction Three: More Competitive Individuals Will Be More Pro-equity/Anti-equality

ATCG's third advantage over equity theory is that it offers insights about what kinds of individuals will most favour the *equity* distribution rule (under which the highest contributors obtain the greatest rewards) as opposed to the *equality* distribution rule (under which everyone receives the same reward). While equity theory makes no predictions about the preference for equity over equality, ATCG predicts that individuals who have more to gain from engaging in competition will be relatively pro-equity and anti-equality. This prediction will be discussed in Sect. 4, where we focus on individual and sex differences.

4 How Cooperation is Affected by Differences Among Individuals, Differences Between Sexes, and Differences Among Resources

In Sect. 3, we sketched a general overview of ATCG's perspective on reciprocity in groups. In this section we will investigate how individuals will vary in their cooperative behavior, depending on their strategic orientation and their competitiveness. We will then discuss ATCG's predictions about how the sexes will differ in terms of cooperative behavior. Finally, we will explain how ATCG's predictions about resource-sharing vary, when different classes of resources – specifically, windfall and surplus resources – are being shared.

4.1 The Frequency Dependence of Cooperation

As noted above, both equity sensitivity and evolutionary theorists have predicted that individuals will vary in the kinds of cooperative strategies they play. However, only evolutionary theory, and not equity sensitivity theory, provides a solid basis for predicting how particular variables will influence this individual variation. ATCG incorporates this evolutionary view and the predictions that it makes. In order to explain this view, we must first describe why the advantageousness of any cooperative strategy is frequency dependent.

Evolutionary game theory (Maynard Smith 1982) suggests that the adaptiveness of a cooperative strategy in a population often depends on the frequency of other strategies in the same population (Boyd and Lorberbaum 1987; Lomborg 1996; Hauert et al. 2002). Consider the following rock-paper-scissors scenario, which is illustrated in Fig. 1.

In a population of free riders (F), reciprocators (R) – who cooperate as long as they can verify that their partners are cooperating – have an advantage, because only they can gain the benefits of cooperation (assuming that the benefits of cooperation are greater than the costs of verifying partner cooperativeness, and that reciprocators can exclude free riders from the benefits of cooperation). Eventually the population will become dominated by reciprocators. Once the reciprocators gain supremacy, however, they become vulnerable to an invasion of 'unconditional cooperators' (U), who always cooperate, even without verifying partner cooperativeness. While unconditional cooperators gain the same benefits from cooperation as reciprocators, they avoid the reciprocators' verification costs (such verification is wasteful in this environment, because there are no free riders). However, the more the unconditional cooperators come to dominate the population,

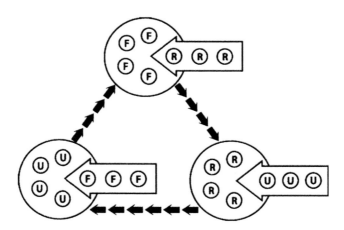

Fig. 1 The cycle of frequency-dependent for three cooperative strategies: free riding (F), reciprocity (R), and unconditional cooperation (U). At the *top* of the diagram, a population dominated by F is invaded by R, who is advantaged over F due to its ability to gain the benefits of cooperation (and to exclude F from these benefits). At the *bottom right*, an R-dominated population is invaded by U, who is advantaged over R due to its ability to gain the benefits of cooperation, without paying the costs of monitoring and verifying partner cooperativeness. At the *bottom left*, a U-dominated population is invaded by F, who is advantaged because it can exploit U's overtrusting cooperativeness. After F becomes dominant, the cycle repeats itself

the more the population becomes vulnerable to an invasion of free riders, because unconditional cooperators are easily exploited (Nowak and Sigmund 1992).

ATCG incorporates the logic of the above rock-paper-scissors scenario, and predicts that the likelihood that a strategy will be pursued in an organization will depend on the frequencies of other strategies in that organization. ATCG is at present agnostic, however, about whether the different strategies in the above scenario represent different individuals that always play the same strategy (i.e., different polymorphisms) or the same individuals played flexible strategies. Some researchers have suggested that the former scenario is more likely, and that fixed polymorphic strategies are maintained in populations because across all social environments of shifting strategy frequencies, each strategy will be adaptive on average (Kurzban and Houser 2005; Cesarini et al. 2008). On the other hand, it seems as though the best possible individual strategy would be a flexible one (Boyd and Lorberbaum 1987) that played (1) reciprocator in a population of free riders, while excluding free riders from the benefits of cooperation, (2) unconditional cooperator in a population of reciprocators, and (3) free rider in a population of unconditional cooperators. To what extent is an individual capable of switching strategies according to this pattern? That question has not yet been thoroughly addressed by research. But regardless of whether individuals are best seen as fixed as opposed to flexible cooperative strategists, ATCG makes three points here that are of particular relevance to managers.

4.1.1 First Point for Managers: Strategic Behavior Can Be Altered

First, even if people are fixed strategists, evidence reviewed above suggests that group members do adjust their cooperative behavior somewhat, depending on how they expect co-members will behave. For example, would-be free riders become more cooperative when they perceive they may be ostracized for free riding, and reciprocators become less cooperative in the presence of free riders. These adjustments may not map on particularly well to the rock-paper-scissors dynamics described above; for example, a free rider who starts acting like a reciprocator out of fear of being ostracized may not be "switching strategies" so much as suspending his free riding until the threat of ostracization has passed. Nevertheless, the fact that members make these adjustments does demonstrate that social influences – especially, imposition of the consequences problem on would–be free riders – can be used to enhance group productivity, as ATCG (but not equity theory) predicts.

4.1.2 Second Point for Managers: Shifts in Employee Cooperative Behavior Can Be Predicted, Based on the Frequencies of Strategies Within an Organization

A second point of relevance to managers is that regardless of whether people are fixed or flexible strategists, the rock-paper-scissors scenario predicts that particular strategies are likely to emerge and become dominant in particular organizational environments. For example, imagine an organization in which insufficient effort is made to monitor employee contributions, and to ensure that the greatest rewards go to the highest contributors to organizational goals. Low contributors can obtain high rewards, for example, by convincing management that they have contributed more than they actually have. Because it is not necessary to actually contribute in order to get ahead, would-be high contributors lose their motivation to contribute, and free riding emerges as the dominant strategy. (Throughout this example, the emergence of a new dominant strategy could be due to either current employees who switch their strategies, or else to an influx of new employees – who may be attracted to the organizational culture because it affords their strategy an advantage).

In order to rectify this situation, management will need to begin neutralizing the free rider advantage by allocating higher rewards to higher contributors. This introduction of fair compensation policies will give reciprocity an advantage over free riding, and reciprocity will become the dominant strategy. Over time, employees will become increasingly trusting that their contributions will be rewarded proportionately. The more they trust in this outcome, the less necessary they should believe it is to constantly monitor and verify that their own benefit-to-contribution ratios are no lower than co-members. Such monitoring efforts are wasteful when everyone else truly is reciprocating, so unconditional cooperation will emerge as the dominant strategy. The more members cooperate unconditionally, however, the more opportunity co-members will have to exploit them. This may explain why, although a high level of trust is generally assumed to be beneficial in organizations (Dirks and Ferrin 2001), "too much" trust appears to be detrimental to work team effectiveness (Langfred 2004). Unverified trust will create fresh opportunities for co-members to adopt free riding techniques, for example to exaggerate the extent of their own unmonitored contribution level. If an organizational climate of too much trust allows free riding to emerge as the dominant strategy, the cycle will have come full-circle, and reciprocity will again need to be restored.

4.1.3 Third Point for Managers: Cooperation is Always Ultimately Vulnerable

The above example contains a practical warning: even in an organization in which rewards are allocated extremely fairly, the stability of cooperation is always ultimately vulnerable. A manager might rightfully take pride in the high levels of trust that he observes in his organization, but he should always keep in mind that climates of unconditional cooperation are vulnerable to being invaded and undermined by free riders. By the same token, however, even an organization that has decayed into a free rider's paradise can be rehabilitated, provided that management is willing to make the effort to change the culture such that individual contributions to organizational goals are monitored and rewarded proportionately.

4.2 Competitiveness and a Preference for Equity over Equality

So far our chapter has focused on one kind of distribution rule in particular: the *equity rule*, which specifies that individuals receive rewards in direct proportion to their contributions. We have focused on this rule because it leads to the most economically productive groups (Deutsch 1975), due to the fact that it most effectively solves problems of cooperation (especially, the free rider problem) that hinder productivity. However there are, of course, other distribution rules in human societies, and two other common ones are the *equality rule*, under which everyone receives the same amount, and the *need rule*, under which the needier receive more (Deutsch 1975; Romaine and Schmidt 2009). Equity and equality have received more research attention than need, and are probably more relevant than need in organizational contexts, so we will focus here on equity and equality.

Whether an individual benefits more from equity or equality depends on that individual's competitiveness, that is, on how much that individual can gain by engaging in competition. Two main factors determine an individual's competitiveness: the individual's sex (as we will discuss in the next section), and the individual's likelihood of winning that competition. A more competitive group member will benefit more from equity than equality because only equity will give him an opportunity to gain, via competitive altruism, an advantage over co-members. For example, an individual who is highly capable of contributing to a group productive effort would stand to be highly rewarded in an equity system, and would do better under equity than under equality. A member who has little ability to engage in competitive altruism, on the other hand, would more likely do better under equality.

Research on how individual competitive ability affects attitudes toward equity and equality has tended to focus on the level of the nation-state or of society as a whole. For example, studies focusing on preferences for national governments that are more oriented towards equity or meritocracy (e.g., capitalism) versus equality (e.g., communism) have found that citizens who are better able to acquire resources, such as higher-income and better-educated citizens, are relatively supportive of the rule of equity (Ritzman and Tomaskovic-Devey 1992; Kunovich and Slomczynski 2007). Further, research on "social dominance orientation" has found that members of ethnic majorities, as well as higher-income individuals, tend to be more generally approving of inequality among groups in society (Pratto et al. 2006). Studies such as these suggest that individuals tend to prefer the distribution rule which advantages them. However, these studies do not directly examine possible relationships between specific biological traits and a pro-equity/anti-equality orientation.

ATCG offers novel predictions here: pro-equity/anti-equality sentiment will be expressed relatively highly by individuals who display traits that would have enhanced individual competiveness in ancestral environments. In making this prediction, ATCG could potentially cast new light on the issue of who prefers equity. For example, ATCG predicts that males with relatively great upper body strength will be relatively pro-equity/anti-equality. The logic of this prediction is similar to that used by Sell et al. (2009), who show that males with greater upper body strength express more support for political aggression (e.g., for military action by their own country). Sell et al. explain this result by noting that in ancestral environments, stronger males could have benefited relatively highly from the use of aggression. Of course, even though upper body strength has little impact on who wins wars in modern environments, the evolved psychology persists. Similarly, stronger males in ancestral environments would have had more to gain from equity and more to lose from equality, because their physical power would have made them relatively capable of contributing to group productive efforts. Therefore, ATCG predicts them to be relatively pro-equity and anti-equality in modern environments, even though physical strength is, in many modern organizations, less important than it was ancestrally for engaging in competitive altruism.

Besides physical strength, other ancestral correlates of competitiveness that ATCG predicts will relate positively to pro-equity/anti-equality orientation include testosterone level, and measures of good health and physical condition such as physical attractiveness and bilateral facial and bodily symmetry. Higher testosterone levels are associated with increased competitive status-seeking behavior in males (Dabbs 1997, 1998), and physical attractiveness and symmetry are both used as general indexes of biological quality (Gangestad et al. 1994; Brown et al. 2008). All of these variables have been shown to affect some aspects of behavior in economic games. For example, more symmetrical males make lower offers in an economic game (Zaatari and Trivers 2007), while higher-testosterone men are more likely to reject low offers (Burnham 2007). Physical attractiveness has shown no consistent relationship with behavior in these games (for inconsistent results see Mulford et al. 1998; Solnick and Schweitzer 1999; Takahashi et al. 2006). Taken together, these results do not allow one to assess whether these physical correlates of ancestral competitiveness are associated (be it positively or negatively) with level of "general cooperativeness", and they do not test the hypothesis that these physical correlates are associated positively with pro-equity/anti-equality orientation. However, these results do imply that there are links between these physical correlates and the psychological mechanisms which govern cooperative behavior, and ATCG suggests some compelling hypotheses about what these links should be, and how they should impact support for the equity rule in organizations.

4.3 Sex Differences

So far in Sect. 4 we have focused on individual difference variables that affect cooperativeness in both sexes. Now we will examine differences in cooperativeness that distinguish the sexes from each other.

ATCG incorporates the standard evolutionary approach to explaining sexually dimorphic traits, and thus provides a solid basis for predicting sex differences in cooperative behavior. According to the theory of parental investment and sexual selection (Darwin 1871; Trivers 1972), sex differences evolve because the sexes are selected to make different-sized investments in the production of offspring. In most species, males are the lesser-investing sex; for example, while the minimum investment that most male mammals must make in order to reproduce is a trivial amount of time and sperm, most female mammals must make a minimal investment of a long period of gestation and lactation. As a result, males have the potential to reproduce at a much faster rate than do females, and the reproductive success of males (unlike that of females) is limited mainly by mating opportunities. Because mating opportunities benefit males more than females, and because higher status males get more mating opportunities, selection on males tends to strongly favour the ability to succeed in status competition. Therefore in most species, especially mammals and primates, (including humans) males compete for status more vigorously than do females (Daly and Wilson 1988; Kruger and Nesse 2006, 2007; Graves, 2010). And just as males are, on average, better-designed than females for status competition, females are, on average, better-designed than males for parental investment.

One implication of these evolved sex differences is that male and female employees, in evaluating the fairness of their benefit-to-contribution ratios, will tend to differ in the forms of benefit they most value. Because females are relatively more oriented towards parental investment, family-friendly policies tend to be valued more by females than by males (Scandura and Lankau 1997; Kim 2008). Benefits that come in the form of generous parental leave policies and flexible work schedules, for example, will be valued more highly by females than by males.

An even more important result of these sex differences is that human males (like the lesser-investing sex in many species) should tend to be more motivated than females to compete for social status. Males manifest this tendency during childhood and continue to display it throughout their adult lives (Geary 2002; Browne 2006). Studies in experimental psychology and economics have routinely found that males are more interested than females in competitive behaviour (review in Croson and Gneezy 2009). For example, when engaged in tasks such as solving puzzles and running on a track, male performance is enhanced when the tasks are performed in competition with others, while female performance is not (Gneezy et al. 2003; Gneezy and Rustichini 2004); and when given a choice about what kind of compensation scheme they prefer, males are more likely than females to choose a competitive scheme (e.g., winner take all) as opposed to a non-competitive one (e.g., piece rate) (Niederle and Vesterlund 2007). Male competitiveness is also evident in studies that have focused explicitly on cooperation. Van Vugt et al. (2007) found that males increased their in-group cooperation significantly in response to competition from rival groups, whereas females were relatively unaffected by this competition.

The increased competitiveness of human males should make them more pro-equity and anti-equality, for reasons outlined in the previous section of this chapter: because ancestral males had more to gain than females from status competition, they also had more to gain than females from the rule of equity and less to gain from the rule of equality. The fact that males do tend to be more pro-equity than females, and that females tend to be more pro-equality than males, has been recognized for decades. Studies have found consistently that when allocating resources, males tend to use the equity rule and females tend to use the equality rule (Vinacke 1969; Major and Deaux 1982; review in Inness et al. 2004). This sex difference has usually been explained in terms of different socialization pressures on males and females (Inness et al. 2004). However, because ATCG explains variation in pro-equity/anti-equality orientation in terms of variation in competitiveness, as opposed to sex differences per se, ATCG predicts not just between-sex differences in this orientation, but also within-sex differences depending on other factors (as noted above). Further, because ATCG attributes sex difference in pro-equity/anti-equality orientation primarily to biological adaptation, as opposed to socialization, it predicts that this difference would be difficult to eradicate via socialization alone. Further evidence against the socialization hypothesis is that differences in cooperative behavior between boys and girls emerge at a very young age (Ellis et al. 2008). For example, boys more often play team games involving larger groups, are angrier when rules are broken, and have more transient friendships, whereas girls have more exclusive friendships. Although the sex difference in competitive status-striving has occasionally been reflected upon in the mainstream organizational behaviour literature (for example, in the context of salary negotiation [Stevens et al. 1993]), it is widely underappreciated in the field (Sandelands 2002). Which factors may account for the neglect of this sex difference? It has not been due to a failure on the part of organizational researchers to appreciate the general importance of status enhancement as an incentive in organizations; indeed, they have appreciated its importance for decades (Clark and Wilson 1961). Nor has it been due to a general reluctance among organizational researchers to investigate sex differences; indeed, according to a review by Ely and Padavic (2007), no less than 131 articles discussing sex differences appeared in the top four management journals between 1984 and 2003.

Instead, neglect of this sex difference has probably been due to two other factors: first, the general political thorniness of the topic (see below); and second, the fact that evolutionary considerations have not been a traditional component of any topic in organizational behavior, including sex differences. For example, of those 131 management articles on sex differences, none were recorded by Ely and Padavic as having taken an evolutionary theoretical perspective. It is no coincidence that the field's most extensive and straightforward discussions of sex differences in status-striving have appeared in a special issue of *Journal of Organizational Behavior* devoted to Darwinian perspectives on organizations (Browne 2006; Colarelli et al. 2006). Organizational researchers would benefit by taking a more evolutionary perspective on this topic, as there is a clear Darwinian rationale for why males should be relatively preoccupied with competition and status, and this sex difference probably generates a variety of important effects in organizational contexts.

4.3.1 Negative Reactions to Status Reductions, Especially Among Males

One of these important effects is that employees, and particularly male employees, should be sensitive to perceived social slights regarding the value of their contributions to cooperative endeavors. Evolutionary psychologists have long recognized that males are relatively likely to react negatively and sometimes violently to insults to their status, even when these insults seem relatively trivial (Daly and Wilson 1988; Goldstein 2002; Nisbett and Cohen 1996; Wrangham and Wilson 2004). The social dynamics of a typical organization will provide regular opportunities for an employee to feel that his or her status has been slighted in some way. Such insults may be explicit, for example being demoted, fired, or passed over for a promotion, but in group cooperative interactions they will more often be subtle, for example sensing that the recommendations you made in a meeting were ignored, or that your contributions to a group project were not adequately recognized. Differences in how negatively males and females react to such insults could lead to sex differences in variables that are important to organizational behavior researchers such as motivation, job satisfaction, and desire for retributive justice.

The potential of status reductions to elicit strong negative reactions, particularly among males, is one reason why status must be allocated with great care. Although status rewards may often seem relatively cheap to administer compared to other kinds of incentives (e.g., financial ones), status is nevertheless a scare resource. Status allocation events are zero-sum games, as any enhancement in the rank of one particular member will produce a drop in the *relative* status of at least one co-member (relative, that is, to the ascendant member), and thus may be perceived as insulting by the co-member(s). To help minimize the chances that a status reallocation event will be perceived as insulting, care should be taken to convince all group members that the reallocation has been equitably based on the extent to which members have been contributing to group goals. Peer reviews might even be used in the judgment, to generate the impression that the decision reflects a common census rather than arbitrary favoritism.

4.3.2 Positive Reactions to Status Enhancement, Especially Among Males

The flip side of males reacting more negatively to status-lowering insults and demotions is that they should also be relatively motivated to strive for status-enhancing rewards. Such rewards could include material status symbols like a higher salary or bigger office, but could also include social indicators such as public recognition for one's achievements or a higher assigned rank in an office hierarchy. The view that males should on average be relatively motivated to chase such rewards implies that the underrepresentation of females in top management positions may be due not just to sexist discrimination, but to a reduced motivation on the part of females to compete aggressively for these jobs (Browne 2006; this issue is also relevant to female political candidates, e.g., Clift and Brazaitis 2003). This observation may seem controversial, as it would seem to suggest that women do not desire such positions as strongly as do men, which might seem to justify their underrepresentation. However, a few considerations must be kept in mind here.

First, as with many scientific statements about mean group differences, this is probably a case of overlapping normal distributions, which is consistent with the expectation that many females will be *more* status-oriented than many men. Second, predicting that males will on average be more motivated to compete for high-status positions is not the same thing as predicting that they will be more effective on average in such positions; desiring a job is not the same thing, of course, as being competent to perform it. Accordingly, the observation that males tend to more competitively pursue status says nothing about the desirability of male overrepresentation in top management (indeed, it gives us reasons to assess it more critically). This observation does suggest, however, which steps an organization might take in order to increase female representation in high-status positions. In particular, it suggests that an open competition for such jobs, in which an organization waits to see which candidates throw their hat into the ring and most aggressively promote themselves, might not be the best way to attract the most qualified female candidates (or indeed many qualified male candidates). Such competitions may self-select for a large pool of males, and females who are relatively male-like in terms of competitive status-striving (Rhoads 2004). However, a larger pool of qualified females might be generated if such candidates are actively scouted out and recruited, instead of being expected to aggressively pursue the jobs on their own.

4.4 Different Sharing Expectations for Windfall and Surplus Resources

We will conclude Sect. 4 by pointing out that expectations about how a group's resources should be shared will be influenced not just by fairness considerations and by differences among individuals and between sexes, but also by the abundance and availability of the resource. In discussing ATCG's predictions about resource-sharing so far, we have been focusing on resources that are deliberately produced by concerted organizational effort. In these situations, as we have seen, the prevailing view of fairness tends to be that only someone who contributed to production should receive a share of the resource, and higher contributors should receive larger shares. ATCG identifies two kinds of resources, however, that people tend to believe should be shared more widely, generously and equally.

The first of these resources are windfall resources, that is, resources that are unpredictable in terms of availability. ATCG agrees with the perspective that when the availability of a resource is relatively unpredictable, individual-level selection favors widespread voluntarily sharing (Kaplan and Hill 1985; Andras et al. 2007). This sharing rule appears to be the product of a risk-reduction psychological adaptation: if a resource's availability is unpredictable, then chance determines who acquires it. Thus, any one person is just as likely to benefit from the widespread sharing rule as to be obligated by it. Support for this theory has been produced in studies such as Kaplan and Hill (1985) and Kaplan et al. (1990), who found that more unpredictable resources were shared more widely by Ache foragers. Similarly, Kameda et al. (2002) found that in a series of laboratory and vignette experiments, people who acquired money as the result of chance were more willing to share it widely, and were expected by others to share it more widely.

Although the evidence in favour of windfall resources being widely shared is compelling, some research suggests that other factors can emerge as being more important influences on how widely a resource is shared. Bliege Bird et al.'s (2002) study of Meriam foragers suggests that a resource's abundance, as opposed to its unpredictability, is a more important predictor of how generous people are with it. In their study, when an individual possessed a surplus of a food resource such as fish or turtle, he was more likely to share it widely. ATCG would predict this result, because the less an individual needs to consume a resource himself, the more he can afford to exchange it for other resources, such as social status. For example, Bliege Bird et al. (2002) suggest that sharing allows individuals to broadcast a costly signal of the qualities that enabled them to forage successfully; thus, their sharing increases their social status by making them seem more attractive to potential mates and allies.

ATCG's perspective on windfall and surplus resources can help illuminate some practical issues about how the fairness of compensation procedures are evaluated in organizations. Managers should keep in mind that when organizations acquire resources that are unexpected, or more than the organization is perceived to "need", employees will probably feel relatively entitled to a share of these resources. If an umbrella-making company has a particularly profitable quarter due to a freakishly rainy summer, it would good for employee satisfaction to widely distribute the benefits of this windfall. And if a company's profits have far exceeded its budgeted needs, then widespread sharing with employees would again be well-advised. What's more, managers who hoard resources for themselves will be perceived as particularly selfish if these resources are of the windfall and/or surplus kind. Consider, for instance, the recent public outrage over the size of banker bonuses. The unpredictable quality of bonuses probably makes the public regard them to some extent as windfall resources. Moreover, bonuses are perceived as surplus – not needed for the bank's operating costs or to pay the bankers' already-generous salaries. These bonuses are perceived as being concentrated in the hands of a few elite earners, as opposed to being shared generously throughout a larger community – not shared, for example, with the society which kept many of the banks afloat throughout the crisis (although these bonuses are usually taxed, being taxed is not perceived as voluntary sharing), or even with lower-level employees of the banks themselves. Thus banker compensation, which the public already perceived as basically unfair (e.g. due to outsized rewards, and as discussed in Sect. 3, the practice of "reward for failure"), seems even more unfair because it often takes the form of unpredictable surpluses that are not voluntarily shared.

5 Conclusion

The Adaptationist Theory of Cooperation in Groups (ATCG) is a synthetic theory that draws together the contributions of a large number of researchers. Most of these researchers have been able, by adopting an individual-level adaptationist perspective, to make predictions about cooperation in groups that go beyond those that are made by existing theories in social and organizational science. That said, ATCG also shares predictions with several previous theories. In this conclusion, we will briefly review some of the main ways in which ATCG compliments and diverges from existing theories of cooperation in groups.

First of all, it may seem ironic, but the theory of cooperation that ATCG probably has the least in common with is another evolutionary theory, the purely group selectionist perspective (Gintis 2000). All of ATCG's predictions follow from the basic premise that cooperation evolved because individual cooperators receive fitness advantages; without this premise, ATCG has no reason to predict behavioral dynamics such as reciprocity, competitive altruism, free riding, the frequency dependence of cooperative strategies, and individual and sex differences in cooperative behavior. Further, although a multilevel selectionist perspective (Wilson and Wilson 2007) could accommodate these individual-level processes better than a purely group selectionist process could, we see no added value, in terms of improving ATCG's predictive power, in adopting a multilevel perspective at this stage of theory development.

ATCG has a good bit more in common with equity theory (Adams 1963), with its focus on input-to-outcome (benefit-to-contribution) ratios, and with equity sensitivity theory (Huseman et al. 1985), which recognizes individual variation in the preference for equity. However, ATCG improves on equity theory's ad hoc and minimal attention to the free rider problem by recognizing this problem as the central impediment to productivity in groups. Further, because equity theory and equity sensitivity theory focus on the internal emotional regulation of cooperative behavior, they do not offer clear solutions to the free rider problem; ATCG on the other hand does offer solutions, by predicting that free riding will be mitigated by imposition of external social consequences (or by cues which suggest that such consequences are forthcoming). And while equity sensitivity theory predicts that different kinds of cooperative strategies will exist in a population, ATCG goes much further by predicting the dynamics of the process by which any one cooperative strategy can emerge as dominant in an organization, depending on the frequencies of other strategies.

ATCG also predicts that individuals with greater competitive ability should do better under equity systems as opposed to equality systems, and so should hold relatively pro-equity/anti-equality attitudes. With this prediction, ATCG distinguishes itself further from equity theory and equity sensitivity theory, but finds some common ground with theories which predict that individuals who are better able to compete for resources in modern societies will exhibit more support for meritocracy and social inequality (Ritzman and Tomaskovic-Devey 1992; Kunovich and Slomczynski 2007; Pratto et al., 2006). However, ATCG goes beyond these theories as well, by predicting that traits that were conducive to competitive ability in ancestral environments should lead to increased pro-equity/anti-equality orientation in modern environments, regardless of the extent to which these traits increase competitive ability in modern environments. By defining competitive ability in terms of ancestrally-relevant criteria, ATCG can identify novel variables (e.g., aspects of biological formidability such as strength and attractiveness) that may impact preferences for equity over equality.

ATCG also has features in common with theories that have recognized the centrality of the free rider problem (Olson 1965; Hardin 1968). However because ATCG focuses on the evolutionary dynamics that allow the free riding strategy to either flourish or perish, it has arrived at predictions about this problem that other theories have not made. For example, ATCG predicts that organizations will be most vulnerable to an invasion of the free riding strategy when levels of trust within the organization are at their highest, and least vulnerable when reciprocal altruism has been allowed to emerge as the dominant strategy within the organization. ATCG also places a uniquely strong emphasis on solutions to the free rider problem such as punishment and ostracism of free riders, and positive assortation among cooperators, and makes a variety of novel predictions about how these solutions will work. For example, ATCG predicts that because higher contributors are relatively personally disadvantaged by free riders, they will be relatively likely to detect them and advocate their punishment. It also predicts that if you allow people to choose their own interaction partners as they assort into cooperative groups, then more cooperative members will mutually choose one another while excluding less cooperative members. Finally, ATCG predicts that cues that in ancestral environments would have indicated that one's cooperative behavior was being monitored, such as eye-like depictions, will increase cooperative behavior in modern environments, even though people rationally "know" that these depictions cannot actually see.

ATCG focuses on the centrality of social status as a second-order benefit of cooperation, and on the fact that in a well-managed group in which reciprocity is the dominant strategy, group members are in competition with one another to contribute the most to group goals. It therefore makes predictions about the relationship between cooperation and status that other theories have not explicitly made. Namely, ATCG predicts that through the process of competitive altruism, the highest contributors will achieve the highest social status within the group. Further, because the competitive altruist's ultimate goal is to compete for high status, and his altruistic efforts are just a means to that end, there is always the risk that he will put his own competitive goals ahead of the group's actual best interests, and as a result end up harming the group (e.g., by finagling a high-status role that someone else could have performed more competently).

ATCG's theoretical foundations in evolutionary biology, which incorporate parental investment and sexual selection theory (Darwin 1871; Trivers 1972), provide a solid basis on which to predict sex differences that are highly relevant in organizational contexts, such as men's relatively strong interest in competitive status striving and women's relatively strong interest in parental investment. Some implications of these sex differences have been explained by other social science theories, for example, the fact that males are more pro-equity/anti-equality than females has been explained in terms of socialization pressures. ATCG's perspective on these sex differences, however, suggests that they would not be as easy to eradicate as most socialization theories would predict, and furthermore offers specific ways to manipulate these concerns for the good of the organization. Other implications of these sex differences – for example, ATCG's prediction that males will react more negatively than females to status reductions – do not seem to be clearly specified by any other existing theory.

Finally, because ATCG adopts the view that people are adapted to share windfall resources more widely than predictable, deliberately produced resources (Kaplan and Hill 1985), and to share surplus resources more widely than essential resources (Bliege Bird et al. 2002), it predicts how the sharing expectations that emerge in organizations will be affected by resource predictability and availability. These predictions do not seem to be made by any existing theory in organizational science.

Before ending, if we are permitted a more speculative and ambitious claim, it may be no coincidence that the Darwinian focus on individual selection resonates with the economic self-interest model that underlies the insights of Adam Smith and free-market capitalism. Neither justifies the other, of course (that would be the naturalistic fallacy), but they appear to share some fundamental characteristics in common. An interesting question for future research is whether, perhaps, free-market capitalism has succeeded where communism has failed because human brains are better adapted to the former.

In conclusion, we hope we have shown in this chapter how the work of many evolutionary researchers can be pulled together in order to produce a model of human cooperation in groups that is relatively coherent, predictive, and useful in terms of its applied value to real-life organizations. By highlighting the features that ATCG shares in common with existing theories, as well as the novel predictions that ATCG makes, we have tried to demonstrate that the individual-level adaptationist perspective has contributed to scientific advancement in our understating of organizational cooperation. We trust that this perspective will continue to generate new insights about such cooperation in the future, and that it will ultimately lead to a further refined and comprehensive theory.

References

Adams JS (1963) Toward an understanding of inequity. J Abnorm Soc Psychol 67(5):422–436
Adams JS (1965) Inequity in social exchange. In: Berkowitz L (ed) Advances in experimental social psychology, vol 2. Academic, New York, pp 267–299
Akan OH, Allen RS, White CS (2009) Equity sensitivity and organizational citizenship behavior in a team environment. Small Group Res 40(1):94–112
Albanese R, Van Fleet DD (1985) Rational behavior in groups: the free-riding tendency. Acad Manage Rev 10:244–255
Alexander RD (1987) The biology of moral systems. Gruyter, Hawthorne
Andras P, Lazarus J, Roberts G (2007) Environmental adversity and uncertainty favour cooperation. BMC Evol Biol 7:240
Andreoni J (1988) Why free ride? J Public Econ 37:291–304
Barclay P, Willer R (2007) Partner choice creates competitive altruism in humans. Proc R Soc Lond B 274:749–753
Bateson M, Nettle D, Roberts G (2006) Cues of being watched enhance cooperation in a real-world setting. Biol Lett 3:412–414
Betzig LL (1986) Despotism and differential reproduction. Aldine, New York

Bliege Bird RL, Bird DW, Kushnick G, Smith EA (2002) Risk and reciprocity in Meriam food sharing. Evol Hum Behav 23:297–321
Boehm C (2001) Hierarchy in the forest: the evolution of Egalitarian behavior. Harvard University Press, Cambridge
Bolino MC, Turnley WH (2008) Old faces, new places: equity theory in cross-cultural contexts. J Organ Behav 29:29–50
Boyd R, Lorberbaum JP (1987) No pure strategy is evolutionarily stable in the repeated Prisoner's Dilemma game. Nature 327:58–59
Boyd R, Richerson PJ (1988) The evolution of reciprocity in sizable groups. J Theor Biol 132:337–356
Brown WM, Price ME, Kang J, Pound N, Zhao Y, Yu H (2008) Fluctuating asymmetry and preferences for sex-typical bodily characteristics. Proc Natl Acad Sci USA 105:12938–12943
Browne KR (2006) Evolved sex differences and occupational segregation. J Organ Behav 27:143–162
Burnham TC (2007) High-testosterone men reject low ultimatum game offers. Proc. R. Soc. B 274:2327–2330, doi:10.1098/rspb.2007.0546
Burnham T, Hare B (2007) Does involuntary neural activation increase public goods contributions in human adults? Hum Nature 18:88–108
Buss DM (1989) Sex differences in human mate preferences: evolutionary hypotheses tested in 37 cultures. Behav Brain Sci 12:1–49
Cesarini D, Dawes CT, Fowler JH, Johannesson M, Lichtenstein P, Wallace B (2008) Heritability of cooperative behavior in the trust game. Proc Natl Acad Sci 105:3721–3726
Chagnon NA (1979) Is reproductive success equal in egalitarian societies? In: Chagnon NA, Irons W (eds) Evolutionary biology and human social behavior: an anthropological perspective. Duxbury, North Scituate, pp 374–401
Chagnon NA (1988) Life histories, blood revenge, and warfare in a tribal population. Science 239:985–992
Cinyabuguma M, Page T, Putterman L (2005) Cooperation under the threat of expulsion in a public goods experiment. J Public Econ 89:1421–1435
Cinyabuguma M, Page T, Putterman L (2006) Can second-order punishment deter perverse punishment? Exp Econ 9(3):265–279
Clark PB, Wilson JQ (1961) Incentive systems: a theory of organizations. Adm Sci Q 6:129–166
Clift E, Brazaitis T (2003) Madam President: women blazing the leadership trail. Routledge, New York
Colarelli SM, Spranger JL, Hechanova R (2006) Women, power, and sex composition in small groups: an evolutionary perspective. J Organ Behav 27:163–184
Colquitt JA, Greenberg J, Zapata-Phelan CP (2005) What is organizational justice? A historical overview. In: Greenberg J, Greenberg J, Colquitt JA (eds) Handbook of organizational justice. Lawrence Erlbaum Associates, Mahwah, pp 3–56
Cooper J (2007) Cognitive dissonance: 50 years of a classic theory. Sage, New York
Cosmides L, Tooby J (2005) Neurocognitive adaptations designed for social exchange. In: Buss DM (ed) The handbook of evolutionary psychology. Wiley, Hoboken, pp 584–627
Croson R (2007) Theories of commitment, altruism and reciprocity: evidence from linear public goods games. Econ Inq 45:199–216
Croson R, Gneezy U (2009) Gender differences in preferences. J Econ Lit 47(2):448–474
Dabbs JM (1997) Testosterone, smiling, and facial appearance. J Nonverbal Behav 21:45–55. doi:10.1023/A:1024947801843
Dabbs JM (1998) Testosterone and the concept of dominance. Behav Brain Sci 21:370–371
Daly M, Wilson M (1988) Homicide. Gruyter, New York
Darwin C (1859) On the origin of species. Murray, London
Darwin C (1871/1981) The descent of man, and selection in relation to sex. Princeton University Press, Princeton

Davies APC, Shackelford TK (2008) Two human natures: how men and women evolved different psychologies. In: Crawford C, Krebs D (eds) Foundations of evolutionary psychology. Lawrence Erlbaum, New York, pp 261–280

Deutsch M (1975) Equity, equality, and need: what determines which value will be used as the basis of distributive justice? J Soc Issues 31:137–149

Diehl M, Stroebe W (1987) Productivity loss in brainstorming groups: toward the solution of a riddle. J Pers Soc Psychol 53:497–509

Diekmann KA, Samuels SM, Ross L, Bazerman MH (1997) Self-interest and fairness in problems of resource allocation: Allocators versus recipients. J Pers Soc Psychol 72:1061–1074

Dirks KT, Ferrin DL (2001) The role of trust in organizational settings. Organ Sci 12:450–467

Douglas C, Gardner WL (2004) Transition to self-directed work teams: implications of transition time and self-monitoring for managers' use of influence tactics. J Organ Behav 25:47–65

Dugatkin LA (1997) Cooperation in animals. Oxford University Press, New York

Ehrhart K, Keser C (1999) Mobility and cooperation: on the run. Working Paper 99 s-24, CIRANO, Montreal

Ellis L, Hershberger SL, Field EM, Wersinger S, Pellis S, Hetsroni A, Geary D, Palmer CT, Karadi K, Hoyenga KB (2008) Sex differences: summarizing more than a century of scientific research. Psychology Press, Oxford

Ely R, Padavic I (2007) A feminist analysis of organizational research on sex differences. Acad Manage Rev 32:1121–1143

Emerson RM (1962) Power-dependence relations. Am Sociol Rev 27:31–41

Fehr E, Gächter S (2000) Cooperation and punishment in public goods experiments. Am Econ Rev 90:980–994

Fehr E, Rockenbach B (2002) Detrimental effects of sanctions on human altruism. Nature 422:137–140

Festinger L (1957) A theory of cognitive dissonance. Row, Peterson, Evanston

Fischbacher U, Gächter S, Fehr E (2001) Are people conditionally cooperative? Evidence from a public goods experiment. Econ Lett 71:397–404

Gangestad SW, Thornhill R, Yeo RA (1994) Facial attractiveness, developmental stability and fluctuating asymmetry. Ethol Sociobiol 15:73–85

Geary DC (2002) Sexual selection and sex differences in social cognition. In: McGillicuddy-De Lisi AV, De Lisi R (eds) Biology, society, and behavior: the development of sex differences in cognition. Ablex/Greenwood, Greenwich, pp 23–53

Gintis H (2000) Strong reciprocity and human sociality. J Theor Biol 206:169–179

Gintis H, Bowles S, Boyd R, Fehr E (2003) Explaining altruistic behavior in humans. Evol Hum Behav 24:153–172

Gneezy U, Rustichini A (2004) Gender and competition at a young age. Am Econ Rev 94(2):377–381

Gneezy U, Niederle M, Rustichini A (2003) Performance in competitive environments: gender differences. Q J Econ 118(3):1049–1074

Goldstein MA (2002) The biological roots of heat-of-passion crimes and honor killings. Polit Life Sci 21:28–37

Govindarajan V, Gupta AK (2001) Building an effective global business team. MIT Sloan Manage Rev 42:63–71

Graves BM (2010) Ritualized combat as an indicator of intrasexual selection effects on male life history evolution. Am J Hum Biol 22:45–49

Greenberg J (1983) Overcoming egocentric bias in perceived fairness through self-awareness. Soc Psychol Q 46:152–156

Haley KJ, Fessler DMT (2005) Nobody's watching? Subtle cues affect generosity in an anonymous economic game. Evol Hum Behav 26:245–256

Hall K (2007) Speed lead: faster, simpler ways to manage people, projects and teams in complex companies. Nicholas Brealey Publishing, London

Hamilton WD (1964) The genetical evolution of social behavior, I-II. J Theor Biol 7:1–52

Hardin G (1968) The tragedy of the commons. Science 162:1243–1248
Hardy C, Van Vugt M (2006) Nice guys finish first: the competitive altruism hypothesis. Pers Soc Psychol Bull 32:1402–1413
Hauert Ch, De Monte S, Hofbauer J, Sigmund K (2002) Replicator dynamics in optional public goods games. J Theor Biol 218:187–194
Henrich J (2004) Cultural group selection, coevolutionary processes and large-scale cooperation. J Econ Behav Organ 53:3–35
Huseman RC, Hatfield JD, Miles EW (1985) Test for individual perceptions of job equity: some preliminary findings. Percept Motor Skill 61:1055–1064
Huseman RC, Hatfield JD, Miles EW (1987) A new perspective on equity theory: the equity sensitivity construct. Acad Manage Rev 12:222–234
Inness M, Desmarais S, Day A (2004) Gender, mood state, and justice preference: do mood states moderate gender-based norms of justice? Br J Soc Psychol 44:463–478
Johnson DDP, Price ME, Takezawa M (2008) Renaissance of the individual: reciprocity, positive assortment, and the puzzle of human cooperation. In: Crawford C, Krebs D (eds) Foundations of evolutionary psychology. Lawrence Erlbaum, New York, pp 331–352
Kameda T, Takezawa M, Tindale RS, Smith CM (2002) Social sharing and risk reduction – exploring a computational algorithm for the psychology of windfall gains. Evol Hum Behav 23:11–33
Kaplan H, Hill K (1985) Food sharing among Ache foragers: tests of explanatory hypotheses. Curr Anthropol 26:223–246
Kaplan H, Hill K, Hurtado AM (1990) Risk, foraging and food sharing among the Ache. In: Cashdan E (ed) Risk and uncertainty in tribal and peasant economies. Westview Press, Boulder, pp 107–143
Keeley LH (1996) War before civilization: the myth of the peaceful savage. Oxford Univ. Press, Oxford
Kelly RL (1995) The foraging spectrum: diversity in hunter-gatherer lifeways. Smithsonian, Washington, DC
Kidwell RE, Bennett N (1993) Employee propensity to withhold effort: a conceptual model to intersect three avenues of research. Acad Manage Rev 18:429–456
Kim S (2008) Women and family-friendly policies in the Korean government. Int Rev Adm Sci 74:463–476
Kruger DJ, Nesse RM (2006) An evolutionary life-history framework for understanding sex differences in human mortality rates. Hum Nature 17:74–97
Kruger DJ, Nesse RM (2007) Economic transition, male competition, and sex differences in mortality rates. Evol Psychol 5:411–427
Kunovich S, Slomczynski KM (2007) Systems of distribution and a sense of equity: a multilevel analysis of meritocratic attitudes in post-industrial societies. Eur Sociol Rev 23:649–663
Kurzban R, Houser D (2005) Experiments investigating cooperative types in humans: a complement to evolutionary theory and simulations. Proc Natl Acad Sci 102:1802–1807
Lakatos I (1978) The methodology of scientific research programmes, volume 1. Cambridge University Press, Cambridge
Langfred CW (2004) Too much of a good thing? Negative effects of high trust and individual autonomy in self-managing teams. Acad Manage J 47:385–399
Ledyard JO (1995) Public goods: a survey of experimental research. In: Kagel JH, Roth AE (eds) The handbook of experimental economics. Princeton University Press, Princeton, pp 111–194
Lee RB (1993) The Dobe Ju/'hoansi. Harcourt Brace, New York
Lee RB, DeVore I (1968) Man the hunter. Aldine de Gruyter, New York
Leung K, Tong K, Ho SS (2004) Effects of interactional justice on egocentric bias in resource allocation decisions. J Appl Psychol 89:405–415
Lomborg B (1996) The evolution of social structure in the iterated prisoner's dilemma. Am Sociol Rev 61:278–307
Major B, Deaux K (1982) Individual differences in justice behavior. In: Greenberg J, Cohen RL (eds) Equity and justice in social behavior. Academic, New York, pp 43–76

Maynard Smith J (1982) Evolution and the theory of games. Cambridge University Press, Cambridge

Miles EW, Hatfield JD, Huseman RC (1989) The equity sensitivity construct: potential implications for worker performance. J Manage 15:581–588

Miner JB (2003) The rated importance, scientific validity, and practical usefulness of organizational behavior theories: a quantitative review. Acad Manage Learn Educ 2:250–268

Mowday RT, Colwell KA (2003) Employee reactions to unfair outcomes in the workplace: the contributions of Adams's equity theory to understanding work motivation. In: Porter LW, Bigley GA, Steer RM (eds) Motivation and work behavior, 7th edn. McGraw-Hill, Boston, pp 65–82

Mulford M, Orbell J, Shatto C, Stockard J (1998) Physical attractiveness, opportunity, and success in everyday exchange. Am J Sociol 103:1565–1592

Niederle M, Vesterlund L (2007) Do women shy away from competition? Do men compete too much? Q J Econ 122(3):1067–1101

Nikiforakis N (2008) Punishment and counter-punishment in public good games: can we really govern ourselves? J Public Econ 92:91–112

Nisbett RE, Cohen D (1996) Culture of honor: the psychology of violence in the south. Westview Press, Denver

Nowak M, Sigmund K (1992) Tit-for-tat in heterogeneous populations. Nature 355:250–253

Olson M (1965) The logic of collective action: public goods and the theory of groups. Harvard University Press, Cambridge

Ostrom E (1990) Governing the commons: the evolution of institutions for collective action. Cambridge University Press, New York

Ostrom E (2000) Collective action and the evolution of social norms. J Econ Perspect 14:137–158

Page T, Putterman L, Unel B (2005) Voluntary association in public goods experiments: reciprocity, mimicry and efficiency. Econ J 115:1032–1053

Pratto Felicia, Sidanius Jim, Levin Shana (2006) Social dominance theory and the dynamics of intergroup relations: taking stock and looking forward. Eur Rev Soc Psychol 17(1):271–320

Price ME (2003) Pro-community altruism and social status in a Shuar village. Hum Nature 14:191–208

Price ME (2005) Punitive sentiment among the Shuar and in industrialized societies: cross-cultural similarities. Evol Hum Behav 26:279–287

Price ME (2006a) Monitoring, reputation and "greenbeard" reciprocity in a Shuar work team. J Organ Behav 27:201–219

Price ME (2006b) Judgments about cooperators and freeriders on a Shuar work team: An evolutionary psychological perspective. Organizational Behavior and Human Decision Processes 101:20–35

Price ME, Cosmides L, Tooby J (2002) Punitive sentiment as an anti-free rider psychological device. Evol Hum Behav 23:203–231

Rhoads SE (2004) Taking sex differences seriously. Encounter Books, San Francisco

Rielly RJ (2000) Confronting the tiger: small unit cohesion in battle. Mil Rev 80:61–65

Rietzschel EF, Nijstad BA, Stroebe W (2006) Productivity is not enough: a comparison of interactive and nominal brainstorming groups on idea generation and selection. J Exp Soc Psychol 42:244–251

Ritzman RL, Tomaskovic-Devey D (1992) Life chances and support for equality and equity as normative and counternormative distribution rules. Soc Forces 70(3):745–763

Roberts G (1998) Competitive altruism: from reciprocity to the handicap principle. Proc R Soc Ser B Bio 265:427–431

Romaine J, Schmidt AB (2009) Resolving conflicts over employee work schedules: what determines perceptions of fairness? Int J Confl Manage 20(1):60–81

Sandelands LE (2002) Male and female in organizational behavior. J Organ Behav 23:149–165

Scandura TA, Lankau MJ (1997) Relationships of gender, family responsibility and flexible work hours to organizational commitment and job satisfaction. J Organ Behav 18:377–391

Sell A, Tooby J, Cosmides L (2009) Formidability and the logic of human anger. Proc Natl Acad Sci 106(35):15073–15078

Sheldon KM, Sheldon MS, Osbaldiston R (2000) Prosocial values and group-assortation within an N-person prisoner's dilemma. Hum Nature 11:387–404

Shinada M, Yamagishi T, Ohmura Y (2004) False friends are worse than bitter enemies: "Altruistic" punishment of in-group members. Evol Hum Behav 25:379–393

Silk JB (2005) The evolution of cooperation in primate groups. In: Gintis H, Bowles S, Boyd R, Fehr E (eds) Moral sentiments and material interests. MIT Press, Cambridge, pp 43–73

Smith EA (2004) Why do good hunters have higher reproductive success? Hum Nature 15:343–364

Solnick SJ, Schweitzer M (1999) The influence of physical attractiveness and gender on ultimatum game decisions. Organ Behav Hum Decis Process 79:199–215

Stevens JR, Hauser MD (2004) Why be nice? Psychological constraints on the evolution of cooperation. Trends Cogn Sci 8:60–65

Stevens C, Bavetta AG, Gist ME (1993) Gender differences in the acquisition of salary negotiation skills: the role of goals, self-efficacy, and perceived control. J Appl Psychol 78:723–735

Takahashi CT, Yamagishi ST, Tanida S, Kiyonari T, Kanazawa S (2006) Attractiveness and cooperation in social exchange. Evol Psychol 4:300–314

Takezawa M, Price ME (2010) Revisiting "The evolution of reciprocity in sizable groups": Continuous reciprocity in the repeated N-Person prisoner's dilemma. Journal of Theoretical Biology 264:188–196

Thompson LL, Loewenstein G (1992) Egocentric interpretations of fairness and interpersonal conflict. Organ Behav Hum Decis Process 51:176–197

Titmuss RM (1970) The gift relationship: from human blood to social policy. George Allen and Unwin, London

Tooby J, Cosmides L, Price ME (2006) Cognitive adaptations for n-person exchange: the evolutionary roots of organizational behavior. Managerial Decis Econ 27:103–129

Treanor J (2009) RBS record losses raise prospect of 95% state ownership. The Guardian 26 February 2009

Trivers R (1971) The evolution of reciprocal altruism. Q Rev Biol 46:35–57

Trivers RL (1972) Parental investment and sexual selection. In: Campbell B (ed) Sexual selection and the descent of man, 1871–1971. Aldine, Chicago, pp 136–179

Trivers R (2006) Reciprocal altruism: 30 years later. In: Kappeler PM, van Schaik CP (eds) Cooperation in primates and humans. Springer, Berlin, pp 67–83

Van Vugt M, De Cremer D, Janssen D (2007) Gender differences in competition and cooperation: the male warrior hypothesis. Psychol Sci 18:19–23

Vinacke WE (1969) Variables in experimental games: toward a field theory. Psychol Bull 71(4): 293–318

Vollan B (2008) Socio-ecological explanations for crowding-out effects from economic field experiments in southern Africa. Ecol Econ 67:560–573

Walster E, Walster GW, Berscheid E (1978) Equity: theory and research. Allyn & Bacon, Boston

West SA, Griffin AS, Gardner A (2007) Evolutionary explanations for cooperation. Curr Biol 17: R661–R672

Williams GC (1966) Adaptation and natural selection: a critique of some current evolutionary thought. Princeton University Press, Princeton

Wilson EO (1975) Sociobiology: the new synthesis. Belknap Press of Harvard University Press, Cambridge

Wilson DS, Sober E (1994) Reintroducing group selection to the human behavioural sciences. Behav Brain Sci 17(4):585–654

Wilson DS, Wilson EO (2007) Rethinking the theoretical foundation of sociobiology. Q Rev Biol 82:327–348

Wrangham RW, Wilson ML (2004) Collective violence: comparisons between youths and chimpanzees. Ann NY Acad Sci 1036:233–256

Yamagishi T (1986) The provision of a sanctioning system as a public good. J Pers Soc Psychol 51:110–116

Zaatari D, Trivers R (2007) Fluctuating asymmetry and behavior in the ultimatum game in Jamaica. Evol Hum Behav 28:223–227

Caveman Executive Leadership: Evolved Leadership Preferences and Biological Sex

Gregg R. Murray and Susan M. Murray

Abstract There is increasing recognition that human behavior in general, and business behavior in particular, is subject to social and biological effects. This research investigates the well-known but unsatisfactorily explained advantage that males have over females in obtaining executive leadership. We argue that environmental-cultural explanations are incomplete and propose an explanation that adds to the emerging evidence that behavior is subject to evolutionary effects. More specifically, we take the perspective of evolutionary psychology in this research. The explanation presented here is grounded in the evolutionary theory of natural selection such that a psychological adaptation for a preference for male leaders evolved to promote individual survivability in the violent ancestral history of humans. We present convergent interdisciplinary findings as well as supporting evidence from three studies with distinct research designs, domains, and perspectives of analysis to strengthen the validity of our argument. In all, this research offers a more complete theoretical explanation for male predominance in executive leadership and provides an additional theoretical approach to the investigation of modern biases that have been costly to the business community.

Keywords Business leadership · Political leadership · Biological sex · Formidability · Physical stature · Leadership preferences · Gender bias

Despite the rejection of evolutionary theory by social scientists for most of the twentieth century (Saad 2008), emerging evidence suggests that behavior is shaped by evolutionary adaptation, genetic inheritance, and genotypic-environmental

G.R. Murray (✉)
Department of Political Science, Texas Tech University, Lubbock 79409 TX, USA
e-mail: g.murray@ttu.edu

S.M. Murray
Rawls College of Business, Texas Tech University, Lubbock 79409, TX, USA
e-mail: susan.murray@ttu.edu

interaction (e.g., Buss 2005; Lawrence and Nohria 2002; Mayr 2001; Scarr and McCartney 1983). For example, research shows that attention-deficit/hyperactivity disorder is highly heritable (Spencer et al. 2002), that female self-grooming and ornamentation increase near ovulation (Haselton et al. 2007), that mothers invest differentially in children based on maternal resources and the children's perceived reproductive risk (Beaulieua and Bugental 2008), and that brain cells known as mirror neurons facilitate empathic responses (Carr et al. 2003). Biological and evolutionary connections have also been made in the business sciences. For instance, research shows that financial risk taking in men is associated with salivary testosterone and facial masculinity (Apicella et al. 2008), that occupational segregation by sex is partially the result of an imbalance in supply driven by evolutionary adaptations that point females and males toward different occupational preferences (Browne 2006), that genetic factors account for up to 30% of the variance in leadership role occupancy as well as contribute to personality traits related to leadership (Arvey et al. 2006), and that a wide range of consumer behaviors are ultimately the products of one or more key adaptive forces such as survival and reproduction (Saad 2007).

The empirical arena of this investigation is a biological trait that has been related to leadership status: biological sex. Our interest is piqued by the well-known but unsatisfactorily explained advantage males have over females in obtaining executive leadership. A review of international business and government leadership indicates that females are highly unlikely to head large companies or hold chief executive power in government. In 2008, for instance, only 6% of Canada's *Financial Post* 500 largest companies were headed by female chief executive officers (CEOs), which represented the largest proportion of female CEOs among a number of the major national business indices. Similarly, in 2008 only 7% of government leaders worldwide in an executive position were female (Thames and Williams 2009).

While it is provocative to note the relative advantage males hold in obtaining executive leadership, we are left to speculate how biological sex could matter in issues of leadership. We argue that environmental-cultural explanations such as socialization (Bem 1981; Eagly 1987) and organizational culture (e.g., Deal and Kennedy 2000) are incomplete. We propose an explanation that adds to the emerging evidence that human behavior is subject to evolutionary effects. We take the perspective of evolutionary psychology in this research. Evolutionary psychology studies universal human behavior that is related to domain-specific psychological mechanisms that evolved to solve adaptive problems faced in human ancestral times regarding survival and reproduction (Tooby and Cosmides 1992). It suggests that human behavior is the sum of environment and evolutionary adaptation (Buss 1989).

The explanation for the relationship between biological sex and leadership presented here is grounded in the evolutionary theory of natural selection (Darwin 1859). Specifically, we suggest that there is a preference for formidable leaders, which reflects a psychological mechanism that evolved to promote survivability in the violent ancestral history of humans. In particular, ancestors who selected allies who were physically formidable, a cue that was easily available about individuals in ancestral times and still is today (Sell et al. 2008), were more likely to survive because potential opponents received a cue about the likely high costs of a physical confrontation (Sell et al. 2008), which was common in ancestral times (e.g., Chagnon 1997). The preference for physically formidable leaders may help explain the nearly universal advantage that males, who throughout human history have tended to be larger (Geary 1998) and stronger (Lassek and Gaulin 2009), have held over females in the acquisition of executive leadership power. Current research suggests there are as many as eight commonly held leadership prototype dimensions in the modern context (i.e., sensitivity, dedication, tyranny, charisma, attractiveness, intelligence, strength, and masculinity) (Offermann et al. 1994; Johnson et al. 2008). Arguments that physical features may prime components of these prototype dimensions (Lord and Emrich 2000) as well as the glacial speed of evolution and the easy use of physical size as a cue (Sell et al. 2008) suggest that leader traits that were important in the human evolutionary environment likely exert influence still today (Foley 1997; Tooby and Cosmides 1992).

In support of our arguments, we first present a review of the literature from diverse disciplines that documents the relationships between leadership and physical formidability and then leadership and biological sex. The manifestation of the relationship in diverse social contexts, including both human and non-human animals, challenges environmental-cultural explanations and is consistent with an evolutionary explanation. Next, we present three studies with distinct research designs, domains, data, and perspectives of analysis to test our argument. Supportive findings from unrelated sources of data and analysis would strengthen the validity of our argument by suggesting that the results are not an artifact of flawed research designs or data. We conclude with a discussion of the contributions of this research, which include a more complete theoretical explanation for the relationship between biological sex and leadership and the proffer of an additional theoretical approach to the investigation of persistent modern biases, such as sexism, that have been costly to the business community and society in general.

1 Physical Formidability and Leadership

Evidence suggests that the selection of corporate and government executive leaders is often related to the physical stature of the leaders (Simonton 1994). The scholarship that informs our argument begins with literature that documents the robust association between physical formidability and leadership. Formidability here is defined as the potential to hold resources by inflicting costs on competitors (Sell et al. 2008). Convergent literature from anthropology, economics, non-human animal behavior, and psychology demonstrates that the influence of physical stature on leadership status manifests itself in varied environments, both human and non-human, and, consequently, cannot be wholly socially constructed. The review continues with literature that documents the relationship between biological sex and leadership then concludes with literature that establishes an evolutionary basis for a relationship between biological sex and leadership via physical formidability.

Anthropological evidence back to pre-Columbian times relates physical stature to social rank. Brown and Chia-yun propose that the term "big man", used widely across time, is a cultural manifestation of "a pervasive feature of nature: the tendency among humans (and animals) for rank or social stature to correlate with physical stature" (1993, 10). Although it is not certain that their usage refers exclusively to physical stature, Boehm (1999), Chagnon (1997), Diamond (1999), and Meggitt (1977) similarly use the term "big man" to identify individuals who dominate decision making in their domains of expertise. Angel (1971) and Haviland (1967, 321), on the other hand, unequivocally related "political control" to greater physical stature based on skeletal measurements at pre-classical Greek and ancient Mayan excavations.

Studies of non-human animal behavior suggest a positive association between physical size and social rank. For example, the relationship has been detected in a wide range of animals from chimpanzees, gorillas, and baboons (De Waal 2005, 2007; Johnson 1987; Willhoite 1976), to African elephants, reindeer, and Red Deer (Archie et al. 2006; Clutton-Brock et al. 1982; Holand et al. 2004), and even to varieties of birds, fish, and ants (Heinze and Oberstadt 1999; Searcy 1979; Whiteman and Cote 2004). This scholarship suggests that height serves as a cue for an opponent's strength and power when non-human animals face fight-or-flight decisions (Freedman 1979). The presence of this relationship in non-human animals underscores the assertion that this relationship is not wholly induced by human culture. As such, it is most likely a trait that results at least partially from evolutionary pressures on social animals, which will be detailed later.

Studies of modern humans, too, have documented an association between size and value. For instance, objects such as paper disks and index cards displaying symbols with high value are perceived as larger than identically sized disks and index cards displaying symbols with lesser value (Bruner and Postman 1948; Dukes and Bevan 1952). A similar association was found in humans indicating that individuals with greater authority status are perceived as taller than he or she actually is (Dannenmaier and Thumin 1964; Wilson 1968) and, conversely, that taller individuals are perceived as having higher professional status than those with lesser stature (Jackson and Ervin 1992). Research in the U.S. and Sweden indicates that taller males are more successful in terms of professional and educational achievement (Cernerud 1995; Gillis 1982; Magnusson et al. 2006; Persico et al. 2004). And in the political domain, winners of national elections are perceived as being taller after the election than before the election (Higham and Carment 1992), and ideal national leaders are described as having greater physical stature than the typical citizen of their country (Murray and Schmitz forthcoming).

The evidence that this behavior appears across a multitude of distinct cultures suggests that it cannot be explained by cultural construction alone and, therefore, is most likely at least partially explained by evolutionary adaptation. Proponents of a cultural explanation would need to show how the seemingly universal advantage could be learned in and emerge from such diverse social contexts as those experienced by, for example, ancient Mayans (Haviland 1967), pre-classical Greeks (Angel 1971), non-human animals (e.g., De Waal 2007), and modern humans (e.g., Persico et al. 2004).

2 Biological Sex and Leadership

Literature from diverse disciplines including anthropology, economics, non-human animal behavior, and psychology also documents a non-trivial relationship between biological sex and leadership. This review demonstrates that the nearly universal advantage males hold in obtaining leadership cannot be wholly socially constructed due to the varied environments, both human and non-human, in which males dominate public leadership.

Studies from a number of disciplines show that the likelihood of rising to positions of power is strongly related to biological sex. Research in non-human animal behavior suggests such a relationship. Although a small number of non-human animal groups tend to be female-led such as African elephants (Archie et al. 2006), spotted hyaenas (Mills and Hofer 1998), lemurs (Waeber and Hemelrijk 2003), and bonobos (Parish 1994), males dominate females nearly universally in primate and mammal groups (Kappeler 1993). Male dominance has been documented in a wide range of non-human animals from chimpanzees and gorillas (De Waal 2005, 2007; Watts 1996) to feral horses (Boyd and Keiper 2005), wolves (Mech 2000), and even coral-reef fish (Robertson 1972). It is important to note that the presence of this relationship in non-human animals underscores the assertion that this relationship is not wholly induced by human culture. As such, it is most likely a trait that results from evolutionary forces on social animals.

Anthropological and archaeological evidence suggests that human males have dominated in the public sphere dating back at least to pre-Columbian times (Bamberger 1974; Brown 1991; Fox 1983; Ortner 1974; Peterson and Wrangham 1997). Table 1 reports the percent of female leaders across a wide variety of human cultures, both ancient and modern. It shows, for instance, that only five of the 209 Egyptian pharaohs in the 3,000 years from 3100 BCE to 30 BCE were female, while only four of the 187 Roman emperors between 30 BCE and 1453 CE were female (Tapsell 1983). Asian civilizations have been predominantly patriarchal and patrilineal (Jay 1996), as indicated by the few female empresses in the twenty-one centuries of Imperial China (221 BCE to 1912 CE) (Yang 1960) and ten empresses in the twenty-six centuries of Imperial Japan (660 BCE to present) (Tapsell 1983). Historic Europe has also manifested a male-dominated culture, for example, through the monarchies of Belgium, England, France, and Spain. In terms of religion, none of the 302 popes has been female (40 CE to present) (Tapsell 1983), and Islam has been found to be just as male dominated as Christianity (Keegan 1993; Haj 1992).

The relationship between leadership and biological sex is well documented in modern times, too. For instance, females are unlikely to appear in executive

Table 1 Percent female executive leaders by macro-culture

Macro-cultures	Time period	% female	N female	N total
Business domain				
Australia (ASX200)	2008	2	4	200
Australia (ASX200)	2006	3	6	200
Australia (ASX200)	2003	3	6	200
Canada (*Financial Post* 500)	2008	6	30	500
Canada (*Financial Post* 500)	2006	4	21	500
Canada (*Financial Post* 500)	2004	4	20	500
Canada (*Financial Post* 500)	2002	3	14	500
Europe (FTSE300)	2008	2	7	300
Global *Fortune* 500	2008	2	12	500
Global *Fortune* 500	2007	2	10	500
Global *Fortune* 500	2006	1	7	500
Global *Fortune* 500	2005	1	6	500
S. Africa (JSE)	2008	4	13	400
S. Africa (JSE)	2007	3	8	400
S. Africa (JSE)	2006	2	7	400
S. Africa (JSE)	2005	2	8	400
S. Africa (JSE)	2004	2	7	400
U.S. *Fortune* 500	2008	2	12	500
U.S. *Fortune* 500	2005	2	8	500
U.S. *Fortune* 500	2002	1	6	500
U.S. *Fortune* 500	2000	0	2	500
U.S. *Fortune* 1000	2008	2	24	1000
U.S. *Fortune* 1000	2007	3	25	1000
U.S. *Fortune* 1000	2006	2	20	1000
Government domain				
Worldwide	20th Century	1	27	1941
Anglo-America	20th Century	1	1	167
Austral-New Zealand	20th Century	1	2	140
Balkans	20th Century	1	1	83
Central Asia	20th Century	5	7	140
E. Asia	20th Century	0	0	114
Eurasia	20th Century	1	1	89
Euroafrica	20th Century	0	0	68
Europe	20th Century	1	4	479
Latin America/Caribbean	20th Century	3	8	250
Middle East	20th Century	1	1	105
N. Africa	20th Century	0	0	46
Southeast Asia	20th Century	1	1	120
Sub-Saharan Africa	20th Century	1	1	140
Belgian Monarchy	1,831 CE-PRESENT	0	0	7
Incan Empire	1,200–1,572 CE	0	0	18
Danish Monarchy	936 CE-PRESENT	4	2	53
British Monarchy	400 CE-PRESENT	10	7	67
Roman Emperors	31 BCE-1453 CE	2	4	187
Imperial China	221 BCE-1912 CE	0	1	~400
Maurya Empire	322–185 BCE	0	0	9
Imperial Japan	660 BCE-PRESENT	8	10	128
Egyptian Pharaohs	3100–30 BCE	2	5	209

Note: Twentieth century results for government domain from Ludwig (2002)

leadership positions in the business arena. Although the number of female executive leaders has increased over previous decades, Table 1 reports that in 2008 only 4% of South Africa's 400 JSE-listed companies and 2% of Australia's ASX 200 companies were headed by a female CEO. In the same year, only 2% of the Global *Fortune* 500, U.S. *Fortune* 500, and Europe's FTSE 300 were headed by a female CEO.

Females are also unlikely to obtain executive leadership positions in the governmental arena (e.g., Adler 1996). Ludwig (2002) reports that only 1.4% of all government national leaders worldwide with chief executive power in the twentieth century were female ($n = 1{,}941$ leaders in 199 countries). Similarly, but focusing instead on duration in office, Thames and Williams (2009) indicate that females have held executive government positions just 2.1% of the time since World War II ($n = 292$ leader years out of 13,758 total leader years). Cross-culturally, of Ludwig's 13 geographic regions reported in Table 1, only Central Asia reached 5% female national leaders in the twentieth century. Even in the least masculine countries females are highly unlikely to serve as head of state or government. For example, in Hofstede's (2001) ten least masculine countries, only 3.0% ($n = 6$) of national government executive leaders since World War II have been female (Thames and Williams 2009), despite a mean year of achievement of women's suffrage in those countries of 1923.[1] Similarly, in the GLOBE study's 11 societies with the greatest gender egalitarianism (i.e., lowest level of male dominance) (Emrich et al. 2004), only 1.1% ($n = 2$) of national government executive leaders since World War II have been female (Thames and Williams 2009).[2]

It is important to note that a behavior that appears across a multitude of distinct cultures cannot be explained by cultural inducement alone and, therefore, is most likely at least partially explained by evolutionary adaptation. More specifically, the logic of cross-cultural analyses used in evolutionary psychology (e.g., Buss 1989) suggests that human behavior is the sum of culture and evolutionary adaptation. Scholars of evolutionary psychology argue that a universal behavior cannot be explained by culture since the same behavior appears across cultures; therefore, an evolutionary adaptation is a likely explanation of the behavior. Table 1 shows that in no case does female executive leadership exceed 10% (British Monarchy). This review shows that males hold a strong leadership advantage in both the business and government domains and across a wide variety of cultures and epochs as well as across a wide variety of non-human animal groups. Proponents of cultural explanations such as gender-role socialization (Bem 1981; Eagly 1987), the "glass ceiling"

---

[1] The ten least masculine countries according to Hofstede's cultural dimension of masculinity, listed in order of decreasing masculinity, are: Thailand, Portugal, Estonia, Chile, Finland, Costa Rica, Denmark, The Netherlands, Norway, and Sweden.

[2] The 11 GLOBE societies with the least male dominance in practice, listed in order of decreasing male dominance, are: Singapore, Canada, Albania, Sweden, Kazakhstan, Namibia, Denmark, Slovenia, Poland, Russia, and Hungary. We noted 11 societies because the countries ranked 10th and 11th on the list had identical scores. Sweden and Denmark are the only two countries that appear on both the Hofstede and GLOBE lists.

(e.g., Boatwright and Forrest 2000), organizational culture (e.g., Deal and Kennedy 2000), and the "double bind" (e.g., Oakley 2000) would need to show how the nearly universal male advantage could be learned in and emerge from such diverse social contexts as those experienced by Imperial China (Yang 1960), chimpanzees (De Waal 2007), feral horses (Boyd and Keiper 2005), and modern humans. We suggest that the evolutionary theory of natural selection (Darwin 1859) offers some explanatory leverage on this near-universal phenomenon.

3 Evolution and Leadership

The theory of natural selection (Darwin 1859) suggests that evolution shaped humans with traits that were useful to ancestral humans for their interactions with their physical and social environments. In particular, it indicates that physical and psychological (i.e., cognitive, emotional, and motivational) characteristics emerged because they resulted in a greater likelihood of survival and/or reproduction of an individual in human ancestral history (Crawford 2008; Mayr 2001). Given the typically glacial speed of evolution, the modern human brain, like other parts of the modern human body, still reflects the hominids living in the environment of evolutionary adaptedness (Foley 1997; Tooby and Cosmides 1992). Instincts acquired through evolution in human ancestral times, then, manifest themselves in modern life, even when seemingly irrational in the context of the twenty-first century (e.g., Henrich and Gil-White 2001; Little et al. 2007). For example, the nearly universal fear of snakes (LoBue and DeLoache 2008), which are rarely encountered in modern society, and the preference for sweet and fatty foods (Nesse and Williams 1994), which are unhealthy additions to modern diets, persist today but evolved to promote survival in times when snakes were common threats and adequate caloric intake was uncertain. Following this logic, it is reasonable to argue that modern preferences for leader characteristics reflect adaptive solutions to problems encountered in human ancestral times (Van Vugt et al. 2008). This suggests that individuals discount aspects of modern, large-scale society and make leadership decisions using cues that were useful to ancestral humans in evolutionary, small-scale societies (Henrich and Gil-White 2001; Little et al. 2007).

So what was the social context for leaders in the environment of evolutionary adaptedness? The human species has lived over 99% of its existence in hunter-gatherer "tribes" of 5–150 people (Diamond 1999). Conflict and warfare were common (e.g., Chagnon 1997; Van Vugt et al. 2008) as individuals and groups competed over land, food, and status (Petersen et al. 2008). Because groups are more likely to survive intergroup conflict when a centralized command or leader emerges (Keegan 1993) and because of the violent environment, leadership in ancestral times was gained through qualities that included fighting skills and strength (Diamond 1999).

Modern leadership preferences reflect these ancestral forces through a number of characteristics. First, in social interactions, individuals establish stable dominance hierarchies quickly, even based on "first-glance impressions" that occur before any verbal interaction (Kalma 1991). Humans have the ability to assess visually a person's formidability, as indicated by strength and fighting skills, with strength and fighting skills being strongly statistically related and height being a statistically meaningful cue for both (Sell et al. 2008). Second, individuals tend to prefer more dominant leaders when threat is greater (Little et al. 2007; McCann 2001). This is consistent with findings that individuals with greater physical stature, as indicated by relative height, are more likely to be perceived as capable and competent (Hensley 1993). It is also consistent with findings that individuals with greater physical stature are more likely to be respected and feared by potential opponents (Gregor 1979). Both of these findings reflect psychological tendencies that affect individual behavior in terms of both intra- and intergroup competition. For example, social group members tend to prefer individuals with greater physical stature as economic and political allies (Ellis 1995) and, therefore, as group leaders (Murray and Schmitz forthcoming). These preferences are consistent with findings in studies of chimpanzees and other primates that indicate that the social rank of group members often depends on the social rank of their allies. This literature on dependent rank (De Waal 2007) indicates that individuals know who a powerful ally will support in a conflict and the likely outcome of the conflict, so the powerful ally's presence sends a cue to his or her associate's opponent to submit to the associate before the conflict starts. Third, archeological evidence suggests that males have been physically larger than females in all human hominid ancestors dating back three to four million years (Geary 1998). This translates in current times to men having on average 61% more muscle mass (Lassek and Gaulin 2009) and 50–100% more upper-body strength (Pheasant 1983) than women, with male and female distributions in upper-body strength and muscle mass overlapping by less than 10% (Lassek and Gaulin 2009). Fourth, and finally, research indicates that males are strongly preferred over females during intergroup competition and that males are more instrumental in raising group investment than females during intergroup competition (Van Vugt and Spisak 2008), which is consistent with evidence that throughout history males have been more likely to serve as combatants in wars and other intergroup conflict than females (Goldstein 2003; Keegan 1993).

4 Hypotheses

In an effort to evaluate the potential evolutionary relationship between biological sex and leadership, this research tests hypotheses that assess preferences for female versus male leaders as well as physical formidability. We expect threat to trigger a preference for male versus female leadership. More specifically, evolutionary adaptations solve problems encountered in the environment of evolutionary adaptedness (Foley 1997; Tooby and Cosmides 1992) wherein a wide range of threats was present. In the ancestral environment humans frequently faced threats such as conflict and war (e.g., Chagnon 1997; Diamond 1999; Van Vugt et al. 2008) as individuals and groups competed for resources necessary for survival (Petersen et al. 2008). As a result of the violent ancestral environment, leadership was gained through qualities that included fighting skills and strength (Diamond 1999), which are characteristics for which males are significantly advantaged over females (Goldstein 2003; Kappeler 1993; Keegan 1993; Lassek and Gaulin 2009; Pheasant 1983). This evolutionary context and the typically glacial speed of evolution, then, imply a psychological adaptation for individual survivability manifested even in modern times that favors male leaders due to males' greater physical formidability relative to that of females (Ellis 1995; Gregor 1979; Little et al. 2007; McCann 2001). This logic implies the following hypothesis in study 1:

H_1: *Economic threat triggers increased support for male executive leadership relative to female executive leadership in the domain of government.*

It implies in study 2:

H_{2a}: *Economic threat triggers an increased preference for male executive leadership in the domain of business.*
H_{2b}: *Economic threat triggers an increased preference for more physically formidable executive leaders in the domain of business.*
H_{2c}: *Economic threat in the domain of business triggers an increased preference for male executive leaders that is associated with physical formidability.*

It implies in study 3:

H_{3a}: *National security threat triggers an increased preference for male executive leadership in the domain of government.*
H_{3b}: *National security threat triggers an increased preference for more physically formidable executive leaders in the domain of government.*
H_{3c}: *National security threat in the domain of government triggers an increased preference for male executive leaders that is associated with physical formidability.*

5 Data, Methods, and Empirical Analyses

The hypotheses are tested via three studies that use different experimental research designs and analyses of the two domains of business and government. In each study, individual (i.e., follower) preferences regarding the biological sex of leaders serves as the primary measure of interest. Studies 2 and 3 also assess the role of physical formidability in leadership preferences. This strategy of triangulation, which employs independent data and analyses, reduces the likelihood that findings are the result of flawed data or analysis and, therefore, increases confidence in the findings (Klass 2008). Convergent evidence from these studies would significantly strengthen the validity of the assertion that biological sex matters in issues of executive leadership via a preference for more physically formidable leaders.

5.1 Study 1: Support for a Government Executive Leader by Economic Threat and Biological Sex of the Leader

The first study is designed to assess individual (i.e., follower) support for a presidential candidate when the biological sex of the candidate and economic threat are experimentally manipulated. The evolutionary argument presented here suggests that threat, in this case national economic weakness, triggers increased support for a male leader relative to a female leader. While economic insecurity does not represent the same intensity of threat to modern humans that the violent environment represented to ancestral humans, it does represent the possibility of reduced resources relevant to survival such as food and shelter; therefore, it is reasonable to conclude that this type of threat could trigger a similar response.

These data were collected in October 2009 from citizens of Lubbock County, Texas (USA), who were called and appeared for jury duty. The county randomly selects these individuals from lists of licensed drivers and registered voters who are 18 years old or older and eligible to vote in Lubbock County. Subjects were recruited to the study through voluntary participation while they awaited assignment to a trial or dismissal. Although the jury pool provides a sample of subjects from a limited geographic area, the resulting sample is more representative than the typical college student subject pool. The Lubbock County Board of Judges approved the use of the jury pool for these research purposes. Court personnel did not participate in the administration or processing of the surveys or data.

The sample included 292 subjects. They ranged in age from 22 to 84 ($M = 48.1$, $SD = 13.2$), with 18 subjects who did not report age. There were slightly more female ($n = 149$, 51%) than male ($n = 142$) subjects, with one subject who did not report gender. About 74% ($n = 207$) indicated that the racial or ethnic group that best describes them is white or Caucasian, 19% ($n = 54$) indicated Hispanic or Latino/Latina, and 5% ($n = 13$) indicated black or African American. The remaining subjects ($n = 5$) indicated that Asian, American Indian, other group, or some combination of racial-ethnic groups best describes them, while 13 subjects did not report race/ethnicity. Slightly more than one in three subjects ($n = 101$) reported that the highest level of education they had achieved is high school degree or less, 29% ($n = 85$) reported some college, 27% ($n = 78$) reported receiving a college degree, and 9% ($n = 27$) reported receiving a graduate degree; one subject did not report education. About 12% ($n = 34$) of subjects reported that their total family annual income is less than US \$25,000, 28% ($n = 76$) reported income between US \$25,000 and \$49,999, 28% ($n = 76$) reported income between US \$50,000 and \$89,999, and 22% ($n = 60$) reported US \$90,000 or more; 46 subjects refused to report their income.

Using a between-subjects posttest-only 2×2 design, subjects read a vignette about a presidential candidate, then indicated how likely or unlikely they were to support the candidate for president using a 7-point scale, where one indicated that the subject was "very unlikely" to support the candidate and 7 indicated that the subject was "very likely" to support the candidate. The president is the chief executive of the national government in the United States. See Appendix A for details. Subjects were randomly assigned to one of four treatment groups. The manipulations are condition of the country's economy (i.e., "strong" versus "weak"), which represents the threat and non-threat environments, and biological sex of the candidate (i.e., "Joan" versus "John"). The measure of interest is the likelihood of supporting the presidential candidate given the threat condition and biological sex of the candidate; that is, the interaction between the threat environment and the candidate's biological sex. The treatment groups are:

T_1: Senator Joan Harper and "the country's economy is strong". ($n = 73$)
T_2: Senator Joan Harper and "the country's economy is weak". ($n = 72$)
T_3: Senator John Harper and "the country's economy is strong". ($n = 76$)
T_4: Senator John Harper and "the country's economy is weak". ($n = 71$)

The expectation is that subjects are more likely to support the male candidate relative to the female candidate under conditions of economic threat than under conditions of economic non-threat (i.e., $[T_4 - T_2] > [T_3 - T_1]$).

Subjects completed manipulation checks, which suggest that the threat and candidate-gender manipulations were successful. Regarding the threat manipulation, the subjects were asked to indicate their agreement, from completely disagree (coded 1) to completely agree (coded 7), with the statement: "As indicated above, the country's economy was described as 'weak and declining.'" The manipulation check was significant ($t[255] = -5.5$, $p < .001$, one-tailed test) such that when subjects read the threat treatment (i.e., weak economy) they were more likely to agree with the statement ($M = 4.9$, $SD = 1.6$) than when they read the non-threat treatment (i.e., strong economy) ($M = 3.6$, $SD = 2.0$). Regarding the manipulation of candidate gender, the subjects were asked to indicate their agreement, from completely disagree (coded 1) to completely agree (coded 7), with the statement: "The candidate described above was female." The manipulation check was significant ($t[260] = 17.6$, $p < .001$, one-tailed test) such that when subjects read the female candidate treatment they were more likely to agree with the statement ($M = 6.1$, $SD = 1.7$) than when they read the male candidate treatment ($M = 2.4$, $SD = 1.7$).

Table 2 reports the results of a two-way ANOVA, which estimates main effects for the economic-threat and candidate-gender manipulations and their interactive effects on support for the candidate. Neither the main effect of the economic-threat manipulation nor candidate-gender manipulation is statistically significant (threat: $F[1,278] = 1.24$, $p = .27$; candidate gender: $F[1,278] = 2.32$, $p = .13$). Consistent with the expectation, the interaction of economic threat and candidate gender,

Table 2 Support for presidential candidate by manipulations of economic threat and candidate sex (ANOVA)

	F	p	η^2
Economy	1.24	.27	< .01
Candidate sex	2.32	.13	< .01
Economy × candidate sex	2.94	.09	.01

Note: $n = 282$

Table 3 Mean support for female and male candidate by economic condition

	Economy	
Candidate sex	Strong	Weak
Female	3.8	3.7
Male	3.7	4.3
$F\ (1,278)$	.02	5.10
p	.89	.02

Note: $n = 282$

however, approaches conventional levels of statistical significance ($F[1,278] = 2.94$, $p = .09$).

To actually test hypothesis 1, though, the simple main effects of the interaction must be evaluated. That is, the relationship between candidate support and candidate gender must be evaluated separately for the threat (i.e., weak economy) and non-threat (i.e., strong economy) treatments. Table 3 reports the mean values of candidate support for the interaction, which represents the four treatments. As expected, support for the male candidate relative to the female candidate is significantly greater under conditions of threat (female: $M = 3.7$, $SD = 1.5$; male: $M = 4.3$, $SD = 1.9$; $F[1,278] = 5.10$, $p = .02$) but not under conditions of non-threat (female: $M = 3.8$, $SD = 1.6$; threat: $M = 3.7$, $SD = 1.6$; $F[1,278] = .02$, $p = .89$). This result supports hypothesis 1.

It is reasonable to consider whether these results are robust across subject gender. That is, might female subjects be more likely to evaluate favorably female candidates and male subjects be more likely to evaluate favorably male candidates? Evidence regarding the effect of subjects' gender on their identification of gendered leadership prototypes is mixed (Johnson et al. 2008). Analyses of the 3-way ANOVA (subject sex by candidate sex by economic condition) suggest that subject sex does not moderate the 2-way interaction between candidate sex and economic condition. The F-test of the 3-way interaction is not statistically significant ($F[1,273] = .12, p = .72$) nor are tests of simple main effects for the 2-way interactions for female subjects ($F[1,273] = .64$, $p = .42$) or male subjects ($F[1,273] = 1.73, p = .19$).

These findings indicate that, as expected, threat triggers greater support for male leaders relative to female leaders. As such, we conclude that these results support hypothesis 1. While these results partially support the evolutionary argument presented here, they do not allow us to assess the role of physical formidability in these preferences. The next two studies are designed to capture the role of physical formidability and biological sex in leadership preferences.

5.2 Study 2: Biological Sex and Physical Formidability of Individuals' "Ideal" Chief Executive Officer

This study is designed to capture attitudes toward the biological sex and physical formidability of a preferred business leader when an individual (i.e., follower) is experiencing experimentally manipulated conditions of threat, in this case job security related to the financial profitability or decline of the individual's employer. Following the evolutionary argument, hypothesis 2a asserts that increased threat to the individual via the company triggers an increased preference for a male leader and, conversely, a decreased preference for a female leader. Hypothesis 2b asserts that increased threat to the individual via the company triggers an increased preference for a more physically formidable leader, while hypothesis 2c asserts that increased threat to the individual via the company triggers an increased preference for a male leader that is associated with physical formidability. While job insecurity does not represent the same intensity of threat to modern humans that the violent environment represented to ancestral humans, economic insecurity does represent the possibility of reduced resources relevant to survival such as food and shelter; therefore, it is reasonable to conclude that this type of threat could trigger a similar response.

The data were collected in October 2009 at a large American public university using paper-and-pencil survey instruments from samples of students enrolled in introductory political science classes. These classes are required for graduation, so students in these classes represent a diverse range of majors. Participation was voluntary. Student subjects received extra credit on a class assignment for completing the instrument. The sample included 419 subjects. Subjects ranged in age from 16 to 50 ($M = 19.2$, $SD = 2.5$), with one subject who did not report age. There were more males ($n = 245, 59\%$) than females ($n = 173$), with one subject who did not report gender. Almost 66% ($n = 274$) indicated that the racial or ethnic group that best describes them is white or Caucasian, 20% ($n = 83$) indicated Hispanic or Latino/Latina, and about 5% indicated black or African-American ($n = 21$) or Asian ($n = 23$). The remaining subjects ($n = 15$) indicated that other group or some combination of racial-ethnic groups best describes them, while three subjects did not report race/ethnicity.

Using a between-subjects posttest-only 2×2 design, subjects were asked to complete two verbal descriptions: (1) the "ideal chief executive officer" "who will be taking over [the company you work for] next month" and (2) the "the typical employee of this company". Subjects also completed a drawing of a meeting of the CEO and employee "to get as complete a description" of subjects' perceptions as possible. See Appendix B for details. Subjects were randomly assigned to one of four treatment groups with the manipulation of interest being the company's financial condition, which represents the threat (T_1) and non-threat (T_2) environments, and the second manipulation being the order in which the individuals were described, either CEO or employee first, which represents a check for question-order effects. The treatment groups are:

T_{1a}: The company is "declining and fears bankruptcy in the near future", CEO described first ($n = 102$).

T_{1b}: The company is "declining and fears bankruptcy in the near future", employee described first ($n = 104$).

T_{2a}: The company is "growing and expects continued profitability in the near future", CEO described first ($n = 108$).

T_{2b}: The company is "growing and expects continued profitability in the near future", employee described first ($n = 105$).

Following hypothesis 2a, the expectation is that subjects are more likely to ideate a male CEO and, consequently, less likely to ideate a female CEO when the company is declining and fears bankruptcy (T_1) than when the company is growing and profitable (T_2). According to hypothesis 2b, the expectation is that subjects are more likely to ideate a more physically formidable CEO when the company is threatened (T_1) than not threatened (T_2). And following hypothesis 2c, the expectation is that subjects are more likely to associate physical formidability with male leadership when the company is threatened (T_1) than not threatened (T_2).

Subjects completed manipulation checks, which suggest that the threat manipulation was successful. About half of the subjects ($n = 219$, 53%) were asked to indicate their agreement, from completely disagree (coded 1) to completely agree (coded 7), with the statement: "The company indicated above was described as 'declining' and 'failing' ". This manipulation check was significant ($t[217] = -14.3$, $p < .001$, one-tailed test) such that when subjects read the threat treatment (T_1) they were more likely to agree with the statement ($M = 5.0$, $SD = 1.6$) than when they read the non-threat treatment (T_2) ($M = 2.2$, $SD = 1.3$). The remaining subjects ($n = 196$, 47 %) were asked to indicate their agreement, from strongly disagree (coded 1) to strongly agree (coded 7), with the statement: "As indicated above, the company you imagined working for is successful". This manipulation check was significant ($t[194] = -7.5$, $p < .001$, one-tailed test) such that when subjects read the threat treatment (T_1) they were more likely to disagree with the statement ($M = 1.8$, $SD = 0.9$) than when they read the non-threat treatment (T_2) ($M = 3.2$, $SD = 1.6$). The check for question-order effects shows that the order of descriptions did not bias the results. A difference of proportions test indicates no statistical difference ($z = .2$, $p = .81$, two-tailed test) in the ideation of a male CEO between subjects asked to describe the CEO or the employee first, and an ANOVA indicates no statistical difference ($F[1,311] = .08$, $p = .78$) in the formidability of the CEO between subjects asked to describe the CEO or employee first.

After completing the descriptions, subjects were asked to answer a number of questions about the CEO and employee, including a question about the CEO's biological sex. While analyses of the verbal descriptions are not reported here, these descriptions help to fix the characteristics of the CEO in the subject's mind prior to answering the questions. That is, they serve as a commitment of the respondent to the description of the ideated CEO that is designed to prevent respondents from socially reacting to the follow-up questions.

The results in Table 4 support hypothesis 2a. As expected, significantly more subjects ideated a male CEO under the threat treatment (88%) than under the non-threat treatment (79%) ($z = -2.5$, $p < 0.01$, one-tailed test). Put otherwise, the percent of subjects who ideated a *female* CEO *decreased* by 53% from the non-threat (15%) to threat (7%) treatments ($z = 2.4$, $p < 0.01$, one-tailed test).

Again, it is reasonable to consider whether these results are robust across subject gender. While these data suggest that female subjects are less likely to ideate a male CEO than male subjects (78 versus 87%), under the threat treatment both sexes are more likely to ideate a male CEO. The table shows that significantly more male subjects ideated a male CEO under the threat treatment (91%) than under the

Table 4 Percent male ideal CEO by treatment (threat condition)

	Failing company (T_1)	Growing company (T_2)	$n\ T_1, T_2$	z	p^a
All subjects	88%	79%	206, 213	−2.5	< .01
Female subjects	83	74	78, 95	−1.5	.06
Male subjects	91	83	127, 118	−1.7	.04

[a]One-tailed test

non-threat treatment (83%) ($z = -1.7$, $p = 0.04$, one-tailed test). It also suggests that more female subjects ideated a male CEO under the threat treatment (83%) than under the non-threat treatment (74%) ($z = -1.5$, $p = 0.06$, one-tailed test). Put otherwise, the threat condition is associated with a 9-percentage-point increase for female subjects and an 8-percentage-point increase for male subjects, which suggests that the gender of the subject does not moderate the effect of the threat manipulation.

Like study 1, these results indicate that threat increases the preference for male leadership. The argument presented here, though, suggests that this preference is a vestige of evolutionary forces in the violent human ancestral environment and is, therefore, associated with a preference for more physically formidable leaders that is triggered by threat. This leads to the expectation that in the drawing of the meeting between the CEO and employee that the CEO will be relatively more physically formidable than the employee under the threat treatment than under the non-threat treatment. Further, it leads to the expectation that the preference for a male CEO will be associated with greater physical formidability. We assess relative physical formidability by measuring the difference in vertical height of the CEO and employee in the drawing task. While bulk or strength may also represent formidability, we choose height due to its utility as a cue for formidability (Sell et al. 2008) and its ease of use with the drawing task. For all subjects who completed valid drawings ($n = 313$), the relative height of the CEO compared to the employee ranges from the CEO being 30% shorter to 90% taller ($M = .13$, $SD = .21$), with eight outliers equal to or greater than three standard deviations ($z = 3.1$–6.9) removed from the analysis.

The results of an ANOVA, which estimates the effect of the threat manipulation on the relative height of the CEO compared to the employee, suggest no association between the threat and CEO formidability ($F[1,311] = .09$, $p = .77$). More specifically, the results suggest that the CEO is 12% taller ($M = .12$, $SD = .22$) than the employee under the threat treatment and 13% taller ($M = .13$, $SD = .21$) under the non-threat treatment; the difference is not statistically significant ($t[313] = .30$, $p = .62$, one-tailed test). These results indicate that this type of economic threat does not trigger a preference for leaders with greater physical formidability. These results fail to support hypothesis 2b. But is physical formidability associated with male leadership? The results of two ANOVAs, which estimate the effect of the threat manipulation on the relative height of the CEO separately for ideated male and female CEOs, suggest there is no association between threat and physical formidability for male leaders ($F[1,265] = .02$, $p = .90$) or female leaders ($F[1,31] = 1.29$, $p = .26$). These results fail to support hypothesis 2c.

These results for study 2 indicate that subjects are more likely to ideate a male leader at the expense of female leadership under conditions of threat, but not under conditions of non-threat. This supports hypothesis 2a. They fail, though, to confirm the argument that the preference for a male leader may be related to a preference for more physically formidable leaders triggered by threat (hypotheses 2b and 2c). Study 3 tests these relationships in the government domain.

5.3 Study 3: Biological Sex and Formidability of Individuals' "Ideal" National Political Leader

This study is designed to capture attitudes toward the biological sex and physical formidability of a preferred national political leader when an individual (i.e., follower) is experiencing experimentally manipulated conditions of threat, in this case national conditions of war or peace. Following the evolutionary argument, hypothesis 3a asserts that increased threat to the individual via national security triggers an increased preference for a male leader and, conversely, a decreased preference for a female leader. Hypothesis 3b asserts that increased threat to the individual via national security triggers an increased preference for a more physically formidable leader, while hypothesis 3c asserts that increased threat to the individual via national security triggers an increased preference for a male leader that is associated with physical formidability. While war does not represent the same threat to modern humans that the violent ancestral environment represented to ancestral humans, modern warfare does pose a meaningful threat to the survival of citizens of nations at war; therefore, we suggest that it is reasonable to conclude that the threat of war could trigger a similar response.

The data were collected in July 2009 at a large American public university using paper-and-pencil survey instruments from samples of students enrolled in introductory political science and accounting classes. The political science classes are required of all university students for graduation and the accounting classes are required of all business students for graduation, so students in these classes represent a diverse range of individuals. Participation was voluntary. Student subjects received extra credit on a class assignment for completing the instrument. The sample included 96 subjects. Subjects ranged in age from 18 to 41 ($M = 21.3$, $SD = 2.6$). There were more males ($n = 49$, 51%) than females ($n = 47$). About 79% ($n = 76$) indicated that the racial or ethnic group that best describes them is white or Caucasian, 10% ($n = 10$) indicated Hispanic or Latino/Latina, and less than 5% indicated black or African-American ($n = 4$) or Asian ($n = 3$). The remaining subjects ($n = 3$) indicated that some other racial-ethnic group best describes them.

This study is similar in design to study 2. Using a between-subjects posttest-only 2×2 design, subjects were asked to complete two descriptions: (1) the "ideal national leader of your country" and (2) the "the typical citizen from your country".

Each description consisted of individual verbal descriptions of the leader and citizen as well as individual drawings of the leader and citizen "to get as complete a description" of subjects' perceptions as possible. Each description also included a verbal description and drawing of a meeting of the leader and citizen. See Appendix C for details. Subjects were randomly assigned to one of four treatment groups with the manipulation of interest being the nation's state of war or peace, which represents the threat (T_1) and non-threat (T_2) environments, and the second manipulation being the order in which the individuals were described, either national leader or citizen first, which represents a check for question-order effects. The treatment groups are:

T_{1a}: The "country is experiencing a time of war", leader described first ($n = 23$).
T_{1b}: The "country is experiencing a time of war", citizen described first ($n = 25$).
T_{2a}: The "country is experiencing a time of peace", leader described first ($n = 24$).
T_{2b}: The "country is experiencing a time of peace", citizen described first ($n = 24$).

Following hypothesis 3a, the expectation is that subjects are more likely to ideate a male national leader and, consequently, less likely to ideate a female national leader when the country is experiencing a time of war (T_1) than when the country is experiencing a time of peace (T_2). According to hypothesis 3b, the expectation is that subjects are more likely to ideate a more physically formidable leader when the country is threatened (T_1) than not threatened (T_2). And following hypothesis 3c, the expectation is that subjects are more likely to associate physical formidability with male leadership when the country is threatened (T_1) than not threatened (T_2).

Subjects did not complete a manipulation check of the threat treatments, but the manipulation check in study 2, which employed similar tasks, suggests that the treatments were likely successful. The check for question-order effects suggests that the order of descriptions did not bias the results. A difference of proportions test indicates no statistical difference ($z = -1.0$, $p = .30$, two-tailed test) in the ideation of a male national leader between subjects asked to describe the leader or citizen first, and an ANOVA indicates no statistical difference ($F[1,72] = 2.04$, $p = .15$) in the formidability of the national leader between subjects asked to describe the leader or citizen first. After completing the descriptions, subjects were asked to answer a number of questions about the national leader and citizen, including a question about the leader's biological sex. Like study 2, analyses of the verbal descriptions are not reported here.

The results in Table 5 are supportive of hypothesis 3a. The table suggests that more subjects ideated a male national leader under the threat treatment (94%) than

Table 5 Percent male ideal national leader by treatment (threat condition)

	War (T_1)	Peace (T_2)	$n\ T_1, T_2$	z	p^a
All subjects	94%	83%	48, 48	−1.6	.06
Female subjects	88	81	16, 31	−.6	.28
Male subjects	97	88	32, 17	−1.2	.11

[a]One-tailed test

under the non-threat treatment (83%) ($z = -1.6$, $p = 0.055$, one-tailed test). Put otherwise, the percent of subjects who ideated a male national leader increased by 13% from the peace treatment to the war treatment.

Once again, it is reasonable to assess whether subject gender moderates the effect. While these data suggest that female subjects are less likely to ideate a male national leader than male subjects (83 versus 94%), under the threat treatment both sexes appear to be more likely to ideate a male leader. The table shows that about 7% more female subjects and 9% more male subjects ideated a male leader under the threat treatment than under the non-threat treatment, but in neither case is the increase distinguishable from zero, most likely due to the small sample size. Regardless, the similar effects suggest that the gender of the subject does not moderate the effect of the threat manipulation.

Like studies 1 and 2, the results suggest that threat increases the preference for male leadership. The evolutionary approach presented here, though, suggests that in the drawing of the meeting between the leader and citizen that the leader will be relatively more physically formidable than the citizen under the threat treatment than under the non-threat treatment. Further, it suggests that the preference for a male leader will be associated with greater physical formidability. Again, relative physical formidability is assessed by measuring the difference in vertical height of the leader and citizen in the drawing task. For all subjects who completed valid drawings ($n = 72$), the relative height of the leader compared to the citizen ranges from the leader being 22% shorter to 105% taller ($M = .15$, $SD = .29$), with two outliers equal to or greater than three standard deviations ($z = 4.3, 6.6$) removed from the analysis.

The results of an ANOVA, which estimates the effect of the threat manipulation on the relative height of the national leader compared to the citizen, are suggestive of an association between the threat and leader formidability ($F[1,70] = 2.88$, $p = .09$, $\eta^2 = .04$). More specifically, the results indicate that the leader is 20% taller than the citizen ($M = .20$, $SD = .37$) under the threat treatment and 9% taller ($M = .09$, $SD = .16$) under the non-threat treatment. A test of the direction of the effect indicates that the difference is in the expected direction and statistically significant ($t[72] = -1.73$, $p = .04$, one-tailed test). These results support the argument that threat triggers a greater preference for more physically formidable leaders, as suggested in hypothesis 3b.

But is physical formidability associated with male leadership? The small number of ideated female leaders ($n = 6$) prevents us from evaluating the effect for female leaders, but the results of an ANOVA that estimates the effect of the threat manipulation on the relative height of the leader for ideated male leaders are suggestive of an association between threat and physical formidability for male leaders ($F[1,62] = 2.71$, $p = .10$, $\eta^2 = .04$). In particular, the results suggest that the male leader is 21% taller than the citizen ($M = .21$, $SD = .39$) under the threat treatment and 8% taller ($M = .08$, $SD = .14$) under the non-threat treatment. A test of the direction of the effect indicates that the difference is in the expected direction and statistically significant ($t[64] = -1.77$, $p = .04$, one-tailed test). These results partially support the argument that threat triggers an increased preference for male executive leaders that is associated with physical formidability, but we are unable to confirm that the effect is not also present for female executive leaders. As such, hypothesis 3c is only partially supported.

These results for study 3 are suggestive that, as expected, subjects are more likely to ideate a male leader under conditions of threat, as asserted in hypothesis 3a. They also suggest that threat triggers a preference for more physically formidable leaders, as asserted in hypothesis 3b, but they only partially support an association between a preference for male leaders and physical formidability, as asserted in hypothesis 3c.

6 Summary of Results

This research was designed to investigate why males hold a nearly universal advantage over females in obtaining executive leadership. The evolutionary argument presented here indicates that violent forces in the evolutionary environment led to a psychological adaptation for more physically formidable leaders, which even in modern times advantages males over females in obtaining leadership. Three broad expectations emerge from this argument. First, threat triggers a greater preference for male leaders versus female leaders (i.e., hypotheses 1, 2a, and 3a). Second, threat triggers a greater preference for more physically formidable leaders (i.e., hypotheses 2b and 3b). Third, threat triggers a greater preference for male leaders that is associated with physical formidability (i.e., hypotheses 2c and 3c).

Table 6 presents a summary of the findings related to each expectation by study. It shows that all three studies indicate that threat triggers a greater preference for male leaders. This preference is consistent across the business and government domains. Study 1 does not assess physical formidability, but study 3 indicates that threat triggers a greater preference for more physically formidable leaders in the domain of government, while study 2 does not show the same effect in the domain of business. Study 3 partially supports an association between a preference for male leadership and physical formidability in the domain of government, but study

Table 6 Summary of findings by expectation and study

Expectation	Study		
	1: Government/economy	2: Business	3: Government/war-peace
Threat increases preference for male leaders	S	S	S
Threat increases preference for formidable leaders	–	NS	S
Threat increases preference for male leaders/formidability	–	NS	PS

Note: S supported, PS partially supported, NS not supported

2 does not in the domain of business. In the case of study 3, the small number of ideated female leaders limited the analysis.

These results reflect some of the limitations of this research to address in future research. The subjects are not broadly representative geographically or, particularly in studies 2 and 3, which use college students, in age and education. The results in study 2 compared to study 3 in terms of physical formidability may reflect a lack of effect in the business domain, which would weaken the evolutionary argument. Alternatively, they may reflect a flawed treatment in study 2 that did not adequately capture a relationship between economic threat and survival, or they may reflect the fact that for most college students job insecurity does not threaten survival while war, which is tends to be fought by young people, does.

Future research should also consider the effect of the emergence of individual leaders versus the effect of people's preferences for leaders. The studies presented here focus on the preferences individuals hold regarding who leads them, while other research focuses on the types of individuals who put themselves forward as leaders. If certain types of people are more likely to compete for leadership positions and other types are less likely, then the pool of potential candidates from which leaders are drawn is unlikely to be representative of the group to be led. For instance, research shows that taller males are more likely to express interest in running for a leadership position in an organization, which corresponds with findings that major candidates for national office tend to be taller than the typical citizen (Murray and Schmitz forthcoming). Similarly, males are more likely than females to seek prestige and dominance (e.g., Kenrick et al. 2004), which may be related to, among other things, males' greater level of testosterone (Zyphur et al. 2009) and its association with status seeking (Newman et al. 2005). From the perspective of leadership emergence, the first study suggests that individuals with greater physical stature are more likely to put themselves forward for leadership positions, while the second suggests that males are more likely to put themselves forward for leadership positions.

7 Discussion and Conclusion

A vast body of literature suggests that the nearly universal advantage males hold over females in obtaining executive leadership cannot be wholly socially constructed. Proponents of cultural explanations would need to show how this advantage manifested in modern humans could result from such diverse social contexts as those experienced in 3,000 years of ancient Egypt (Tapsell 1983) and twenty-one centuries of Imperial China (Yang 1960) as well as in the preponderance of non-human animals such as chimpanzees (De Waal 2007), feral horses (Boyd and Keiper 2005), and coral-reef fish (Robertson 1972).

While the nearly universal manifestation of the effect supports arguments regarding an evolutionary factor in the female disadvantage in obtaining executive leadership, it does not necessary confirm the evolutionary argument presented here. The key components of this argument are threat and physical formidability.

Cultural and evolutionary explanations can be difficult to disentangle from each other, so it is conceivable that cultural explanations could explain the reported bias toward male leaders in response to threat. For instance, socialization-based theories such as social role theory (Eagly 1987) and gender schema theory (Bem 1981) could be used to argue that individuals are socialized to expect males and not females to respond to threat. But these arguments do not as comprehensively explain, for instance, either the positive association between physical formidability and threat or the association manifested between male leadership, physical formidability, and threat in study 3.

We suggest that the convergent evidence from the literature presented as well as these studies and their different research designs, domains, data, and analyses support the assertion that biological sex matters in issues of executive leadership via a preference for more physically formidable leaders. The contribution of this research extends, though, beyond merely demonstrating a relationship between biological sex, physical formidability, and leadership. First, it offers a more complete theoretical explanation for this phenomenon. Environmental-cultural arguments alone cannot explain how the seemingly universal leadership advantage of males could emerge from the diverse social contexts reviewed here. In terms of evolutionary theory, the relative advantage of male leaders may be partially explained as a probabilistic artifact of the fighting skills and strength often used to gain leadership in the violent human ancestral environment. Although individuals in the modern context reference a number of dimensions when thinking of prototypic leadership (Offermann et al. 1994; Johnson et al. 2008), the slow speed of evolution and the cognitive efficiency of physical size as a cue (Sell et al. 2008) suggest that leader traits that were useful in the evolutionary environment likely play a role still today (Foley 1997; Tooby and Cosmides 1992). Second, this research demonstrates that evolutionary theory may provide an additional approach to the investigation of modern biases such as sexism that are related to seemingly inconsequential traits and that have been costly to the business community and society in general. Culture-only explanations and approaches create expectations that have left many citizens unsatisfied with progress toward greater equality. This research implies that the bias in favor of male leaders may have an evolutionary component that has made it difficult to extinguish. Evolutionary theory may give policy makers in both the private and public sectors informational leverage that could be useful not for justifying the status quo, but for more comprehensively understanding and possibly addressing some of the most divisive and costly issues in society.

Appendix A: Support of Presidential Candidate Vignette Study (Study 1)

Senator Joan [John] Harper has been selected by her [his] party to run for president of the United States. Sen. Harper has served in the US Senate for two terms. Like most national politicians, the senator has a long list of political achievements.

She [He] has been the chair of the Senate Armed Services committee for four years, is credited with leading congressional negotiations over a major tax reform bill, and sponsored legislation to improve the financing of public education. Harper is usually among the moderate members of the Senate. For example, the senator recently supported bills designed to reduce the emission of air pollutants by factories and to extend tax credits given to small businesses, and opposed a bill that would have made it easier for people to get military-style assault weapons. Before being elected to the US Senate, Harper served four terms in the US House of Representatives and practiced law for several years. Supporters and opponents agree that Harper is intelligent and articulate with proven leadership skills. The senator has been married for 32 years and has two adult children.

Respected experts say that the country's economy is strong and growing [weak and declining]. The opposition party has not yet selected its nominee to run against Harper, but the two front runners are ideologically different from the senator, with one being slightly more liberal than the moderate Harper and the other being slightly more conservative.

Instrument Item 5. How likely or unlikely would you be to support Joan [John] Harper for president in the upcoming election?

Very Unlikely (1) to Very Likely (7)

Appendix B: Chief Executive Officer Description Task (Study 2)

Task 1. You have started your career, and the company you work for is growing and expects continued profitability [is declining and fears bankruptcy] in the near future. A new CEO (chief executive officer) will be taking over next month. Create in your mind the ideal CEO of this company. This should not be a real person but should be a fictitious person that has all the characteristics you want in the perfect CEO of your company. What are this person's professional qualities and characteristics? What are this person's personal qualities and characteristics?

Write down as many details as possible that come to mind about this person. Take about half a minute to complete this description.

Task 2. Thinking still about your career and the successful [failing] company you work for, create in your mind the typical employee of this company. This should not be a real person but should be a fictitious person that has all the characteristics of the average employee of your company. What are this person's professional qualities and characteristics? What are this person's personal qualities and characteristics?

Write down as many details as possible that come to mind about this person. Take about half a minute to complete this description.

Task 3. Think about the typical employee meeting your ideal CEO of your successful [failing] company. To give us as complete a description as possible, draw a picture of that meeting in the space below. Both individuals should be standing in your picture. Include any details that are important to your image of this meeting. Clearly label the employee and CEO in the picture.

Artistic ability does not matter. Stick figures are fine if you run short of time and/or artistic ability. Take about one minute to complete this drawing.

Instrument Item 6: What is the gender of the CEO you described?

a. Female   b. Male

Measurement in Drawing Studies (Study 2 and 3)

We expect that subjects are more likely to draw leaders that are larger than followers under conditions of threat. The primary measure is the relative difference in vertical size of the leader and follower in the "meeting" drawing. We define "larger" as the vertical distance between the highest and lowest points of each figure, with the distance being measured as a vertical line that is at a 90° angle to the ground. The highest point of a figure includes the top of the head in simple figures but includes extensions such as hair, hats, and bows in more complex figures. Drawings in which the difference between the citizen and leader is less than 1 mm are coded as no difference. Drawings in which both figures are not standing or in which the difference is incomprehensible (e.g., figures are sitting around a table or dismembered or only one figure was drawn) are disqualified as non-responsive.

Appendix C: National Leader Description Task (Study 3)

Task 1. Imagine that your country is experiencing a time of war [peace]. Create in your mind the ideal national leader of your country, such as a president or prime minister, during a time of war [peace]. This should not be a real person but should be a fictitious person that has all the characteristics you would want in the perfect leader of your country. What are this person's personal qualities and characteristics? What are this person's political qualities and characteristics?

Write down as many details as possible that come to mind about this person.

Task 2. Thinking still about your ideal national leader during a time of war [peace], draw a picture of that person on this sheet of paper. The national leader should be standing in your picture. Include any details that are important to your image of this person.

Artistic ability does not matter. Stick figures are fine if you run short of time and/or artistic ability.

Task 3. Create in your mind the typical citizen from your country during a time of war [peace]. This should not be a real person but should be a fictitious person that has all the characteristics of the average citizen in your country. What are this person's personal qualities and characteristics? What are this person's political qualities and characteristics?

Write down as many details as possible that come to mind about this person.

Task 4. Thinking still about the typical citizen during a time of war [peace], draw a picture of that person on this sheet of paper. The citizen should be standing in your picture. Include any details that are important to your image of this person.

Artistic ability does not matter. Stick figures are fine if you run short of time and/or artistic ability.

Task 5. Think about the typical citizen meeting your ideal national leader during a time of war [peace]. Write down as many details as possible that come to mind about this meeting.

Task 6. Thinking still about the typical citizen meeting your ideal national leader during a time of war [peace], draw a picture of that meeting on this sheet of paper. Both individuals should be standing in your picture. Include any details that are important to your image of this meeting. Clearly label the citizen and national leader in the picture.

Artistic ability does not matter. Stick figures are fine if you run short of time and/or artistic ability.

Instrument item 9. What is the gender of the national leader you described?

a. Female   b. Male

References

Adler NJ (1996) Global women political leaders: an invisible history, an increasingly important future. Leadership Quart 7:133–161

Angel JL (1971) The people. Smithsonian Institution Press, Washington, DC

Apicella CL, Dreber A, Campbell B, Gray PB, Hoffman M, Little AC (2008) Testosterone and financial risk preferences. Evol Hum Behav 29:384–390

Archie EA, Morrison TA, Foley CAH, Moss CJ, Alberts SC (2006) Dominance rank relationships among wild female African elephants, Loxodonta africana. Anim Behav 71:117–127

Arvey RD, Rotundo M, Johnson W, Zhang Z, McGue M (2006) The determinants of leadership role occupancy: genetic and personality factors. Leadership Quart 17:1–20

Bamberger J (1974) The myth of matriarchy: why men rule in primitive society. In: Rosaldo MZ (ed) Women, culture, and society. Stanford University Press, Stanford, pp 263–280

Beaulieua DA, Bugental D (2008) Contingent parental investment: an evolutionary framework for understanding interaction between mothers and children. Evol Hum Behav 29(4):249–255

Bem SL (1981) Gender schema theory: a cognitive account of sex typing. Psychol Rev 88:354–364

Boatwright KJ, Forrest L (2000) Leadership preferences: the influence of gender and needs for connection on workers' ideal preference for leadership behaviors. J Leadersh Organ Stud 7 (2):18–34

Boehm C (1999) Hierarchy in the forest: the evolution of egalitarian behavior. Harvard University Press, London

Boyd L, Keiper R (2005) Behavioural ecology of feral horses. In: Mills DS, McDonnell SM (eds) The domestic horse: the origins, development and management of its behaviour. Cambridge University Press, New York, pp 55–82

Brown DE (1991) Human universals. McGraw Hill, New York

Brown DE, Chia-yun Y (1993) 'Big man' in universalistic perspective. Manuscript, University of California at Santa Barbara

Browne KR (2006) Evolved sex differences and occupational segregation. J Organ Behav 27:143–162

Bruner JS, Postman L (1948) Symbolic value as an organizing factor in perception. J Soc Psychol 27:203–208

Buss DM (1989) Sex differences in human mate preferences: evolutionary hypotheses tested in 37 cultures. Behav Brain Sci 12:1–49

Buss DM (2005) Handbook of evolutionary psychology. Wiley, Hoboken

Carr L, Iacoboni M, Dubeau M, Mazziotta JC, Lenzi GL (2003) Neural mechanisms of empathy in humans: a relay from neural systems for imitation to limbic areas. Proc Natl Acad Sci USA 100(9):5497–5502

Cernerud L (1995) Height and social mobility. Scand J Soc Med 23:28–31

Chagnon NA (1997) The Yanomamo. Wadsworth, London

Clutton-Brock TH, Guinness FE, Albon SD (1982) Red deer: behaviour and ecology of two sexes. University of Chicago Press, Chicago

Crawford C (2008) Adaptations, environments, and behavior: then and now. In: Crawford C, Krebs D (eds) Foundations of evolutionary psychology. Lawrence Erlbaum Associates, New York, pp 191–214

Dannenmaier WD, Thumin FJ (1964) Authority status as a factor in perceptual distortion of size. J Soc Psychol 63:361–365

Darwin C (1859) On the origin of species by means of natural selection, or the preservation of favoured races in the struggle for life. John Murray, London

De Waal F (2005) Our inner ape. Riverhead Books, New York

De Waal F (2007) Chimpanzee politics: power and sex among apes. Johns Hopkins University Press, Baltimore

Deal TE, Kennedy AA (2000) Corporate cultures: the rites and rituals of corporate life. Perseus Publishing, Cambridge

Diamond J (1999) Guns, germs, and steel: the fates of human societies. W. W. Norton, New York

Dukes WF, Bevan W (1952) Size estimation and monetary value: a correlation. J Psychol 34:43–53

Eagly AH (1987) Sex differences in social behavior: a social-role interpretation. Erlbaum, Hillsdale

Ellis BJ (1995) The evolution of sexual attraction: evaluative mechanisms in women. In: Barkow JH, Cosmides L, Tooby J (eds) The adapted mind: evolutionary psychology and the generation of culture. Oxford University Press, New York, pp 267–288

Emrich CG, Denmark FL, Den Hartog DN (2004) Cross-cultural differences in gender egalitarianism. In: House RJ, Hanges PJ, Javidan M, Dorfman PW, Gupta V (eds) Culture, leadership, and organizations: the GLOBE study of 62 societies. Sage, Thousand Oaks, pp 323–394

Foley R (1997) The adaptive legacy of human evolution: a search for the environment of evolutionary adaptedness. Evol Anthropol 4(6):194–203

Fox R (1983) Kinship and marriage: an anthropological perspective. Cambridge University Press, Cambridge

Freedman DG (1979) Human sociobiology: a holistic approach. Free Press, New York

Geary D (1998) Male, female: the evolution of human sex differences. American Psychological Association, Washington, DC

Gillis JS (1982) Too tall, too small. Institute for Personality and Ability Testing, Champaign

Goldstein JS (2003) War and gender: how gender shapes the war system and vice versa. Cambridge University Press, Cambridge

Gregor T (1979) Short people. Nat Hist 88:14–19

Haj S (1992) Palestinian women and patriarchal relations. Signs 17(4):761–778

Haselton MG, Mortezaie M, Pillsworth EG, Bleske-Rechek A, Frederick DA (2007) Ovulatory shifts in human female ornamentation: near ovulation, women dress to impress. Horm Behav 51:40–45

Haviland WA (1967) Stature at Tikal, Guatemala: implications for ancient Maya demography and social organization. Am Antiquity 32:316–325

Heinze J, Oberstadt B (1999) Worker age, size, and social status in queenless colonies of the ant Leptothorax gredleri. Anim Behav 58:751–759

Henrich J, Gil-White FJ (2001) The evolution of prestige: freely conferred deference as a mechanism for enhancing the benefits of cultural transmission. Evol Hum Behav 22(3):165–196

Hensley WE (1993) Height as a measure of success in academe. Psychology 30:40–46

Higham PA, Carment DW (1992) The rise and fall of politicians: the judged height of Broadbent, Mulroney, and Turner before and after the 1988 Canadian federal election. Can J Behav Sci 24:404–409

Hofstede G (2001) Culture's consequences, comparing values, behaviors, institutions, and organizations across nations. Sage Publications, Thousand Oaks

Holand Ø, Gjøstein H, Losvar A, Kumpula J, Smith ME, Røed KH, Nieminen M, Weladji RB (2004) Social rank in female reindeer (Rangifer tarandus): effects of body mass, antler size and age. J Zool 263:365–372

Jackson L, Ervin K (1992) Height stereotypes of women and men: the liabilities of shortness for both sexes. J Soc Psychol 132:433–445

Jay JW (1996) Imagining matriarchy: 'Kingdoms of women' in Tang China. J Am Orient Soc 116(2):220–229

Johnson JA (1987) Dominance rank in juvenile Olive Baboons, Papio Anubis: the influence of gender, size, maternal rank, and orphaning. Anim Behav 35:1694–1708

Johnson SK, Murphy SE, Zewdie S, Reichard RJ (2008) The strong, sensitive type: effects of gender stereotypes and leadership prototypes on the evaluation of male and female leaders. Organ Behav Hum Decis Process 106:39–60

Kalma A (1991) Hierarchisation and dominance assessment at first glance. Eur J Soc Psychol 21:165–181

Kappeler PM (1993) Female dominance in primates and other mammals. In: Gordon PP, Klopfer PH, Thompson NS (eds) Perspectives in ethology, vol 10, Behavior and evolution. Springer, Germany, pp 143–158

Keegan J (1993) A history of warfare. Key Porter Books, Toronto

Kenrick DT, Trost MR, Sundie JM (2004) Sex-roles as adaptations: an evolutionary perspective on gender differences and similarities. In: Eagly AH, Beall AE, Sternberg RJ (eds) The psychology of gender. Guilford, New York

Klass GM (2008) Just plain data analysis: finding, presenting, and interpreting social science data. Rowman and Littlefield, New York

Lassek WD, Gaulin SJC (2009) Costs and benefits of fat-free muscle mass in men: relationship to mating success, dietary requirements, and native immunity. Evol Hum Behav 30(5):322–328

Lawrence PR, Nohria N (2002) Driven: how human nature shapes our choices. Jossey-Bass, San Francisco

Little AC, Burriss RP, Jones BC, Roberts SC (2007) Facial appearance affects voting decisions. Evol Hum Behav 28:18–27

LoBue V, DeLoache J (2008) Detecting the snake in the grass: attention to fear-relevant stimuli in adults and young children. Psychol Sci 19(30):284–289

Lord RG, Emrich CG (2000) Thinking outside the box by looking inside the box: extending the cognitive revolution in leadership research. Leadership Quart 11:551–579

Ludwig AM (2002) King of the mountain: the nature of political leadership. University Press of Kentucky, Lexington

Magnusson PK, Rasmussen F, Gyllensten UB (2006) Height at age 18 years is a strong predictor of attained education later in life: cohort study of over 950, 000 Swedish men. Int J Epidemiol 35:658–663

Mayr E (2001) What evolution is. Basic Books, New York

McCann SJH (2001) Height, societal threat, and the victory margin in presidential elections (1824–1992). Psychol Rep 88:741–742

Mech LD (2000) Leadership in wolf, *Canis lupus*, packs. Can Field Nat 114(2):259–263

Meggitt MJ (1977) Blood is their argument: warfare among the Mae Enga tribesmen. Mayfield, Palo Alto

Mills MGL, Hofer H (1998) Hyaenas. IUCN, Switzerland

Murray GR, Schmitz JD (forthcoming) Caveman politics: evolutionary leadership preferences and stature. Social Science Quarterly

Nesse R, Williams GC (1994) Why we get sick: the new science of Darwinian medicine. Vintage Books, New York

Newman ML, Sellers JG, Josephs RA (2005) Testosterone, cognition, and social status. Horm Behav 47:205–211

Oakley JG (2000) Gender-based barriers to senior management positions: understanding the scarcity of female CEOs. J Bus Ethics 27:321–334

Offermann LR, Kennedy JK, Wirtz PW (1994) Implicit leadership theories: content, structure, and generalizability. Leadership Quart 5:43–58

Ortner SB (1974) Is female to male as nature is to culture? In: Rosaldo MZ (ed) Women, culture, and society. Stanford University Press, Stanford, pp 67–87

Parish AR (1994) Sex and food control in the uncommon chimpanzee: how Bonobo females overcome a phylogenetic legacy of male dominance. Ethol Sociobiol 15:157–179

Persico N, Postelwaite A, Silverman D (2004) The effect of adolescent experience on labor market outcomes: the case of height. J Polit Econ 112:1019–1053

Petersen MB, Delton AW, Robertson TF, Tooby J, Cosmides L (2008) Politics of the evolved mind: political parties and coalitional reasoning. Paper presented at the Midwest Political Science Association annual conference, Chicago

Peterson D, Wrangham R (1997) Demonic males: Apes and the origins of human violence. Mariner Books, New York

Pheasant ST (1983) Sex differences in strength: some observations on their variability. Appl Ergon 14:205–211

Robertson DR (1972) Social control of sex reversal in a coral-reef fish. Science 177(4053):1007–1009

Saad G (2007) The evolutionary bases of consumption. Lawrence Erlbaum Associates, Mahwah

Saad G (2008) The collective amnesia of marketing scholars regarding consumers' biological and evolutionary roots. Market Theory 8(4):425–448

Scarr S, McCartney K (1983) How people make their own environments: a theory of genotype - environment effects. Child Dev 54(2):424–435

Searcy WA (1979) Morphological correlates of dominance in captive male red-winged blackbirds. Condor 41:417–420

Sell A, Cosmides L, Tooby J, Sznycer D, von Rueden C, Gurven M (2008) Human adaptations for the visual assessment of strength and fighting ability from the body and face. Proc Roy Soc B Biol Sci 276:575–584

Simonton DK (1994) Greatness: who makes history and why. Guilford, New York

Spencer TJ, Biederman J, Wilens TE, Faraone SV (2002) Overview and neurobiology of attention-deficit/hyperactivity disorder. J Clin Psychiatry 63(12):3–9

Tapsell RF (1983) Monarchs, rulers, dynasties, and kingdoms of the world. Facts on File Publications, New York

Thames F, Williams M (2009) Female executive and legislative leaders. Unpublished raw data

Tooby J, Cosmides L (1992) Psychological foundations of culture. In: Barlow J, Cosmides L, Toody J (eds) The adapted mind: evolutionary psychology and the generation of culture. Oxford University Press, New York, pp 19–136

Van Vugt M, Spisak BR (2008) Sex differences in the emergence of leadership during competitions within and between groups. Psychol Sci 19:854–858

Van Vugt M, Hogan R, Kaiser RB (2008) Leadership, followership, and evolution. Am Psychol 63(3):182–196

Waeber PO, Hemelrijk CK (2003) Female dominance and social structure in Alaotran gentle lemurs. Behaviour 140:1235–1246

Watts DP (1996) Comparative socioecology of gorillas. In: McGrew WC, Marchant LF, Nishida T (eds) Great ape societies. Cambridge University Press, Cambridge, pp 16–28

Whiteman EA, Cote IM (2004) Dominance hierarchies in group living cleaning gobies: causes and foraging consequences. Anim Behav 67:230–247

Willhoite FH (1976) Primates and political authority: a biobehavioral perspective. Am Polit Sci Rev 70:1110–1126

Wilson PR (1968) Perceptual distortion of height as a function of ascribed academic status. J Soc Psychol 74:97–102

Yang L (1960) Female rulers in Imperial China. Harvard J Asiat Stud 23:47–61

Zyphur MJ, Narayanan J, Koh G, Koh D (2009) Testosterone-status mismatch lowers collective efficacy in groups: evidence from a slope-as-predictor multilevel structural equation model. Organ Behav Hum Decis Process 110:70–79

Leadership in Organizations: An Evolutionary Perspective

Brian R. Spisak, Nigel Nicholson, and Mark van Vugt

Abstract In this chapter we discuss the potential of evolution to serve as a framework for unifying our understanding of leadership. From this perspective we consider the ultimate origins and functions of leadership, the role of co-evolution, and methods for testing evolution-based leadership hypotheses. To begin, we examine evolutionarily stable situation dynamics in the environment (e.g., intergroup conflict) that may have selected for (1) leadership behavior as well as (2) corresponding human traits intended to signal potential leadership ability and use this argument to support the notion of context-specific "cognitive leadership prototypes". Particular attention is also given to the role of the follower and the specific pressures encouraging "followership investment". In addition, co-evolution logic is used to examine the intricate relationship between the environment, human culture, and the emergence of certain leadership styles. Next, we discuss five methods for testing an evolution-based hypothesis of leadership and followership. Finally, we highlight practical implications which include appreciating the role of the follower, the impact of social constructs on modern leadership, the benefits of distributed leadership, and the importance of feminine leadership styles. Also, for consideration throughout the chapter, organizational examples are provided such as the homogenization of corporate culture and the current role of monarchies in Western society.

B.R. Spisak (✉)
Department of Social and Organizational Psychology, VU University Amsterdam, Van der Boechorststraat 1, Room 1B-09, 1081 BT Amsterdam, The Netherlands
e-mail: BR.Spisak@psy.vu.nl

N. Nicholson
Organisational Behaviour, London Business School, Regent's Park, London NW1 4SA, UK
e-mail: nnicholson@london.edu

M. van Vugt
Department of Social and Organizational Psychology, VU University Amsterdam, Van der Boechorststraat 1, Room 1B-57, 1081 BT Amsterdam, The Netherlands
e-mail: m.van.vugt@psy.vu.nl

Keywords Evolution · Leadership · Followership · Prototype · Heuristic · Emergence · Investment · Co-evolution · Gender · Coordination · Cooperation · Conflict

Leadership is a universal phenomenon – it seems to be visible in all cultures and at all known historical periods, though taking quite different forms across times and places (Brown 1991). It is also one of the great obsessions of our times. Political leadership remains an area of keen public focus, on which the hopes and fears are pinned of many societies and groups. In business, leadership remains the hottest of topics. A brief perusal of business bookshelves will quickly reveal that more volumes appear with the word "leadership" in the title than any other domain of management. It is big business in education and consulting where corporations devote large budgets to new and better ways of finding, developing, and retaining leadership talent.

It is curious that little attention is given to fundamental questions, such as what is leadership? Is it a trait or ability, a position in a social system, or process of influence that takes place in groups? Arguably it is all three, but failure to make such distinctions is a possible reason for the unending stream of books on the subject and the lack of a unifying perspective on the topic (cf. Nicholson 2005a, b; Van Vugt et al. 2008a). This chapter takes a fresh look at the topic and aims to lay the platform for a more unifying perspective by considering the evolutionary origins and functions of leadership, how a co-evolutionary framework explains its different manifestations, and how to test evolutionary hypotheses of leadership.

1 The Evolutionary Origins of Leadership

A neo-Darwinian perspective commences by considering the fitness enhancing properties of leadership capability before considering its likely ontogeny and subsequent adaptation over time. The answer to the first question lies in the social nature of our species and the need for coordination to achieve essential fitness-enhancing goals. Social coordination can be achieved in many ways, but one of the most efficient is for an individual to perform the role of leader and for others to be followers. Leadership coordination can have different manifestations, or styles, from despotic to democratic leadership and anything in between. We shall discuss these manifestations later in this chapter. Our first goal is to consider the logic of leadership emergence.

Which evolutionary pressure(s) selected for our ability to coordinate via leadership and followership and what corresponding phenotypic and genotypic changes occurred in human evolution? Previous research on this topic suggests selection pressures associated with a nomadic hunting and gathering lifestyle – the way ancestral hominids have lived for at least several millions of years, and our own species, homo sapiens, for around 240,000 years until the advent of agriculture more than 10,000 years ago (Van Vugt et al. 2008b). Adaptations for leadership and importantly followership may have laid the foundations for the increase in the scale and social complexity of human societies across history and this development in turn affected the manifestation of leadership. Our view is that humans evolved in environments that were characterized by natural oscillations in the availability of reproductively relevant resources as well as changing climates and geographies, which created selection pressures on forming highly effective groups to solve various coordination problems.

The main idea is that these coordination problems should center on the basic needs for genetic replication (i.e., resource attainment and creating environments conducive to rearing offspring) and exert a sufficiently consistent and recurring selection pressure. We consider four behavioral dynamics to be essential for human survival and reproductive success: (1) resource attainment, (2) group movement, (3) internal peacekeeping, and (4) intergroup relations. As we shall discuss, these problems arise and induce pressures for leadership emergence when there is an asymmetry of available resources and reproductively favorable environments.

First, vital to our survival is the attainment of sufficient levels of caloric intake and hydration (i.e., food and water), and establishing shelter with access to these necessities. Living in groups is a strategy that humans, pre-humans, and other species have evolved for this purpose. We argue that this fundamental requirement has shaped human group psychology. Yet the benefits that come with numbers also yield a cost in the form of coordination problems, three of which are described below.

The second recurrent environmental problem is group movement. Whereas resource attainment is a matter of maximizing opportunity *within* a particular environment, group movement concerns the transition *between* viable habitats. For the majority of human history groups have needed to be nomadic or at least semi-nomadic to follow changing patterns of migrating prey, vegetation, and sources of water (Diamond 1997). For example, during particular times of the year (e.g., dry seasons) waterholes can dry-up necessitating transition to less arid conditions.

Third is the need for cooperation. This introduces a controversial topic in evolutionary theory – group selection. It has been theoretical orthodoxy that selection (natural and sexual) is driven by the survival and reproduction of the biological replicators that define our phenotypic identity – the gene (Dawkins 1976). Yet selection does not operate on the genotype but on the phenotype and recently there have been persuasive arguments for what is called "group selection", the idea that the group context creates a framework for the selection of those phenotypes that are congruent with the needs of the group, i.e. members of a collective prosper because of their relationship to the existing configuration of attributes, which collectively enable the group to master its environment (Sober and Wilson 1998; Wilson et al. 2008). Given the conflict between self-interest and self-sacrifice for the group, there are continual threats to cohesion in the form of free riding and other rule violations that threaten harmony within the group (De Cremer and Van Vugt 2002; O'Gorman et al. 2008). Subsequently, there is a need for internal peacekeeping and we suggest this selected for specific attributes to create and maintain a stable social environment and cohesive social group. Later we shall argue that the forces for selection include a group's culture – a process that is identified as "co-evolution".

Fourth, is a concern for the management of intergroup relations, since humans have existed for most of their history in extended clan formations, in which the kinship ties between subgroups may be quite weak. This requires the regulation of interrelations among the sub-groups of large aggregations, as well as periodic interactions with true out-groups of strangers. These interactions can either be hostile or peaceful. Inter-group raiding and trading were the common forms of such exchanges (Van Vugt 2009; Wrangham and Peterson 1996). Thus there is a need to mobilize for warfare, and for the politics and diplomacy of coalition formation and peacekeeping. These needs also have shaped how we organize and which attributes are favored among members to successfully prosecute and support the strategic goals of the group.

In this chapter, we develop the idea that these coordination problems have unique requirements and that they selected for mechanisms to coordinate group life such as a set of mechanisms that made it possible for individuals to form leadership-followership relations.

The increased importance of the social group as a buffer against environmental fluctuations (e.g., sharing food during shortages) selected for social adaptations to reap the benefits and avoid the costs of group living. The major outcome of this evolutionary trajectory was the expansion of the neocortex, dubbed as the social brain hypothesis (Dunbar 1998). One of the core pressures behind the expansion of the social brain may be group size increases and the associated problems of social coordination. Groups that successfully work together and suppress internal conflict increase the overall fitness of its members (Wilson et al. 2008). As fitness increases populations grow and there will be selection on traits to manage larger social networks more effectively. Those individuals, and consequently groups, maintaining larger and more integrated networks are likely to have greater access to scarce resources through opportunities for sharing and success in conflicts between groups. Given the positive correlation between group size and neocortex size across primate species (Dunbar 2004), the need to coordinate group efforts in oscillating environments selected for the increased mental capacity which made leadership and followership possible on a much larger scale than ever before.

It is important to note that leadership, as an element in the systemic social solution to these challenges, is not a unique feature of human evolution (Van Vugt and Kurzban 2007). Ants, bees, birds, lions, and other social species show basic patterns of leadership and followership to solve coordination problems. In some of the most primitive cases, such as the waggle dance of bee scouts to recruit followers, the behavior is likely an evolutionary elaboration of the same mechanism that makes it possible for an army of soldiers to follow the orders of a single general. Comparative studies of other social mammals, such as chimpanzees, wolves, and elephants, indicate that leadership has varying functions in different species (Van Vugt 2006). Dominance hierarchies, politics, and coordination via power, coalition, and exchange have been reliably recorded among other primates, especially the Great Apes (De Waal 1989a, b; Silk 2007). However, humans have evolved characteristics for adaptation to a wide range of environments and living conditions, and thus require behavioral plasticity, i.e. a greater array of social responses and flexible strategies. The emergence of language in humans greatly enhanced the opportunity to lead large groups. Other communication systems (such as pheromones in social insects) might be just as reliable and effective however.

2 Leadership Emergence

To unravel dynamics of leader emergence requires us to examine three essential elements of leadership: Situation, Processes, and Qualities – the SPQ Model (Nicholson 2010). The adaptive challenge of leadership originates from the demands of what we can call leadership "situations" (the S factors). Any situation that could benefit from coordination by an agent is potentially a leadership situation. In modern organizational life these are identified as nodes or statuses in a hierarchy, though ostensibly egalitarian contexts are also potential leadership situations. Thus in a wide array of situations there is potentially a manifest benefit from leadership "processes" (the P factors). A leadership process is any behavior that directs and coordinates group effort. Even in a rigid hierarchy where behavior is coordinated by rules and operating procedures there is still a need for leadership processes to manage exceptions and to direct the application of systemic processes. Leadership processes thus embrace a variety of behaviors from the directive to the consensus-seeking. This makes influence in all its forms primarily a leadership process (Hollander 1978), including all the behaviors that are preparatory to influence or the exercise of power. The model thus implies that a prior need, and key leadership skill, is the ability to understand the current demands facing the group and to anticipate and imagine future situations. Thus leadership processes potentially embrace all human behaviors that can serve the goal of direction and achieving coordination. The key task therefore is to identify which critical situations require leadership and to determine whether there are individuals capable of performing these behaviors.

This brings us to leadership "qualities" (the Q factors). The model accords a central role to stable individual differences in leadership emergence, effectiveness, and derailment (Judge et al. 2002; Lord and Hall 1992). It is evident that human individuals are not all equally capable of enacting leadership processes as a function of differences in cognitive capabilities (perception and understanding), action capabilities (physical attributes and skills), and motivational capabilities (drives and interests). The science of behavior genetics tells us that many of these qualities have a substantial heritable component and achieve stability as traits by early adulthood (Arvey et al. 2006; Johnson et al. 1998). Evolutionary theory is interested in why such individual variations should arise.

Frequency dependent selection operates on many attributes, including psychological traits (Nettle 2006). This is the idea that there is comparative advantage in having a profile of attributes that differentiates us from other individuals in achieving reproductive success. A simple example would be the idea that in a world full of "followers" a minority who are capable of leading will secure benefits from performing that role, and conversely, in a world full of "leaders" there will be rewards for those who are happy to be "followers". This logic extends to the widest range of human attributes, resulting in the array of human types that can be found in every community. There is evidence that the more social a species is, the more differentiation there is in terms of personality (Penke et al. 2007). In humans the extreme variety of human personality types affords two key opportunities.

One is mate selection. At a psychological level human attribute diversity offers the chance for bonding on the basis of mutual gratification of needs (Buss 2003) and at a biological level the union of optimally differentiated immune systems, giving their offspring better life chances in the face of evolving pathogens (Williams 1975). The second is a comparative advantage in the social economy of the human group, with the possibility for the individual to bring a unique profile of skills and orientations to the service of the group (division of labor). Within the latter context leadership can be seen as a social role that is needed, along with many others, by the group, though, as we have observed, the nature of the desired leadership profile will vary according to the structure, culture, and challenges facing the group: what we have called the leadership situation. Thus we reason that the forces of selection result in the occurrence of human types who are more suited to leadership roles than others (Van Vugt 2006).

In terms of followership, if leadership is crucial to the survival of human groups we would expect humans to have evolved a suite of cognitive adaptations to recognize a leadership situation and identify an appropriate potential leader (i.e., those who followed bad leaders would have died out), and because what constitutes good leadership might vary from one situation to the next this mechanism probably consists of a set of heuristics or "if-then" rules. For instance, *if* the group is at war with another group *then* individuals would follow a leader with different characteristics and abilities than if the group is brokering peace.

As Buss (1991) argues, individual differences exist in part to maximize opportunities for cooperation. For example, leadership situations can favor prototypes not only between the sexes (i.e., men for war and women for peace – Van Vugt and Spisak 2008), but also within (e.g., *masculine* men for conflict and *feminine* men for peace). In fact, unpublished research by Spisak and Van Vugt highlights other forms of novel leadership emergence to challenge traditional male-female views (e.g., *masculine women* preferred over *feminine men* as leaders during intergroup conflict). This research will be discussed in more detail in the "Testing Evolutionary Hypothesis about Leadership" section of this chapter

Specific traits aside, the repetitive dynamics of these problems over time would have selected for a set of cognitive leadership prototypes that individuals with particular features would match better than others. A "cognitive leadership prototype" can be thought of as a set of traits and characteristics that reliably predict leadership ability in specific situations and these evolved prototypes are likely to be activated automatically and spontaneously when such situations arise (cf. leader categorization theory; Lord and Maher 1991). This is analogous to competitive sports. The requirements to be a successful horse jockey are quite different relative to that of a master Sumo wrestler and they come with a different set of physical and perhaps psychological traits and it would not be difficult to assess those individuals best suited for either role.

The key to understanding leadership prototypes is identifying critical leadership situations that have been recurrent and stable enough to exert sufficient selective pressure for cognitive leader prototypes to have evolved. As we have already mentioned, these demands can include resource attainment, group movement, internal peacekeeping, and intergroup relations. Within each of these challenges are tasks that must be accomplished to effectively address the problem and we believe that leadership may have served such functions.

In hunter gatherer communities four tasks may be identified that are essential for the adaptive capability and survival of the group and these correspond nicely to the coordination problems that we have discussed earlier (Nicholson 2005a; Van Vugt 2006): (1) Food-sharing allocations, which equates to the essential task of governance (resources maintenance); (2) Decisions about where to camp and hunt; what could be called the strategic challenge (group movement); (3) The control of aggressive males; which is in effect a challenge of culture management (peacekeeping); (4) Relations with other groups and communities (intergroup relations). These functions are, to a degree, interdependent around what Drath et al. (2008) identify as the components of leadership effectiveness – DAC – direction, acceptance, and commitment. The four functions we have identified require respectively the qualities associated with vision and planning; justice and integrity; emotional intelligence; and tact and diplomacy. Furthermore, there is no need for all these leadership processes to be possessed by a single individual so long as they are embodied in some social processes within the group.

There are other universals for emergent leadership in ostensibly egalitarian contexts, such as those that generally characterize hunter-gatherer communities (Boehm 1999), which correspond neatly to the results of the cross-cultural studies into desirable and undesirable leadership traits, notably around ethics and integrity, interpersonal skills, and the ability to mobilize positive emotions (Dorfman et al. 2004). These embody the processes by which leaders are accepted as trustworthy, dependable, and competent in finding the solutions to recurring group tasks.

Finally, a prototype for many leadership models is parenting. Every child has experienced one or more examples of adult leadership in familial contexts. Many of these find expression in solely adult decision-making contexts, especially perhaps in family firms where familiar pathologies of parenting are visible (Gordon and Nicholson 2008). But in many other contexts one can observe parental paradigms being replicated – from nurturing and caring to despotism (Kets de Vries 1997). It seems likely that as adults we may retain sensitivity and responsiveness to these paradigmatic forms.

3 Leadership Prototypes

Are there reliable trait differences between individuals that increase their propensity to emerge as leaders in different adaptive situations? For instance, let us consider the ancient and recurrent problem of conflictual intergroup relations

(Keeley 1996; Johnson and Van Vugt 2009). In times of fighting a strong, physically formidable, and aggressive individual would be preferred as leader. Conversely, if the situation requires peacekeeping, the same aggressive behaviors will be a hindrance, and the ability to cooperate, empathize, and communicate will become favored leadership traits. An evolutionary analysis enables us to examine the connection between leadership situations and evolved leadership prototypes by formulating and testing hypotheses about the content of these prototypes.

Research on the 2004 presidential elections between George W. Bush and John Kerry illustrates the point (Little et al. 2007). Researchers took facial images of Bush and Kerry and using face morphing software applied 30% of their facial features to a neutral base face. This process provided them with two images, a "Bush-like" face and a "Kerry-like" face. The important point is that both images contained features of the respective candidates, but only using only 30% of their respective facial features ensured that the composite images were not recognizable as Bush or Kerry, thus eliminating real world voter bias. Next, in the experimental phase, participants were asked to choose between the "Bush-like" and "Kerry-like" face in times of war and peace. Overwhelmingly the "Bush-like" face was voted for in times of war whereas in times of peace the "Kerry-like" face was preferred. Moreover, the "Bush-like" face was rated more masculine and the "Kerry-like" face more feminine.

Saad (2003) points out voters tend to use information shortcuts, such as visual cues, to simplify the rationally complex process of leadership selection. He argues height can serve as a cue for dominance and provides compelling evidence from past U.S. presidential elections. From 1904–1996 the winning candidate has 83% of the time been taller than his rival! Given the United States emphasis on defense it may prompt a prevailing environmental perception of intergroup conflict which elicits the preference for a dominant literally overbearing leader. Consequently, voters may use height as a heuristic for leadership potential in particular situations.

This suggests that followers use physical cues to make judgments on an individual's leadership ability based on the match between the leadership situation (war, peace) and the leadership prototype (aggressive, cooperative), with height and facial masculinity-femininity (in this case) serving as cues. Indeed positive correlations have been observed between facial masculinity and levels of testosterone and between testosterone and aggressive and dominant behaviors (Penton-Voak and Chen 2004; Sellers et al. 2007), suggesting the validity of such cues. In addition, this accords with the SPQ (Situations, Processes Qualities) model, introduced earlier, which argues that relatively invariant yet diverse qualities of individuals (would-be leaders) are the subject of selection by agents (followers, parties, other leaders) in response to different leadership situations in order that these individuals may enact influence processes.

We argue that contemporary leadership is a product of human genetic evolution whereby individuals attend to information that is reliably connected with leadership success in the past. The argument is that those individuals and groups who would pick the right leader for a particular situation – for instance, a masculine-looking leader in war time – would fare better than those picking the wrong leader – a feminine-looking leader during war. Over time this would have led to the formation of a set of distinct cognitive leadership prototypes to cope with different situations and those individuals that would match these prototypes would be more likely to attract followers (e.g., if at war, follow a physically formidable leader).

However, leadership situations are also the subject of socio-cultural development. Co-evolutionary processes maintain group-beneficial equilibria by supporting the emergence of new arrays of prototypes (Henrich 2004; Richerson and Boyd 2005). One possibility is that the leader prototypes that are reminiscent of our ancestral past may be no longer predictive of leadership success in modern society – the idea of a potential "mismatch" (Van Vugt et al. 2008). Given that these prototypes were shaped over several millions of years of living in small egalitarian groups, which are quite unlike modern nations and businesses, one could argue that these prototypes may no longer predict leadership ability and success in complex modern environments. Some instances of leadership derailment are arguably disequilibria of misfitting prototypes (Van Velsor and Leslie 1995). Yet another possibility is that co-evolutionary processes have led to the emergence of new effective prototypes (Richerson and Boyd 2005). The expansion of human groups and the ability of individuals to lead groups containing millions of followers suggest that both prototypes and selection processes are delivering the leaders we need.

Another implication is that aspiring leaders can influence their success by changing the perception of the leadership situation so that they better match the prototype. For example, the interests of a masculine looking leader candidate would be best served if he (a) perceives the environment as containing threat of intergroup hostility, and (b) can persuade others of the reality of this threat. One is reminded of George Bush's campaign in the 2004 US election in which he constantly reminded the American people of the threat of Al Qaeda and with success – he beat Kerry with a comfortable margin. The relationship between leader situations and perceived qualities is not one of mechanistic and passive accidents of fit and misfit – leaders actively seek to promote and sustain situations that favor their styles (Nicholson 2010).

4 A Short Co-Evolutionary History of Leadership

Human culture has followed a co-evolutionary course. Cultural innovations such as the control of fire and the cooking of food led to bodily adaptations of a smaller and more efficient gut in hominids, which in turn facilitated increased ability to trek and hunt (Wrangham 2009). Human social and cultural change has followed a similar pattern with possible implications for leadership. Moving from a hunter-gatherer to an agrarian life style brought about a dramatic change in the fundamentals of human social organization. Not only did it lead to genetic changes in human constitution to allow some groups of modern humans to absorb lactated milk (though many still cannot), and a range of new challenges in the form of pathogens that jump the barrier between domesticated animals and humans, but it changed our relationship to each other (Diamond 1997).

Formerly, the hunter-gatherer lifestyle of our ancestors enforced a loose egalitarianism and leadership roles were distributed among the group (Van Vugt et al. 2008; Whiten 1999). Emergent leaders were mostly transient for populations constantly on the move and they had little if any non-perishable wealth (Coon 1979). The agricultural revolution of some ten millennia ago produced a profound change in every aspect of human culture and society, allowing not only the accumulation of wealth and power but also its transfer between generations. This creates a compelling Darwinian logic for the acquisition and retention of leadership, including across generations because it translates directly into reproductive success (Betzig 1993). Leadership in the world of fixed settlements and centers of power, following the agricultural revolution, allowed the emergence of varieties of despotism. Absolutism was only leavened by the countervailing powers of competing warlords and subsequently, with the education and empowerment of the masses, by the people and their representatives (Van Vugt et al., 2008).

It is interesting to view, as an aside, the model that lies in between the hunter-gatherers and the agrarians: The pastoralists with their semi-nomadic lifestyle. The adaptive model of leadership one finds here is simultaneously more structured and collectivist than either of the others (Hodgson 2001; Saitoti 1986). In these societies one finds again the isomorphism between leadership models and the structure and culture of the collective; the co-evolutionary logic that favors the advancement of individuals who are skilled in the art of intermediation across the rigid boundaries of the social structure. This works for pastoralists because of their rigid age-grade structure and intense collectivism or anti-individualism within age sets (Nicholson 2005a).

In many early tribal societies, leadership follows the so-called Big Man model (Nicholson 2005a; Van Vugt and Ahuja 2010). This concept originated in the ascendance of leaders able to secure the most resources for the tribe (e.g., the best hunters and fishers) and who proved their fitness to lead by their judicious and selfless sharing of surpluses with tribal members (Coon 1979; Kets de Vries 1999). This prototype survives in Africa and elsewhere, where it has become synonymous with a corrupted form of governance where the concentration of power in a one-party state allows its rulers to act out a kleptocratic parody of the Big Man model. The co-evolutionary equilibrium here consists of historical faith in the patronage model of the clan, with a tradition of dependence on the largesse of chieftains, even though it is economically self-defeating.

The co-evolutionary argument that explains these historical shifts owes greatly to human adaptability. The nature of the environmental challenge such as a mobile versus sedentary lifestyle or external threat versus cooperation evokes appropriate social institutions that recalibrate the values attached to individual attributes (e.g., favoring warriors versus peacemakers as leaders). Various forms of selection (natural, social, or sexual selection) then conspicuously favor the prosperity of some leadership prototypes over others. Other systems (e.g., education, culture) may subsequently weigh in to reinforce the bias, which may result in selection at the cultural and perhaps even at the genetic level, such as the claimed differences in leadership style and temperament between northern and southern climes (Hofstede 1982; Kagan 1994).

The co-evolutionary logic applies more locally in sub-cultures, which is what we may regard many organizations as; especially those that have been around long enough to have acquired the attributes that help to keep culture in place: Life-time members, traditions, legends, rituals, selection and de-selection mechanisms, established operating norms and procedures (Pettigrew 1979). There is a long tradition of research on Schneider's ASA "the people make the place" model (Smith 2008), which argues that organizational subcultures homogenize over time by what has been called "elective affinity" (Nicholson 2000). People, including leaders, are attracted to and self-select into organizations that already contain like-minded individuals who have previously elected to join and stay, misfits having deselected themselves. A corollary of this logic is the somewhat paradoxical idea that the freer labor markets become the less diversity there will be in organizations. Indeed, the search for external rather than internal leaders is often a reflection of their desire to drive change from the top.

Of course this is only part of the picture since the co-evolutionary argument also points out the need for communities to be adaptive to their external environment, and excessive homogenization will lead to a loss of adaptability, or "nest fouling" (Astley 1985). For this reason there is often a struggle in established organizations between conservatism and change, the latter being driven by the thrusting nascent businesses who would capture their markets. These are driven by an entrepreneurial spirit, and, indeed, on the ASA principle are peopled with entrepreneurial personalities (Chell et al. 1991). This argument suggests that the continual call for "entrepreneurship" in large corporations is a somewhat futile whistling in the wind, and the best they can do is to acquire such upstarts and capture what they can of the spirit before it departs to more sympathetic environments (Fisher and Koch 2008).

Yet further complication is added by the fact that organizations, to a degree, choose their environments. The work of Pierce and White (1999, 2006) presents a significant argument in this regard, about the relationship between environmental dependence and the internal logic and culture of an organization. Reviewing a field experiment of macaque colonies, which showed that centralized food supplies generated hierarchical structures and "agonic" (competitive) relationships, while decentralized supply fostered egalitarian and cooperative systems, they argued that the same applied in organizations (Pierce and White 1999). A subsequent laboratory experiment with a human population confirmed the expectation (Pierce and White 2006).

The evolutionary implication is that organizational forms and structures are congruent with their environments, and that classic hierarchical structures are adapted to monolithic supply chains. One may deduce that the forces of globalization and dispersed supply chains presage the new and emerging organizational forms we can see around us: networked, modular, temporary, and cooperative (Lewin and Volberda 1999). Yet if organizations can choose their environments it seems likely that members inured to a culture of a particular type will try to preserve it. The death of many organizations seems to follow this pattern – leaders whose vision stems more from their personal needs for certainty than adaptation to a changing world (Hogan et al. in press). It is such dialectics that drive the waves of revolution and consolidation of business cultures over time.

5 The Nature of Followership

In looking at the situational contingencies that have shaped the ontogeny of human leadership one stands above all others in importance – it is the people providing the social context for the emergence of leadership, the followers. The term followership is in danger of misrepresenting the dynamic of the relationship between the leader and the led, by connoting the former as the active agent and the latter as passive responders. The relationship may indeed take this form or indeed the opposite where leaders are the puppets of their followers. What matters is that followership is a surprisingly little understood or discussed aspect of leadership, with an evolutionary approach having much to say about it.

One of the first scholars in the past century to recognize the lack of research and importance of this topic was Mary Parker Follett (Gilbert and Hyde 1988). She provided the following observation of followership in a 1933 lecture at the Department of Business Administration of the London School of Economics, "... let me speak to you for a moment about something of the utmost importance, but which has been far too little considered, and that is the part of the followers in the leadership situation. Their part is not merely to follow, they have a very active role to play and that is to keep the leader in control of a situation" (Follett 1949, p. 41). Researchers continue to lament the lack of work surrounding followership and its origins (e.g., Bjugstad 2004; Brown 1995; Dixon and Westbrook 2003; Nolan and Harty 2001; Van Vugt and Kurzban 2007). Considering the overwhelming amount of time we spend in followership roles, research is needed to reach a deeper understanding of the motives, attributes, and interests of people who consent to being led.

Given that both leadership and followership can vary enormously in their manifestations, does followership have any defining feature? A starting point is to consider followership as a coordinated investment or commitment of time, resources, energy, and so on in a particular leader to achieve a particular goal. This can be termed "followership investment". The act of supporting or submitting to leadership also involves some degree of risk and constraint as the person surrenders part of their autonomy. Likewise, it is implicitly an issue of motivation, and raises the question of what motivates people to invest in a leader.

It is proposed that the decision to invest will be based on an overall cost/benefit analysis which includes the follower's perception of both the situation and the most desirable leader traits for that situation. From an evolutionary perspective, one answer that has been suggested is "that followership emerged in response to specific ancestral problems that were best solved through collective effort coordinated by a leader-follower structure that enhanced individual and group survival" (Van Vugt et al. 2008a; p. 189). This is consistent with the concept that human social groups evolved to address matters of survival as a means of genetic replication. Moreover, it suggests that survival and reproductive success are primary motivators for following. Yet it is also true that followers often do worse than leaders in terms of proximate goals such as wealth (Switzer 1975) as well as reproductive success (Betzig 1986; Chagnon 1997) and because evolution operates on the basis of relative fitness an explanation is needed for why individuals would consent to being followers.

In all social species risk attends those who become separated from the group, so there is some inertial benefit to being a follower, as Darwin recognized in his book *Descent of Man* (p. 105): "With those animals which were benefited by living in close association, the individuals which took the greatest pleasure in society would best escape various dangers, while those that cared least for their comrades, and lived solitary, would perish in greater numbers". In situations where leaders are appointed or hereditary, becoming a leader may be difficult and often the only choice open to followers is to accept their subordinate position or defect to join another group (Van Vugt et al. 2004) this will be based on the follower's calculus of risks and benefits. One may also note that in social groups where leadership is emergent (rather than hereditary or by appointment), the role is typically contested, which also entails risks for leadership contenders. Losers can forfeit their position in a dominance hierarchy and even suffer more direct threats to their fitness, so acceptance of a subordinate status is for many a rational choice (Nicholson 2000). This pattern has been observed in other species such as Gelada monkeys where the loss of a leadership position results in fitness impairment, in some cases the forfeiture of the right to reproduce.

The establishment of dominance hierarchies is the outcome of multiple and serial calculations by group members of the costs, risks, and possible gains of striving for enhancement. In organizations the phenomenon of organizational "plateauing" is the result of two forces – individuals who have lost out in a tournament contest, and those who have elected to contest no further to avoid the risks (Nicholson 1993; Nicholson and De Waal 2005). Thus, attention should focus on how the follower perceives these possible payouts.

Human rational assessment and behavior is ultimately bounded by the availability of information in the environment and our cognitive limitation to analyze this data. Whether followers are selecting their leader or making a choice whether or not to defect from a led group, their decision has the character of bounded rationality (Gigerenzer and Selten 2002), and decisions (such as who to follow) depend greatly on perception driven heuristics (Simon 1957). Specifically, followership investment and collective action depends on how group members filter this information regarding the environment, the leader, fellow followers, and the utility of one behavior over another.

The primary assumption for followership to occur is that individuals are better off staying together than going alone (Van Vugt 2006). A simple game theory model

	Player 2	
	Waterhole A	Waterhole B
Waterhole A (Player 1)	1,1	0,0
Waterhole B	0,0	1,1

Fig. 1 Coordination game (Adopted from Van Vugt 2006)

shows that when coordination benefits exceed the benefits of "going alone", following becomes the optimal choice (see Fig. 1). Suppose there is a dyadic relationship and both group members benefit equally by traveling together for protection to either waterhole A or B. Conversely, neither member gains the benefit of group security if they travel to separate waterholes. This creates an asymmetric value between individual or coordinated behavior, and ultimately favors coordination for resource attainment. That is, when player 1 makes a move then it is in the interest of player 2 to follow 1 wherever he or she decides to go, to either waterhole A or B.

One implication of this simple waterhole example is that activation of followership may only occur when there is a leadership situation and the leader's intentions or qualities become sufficiently salient (i.e., player 1 displaying initiative and making the first move). At this basic level followership may have the character of herding behavior – following what other followers are doing on the basis of the "wisdom of crowds" rule (Surowiecki 2004). This is akin to Ridley's (1994) account of mate choice among sage grouse. At the "lek", males parade their fine feathers for females to choose those which are presumed to indicate good genes, with the result that typically only around 10% of the males father the next generation. However, it seems that females are not making fine discriminations between males, but imitating other females. Research on mate choice copying as a decision rule for humans finds a similar pattern (Waynforth 2007). Using a related heuristic, followers may often choose to follow leaders who have followers, rather than because of a rational analysis of a leader's qualities.

Where there is a choice to follow or go it alone the motive that is often most relevant to following a leader is people's need to belong (as in Darwin's quote). As Baumeister and Leary (1995, p. 497) explain, "The need to belong is a powerful, fundamental, and extremely pervasive motivation". People rally behind a leader because it adds to the cohesion of the group and cohesive groups are safer places to be. Leaders form a focal point for the coordination of groups. They do not have to do much to achieve this. The monarchs of many modern nations have the status of figureheads rather than active leaders yet by acting as the symbols of their nations they contribute to the cohesion and unity of their peoples. The better an individual can fulfill people's belonging needs the more likely they are to attract followers. This is the notion of prototypical group leadership (Hogg 2001). An individual is more likely to emerge as leader if they match the prevailing group norms and values, for instance, when they hold an opinion that matches the majority of group members. From an evolutionary perspective, it is probably safer to follow someone who shares the dominant norms and values in the group because they are likely to promote cohesion and stability.

A second motive is understanding. Following a leader might be an effective strategy for understanding how the world works and for learning new things especially in unpredictable environments. For instance, for humans who inhabit a world that is changing and unpredictable, surrounded by such varied terrain as forests, tundra, and savannah, gathering food is not straightforward; food comes in many forms, each requiring its own gathering technique. If you are going to eat, and therefore to survive, it pays to be versatile and varied in the way you seek out dinner. And so it pays to learn.

One way of learning is through simple trial and error, which is potentially a very costly strategy. It is time-consuming and risky, since errors can be dangerous. It is preferable to acquire heuristics, strategies, skills, and causal reasoning that improves our understanding of how the world works. The more unpredictable environment the more important such learning is. And what better way to learn than from an individual with the expertise and experience to solve particular problems who then emerges as the leader. One of our first experiences with this sort of learning via leadership is often the inter-generational cultural transmission of parent-leader and child-follower. This innate ability to follow and learn is an important component of our theoretical understanding of the evolution of human leadership. A process for testing such ideas is a logical next step.

6 Testing Evolutionary Hypotheses about Leadership: The Male Warrior vs. Female Peacekeeper Hypothesis (MWFP)

It is important to consider how evolutionary hypotheses about leadership can be tested. Many evolutionary hypotheses emerge in the context of discovery but it is in the context of proof that they are supported or falsified. Evolutionary psychology has been accused of weaving together "just so" stories about human social behavior (Nicholson 2005b). Yet like any other psychology discipline evolutionary psychology generates testable hypotheses that can be supported or falsified through empirical research. To test evolutionary hypotheses about leadership requires one to build a nomological network of interconnected predictions and adopt a multi-methodology approach to test these in different leadership domains (Schmitt and Pilcher 2004). Here we give an example of such an evolutionary hypothesis, based on research two of the authors (Van Vugt and Spisak) conducted on leadership and gender differences. The main hypothesis, informed by an evolutionary approach, is that people with masculine traits are more likely to emerge as leaders during intergroup conflict and people with feminine traits during intragroup conflict. We dub this the Male Warrior-Female Peacekeeper Hypothesis (MWFP-hypothesis).

One way to test this hypothesis is through designing a scenario study, for instance, about a mock presidential election (Van Vugt and Spisak 2008). In one scenario participants are told to imagine that their country is at war and in another that their country faces an internal conflict. Here are the scenarios we used in our study:

War scenario

Your country of Taminia is at war with the neighboring country of Robania. It has been an aggressive, costly, and competitive war with no side willing to concede. Recently, Robania has increased their forces and intensified their bombing raids. This has made everyone exceptionally concerned for their safety. You and your fellow citizens are determined to establish dominance over Robania in order to protect the lands, resources, and people of Taminia. Currently, your country is in the middle of a presidential election. Please select the leadership qualities you are most likely to vote for in a war-time situation, and rate your degree of preference.

Peace scenario

Your country of Taminia has fallen into an economic recession and the two major political parties are experiencing internal differences. As a result, the people are strongly divided on what course of action is necessary to restore Taminia. Recently, disagreements between rival party members have become hostile with small pockets of violence occurring throughout the country. This has caused a growing threat of civil war. However, the general consensus is to avoid internal fighting and resolve disputes without hostility. The citizens of Taminia prefer a wise strategy that includes compromise and cooperation. Currently, your country is in the middle of a presidential election. Please select the leadership qualities you are most likely to vote for to resolve internal conflicts peacefully, and rate your degree of preference.

In one study we simply asked them to indicate their preference for a male or female leader. As predicted in the war scenario there was a strong preference for a male candidate (91.1%) and in the peace scenario a female candidate received the majority of the votes (75.6%) – both differences were statistically significant (Van Vugt and Spisak 2008). This suggests that stereotypical traits of men as aggressive and women as cooperative are traits that followers use when making decisions on followership investment.

In the unpublished data mentioned earlier regarding gender differences we looked at variations in the degree of facial *masculinity versus femininity*. Both men and women vary in their masculinity/femininity and these differences are largely the product of the regulation of sex hormones testosterone and estrogen. Consequently, this suggests leadership opportunities and prototypes may be shaped more finely by biological differences in masculinity or femininity.

To test this we masculinized and feminized both male and female composite facial images which yielded four images types: (a) a masculine looking male, (b) a feminine looking male, (c) a masculine looking female, and (d) a feminine looking female (see Fig. 2). These facial types where then presented as forced-choice pairs (masculine-male vs. feminine-female, masculine-male vs. masculine-female, and

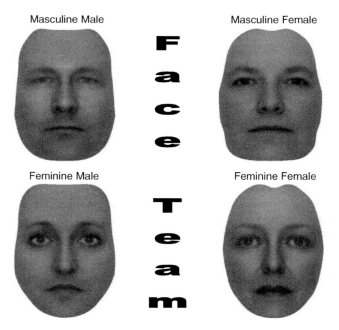

Fig. 2 Examples of masculinzed and femininized face morphs to test evolutionary hypothesis about leadership: The Male Warrior-Female Peacekeeper Hypothesis

so on) with the scenarios cited above and participants were asked to vote for a face they preferred as a leader for each situation. As expected, masculine facial images were voted for more often during war and feminine facial images received the majority of votes during peace. On average masculine face types (both male and female) received 66% of the vote when paired with feminine faces for war and conversely feminine images won 63% of the time during peace.

Furthermore, it appears biological sex was not as strong a predictor of leadership emergence as was masculinity and femininity. For instance we found significant results showing that masculine-looking *female* images were preferred as leaders above feminine-looking *males* during wartime and *feminine-males* over *masculine-females* during peacetime. Also, in the conditions where the facial appearance of gender was constant for the paired faces and biological sex differed (e.g., masculine-male vs. masculine-female for war and feminine-male vs. feminine-female during peace) a probability of chance was observed. These findings offer a very novel approach for understanding the interaction between leadership and gender, and strengthen the need for evolution as a necessary theoretical framework to drive uniquely insightful hypothesis formation in the social sciences. These findings are also reminiscent of the US-presidential study conducted by Little et al. (2007) in which they morphed the Bush and Kerry faces and found that a masculine looking candidate (Bush) was preferred in a situation when the US was facing a war.

A third way to test evolutionary hypotheses about leadership is through economic game experiments. Research by Van Vugt and Spisak (2008) placed participants in groups of five to play a step-level public-goods game. The basic objective of this game is to reach a predetermined degree of collect investment from individual donations of group members. For this particular game each participant was given £3 and if the group investment reached a total of £12 (i.e., an average individual donation of 80%), every player received a £5 bonus in addition to the amount they kept in their private fund. However, if the level is not reached everyone loses their investment and merely keeps the amount remaining in their private fund. This creates an obvious dilemma for each player. Should they donate their funds to the group, trusting that the other members will act accordingly, or opt for a selfish strategy? Fundamentally, a public-goods game is a measure of cooperation, indicting how much individuals are prepared to sacrifice in order to help their group (Hardy and Van Vugt 2006).

Also, players in the Van Vugt and Spisak (2008) game were placed either in an intra- or intergroup conflict situation: One group of participants were told that the aim of the study was to "examine how well individual players are doing in group investment games and compare the results between individual players within each of the groups" (intragroup competition condition) and the second group was advised to "examine how well groups of players from different English universities are doing in these group investment games and compare the results between different universities" (intergroup competition condition). Respectively, the purpose of this manipulation was to make salient a dynamic of either cooperation within the group or the sense of competition between groups. As explained previously in this chapter, it is expected that followers experiencing diverse situation requirements for goal attainment will prefer different leadership traits. Hybrid and control conditions were also part of the design. In addition to manipulating the situation dynamics, teams were assigned either a fictitious male or female leader of the group. Participants were provided with a name and short biography of their fictitious leader. The primary goal of this study was to examine a change in the level of cooperation (i.e., financial investment) as the follower's perceptions of the situation and leader were modified.

As expected, players contributed more to the group fund when (1) a male leader was assigned to intergroup competition and (2) a female leader was paired with the intragroup condition. This suggests that as the demands of the situation shift so do the prototypical preferences of the leader. Moreover, this relationship is in-line with our theoretical understanding of evolved leadership prototypes resulting from coordination problems routinely encountered in our environment. There are a variety of opportunities for further economic games experimentation on the MWFP-hypothesis. For example, does a feminine leader enhance cooperation between groups in an environment where conflict and cooperation are both potential outcomes? Likewise, will cooperation between groups turn into conflict with a masculine leader prototype? Also, will a group perform better or worse in these games when there is a leadership team rather than a single leader? Finally, what can this tell us about application to increase organizational performance or reduce violence between groups?

A fourth way of testing the hypothesis would be to conduct an archival study in which we look at instances of masculine and feminine like leaders in the history of nations or businesses. For instance, this could be done by trait assessment from content analysis of speeches given by these leaders, and rating their photographs in terms of masculinity/femininity. We could then gather data about the situation surrounding the election of these individuals and mark them in terms of either a risk of external conflict or internal conflict. Support for the MWFP-hypothesis would be obtained if there is a higher incidence of male or masculine leaders during external threats and female or feminine leaders during situations in which groups are committed to peaceful relations (post-war settlements).

An initial attempt for such an analysis would be looking at companies that are both relatively old and large to provide a diverse and extensive amount of data and build a highly comprehensive model of organizational evolution. This data should contain personality information about former CEO's and managers and changes in environmental conditions (e.g., economic fluctuations) as well as the company's evolving leadership, culture, mission, and so on over a temporally and geographically sufficient scale. Certain older multinationals can meet these requirements, where their history of leadership reflects the historical impacts of war, depression, the rise of the American middle class, and so on. Many multinationals have also experienced massive expansion across the globe providing opportunities to observe leadership emergence and followership behavior cross-culturally. Such companies provide models to observe and predict changes in organizational leadership consistent with evolutionary hypotheses such as the MWFP-hypothesis.

Fifth, we could use the tools of game theory (Maynard-Smith 1982; Van Vugt et al. 2008) to model the emergence and effectiveness of masculine leaders during war time and feminine leaders during peace time. Using computer simulations we could introduce agents into a space where they interact with other agents. These agents either adopt an aggressive "masculine" strategy (e.g., they make unprovoked attacks against their neighbors) or a peaceful "feminine" strategy (e.g., they cooperate with their neighbors unless the neighbor attacks them and then they retaliate; cf. Tit-for-Tat). By varying aspects of the environment - for instance, is an individual player surrounded mostly by "masculine" or "feminine" players - we can then look at the success of each of these strategies and their increase (or decrease) over many generations. It is the underlying evolutionary strategies of aggression to gain resources (i.e., masculine) or peace to maintain stability for rearing offspring (i.e., feminine) that is of consideration.

Finally, we can use genetics studies to examine which genes are likely to be involved in the male warrior and female peacekeeper syndromes/proclivities. It has been asserted that the gene MAO-A plays a role in the onset of aggressiveness in males by affecting serotonin levels. It has been dubbed the male warrior gene in the popular literature. Males with one variant of this gene are indeed more likely to join youth gangs (Beaver et al. 2009) and make unprovoked attacks in war games (McDermott et al. 2008).

7 Some Conclusions and Implications

From the theory of evolution we glean deeper insight into the origins of leadership and followership in our species. This knowledge can ultimately help to design organizations that work with or around our evolved tendencies to select and follow leaders. We note four implications.

Gender and leadership. The potential of female senior leadership is often overlooked in corporations. Although male leadership is still the norm in most business organizations, reflecting our ancestral biases to select masculine leaders in competitive environments - an overabundance of male leaders in other organizational types such as NGOs which pursue more communal and cooperative not-for-profit bottom-lines is potentially limiting. However, even in competitive market driven organizations excessive masculine leadership can have negative consequences on the for-profit bottom-line.

The logic of co-evolution applies. Earlier we considered the drivers of congruence and incongruence within organizations – between leaders, members, and subcultures – and between organizations and their environments. Human agency, the ability to imagine and bring about future states, is arguably the quality that most distinguishes us from any other species. This drives co-evolution by enabling "purposive organization". We noted from the work of Pierce and White (2006) that external forces may predispose organizations toward hierarchical agonic vs. egalitarian cooperative forms. But we also argued that this may be a matter of choice – there is more than one way to organize to achieve organizational goals. Traditionally, business organizations have been dominated in management and leadership by men, and one can reason that there may be a bias towards electing for forms of organization that give maximum play to the needs of dominant males, dominance hierarchies, focused task allocation, and competitive striving. This suggests that competitive hierarchies, division of labor, and tournament promotion systems arise not so much because they uniquely fit the external environment, but because they are within the comfort zone of their primary agents, masculine-men (Nicholson 2000).

If the forces of globalization and social development are moving organizations in the direction of flatter structures, multitasking, and cooperation, then these are conditions that in the future will require more feminine approaches to leadership. But whether we see an increase in the frequency of female leadership will depend on how men of power will facilitate the evolution of structures towards one that render themselves as less valuable. Leaders currently in these top positions who are less willing to encourage feminine approaches at high levels will ultimately hinder their organizations viability in the global arena. For example recent research has found that testosterone is associated with financial risk-taking (Apicella et al. 2008), which in excess (as we have seen in the global credit crisis) can be harmful for organizations and some have claimed that with more women at the helm of international banks and businesses the economic depression could have been avoided. Increasing female senior leadership is therefore not just a matter of equality but also of common sense.

Corresponding to the dearth of female leadership at senior levels and unsustainable risk-taking is the tendency for masculine leaders to express an abundance of dominant traits. This behavior, though effective for asserting oneself into leadership roles, does not necessarily yield an optimal match between the leader and the situation. As research has shown, imposed dominant leadership can create negativity amongst those expected to follow (Van Vugt et al. 2004), which may also apply when a dominant leader is elected and the follower is not in a position to leave the group (e.g., for economic reasons). A possible solution is establishing mechanisms within the institution to control the proliferation of aggressive individuals – a common task in tribal societies that have predominated throughout our ancestral history (Nicholson 2005a). This may apply to the military, and to a lesser extent, corporations and other establishments that assume a hierarchal structure and/or that measure success through economic competition.

To make the MWFP-hypothesis tangible lets consider the explicit differences between Google and Enron. The so-called "Google Culture" emphasizes a relaxed, nurturing, and cooperative global environment while striving for a "small company feel" – a feminine culture. Their overwhelming success with this culture supports our argument for the advantages of feminine leadership styles in modern and highly connected environments. On the other hand in Enron's leadership and culture, hierarchical and dominant leadership – which one sees predominantly in all male groups - mixed with an artificial environment of hyper-competiveness became a catalyst for the company's infamous accountancy practices and terminal failure. In order for organizations with similar faults to avoid such catastrophic ends they should start by thoroughly digesting the remaining three implications.

The social construction of leadership. Much has been written about the romantic idealization of leadership (Keller 1999; Meindl et al. 1985), which had led to some writers arguing that contemporary forms, including the relative exclusion of women, are due to our suffusion in an ideological orthodoxy. We agree that the imagery of leadership is important, and often followers respond to more the ciphers of leadership, as represented in their PR, than in the reality of their imperfect characters. We also accept that leaders play up to the dominant imagery – akin to gorilla chest beating to demonstrate power – without it actually having to be put to the test. Yet, as in other primates, our displays have underlying utilities that can be tested. The world may be socially constructed through dialogue, contested meanings and imagery, but the meanings are not arbitrary; they are rooted in the underlying values of biological utilities. This is the familiar yet convoluted paths by which proximate goals draw their energy from distal goals (Barrett et al. 2002.), but the form they take follows the rules of translation set by the context.

Thus even in modern society we find tall leaders favored over shorter others, regardless that the distal utility from our ancestral past will never be realized (Judge and Cable 2004), that is, we will almost never have to depend upon our leaders' physical attributes for any supposed benefits they may confer (cf. mismatch hypotheses; Van Vugt et al. 2008). Women are likewise undoubtedly disadvantaged by failing to measure up to the imagery of heroic leadership, though the disconnect between the distal and the proximate in contemporary settings is so complete that this is hopefully a waning source of disadvantage to women's prospects. These, as we have argued, are more due to the unconducive nature of the most senior leadership roles for women in most organizations.

Distributed leadership. Another implication of our contingent evolutionary analysis of leadership and organizational forms is the potential benefits of distributed leadership. In ancestral groups various individuals performed different leadership roles but in modern societies the tendency is to invest power in single individuals. However, there are many examples of co-leadership, and in many large and complex businesses, leaders have critical partnerships that underlie their success (e.g., between Chief Executives, Chairman, Finance Directors, and other significant power holders; Alvarez and Svejenova 2005; Heenan and Bennis 1999; Nicholson 2008; O'Toole et al. 2002). The SPQ logic (Situations, Processes, Qualities) introduced earlier, coupled with our co-evolutionary arguments, suggests that power sharing models should become more frequent as organizations' environments and structures become more complex and uncertain, and their strategies become more demanding. Thus we find organizations such as Google, McKinsey, and Bloomberg that operate with diverse and complex information, with varied and deep client needs, require strong yet fluid networks of internal collaboration and multi-local centers of power.

Understanding followership. A final implication of our evolutionary analysis is appreciating the role of followership. As we have mentioned in this chapter the leadership literature has paid little attention so far to the position and nature of followers (Van Vugt et al. 2008). Organizations that can understand the needs and desires of their followership base may be better equipped to manage their human capital and adjust to change. We propose taking an approach that incorporates our understanding of evolved human behavior to foster a deeper understanding of how followers engage with their organizations. With the exception of particular threats such as intra- or intergroup conflicts it may be best for leaders to leave individuals alone and let them do their jobs with relative autonomy (Van Vugt et al. 2008). Leader-follower dynamics evolved for the purpose of addressing specific group threats in our ancestral environment (Van Vugt et al. 2008) and outside these threats most employees simply wish to be left alone. Managers should recognize and avoid the tendency towards excessive leadership.

In summary, this chapter has offered a novel explanation for the much researched phenomenon of leadership and followership that incorporates a current understanding of human evolution. Given the various sources we have enlisted to develop our argument, it is clear that a complete understanding of leadership, and equally important, followership needs to take a multidisciplinary approach including all the behavioral sciences from psychology to biology. Future work will want to build upon this theoretical framework to clearly define a followership typology that considers our innate tendencies and how that interacts with modern environments. The theory of evolution can provide a means by which to connect these disjointed aspects of our knowledge on leadership and shed new light on a particularly influential component of group and organizational processes.

References

Alvarez JL, Svejenova S (2005) Sharing executive power. Cambridge University Press, Cambridge
Apicella CL, Dreber A, Campbell B, Gray PB, Hoffman M, Little AC (2008) Testosterone and financial risk preferences. Evol Hum Behav 29:384–390
Arvey RD, Rotundo M, Johnson W, Zhang Z, McGue M (2006) The determinants of leadership role occupancy: genetic and personality factors. Leadership Quar 17:1–20
Astley WG (1985) The two ecologies: population and community perspectives on organizational evolution. Adm Sci Q 30:224–241
Barrett L, Dunbar R, Lycett J (2002) Human evolutionary psychology. Palgrave, Basingstoke
Baumeister RF, Leary MR (1995) The need to belong: desire for interpersonal attachments as a fundamental human motivation. Psychol Bull 117:497–529
Beaver KM, DeLisi M, Wright JP, Vaughn MG (2009) Gene environment interplay and delinquent involvement: Evidence of direct, indirect, and interactive effects. J Adolescent Res 24:147–168
Betzig LL (1986) Despotism and differential reproduction: a Darwinian view of history. Aldine, Hawthorne
Betzig L (1993) Sex, succession, and stratification in the first six civilizations: how powerful men reproduced, passed power on to their sons, and used power to defend their wealth, women, and children. In: Ellis L (ed) Social stratification and socioeconomic inequality, vol 1. Praeger, Westport, pp 37–74
Bjugstad K (2004) Internet book search on leadership and followership [Online]Retrieved: http://www.amazon.com.html [15 Oct. 2004].
Boehm C (1999) Hierarchy in the forest: the evolution of egalitarian behavior. Harvard University Press, Cambridge
Brown DE (1991) Human universals. McGraw-Hill, New York
Brown T (1995) Great leaders need great followers: interview with Ira Chaleff, author of Courageous Follower. Industry Weekly 244(16):25
Buss DM (1991) Evolutionary personality psychology. Annu Rev Psychol 42:459–491
Buss DM (2003) The evolution of desire: strategies of human mating. Basic Books, New York
Chagnon NA (1997) Yanomamo. Harcourt, Fort Worth
Chell E, Haworth J, Brearley S (1991) The entrepreneurial personality: concepts, cases and categories. Routledge, London
Coon CS (1979) The hunting peoples. Penguin, New York
Darwin C (1871) The descent of man. Appleton, London
Dawkins R (1976) The selfish gene. Oxford University Press, New York
De Cremer D, Van Vugt M (2002) Intergroup and intragroup aspects of leadership in social dilemmas: a relational model of cooperation. J Exp Soc Psychol 38:126–136
De Waal FBM (1989a) Chimpanzee politics: power and sex among apes. John Hopkins Press, Baltimore
De Waal FBM (1989b) Peacemaking among primates. Harvard University Press, Cambridge
Diamond J (1997) Guns, germs, and steel. Random House, New York
Dixon G, Westbrook J (2003) Followers revealed. Eng Manage J 15(1):19–25
Dorfman PW, Hanges PJ, Brodbeck FC (2004) Leadership and cultural variation: the identification of culturally endorsed leadership profiles. In: House RJ, Hanges PJ, Javidan M, Dorfman PW, Gupta V (eds) Culture, leadership, and organizations: the GLOBE study of 62 societies. Sage, Thousand Oaks, pp 669–722
Drath WH, McCauley CD, Palus CJ, Van Velsor E, O'Connor PMG, McGuire JB (2008) Direction, alignment, commitment: towards a more integrative ontology of leadership. Leadership Quar 19:635–653
Dunbar RIM (1998) The social brain hypothesis. Evol Anthropol 6:178–190
Dunbar RIM (2004) Grooming, gossip, and the evolution of language. Faber & Faber: London
Fisher JL, Koch JV (2008) Born not made: the entrepreneurial personality. Praeger, Westport

Follett MP (1949) The essentials of leadership. Management Publications Trust, Ltd., London
Gigerenzer G, Selten R (2002) Bounded rationality: the adaptive toolbox. MIT Press, Boston
Gilbert GR, Hyde AC (1988) Followership and the federal worker. Public Adm Rev 48(6): 962–968
Gordon G, Nicholson N (2008) Family wars. Kogan Page, London
Hardy CL, Van Vugt M (2006) Nice guys finish first: the competitive altruism hypothesis. Pers Soc Psychol Bull 32:1402–1413
Heenan DA, Bennis W (1999) Co-leaders: the power of great partnerships. Wiley, New York
Heinrich J (2004) Cultural group selection, coevolutionary processes and large-scale cooperation. J Econ Behav Organ 53:3–35
Hodgson DL (2001) Once intrepid warriors. Indiana University Press, Bloomington
Hofstede G (1982) Values survey module (Tech. Paper). Institute for Research on Intercultural Cooperation, Maastricht
Hogan J, Hogan R, Kaiser RB (in press) Management derailment: personal assessment and mitigation. In: Zedeck S (ed) American Psychological Association handbook of industrial and organizational psychology. American Psychological Society, Washington, DC
Hogg MA (2001) A social identity theory of leadership. Pers Soc Psychol Rev 5:184–200
Hollander EP (1978) Leadership dynamics: a practical guide to effective relationships. Free Press Macmillan, New York
Johnson AM, Vernon PA, McCarthy JM, Molso M, Harris JA, Jang KJ (1998) Nature vs nurture: are leaders born or made? A behavior genetic investigation of leadership style. Twin Res 1:216–223
Johnson DDP, Van Vugt M (2009) A history of war: The role of inter-group conflict in sex differences in aggression. Behav Brain Sci 32:280–281
Judge TA, Bono JE, Ilies R, Gerhardt MW (2002) Personality and leadership: a qualitative and quantitative review. J Appl Psychol 87:765–780
Judge TA, Cable DM (2004) The effect of physical height on workplace success and income. J Appl Psychol 89:428–441
Kagan J (1994) Galen's prophesy: temperament in human nature. Basic Books, New York
Keeley LH (1996) Warfare before civilization: the myth of the peaceful savage. Oxford University Press: Oxford
Keller T (1999) Images of the familiar: Individual differences and implicit leadership theories. Leadership Quar 10:589–607
Kets de Vries MRF (1997) The leadership mystique. In: Grint K (ed) Leadership: classical, contemporary and critical approaches. Oxford University Press, Oxford, pp 250–271
Kets De Vries M (1999) High-performance teams: lessons from the Pygmies. Organ Dyn 27:66–77
Lewin AY, Volberda HW (1999) Prolegomena on coevolution: a framework for research on strategy and new organizational forms. Organ Sci 10:519–534
Little AC, Burriss RP, Jones BC, Roberts SC (2007) Facial appearance affects voting decisions. Evol Hum Behav 28:18–27
Lord RG, Hall RJ (1992) Contemporary views of leadership and individual differences. Leadership Quar 3(2):137–157
Lord RG, Maher KJ (1991) Leadership and information processing: Linking perceptions and performance. Unwin Hyman: Boston
Maynard-Smith J (1982) Evolution and the theory of games. Cambridge University Press, Cambridge
McDermott R, Cowden JA, Rosen S (2008) The role of hostile communications in a crisis simulation game. J Peace Psychol 14(2):151–168
Meindl J, Ehrlich SB, Dukerich JM (1985) The romance of leadership. Adm Sci Q 30:78–102
Nettle D (2006) The evolution of personality variation in humans and other animals. Am Psychol 61:622–631
Nicholson N (1993) Purgatory or place of safety? The managerial plateau and organisational agegrading. Hum Relat 46:1369–1389
Nicholson N (2000) Managing the human animal. Texere, London

Nicholson N (2005a) Meeting the Maasai: messages for management. J Manage Inq 14:255–267
Nicholson N (2005b) Objections to evolutionary psychology: reflections, implications and the leadership exemplar. Hum Relat 26:137–154
Nicholson N (2008) Critical leader relationships. Working Paper, London Business School
Nicholson N (2010) Leadership: integrating theory and practice through the SPQ framework. Working Paper, London Business School
Nicholson N, De Waal AW (2005) Playing to win: biological imperatives, self-regulation and trade-offs in the game of career success. J Organ Behav 26:137–154
Nolan JS, Harty HF (2001) Followership ≥ leadership. Education 104(3):311–312
O'Gorman R, Henrich J, Van Vugt M (2008) Constraining free riding in public goods games: designated solitary punishers can sustain human cooperation. Proceedings of the Royal Society B, 276, 323–329
O'Toole J, Galbraith J, Lawler EE (2002) When two (or more) heads are better than one: the promise and pitfalls of shared leadership. Calif Manage Rev 44:65–83
Penke L, Denissen JJA, Miller GF (2007) The evolutionary genetics of personality. Eur J Pers 21:549–587
Penton-Voak IS, Chen JY (2004) High salivary testosterone is linked to masculine male facial appearance in humans. Evol Hum Behav 25:229–241
Pettigrew AM (1979) On studying organizational culture. Adm Sci Q 24:570–581
Pierce BD, White R (1999) The evolution of social structure: why biology matters. Acad Manage Rev 24:843–853
Pierce BD, White R (2006) Resource context contestability and emergent social structure: an empirical investigation of an evolutionary theory. J Organ Behav 27:221–240
Richerson PJ, Boyd R (2005) Not by genes alone: how culture transformed human evolution. University of Chicago Press, Chicago
Ridley M (1994) The Red Queen: sex and the evolution of human nature. Penguin, Harmondsworth
Saad G (2003) Evolution and political marketing. In: Peterson SA, Somit A (eds) Human nature and public policy: an evolutionary approach. Palgrave Macmillan, New York, pp 121–138
Saitoti TO (1986) The worlds of a Maasai warrior: an autobiography. Random House, New York
Schmitt DP, Pilcher JJ (2004) Evaluating evidence of psychological adaptation: how do we know one when we see one? Psychol Sci 15:643–649
Sellers JG, Mehl MR, Josephs RA (2007) Hormones and personality: testosterone as a marker of individual differences. J Res Pers 41:126–138
Silk JB (2007) The strategic dynamics of cooperation in primate groups. Adv Study Behav 37:1–42
Simon HA (1957) Administrative behavior. MacMillan, New York
Smith DB (2008) The people make the place: dynamic linkages between individuals and organization. Erlbaum, New York
Sober E, Wilson DS (1998) Unto others: the evolution and psychology of unselfish behavior, Boston: Harvard University Press
Surowiecki J (2004) The wisdom of crowds: why the many are smarter than the few and how collective wisdom shapes business, economies, societies and nations. Little, Brown, New York
Switzer KA (1975) Peasant leadership: comparisons of peasant leaders in two Colombian states. Int J Comp Sociol 16:291–300
Van Velsor E, Leslie JB (1995) Why executives derail: perspectives across time and cultures. Acad Manage Exec 9:62–73
Van Vugt M (2006) The evolutionary origins of leadership and followership. Pers Soc Psychol Rev 10:354–372
Van Vugt M (2009) Despotism, democracy and the evolutionary dynamics of leadership and followership. Am Psychol 64:54–56
Van Vugt M, Ahuja A (2010) Selected: Why some people lead, why others follow and why it matters; What evolutionary psychology tells us about leadership and what makes an outstanding leader. Profile, London

Van Vugt M, Kurzban RK (2007) Cognitive and social adaptations for leadership and followership: evolutionary game theory and group dynamics. In: Forgas J, von Hippel W, Haselton M (eds) The evolution of the social mind: evolutionary psychology and social cognition, vol 9, Sydney symposium of social psychology. Psychology Press, London, pp 229–244

Van Vugt M, Spisak BR (2008) Sex differences in leadership emergence during competitions within and between groups. Psychol Sci 19:854–858

Van Vugt M, Jepson S, Hart C, De Cremer D (2004) Autocratic leadership in social dilemmas: a threat to group stability. J Exp Soc Psychol 40:1–13

Van Vugt M, Hogan R, Kaiser R (2008a) Leadership, followership, and evolution: some lessons from the past. Am Psychol 63:182–196

Van Vugt M, Johnson D, Kaiser R, O'Gorman R (2008b) Evolution and the social psychology of leadership: the mismatch hypothesis. In: Hoyt C, Forsyth D, Goethals A (eds) Leadership at the crossroads, vol 1, Leadership and psychology. Praeger, West Port, pp 267–282

Waynforth D (2007) Mate choice copying in humans. Hum Nat 18:264–271

Whiten A (1999) The evolution of deep social mind in humans. In: Corballis M, Lea SEG (eds) The decsent of mind. Oxford University Press, Oxford, pp 155–175

Williams GC (1975) Sex and evolution. Princeton University Press, Princeton

Wilson DS, Van Vugt M, O'Gorman R (2008) Multilevel selection theory and major evolutionary transitions: implications for psychological science. Curr Dir Psychol Sci 17:6–9

Wrangham R (2009) Catching fire: how cooking made us human. Basic Books, New York

Wrangham RW, Peterson D (1996) Demonic Males: Apes and the origins of human violence. Houghton Mifflin, New York

Hardwired to Monitor: An Empirical Investigation of Agency-Type Social Contracts in Business Organizations

David M. Wasieleski

Abstract This chapter, grounded in empirical analysis, supports the position adopted by evolutionary psychologists that the human brain is hardwired to solve adaptive problems involving social exchange relationships. First, the evolutionary psychology hypothesis regarding social exchange is presented and explained in terms of its relevance to business. It is argued that the presence of cheater-detection/social-contract neural algorithms is ubiquitous among all members of a human population regardless of formal business training. In Study 1, I test the hypothesis on a sample of 300 business practitioners and students. Additionally, this study examines whether human brain circuits are structured to recognize agency-type arrangements in firms. In a second experiment, the effect of organizational work experience was tested to discover whether there exist moderating factors on the activation of cheater-detection circuits in a business context. It is posited that although corporate agents' minds are biologically evolved to identify violators in social contract situations, the neural circuits responsible for detecting these breaches are influenced by organizational components including, organizational culture, that affect individuals' perceptions of the terms of the exchange. Implications for business practitioners and researchers are offered.

Keywords Agency relationships · Business ethics · Cheating · Evolutionary psychology · Monitoring · Perception · Social contracts

1 Introduction and Purpose

Business firms are an outgrowth of natural processes. Their formation, maintenance, and survival are made possible by the physical, biological, and psychological machinery of nature. Corporations originated for instrumental purposes and

D.M. Wasieleski
Duquesne University, 918 Rockwell Hall, 600 Forbes Avenue, 15282 Pittsburgh, PA, USA
e-mail: wasieleski@duq.edu

served as a means to an end. What may not be easily accomplished by individuals alone may be quite feasible when the efforts of several individuals are combined toward a single purpose or mission. Throughout evolutionary time, individuals achieved goals by entering into exchanges with other individuals in their social group (i.e., tribe or band). Organizations serve a similar purpose for society by facilitating humans' ability to economize—form structures and develop processes that prudently and practically generate benefit from a given level of resources—in their natural world (Frederick 1995).

Organizations are also described as a nexus of contracts, whether they take the form of written agreements or informal understandings (Jensen and Meckling 1976). For any organization to function properly, these binding agreements between two or more parties must be upheld. They are a necessary feature of firms, without which achievement of organizational goals would be impossible (Robinson et al. 1994; Leana and Rousseau 2002). The breaking of agreements between individuals is widely recognized in organizational life as a serious impediment to an efficiently operating organization (Eisenhardt 1989). Breached good faith agreements between two or more individuals are a chronic feature of modern business. Scandals associated with the 2009 financial crisis all involved a broken contract of some sort. Certainly the multitude of people who entrusted their investments with Bernie Madoff did not anticipate that their assets had been used in a Ponzi scheme. This unethical behavior may be traced back to human ancestry (Heinrich 2006). If individuals who form these agreements with each other in organizational settings are biologically equipped to interact contractually in a certain way, it is not difficult to believe that evolutionary forces are in part responsible for the formation and failure of relationships in firms.

In this chapter I describe an empirical research project that tests for the presence of cheater-detection/social-contract neural algorithms in a sample of undergraduate business students, as an extension of the research conducted and led by evolutionary psychologists, Leda Cosmides and John Tooby (Cosmides 1989; Cosmides and Tooby 1999; Tooby and Cosmides 1992; Cosmides and Tooby 2005; Ermer et al. 2006). In their work, they hypothesize that modern-day individuals are 'hardwired' to recognize violators of conditional rules in certain conditions resembling a social contract (i.e., agreements between two parties). Based on the theoretical groundwork laid by evolutionary psychology and other natural science disciplines, I examine whether human brain circuits are able to recognize one specific type of social relationship in firms— agency arrangements. The agency problem—the dilemma of not having an agent behave in the way directed by the principal— "exists in all organizations and in all cooperative efforts—at every level of management in firms..." (Jensen and Meckling 1976: 309) This moral hazard can also take the form of a conflict between various agents within a given firm, such as between executives and the shareholders that they represent (Miller and Whitford 2007). Given its ubiquity in corporations, the agency relationship serves as an interesting, common organizational arrangement in modern-day businesses for this study and thus, is the study's behavioral context. These relationships are thought to pervade management and organization theory (Ross et al. 1997).

In this line of inquiry, the major research question explored is: Assuming that social-contract/cheater-detection algorithms exist among a population of business practitioners, what organizational factors could be responsible for influencing the activation of the social-contract algorithms among members in a business population? Ultimately, the central thesis is: *Although corporate agents' minds are biologically evolved to identify cheaters in social contract situations, the neural machinery responsible for detecting these breaches is influenced by organizational and cultural components that affect the individuals' perceptions of the terms of the exchange.*

Recently, insights from evolutionary psychology have been applied to a variety of organizational contexts. While the usefulness of the approach has been debated (Markoczy and Goldberg 2004; Pava 2009; Sewell 2004), much attention has been given to the applicability of evolutionary theory to cooperative relationships within organizations (Hill and Buss 2006; Loch et al. 2006; Price 2006; Nicholson 2008). The first major goal of this study is to introduce Cosmides and Tooby's approach to the business ethics and organizational behavior fields. Within the field of evolutionary psychology, the Cosmides-Tooby approach to understanding social exchange stems from the simple premise that the human brain is comprised of a series of content-specific programs (i.e., domain-specific) that regulate behavior. They claim that in order to understand culture and human adaptations over time, it is necessary to not think of the brain as a 'blank slate' but rather, as a network of interrelated, specific programs each designed by natural selection to solve particular adaptive problems that faced our ancestors. These ancestrally formed programs still operate in modern human brains and are largely responsible for the formation of human culture. (Cosmides and Tooby 2004) Their research stream has been validated and respected in the evolutionary psychology literature for years (Buss 2009; Dennett 1995; Gaulin and McBurney 2001; Nicholson 1997; Wasieleski and Weber 2009). It has been used to discover how individuals reason through social dilemmas involving cooperation, punishment, reciprocity, and cheating. However, as this current study highlights, the approach taken by Cosmides and Tooby does not tell us the whole story. Aspects of culture, specifically in this study, organizational culture, do influence perceptions and judgments in the brain (Fehr and List 2004; Nicholson 2008). An alternate view of the human brain favors a blank-slate conception (Pinker 2002), which posits that the circuits in the brain are useful across contexts; that information is gathered from multiple domains and derived from perceptions of the environment. Thus, a second goal of this study is to integrate Cosmides and Tooby's content-specific view of the brain with the opposing content-free, or 'domain-general' view of the brain (i.e., absent of any subject matter) within the evolutionary psychology field.

This research utilizes the Integrated Causal Model (ICM) as the conceptual foundation of human behavior, rather than the Standard Social Science Model (SSSM), which has been governing the social science disciplines for decades. Essentially, the SSSM claims that some inference procedures governed by the brain are domain-general, or content-free. In this model, the human brain gathers its knowledge about human behavior and cultural phenomena from perception of direct common human experiences. The model is defined by the reliance on the blank slate, and the exclusive focus on learning, culture, and socialization as explanatory agents of behavior (Tooby and Cosmides 1992). The ICM takes a step back from social science-dominated explanations of behavior and assumes that cultural phenomena are derived from natural manifestations of selection pressures acting upon our prehistoric (i.e., Pleistocene) ancestors. It recognizes that the human mind is composed of domain-specific modules that were selected evolutionarily to solve various adaptive problems. One of these adaptive problems facing our ancestors was cooperation in social exchanges (Cosmides and Tooby 1995; Tooby and Cosmides 1992). These social exchange mechanisms in turn, generate elements of human culture. Thus, the model of human motivation in this paper reflects the social and cultural nature as well as the biological impulses of human beings, as a strategy for finding consistency between evolutionary psychology and cultural explanations of behavior in the corporate world.

Lastly, in this project, I expand Cosmides and Tooby's approach to social contracts, which only involves dyadic exchange partners, by examining the effect of organizational hierarchies on business practitioners' perceptions of violations of rules in a social contract. For the first time in the evolutionary psychology literature, agency-type arrangements to social exchange are introduced and examined in terms of the monitoring of cheating behavior. Modern-day organizational structures are likely to involve power differentials in the ranks of the firm where social contract rules are being evaluated by a third party who acts as an agent of the organization's owner (Hastings and Shaffer 2008). Our Pleistocene ancestors were also placed in social arrangements with power differences (Cummins 1998). While the evolutionary psychology field acknowledges the fact that these hierarchical relationships in social groups were familiar to our ancient predecessors, the field has not explored or empirically tested the operation of neural algorithms—the brain circuits responsible for performing specific tasks—related to social exchanges in this more complex context. This contribution is presented in the current chapter.

The chapter is structured in the following manner: To start, the theoretical background of evolutionary theory and social exchange is presented. Based on that foundation, the evolutionary psychology approach to social exchanges is offered with a focus on the Cosmides and Tooby hypothesis, as defined above.

2 Theoretical Background

As mentioned in the previous section, some of the most important adaptive problems that faced our ancestors were to "navigate the social world" (Cosmides and Tooby 2000b: 1259). Social exchange is defined as cooperation among individuals to achieve mutual benefit (Cosmides and Tooby 1989). In the Pleistocene Era, the period in which modern human minds are thought to have formed, our hominid ancestors lived and operated mainly as hunter-gatherers who were used to life in small groups of no more than 150 individuals (Lee and DeVore 1968; Greenwood and Stini 1977). It was within these small groups that most exchanges took place.

While many of the members of any particular band were likely to be genetically related, humans at this time did cavort with non-kin. For evolutionary psychologists, this is an important point. In dealing with non-kin, individuals had to be able know with whom to engage in social exchanges. Humans' mental capacities and physical capabilities evolved in this small-band context for millennia. "Our species spent over 99% of its evolutionary history as hunter-gatherers in Pleistocene environments" (Cosmides and Tooby 1987: 280). Their position is that ancestral conditions over that formulative period of time have more of an influence on the way humans are designed than do conditions in the modern industrialized age in which we live. According to Cosmides and Tooby, only in recent evolutionary history did humans begin to interact in much larger groups. While other evolutionary theorists dispute this point and believe that our ancestors were accustomed to interacting within larger groups composed of non-kin members (Fehr and Fischbacher 2004), the important point to remember is that modern conditions could not possibly have had the time to manipulate the physical and mental structures of individuals. Contemporary humans are a product of their evolutionary past, and that past was a very different world than it is today. Through natural selection, design structures emerge which offer fitness characteristics, facilitating survival. It zeroes in on an adaptive problem caused by our ancestral environment and addresses the problem with a particular morphological trait. For instance, various physical traits possessed by present-day humans formed because they originally served a survival purpose for our ancestors (e.g., 5-digit hands, sense of smell, bi-pedal ability to walk, etc.).

One of the adaptive problems faced by our ancestors was how to interact with others (kin and non-kin) in small groups. This challenge is not addressed merely by physical adaptations alone. Rather, for two individuals to communicate and engage in a social exchange for some kind of benefit, the human mind would have had to evolve a form that facilitated it to negotiate social interaction functions. In an increasingly social world in the Pleistocene, humans needed to develop the ability to know how to enter into agreements with non-kin, know when to engage in social contracts, and with whom to interact, and with whom to avoid. Today, in the twenty-first Century, human beings still face this challenge, even if the contexts have become more complex. The neural machinery used in the modern world is the same circuitry that evolved in this prehistoric period (Tooby et al. 2008). The next section of this chapter is about this neural circuitry, and why it formed to address social exchanges. Once the evolutionary psychology approach to understanding social contracts is presented, and the Cosmides and Tooby social contract hypothesis is described, I will offer new theoretical links of my own that will expand upon what has already been empirically studied.

2.1 The Evolutionary Psychology Approach to Social Exchanges

Evolutionary psychology is an approach or way of thinking about any field in the psychology paradigm, so that its basic tenets can be applied to sensation, consciousness, learning, motivation, social behavior, and cognition (Gaulin and McBurney 2001). The same natural selection processes that lead to the design of the physical features of organisms' bodies, lead to the design of the structure of the mind as well. Physical forms evolved from the functions they serve for the organism that possess them. Essentially, evolutionary psychology is the integration of evolutionary biology, biological anthropology, and cognitive psychology (Tooby and Cosmides 1992). Evolutionary biology, as a field, can aid in understanding the brain's cognitive architecture by identifying its functional engineering specifications. (Tooby and Cosmides 2000a). Since the design features of the brain are evident and available for observation, the strategy for understanding how the brain works comes from an investigation into the functions which the structure serves.

In their research, Cosmides and her colleagues refute the claim that there is a broad-based general-purpose brain circuitry responsible for all kinds of social exchanges, which simultaneously can account for performance on logical reasoning tasks. She argues that the human cognitive phenotypes have features that seem to be specially engineered for addressing adaptive problems associated with social exchanges. (Cosmides and Tooby 2000b: 1266) Humans' minds are representative of an orchestra of intermingling circuits each responsible for a different task. For instance, humans developed a sense of fear when faced with an aggressive predator. This serves the purpose of avoiding situations that place the individual in dangerous situations. While in the Pleistocene this sense evolved to protect individuals in a much different environment, humans today still have this sense to facilitate avoidance of situations that may cause pain or threaten life. Human minds also developed the sense of disgust, which not only kept individuals from eating poisonous foods, but also deter siblings from mating with each other, so as to prevent birth defects that would threaten survival. This cultural taboo may have biological origins.

Contrary to the assumption that the brain is comprised of a limited number of domain-general, content-independent circuits (Cheng and Holyoak 1985), Cosmides argues for domain-specific, content-dependent mechanisms designed to solve very specific adaptive problems. In other words, the brain is not a malleable "blank slate." Regardless of environmental conditions or type of culture, the same brain phenotype exists in every human. Reasoning about social exchange is controlled by social contract algorithms, which compute the information necessary to engage in and maintain mutually beneficial social relationships. This particular function shall be the focus of the remainder of this chapter.

Using a computational logic—meaning that an individual attempts to calculate the costs and benefits of each exchange with a contracting partner—for analyzing social exchanges (see Marr 1982), Cosmides' focus is on predicting which features the algorithms must have in order to successfully reason through social interactions. Following the cognitive neuroscience agenda, Cosmides attempts to identify and sort the modules in the brain into functionally specific units. For social exchange to occur, potential contracting partners must have the ability to recognize costs and benefits of the exchange. When presented with a decision rule, the algorithms assess these predicted harms and gains as compared to harms and gains associated with not exchanging, or staying with the status quo. In essence, they *compute* whether the contract is beneficial to each person overall.

For social exchange to evolve in a species, reciprocity must be the favored strategy (i.e., Tit-for-Tat) (Trivers 1971; Axelrod 1984; Fehr and Fischbacher 2004). Algorithms designed to enable individuals to reason about social exchange would then favor relationships that were cooperative. Social contract algorithms would also need a sub-routine mechanism designed to detect defectors from the agreed upon reciprocal arrangement. Individuals who cheat on a contract are distrusted in future social exchange relationships. Thus, to be effective social contract algorithms need to include programs that facilitate the ability to obtain fast and accurate information about whether a person has cheated or intends to cheat on a social contract (Cosmides and Tooby 1989). Cheating, in this context is simply a violation of the conditional rule of the social contract, either implied or explicit. Cheating involves not paying a cost when the exchanged benefit was taken. From the first-person perspective, an individual has been cheated when s/he pays the cost but does not receive the agreed upon benefit and vice versa. Closely related to the *benefit derived by cheating* in a relationship is the *intent to cheat*. This variable is the contractor's clearly stated desire to deviate from the contractual terms. If a contracting partner either has a reputation for cheating or there is evidence of the intention to cheat, the cheater-detection algorithms are likely to be activated (Cosmides 1989). It is these two variables that Cosmides believes are the most critical in determining an individual's ability to recognize violators of social contract rules.

The cheater detection subroutine operates on an inference procedure for identifying potential cheaters. Punitive sentiments toward a cheating party involve not contracting with that party in other future encounters (Price et al. 2002; Hastings and Shaffer 2008). Those contractors who accepted a benefit would need to be observed to discover if they paid the required cost. By the same token, contractors who did not pay the required cost would need to be observed to see if they unjustly accepted the benefit. A person looking for cheating contracting partners can ignore individuals who do not take benefits as well as those who pay the cost because such people are not causing direct harm.

Another factor that affected humans' survival involved the structure of social groups in which they lived. Cummins (1998) acknowledged that our predecessors existed in a social world not uncommon to contemporary societies in terms of the dominance hierarchies that naturally form between individuals of varying power (de Waal 1996; Stone 1997; Henrich et al. 2004). Dominance evolved in the human species as dominant individuals had more success obtaining resources such as food and sexual relations. It is not a stretch to imagine that early humans also had to navigate around a socially differentiated hierarchical world. Special reasoning architecture evolved that dealt with repeated adaptive problems specific to social contexts involving individuals within dominance hierarchies (Cummins 1998; Hastings and Shaffer 2008). People in positions of authority often are the ones who create the permissions and duties that subordinates are to follow. Certainly, in business firms it is quite commonplace to have dominance hierarchies in place within typical organizational structures. The present chapter aims to show how this dominance layout in non-dyadic, agency relationships may affect how people recognize rule violations within a company. The empirical study described in this current book chapter focuses on the perspective of the individual with authority to monitor for cheating. Evolutionary psychologists acknowledge other psychological mechanisms that are activated for authoritarianism under conditions of threat (Shaffer and Hastings 2004; Hastings and Shaffer 2008). Forming coalitions and alliances is one such ability that is governed by mental circuits in this context (Hastings and Shaffer 2005). However, the focus in this chapter will be on the social exchange itself.

Norms and collective values are generated from social dominance practices (Cummins 1998) in cultures including permission rules identified by social contracts (e.g., to be fair and just). Maintenance of reciprocally altruistic behavior involves the development of social order rules or norms regardless of culture. Cheating behavior is undesirable and would be sanctioned. When normative standards of behavior in the group are violated, members of the group often punish the violators of the permission rules established by the norms (Fehr and List 2004). The group norms and reciprocity checks essentially protect members of the group from deviant behavior. Thus, research in evolutionary economics has supported the view that given the propensity of human beings to shirk on contracts due to material incentives to do so, individuals will often sacrifice themselves in order to punish the cheaters (Fehr and Gachter 2002). The sanctioning of cheaters of rules can be for self-interested reasons or, for the interests of the group as a whole. The latter reason implies a preference for group survival, common to group selectionism arguments (Wilson 1993). Long-run interests for the group were protected when individual members punished partners who treated the group unfairly (Ridley 1985). This view is controversial among evolutionary scholars and is not dealt with in this chapter. Nevertheless, generally, the tendency to cooperate with those who treat individuals fairly and to sanction those who do not is called strong reciprocity (Fehr and Fischbacher 2003; Wasieleski and Hayibor 2009).

To this point, the theoretical exposition has been presented on evolutionary theory, natural selection, and evolutionary psychology. For the purposes of this book chapter on social contracts in a business context, the aim of the evolutionary psychology approach is limited to one particular adaptive problem—social exchange. Although there are different aspects to social exchange that involve punishment, group protection, and coalition strategies that appeal to authority, my aim in this narrative and subsequent study is to focus on the social-contract/cheater-detection algorithms that Cosmides and Tooby highlight in their research. This serves as a marvelous base from which to work, as their research addresses social contract exchanges involving only two partners. In the next section, I develop a theoretical expansion of their approach by studying a common social contract arrangement in business organizations—one that involves a dominance hierarchy. The first issue that needs to be addressed is that of "perspective" of the monitoring party of the social exchange.

3 Hypotheses Development

3.1 Experiment 1

Research has shown that a person's "perspective" in a social exchange relationship is critical for the activation of the brain's cheater-detection algorithms (Gigerenzer and Hug 1992). Perspective, which means the point-of-view of which a contracting partner is operating under (e.g., is the contracting partner cued into the point-of-view of the owner of the firm, or the manager working for the firm) is a key to the ability to spot cheaters in social exchanges. In other words, an individual must observe their contracting partner as having an ability to cheat in the relationship. Individuals are bounded by the perspective or role in which they are situated, and can only recognize potential cheaters based on the information available to them (Gigerenzer and Seltan 2001). "If a person represents one person in a social contract, and the other party has a cheating option, then a cheater-detection algorithm is activated that searches for information of the kind 'benefit taken and costs not paid' (requirement not met) by the other party" (Gigerenzer and Hug 1992: 165). Evolutionary psychology research on social contracts often uses the Wason selection task (Wason 1968) to measure an individual's ability to detect violators of conditional rules (explained in detail in the Methodology section of this chapter). Subjects completing the task must be cued into a certain party perspective to perceive specific options available to the monitoring agent of the specified actor on the other side of the contract.

The perspective taken by the respondent (i.e., the subject completing the written task) strongly affects the reasoning elicited and the likelihood of triggering the cheater-detection algorithm. The ability to detect the cheating option is paramount to the monitoring agent. In evolutionary psychology, "triggering" of a neural circuit refers to the program in the brain being activated for use in a certain situation. Critical for the activation of a social-contract algorithm with a cheater-detection subroutine (as described by Cosmides and Tooby) is the presence of a contracting partner (or, potential partner) with an ability to breach the rule of the social contract. Unless a person is cued into a particular and clearly defined role in a dyadic social contract and, the other party has a cheating option, the social-contract algorithms do not necessarily get activated.

While *intent to cheat* and *benefit derived by cheating* are the two factors identified as affecting the activation of cheater-detection algorithms, a third variable is examined here: an intervening third party in the social contract relationship of two parties on the activation of the social-contract/cheater-detection algorithms of the monitoring party. Previous research using the Wason selection task to detect cheaters has looked only at direct dyadic social exchanges (Cheng and Holyoak 1985; Cosmides 1985, 1989; Cosmides and Tooby 1992; Gigerenzer and Hug 1992). Unique to this current study is the introduction of a third party to the social contract relationship. Social contracts exist within a given socio-cultural system and the power hierarchies that exist therein. Thus, is there an effect on cheater-detection when an intermediate level of organizational hierarchy is introduced into a social-contract relationship in an organizational setting? Are individuals' minds equipped with the cognitive machinery necessary to monitor cheaters on social contracts when there are more than just two contracting partners? This is what the forthcoming empirical study examines.

Experiment 1 of this chapter focuses on the effects of an agency arrangement on a subject's ability to recognize the cheaters of a conditional social contract rule. First, I simply test whether there would be any substantive difference in the detection of cheaters (i.e., the activation of social-contract/cheater-detection algorithms) in situations that involve a direct relationship between two parties (the owner of a company and the employees completing a task) and in situations that inject an intermediary party between the owner and the employees. This latter situation describes an agent hired to manage the employees completing a task for the owner (Agency Hypothesis). The second part of Experiment 1 then tests whether the agent's *intent to cheat* the owner has any effect on a respondent's ability to recognize the violators of the social contract conditional rule (Honest Incompetence Hypothesis). Thus, only tasks describing the agency relationship are tested in this second part of the first experiment.

3.1.1 Agency Hypothesis

In business, a typical organizational arrangement involves an owner hiring a manager (or, other employee) to operate organizational functions (Jensen and Meckling 1976; Mitnick 1997). The separation of ownership and control in business occurred when owners of companies no longer were able to manage all of their company's affairs (Berle and Means 1932). This kind of hierarchical relationship was not foreign to our Pleistocene ancestors either. Ancestral social structures were not necessarily characteristically dyadic. Hierarchies existed in primitive social group bands and, exchanges in these contexts often involved more than one contracting partner (Beals et al. 1977; Bonner 1980). Of course, power-neutral bands were also commonplace in this era, where social hierarchies were virtually nonexistent. Many of these types of groups were populated with members of the same kin. Even today, certain indigenous tribes in the Amazon Basin live and operate with no discernable social differences among members (Davis 2009). However, the focus of this current research is on the type of social relationship which involves a dominance hierarchy because this type of relationship is typical in business organizations. Agency-type social group arrangements should not be unfamiliar to our Pleistocene-influenced minds, despite the existence of strict egalitarian relationships.

Recently, an alternative conception of the social contract has been developed as an alternative to the purely philosophical and socially constructed view of an exchange. The implicit social contract derived from natural law has pervaded the political philosophy literature for centuries (at least since Thomas Hobbes) and also in the business and society literature in modern writings (Donaldson 1989; Donaldson and Dunfee 1999; Johnson-Cramer and Philips 2005). Evolutionary social contract (ESC) is a much different term, with its roots in evolutionary biology, evolutionary psychology, and cognitive neuroscience. It is a naturally developed tool used to create and sustain mutually beneficial cooperative relationships. More specifically, ESCs are "dynamic social exchange relationships and the biological and social processes that produce them, governed by ancestrally shaped neural circuits...keyed to achieve individual and/or group advantage in a context of social reciprocity" (Frederick and Wasieleski 2002: 290). Social reciprocity moderates self-serving behaviors in social exchanges. Moreover, selection involving risks and potential utility gains of the exchange of favors shapes not only social behavior, but cognitive reasoning (Gaulin and McBurney 2001).

It is important to emphasize that at no point do ESCs reject the idea that self-interested behavior occurs in social exchanges. One aspect of human behavior is indeed individualistic. However, it is not the only explanation of human motives. Although it is acknowledged that seemingly altruistic behavior on behalf of one of the contracting parties is partly due to the fear of being penalized for breaching the contract (Binmore 1994; Fehr and Fischbacher 2004), humans do wish to partake in social exchanges for long-term mutual benefits. Reciprocal altruism is responsible for regulating and constraining social exchanges (Trivers 1971; Frederick and Wasieleski 2002). Reciprocal altruism is not to be confused with strong reciprocity. Reciprocal altruism involves a short-term loss on behalf of a contracting partner in the hopes of long-term gain. In contrast, the strong reciprocator does not necessarily expect any personal gains in the future (Fehr and Henrich 2004).

Unlike the philosophical notion of the social contract, evolutionary social contracts are real relationships between contracting parties. The traditional philosophic concept of abstract social contracts is replaced by one that is rooted in biologically-driven individual and organizational behaviors. ESCs form in response to, and exist within, ecological challenges and are sustained by a need to develop individual and group advantage. ESCs can take a variety of forms depending on the cultural origins of a particular social class system (Fehr and Fischbacher 2004). For example, take a simple labor contract. They imply a need for business to engage employees in a social exchange, and involve actual written documents that outline the form of the relationship. In labor negotiations with management, it is expected that social exchange neural modules in the brain will be activated to determine the dual mutual advantages for each party (Frederick and Wasieleski 2002: 292–293). These components of ESCs are manifested in all social contracts because they describe the natural and biological aspects that underlie and drive human social behavior. When both parties accept the terms of the labor contract, distributive justice is served because each party has conceded to the costs and benefits. However, conceptions of justice and fairness depend greatly on the cultural features of the environment in which the relationship exists (Gintis et al. 2003). For example, some cultures operate on a very distinct class system, where justice and fairness are based primarily on the rank or status of the member of the culture. Members of the Barasana in Northwest Amazon have to deal with social contracts like these, as deference to the shaman is always paramount, and controls every relationship with the culture (Davis 2009). In modern societies where power distance over the culture is low (e.g., Australia), perceptions of justice are different than those societies where power distance is high (e.g., Malaysia) (Hofstede 2001). The latter cultures are more accepting of fairness decisions based on a person's status in the hierarchy.

Business organizations are normally structured as a series of hierarchies and levels of authority and responsibility (Micklethwait and Wooldridge 2003). Principal-agent relationships in business organizations are one such hierarchy. The agent acts on behalf of the principal creating a power differential and a context in which social reciprocity and exchanges take place. The agent's role in each agency relationship is explicitly defined, usually by explicit or even tacit contract arrangements. Understandings of contractual agreements are explicitly discussed, instead of being only tacitly inferred (Frederick and Wasieleski 2002). The obligations of the agent and rules to be followed are originally designed by the practical needs of the principal. Thus, the principal possesses power. The symbiotic-mutualistic impulses are countered by self-seeking, power aggrandizing impulses that are conditioned by the organization's design and prevailing culture. In other words, peoples' intrinsic tendencies to cooperate with one another and be fair in social exchanges are moderated by competing motivations to gain power in relationships (Frederick 1995) and by the dominant organizational culture of an organization (See Victor and Cullen 1988 and Schein 1985).

The present research examines whether this agency-type arrangement makes a difference in respondents' abilities to detect cheaters in a business context by comparing cheater-detection rates on Wason Selection Tasks characterized by a dyadic relationship between principal and employees, and rates on tasks characterized by an agency relationship, in which the principal relies on the agent to monitor the employees' behavior. Since Pleistocene-era ancestors were faced with hierarchical social arrangements, one would not expect a difference in cheater detection rates between the task with an agency arrangement and the task that has direct dyadic relationships. Even though present-day humans are not faced with the same exact conditions and challenges that ancestral humans faced, modern humans still struggle with the psychological adaptations that are now activated in contemporary environments (Buss 2009). Thus, the main hypothesis states:

Hypothesis 1: *The agency relationship will have no effect on cheater detection rates on the Wason Selection Tasks.*

3.1.2 Honest Incompetence Hypothesis

In the agency theory literature, it is acknowledged that not all agents who misbehave intend to do so. The principal has another problem: the honest incompetence of the agent (Hendry 2002). In this case, the agent is not cheating or violating the principal's rules out of economic self-interest. Rather, the agent is not meeting the principal's objectives because s/he is not qualified to do the job or because an honest mistake has been made. Here the moral hazard still technically exists for the principal because the agent is not addressing the owner's interests out of error. The

2008 global financial crisis was caused in part by the issuance of sub-prime mortgages. While many of the mortgage brokers were indeed corrupt and were only interested in making their short-term sales, several of the brokers and underwriters issued mortgages to families who could not afford them because they did not conduct an adequate credit audit of their customers. Some of the loans issued by financial institutions like Bank of America and Chase Bank did not serve the interests of the principal owners of the companies because the individual brokers conducting the transactions did not do their job with proper care. Thus, while agents in the typical relationship are often assumed to be competent and aware, this is certainly not always the case. In fact, incompetence has little to do with expended effort (Nilikant and Rao 1994). Rather, Hendry reminds us that especially in cases where the agent has to make a judgment and cooperate with others, undesirable outcomes are common within organizations.

Incompetence among the agents in firms is partly a function of cognitive limitations, which severely restrict an individual's ability to absorb and process information. Kruger and Dunning (1999) discuss workers in organizations who are unskilled and unaware. Employees who do not possess the skill to perform a task or job at work are not uncommon. However, many employees are not cognizant of the fact that they are ineffective, either because no one ever informs them, or because they possess a high overconfidence bias (Lichtenstein et al. 1982). Some of today's most famous CEOs, like Carla Fiorini of Hewlett-Packard, were ineffective at their jobs. Even as she watched her company's stock price decrease while she was in charge, she never admitted that any failure of the company was her fault. Agents are never able to make judgments based on perfect information. Organization theorists proclaim that individuals are often constrained by bounded rationality and suffer from an inability to have complete information about their environments (Simon 1982). Without perfect information, both contracting parties to an agency relationship perform inefficiently, creating a situation of moral hazard, in which the manager behaves in a manner that is inconsistent with the desires of the owner. But in this situation the owner is unable to monitor what the agent is actually doing (Jacobides and Croson 2001).

Evolutionarily speaking, this too is a problem in that if the specific costs and benefits are not recognized by each party in a social exchange, the social-contract/cheater-detection neuronal algorithms will not be triggered.
In evolutionary psychology terms, this can present a problem to the principal of knowing when purposeful cheating behavior is occurring. When there is no clear intent of the agent to engage in deviant behavior, the cheater-detection algorithms are not likely to be activated, according to Cosmides and Tooby (2004). Thus, monitoring for cheaters would prove to be quite difficult. Hypothesis 2 states:

Hypothesis 2: *The rates of detection of rule violations will be lower on Wason Selection Tasks with content that describes the agent's honest incompetence than on tasks with content that describes the agent's intent to cheat.*

So, Hypothesis 1 addresses whether organizational hierarchy will affect individuals' ability to detect cheaters on a conditional rule. Thus, an agency relationship is examined against a direct relationship between a monitoring owner and his/her employees. The Wason Selection Task structure involves the respondent assuming the role of owner of a company who has hired a manager to monitor the behavior of four employees. Thus, there is an intermediary player in the owner-employee relationship. In the typical social contract structure of the Wason Selection Task, the owner has direct monitoring authority over the four employees, with no intermediary manager (agent). Thus, the agency hypothesis is tested. As stated earlier, no statistically significant differences, or substantive differences are expected because humans' minds should be hardwired to recognize agency-type arrangements in communities.

The next step in this empirical study is to examine the intent of the manager in the organizational setting, and to discover if this has any effect on the respondent's ability to detect violators of the social contract rule. Does the agent intend to cheat the owner, or is the manager incompetent and violates the owner's rule by mistake? Hypothesis 2 examines this question. In this case, two different agency-type arrangement tasks are compared—one that describes the agent as having intent to cheat, and one that describes the agent as committing an unintended error.

3.2 Experiment 2

Experiment 2 examines the population of respondents (to the study) themselves. Here, the subjects completing the empirical instrument are separated into two groups—one with business experience, and one with little or no business training. The reason for this experiment is to determine if the results from Experiment 1 could be interpreted as being influenced by a respondent's understanding of an owner-manager-employees structure. Does experience with business organizations affect how subjects perceive and analyze a cheater-detection task? One additional hypothesis is offered for this experiment.

3.2.1 Populations Hypothesis

In order to examine whether or not socialization and experience have anything to do with the facilitation of the activation of the cheater-detection algorithms—in other words, testing the "blank slate" hypothesis that individuals' minds are a veritable tabula rasa and will form based on past experiences—a separate test has to be conducted comparing two populations. Cheng and Holyoak (1985) posit that individuals possess domain-general reasoning circuits in the brain, which regulate several different tasks. These neural circuits in effect are impressionable, or are moderated by cultural norms and experiences. This pragmatic reasoning hypothesis is counter to Cosmides and Tooby's general social-contract hypothesis that there exist domain-specific circuits in the brain designed to reason through social exchange, including a sub-function of detecting cheaters of social contract conditional rules. This content-general position also conflicts with Pinker's (2002) contention that humans learn from their referent groups and from the experiences accumulated through a lifetime. It presumes that no circuit in the brain is 'hardwired' to complete specific tasks that aid in an individual's survival. Rather, perceptions and interpretation of certain social contracts will be affected by the person's context related to that situation. In 1992, Gigerenzer and Hug tested German engineering students' ability to correctly identify logical rule violations on a version of the Wason Selection Task, compared with a general undergraduate student sample. The authors found that the engineering students made correct identifications of rule violations at a rate significantly higher than with the general undergraduate students. They concluded that experience and education could indeed affect individuals' cognitive abilities on certain tasks.

For business practitioners, business education and socialization through firsthand experience with a business organization is likely to affect their perceptions of hypothetical business scenarios. Organizational cultures do socialize members of the organization (Schein 1985) and could influence employee reasoning and behavior (Weaver and Trevino 1999). Recently, Wasieleski and Weber (2009) demonstrated in their empirical study utilizing the Wason Selection Task that job function may affect an individual's ability to detect violators of rules. Thus, scenarios framed in a business setting may be more familiar to business practitioners than to students who have never had any applied business experience. Could one's familiarity with a business situation perhaps influence the activation of algorithms in the brain that have the primary purpose of detecting cheaters? Or, since the neural circuits are so intensely hardwired to perform specific survival tasks, would experience matter little? Essentially, are Cosmides and Tooby correct in arguing for the latter, or are there moderating effects dictated by culture and experience? Thus, Hypothesis 3 states:

Hypothesis 3: *The rates of detection of rule violations will be lower on business content Wason Selection Tasks among respondents from an undergraduate student population with no practical business experience than the rates elicited among business practitioners.*

According to a strict reading of the Cosmides and Tooby view of social contract reasoning, there should be no significant differences in reasoning between the two populations. The reason for this is that regardless of background, humans' minds are hardwired to look for cheaters when engaging in social contracts with others. In Cosmides' earlier research (1989), she tested unfamiliar problems and contexts in a broad student population. Despite having had no experience with a particular situation as described in the Wason Selection Task, respondents still could identify the violators of a conditional social contract rule. However, the alternate viewpoint that the algorithms in the brain are subject to social and environmental contexts remains compelling. In fact, in more recent research, Cosmides and Tooby (2004) acknowledge that cheater detection can be strongly or weakly activated. This implies a "degree" of activation, almost as if the algorithms are tuning knobs that can be turned up or down. However, never do the authors explain what conditions affect this degree of activation. Given the fact that there are a few conflicting results to their domain-specific hypotheses (mentioned in this section) and that the degree to which there only exist domain-specific reasoning circuits in the brain is a hotly contested issue in evolutionary psychology, it is reasonable to investigate whether background in a particular context actually affects a person's reasoning when asked to consider that context. Cosmides and Tooby also posit that the domain-specific programs are responsible for shaping humans experiences and attributing meaning to those experiences. In effect, these algorithms are greatly involved in shaping human culture. As stated in this chapter, other evolutionary theorists favor the opposite view that culture shapes the functioning of the human brain. In this chapter, I am attempting to support a view that there are domain-specific algorithms, but how and the degree to which they are activated is influenced by organizational culture and experiences.

In the next section, the research design and methodology of the two experiments is described and drawn out. Paramount to understanding the results of the studies is an awareness and comprehension of the instrument—the adapted Wason Selection Task. The nuances and slight differences in the different conditions is important for understanding under what conditions the social-contract/cheater-detection algorithms are activated.

4 Methodology

4.1 Instrument: The Wason Selection Task

P.C. Wason's selection task is the single most studied reasoning problem in psychology (Santamaria et al. 1996). Initially, he manufactured a logical reasoning test to determine the general ability of humans to recognize violations of abstract rules. The task presents the subject with an *If p, then q* conditional rule. This paper-and-pencil test asks respondents to discover when the rule has been violated over four occasions. These occasions are graphically represented by four boxes, or cards (See Fig. 1). For each instance, respondents are given only partial information. Four cards are then shown with values for *p, not-p, q,* and *not-q*. Each occasion is represented by one of the four cards. On one side of the card, the information tells whether or not the antecedent (*p or not-p*) is true, while the other side gives information about whether or not the consequent (*q or not-q*) is true (Wason 1968). The respondent can see only one side of the card for each occasion. Subjects must identify which card or cards they must turn over to determine whether the conditional rule was violated. Logically speaking, a choice of *p* and *not-q* would be the correct response because only "a card with a true antecedent on one side and a false consequent on the other can falsify the rule" (Cosmides 1989).

Originally the Wason selection task was constructed as an instrument to test an individual's logical reasoning ability. Wason (1968) designed an abstract logic task in which letters and numbers were shown in the conditional rule and in individual

You are given the statement:
"If a card has a vowel on one side, then it has an even number on the other side."
(If p, then q)
The cards below have a single number on one side and a single letter on the other.

Which of the cards would you need to turn over to test whether the statement is true or false?

Fig. 1 Standard abstract logic structure Wason task
Source: Manktelow 1999

note cards. There were four cards for each task. One side showed a letter whilst the other side presented a number. Only one side of the card was visible to the respondents. Specifically, respondents were asked to select which cards needed to be turned over in order to find out whether the conditional rule, "If there is an E on one side of the card, then there is a 4 on the other side" was violated. The four cards usually showed an "E," a "4," a "7," and a "D," respectively.

Historically, only 4–10% of respondents reveal the logically correct cards (Cosmides and Tooby 2004). In this scenario, the "E" and the "7" are the necessary cards to verify the integrity of the rule. The "E" must be flipped to figure out whether a "4" appears on the other side of the card because any numeral or letter other than the number "4" would falsify the conditional rule. Respondents must also check to verify the flip side of the card with the "7" visible. An "E" on the back of this card would also falsify the rule. In logical terms, bothering with either of the other two cards cannot disaffirm the conditional rule.

Building on this previous research with the abstract logic tasks centered on understanding the content-dependent cognitive processes in the brain, a group of researchers explored the contexts in which thematic content facilitates performance on selection tasks (Griggs and Cox 1982; Cosmides 1989; Manktelow and Evans 1979; Gigerenzer and Hug 1992; Barrett 1999). Wason suggested that there were principles dictating how people reason but neglected to discover which precise principles would provide consistent results on his task. In terms of reliability and generalizability of the instrument, evolutionary psychologists Cosmides and Tooby have offered a promising approach that accounts consistently for thematic content task performance.

Decades after Wason invented his task, Leda Cosmides (1985, 1989) adapted the original logical task to closely resemble social contract conditional rules in order to test for the existence of cheater-detection algorithms in the human mind. This runs contrary to the availability hypotheses (Kahneman and Tversky 1972) and deductive reasoning accounts which posit that individuals' abilities to reason logically account for the ability to detect violators of rules. Instead of an abstract conditional rule, Cosmides transformed it into a cost-benefit structure of a social contract. If one presents part of the conditional rule in terms of a benefit received (p), and the other part of the rule as a cost paid (q), then in effect, the logical reasoning rule is transformed into a social contract structure (Cosmides 1985). Cards now represent "cost paid" or "not paid" and "benefit accepted" or "not accepted," respectively. If a person has an algorithm designed to "look for cheaters" it would lead that person to select the "cost not paid" card (not-q) and the "benefit accepted" card (p) to find possible cheaters of the conditional rule (p.198) despite the limited information that is otherwise available (See Fig. 2). While respondents on logical tasks correctly selected cards at a very low rate (Wason and Johnson-Laird 1972), cheater detection rates on social contract rules rose to a rate from 60% to 75%. Cosmides (1989), and later, Cosmides and Tooby (2000), inferred from this data that people have cognitive adaptations that enable them to identify cheaters in social exchange situations (Cosmides and Tooby 2000b).

The present study adapts the instrument further to reflect social contract tasks within a business context. The structure illustrated in Fig. 2 is replicated but placed in an organizational setting. Two separate tasks were created to reflect different types of relationships with the firm's owner. One task contained content that reflected an agency-type relationship between an owner of a production firm and a manager of employees' pay bonuses. The other task replicates the situation but manipulates the type of relationship the owner has with his/her employees. This task describes a direct dyadic relationship with employees. Appendix A illustrates both tasks.

This study outlined here acknowledges the importance of perspective for activation of the cheater-detection subroutine. In each of the tasks, the perspective in which the respondent is cued is held constant by telling the story in the second person. A principal and agent were presented in each distributed task, but subjects were asked to assume the role of owner in each variation. Thus, in every task, respondents are cued into the role of the principal (owner). The agent or employee were always the ones being monitored in the scenarios and are always the persons in the task having the opportunity to cheat. This variable was held constant in order to isolate the effects of *intent* and *benefit received by cheating* on cheater detection in the agency relationship. I did not manipulate which party in the exchange

It is your job to enforce the following law:
"If you take the benefit, then you pay the cost." (If p, then q)
The cards below have information about four people. Each card represents one person. One side of a card tells whether a person accepted the benefit and the other side of the card tells whether that person paid the cost.
Indicate only the card or cards you definitely need to turn over to see if any of these people are breaking this law.

Fig. 2 Standard social contract structure Wason task
Source: Cosmides 1985: 197

relationship has the ability to cheat because the objective is to observe the main effects of only these two variables.

Participants were required to complete another task designed to test for the effect of cheater-detection variables—*intent to cheat* and *benefit derived by cheating*—in the agency relationship. Thus, the independent variables necessary to activate the cheater-detection circuits (*intent to cheat* and *benefit derived by cheating*) according to evolutionary psychology theory were omitted from this agency-type task. This manipulation is designed to resemble a situation in which the breach of the conditional rule was caused by an honest error. The general context remained the same. It is the same production-bonus scenario used in the other tasks. This was constructed to test whether the evolutionary psychology hypothesis championed by Cosmides and Tooby was replicated in a business, agency-type context. (See the "Honest Incompetence Task" in the Appendix for the manipulation of the *intent to cheat* and *benefit derived by cheating* variables).

4.2 Experiment 1

4.2.1 Research Design and Sample

This first experiment tested Hypotheses 1 and 2. A between-subjects research design was used in this experiment to avoid any transfer effects and contamination that may result from respondents seeing all variations of the independent variables. Prior studies using versions of the Wason selection task have utilized a similar design (Cosmides 1985, 1989; Sugiyama et al. 2002).

Student convenience samples were used for this phase of the research project. Previous research using the Wason selection task used student convenience samples for testing the existence of content-dependent algorithms (Cosmides 1985; Cosmides 1989; Gigerenzer and Hug 1992; Price et al. 2002). Moreover, since social-contract algorithms with a cheater-detection subroutine are thought to be universally hardwired in the species (Cosmides and Tooby 2000a), the type of population used should matter little. One hundred thirty-seven undergraduate business student participants were surveyed and completed the task (average age was 20.81). Subjects were all taken a mid-western United States university. Voluntary participation was requested of students in classroom settings.

4.2.2 Results

The research tested variables necessary for the activation of cheater-detection algorithms in business social contract scenarios. To assess the rates of cheater-detection in each of the tasks, a percentage of the subjects who chose the *not-q* and *p* cards only was calculated. See Table 1 for the frequency of *p* and *not-q* choices across the tasks, as well as the rates of cheater-detection and the corresponding

Table 1 Summary results for experiment 1: Undergraduate sample comparison of cheater-detection rates—manipulating agency variable

	Entire population
Agency task with intent and benefit	59.5%
	25/42
Direct dyadic social contract task	57.8%
	37/64
Agency task compared with dyadic social contract task	**z = 0.1748**
	N.S.

z-tests for this part of the study (one-tailed). Once the percentages were determined, tests for statistical significance of differences between the rates of cheater-detection between the groups were performed using z-tests.

The first empirical test involves comparing the rate of cheater-detection on tasks with content specifying an agency-type organizational arrangement against tasks with content specifying only a dyadic social contract relationship with no hierarchical relationship described. In this part of the study, both tasks contain content that specifies both *intent to cheat* and *benefit received by cheating*. The agency hypothesis (Hypothesis 1) states there should be no difference in cheater-detection rates due to the inclusion of the agency variable. In other words, rates of identifying the violators of the conditional rule between respondents completing a task containing content that describes an agency relationship and respondents completing a task containing content that describes a direct social contract relationship should not be significant. *Hypothesis 1 is supported*. The rates of cheater-detection between the two conditions were very similar (59.5% for the agency-type task versus 57.8% for the direct social contract arrangement) ($z = 0.1748$; $p = 0.00001$). This result indicates that imposing an agency-type arrangement into the business production task scenario had a negligible effect on respondents' ability to detect the violators of the social contract conditional rule.

Rates of cheater detection were also compared between two agency-type tasks. Table 2 shows the results of the z-test comparing these percentages. Hypothesis 2 predicted that respondents completing tasks with the independent variables *intent to cheat* and *benefit derived from cheating* included in the content would elicit rates of cheater detection higher than respondents completing tasks without those variables included in the content. In other words, on tasks with honest incompetence described, individuals are less likely to detect the violators of the conditional rule. As illustrated, *Hypothesis 2 is supported* ($z = 2.03$; $p = 0.021$). This test was run to examine whether individuals are as adept at identifying cheaters of social contract rules when the agent hired to monitor employees cheated the owner by mistake. Thus, one of Cosmides' key factors for the activation of the social-contract/cheater-detection algorithms—*intent to cheat*—is removed. This current study supports the notion that an agency-type arrangement within a social contract scenario has no effect on an individual's cheater-detection ability. As hypothesized, since ancestral environments often featured hierarchical relationships within groups and tribes, the evolved mind should be familiar with these kinds of social

Table 2 Summary results for experiment 1: undergraduate sample comparison of cheater-detection rates—manipulating intent and benefit

	Entire population
Agency task with intent and benefit	*59.5%*
	25/42
Agency task absent intent and benefit	*35.4%*
	11/31
Agency task compared with dyadic social contract task	**z = 2.03**
	p = 0.021

exchanges. So, I wanted to examine the agency-type arrangement in more detail, since this type of task has never been studied before in the literature. Despite the added layer of management in the agency-type task, Cosmides and Tooby's theory is robust in that the *intent to cheat* must be present in order for the cheater-detection algorithms to be activated. At least, the results in this present study show that activation rates were much higher in the *intent to cheat* condition.

4.3 Experiment 2

4.3.1 Research Design and Sample

The design from the first experiment is replicated here but placed in the hands of business practitioners, rather than undergraduate business students. Once again a between-subject design was used. Each respondent only received one task. Full-time business practitioners with at least two years of full-time business experience were obtained from a convenience sample of Master of Business Administration students enrolled at an accredited mid-western graduate business school. Surveys were completed during class time on a voluntary basis. Two hundred and two part-time (night) graduate business students were surveyed and given the same tasks as described in Experiment 1. Eight responses had to be discarded due to insufficient information regarding work experience. The average age of the practitioner sample was 26.1 years. Hypotheses 1 and 2 were tested again with the business practitioner sample first. Then, Hypothesis 3 was tested to see if there are any differences between populations.

4.3.2 Results

Seventy-four business practitioners were administered the *intent to cheat* and *benefit derived by cheating* version of the direct social contract business scenario task. In this version, the owner directly monitors the employees, without any intermediary manager. This group of respondents was cued into the role of owner and was asked if any of the four employees could have broken the conditional rule.

Of the 74 respondents, 43 correctly selected the *p* and *not-q* cards (58.1%). In prior research using social contract Wason Selection Tasks, this percentage is in line with the average results (Cosmides 1989). Even though the tasks used in this study are unique adaptations of the social contract structure, the rates elicited here fall into the average range of respondents choosing *p* and *not-q* cards (58–75%). In the second condition, in which the task included the factors theoretically necessary for cheater-detection circuit activation (*intent* and *benefit derived from cheating*), but also included an agent who may be purposely breaking the rule, 52.5% of those responding to this task correctly selected the cheater-detection cards (31 out of 59). Finally, in the condition in which neither the intent nor the benefit was explicitly stated, but the task was framed as an agency situation, only 22 out of 61 respondents selected *p* and *not-q* cards (36.1%). Given the fact that the two critical factors cited by Cosmides and Tooby are absent, this is not a surprising percentage (Table 3 and 4).

When comparing these percentages using simple z-tests for two proportions, let us first see if the business practitioners experienced any difficulty with tasks that were framed with an intermediary manager (with the intent to cheat the owner) versus a direct social contract relationship with the employees, by revisiting Hypothesis 1. With the business practitioners the result is similar to the result with the undergraduate students. There is no statistically significant difference in cheater-detection rates between the two tasks (z-value: 0.516; p = 0.694). Thus, in this population, *Hypothesis 1 is supported*. When comparing two agency-type tasks—one with the manager described as having the *intent to cheat* and also being able to derive *benefit from cheating*, and the other task with the agent making an honest mistake—another similar result is found. Business practitioners and undergraduate students with no full-time business experience each elicited higher rates of cheater-detection when intent and benefit were presented (z-value = 2.373;

Table 3 Summary results for experiment 2: business practitioner sample comparison of cheater-detection rates—manipulating agency variable

	Entire population
Agency task with intent and benefit	52.5%
	31/59
Direct dyadic social contract task	58.1%
	43/71
Agency task compared with dyadic social contract task	**z = 0.516**
	p = 0.694

Table 4 Summary results for experiment 2: business practitioner sample comparison of cheater-detection rates—manipulating intent and benefit

	Entire population
Agency task with intent and benefit	52.5%
	31/59
Agency task absent intent and benefit	36.1%
	22/61
Agency task compared with dyadic social contract task	**z = 2.373**
	p = 0.009

Table 5 Summary results for experiment 2: comparison of business practitioners and undergraduate students

	Entire population
Undergraduate sample	59.5%
	25/42
Business practitioner sample	52.5%
	31/59
Compared for agency task including intent and benefit variables	**z = 0.495**
	p = 0.690

p = 0.009). Thus, with the business practitioner sample, *Hypothesis 2 is supported*. Table 5 shows the results.

Hypothesis 3 states that the rates of cheater-detection will be lower on business content Wason Selection Tasks among respondents from an undergraduate student population with no practical business experience than the rates elicited among business practitioners with formal training. It was important to not only examine rates when the tasks are manipulated, but also to examine what happens to rates of detection when the respondent sample is changed. Does the experience that several years of full-time work experience make respondent more adept at identifying the rule violators on the task? It appears not. When comparing cheater-detection rates at a 95% confidence level on the task with no manager in the scenario, there is no statistically significant difference (z = −0.054; p = 0.478). On the task with a manager who intends to cheat the owner, the result is much of the same (z = 0.495; p = 0.690). Again, there is no difference between the two populations. Finally, when the agency, honest incompetence task is examined, there is no significant difference between the two groups (z = −0.135; p = 0.446). Thus, *Hypothesis 3 is rejected*. Cheater-detection does not seem to be affected by real-world, practical business experience. A discussion as to the meaning of the results in theory and in practice follows (Table 5).

5 Discussion and Future Theoretical Directions

In summary, the agency hypothesis that states there should be no difference in cheater-detection rates from groups responding to tasks with a direct social contract relationship described and rates from groups responding to tasks with an agency-type arrangement described, is supported. This result remained unchanged when examining undergraduate students with no practical business experience or business practitioners with years of direct business experience. The second hypothesis, the honest incompetence hypothesis, states that rates of cheater detection will be higher on agency tasks that describe the manager as having intent to cheat than on agency tasks that describe the manager as making an honest mistake. Indeed, this is what was found for both the undergraduate group and the business practitioner group. When rates of cheater detection between the populations was compared—testing Hypothesis 3—no significant differences were found between the groups on any of the tasks. Thus, H3 was not supported. The findings of these studies are significant for the evolutionary psychology scholars, as well as for business practitioners.

The results do not refute the evolutionary psychology hypothesis that individuals' ability to detect violators of social contract rules is hardwired in the neural architecture of the brain. This is the hypothesis that is favored by Cosmides and Tooby. Thus, with the findings of this present study, additional support is provided for the existence of domain-specific (cheater-detection) algorithms in the brain. More importantly, the agency-type relationship does not seem to have an effect on the ability to detect rule violations on the Wason Selection Task. However, the conventional position needs to be tempered with the inclusion of moderating organizational influences. Rates of cheater detection were consistent with past research in the field despite the manipulation of the agency relationship and the intention to cheat. When the brain is viewed as a symphony of interacting brain circuits subject to perceptions of environmental cues, insights into human behavior can be fostered. The point at which interdependence of nature and nurture exists is at the level of evolved psychological mechanisms in the brain.

The study presented in this chapter is the first to examine this agency variable on cheater detection. The agency hypothesis addresses a cultural influence on Pleistocene circuits. As noted earlier, hierarchical relationships should be familiar to contemporary minds since social groups were organized along power lines in hunter-gatherer days. Corporations are organized in terms of agency-type relationships, where one person acts on another's behalf. Cosmides and Tooby (2004) acknowledge that even though these hierarchical relationships are familiar to our anciently formed minds, the agency relationship in particular may suppress the triggering of the cheater-detection algorithms because whom is being cheated is often not clear. Agents who are not aware of the company's costs and benefits and cannot determine how the company is affected by an employee's behavior are less likely to spontaneously attend to possible cases of cheating by those employees or other stakeholders.

Thus, an individual's perspective in a business social contract scenario could be a significant factor contributing to the results of the present study. Perhaps cheater detection is affected by the social structure of the corporation. Reciprocity in evolutionary theory is typically analyzed in terms of equitable relationships. Cosmides' stated evolved algorithms for reciprocity do not take into account the true context of an agency relationship—one based on a difference in power and social status. Recall that the respondents in both experiments were all cued into the perspective of the owner of the manufacturing firm. This owner has the power to award bonuses and was the person responsible for constructing the social contract conditional rule, on which the exchange relationship is based. Future studies should attempt to cue respondents into the subordinate role to examine whether the change of perspective has an effect on cheater detection.

Why then does cheating behavior so often go undetected in the modern business world? The recent transgressions of executives at Bank of America, AIG, Fanny Mae, and Freddy Mac that cheated many of their customers out of fair mortgage contracts are not isolated incidents. One explanation may involve the power structure of organizations. The social order discussed in the previous paragraph is a part of corporate culture that often constrains the behavior of individuals. Cummins (1999) posits that social rules and differences in rank in social groups affected the evolution of cognitive functions in the brain. Her deontic reasoning theory suggests that humans have ancestrally formed cognitive circuits that are responsible for checking for social norm compliance (Fiddick and Cummins 2001). The social norms include the structuring of social groups along power and dominance lines. The preservation of an individual manager's power is a key goal of an organizational culture (Frederick 1995). Due to the highly interactive nature of the neural algorithms, Fiddick and Cummins (2001) studied whether individuals in a position of power would perceive cheating to be a less severe issue than individuals who do not possess power. In a ledger task, they cued respondents into roles of boss or subordinate (but did not use a business population) and evaluated their tolerance to cheating. They found that people cued to the higher rank were more tolerant of cheating than people cued to a lower rank. Individuals in the higher-ranking role even felt that they are more fairly treated than the individuals cued to the lower-ranking role. One possible reason for this might be that many individuals who reach the upper echelons of business organizations do so by cheating, lying, and stealing. Hence, they are less likely to care about cheating transgressions when committed by others given that they recognize that such behaviors as central to their ascendancy.

This power-aggrandizing behavior is also believed to be hardwired into humans' brains (Frederick 2004). Power-aggrandizement was a means of survival, just as is the detection of cheaters. It is not difficult to see examples of the abuse of power in modern business organizations. At the beginning of this century, corporate executive crime was rampant and a chronic problem. Chief Executive Officers like Jeffrey Skilling of Enron, Bernard Ebbers of WorldCom, and Dennis Kozlowski, of Tyco (to name but a few), all were caught cheating their companies. Their behavior caused the demise of their companies, the loss of all stock value to their shareholders, and thousands of lost jobs. This latter consequence was also associated with vanishing pensions and health benefits. Thus, executives like these men did not honor their social contracts with multiple stakeholder groups. The repercussions of this abuse of power were widespread and dire.

This finding certainly provides some insight into why implicit contracts in organizations deteriorate over time (Robinson et al. 1994), but what does it tell us about cheater detection? Future research in this area of evolutionary psychology should test these findings against Barrett's (1999) claim that the cheater-detection algorithms are activated incrementally. If there is an interaction among different circuits in the brain and if these circuits are influenced by cultural factors, then the effects of perceptions of role power differentials on the activation of cheater-detection mechanisms need to be examined.

Other cognitive circuits that should be examined in order to obtain a fuller understanding of how the algorithms in the brain interact involve heuristics. In attempting to detect specific instances of cheating in a particular context, owners and managers are not only equipped with cognitive machinery hardwired to monitor the costs and benefits of exchanges in a social contract, but they may also utilize certain mental shortcuts when making decisions. According to Tversky and Kahneman, intuitive judgments related to perception and active reasoning (cognitive heuristics) may be related to evolutionary history (Kahneman 2003). For instance, the availability of information relating to the rule violations may influence a person's ability to detect contractual breaches (Tversky and Kahneman 1973). In other words, according to the availability heuristic, if a manager has had a prior experience of cheating by employees, and that experience cost the firm a large amount of money, then that manager may overestimate the frequency with which cheating takes place in the workplace. Thus, s/he may be biased when completing the task. Individuals will typically retrieve information from experience regarding an event and use that experience to make judgments about the probability of future similar events. Any prior instance of cheating experienced by an employer may influence perceptions of potential violators of company rules (Hayibor and Wasieleski 2008). Future research should examine how heuristics like this one affect individuals' perceptions of cheating in the workplace.

6 Implications for Practitioners

For managers in a real organizational environment, there are lessons to be learned from the study in this chapter. It is particularly interesting and perhaps significant that undergraduate business students with little or no full-time work experience consistently demonstrated equally high rates of cheater-detection than the business practitioner MBAs when both *intent* and *benefit* were present, and in the direct social contract condition (contrary to Hypothesis 3). Nonetheless, the results obtained here are exactly what Cosmides and Tooby would expect. Cheater-detection, as a domain-specific function of the brain, is hardwired to regulate social exchanges even among modern-day individuals. Business education and experience with a particular business situation appear to have little or no effect on cheater-detection. Individuals may just be innately effective at identifying the violators of social contract rules. This finding is important for business practitioners. No matter whether an employee is newly hired from college, or is tenured at the company for years, when certain conditions are present, individuals are able to detect cheaters fairly effectively. Thus, any manager (new or old) who is given the responsibility at work to monitor an employee's behavior for cheating the company would be better at detecting violators if the manager was informed about what sort of benefit the employee could gain by cheating. If the employee benefits by cheating on the social contract and the manager assumes that the employee may have intent to cheat, then it is more likely the manager will recognize situations in which the employee broke the rules. The lesson learned here is that instead of using only control mechanisms in an organization to mitigate cheating behavior (e.g., penalties for wrongdoing) by employees, managers should develop an understanding of the way individuals' minds are developed, and work *with* that knowledge to create conditions that help people monitor for undesirable behavior.

Lack of specification of the principal's objectives has been identified as another contributing factor to agent breaches of contract (Hendry 2002). While tasks may be specified to the agent, the owner may not be able to effectively communicate all the information related to a task in a specific situation and environment. This is another symptom of bounded rationality and could lead to violations of conditional rules in the workplace. To reduce the incidence of ethical breaches of social contracts, owners and managers should pay attention to the fact that their agent's minds are not only designed to recognize cheaters when specific conditions are present, but that individuals' minds are limited by heuristics and cognitive biases. Knowing that the specificity of the task is critical for brain circuits designed to monitor ethical breaches of rules, employers need to make such rationales and tasks explicit to their employees. For example, if owners were to explain to the managers responsible for monitoring employees' behavior how the organization is affected by cheating on the social contract, then perhaps more cheaters would be caught. If a manager in an agency relationship does not see why the conditional rule of the social contract is in place, or does not understand its purpose, then s/he is less likely to recognize when the rule is being broken. Perhaps more brokers who issued unfair mortgages to customers would have been caught earlier if the managers realized the long-term effects the risky loans have on the issuing company, the customers, and the overall economy. (See Ermer et al. 2008)

In conclusion, it is important for business practitioners to factor into their decision-making the functioning of the evolved human mind. If we are to agree with the evolutionary psychology position that human minds are hardwired to detect violators of social contract conditional rules, then the implications for business may revolve around the issue of framing. If, indeed human minds are designed to identify cheaters on social contract-type rules, then it may be important for corporations to provide rationales to managers for the existence of particular policies. These company policies may be better served if framed in terms of social contract rules. Moreover, the benefits and costs must be clearly outlined to the agent who is monitoring the exchange (Cosmides and Tooby 2004). One's natural ability to identify rule violators is dependent on the perception of these costs and benefits. Thus, it is critical for corporations to recognize the factors that facilitate the effective monitoring of social exchanges in order to ultimately decrease the frequency of rule violations.

Appendices

Direct Arrangement Task

You are the owner of DMW Company, a manufacturer of cell phones. Your company's financial situation is dire. You discuss this problem with your employees, explaining that DMW will go out of business if production rates stay the same. To fix the problem, the employees suggest, and you agree to, the following new rule:

If an employee is to receive a pay bonus, then that employee must produce more than 1,000 units in a week.

This is the only way an employee can earn a bonus in your company.

At first things seem to be going well. But then you hear that some of the employees may be breaking this new rule. As owner, you want to check to see if any employees are breaking the rule.

The documents below tell about four employees in DMW's plant: Ed, Bob, Pete, and Tom. But some papers fell on top of them, so you can only see half of each document.

Each document tells what happened last week with one of these employees. The top tells how many units that employee produced last week, and the bottom tells whether or not that employee got a pay bonus last week.

Some of these employees may be breaking the new rule. Which document(s) would you definitely need to uncover to find out if any of these employees have broken the rule: *"If an employee is to receive a pay bonus, then that employee must produce more than 1,000 units in a week."*? (Don't choose any more documents than are absolutely necessary.)

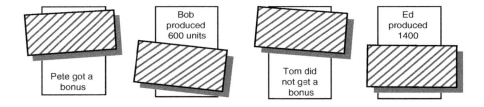

Agency-Type Arrangement

The paragraph in boldface above is interchanged with the paragraph below to reflect the agency relationship in this task.

You have hired a new manager whose job it is to enforce this rule. Each time a bonus is paid, the manager also earns a small bonus. At first things seem to be going well. But then you hear that your manager is crafty, and may be breaking this new rule on purpose. He would benefit by breaking it. As owner, you want to check to see if the manager ever breaks the rule.

Note: The card choices and rule are the same on all tasks.

Honest Incompetence Task (Agency relationship)

You are the owner of DMW Company, a manufacturer of cell phones. Your company's financial situation is dire. You discuss this problem with your employees, explaining that DMW will go out of business if production rates stay the same.

To fix the problem, the employees suggest, and you agree to, the following new rule:

If an employee is to receive a pay bonus, then that employee must produce more than 1,000 units in a week.

This is the only way an employee can earn a bonus in your company.

You have hired a new manager whose job it is to enforce this rule. At first things seem to be going well. But then you hear that your manager is absent-minded, and may be breaking this new rule by accident. As owner, you want to check to see if the manager ever breaks the rule.

The documents below tell about four employees in DMW's plant: Ed, Bob, Pete, and Tom. But some papers fell on top of them, so you can only see half of each document.

Each document tells what happened last week with one of these employees. The top tells how many units that employee produced last week, and the bottom tells whether or not that employee got a pay bonus last week.

The absent-minded manager may be breaking the new rule by accident. Which document(s) would you definitely need to uncover to find out if the manager has ever broken the rule: *"If an employee is to receive a pay bonus, then that employee must produce more than 1,000 units in a week."*? (Don't choose any more documents than are absolutely necessary.)

References

Axelrod R (1984) The Evolution of Cooperation. New York: Basic Books

Barrett HC (1999) Guilty minds: How perceived intent, incentive, and ability to cheat influence social contract reasoning. 11th Annual meeting of the human behavior and evolution society, Salt Lake City, Utah

Beals RL, Hoijer H, Beals AR (1977) An introduction to anthropology, 5th edn. Macmillan Publishing Company, New York

Berle AA and Means GC (1932) The Modern Corporation and Private Property. 1991 Transaction Publishers, New Brunswick and London, U.K. (ed.), New York: The Macmillan Company

Binmore K (1994) Game theory and the social contract, volume 1: playing fair. MIT Press, Cambridge

Bonner JT (1980) The evolution of culture in animals. Princeton University Press, Princeton

Buss DM (2009) The great struggles of life: Darwin and the emergence of evolutionary psychology. Am Psychol 64(2):140–148

Cheng PW, Holyoak KJ (1985) Pragmatic reasoning schemas. Cognition 17:391–416

Cosmides L (1985) Deduction or Darwinian algorithms? An explanation of the elusive content effect on the wason selection task. Doctoral Dissertation, Department of Psychology, Harvard University: University Microfilms, #86-02206

Cosmides L (1989) The logic of social exchange: has natural selection shaped how humans reason? Studies with the Wason selection task. Cognition 31:187–276

Cosmides L, Tooby J (1987) From evolution to behavior: evolutionary psychology as the missing link. In: Dupre J (ed) The latest on the best: essays on evolution and optimality. MIT Press, Cambridge, pp 277–306

Cosmides L, Tooby J (1989) Evolutionary psychology and the generation of culture, part II. Ethol Sociobiol 10:51–97

Cosmides L, Tooby J (1992) Cognitive adaptations for social exchange. In: Barkow, Jerome H, Cosmides Leda, Tooby John (eds) The adapted mind: evolutionary psychology and the generation of culture. Oxford University Press, New York, pp 19–136

Cosmides L, Tooby J (1995) From function to structure: the role of evolutionary biology and computational theories in cognitive neuroscience. In: Gazzaniga MS (ed) The cognitive neurosciences. MIT Press, Cambridge, pp 1199–1210

Cosmides L, Tooby J (1997) Dissecting the computational architecture of social inference mechanisms. In: Chichester (ed) Characterizing human psychological adaptations. Wiley, Chichester, pp 132–161

Cosmides L, Tooby J (1999) Toward an evolutionary taxonomy of treatable conditions. J Abnorm Psychol 108(3):453–464

Cosmides L, Tooby J (2000a) The cognitive neuroscience of social reasoning. In: Gazzaniga MS (ed), The Cognitive Neurosciences. 2nd Ed. Cambridge, MA: MIT, 1259–1270

Cosmides L, Tooby J (2000b) Introduction. In: Gazzaniga MS (ed), The Cognitive Neurosciences. Cambridge, MA: MIT, 1–8

Cosmides L, Tooby J (2004) Knowing thyself: the evolutionary psychology of moral reasoning and moral sentiments. In: Edward Freeman R, Patricia Werhane H (eds) Business, Science, and Ethics, The Ruffin Lecture Series 4. Society for Business Ethics, Charlottesville, pp 93–128

Cosmides L, Tooby J (2005) Neurocognitive adaptations designed for social exchange. In: Buss DM (ed) Handbook of evolutionary psychology. Wiley, Hoboken, pp 584–627

Cosmides L, Tooby J, Barkow JH (1992) Introduction: evolutionary psychology and conceptual integration. In: Barkow, Jerome H, Cosmides, Leda, Tooby John (eds) The adapted mind: evolutionary psychology and the generation of culture. Oxford University Press, New York, pp 1–18

Cummins DD (1998) Social norms and other minds: the evolutionary roots of higher cognition. In: Cummins D, Allen's C (eds) The evolution of mind. Oxford University Press, New York, pp 30–50

Cummins DD (1999) Cheater detection is modified by social rank: the impact of dominance on the evolution of cognitive functions. Evol Hum Behav 20:229–248

Davis W (2009) The wayfinders: why ancient wisdom matters in the modern world. Anansi, Toronto

Dennett DC (1995) Darwin's dangerous idea: evolution and the meanings of life. Touchstone, New York

de Waal F (1996) Good Natured: The Origins of Right and Wrong in Humans and Other Animals. Cambridge: Harvard University Press

Donaldson T (1989) The ethics of international business. Oxford University Press, New York

Donaldson T, Dunfee TW (1999) Ties that bind. Harvard Business School Press, Boston

Eisenhardt KM (1989) Agency theory: an assessment and review. Acad Manage Rev 14(1):57–74

Ermer E, Guerin SA, Cosmides L, Tooby J, Miller MB (2006) Theory of mind broad and narrow: reasoning about social exchange engages ToM areas, precautionary reasoning does not. Psychol Press 1(3–4):196–219

Ermer E, Cosmides L, Tooby J (2008) Relative status regulates risky decision making about resources in men: evidence of the co-evolution of motivation and cognition. Evol Hum Behav 29:106–118

Fehr E, Fischbacher U (2003) The nature of human altruism. Nature 425:785–791

Fehr E, Fischbacher U (2004) Third-party punishment and social norms. Evol Hum Behav 25:63–87

Fehr E, Gachter S (2002) Altruistic punishment in humans. Nature 415:137–140

Fehr E, Heinrich J (2003) Is strong reciprocity a maladaptation? On the evolutionary foundations of human altruism. In: Hammerstein P (ed) Genetic and cultural evolution of cooperation. Dahlem Workshop Reprint 90, Cambridge, MA, 55–82

Fehr E, Heinrich J (2004) Is strong reciprocity a maladaptation? On the evolutionary foundations of human altruism. Working paper

Fehr E, List J (2004) The hidden costs and returns of incentives: turst and trustworthiness among CEOs. J Eur Econ Assoc 2:743–771

Fehr E, Fischbacher U, Gachter S (2002) Strong reciprocity, human cooperation and the enforcement of social norms. Hum Nat 13:1–25

Fiddick L, Cummins DD (2001) Reciprocity in ranked relationships: does social structure influence social reasoning? J Bioecon 3:149–170

Frederick WC (1995) Values, nature, and culture in the american corporation. Oxford University Press, London

Frederick WC (2004) The evolutionary firm and its moral (dis)contents. In: Edward Freeman R, Patricia Werhane H (eds) Business, Science, and Ethics, The Ruffin Lecture Series 4. Society for Business Ethics, Charlottesville, pp 145–176

Frederick WC, Wasieleski DM (2002) Evolutionary social contracts. Bus Soc Rev 107(3):283–308

Gaulin SJC, McBurney DH (2001) Psychology: an evolutionary approach. Prentice Hall, Upper Saddle River

Gigerenzer G, Hug K (1992) Domain-specific reasoning: social contracts, cheating, and perspective change. Cognition 43:127–171

Gigerenzer G, Selten R (eds) (2001) Bounded rationality: The adaptive toolbox. Cambridge, MA: MIT Press

Gintis H, Bowles S, Boyd R, Fehr E (2003) Explaining altruistic behavior in humans. Evol Hum Behav 24:153–172

Greenwood DJ, Stini WA (1977) Nature, culture, and human history: a bio-cultural introduction to anthropology. Harper and Row, New York

Griggs RA, Cox JR (1982) The elusive thematic-materials effect in Wason's selection task. Brit J Psychol 73:407–420

Hastings BM, Shaffer BA (2005) Authoritarianism and sociopolitical attitudes in response to threats of terror. Psychol Rep 97:623–630

Hastings BM, Shaffer B (2008) Authoritarianism: the role of threat, evolutionary psychology, and the will to power. Theor Psychol 18(3):423–440

Hayibor S, Wasieleski DM (2008) Moral Recall: Examining the Effects of the Availability Heuristic on Perceptions of Moral Intensity. Journal of Business Ethics 84:151–166

Heinrich J (2006) The evolution of cooperative institutions: tackling the problem of equilibrium selection. Science 312:60–61

Hendry J (2002) The principal's other problems: honest incompetence and the specification of objectives. Acad Manage Rev 27(1):98–113

Henrich J, Boyd R, Camerer C, Fehr E, Gintis H (2004) Foundations of human sociality. Oxford University Press, Oxford

Hill SE, Buss DM (2006) Envy and positional bias in the evolutionary psychology of management. Manage Decis Econ 27:131–143

Hofstede G (2001) Culture's consequences: comparing values, behaviors, institutions, and organizations across nations, 2nd edn. SAGE Publications, Thousand Oaks

Jacobides MG, Croson DC (2001) Information policy: shaping the value of agency relationships. Acad Manage Rev 26(2):202–223

Jensen MC, Meckling WH (1976) Theory of the firm: managerial behavior, agency costs, and capital structure. J Financ Econ 3:305–360

Johnson-Cramer M, Phillips RA (2005) "Stakeholders", in Carl Mitcham (ed.), Encyclopedia of Science, Technology, and Ethics. (Detroit: Macmillan Reference)

Kahneman D (2003) Maps of bounded rationality: a perspective on intuitive judgment and choice. Am Econ Rev 93(5):1449–1475

Kahneman D, Tversky A (1972) Subjective probability: A judgment of representativeness. Cognitive Psychology 3:430–454
Kruger J, Dunning D (1999) Unskilled and unaware of it: how difficulties in recognizing one's own incompetence lead to inflated self-assessments. J Pers Soc Psychol 77(6):1121–1134
Leana C, Rousseau DM (eds) (2002) Relational wealth: the advantages of stability in a changing economy. Oxford University Press, Oxford
Lee R, DeVore I (eds) (1968) Man the hunter. Aldine, Chicago
Lichtenstein S, Baruch F, Phillips LD (1982) Calibration of probabilities: the state of the art to 1980. In: Daniel Kahneman, Paul Slovic, Amos Tversky (eds) Judgment under uncertainty: heuristics and biases. Cambridge University Press, Cambridge, pp 306–334
Loch CH, Galunic DC, Scheider S (2006) Balancing cooperation and competition in human groups: the role of emotional algorithms and evolution. Manage Decis Econ 27:217–233
Manktelow K (1999) Reasoning and thinking. Psychology Press, East Sussex
Manktelow K, St Evans JBT (1979) Facilitation of reasoning of realism: effect or non-effect? Br J Psychol 70:477–488
Markoczy L, Goldberg J (2004) Yabba-dabba-doo! A response to unfair accusations. Hum Relat 57(8):1037–1046
Marr D (1982) Vision: a computational investigation into the human representation and processing of visual information. Freeman, San Francisco
Micklethwait J, Wooldridge A (2003) The company: a short history of a revolutionary idea. Modern Library, New York
Miller GJ, Whitford AB (2007) The principal's moral hazard: constraints using incentives in hierarchy. J Publ Adm Res Theor 17(2):213–234
Mitnick BM (1997) Agency theory. In: Patricia Werhane H, Edward Freeman R (eds) The Blackwell encyclopedia dictionary of business ethics. Blackwell Business, Malden, pp 11–17
Nicholson N (1997) Evolutionary psychology: toward a new view of human nature and organizational society. Hum Relat 50(9):1053–1078
Nicholson N (2008) Evolutionary psychology, organizational culture, and the family firm. Acad Manage Perspect 4:73–84
Nilikant V, Rao H (1994) Agency theory and uncertainty in organizations evaluation. Organ Stud 15:649–672
Pava ML (2009) The exaggerated claims of evolutionary psychologists. J Bus Ethics 85:391–401
Pinker S (2002) The Blank Slate: The Modern Denial of Human Nature. New York: Viking
Price ME (2006) Monitoring, reputation, and 'greenbeard' reciprocity in a Shuar work team. J Organ Behav 27:201–219
Price M, Tooby J, Cosmides L (2002) Punitive sentiment as an anti-free rider psychological device. Evol Hum Behav 23:203–231
Ridley M (1985) The problems of evolution. Oxford University Press, Oxford
Robinson S, Kraatz M, Rousseau DM (1994) Changing obligations and the psychological contract: a longitudinal study. Acad Manage J 37:137–152
Ross WT Jr, Anderson E, Weitz B (1997) Performance in principal-agent dyads: the causes and consequences of perceived asymmetry of commitment to the relationship. Manage Sci 43(5):680–704
Santamaria C, Garcia-Madruga JA, Carretero M (1996) Univeral connectives in the selection task. Q J Exp Psychol 49A(3):814–827
Schein EH (1985) Organizational Culture and Leadership. San Francisco: Jossey-Bass
Sewell G (2004) Yabba-dabba-doo! Evolutionary psychology and the rise of Flintstone psychological thinking in organization and management studies. Hum Relat 57(8):923–955
Shaffer BA, Hastings BM (2004) Self-esteem, authoritarianism, and democratic values in the face of threat. Psychol Rep 95:311–316
Simon HA (1982) Models of bounded rationality: behavioral economics and business organization. MIT Press, Cambridge
Stone L (1997) Kinship and gender. Harper-Collins, Boulder

Sugiyama LS, Tooby J, Cosmides L (2002) Cross-cultural evidence of cognitive adaptations for social exchange among the Shiwiar of Ecuadorian Amazonia. Proc Natl Acad Sci 99(17):11537–11542

Tooby J, Cosmides L (1992) The psychological foundations of culture. In: Barkow, Jerome H, Cosmides, Leda, Tooby, John (eds) The adapted mind: evolutionary psychology and the generation of culture. Oxford University Press, New York, pp 19–136

Tooby J, Cosmides L (2000) Mapping the evolved functional organization of mind and brain. In: Gazzaniga MS (ed) The cognitive neurosciences. MIT Press, Cambridge, pp 1185–1196

Tooby J, Cosmides L, Sell A, Lieberman D, Sznycer D (2008) Internal regulatory variables and the design of human motivation: a computational and evolutionary approach. In: Elliot A (ed) Handbook of approach and avoidance motivation. Larence Erlbaum Associates, Mahwah

Trivers R (1971) The evolution of reciprocal altruism. Q Rev Biol 1971(46):33–57

Tversky A, Kahneman D (1973) Availability: a heuristic for judging frequency and probability. Cogn Psychol 5:207–232

Victor B, Cullen JB (1988) "The Organizational Bases of Ethical Work Climates". Administrative Science Quarterly 33(1):101–125

Wasieleski DM, Hayibor S (2009) Evolutionary psychology and business ethics research. Bus Ethics Quart 19(4):587–616

Wasieleski DM, Weber J (2009) Does job function influence ethical reasoning? An adapted Wason task application. J Bus Ethics 85:187–199

Wason PC (1968) Reasoning about a rule. Q J Exp Psychol 20:273–281

Wason PC, Johnson-Laird PM (1972) The psychology of reasoning: structure and content. Harvard University Press, Cambridge

Weaver G, Trevino LK (1999) Compliance and values-oriented programs: influences on employees' attitudes and behavior. Bus Ethics Quart 9(2):315–336

Wilson JQ (1993) The moral sense. Free Press, New York

The Role for Signaling Theory and Receiver Psychology in Marketing

Bria Dunham

Abstract Within marketing contexts, messages are effective when consumers find them both believable and relevant. An understanding of signaling theory and signal design features, derived from the study of animal and human behavioral ecology, can help marketers overcome the first challenge of crafting believable signals. Effective signals must fundamentally overcome the skepticism of receivers and generally accomplish this by linkage, either through identity or costliness, to the underlying quality being signaled. An understanding of receiver psychology, which involves appeals based on innate preferences that derive from shared human evolutionary history, can help marketers overcome the second challenge of rendering signals attractive and meaningful to consumers. Sensory bias, sexual stimuli, neoteny, and status all offer ripe opportunities for marketers to appeal to the innate preferences of consumers broadly or to specific targeted demographics. The following chapter provides an overview of signaling theory and receiver psychology as grounded in the evolutionary disciplines, with examples and applications that extend to the business world.

Keywords Signaling theory · Receiver psychology · Sensory exploitation · Signal cost · Consumer skepticism · Advertising · Marketing

1 Introduction

Why are black iPhones sold with white earbuds? There are many possible explanations. Perhaps Apple has such a backlog of white earbuds that it was convenient to package them with black iPhones so as to use the existing inventory. Possibly white earbuds are cheaper or easier to produce. Maybe manufacturing black earbuds

---

B. Dunham
Public Health, New York University, 240 Greene Street, 2nd Floor, NY 10003, New York
e-mail: bd411@nyu.edu

has never occurred to decision-makers in the Apple product design department. We could develop a number of similar suggestions, but none of these inventory- and production-oriented explanations are particularly convincing: such a large and successful company as Apple surely would consider the possibility of distributing handheld gadgets with matching earphones and would surmount any minor production and inventory obstacles to do so if matching the earphone color to the color of the device would be a strategic selling point.

A more compelling explanation is that white earbuds serve a signaling function, related to the popularity and status associated with the iPod prior to the release of the iPhone. The iPod was initially released in 2001, has generated many different iterations and spin-off versions, and has dominated the market for handheld digital media players. White hardware has become a distinguishing feature of many Apple products. The clean, crisp whiteness of the iPod is a highly conspicuous design feature, as iPods are routinely exhibited on sidewalks, school buses, and subways as their owners make their daily commutes. The distinctive white earbuds, as an extension of the iPod, help reinforce the brand awareness by their visibility even when the music player itself is tucked away in a pocket or bag. Although the design of the headphones has changed several times over the history of the iPod, they have consistently been white, small, and designed to fit inside the ear. When Apple began to offer iPods in different colors, they still came packaged with white earbuds. The iPhone was first released in 2007, following a massive marketing and media blitz. Upon the release of the iPhone, consumers were already largely familiar with the similar iPod as both an entertainment device and marker of status; the iPhone release may have "piggybacked" on this consumer familiarity. All iPhone models to date have been available in black casings; some models have also been available in white. By including the iconic white earbuds with each iPhone purchase regardless of the device color, Apple facilitates their customers' conspicuous status display and thus reinforces their own brand visibility. Telltale white earbuds indicate to passersby that the bearer ascribes to certain notions of coolness and style, engages willingly in some degree of conspicuous consumption, has the necessary resource control to afford a portable Apple device (and the accompanying service plan, in the case of the iPhone itself), and presumably enjoys music. That's a lot of information content for less than an ounce of plastic and wire.

The black iPhone-white earbud phenomenon fits into a broader framework of signaling theory, which itself is informed by theoretical biology. The swell of evolutionary thought in fields relating to human behavior, from medicine to economics to law, can also equip businesses with targeted insights into consumer psychology and desires. Graduate study in business, however, largely omits these insights, leading to the argument that much of marketing and consumer behavior research is antibiological in nature (Miller 2009; Saad 2007, 2008; Saad and Gill 2000). Database and index searches for signaling theory terminology, or key terms from evolutionary psychology, in business sources provide scant results. Miller (2009) surveyed the three main journals in marketing—*Journal of Marketing*, *Journal of Marketing Research*, and *Journal of Consumer Research*—noting that although a small number of papers addressed how signaling theory can be used to communicate information about a company's traits to consumers, no results addressed how consumption could communicate information about purchasers' traits to other people. Saad (2006) noted that *Journal of Consumer Research* abstracts for a 28-year period yielded only one result for "biology", one for "evolutionary psychology", and none for "Darwin". It is safe to assume that evolutionary approaches have been underutilized thus far in consumer behavior research and marketing, thus suggesting that the field is ripe for new evolutionary insights. This chapter provides a crash course in signaling theory and reviews the extant literature on its use and usefulness in marketing, advertising, and other business disciplines. In particular, this article will address signals, cues, and indices as packets of information transmission from producers or marketers to consumers; will delineate the uses and limitations of signaling theory within marketing; and will discuss appeals to the evolved receiver psychology of consumers.

Biological signaling theory is based in the study of animal behavior. Human behavioral ecologists and evolutionary psychologists have taken this framework and applied signaling theory to understanding human interactions from an evolutionary perspective (Cronk 2005; Iredale et al. 2008; Smith and Bliege Bird 2000). Some of applications of signaling theory to contemporary human behavior have direct relevance to economic transactions (e.g., Miller 2009). However, most references to signaling theory in business contexts refer to economic signaling, which differs from signaling theory as used by biologists, ethologists, and human behavioral ecologists. Economic signaling theory focuses on what business scholars consider costly signals of quality (e.g., Dawar and Sarvary 1997; Cai et al. 2002), but does not integrate an evolutionary perspective or investigate how the signal itself has evolved over time due to receiver feedback loops. Both long- and short-term marketing strategies can profit from an understanding of how signal design can overcome consumer skepticism and how certain types of signals can appeal to consumers' evolved preferences.

Economic signaling theory focuses on costliness in a purely financial sense whereas biological signaling theory considers the cost of signal production and maintenance in terms of survival and reproductive success. While "cost" may seem intuitively financial in business contexts, it is important to distinguish costliness in the evolutionary sense from the property of being expensive. Financial cost can be evolutionarily costly, but only when the cost is so high as to present a real and imminent threat to the survival of the business in the case of dishonest signaling or where the cost is so truly prohibitive that it would be impossible, not merely inadvisable, to signal falsely. Adopting this evolutionary approach to costly signaling, rather than the conventional business model that costly signals are those that are financially expensive, may elucidate the important role that signaling can play between different parties engaged in business enterprises.

Within the business disciplines, marketing is an intuitive arena for the application of signaling theory. In fact, biologists, anthropologists, and psychologists working from a signaling theoretical perspective have long co-opted marketing terminology in discussing the signals that people and other organisms send to each other. A peacock's tail or a man's facial symmetry are spoken of as "advertisements" of their quality as mates, as are elements of the external environment under the domain of the organism, such as a bowerbird's bower or lawyer's flashy sports car. These latter elements are part of what Dawkins terms "the extended phenotype" (1982) and may be most instructive for examining the utility and disutility of conspicuous consumption for mate-seekers. Recent substantial work on the evolution of consumer behavior has already incorporated insights from signaling theory (e.g., Griskevicius et al. 2010; Miller 2009; Saad 2007; Saad and Vongas 2009) and sex differences in evolved preferences and neurobiology (e.g., Pace 2009). Marketers can use the notion of the extended phenotype and knowledge about evolved preferences to guide product promotion efforts that appeal to consumers' own signaling motivations.

Despite laws regulating truth in advertising, marketing is not readily believed to be honest, as the field's objective is to present a positive impression of a product in order to increase sales and generate a profit for the company in question, both in short- and long-term contexts. Indeed, consumers are skeptical even after positive verification of advertising claims that appear too good to be true, which suggests that consumer skepticism may be an adaptive response to dishonesty in advertising (Koslow 2000). An examination of signal forms and routes to signal reliability may assist marketers in determining which types of signaling are appropriate and efficient for their particular aims.

2 The Basics of Signaling Theory

From an evolutionary psychological perspective, the first challenge in marketing is to render an advertisement, brand, or other marketing device as believable in the hopes of transforming audience members into actual consumers of the marketed good or service. Examining the different routes to signal reliability within biological systems provides a framework for identifying the opportunities to boost either actual signal reliability or the consumers' perceptions of signal reliability. This approach can also identify the limitations of classic biological signaling theory in marketing and can illuminate opportunities to use signals to appeal directly to different aspects of receiver psychology.

Signaling theory investigates the transmission of information from one individual, called a sender, to another individual, called a receiver. Biologists, human behavioral ecologists, and evolutionary psychologists attempt to explain signaling theory using an evolutionary framework, while economists and marketers apply signaling theory to patterns within commerce and business. These approaches are not as disparate as they may at first seem. An evolutionary perspective could equip marketers and economists to better understand signal design while an understanding of signaling within the business world could aid biologists in contextualizing and explaining their research to broader audiences. A signal is any physical or behavioral trait of an individual that has evolved to influence the behavior of others, and which is effective because the receiver's response has also been shaped by selection (Maynard Smith and Harper 2003). These signals convey information about the sender's characteristics (e.g., Zahavi 1975) or decrease the receiver's uncertainty regarding the sender's own future behavior (Krebs and Dawkins 1984).

Signaling theory is essentially about communication in a very broad sense; indeed, it is the dominant theoretical perspective within the scientific study of animal communication. According to classic biological signaling theory, signals are designed by selection and produced by a sender to meet a specific need. Applying signaling theory outside of biological phenomena demonstrates that evolution is not the only signal designer. Humans, including marketing professionals, design many signals for personal and professional uses disconnected from biological evolution. Basic principles of signaling theory are instructive for understanding effective and efficient signal design and routes to signal reliability, regardless of whether the signals are designed by evolution or by people. As people are themselves designed by evolution, one should expect that man-made signals should largely congrue with Darwinian realities.

Signal transmission depends not only upon a sender and a message sent, but also upon a receiver whose understanding of the world is such that the signal can be properly interpreted to evoke the appropriate response. The conspicuousness of a signal, the degree to which it is stereotyped, redundant features, and alerting characteristics all enhance the likelihood that a receiver will detect a signal (Wiley 1983). Signaling happens when one individual has information that a second individual does not, and where the sending organism benefits from producing the signal due to its effect on the receiver. Often the receiver benefits from this information as well. Krebs and Dawkins (1984) cast senders as manipulators, who alter the behavior of others to their own advantage, and receivers as mind-readers, who anticipate signalers' future behavior and react accordingly. Within a business context, marketers are manipulators who transmit advertisements to entice consumers to buy goods and services, and those same consumers are mind-readers that interpret the actual utility of the product for their particular circumstances, although they may be persuaded by the content and style of the advertisement, or signal, itself.

Signals, in an evolutionary sense, are not arbitrary. Honest signals contain a link to the underlying attribute being communicated, generally either by an inherent and unfakeable connection to the quality being signaled or by costliness; an awareness of this link can be useful in guiding current and future interactions between individuals. However, not all signals are honest. Under certain circumstances, senders may benefit from manipulating the behavior of receivers by use of dishonest signaling, even when this manipulation is not in the best interest of receivers. Systems can be evolutionarily stable in the presence of dishonest signaling so long as signals are honest on average (Johnstone and Grafen 1993; Kokko 1997). As such, routes to signal reliability and anti-deception strategies are important topics within theoretical and empirical investigation of signaling phenomena.

3 Different Routes to Signal Reliability

Any signal must necessarily overcome the skepticism of receivers in order for the sender to accrue the benefit of its production. One way of overcoming receiver skepticism relies on the design of the signal itself and the reasons why that signal may be perceived as honest. Reliability can be ensured by any of three central criteria: (1) where production of the signal would be prohibitively costly for a sender of low quality; (2) where the sender would not gain from falsely producing the signal, even if the signal were cost-free, particularly where the sender and receiver have a common interest; and (3) where the signal cannot be faked (Maynard Smith and Harper 2003). In addition to these three routes to signal reliability, signals may also be honest due to high punishment costs or reputational effects in social species, including humans (Maynard Smith and Harper 2003). Further explanation and evolutionary examples of routes to signal reliability follow, divided into signal forms whose reliability is contingent upon cost and signal forms whose reliability is based on the intrinsic link between signal and the underlying quality.

3.1 Costliness

Much discussion of the honesty or reliability of signals revolves around costly signaling. Cost in the signaling sense generally does not mean financial costliness, although there are some exceptions; rather, it refers to a mixture of strategic and efficacy costs involved in the production and transmission of the signal (Krebs and Dawkins 1984). Efficacy costs are the baseline costs necessary to ensure that the signal may be reliably perceived and interpreted. In contrast, strategic costs, such as the increased predation risk for a peacock due to his lovely but cumbersome tail or the increased burden to immune response in a man with high testosterone, are prohibitive for the sender; these are generally the costs entailed when researchers refer to "costly" signals. The presence of strategic costs in a signaling system increases, but does not completely ensure, honesty because the cost to a dishonest signaler is higher than the benefit, either due to a reduction in bodily resources for somatic needs or an increased vulnerability to parasites, pathogens, and predators. Essentially, the presence of costs that would be too dear for a signaler of low quality to produce assures the receiver of the signal's veracity due to the prohibitive nature of the cost.

A discussion of efficacy costs in marketing may be broached by reference to media saturation. The average consumer is exposed to over 60,000 words from the mass media daily, including such a bulk of advertisements that consumers will often disregard nearly all information received due to the impossibility to cognitively process so many stimuli (Herbig and Kramer 1994). As businesses have a vested interest in inducing consumers to perceive, process, and retain advertising messages about their products, it is useful to examine the design features that ensure this transmission and retention. In terms of signal design features, detectability and discriminability both rely on efficacy costs, as an efficacy cost is simply the minimal expenditure for effective transmission. A receiver's ability to perceive a stimulus and distinguish it from its surroundings is essential for that signal's transmission. An example of a particularly detectable and discriminable advertisement is the iconic large Citgo advertisement in Boston's Kenmore Square, which is far more attention-grabbing than the myriad conventional billboards in the area. Memorability, in contrast, derives from the salience of the stimulus and is not ensured by attempts to make that signal more detectable or discriminable. Strategic costs may contribute to memorability, but so do all other features of signal design that increase conspicuousness or significance to the receiver (Guilford and Dawkins 1991). Marketing has many routes to signal memorability: association with familiar cultural touchstones or persons, distinctive and ubiquitous logos that appeal to the senses, and so forth. Discordance can also enhance the memorability of an advertising message: commercials for the sandwich franchise Quiznos, for example, feature eccentric mascots with incongruent physiques, such as "Baby Bob", a talking baby with an oversized head, and the "spongmonkeys", two prosimian primates with oversized human facial features who sing that they "love the subs". The "spongmonkeys" in particular have precipitated an unprecedented amount of viewer and consumer mail to Quiznos's corporate office (Stevenson 2004). Trey Hall, Chief Marketing Officer for Quiznos, reports that the "spongmonkey ads" were launched to increase consumer awareness of the brand through being "dramatic" with a limited advertising budget; this goal is largely considered to have been met (Stevenson 2004). Memorability may be the most significant of the three efficacy costs for classical advertising aims, but detectability and discriminability should also be considered, particularly in light of advertising clutter (Pieters et al. 2007; Rotfield 2006).

The classic example of a heavy strategic cost is a handicap signal. Handicaps are the flashy stars of signaling theory: showy exhibitions of quality that weaken the sender by virtue of their cost. For example, a large tail both requires valuable somatic resources and encumbers a peacock's ability to evade predators. Zahavi (1975) proposed that these extravagances are signals to peahens, which could use the tail as a reliable signal of the peacock's health or genetic quality. Such an imposing cost would make faking the signal prohibitively costly, thus ensuring signal honesty. Handicaps are generally considered to be an extreme form of costly signaling. Other costly signals in nonhuman species include food and alarm calls, as the caller incurs an increased predation risk or reduces his own access to a resource in order to warn group members of danger or call individuals to share in a food source. The specific signaling function varies dramatically by species, with some examples best explained by reference to kin selection and some that seem to represent an increased status effect for the caller or increased observed ownership of a portion of the shared resource (Searcy and Nowicki 2005). As a human example, Meriam islanders use turtle hunting as a costly signal of male fitness and resource control, which varies by the specific role undertaken in the hunt and the type of expedition (Smith and Bliege Bird 2000, 2003; Smith et al. 2003). With costly and handicap signals, individuals who are of insufficient quality to signal a feature would find it very difficult to convincingly do so, as such signaling demands greater metabolic resources than the sender has in reserve or because the deficiency would be obvious to receivers.

In humans, muscularity may serve as a handicap signal of physical strength, particularly weightlifting ability. Further, some degree of male muscularity is considered attractive in both heterosexual (Frederick and Haselton 2007) and homosexual (Swami and Tovée 2008) contexts, rendering it adaptively relevant to observers, although individual preferences vary. Increased muscle mass is both the result and the facilitator of regular weightlifting activity. A person's degree of muscularity does change over time and enacts strategic costs, in terms of somatic resources and opportunity costs of time spent engaged in athletic activities, to ensure its maintenance (Sugawara et al. 2002). Individuals with lesser weightlifting ability would be unable to develop muscles suggesting considerably greater strength than they possessed, and any attempt to circumvent this system by use of a false signal such as a muscle suit would likely be met by injury or ridicule when the false signaler attempted to lift a heavy load. Even in cases where steroids or other muscle enhancing substances are used to grow bulkier muscles than the individual would have otherwise developed, the muscularity itself still serves as a signal of weightlifting ability but not as a reliable signal of underlying physiology.

Existing scholarship on handicap signaling in business journals has conflated the evolutionary notion of costliness with financial costliness (Ambler and Hollier 2004), or with behaviors that do not entail debilitating costs to the signaler (Deutsch Salamon and Deutsch 2006). Although a corporation, firm, or business can be interpreted as an individual signaler in a business context, that entity must withstand a relevant survival cost in order for a costly signal to be considered reliable. These inquiries do identify relevant signals in business contexts, but neither provides a clear example of a Zahavian handicap. Two key complications arise in applying the handicap hypothesis to marketing: (1) financial costliness does not carry a penalty of the same form or magnitude as evolutionary costliness, and (2) high advertising budgets do not functionally render the signal more reliable, although they may be perceived as such by viewers. The very fact that high advertising expenditures are perceived as more reliable signs of quality by potential consumers (Kirmani and Wright 1989), in spite of the differences between financial and evolutionary costliness, underscores the usefulness of understanding signaling theory within business contexts. True handicap signals should be exceedingly rare in business contexts due to loss aversion by business owners and shareholders. The exorbitant costs associated with handicap signaling, along with the severe and survival-threatening risks of signaling when the business is not truly equipped to bear the cost of that signal, discourage the use of handicaps in commercial enterprises. Certain forms of money-back guarantees, particularly those for high-cost products and where consumers can return a product due to dissatisfaction rather than proof of a physical defect, may represent a legitimate handicap business signal in that the financial cost may be too great for businesses with products of insufficient quality to bear and remain solvent. However, most money-back guarantees are either for lower-cost products, where customers may be less inclined to spend the opportunity cost to obtain a refund, or require that the customer show substantial evidence of a defect, as with lemon laws for new vehicle purchases. These limited money-back guarantees, in contrast to satisfaction guarantees for high-cost goods, are insufficiently costly as signals to constitute a true handicap.

The possession of an honors degree from a highly esteemed university provides a potential employer with an expensive testament to the applicant's quality (Spence 1973). Earning such a degree reflects intelligence, conscientiousness, and the base resources to have been adequately prepared for college and then to have been able to afford its cost. According to Frank (2007), attorneys drive cars that signal competence and past successes to their current or prospective clients. This induces lawyers to spend ever more money to maintain their status, resulting in a signaling arms race of BMWs and Mercedes. The most successful lawyers end up with the most expensive cars, although many less successful lawyers may have spent disproportionately in order to ensure future work. Chemistry professors, in contrast, have no career-based incentive to signal success by ever more expensive automobiles, as their variance in salary is lower than that of attorneys and the granting institutions and deans that determine those salaries are rarely aware of which cars professors drive. The disproportionately nice cars driven by real estate agents may also serve a similar signaling function in providing the agents with an opportunity to display their own extended phenotype. Homebuyers might then transfer luxurious qualities about the realtor's car to the property, even though these two entities are largely independent of each other. Organic certification serves as a costly signal of a particular set of food production criteria, which is itself associated with ecological consciousness and health-related concerns. The process of becoming certified as an organic food producer is time-consuming, financially costly, and bureaucratically tangled. Due to the onerous nature of the process, many small producers with sustainable practices opt out of formal certification. Large-scale organic agribusiness, which must follow the letter of organic certification but not necessarily the spirit, is a lucrative industry that convincingly signals certain information about food production to consumers that are disconnected from a more immediate interaction with the producer.

Under certain circumstances, signals that are not costly can nonetheless be reliably honest. Minimal cost signals may be evolutionarily stable where senders and receivers rank their preferences for outcomes in the same order, where dishonest signaling is punished, where senders and receivers have overriding common interests, where senders would not benefit by signaling falsely, or where they solve coordination problems between individuals that expect repeated interactions (Maynard Smith and Harper 2003). Within the business realm, low-cost signals could be functional when corporations anticipate ongoing professional relationships, where failures affect both parties equally, and generally where the relationship between entities is highly cooperative. Within the animal kingdom, an obscure but illustrative example of a minimal cost signal comes from the mating behavior of *Drosophila subobscura*. When approached by a new male, a mated female extrudes her ovipositor to signal that she has already been inseminated. The male then ceases what would otherwise be a lengthy courtship display. Both parties have an interest in the cessation of unsuccessful courtship, and by use of this minimal cost signal, the female communicates sufficient information for the common interest to be recognized and for the male to move on to a more receptive potential mate (Maynard Smith 1956). Some forms of commitment signaling in human courtship consist of minimal cost signals, such as wearing a romantic partner's fraternity pin or letter jacket. This form of signaling carries a low strategic cost for both the donor and donee of the object but conveys salient information about the relationship to outside parties. In these examples, a woman will visibly wear an article that her suitor likely already owned independently of their relationship. This form of signaling in courtship contrasts somewhat with the costs entailed in engagement rings worn by women and wedding rings worn by both parties in a relationship. These rings are intrinsically linked to the courtship itself, having been purchased or handed down within a family to commemorate that particular relationship, and do generally involve some degree of cost in their purchase, although this cost is highly variable (see Cronk and Dunham 2007 for a discussion of the signaling value of engagement rings).

Minimal cost signals aren't particularly attention grabbing, either for receivers or for academics working on signaling topics. Nonetheless, they represent a significant category within signaling theory and are relevant for marketers precisely because of their low cost in an evolutionary sense. Few business signals should be expected to be truly costly, in the sense of imposing such an undue burden that a dishonestly signaling business would be exterminated by the market, simply because the cost involved in transmitting the signal could be devoted to other business expenses. Furthermore, boards of directors and stockholders would rarely be expected to idly approve of such risky endeavors. Success in business industries is rarely as "all or nothing" as it is in biological signaling systems, such as mating and evasion of predators. One business example of a minimal cost signal is the near ubiquitous grocery or department store posting that guide dogs are permitted. This signal in stores that otherwise have no-pet policies is advantageous to store owners and managers for three key reasons, even though the primary beneficiaries of such policies are blind individuals and seeing-eye dogs who cannot read the signs. The first reason is that this decreases the possibility that a customer who does not immediately recognize an animal in the store as a guide animal will mistakenly assume that the anti-pet policy is not actively enforced. The second is to reassure individuals who would presume that an absolute prohibition against all animals would be discriminatory (Frank 2007). The third, not addressed by Frank, is that not all individuals with service animals are themselves blind, as guide animals may be used to help people with a range of different disabilities. In all of these cases, the costs of presenting the signal are minimal and the benefits, while small, are great enough to offset the very low cost. As such, minimal cost signals in business contexts do not "handicap" the signaler and may be of particular use to marketers due to their low risk profiles and palatability to stockholders. Exploring the routes to reliability with minimal cost signals, particularly in regards to emphasizing confluences of interests between businesses and consumers, will allow marketers to craft minimal cost signals tailored specifically to the aims of a particularly company. Investments in local social programs, such as hosting book drives or donating day-old pastries to a soup kitchen, constitute a straightforward minimal cost signal that individual businesses or franchises could undertake to signal their community involvement and shared sense of purpose to consumers; tasteful promotion of these activities by marketers could enhance the stature of the business to a larger consumer base. Other minimal cost signals may be more appropriate for other marketing aims or within different industries.

Beyond its intuitive applicability to marketing and advertising, signaling theory may help interpret interactions in other business contexts. Market share repurchases, where corporations buy back their own shares on the stock market or from individual shareholders to increase the company's equity, are potential opportunities for companies to signal their confidence in their own value and their belief that the current market price is below the true value. Firms that frequently repurchase their own shares are larger, have a more stable operating budget, and tend to pay higher dividends (Jagannathan and Stephens 2003). Firms that announce open market share repurchases but then do not actually themselves repurchase the shares tend to be smaller and to attract less attention from analysts than do firms that follow through with repurchases (Bhattacharya and Dittmar 2008). In this manner, firms' willingness to announce and to follow through with repurchases may transmit signals to current stockholders, potential stockholders, and consumers of the firms' products.

Another opportunity for signaling in a non-marketing business context is organizational citizenship behavior within companies. Salamon Deutsch and Deutsch (2006) argue that organizational citizenship behavior, wherein employees perform tasks beyond their job descriptions for the benefit of the company and their coworkers, represents a handicap signal to convey the senders' underlying competitive qualities and skills. However, organizational citizenship behavior is relatively easy to fake in comparison to the sorts of handicap signals seen in biological systems. Individuals could sacrifice time and energy that they could otherwise spend outside of work. Furthermore, the penalty for insufficient signaling is likely not so severe as to cause a risk to survival in the corporate environment. It may be more instructive to consider organizational citizenship behavior as a signal of variable costliness that conveys commitment to the corporation. Organizational citizenship behavior may not give as much information about the intrinsic qualities of the workers, including their job skills, as it does about their high valuation of the company and willingness to personally sacrifice for the benefit of the team. In markets where actors know each other and have an expectation of future interaction, as between firms and contractors, reputational effects may accrue from dishonest communication (Phalen 1998). Thus signals may be expected to be honest, even in the absence of efficacy or strategic costs in the production of that signal, because the penalty for dishonest signaling is so punitive as to be prohibitive.

3.2 Identity

Costliness is only one route to signal reliability, although it is the one most frequently examined by researchers studying biological signaling phenomena.

If signals can influence the behavior of other individuals, why don't people signal falsely to induce the desired response? In addition to the constraints on signal honesty due to cost, potential for punishment, and lack of benefit for dishonest signaling, certain signals can be honest due to an intrinsic link to the quality represented and sheer impossibility to be faked, in contrast to an exorbitant cost that would render attempts to falsely signal foolhardy, yet technically possible. Cues and indices provide reliable transmissions of information to receivers due to these immutable connections.

Cues are defined very broadly as any animate or inanimate feature that can be used by an organism to inform and guide future action (Hasson 1994; Maynard Smith and Harper 2003). This distinguishes cues from signals, as signals can be activated and de-activated, whereas cues are fixed at a point in time (Maynard Smith and Harper 2003). The crucial distinction between signals and cues is that signals evolved due to their effect on others and cues did not. Specifically, signals evolved because they influenced the knowledge of receivers about senders, even at a cost to the senders' somatic fitness. Cues, in contrast, do not entail a somatic cost, may not be heritable, may evolve due to natural selection rather than the effect on the receiver, and may be maintained despite offering receivers more information than is necessarily in the best interest of senders (Hasson 1997). Cues are, therefore, linked to the quality being perceived by an observer in a more direct and unfakeable manner than are signals. As cues are intrinsic, unfakeable, and offer few opportunities to bias consumer behavior to the benefit of the business entity, their applications should be relatively rare in marketing contexts but cues should be highly attended to and perceived as reliable by consumers. The following examples of cues in biological and business contexts may clarify cues as a side note to signaling phenomena.

An animal example of a cue is the weight difference in funnel-web spiders, which determines whether an interloper will instigate or retreat from a contest (Reichert 1978; Maynard Smith and Harper 2003). The act of vibrating the web is an index, but the size difference itself did not evolve due to receiver psychology and is fixed at a specific point in time. In women, facial masculinity may serve as a cue of sexual attitudes and behavior due to the underlying association of both with testosterone (Boothroyd et al. 2008; Campbell et al. 2009). This cue did not evolve to serve the purposes of the sender; indeed, it may be contrary to the information that a woman would prefer to convey and is relatively fixed at one point in time; in fact, women may attempt to circumvent the cue by use of cosmetics (Cronk et al. 2003). Within a business context, the crowdedness of a parking lot or dining room is a cue to potential customers of the popularity, and by extension the quality, of an establishment. It is a feature of the environment that conveys information about the establishment to passersby. Management may attempt to circumvent the parking lot cue by asking staff to park directly by the entrance rather than reserving the prime parking spaces for customers, but it is rather difficult to convincingly fake the crowded dining room cue by placing mannequins in seats. Other business applications of cues are mandatory guidelines for listing nutritional information on foods, posting health department ratings in restaurants, and providing OHSA information on chemicals or other hazardous materials in workplace environments. These cues, as they cannot legally or logistically be faked by business owners who might benefit by transmitting a different message, are reliable due to the direct information content of the cue.

Indices are unfakeable because they are causally dependent upon the trait being signaled (Maynard Smith and Harper 2003). Unlike cues, indices are signals that organisms actively produce and from which they accrue benefits; they are not passive and cannot be neutral or negative as cues may be. Unlike handicaps and other costly signals, they have no strategic costs. The stotting of Thomson's gazelles provides a clear illustration of an index (Caro 1986; Fitzgibbon and Fanshawe 1988). Upon spying a cheetah or predatory canine, a fit gazelle will leap repeatedly in place, displaying his awareness that a predator is in the vicinity. Stotting, in effect, lets the predator know that that particular gazelle is prepared to flee and that perhaps another gazelle would make a more vulnerable meal. Collaborative human music and dance performances may signal important information to members of the group and to outside parties. In particular, the degree of successful collaboration may signal the strength of the social coalition to outgroup members and smooth the way for intergroup encounters (Hagan and Bryant 2003). In this manner, group cohesiveness in musical performance is an index of group social cohesiveness; it is unfakeable, linked to identity, and has no particular strategic cost for its production although it carries an efficacy cost of learning and performing the selection.

Local agricultural status, as evidenced through participation in producers-only farmers' markets or through signage at a third party retail grocer, may serve as an index of local production. Local production is itself highly desirable to a subset of consumers due to its associations with ecological consciousness, sustainable practices, and support of small-scale local businesses. Indeed, purchases of ecologically conscious products may serve as a signal of altruism towards the planet and its inhabitants, and thus can be motivated by status-enhancing primes (Griskevicius et al. 2010). A growing interest in sustainable eating and in supporting local farmers has contributed to the popularity of farmers' markets and in supermarket signage to note the provenance of wares. Some farmers' markets allow resale of produce grown far away, but producers-only farmers' markets self-evidently limit vending space to producers within convenient driving distance. As such, consumers have a reasonable assurance that the food was produced locally. Many vendors increase consumer confidence in their business ideology by providing information about their farm or dairy, ranging from distributing literature to displaying pictures to inviting visitors to the farms. These low-cost marketing materials signal to customers that the vendors are ideologically attractive, in the sense of representing small family businesses, practicing sustainable farming techniques, limiting the use of certain materials in food production, or some combination of these.

Some signals may be maladaptive or inefficient, although these should generally be limited over time due to negative selection pressures; cues, however, can remain stable over time despite possible disadvantages to senders. Signals from marketers may contradict the foundational message of their product. Miller (2009) provides the "right hand ring" advertisement series from the DeBeers diamond cartel as an example of this. At a minimum, an engagement ring, diamond or otherwise, signals the intentions of a woman and her suitor to wed. Differences in the proportional costs of engagement rings indicate that they also signal information about male and female mate value, as well as features of the courtship (Cronk and Dunham 2007). Miller (2009) argues that the emergence of single, successful women buying ornate diamond rings to wear on their right hands, wrapped up in an advertising campaign that appeals simultaneously to notions of empowerment and entitlement, undermines the base functional signal of engagement rings as a marker of betrothed status. If observers do indeed cease to differentiate between right and left hand rings, this marketing campaign may have undermined DeBeers's own best interest by lessening the signaling prominence of diamond engagement rings.

Table 1 reviews and defines each signal type, the strategic cost associated with producing the signal, a nonhuman example, a human example from a non-business context, and a human example from a business context.

4 The Role of Sensory Bias and Receiver Psychology in Signal Design, and How This Matters for Marketers

The appeal to receiver psychology, through either manipulating evolved preferences or by reducing skepticism, is the crux of signaling theory. Much of signaling focuses on exploiting the sensory and psychological biases of receivers rather than on convincing those receivers of a signal's honesty (Enquist and Arak 1998; Guilford 1997; Ryan 1998). Examining signal design from the standpoint of receiver psychology facilitates explanations that are not contingent upon sheer costliness but rather focus upon exploitation of innate or evolved preferences, such as those for symmetry (van Valen 1962), neoteny (Hinde and Barden 1985), and the color red (Adams and Osgood 1973). Within the business realm, attention to evolved preferences that capitalize upon sensory bias can guide both product design and marketing efforts (Saad 2006). Presenting signal messages that appeal to the receiver psychology of consumers and that serve as an inducement to buy represents the second major challenge facing marketers from an evolutionary psychological perspective. Precisely because so many signals used in marketing can be faked, due to the low costs in an evolutionary sense of dishonest signaling and the rarity of truly unfakeable cues and indices, appeals to receiver psychology through the five senses may equip marketers with tools derived from evolutionary psychology to better position products and attract consumers.

4.1 Sight and Sound: The Obvious Targets

The available advertising venues in Western society are particularly amenable to pitches that exploit the senses of sight and sound (see Saad 2004 for a discussion of

Table 1 Types of signals

Type	Definition	Strategic cost	Nonhuman example	Human nonbusiness example	Business example
Index	Unfakeable signal causally dependent on the trait displayed	None	Stotting in Thomson's gazelles (Caro 1986)	Music and dance ability as index of group cohesion (Hagan and Bryant 2003)	Local farming status
Costly	Reliable signal due high strategic costs	High	Food and alarm calls (Searcy and Nowicki 2005)	Turtle hunting by Meriam islanders (Smith and Bliege Bird 2000, 2003)	Organic certification; job market signaling (Spence 1973)
Handicap	Signal testing an individual with a cost that negatively impacts survival (Zahavi 1975)	High	Peacocks' tails (Zahavi 1975)	Muscularity as signal of strength	Should be very rare in business contexts; may include certain money-back guarantees
Minimal cost	Signal conferring no or minimal cost; may be reliable due to common interests, reputational effects, or risk of punishment	Low	Ovipositor display in *Drosophila subobscura* (Maynard Smith 1956)	Some forms of commitment signaling in courtship, such as wearing a fraternity pin or letter jacket	Guide dog posting (Frank 2007)
Cue	Feature of the world that can be used as a guide to future action (Hasson 1994). Cues are not signals	None	Weight difference in funnel-web spiders (Reichert 1978)	Female facial masculinity as a cue of sociosexuality (Boothroyd et al. 2008; Campbell et al. 2009)	Crowded parking lots or dining room as cue of popularity

advertising images from an evolutionary perspective). Commercial images proliferate on the many flat surfaces of the modern city, from buses to newsstands to Times Square billboards. The standard "hour-long" network television program is actually about 42 min long, with the remaining 18 min consisting of commercial programming; consumer attention wanes with increased commercial length and when high information content is paired with low entertainment context (Woltman Elpers et al. 2003). Radio programs shuffle between music, announcer comments, and yet more advertisements. Indeed, one indirect measure of the strength of the economy itself is the thickness of mainstream fashion magazines, as their heft is directly proportional to the number of ads sold (Johnson 2009; Smith 2009).

Humans are highly visual organisms. Visual dominance is a highly derived trait, being more significant for primates than most other mammals and a particularly essential trait in the human adaptive toolkit when compared to the sensory lives of other primates (in contrast, most mammals rely proportionately more heavily on olfactory cues and less on sight than we do). The approximately 120 million rods and seven million cones in the human eye allow for a rich visual perception of the external environment. Contemporary optometry extends this acuity to sufferers of myopia, hyperopia, astigmatism, and cataracts. Although relatively little can be done for macular degeneration or color-blindness, the wealth and history of treatments for vision defects reflects the importance of sight for humans' navigation of the world. Stronger evidence for vision as a key component within the human sensory toolbox, which is less subject to the history of technological development, are shifting preferences for visual novelty and familiarity in human infancy (e.g., Wetherford and Cohen 1973) and the speed with which humans can complete certain visual detection tasks (e.g. Thorpe et al. 1996). Given the importance of vision in one's perception and assessment of the physical world, appeals to vision are salient in business contexts.

Capitalizing upon the role of visual stimuli in advertising, marketers have heavily studied the use of color, albeit usually without an evolutionary bent. For example, Anglo-Canadian mall shoppers associated green plants with positive evaluations of merchandise whereas Franco-Canadian shoppers showed a similar preference for merchandise positioned near yellow or red flowers (Chebat and Morrin 2007). Color preferences also play a role in mate choice, both in humans and across species. Elliot and Niesta (2008) noted the presence of red coloration in sexual swellings and other estrous-related changes in non-human primates, along with historical and literary associations between red and sex, in their investigation of men's preferences for red color in mating contexts. Stephen et al. (2009) found that research subjects choose to experimentally increase the amount of red pigmentation in stimulus figures of human female faces. This increased red pigmentation mimicked the effect of highly oxygenated blood and increased perceptions of health, as well as the increased facial hue due to sexual arousal. However, preferences for and affective reactions to color are context-dependent. Due to its associations with failure, men are averse to red in competitive contexts (Hill and Barton 2005; Elliot et al. 2007) but view red positively in romantic contexts (Elliot and Niesta 2008). Further, color associations, like many other associations elicited by marketers, vary cross-culturally and may well deserve more detailed consideration in global marketing campaigns (Saad 2006). In biological systems, aposematic coloration can serve as a warning signal to predators of the noxious taste of a particular prey species. Non-venomous species mimic venomous species via Batesian mimicry, thus lessening their predation risk due to the predatory species' disinclination to risk a deadly meal. As such, aposematism does not serve as a reliable signal in biological systems, yet it is one that may often be heeded despite its unreliability due to the high cost to a predator who fails to heed the warning when necessary. Evolutionary theory does not uniformly project that bright coloration should be attractive and desirable, but rather that bright coloration would tend to be attention-grabbing in contrast to milder colorations that are not associated with ripe fruits, sexual arousal, or deadly repasts.

Sound is also a crucial sense both for survival in nature and success in advertising markets. Evolutionarily speaking, food and alarm calls are signals that audibly capture the attention of the intended receiver; they are risky because they also capture the attention of unintended receivers, including potential predators and rivals (Searcy and Nowicki 2005). The attention-seizing property of auditory signals is also relevant for marketers. The increased volume of television commercials, as compared to the volume of regular programming, may represent an efficacy cost. A suddenly blaring television doesn't cue a viewer in to the effectiveness of the touted message, but it may earn the advertiser a few seconds of attention before the viewer can grab the remote control to lower the volume. In contrast to the perhaps unwanted distraction of a suddenly loud television advertisement, music and the appreciation thereof play roles in social life and personal enjoyment in many cultures. Particularly, the production of music may signal creativity in courtship (Miller 2000) and listening to music is a significant part of many ritualized gatherings, from weddings to funerals. Unsurprisingly, marketers exploit people's affective responses to music by incorporating familiar songs or catchy jingles into commercials and by playing muzak or other audio in retail settings. The most salient musical selection to accompany an advertisement is highly context-dependent, may influence shopping behavior through both direct effects on mood and interaction effects with other elements of the advertisement, and is likely to be shaped both by environment and evolved psychology (Bruner 1990). Bruner (1990) argues that "[m]usic is likely to have its greatest effect when consumers have high affective and/or low cognitive involvement with the product" (pp. 101); listing examples of products that fall into this category as types of clothing or accessories, plus alcoholic beverages. He distinguishes these from products where individuals have a higher cognitive involvement and perhaps a lower cognitive involvement, such as appliances, vehicles, technological gadgetry, and insurance. Music may therefore be a peripheral cue for persuasion within the Elaboration Likelihood Model, affecting consumers by the emotional attachments they feel towards music rather than by cognitive processing of information claims. The products with which consumers have high-affective and low-cognitive involvement, and therefore those that may be most effectively marketed with use of music, may serve a signaling function to others, as clothing and alcoholic beverages are often prominent markers of personality in social settings. This contrasts with products that have low affective and high cognitive appeals, such as appliances, as these objects are predominantly intended for private use and are less effectively marketed with use of music. Further, products can serve as advertisements for the music that ostensibly itself advertises the product, sometimes intentionally and sometimes incidentally. The increased familiarity of a Coldplay or Chairlift song after being featured in a heavily aired Apple commercial underscores this cycle.

4.2 Scent, Taste, and Touch: The Senses That Try to Get Away

Sight and sound are easily manipulated in advertisements due to the nature of the media. Scent, taste, and touch are more elusive. Advertisements may compensate, in part, by using descriptive terminology that evokes the smell of freshly washed laundry or a spring meadow. They may describe the flavor of a juicy hamburger, complete with a diner's moans of appreciation and hyper-enlarged visual detail to show the crispness of the lettuce and tomato between a sizzling meat patty and fluffy bun. They may use lighting and ripples to show the sheen of satin when promoting a luxury sedan or bodywash, neither of which actually involve the haptic feel of satin. Despite all the language ploys that advertisers may use to evoke these senses, it is far more difficult to directly engage the senses of scent, taste, and touch in consumers. Furthermore, such direct engagement generally requires a greater expenditure in terms of cost and effort per audience member reached.

Romantics speak of scent as the most sentimental of the senses, reflecting on how certain scents waft the smeller back to childhood at grandmother's house or a long-since-visited café. Memory elicitation due to odor recognition is particularly strong and may represent a separate memory system (Herz and Engen 1996). Pleasant ambient scents are associated with improved product evaluations when the scents are congruent with the product category; further, incongruent scents do not result in devalued product perceptions (Bosmans 2006). Businesses increasingly use ambient scents in retail and service environments that are not emanated by the products themselves (e.g., Bosmans 2006). Despite the evocative power of scent, it is rarely directly used in marketing outside of the retail environment. When scent is used in marketing, the scent usually *is* the product, as in the cases of department store perfume samples and magazine cologne inserts. Some innovative marketing strategies get the scent of the product into novel advertising opportunities, such as the use of a citrusy smell to advertise anti-dandruff shampoo at bus stops (Roberts 2005, pp. 123). The most frequently encountered exception to the scent-identity marketing pattern is the use of freshly-baked cookies, or, more often, scented candles that smell like freshly baked cookies, by realtors whose intention is to sell houses rather than to sell cookies or candles. This cookie effect has been extended beyond its use to market properties. In an experimental setting, women in a room that smelled like chocolate chip cookies were more likely to express a desire to make an unplanned sweater purchase while on a limited budget than were women in a room without the cookie scent (Xiuping 2008). Marketers may thus use scents to signal associations to consumers in the hopes of building upon existing preferences. This use could best be thought of as a minimal cost signal with limited reliability, as the connection between the scent and the product is not ensured by either costliness or any inherent, intrinsic link.

Marketers may do well to attend to previous work on the evolutionary basis of scent preferences. From an evolutionary standpoint, our preferences for certain types of scents may derive from our more general disgust-based aversion to putrefaction and biological waste, consistent with a pathogen-avoidance domain (Tybur et al. 2009), coupled with preferences for fruits that smell ripe. This aversion is deeply rooted and likely predates culture in humanity's evolutionary past (Curtis 2007) and is particularly concerned with eating or otherwise orally coming in contact with "contaminated" objects, such as those containing traces of feces (Rozin and Fallon 1987). As such, most pleasant smells may be pleasant not because of what they represent, but rather because of the absence of decay that they signal. Evolutionary theory does not clearly predict whether an individual would prefer floral or fruity scents, as not every preference is rooted in an evolutionary mechanism. Evolution does, however, contribute to scent's role in sexual attraction and arousal. Evolutionary psychologists have further demonstrated that women have mating preferences based strictly on scent, in the absence of other inputs, for more masculine men, men with heterozygous major histocompatibility complex genes (MHC), and more symmetrical men (e.g., Gangestad and Thornhill 1998; Thornhill et al. 2003), which themselves are mediated by menstrual cycle effects and women's partnership status. These preferences may be exploited not only by marketers but also in product design itself. Consumers use perfumes not to mask their own body odors but rather to enhance and augment their natural scents and to hypothetically signal their own MHC to potential mates (Milinski and Wedekind 2001; Havlicek and Roberts 2009). Awareness of consumers' own signaling aims in perfume use can guide both the development of new fragrances and the marketing promotion of these, hinging upon the implication of scents that smell like the bearer, only enhanced.

Taste is another sense with a deep evolutionary heritage in humans. In the environment of evolutionary adaptedness (EEA), preferences for sweet and fatty foods helped humans stay alive. Due to the scarcity of foods containing these tastes in the ancestral environment and the associated vitamin, mineral, and nutrient content of these foods, individuals who sought out berries or consumed game animals at least occasionally had survival and reproductive advantages over those who did not. Sugars and fats are by no means limited in the contemporary Western diet. The widespread obesity rates of America and much of the developed world are largely due to our innate preferences for flavors that would have been painstaking to seek out in the EEA but that are amplified exponentially in the heavily processed packages within easy reach on the grocery store shelf. Substantial quantities of high-fructose corn syrup and hydrogenated vegetable oils have made their way into the American diet as a result of these ancient preferences, despite the lack of these chemical compounds in the Pleistocene. These preferences are well-recognized by food designers, regardless of their interest in the adaptive significance of such foods. Marketers may therefore signal the "richness" and "decadence" of certain foods in order to tap into these evolutionarily designed preferences. Handled deftly, this may be of special use in targeting health-conscious consumers, who may seek gustatory indulgence paradoxically presented in a low-calorie, low-fat shell.

As with appeals to the other four senses, marketers may benefit from attending to the role of touch in receiver psychology. Innate preferences for certain types of touch may be related to our shared evolutionary history as group-living primates. Humans are distinct in living in such large, geographically-dispersed social groups, which was first facilitated by grooming and then the evolution of language (Dunbar 1996). As such, our preferences for luxurious textures may be an outgrowth of tactile comforting from relatives and other group members. Roberts (2005) argues that touch is missing from much of product design and links the physical sensation of touching people with selling products. A series of experiments of questionable moral and ethical standards established that isolated rhesus monkeys preferred tactile contact with wire "mothers" covered in terrycloth to that of uncovered wire "mothers" that provided milk (Harlow and Zimmermann 1959). The close association between physical touch and social bonding should not seem surprising in a society that craves bed linens with high thread counts and welcomes recommendations from sommeliers who speak of wine's "mouthfeel". Under experimental conditions, waitstaff that physically touch their clients increase their tips by more than 3% in comparison to waitstaff that do not touch the customers during interactions (Lynn et al. 1998b). Similarly, retail customers spent more on products and shopped for longer periods of time after having been touched by sales staff (Hornik 1992). Manipulations of tactile sensations to increase consumer spending may best be invoked in retail environments where consumers could both physically handle the merchandise and be themselves touched by sales associates and product representatives. This is especially illustrated in cosmetics departments where crisply dressed sales staff offer complimentary makeovers.

Many of the applications of signaling theory to marketing and advertising may be most effective in direct interpersonal encounters. Human psychology evolved within a context of dyads and small groups, not within a context where information is spread by an impersonal mass media blitz. This is not to say that large advertising campaigns cannot benefit from the applications of signaling theory and consideration of receiver psychology. Indeed, understanding innate preferences and the evolutionary rationale for how they manifest themselves may be very instructive for marketers. But the highest potential impact per contacted consumer may come from the incorporation of multiple senses and signals, which is most easily managed via face-to-face interaction. Indeed, the senses of taste, touch, and scent cannot be manipulated by standard print and video advertisements, although perfume inserts and glossy pages are limited substitutes for specific goods. Consumers' inability to touch the merchandise presents a challenge for internet retailers; this effect is greater for female shoppers and for products whose quality can best be assessed by use of tactile cues (Citrin et al. 2003).

5 Receiver Psychology Beyond the Senses

Appeals to receiver psychology in marketing contexts extend past innate preferences tied to the five senses. As such, it may be instructive to examine elements of our evolutionary history that predict consumer preferences. The broad domains that may be most useful for marketers are sexual appeal, solicitive behaviors towards children, and risk aversion.

The notion that "sex sells" is perhaps the most widely recognized message in popular advertising (Saad 2004, 2007, Chap. 4). In its more explicit forms, the use of sexuality in advertising is met with reactions ranging from blasé acceptance to organized resistance to active encouragement. Roberts (2005) explicitly applies romantic and sexual contexts to the relationship between customers and their favored brands, arguing that successful brands forge these relationships by the use of mystery, sensuality, and intimacy.

Why does sex sell? The simple answer is because sex is pleasurable and continually, rather than cyclically, interesting. Why is sex pleasurable and interesting? Sex is pleasurable and interesting because human psychology and physiology have evolved to make it so. Why did human psychology and physiology evolve to make sex so pleasurable and interesting? That's a somewhat more complicated question, with responses that relate to increased genetic representation in future generations, provisioning, social cohesion, the division of labor, and a host of other factors. Within that tangle of responses, however, is a commonly accepted argument that men and women exhibit certain differences in sexual interest and behavior that are consistent with divergent evolutionary strategies but convergent goals once constraints, such as monogamy or mutual investment in offspring, are included in the system. Attending to these sex differences in biology and behavior can guide marketing efforts (Pace 2009). In a different business domain, receiver biases impact hiring decisions, with Human Resource (HR) professionals of prime reproductive age preferring attractive opposite-sex applicants in an experimental setting. Female college students preferentially chose less-attractive female hirees in an experimental setting that tested intrasexual competition, but this finding was not replicated in the sample of trained HR managers (Luxen and van de Vijver 2006).

Another appeal to receiver psychology is the emphasis of neotenous characteristics in both human and non-human advertising stimuli. Neoteny isn't as immediately recognizable as sex appeal in terms of features exaggerated and emphasized by advertising. Nevertheless, neoteny, or the presentation of juvenile features, plays a substantial role both in marketing and in product design. Due to the high altriciality of human infants, people are highly solicitive of children and are especially attuned to helpless, childlike features in the external environment. This solicitive behavior endures even when the childlike features have no actual relationship to a human infant, much less to one's own offspring. One example of a neotenous consumer good is the teddy bear, heavily represented in gift shops and bedrooms across Western society. The evolution of the teddy bear has progressed from a realistic bear-like appearance with an elongated snout to the current incarnation of a large-headed, large-eyed, smaller snout, cuddly being that in many ways holds greater resemblance to a human infant than a member of the *Ursidae* family (Hinde and Barden 1985). In addition to teddy bears, Cabbage Patch Kids and Mickey Mouse may owe part of their success to consumers' innate preferences for neotenous features (Lynn et al. 1998a). Crafting advertisements that include neotenous features may appeal to the child-solicitive elements of evolved human psychology. Lynn et al. (1998a) note that the neotenous appeal of the Pillsbury Doughboy and the Campbell Soup Kids may be particularly attractive to consumers despite the characters' roles as spokespersons rather than as the product available for purchase.

An important lesson from marketing, particularly as it relates to ecologically-conscious behavior, is that people are more inclined to behave in certain ways when they are made aware that others engage in those same activities (Cialdini 2003; Goldstein et al. 2008), which is itself perhaps related to human group dynamics and desires to conform. However, this may vary by context and the effectiveness of an advertising message is linked to the broader piece of media within which it is displayed. Griskevicius et al. (2009) demonstrated that appeals to an establishment's popularity are more persuasive when audiences have been primed with a fear condition related to survival as compared to a romantic condition; the converse is true for appeals to a service's distinctive and under-discovered allure. Further, fear conditions rendered advertisements emphasizing an undiscovered gem of an establishment less persuasive than a control advertisement, and romantic desire primes rendered advertisements that emphasized an establishment's popularity less effective than a control advertisement. These findings are consistent with evolved predispositions to band together for the sake of individual self-interest when danger threatens (e.g., Hamilton 1971; Palley 1995) or to distinguish oneself as distinctive in romantic and sexual competition (e.g., Miller 2000). The authors suggest that the first 15 seconds of a video advertisement could be used to elicit an emotional response that would render the message of the advertisement more persuasive and the product itself more attractive, depending upon whether the problem and the appeal offered a solution to the adaptive problem represented by the emotion.

6 The Consumer as Signaler

Beyond the signals conveyed by a corporation or an advertising firm to entice and retain customers, the role of the consumer him- or herself as a signaler is germane for a discussion of signaling theory in marketing. Both specific commercial goods and consumption more generally can signal qualities about the purchaser to other individuals such as potential romantic partners, rivals, and colleagues; business entities may wish to consider consumers' signaling motivations as product pitches are formulated. Miller (2009) presents the argument that most human buying patterns can be reduced to attempts to signal general intelligence and the Big Five personality traits, which are Openness, Conscientiousness, Agreeableness,

Stability, and Extraversion. With this view in mind, it may behoove marketers to attend to the qualities that potential consumers would want to transmit and to ways to convey through advertising that their products would serve as an effective and efficient signal of these traits.

Insofar as marketing emphasizes the signaling capacity of products themselves, in terms of their usefulness for attracting mates and impressing others, the signals upon which the field focuses may be inefficient. Miller (2009) argues that modern marketing overly relies on signals of wealth, status, demographics, and taste along with a concurrent lack of attention to reproductively relevant qualities such as kindness, creativity, and humor. Although these attractive qualities largely relate to the Big Five personality factors and general intelligence, marketers tend to ignore them in pursuit of faddish notions that do not have a long history of empirical support (Miller 2009). However, insights from evolutionary psychology would still encourage marketers to attend to certain elements beyond personality, including resource control in males and reproductive potential in females, which marketers indeed do en masse. In routine social encounters, the most effective way for a woman to convey her reproductive potential is to emphasize her appearance. This aim can be accomplished either through her behavior of actively calling certain physical features to attention, such as through the use of low-cut blouses, or through accentuating products, such as cosmetics. Preference matching on the Big Five personality traits, either through mating or commercial markets, is driven by assortative pairing wherein like attracts like and greater mate similarity is associated with higher marital satisfaction (Gaunt 2006). Preferences for signposts of fertility, status, dominance, and resource control are not as individually variable as are preferences for personality traits; these are roughly stable within and across societies. The signaling value of products to convey personality attributes should not be discounted, but neither should the relevance of classically desirable mate characteristics.

Advertising makes vague allusions to the signaling value of products rather than overt claims. It is rare to find a commercial that explicitly assures increases in reproductive success to smart-thinking customers who snap up the touted product. A contributing factor to this phenomenon may be plausible deniability both on the part of the advertiser if confronted with angry lovelorn customers and on the part of the consumer if confronted with a suspicious or jealous spouse (Miller 2009). The additional mating opportunities that may accrue from the exhibition of a fancy sports car or cosmetics are generally alluded to in the subtext of ads, not as the surface message.

Consumption of luxury goods can serve as a signal of social status; this ties directly into an examination of signal cost. The waste inherent in costly signaling stands in contrast to the neoclassical economic view of humans as rational actors. Due to this paradox, some of the earliest investigations into the signaling power of commercial activity and consumption dealt with the pursuit of luxury. Predating formal signaling theory, John Stuart Mill (1848) noted that luxury item are purchased for the sake of the owner's reputation, accruing from the costliness of the product, which makes them an appropriate good for taxation. Thorstein Veblen's (1899) notion of conspicuous consumption, widely cited across the social sciences, further considered costliness and ostentatious display of wealth as signals of status.

Luxury consumption considerably hampers future consumption opportunities (Frank 1999), yet luxury goods are distinctively high in signaling capacity due to their considerably high financial cost, recognizability, and desirability. This results in a market of aspirational customers, but multiple scholars have noted the risk inherent when luxury manufacturers attempt to increase their sales by offering several lower-cost products or a more affordable product line (e.g., Saad 2007; Thomas 2007). The deceptive signaling function of greater resource control is met through both the secondhand luxury market, such as through consignment boutiques, and the consumption of counterfeit luxury goods. The Asian market is particularly robust for both genuine and counterfeit luxury goods (Thomas 2007). Young unmarried Japanese women in particular, who often continue to reside with their parents until they get married and while working office jobs, spend exorbitantly on luxury clothing and accessories, which they maintain meticulously (Muller 2006; Thomas 2007). Counterfeit goods may be more readily assumed to be legitimate in underdeveloped nations, where the population is not as familiar with the details and physical appearance of genuine luxury goods as are consumers in more developed nations (van Kempen 2003); the ecological context-dependence of perceiving this deception underscores the relevance of evolutionary psychology for understanding the phenomenon (Saad 2007).

A final manifestation of consumers as signalers concerns the recent consumer interest in ecologically-conscious products. Griskevicius et al. (2010) noted that experimental subjects reported preferences for purchasing environmentally-conscious products when they were primed in a status-seeking condition and when green products were more, not less, expensive than their non-green counterparts. This finding contrasts with rational economic theory but is highly consistent with signaling theory. Products that directly appeal to consumers' desires to signal their resource control and altruism practically market themselves, so long as their visibility is such that consumers are aware of their availability. Marketing campaigns can profit from further emphasizing these functional and evolutionarily-undergirded components, such as by showing consumers in a context where others note and appreciate the "greenness" and altruism of the purchaser. Griskevicius et al. (2010) advocate that marketing efforts for ecologically-conscious products should clearly link the products to status, through either association with high-status celebrity endorsers or by showcasing the products at prestigious events, especially when products have high development costs (e.g., green cars). However, lower-cost "green" products should not be linked to status in marketing campaigns due to their inability to signal wealth.

The motivations of consumers to boost their own signaling power manifests in different ways depending on the specific aims and resources of individual consumers. Women seeking mates may gravitate towards products to signal their fertility, men seeking mates may choose flashy status objects that demonstrate their resource control, and mate seekers of both sexes are likely to choose products that signal aspects of personality and taste. Those consumers less directly motivated by mating aims may still make similar purchasing decisions, both because our evolved predispositions run deeper than our proximate goals and because the same sorts of products may enhance our status among friends, neighbors, and associates more generally. Recognizing a product's signaling potential not only *to* a consumer but *for* a consumer may help marketers better identify effective advertising strategies.

7 Evolution and Marketing in a Recession

As of the time of this writing, the global economic climate is in a tailspin. The New York Stock Exchange plummeted in September 2008 as major US and international financial institutions plummeted into dire financial straits and the economy has yet to make a full recovery by March 2010. Repercussions have been substantial on a global scale. For example, the Icelandic krona is so devalued that half of the nation's businesses became insolvent and 15% of Icelanders found themselves with negative equity (Cendrowicz 2009). Unemployment is staggeringly high. What is the role for marketing in such a bleak economic landscape and what can we learn about it from an understanding of our evolutionary past?

Recession pricing has become a common selling point within the service industry, for everything from steak (Spano 2009) to vacations (Engle 2009) to prostitution (BBC 2009). Perhaps marketers are onto something with this straightforward acknowledgment of the dismal economic climate. Recession pricing, itself perhaps a last ditch measure to ensure some sales in a dire economy, also has the role of signaling to consumers that we, as a society, are in this together and that the commercial establishment recognizes their customers' own needs and limitations at this time. Such signaling of commitment and connection may prove to have been a successful long-term strategy to ensure customer loyalty when the economy improves, assuming that the business is able to weather this storm (see Palmer 2000 for application of game-theoretic models to an evolutionary view of relationship marketing between business entities and consumers).

Advertising is generally more subject to economic fluctuations than other areas of business and cyclicity of advertising expenditures varies by country as well as by company, with countries that show more fluctuations in advertising expenditures experiencing slower overall advertising market growth (Deleersynder et al. 2009). Increasing advertising expenditures for consumer products during a recession is associated with greater corporate benefits than increases in advertising expenditures when the economy is not in a recession (Frankenberger and Graham 2003) and advertising expenditures that run counter to cyclical predictions are associated with greater success for the company (Srinivasan et al. 2005). Frankenberger and Graham (2003) argue that firms should generally increase advertising expenditures during a recession if it is financially feasible to do so, but also note that repercussions of cutting advertising budgets will mostly be limited to the recession year itself, rather than extending into the firm's future profits.

8 Conclusion

A signaling theoretical approach to marketing, incorporating different routes to signal reliability and sources of salience due to receiver psychology, can further equip existing efforts to understand strategic marketing opportunities. Insights from signaling theory can help marketers understand how to overcome the skepticism of potential consumers about their product claims and also understand how those very same customers could use the marketed products in their own signaling efforts.

As most signals in advertising contexts are unlikely to be "handicaps" in the evolutionary sense, given the prohibitive costs entailed and the likely reticence of stockholders to stand idly by when their profits are placed at risk, marketers may do best to consider alternate routes to signal reliability and the importance of receiver psychology. At minimum, an advertising message must be detectable, discriminable, and memorable in order to be effective. Attempts to enhance memorability and persuade consumers towards a purchase can take multiple forms: increasing signal cost (even if not by such a degree as to constitute a handicap), exploiting sensory perceptions, appealing to consumers' evolved predispositions, or demonstrating the signaling value of the product for consumers themselves.

Appeals to memorability are tied up in the costliness of signals transmitted by business entities. Consumers attend to signals about a company's quality, as do shareholders and competitors, although it would seem that the company's reputation is not as relevant to consumers as the value of the particular product. Frank (2007) argues that including the phrase "As Seen on TV" in magazine and newspaper advertisements serves as a signal of confidence in the product to potential consumers, as it draws their attention to the fact that the item has been promoted in a potentially more expensive medium than the one that they are currently perusing. In contrast to a costly signaling function, noting in a print advertisement that a product was sold on television could serve a memorability function, cueing in the reader to a recognition of having seen the product before and evoking recollections of aired demonstrations or testimonials. Gandolfi et al. (2002) explicitly apply biological signaling theory to understanding why firms spend so much money on advertising without a substantial informative content. In this perspective, the function of expensive advertising is to convince the public that the firm is sufficiently successful to bear the costs of the signal, thus conveying that the business entity will not attempt to sell sub-standard merchandise, as doing so would carry too great of a reputational penalty. Alternately, such expenditures may simply serve to increase the appeal and memorability of the product without serving as a testament to the product's quality, as there is no intrinsic link between the product quality and advertising expenditures. The increase in viewer perception of quality with increased advertising expenditures (Kirmani and Wright 1989), while certainly relevant from the standpoint of receiver psychology, does not lead to a sufficient survival risk for the business as the result of viewer backlash due to product dissatisfaction.

Marketing is in the complex position of signaling to multiple audiences simultaneously, some of which may be at cross-purposes with each other. It may be useful to look at signaling in marketing across nested levels. Advertisements themselves serve as communication from suppliers to varied audiences, including consumers, stockholders, and their own employees. The purchased items themselves equip individuals to signal qualities to prospective mates, associates, and rivals. The primary audience of an advertisement is the potential consumer, but shareholders, competitors, and company staff also receive the signal. The salient information for the consumer concerns the product's specific value, defined in a myriad of factors related to quality, cost, preference-matching, and its own capacity to signal to others. The salient information for shareholders, competitors, and company staff, in contrast, is the brand. In pursuit of these aims, companies may spend excessively on advertisements simply to signal their ability to withstand the costs of such wastefulness (e.g., Ambler and Hollier 2004).

In biological systems, signals do not generally occur singly; rather, they are often transmitted at the same time as a receiver observes other qualities about an organism. For example, "beauty" may represent a cohesive integration of multiple human traits, with mate decisions partially based upon assessment of this combined quality (Fink and Penton-Voak 2002). If multiple traits coalesce to give a cohesive insight into the immune response of a potential mate, such a combined signal might be more reliable than individual signals, which might be easier to fake. Alternately, transmission of multiple signals may represent an attempt by senders to interfere with reception of competing signals and where receivers develop fine-tuned abilities to separate the honest, salient features from the noise (Lozano 2009). Marketers would do well to consider the consolidated and nested nature of most signaling phenomena. Of course, any individual marketing message is likely to contain multiple signals, some of which may reinforce other signals and others of which may relate to different aims or appeals to receiver psychology. A given advertisement, for example, could simultaneously signal a message regarding the firm's resource control and confidence in the product (in terms of the production and distribution costs), a message regarding attractive qualities of the product itself (such as direct or implied appeals to its popularity, distinctiveness, or utility), and a message obliquely linking the product to the ascribed or aspirational traits of the consumer (such as appeals that imply sexual success or increased status for the bearers of such goods). Whether the transmission of multiple signals results in a more convincing message or a more competitive message, it would seem that multiple signals or signals that exploit multiple elements of receiver psychology would be more effective in marketing than lone signals.

Individual consumers can show resistance to even impeccably-designed marketing signals and can subvert the signaling message of their own purchases. Strongly anti-consumerist mores nullify the impact of a highly-recognizable logo. Oversized bright green Panasonic headphones are fully compatible with Apple iPhones and send a rather different message to observers than do the iconic white earbuds resting on a shelf at home. Evolutionary psychology cannot give any answers to how *every* person or *any given* individual will react to a marketing message; rather, it can offer insights on how populations will tend to behave as a result of our collective evolutionary past. As such, insights from evolutionary psychology offer a promising avenue of opportunity for marketers seeking to increase their market success by attending to innate consumer preferences.

Acknowledgements I wish to thank Gad Saad for constructive editorial remarks on the content and organization of this chapter. I would further like to thank Lee Cronk, Rolando de Aguiar, Frank Batiste, and Helen Wasielewski for providing comments on an early version of this manuscript as members of the Rutgers University Human Behavioral Ecology Laboratory. Jennifer Trivedi and Mark Murphy provided useful feedback during revisions and Mike Murphy offered useful discussions of business phenomena.

References

Adams FM, Osgood CE (1973) A cross-cultural study of the affective meanings of color. J Cross Cult Psychol 4(2):135–156
Ambler T, Hollier EA (2004) The waste in advertising is the part that works. J Advertising Res 44(4):375–389
BBC (2009) Brothel offers 'green' discount. BBC News, July 14. http://news.bbc.co.uk/2/hi/europe/8149334.stm
Bhattacharya U, Dittmar AK (2008) Costless versus costly signaling: Theory and evidence. Working Paper from the Indiana School of Business. Available at SSRN: http://ssrn.com/abstract=250049 or doi:10.2139/ssrn.250049
Boothroyd LG, Jones BC, Burt DM, DeBruine LM, Perrett DI (2008) Facial correlates of sociosexuality. Evol Hum Behav 29(3):211–218
Bosmans A (2006) Scents and sensibility: when do (in)congruent ambient scents influence product evaluations. J Market 70(3):32–43
Bruner GC (1990) Music, mood, and marketing. J Market 54(4):94–104
Cai CX, Duxbury D, Keasey K (2002) A new test of signaling theory. Finance Lett 5(2):1–5
Campbell L, Cronk L, Simpson J, Milroy A, Wigington T, Dunham B (2009) The association between men's ratings of women as desirable long-term mates and individual differences in women's sexual attitudes and behaviors. Pers Individ Differ 46(4):509–513
Caro TM (1986) The functions of stotting in Thompson's gazelles. Anim Behav 34:663–684
Cendrowicz L (2009) Iceland's urgent bid to join the EU. Time, June 17. http://www.time.com/time/world/article/0,8599,1911188,00.html
Chebat J-C, Morrin M (2007) Colors and cultures: exploring the effects of mall décor on consumer perceptions. J Bus Res 60(3):189–196
Cialdini RB (2003) Crafting normative messages to protect the environment. Curr Dir Psychol Sci 12(4):105–109
Citrin AV, Stem DE Jr, Spangenberg ER, Clark MJ (2003) Consumer need for tactile input: an internet retailing challenge. J Bus Res 56(11):915–922
Cronk L (2005) The application of animal signaling theory to human phenomena: some thoughts and clarifications. Soc Sci Inf/Information sur les Sciences Sociales 44(4):603–620
Cronk L, Dunham B (2007) Amounts spent on engagement rings reflect aspects of male and female mate quality. Hum Nat 18(4):329–333
Cronk L, Campbell L, Milroy A, Simpson JA (2003) Cosmetics as a signaling system. Paper presented at the annual meeting of the American Anthropological Association, New Orleans
Curtis VA (2007) Dirt, disgust, and disease: a natural history of hygiene. J Epidemiol Community Health 61(8):660–664
Dawar N, Sarvary M (1997) The signaling impact of low introductory price on perceived quality and trial. Market Lett 8(3):251–259

Dawkins R (1982) The extended phenotype. Oxford University Press, Oxford
Deleersynder B, Dekimpe MG, Steenkamp J-BEM, Leeflang PSH (2009) The role of national culture in advertising's sensitivity to business cycles: an investigation across continents. J Market Res 46(5):623–636
Deutsch Salamon S, Deutsch Y (2006) OCB as a handicap: an evolutionary psychological perspective. J Organ Behav 27(2):185–199
Dunbar R (1996) Grooming, gossip, and the evolution of language. Harvard University Press, Cambridge
Elliot AJ, Niesta D (2008) Romantic red: red enhances men's attraction to women. J Pers Soc Psychol 95(5):1150–1164
Elliot AJ, Maier MA, Moller AP, Friedman R, Meinhardt J (2007) Color and psychological functioning: the effect of red on performance attainment. J Exp Psychol Gen 136(1):154–168
Engle J (2009) A bad economy adds up to good vacation deals. Los Angeles Times, July 19. http://www.latimes.com/business/investing/la-tr-money19-2009jul19,0,7263187.story
Enquist M, Arak A (1998) Neural representation and the evolution of signal form. In: Dukas R (ed) Cognitive ecology: the evolutionary ecology of information processing and decision making. University of Chicago Press, Chicago, pp 21–88
Fink B, Penton-Voak IS (2002) Evolutionary psychology of facial attractiveness. Current Directions in Psychological Science 11(5):154–158
Fitzgibbon CD, Fanshawe JH (1988) Stotting in Thompson's Gazelles: An honest signal of condition. Behavioral Ecology and Sociobiology 23(2):69–74
Frank RH (1999) Luxury fever: why money fails to satisfy in an era of excess. The Free Press, New York
Frank RH (2007) Decoding marketplace signals. In: The economic naturalist. Basic Books, New York, pp 133–148
Frankenberger KD, Graham RC (2003) Should firms increase advertising expenditures during recessions? Marketing Science Institute Report No. 03-115
Frederick DA, Haselton MG (2007) Why is muscularity sexy? Tests of the fitness indicator hypothesis. Pers Soc Psychol Bull 33(8):1167–1183
Gandolfi AE, Gandolfi AS, Barash DP (2002) Economics as an evolutionary science: from utility to fitness. Transaction Publishers, New Brunswick
Gangestad SW, Thornhill R (1998) Menstrual cycle variations in women's preferences for the scent of symmetrical men. Proc R Soc Lond B 265:927–933
Gaunt R (2006) Couple similarity and marital satisfaction: are similar spouses happier? J Pers 74(5):1401–1420
Goldstein NJ, Cialdini RB, Griskevicius V (2008) A room with a viewpoint: using social norms to motivate environmental conservation in hotels. J Consum Res 35(3):472–482
Griskevicius V, Goldstein NJ, Mortensen CR, Sundie JM, Cialdini RB, Kenrick DT (2009) Fear and loving in Las Vegas: evolution, emotion, and persuasion. J Market Res 46:384–395
Griskevicius V, Tybur JM, Van den Bergh B (2010) Going green to be seen: status, reputation, and conspicuous conservation. J Pers Soc Psychol 98(3):392–404
Guilford T (1997) The extravagance of animal signals. J Biol Educ 31(1):24–28
Guilford T, Dawkins MS (1991) Receiver psychology and the evolution of animal signals. Anim Behav 42(1):1–14
Hagan EH, Bryant GA (2003) Music and dance as a coalition signaling system. Hum Nat 14(1):21–51
Hamilton WD (1971) Geometry for the selfish herd. J Theor Biol 31(2):295–311
Harlow HF, Zimmermann RR (1959) Affectional responses in the infant monkey: orphaned baby monkeys develop a strong and persistent attachment to inanimate surrogate mothers. Science 130(3373):421–432
Hasson O (1994) Cheating signals. J Theor Biol 167(3):223–238
Hasson O (1997) Toward a general theory of biological signaling. Journal of Theoretical Biology 185(2):139–156

Havlicek J, Roberts SC (2009) MHC-correlated mate choice in humans: a review. Psychoneuroendocrinology 34(4):497–512

Herbig PA, Kramer H (1994) The effect of information overload on the innovation choice process: Innovation overload. Journal of Consumer Marketing 11(2):45–54

Herz RS, Engen T (1996) Odor memory: review and analysis. Psychon Bull Rev 3(3):300–313

Hill RA, Barton RA (2005) Red enhances human performance in contests. Nature 435(7040):293

Hinde RA, Barden LA (1985) The evolution of the teddy bear. Anim Behav 33(4):1371–1373

Hornik J (1992) Tactile stimulation and consumer response. J Consum Behav 19(3):449–458

Iredale W, van Vugt M, Dunbar R (2008) Showing off in humans: male generosity as a mating signal. Evol Psychol 6(3):386–392

Jagannathan M, Stephens C (2003) Motives for multiple open-market repurchase programs. Financ Manage 32(2):71–91

Johnson S (2009) Fashion mags in a fix. Marketing, Aug 19, 8

Johnstone RA, Grafen A (1993) Dishonesty and the handicap principle. Animal Behaviour 46(4):759–764

Kirmani A, Wright P (1989) Money talks: perceived advertising expense and expected product quality. J Consum Res 16(3):344–353

Kokko H (1997) Evolutionarily stable strategies of age-dependent sexual advertisement. Behav Ecol Sociobiol 41(2):99–107

Koslow S (2000) Can the truth hurt? How honest and persuasive advertising can unintentionally lead to increased consumer skepticism. J Consum Aff 34(2):245–268

Krebs JR, Dawkins MS (1984) Animal signals: mind-reading and manipulation. In: Krebs JR, Davies NB (eds) Behavioural ecology: an evolutionary approach, 2nd edn. Sinauer, Sunderland, pp 380–402

Lozano GA (2009) Multiple cues in mate selection: The sexual interference hypothesis. Bioscience Hypothesis 2(1):37–42

Luxen MF, van de Vijver FJR (2006) Facial attractiveness, sexual selection, and personnel selection: when evolved preferences matter. J Organ Behav 27(2):241–255

Lynn M, Kampschroeder K, Perriera T (1998a) Evolutionary perspectives on consumer behavior: an introduction. Paper presented at the twenty-sixth annual conference of the Association for Consumer Research, Montreal, Canada

Lynn M, Le M-K, Sherwyn DS (1998b) Reach out and touch your customers. Cornell Hotel Restaur Adm Q 39(3):60–65

Maynard Smith J (1956) Fertility, mating behavior and sexual selection in *Drosophila subobscura*. J Genet 54:261–279

Maynard Smith J, Harper D (2003) Animal signals. Oxford University Press, Oxford

Milinski M, Wedekind C (2001) Evidence for MHC-correlated perfume preferences in humans. Behav Ecol 12(2):140–149

Mill JS (1848) Principles of Political Economy with some of their Applications to Social Philosophy. Ed. Ashley, WJ. 7th ed, 1909. Library of Economics and Liberty. http://www.econlib.org/library/Mill/mlP.html

Miller G (2000) The mating mind: how sexual choice shaped the evolution of human nature. Random House, New York

Miller G (2009) Spent: sex, evolution, and consumer behavior. Viking, New York

Muller K (2006) Japanland: a year in search of Wa. Rodale, New York

Pace E (2009) The X and Y of buy: sell more and market better by knowing how the sexes shop. Thomas Nelson, Nashville

Palley TI (1995) Safety in numbers: a model of managerial herd behavior. J Econ Behav Organ 28 (3):443–450

Palmer A (2000) Co-operation and competition: a Darwinian synthesis of relationship marketing. Eur J Market 34:687–704

Phalen PF (1998) The market information system and personalized exchange: business practices and the market for television audiences. The Journal of Media Economics 11(4):17–34

Pieters R, Wedel M, Zhang J (2007) Optimal feature advertising design under competitive clutter. Manage Sci 53(11):1815–1828

Reichert SE (1978) Games spiders play. Behav Ecol Sociobiol 3:135–162

Roberts K (2005) Lovemarks: the future beyond brands. Powerhouse Books, New York

Rotfield HJ (2006) Understanding advertising clutter and the real solution to declining audience attention to mass media commercial messages. J Consum Market 23(4):180–181

Rozin P, Fallon AE (1987) A perspective on disgust. Psychol Rev 94(1):23–41

Ryan M (1998) Sexual selection, receiver biases, and the evolution of sex differences. Science 281 (5385):1999–2002

Saad G (2004) Applying evolutionary psychology in understanding the representation of women in advertisements. Psychol Market 21(8):593–612

Saad G (2006) Applying evolutionary psychology in understanding the Darwinian roots of consumption phenomena. Managerial Decis Econ 27(2–3):189–201

Saad G (2007) The evolutionary bases of consumption. Lawrence Erlbaum Associates, Mahweh

Saad G (2008) The collective amnesia of marketing scholars regarding consumers' biological and evolutionary roots. Market Theory 8(4):425–448

Saad G, Gill T (2000) Applications of evolutionary psychology in marketing. Psychol Market 17 (12):1005–1034

Saad G, Vongas JG (2009) The effect of conspicuous consumption on men's testosterone levels. Organ Behav Hum Decis Process. doi:10.1016/j.obhdp. 2009.06.001

Searcy WA, Nowicki S (2005) The evolution of animal communication: reliability and deception in signaling systems. Princeton University Press, Princeton

Smith SD (2009) The ad page recession. Womens' Wear Daily, July 22, 1

Smith EA, Bliege Bird RL (2000) Turtle hunting and tombstone opening: public generosity as costly signaling. Evol Hum Behav 21(4):245–261

Smith EA, Bliege Bird R (2003) Costly signaling and cooperative behavior. In: Bowles S, Boyd R, Fehr E, Gintis H (eds) Moral sentiments and material interests: on the foundations of cooperation in economic life. MIT Press, Cambridge

Smith EA, Bliege Bird R, Bird DW (2003) The benefits of costly signaling: Meriam turtle hunters. Behav Ecol 14(1):116–126

Spano S (2009) High-end New York restaurants offer meal deals during recession. Los Angeles Times, July 2. http://travel.latimes.com/articles/la-tr-nycrestaurants5-2009jul05

Spence AM (1973) Job market signaling. Q J Econ 87(3):355–374

Srinivasan R, Rangaswamy A, Lilien GL (2005) Turning adversity into advantage: does proactive marketing during a recession pay off? Int J Res Market 22(2):109–125

Stephen ID, Coetzee V, Law Smith M, Perrett DI (2009) Skin blood perfusion and oxygenation color affect perceived human health. PLoS ONE 4(4):e5083. doi:10.1371/journal. pone.0005083

Stevenson S (2004) The creatures from the sandwich shop: behind the singing rodents in the Quiznos ad. Slate, Feb 23. http://www.slate.com/id/2095868/

Sugawara J, Miyachi M, Moreau KL, Dinenno FA, DeSouza CA, Tanaka H (2002) Age-related reductions in appendicular skeletal muscle mass: association with habitual aerobic exercise status. Clin Physiol Funct Imaging 22(3):169–172

Swami V, Tovée MJ (2008) The muscular male: a comparison of the physical attractiveness preferences of gay and heterosexual men. Int J Mens Health 7(1):59–71

Thomas D (2007) Deluxe: how luxury lost its luster. Penguin, New York

Thornhill R, Gangestad SW, Miller R, Scheyd G, McCollough JK, Franklin M (2003) Major histocompatibility complex genes, symmetry, and body scent attractiveness in men and women. Behav Ecol 14(5):668–678

Thorpe S, Fize D, Marlot C (1996) Speed of processing in the human visual system. Nature 381 (6582):520–522

Tybur J, Lieberman D, Griskevicius V (2009) Microbes, mating, and morality: individual differences in three functional domains of disgust. J Pers Soc Psychol 97(1):103–122 van Kempen L (2003) Fooling the eye of the beholder: deceptive status signalling among the poor in developing countries. J Int Dev 15(2):157–177

van Valen L (1962) A study of fluctuating asymmetry. Evolution 16(2):125–142

Veblen T (1899) The theory of the leisure class. AM Kelley, New York

Wetherford MJ, Cohen LB (1973) Developmental changes in infant visual preferences for novelty and familiarity. Child Dev 44(3):416–424

Wiley RH (1983) The evolution of communication: Information and manipulation. In Communication. Eds. Halliday, TR, & Slater, PJB. Blackwell, Oxford, pp. 82–113

Woltman Elpers JLCM, Wedel M, Pieters RGM (2003) Why do consumers stop viewing television commercials? Two experiments on the influence of moment-to-moment entertainment and information value. J Mark Res 40(4):437–453

Xiuping L (2008) The effects of appetitive stimuli on out-of-domain consumption impatience. J Consum Res 34(5):649–656

Zahavi A (1975) Mate selection: a selection for a handicap. J Theor Biol 539(1):205–214

Cue Management: Using Fitness Cues to Enhance Advertising Effectiveness

Patrick Vyncke

Abstract Current thinking on advertising processing highly parallels contemporary psychological theory and research revealing that there are two distinct brain systems at work in human information processing and decision making: System 1 (S1, evolutionarily old, unconscious/preconscious, automatic, fast, and intuitive) and System 2 (S2, evolutionarily recent, conscious, controlled, slow, and reflective).

Indeed, state-of-the-art models of advertising processing equally distinguish two different persuasive routes: one in which the consumer focuses on product/brand attribute information and in which he/she engages in elaborated information processing (S2), and one in which she/he processes the ad only superficially in terms of a handful of meaningful "cues" (S1). Regarding S2 advertising processing, means-end-chain theory offers a sound theoretical framework. However, regarding S1 advertising processing the question remains: What constitutes a meaningful cue?

Here, I will argue that both the idea of evolutionary old systems like the S1 systems (evolved "mental organs") and the idea of cues activating them ("fitness cues") are central to evolutionary psychology. I will also present the results of a large scale experiment investigating the impact these cues can have on ad-likeability scores (as indicators of the advertising effectiveness). This experiment equally reveals the value of evolutionary psychology as a sound perspective for cue management practices.

Keywords Evolutionary psychology · Fitness cues · Advertising management · Cue management · Ad-likeability · Advertising processing · Advertising effectiveness

P. Vyncke
Department of Communication Sciences, Ghent University, Korte Meer 7-9-11, B-9000 Ghent, Belgium, 0032/2646890
e-mail: Patrick.Vyncke@UGent.be

Introduction

Current thinking on both advertising processing and consumer behavior is being revolutionized by psychological research which reveals that there are two distinct brain systems at work in human information processing and decision making (cf. Evans et al. 1996; Fine 2006; Gigerenzer 2000, 2007; Gigerenzer et al. 1999; LeDoux 1998; Montagu 2006; Myers 2002; Reber 1993; Stanovich 1999, 2004; for a good overview, see Frankish and Evans 2009). On the one hand, System 1 (S1) can be characterized as being evolutionarily old, unconscious/preconscious, automatic, fast, and intuitive. On the other hand, System 2 (S2) can be labeled as evolutionarily recent, conscious, controlled, slow, and reflective.

Until recently most research on consumer behavior has been (implicitly) framed in a S2 perspective, studying consumers as very rational human beings. However, we are now witnessing a revolutionary takeover of the field by researchers focusing their attention on S1 and the corresponding intuitive, irrational, gut-feeling-driven decisions consumers constantly make in their everyday life (Ariely 2009; Gigerenzer 2007; Hallinan 2009; Lunn 2008; Shermer 2008; Sutherland 2007).

As for advertising processing, the state-of-the-art models that currently dominate the literature – like the Elaboration Likelihood Model – generally distinguish two different persuasive routes and also point towards a dual-processing system in the brains of targeted consumers. One route strongly parallels S2. Taking this route, the consumer focuses on the content of the ad (relevant product/brand attribute information) and engages in extensive and – mostly – conscious elaborated information processing. The other route strongly resembles S1. Here the consumer processes the ad only superficially, quickly, and quasi-automatically in terms of a handful of meaningful cues. A sound theoretical framework has been created around S2 advertising processing, in terms of means-end-chain theory. However, regarding S1 advertising processing the question remains: What constitutes a meaningful cue?

In this chapter, I will introduce the idea of cue management as a form of advertising management which focuses on S1 advertising processing and therefore on the manipulation of advertising cues. As such, cue management can be opposed to means-end-chain management (MEC management, which focuses on S2 advertising processing) as two distinct forms or prototypes of advertising management. Contrary to MEC management, cue management currently lacks a strong theoretical foundation. I will argue that both the idea of evolutionary old brain systems like S1 (evolved "mental organs"), and the idea of cues activating those systems ("fitness cues") are central to evolutionary psychology. Therefore evolutionary psychology can provide a framework for cue management purposes.

Firstly, I will synthesize the essence of the Elaboration Likelihood Model. Secondly, based on this model, I will make a distinction between cue management and MEC management as two distinct forms or prototypes of advertising management. Thirdly I will link these two types of advertising management to the S1/S2 information and decision making systems within our brains to make it clear that cue management appeals to the older and more emotional S1 system, whereas MEC management engages the newer and more rational S2 system. Fourthly, I will argue that a framework to answer the question of what constitutes a meaningful cue can be found within the new science of evolutionary psychology. Finally, I will present the results of my experiment investigating the impact of fitness cues on ad-likeability scores (as predictors of the advertising effectiveness to be expected). My conclusion will be a suggestion for cue management to be developed as a new and legitimate form of advertising management based on evolutionary psychology.

1 The Elaboration Likelihood Model (ELM)

Thinking on advertising processing (for a very good overview, see Vakratsas and Ambler 1999) has come a long way since the old AIDA (Attention Interest Desire Action) model (Strong 1925:76, but attributed to E. St. Elmo Lewis in 1898). Since this preliminary yet seminal model, a myriad of other models have been proposed. Perhaps the two most influential (as measured by their appearance in standard textbooks on advertising management and before the Elaboration Likelihood Model was developed) were the Hierarchical Learning Model (a Think – Feel – Do model, see Lavidge and Steiner 1961) and the Low Involvement Model (a Think – Do – Feel Model, see Krugman 1965, 1977) – referred to by Jones (1990) as the strong and weak theories of advertising. Yet countless other models also arose, so that by the 1970s the field of persuasion was often characterized as replete with conflicting theoretical models and empirical findings, and lacking any coherent, unifying theory (Bagozzi et al. 2002:107).

In the 1980s, the introduction of the Elaboration Likelihood Model (ELM, see Fig. 1) by Petty and Cacioppo (1981, 1986) provided such a coherent, unifying theory. As Bogazzi et al. (2002:107) remark, the ELM was a radically new model:

> An examination of the persuasive theories advanced through the 1970s reveals that all share the similarity of offering *a* [their italics] process by which attitudes are changed. The process hypothesized to guide persuasion differs, albeit, for each theory. (...) In stark theoretical contrast to these prior conceptualizations, the ELM hypothesizes that attitudes can be changed as a result of *different psychological processes* [their italics].

Indeed, the ELM groups the various processes by which the attitudes of the consumer can be changed through an advertising campaign into two conceptually distinct groups: those processes in which attitudes are changed as a result of effortful elaboration (referred to as the **central route** of persuasion) versus those processes in which attitudes are changed as a result of relatively non-thoughtful processes (referred to as the **peripheral route** of persuasion). The ELM predicts that a person's *motivation* and *ability* influence which of the two processes is most likely to guide persuasion. When individuals possess both motivation and ability, they are more likely to be persuaded by thoughtful elaboration on issue-relevant

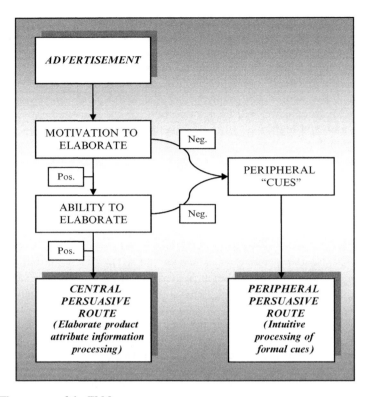

Fig. 1 The essence of the ELM

persuasive information (in the case of advertising: product/brand attribute information). That is, they are likely to consider the information presented, generate thoughts and feelings in response to that information, and change their attitudes as a function of these cognitive processes. However, sometimes – perhaps even most of the time (cf. infra) – consumers do not possess both motivation and ability to elaborate on the content of the ad. The ELM posits that, under these conditions, consumers' attitude change is most likely to be mediated by processes that do not entail thoughtful consideration of issue-relevant information (that is, elaboration). Instead, in those cases, individuals are likely to rely on associative processes such as classical conditioning (Gorn 1982; Stuart et al. 1987) or mere exposure (Zajonc 1980, 1984; Zajonc and Markus 1982), and less effortful inference processes such as heuristic shortcuts (Chaiken 1980) dealing only with peripheral cues presented in the ad, rather than with the issue-relevant information (product/brand attribute information) provided by the ad (Bagozzi et al. 2002:108–109).

The motivation and ability of the consumer are therefore hypothesized to determine which process underlies persuasion. The ELM advances the notion that these two factors influence the *likelihood* that an individual will *elaborate* persuasive information (that is, elaboration likelihood). However, as Bagozzi et al. (2002:112) note:

> It is important to note that elaboration likelihood is conceptualized as a continuum, rather than as two discrete states (...). As individuals move from one end of the continuum to the other, the amount of effort they expend on thoughtfully considering the issue-relevant information ranges from none at all to scrutinizing and considering all information.

2 Means-End-Chain Management and Cue Management

Nevertheless, the ELM enables us to make a distinction between two prototypical forms of advertising management (that is, the process of planning, implementing, and evaluating an advertising campaign) (see also Mitchell and Olson 1981; Shimp 1981): one with a focus on the central route (trying to create a positive brand-likeability by providing the consumer with relevant information about the product/brand's attributes), and one we could call "cue management," with a focus on the peripheral route (trying to enhance the brand-likeability by creating ads with a high ad-likeability by way of inserting the right cues in the ad).

When the advertising manager wants to design an advertising campaign in which the central route prevails, a specific theoretical framework is at his/her disposal: means-end-chain theory (MEC theory). MEC theory was originally developed for relating consumers' product knowledge to their self-knowledge (Gutman 1982; Olson and Reynolds 1983). Knowledge is presumed to be organized in a hierarchy, with concrete thoughts linked to more abstract thoughts in a sequence progressing from *means* to *ends*. As Gutman (1982:60) points out:

> Means are objects or activities in which people engage. Ends are valued states of being such as happiness, security, or accomplishment. A means-end chain is a model that seeks to explain how a product or service selection facilitates the achievement of desired end states.

As such, MEC theory comes down to a radical extension of early approaches to the topic of product meaning. These tended to be from the product attribute perspective, whereby meaning was tied to the physical, observable characteristics of the product. As such, they failed to recognize any type of personal meanings derived from those attributes. Within MEC theory, product meaning was first expanded to take into account both the functional and the nonfunctional benefits that attributes represented for the consumer. The focus was subsequently broadened further to cover yet higher levels of abstraction, that is, personal values. In essence, MEC theory comes down to the application of the personal values perspective to consumer understanding. To the advertising manager, MEC theory is an invaluable resource in defining which "issue-relevant information" to include in the ad for two reasons: (1) rather than concentrate on a particular level of product or brand meanings, it incorporates all levels into a conceptual framework, and (2) it focuses on the associations (i.e., derived meanings) between the levels. These associational linkages provide an understanding of how consumers interpret product attributes (*means*) as representing benefits to them (referred to as *consequences*) and how

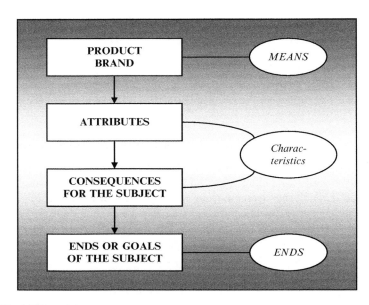

Fig. 2 The MEC model

these benefits are ultimately translated into personal values (*ends*) (see Fig. 2). It is this associational element of the MEC model that offers keen insight into the meanings that consumers derive from products and ads (Batey 2008:21–22).

The relationship of means to ends is of course many-to-many, since a given end can be achieved by more than one alternative means, and a given means could be serving any of several ends. To illustrate this with an example, one can imagine the following MEC in the brain of a particular consumer, built around the concept of *practicing sports* (Fig. 3)

It is obvious that MEC theory constitutes a sound framework for MEC management, since it enables the advertising manager to investigate and specify which "issue-relevant information" (cf. the ELM) should be included in the advertising campaign when the focus is on the central route of persuasion. Moreover, the advertising manager can rely on specific research methods that have been proposed in addition to the MEC model (Pieters et al. 1995). However, sometimes – perhaps even most of the time – consumers don't have the motivation *and* the ability to elaborate on the issue-relevant information contained in the ad. Indeed, it can be expected that the average consumer, in dealing with the average ad in an average market, more often takes the peripheral rather than the central route, since she/he generally lacks the motivation and/or ability for effortful elaboration. Low motivation may be due to a high level of product homogenization (making brands undifferentiated in terms of technical/functional attributes), to widespread quality guarantees (erasing differences in terms of general product quality), to the fact that the consumer knows that advertising does not offer neutral, unbiased (and therefore valuable) information, and to the consumer's previous brand experiences.

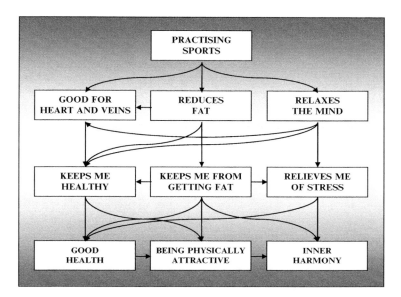

Fig. 3 An example of a concrete MEC

Low ability to elaborate may be due to the complexity of the contemporary marketing scene confronting the consumer, with countless ads for countless brands, the limited time that a consumer has available for processing ads, the often distracting environment in which she/he is exposed to the ad, or the unfortunate timing of the exposure of the consumer to the ad. Having to deal with a consumer who lacks either the motivation or the ability to elaborate on the ad, it makes little sense for the advertising manager to design an ad based on MEC management. In these situations, it would make more sense to insert meaningful cues in the ad that can impact consumers' attitudes. I will call this (proto)type of advertising management cue management, so as to distinguish it from MEC management as the other (proto) type of advertising management – at least as suggested by the ELM. Figure 4 shows an example of how an ad for toothpaste for kids could look like when conceived from a MEC management perspective versus a cue management perspective.

Notice that, in the first ad, the advertising manager provides the consumer with issue-relevant information that enables him/her to make a connection between concrete product attributes (alpha enzyme complex), consequences (having white teeth), and his/her personal values (looking good). The ad stimulates elaborate processing: Do I want a toothpaste that makes my children's teeth white or do I rather want a toothpaste that keeps their teeth healthy? What is an enzyme complex? Should I do the test? In the cue management version of the ad (the lower version), the advertising manager simply wants the consumer to make a connection between the cue (a cute child) and the brand, so that the positive emotions or feelings elicited by the cue get transferred to the brand, thus influencing brand-likeability in a rather non-thoughtful way.

Fig. 4 An example of an ad campaign for toothpaste for kids. The first is an ad conceived from a MEC management perspective. The second is an ad conceived from a cue management perspective

Contrary to MEC management, cue management still lacks a sound theoretical framework. Indeed, until recently, most work on advertising processing has been focused on S2 processes using the MEC framework. The concept of "advertising cues" has hardly been given any serious attention (although much research has been done on the impact of specific cues such as music, celebrities, humor, etc.). The concept of "cues" was actually first used by Lorenz (1939). Hasson (1994) defines a Lorenzian cue as any feature of the world, animate or inanimate, that can be used by an animal as a guide to future action. I will argue that evolutionary psychology can provide a refined framework for understanding the workings of these cues. Before I turn to the central question of cue management – that is, what constitutes a meaningful cue for a given target audience – I will first consider how the ELM perspective fits into a broader perspective on human information processing and decision making. This will enable us to clarify the link between cue management and evolutionary psychology.

3 The Two Minds of the Consumer

Thus far, I have outlined how the ELM posits that consumers' attitudes can be formed and/or changed by one of two psychological processes. Attitudes can be changed as a result of relatively effortful consideration of the issue-relevant information central to the persuasive message, in which case the subsequent attitudes are the result of cognitive responses to that information. These processes are at the core of what I have called MEC management. Attitudes can alternatively be changed as a result of relatively non-thoughtful processes, in which case the subsequent attitudes are the result of pairing the attitude with a cue that is not diagnostic of the central merits of the persuasive information. These processes are at the core of what I have called cue management. As Bagozzi et al. point out, it is crucial to understand that these two (groups of) processes are fundamentally "qualitatively different" (Bagozzi et al. 2002:119).

Over the past decade, an exciting body of work on human information processing and decision making has explored this idea of a fundamental duality in the human mind in greater detail. Researchers – working on various aspects of human psychology, including deductive reasoning, decision making, and social judgment – have accordingly developed "two mind" theories. As Frankish and Evans (2009:1) put it: "These theories come in different forms, but all agree in positing two distinct processing mechanisms for a given task, which employ different procedures and may yield different, and sometimes conflicting, results". Typically, one of the processes is characterized as fast, effortless, automatic, nonconscious, heavily contextualized, and undemanding of working memory, and the other as slow, effortful, controlled, conscious, decontextualized, and demanding of working memory. These theories then claim that human cognition is composed of two multi-purpose reasoning systems, usually called System 1 and System 2 (S1 and S2), the operations of the former having fast-process characteristics, and those of the latter having slow-process ones (Evans et al. 1996; Stanovich 1999, 2004). In their overview article, Frankish and Evans (2009:15) neatly summarize the differences between S1 and S2 as put forward by the different authors of "two mind" theories. An overview of the most salient characteristics is given in Table 1.

Obviously there are considerable parallels between, on the one hand, S1 information processing and the peripheral persuasive route of the ELM (as a very direct and spontaneous information processing route), and on the other hand between S2 information processing and the central persuasive route of the ELM (as a more elaborated information processing route). This means that cue management must be targeted at the S1 system, tapping into this evolutionarily old system of meaning and decision making. It is precisely one of the great merits of evolutionary psychologists that these researchers pay special attention to this evolutionarily old information processing

Table 1 Features attributed by various theorists to S1 and S2

System 1	System 2
Evolutionarily old	Evolutionarily recent
Unconscious, preconscious	Conscious
Implicit knowledge	Explicit knowledge
Automatic	Controlled
Fast	Slow
Parallel	Sequential
High capacity	Low capacity
Intuitive	Reflective
Associative	Rule-based

Source: adapted from Frankish and Evans (2009)

system. Central to the field of evolutionary psychology (EP) are the concepts of "mental organs" and "fitness cues" activating those organs. Together these concepts can make up an EP framework for cue management purposes.

4 Evolutionary Psychology as a Framework for Cue Management

EP is the study of the functioning of the mind (or, if you wish, of human nature) in light of the process of evolution by natural selection. As Buss (1999:47) remarks:

> If humans have a nature and evolution by selection is the causal process that produced that nature, then the next question is what great insights into human nature can be provided by examining our evolutionary origins.

Darwinian theory states that the core of all animal natures, including humans', consists of a large collection of adaptations. EP tends to focus on one special subclass of the adaptations that comprise human nature – psychological adaptations. Similarly to how evolutionary biology distinguishes within the very complex human body several organs or organic parts that have clear and specific adaptive functions, so does EP try to draw up a map of the extremely complex human mind, by distinguishing different evolved psychological adaptations that constitute it. Metaphorically, these evolved adaptive psychological mechanisms are often called "mental organs". EP then attempts to analyze the human mind as a collection of mental organs. It studies the contexts that activate these mental organs, and it deals with the behaviors generated by those mechanisms.

According to Buss (1999:47–51), a mental organ consists of a set of processes inside a living organism, with the following properties:

- An evolved psychological mechanism exists in the form that it does because it solved a specific problem of survival or reproduction recurrently over evolutionary history. (...)
- An evolved psychological mechanism is designed to take in only a narrow slice of information. (...)
- The input of an evolved psychological mechanism tells an organism the particular adaptive problem it is facing. (...)
- The input of an evolved psychological mechanism is transformed through decision rules into output. (...)
- The output of an evolved psychological mechanism can be physiological activity, information to other psychological mechanisms, or manifest behavior. (...)
- The output of an evolved psychological mechanism is directed toward the solution to a specific adaptive problem.

According to Buss, EP mechanisms almost invariably do their job out of consciousness, which reminds us of the characteristics of S1. But especially important here is the second characteristic mentioned by Buss. It means that we can now understand the cue concept in terms of the narrow slices of information activating mental organs by telling an organism the particular adaptive problem it is facing. Recently, in his evolutionary perspective on consumer behavior, Miller (2009) has introduced the concept of "fitness cues" to highlight the fitness relevance of those cues. I will quote him here at length (Miller 2009:55–56):

> Fitness cues (...) are features of an individual's environment that convey useful information about local fitness opportunities – ways to increase one's survival chances or reproductive success. Darkness is a cue for danger (reduced survival chances), so it induces fear and shelter seeking. For predators, the scent of prey is a cue for food (increased survival chances), so it motivates pursuit, attack, and ingestion. For males, the cues that identify fertile females of their own species carry information about mating opportunities (increased reproductive success), so they motivate pursuit, courtship, and copulation. Our perceptual systems have evolved to pay the most attention to these sorts of fitness cues, because, in evolutionary terms, they are the only things worth noticing about one's world. (Natural selection cannot favor animals' responding to any cues that do not identify an opportunity to promote their survival and reproduction.) Further, animals evolve motivation systems to surround themselves with positive, fitness-promoting cues (which evolve to "feel good"), and to avoid negative, fitness-threatening cues (which evolve to "feel bad"). At the evolutionary level, animals are always under selection to survive and reproduce. But at the subjective level, they are always motivated to chase the fitness cues that feel good – not because they consciously understand that natural pleasures are associated with evolutionary success, but because they have been shaped to act as if they understood that association unconsciously.

According to Miller, we therefore all have a deep and abiding interest in pursuing fitness cues that were associated with better survival, social, sexual, and parental prospects in prehistory. In my opinion, and following Miller, advertising cues can therefore be understood as fitness cues, that is, as those small pieces of advertising information that – within the peripheral persuasive route of the ELM – draw the attention of the consumer and are quickly and unconsciously judged to be either relevant or attractive from a fitness-promoting perspective. An affective reaction – enhancing ad-likeability, and therefore advertising effectiveness – is the corresponding result. It is precisely because a cue is fitness promoting that (a) it is worthy of our attention, (b) it is (generally unconsciously) judged to be relevant and/or attractive, and (c) it "works" by eliciting affective or emotional reactions (we feel good or we feel bad). Therefore, Miller's concept of fitness cues seems to correspond exactly to the functioning of cues in peripheral persuasion.

If one rereads the EP literature from this fitness cue perspective, it becomes evident that specific fitness cues seem to activate the evolved mental organs. Thus, food choice modules are activated by cues of high caloric value such as a sweet or fatty taste. Kin investment is guided by cues of genetic relatedness, such as facial similarities or the fact that one is raised together with others by the same parents. Parental investment is activated by cues such as a crying baby. Reciprocal altruism is guided by reputational cues such as helping people in need or cheater-detecting cues such as speech errors, hesitations, shorter speaking turns, raised vocal pitch, or self-touching behavior. Mate choice is guided by a plethora of cues defining male and female attractiveness or charm (to which we will return within our research project).

These few examples also make it clear that the idea of "fitness-promoting cues" has to be understood in an evolutionary context, that is, as cues that promoted fitness in the Environment of Evolutionary Adaptedness (EEA). Indeed, evolutionary science has made it clear that different environments pose different adaptive problems and so require different adaptations. To understand any particular adaptation, one therefore must know something about the environment in which it evolved. Our EEA has to be situated in the East African savannas, where we lived from about 6 million years ago (after the human lineage split from that of the chimpanzee) until about 100,000 years ago. Around 100,000 years ago, some of our ancestors began to emigrate out of Africa, and eventually colonized the whole world. But 100,000 years is only about 5,000 generations – too short a time for evolution to produce any major changes. This means that we are all "stone agers living in the fast lane" (Evans and Zarate 1999:45–46). We all have a Stone Age mind adapted to living in the EEA. Again, the parallel with S1 as an evolutionarily old system is striking.

The result is that many forms of current consumption behavior (and many forms of behavior in general) – which were quite adaptive in the EEA – now have simply become maladaptive and even sometimes just plain hazardous. An illustrative case can be found in our food preferences for sweet and fatty foods. What was adaptive in the EEA (where those food resources were scarce) has become maladaptive in today's modern society (where those food resources are abundant). The case illustrates that even when we know that fat and sugar are unhealthy for us, we cannot help responding to the corresponding cues. Indeed, fitness cues work through *primary affective reactions* without much rational cognition involved. Again, the parallels with our earlier description of S1 information processing and decision making – and therefore with the peripheral ELM route – are obvious.

In line with EP principles, one can then think of concrete adaptive problems our ancestors faced recurrently, work out the mental organs that evolved to solve those problems, and then start mapping the specific fitness cues that activate those mental organs. These fitness cues can then function as concrete cues in ads, eliciting affective reactions through a process of S1 information processing and decision making, that is, a process of unconscious, fast, intuitive, automatic evaluation of the relevance and/or attractiveness of those cues. It is in this sense that EP can provide both academics and practitioners with a concrete framework for studying and using cues in the context of cue management as a specific form of advertising management. In the final section of this paper, I will test this EP perspective on cue management in a large scale experiment.

5 Exploring the Impact of Fitness Cues on Ad-Likeability

In this last section, I demonstrate the fruitfulness of the EP perspective for cue management through a research project investigating the impact of fitness cues on advertising likeability. Of course, one cannot investigate all fitness cues in any single project, so I have focused on one of the most investigated of the evolved mental organs, namely the mating module. Among the fitness cues that activate these mental organs are the cues that define sexual attractiveness.

Cues of Sexual Attractiveness

Human sexual bonding is indeed one of the key research areas of EP. Since perhaps no other aspect of human behavior has such profound implications on gene replication into the next generation, the extensive interest of EP in this particular aspect of the human mind should be of no surprise. Moreover, it is here (more than with any other aspect of human behavior) that the major differences in male and female thinking and feeling are to be found since, indeed, the recurrent problems our ancestors faced in finding a suitable mate were quite different for the two sexes.

The most influential theoretical model that has been proposed to explain sexual differences in mating behavior is the parental investment model (Trivers 1972). This model states that, within sexually reproducing species, the sex that provides the greater parental investment will be the more sexually choosy and restrained one. Whenever the two sexes within a species provide a differential amount of parental investment in offspring, this should translate into differences in mating behavior including the mating characteristics – or fitness cues – sought in ideal suitors, and the proclivity to engage in short-term versus long-term mating. For *Homo sapiens*, because females provide exceptionally higher parental investment (although we are a species with considerable paternal parental investment), this yields a wide range of psychosexual behaviors that are sex-specific (Saad 2007:61).

What, then, are the cues that make up male and female charm? Although there is much dispute about the precise meaning of some of these cues, there is also substantial agreement that some key features are central to male and female charm. I will limit myself here to some visual cues that are supported by robust empirical findings.

General Cues of Sexual Charm

One set of cues that both men and women share in common are those that signal "good genes". Since DNA testing kits were unavailable in the Pleistocene, both men and women tended to rely on cues of good health as indicators of good genes. Relevant cues then include a smooth skin, white teeth, lustrous and shiny hair, clear eyes, and a healthy skin color (not pale or grey, but displaying a healthy blush). Not all cues are that obvious, however, if you don't investigate their meaning from an EP perspective. Symmetry of the face and the body, for instance, functions as a cue of attractiveness, since it is an indication of health. Indeed, this kind of symmetry correlates with a normal genetic development as well as with a sound immune system, since many disfiguring diseases yield facial or bodily asymmetry.

Since health as an indicator of good genes was important for both sexes, these cues are part of both male *and* female sexual attractiveness. Also, psychological cues such as kindness or general intelligence offered clear adaptive advantages for both sexes, and thus have become part of the sexually attractive make-up of *both* males and females. Yet in many aspects, male and female sexual charms are distinct. As Saad neatly summarizes (Saad 2007:63):

> Two universal and robust findings are that men place a greater premium on youth and beauty whereas women place greater importance on social status and ability to acquire, retain, and share resources. The reason for this pervasive sex difference is that mating preferences cater to sex-specific evolutionary problems.

Cues Central to Male Charm

The main aspect in which male charm differs from female charm is through cues to available or potentially available resources. As Bridgeman (2003:99–103) points out, given the harsh circumstances in which women had to raise their offspring in the EEA, this resource aspect of male charm should not surprise us. Indeed, choosing males based on their ability to acquire, protect, and share resources – and therefore on their status position – is a ubiquitous female mating strategy across a diverse range of species. Also note that, since it takes time for a man to acquire status and (corresponding) resources, this is one reason why women tend to prefer slightly older males, other things being equal. Bridgeman (2003:99) also notes that it is not only social standing that defines the male charm in this respect. Demonstrating skill in hunting (sometimes formalized in games, sports, or rituals) is also important. Together with the protection that a male can offer a female and her offspring (against predators or assaults), this explains why cues to physical strength have also become crucial elements of male charm. Finally, this resource aspect also explains why other valued traits in males are characteristics such as romantic dedication, loyalty, and child-friendliness.

Cues Central to Female Charm

The male is also making a difficult decision in estimating the reproductive capacity of his potential wife for the next two decades, but again nature provides *cues* that help to inform his decision, as Bridgeman (2003:104) points out. One set of cues is those that constitute female physical beauty. Indeed, EP has found that what men find attractive in the appearance of women is a series of cues that enable them to assess a woman's reproductive potential. Therefore, cues such as youth and health are highly valued by males in females.

Again, not all cues are that obvious unless they are investigated from an EP perspective. A waist-to-hip ratio (WHR) of about 0.70, for instance, can only be understood as a cue defining the female charm if one knows that women with a WHR near the optimum of about 0.70 are more likely to be highly fertile than women with much larger or smaller ratios (i.e., the obese, the pathologically thin, and the sexually immature).

Yet there is also a remarkably dubious aspect to what makes females attractive to males. This is sometimes referred to as the Madonna/Whore dichotomy. On the one hand, in many cultures, males tend to be attracted to virginity as an indication of chastity. Its appeal rests in being an extreme cue of sexual faithfulness. The problem males faced in the EEA (where no paternity testing kits were available), was that they risked – in the light of a sexually unfaithful partner –investing their resources in offspring that were not theirs. Therefore, on the one hand, men tend to attach high value to chastity, adopting a Madonna archetype as a standard for the ideal (long-term) partner. On the other hand, men have to invest only very limited resources – and therefore run very little risk – in short-term mating occasions (think of the typical one-night stand). The risks women run on such occasions are much greater (or at least they were in the Pleistocene, given that these short sexual encounters could well end up in pregnancy). Males therefore tend to have a less restrictive attitude toward these forms of short-term sexual mating (at least for themselves). This can sometimes lead them to adopt a Whore archetype as a standard for the ideal (short-term) sexual partner, as reflected in the consumption of pornography, or in the interest men show in cues of female sexual willingness and/or sexual arousal.

Manipulating Ads

In my experiment, I investigated most of these cues that make up male and female charm to learn what effect these cues have in an advertising context. Some authors (for an in-depth discussion, see Saad 2004, and especially Saad 2007:123–162) have already shown that many of these cues frequently and universally appear in ads, suggesting that advertising strategists and creative directors use their intuitive knowledge of these cues to enhance advertising effectiveness. With my experiment, I wanted to discover whether the cues I've discussed did indeed have a real and measurable impact on advertising effectiveness.

I created a total of 80 sets of ads consisting of one neutral version and one manipulated version – that is, an ad version in which cues consisting of male or female charm were either inserted or enhanced – containing the following EP fitness cues for sexual attractiveness:

- Cues that are part of both male and female charm: cues of good health and kindness (19 ad sets)
- Cues of male attractiveness: cues of available resources/material wealth/high status; cues of physical strength; cues of a slightly older age; and cues of romantic dedication and child-friendliness (14 sets)

- Cues of female attractiveness: cues of reproductive potential, such as youthfulness or specific fertility cues such as a 0.70 WHR or large breasts; cues of sexual willingness and/or sexual arousal (31 sets: it was easier to manipulate ads featuring female models, since the female charm is more visually defined than the male charm)
- Combinations of several cues: to learn whether these combinations result in much higher effectiveness scores than single cues (eight sets). I hypothesized that perhaps a single cue manipulation (e.g., enlarging the female ad model's breasts) would have little impact, or at least that combinations of cues (e.g., enlarging the female model's breasts, but also giving her a 0.70 WHR, making her hair more shiny and lustrous, whitening her teeth, and giving her a healthy blush) would have a higher impact on advertising effectiveness measures
- "Reversed" cues (cues of male sexual attractiveness enhanced in female models and vice versa) (four sets). Since we were interested in checking the sex-specificity of certain cues, we also created these "sex-reversed" ad sets. For instance, I not only created ad sets in which the male model showed enhanced cues of physical strength, but also ad sets in which the female model showed these same typically male cues. Or, in other words, I not only manipulated a female model's WHR to reflect the 'ideal' WHR of 0.70, but also created ad sets in which we gave the male model a WHR approaching the 0.70 level. Figures 5 and 6 illustrate a straight and a reversed cue manipulation.
- Finally, there were four sets with no or neutral manipulations (as a reliability check). Two ad sets showed exactly the same ad on both the left and the right side of the screen. This way I was able to check whether indeed these ad sets yielded 50% of respondents choosing the left ad version and 50% choosing the right ad version, as expected by chance. The neutral manipulations were black versus brown hair of the ad model, and green versus blue eyes of the ad model. Since these manipulations don't deal with fitness cues, they are expected to have no impact on the ad effectiveness measure.

Fig. 5 WHR approaching the 0.70 level in the left (manipulated) version of the ad

Fig. 6 "Reversed cue" (WHR approaching 0.70 level) in the right (manipulated) version of the ad

Most cue manipulations were created using Photoshop CS3. This sophisticated picture manipulation software enabled me to slightly whiten the teeth, enlarge the breasts by a few inches, make the skin look a little paler or the lips a little more reddish, place greater emphasis on the male model's abdominal muscles, etc. All ad sets can be viewed and downloaded from the website of C.R.E.A.T.I.V.E. (Centre for Research on the Effectiveness of Advertising Techniques, Innovations, Values and Emotions – a research center based at Ghent University, Belgium): http://www.ugentcreative.eu/.

The Experiment

All 80 ad sets were integrated into a self-running PowerPoint presentation and copied onto a CD-ROM. Two versions of the presentation were made: one AB-version and a mirrored BA-version. Half of the respondents got the AB-version, the other half got the mirrored BA-version. This means that if in an ad set the manipulated version was displayed on the right side of the computer screen for half of the respondents, it was displayed on the left side of the computer screen for the other half of the respondents. This procedure enabled me to avoid order effects due to respondents systematically picking the left or the right ad version as the most appealing one because they don't notice any difference at a conscious level. The two ad sets with no manipulations enabled me to check whether indeed I had succeeded in avoiding this order effect. During the self-running presentation, each ad set – consisting of a neutral and a manipulated version of the same ad – was shown for only 3 s, thus enabling an average (maximum) exposure time of 1.5 s per ad, which resembles the time an average consumer pays to an average print ad. All participants viewed all 80 ad sets.

Three-hundred and seventy respondents took part in the experiment: 185 males and 184 females (one missing value), aged between 14 and 71 years old, with an average age of 35.63 years. All respondents received the self-running PowerPoint on CD-ROM (containing all 80 ad sets) so that they could view the slideshow in the privacy of their own home in the absence of the researcher. For each viewed ad set, each respondent indicated which version (left or right) they considered the most appealing. Even if they did not notice a difference between the two versions of the same ad, they still had to indicate on their answer form – within the 5 s that the computer screen turned black in-between two ad sets – either the left or the right version of the ad as the most appealing. This "forced choice ad preference" measure was used to find out if the inserted or enhanced cues in the manipulated ad version had an impact on the likeability of the ad. Ad-likeability is considered by several authors as a valid – some say even the most valid single – predictor of advertising effectiveness. Indeed, authors such as Biel (1990), Haley and Baldinger (1991), and Dröge (1989) argue that ad-likeability highly correlates with brand preference, and that attitudes toward the ad affect attitudes toward the brand, especially in non-elaborate situations – which is exactly what I am investigating: the processing of cues in the peripheral ELM route (for a meta-analysis, see Brown and Stayman 1992). Brown (1991) also suggests that ad-likeability has a long-term effect. Furthermore, from the perspective of cue management, ad-likeability is the most direct measure of the impact that a specific cue has in terms of advertising effectiveness. Indeed, as I have pointed out, the management of advertising cues aims at creating primary affective reactions that impact brand-likeability through a positive ad-likeability.

Generally, ad-likeability is measured on a scale ranging from 0 to 10 or from "very much dislike" to "very much like". However, I opted for "forced choice ad preference" as a measure of ad-likeability, since my pre-testing of the material revealed that often respondents did not consciously perceive any difference between two ads in an ad set. Indeed, most manipulations were very subtle and would probably not be captured by more traditional ad-likeability measures. That these manipulations nevertheless had a clear impact on ad-likeability will, however, soon be revealed by the obtained findings. One might argue that scaled ad-likeability measures seem to correspond more with S2 processing (since they are based on a more conscious, time-consuming, reasoned deliberation), while our forced choice preference measure allowed us to also detect S1 differences in ad-likeability (since it is based on fast, intuitive, and often unconscious feelings). As Vakratsas and Ambler (1999:32) point out: "The absence of cognition suggested by pure affect models is difficult to show, because cognition usually intervenes in measurement. Asking about feelings brings cognitive processes into play and induces cognitive bias". It is exactly this cognitive bias that I sought to avoid with my "forced choice ad preference" measurement method, since it is S1 processing that cue management researchers are interested in.

Results

Tables 2–7 show the results of the experiment. Each table has the same structure:

- The first column provides the ad set number. Notice that 140 ad sets were part of the PowerPoint presentation, although I created only 80 ad sets specifically for

Table 2 Ad preferences regarding neutral manipulations or no manipulations at all

Ad set No.	Manipulation: which fitness cues are enhanced?	percentages of respondents preferring the ad with the enhanced fitness cues				
		Total	Sign.	Male	Female	Sign.
44	No manipulation at all	49.7	No	51.1	48.6	0.34
67	No manipulation at all	48.9	No	51.9	46.2	0.16
15	Brown versus black hair (as a neutral manipulation)	51.6	No	48.1	55.4	0.10
51	Green versus blue eyes (as a neutral manipulation)	46.6	No	47.3	46.2	0.46

Table 3 Ad preferences regarding non-sex-specific cues of sexual attractiveness

Ad set NR.	Manipulation: which fitness cues are enhanced?	Percentages of respondents preferring the ad with the enhanced fitness cues				
		Total	Sign.	Male	Female	Sign.
Good health of the male model						
03	Clear skin/bags under the eyes removed	71.7	Yes	66.8	77.0	0.02
06	Slightly whitened teeth	64.8	Yes	60.3	69.0	0.05
20	Lower belly fat	63.7	Yes	64.3	62.8	0.43
28	Bags under the eyes removed/brighter eyes: fresh (versus tired)	62.7	Yes	57.8	67.4	0.04
124	Low BMI model (versus overweight model)	96.2	Yes	94.6	97.8	0.08
Good health of the female model						
05	Bags under the eyes removed/brighter eyes: fresh (versus tired)	75.4	Yes	69.2	81.5	0.00
07	Low (versus higher) BMI	92.4	Yes	91.8	92.9	0.42
11	Healthy tanned (versus pale) skin color	87.8	Yes	89.2	86.4	0.26
17	Healthy blush, red lips – no seductive pose	57.6	Yes	54.6	60.3	0.16
38	Bags under the eyes removed/brighter eyes: fresh (versus tired)	54.3	Yes	55.1	53.8	0.44
47	Facial symmetry (versus asymmetry)	63.5	Yes	61.1	65.8	0.21
55	Clear skin (versus birth marks)	75.7	Yes	74.6	76.6	0.37
58	Healthy tanned (versus pale) skin color	79.4	Yes	78.9	79.8	0.47
65	Brighter eyes through darker iris	65.7	Yes	65.9	65.6	0.51
78	Smooth skin (versus slightly pockmarked skin)	80.0	Yes	78.4	81.5	0.27
79	Slightly whitened teeth	57.2	Yes	57.3	57.1	0.52
118	Long lustrous hair	67.8	Yes	66.5	69.0	0.34
131	Clear skin (versus tainted skin)	57.0	Yes	64.3	50.0	0.00
Kindness						
77	Smiling face (versus serious face) of the female model	85.1	Yes	83.8	86.4	0.29

Table 4 Ad preferences regarding cues of male sexual attractiveness

Ad set NR.	Manipulation: which fitness cues are enhanced?	Percentages of respondents preferring the ad with the enhanced fitness cues				
		Total	Sign.	Male	Female	Sign.
Available resources / material wealth / high status						
10	High status (versus casual) clothing (on beach)	56.4	Yes	51.4	61.2	0.04
114	High status (versus casual) clothing (same ad without background)	66.8	Yes	64.9	68.5	0.27
127	High status attribute (watch)	71.1	Yes	75.1	66.8	0.05
128	High status (versus casual) clothing	66.5	Yes	57.8	75.0	0.00
Physical strength						
24	Masculized face (pronounced chin and cheeks, heavier eyebrows)	64.9	Yes	67.7	62.5	0.18
40	Longer, taller body	58.4	Yes	57.4	59.8	0.36
91	Pronounced muscles on torso (biceps, six pack)	60.4	Yes	61.4	59.2	0.38
99	Longer, taller body	63.0	Yes	63.8	62.0	0.40
140	Pronounced muscles on torso (biceps, six pack)	83.5	Yes	82.2	84.8	0.30
Slightly older age / maturity						
16	Young to middle-aged model, but with slightly gray hair	34.6	Yes	32.4	37.0	0.22
80	Young to middle-aged model, with beard (versus no beard)	28.0	Yes	30.3	25.8	0.20
Romantic dedication						
112	Female model with (versus without) dedicated partner	71.4	Yes	57.3	85.3	0.00
134	Dedicated, romantic couple (versus couple just walking together)	64.8	Yes	58.4	71.0	0.01
Child-friendliness						
113	Male model taking care of baby (versus returning from fishing)	58.9	Yes	49.2	68.5	0.00

this study. Indeed, I used this experiment to simultaneously explore some other topics of interest (e.g., the impact of direct versus indirect gaze of the model, MEC manipulations of slogans, inserting subliminal stimuli in ads, etc.), the results of which will be published elsewhere. Using multiple manipulations made it more difficult for the respondent to consciously "detect" the specific EP fitness cue manipulations during the three-second exposure to each ad set.

- In the second column, I describe the specific cue manipulation.
- The third column shows which percentage of the total population preferred the manipulated ad version, that is, the version with the enhanced or inserted fitness cues. Percentages above 50% indicate that the cue was effective in raising the ad-likeability (since this means that more than 50% of the respondents preferred the ad with the enhanced or inserted EP cue to the ad without the EP fitness cue).
- In the fourth column, I indicate by Yes or No whether the deviation from the normally expected 50/50% ratio (of respondents choosing either the neutral or the manipulated version) as reported in the third column is statistically significant as calculated by a percentage test.

Table 5 Preferences regarding cues of female sexual attractiveness

Ad set NR.	Manipulation: which fitness cues are enhanced?	Percentages of respondents preferring the ad with the enhanced fitness cues				
		Total	Sign.	Male	Female	Sign.
Reproductive potential: youth						
09	Blond (versus brown) hair as a juvenile trait	56.5	Yes	58.9	54.4	0.22
31	Full black (versus slightly gray) hair	61.4	Yes	62.2	60.3	0.40
36	Neonatal traits – rounder cheek bones	55.3	Yes	54.6	56.3	0.41
42	Smaller buttocks	58.4	Yes	50.8	65.8	0.00
46	Neonatal traits – enlarged eyes	52.8	No	50.5	54.9	0.23
50	Smaller buttocks	64.6	Yes	60	69	0.04
53	Blond (versus brown) hair and light (versus dark) eyes	55.3	Yes	52.4	57.9	0.17
62	Smooth skin (versus wrinkles and crow's feet)	89.2	Yes	88.1	90.2	0.32
63	Smooth skin (versus slight wrinkles) and whiter teeth	64.0	Yes	63.8	64.1	0.52
72	Longer legs (as a juvenile trait)	61.8	Yes	60.9	63.0	0.37
73	Blond (versus brown) hair as a juvenile trait	65.9	Yes	63.0	68.5	0.16
76	Neonatal traits – small nose	50.7	No	50.0	51.6	0.42
86	Neonatal traits – enlarged eyes	43.2	Yes	47.6	39.1	0.06
Reproductive potential: fertility						
21	Reduced WHR (0.70), large breasts	67.1	Yes	66.7	67.4	0.49
29	Large breasts	74.1	Yes	78.4	69.6	0.04
33	Feminized face (nose, chin, cheek bones, eyebrows)	76.2	Yes	70.3	82.1	0.01
35	Large breasts	55.9	Yes	65.4	46.2	0.00
57	Reduced WHR of 0.70	57.5	Yes	62.7	51.9	0.02
82	Feminized face (nose, chin, cheek bones, eyebrows)	62.4	Yes	62.7	62.0	0.48
95	Reduced WHR of 0.70	57.6	Yes	52.4	62.5	0.03
101	Reduced WHR of 0.70	70.7	Yes	70.8	70.5	0.52
104	Large breasts	66.2	Yes	66.5	65.8	0.49
Sexual willingness and/or arousal						
25	Blush, red lips, a come-hither smile	75.5	Yes	75.1	75.8	0.49
41	Blush, red lips, seductive pose	55.4	Yes	51.9	59.2	0.09
56	Full and swollen lips	54.9	Yes	60.0	49.5	0.03
60	Extremely low-necked dress	57.3	Yes	73.0	41.3	0.00
64	Full red lips	45.1	Yes	53.5	37.0	0.00
68	Extremely low-necked dress	64.1	Yes	69.2	58.7	0.02
129	Full red lips	52.4	No	56.2	48.9	0.10
132	Full blush, seductive pose	46.2	Yes	43.5	49.2	0.16
Child-friendliness						
88	Parental care	57.9	Yes	48.1	67.6	0.00

- In the fifth and sixth columns, I report the percentages of males and females choosing the manipulated version as the most appealing one.
- In the seventh and last column, I report the significance level (one-sided Fisher exact test) of these male/female differences.

In all tables, I have marked in grey the results that do not agree with the EP perspective. Notice that, in general, one should not expect sex differences to occur,

Table 6 The impact of combined cues

Ad set NR.	Manipulation: which fitness cues are enhanced?	Percentages of respondents preferring the ad with the enhanced fitness cues				
		Total	Sign.	Male	Female	Sign.
71	Female model with clear skin, whitened teeth, enlarged pupils, healthy blush, glossy lips, more symmetrical face	66.4	Yes	64.9	67.8	0.32
94	Female model with extremely low-necked dress, blush, red lips	56.8	Yes	74.1	39.7	0.00
98	Female model with glossy lips, enlarged pupils, blush	47.2	No	48.6	45.9	0.34
106	Male model with fewer wrinkles, lighter hair, brighter eyes, red and fuller lips	78.1	Yes	73.5	82.6	0.02
108	Male model with fewer wrinkles, clearer skin, more symmetrical face, brighter eyes	55.7	Yes	54.1	57.6	0.28
110	Female model with lighter hair, fewer wrinkles, healthy blush, red and fuller lips	74.3	Yes	72.0	76.5	0.19
119	Female model with clearer skin, brighter eyes, glossy lips and more symmetrical face	78.6	Yes	76.8	80.4	0.23
125	Female model with large breasts, reduced 0.70 WHR, blush, red lips	38.2	Yes	46.5	30.1	0.00

Table 7 The impact of "reversed" cues

Ad set NR.	Manipulation: which fitness cues are enhanced?	Percentages of respondents preferring the ad with the enhanced fitness cues				
		Total	Sign.	Male	Female	Sign.
18	Female model with enhanced arm muscles and breasts reduced	39.8	Yes	45.1	34.2	0.02
87	Female model showing high-status cues (jewelry)	67.3	Yes	64.3	70.7	0.12
97	Female model with enhanced muscles in arms, belly, and legs	21.9	Yes	28.1	15.8	0.01
116	Male model with reduced WHR of 0.70	45.3	Yes	45.1	45.7	0.50

since an attractive same-sex model is preferred as a model you want to identify with, and an attractive opposite-sex model is preferred as a model you want to be looking at. However, in my comments I will go into greater detail wherever sex differences (cues that work for one sex, but not for the other sex) occur.

The results for the ad sets with no or neutral cue manipulations are shown in Table 2. Indeed, as a check on the reliability of the experimental design (to find out if I had succeeded in avoiding order effects, cf. supra) I included two ad sets with no manipulations at all. In both cases there were no significant deviations from the expected percentages (that is, 50% respondents opted for the left version of the ad, and 50% opted for the right version). We also added two meaningless manipulations, in the sense that no EP theory or research has yet revealed that the cues of brown versus black hair or green versus blue eyes are meaningful fitness cues. As Miller (2009:56) points out, only fitness-related cues can succeed in drawing our attention and eliciting affective reactions: "Natural selection cannot favor animals' responding to any cues that do not identify an opportunity to promote their survival and reproduction". Our findings confirm Miller's point. No significant preferences for either cue were found.

The results for the cues of general sexual attractiveness are summarized in Table 3. Notice that all fitness cues succeeded in substantially enhancing the ad preference scores, sometimes yielding more than 90% of the respondents opting for the manipulated ad. For some ad sets, sex differences did occur, but in all cases (except ad set 05) this only points towards an occasionally increased sensitivity to these general cues of sexual attractiveness when the advertised model is of the opposite sex. However, in most cases this cue sensitivity is equally high for both sexes and independent of the sex of the advertised model. Most importantly, however, no cues were found to have a positive impact on the ad-likeability scores of one sex, yet a negative impact on the scores of the other sex. This means that all results were in line with the EP framework.

The results for the sex-specific cues of male sexual attractiveness are summarized in Table 4. Again, all fitness cues – except the cues for an older age – succeeded in augmenting the ad preference scores well above the expected 50% chance level. The cues for "a slightly older age" (a slight graying of the hair, and a beard, as cues of sexual maturity) are of course debatable. Moreover, what comprises "a slightly older age" is of course wholly dependent on the age of the (female) respondents. In general, no sex differences were found, as men want to identify with attractive male models, and women prefer to look at attractive male models. In some ad sets, however, male attractiveness had more effect on female ad-likeability than on male ad-likeability. As with the results of Table 3, this probably indicates an occasional higher sensitivity to cues of sexual attractiveness when the advertised model belongs to the opposite sex. Yet in one ad set it was the other way around, namely ad set 127, featuring Brad Pitt. The manipulated ad with an expensive watch as a social status cue appealed more strongly to the males than to the females (although it must be stressed that both sexes preferred the manipulated ad version containing the fitness cue). Perhaps Brad Pitt's very attractive face drew too much attention from the female respondents, making them focus less on the social status cue, leading in turn to lower preference scores? Remember that the ads were only shown for 3 s. Of course, since I didn't go into that much detail with my respondents, the true nature of these sex differences is hard to explain, and much more research is needed here. Different aspects of the ad – sometimes perhaps even small details – may also be responsible for some of these sex differences or for making some cues more or less effective than others. Consider, for instance, ad set 128 showing a young male in front of a sporty vehicle. In the manipulated ad version he is wearing a suit (as a cue of higher social status); in the neutral version he is wearing very casual clothing. Female respondents go for the cues of high status, with 75% choosing the manipulated ad as the most appealing one. Males also go for the suit ad, but 42.2% nevertheless found the ad with the casual clothing the most appealing one. Perhaps the male respondents (with males being more involved with cars as a product category) focused more on the sporty yet rather cheap nature of the vehicle and therefore chose the neutral ad with the casual – and therefore sporty and cheaper – clothing style of the owner. Perhaps they judged this ad to have higher internal consistency and therefore picked the neutral version as the "better" one. The important thing is, however, that in both ad set 127 and ad set 128 *both* sexes showed a preference for the manipulated ad version containing the (enhanced or inserted) fitness cues of male social status. This means my research findings were completely in line with the EP perspective. This even holds for the considerable sex differences regarding the cues of romantic dedication and child-friendliness, which – in line with EP predictions – are especially appealing to the female respondents.

The results for the sex-specific cues of female sexual attractiveness are summarized in Table 5. In general, these fitness cues succeeded in substantially raising the preferred ad score above the 50% chance level. However, notable exceptions are the ad sets including what I have called "neonatal" cues (smaller nose and enlarged eyes). In ad sets 46 and 76 these cues had no effect, while in set 86 the enlarged eyes even lowered the expected ad preference score below the 50% level. It is unclear to me what the explanation for these anomalies might be, just as it is often unclear why sometimes certain cues do appeal more to one sex or the other, or even don't appeal more to one sex or the other (as with ad set 25 where I had expected a more pronounced male preference for these cues). Further research is needed, but these anomalies clearly demonstrate that cues should not be understood as simple stimuli that automatically yield consistently high impact scores in any context and in an equal matter for both sexes. Cues can be more or less pronounced, cues always work within a context, and perhaps cues can be better understood in a semiotic (that is, meaning making) perspective than when one looks at cues merely from an information processing perspective. The "buy button" idea that one often comes across in reading popular literature on neuromarketing is surely not supported by my findings, although these findings are strongly in line with EP predictions.

However, some significant differences that arose between the male and female respondents make sense from an EP perspective, for instance, the male/female differences that arise in their reactions towards certain cues to fertility (such as large breasts) and especially towards cues of sexual willingness and arousal (such as full and swollen red lips, extremely lowed-necked dresses, etc.). While these cues often increased the male ad preference scores far above the 50% level, they lowered the female ad preference scores below that level with equal frequency. In order to understand these results, I can refer to the Madonna/Whore dichotomy (cf. supra). This is reflected here in the likeability scores toward ads featuring female models showing "whorish" cues of (short-term) sexual willingness: appealing to men, but not making women want to identify themselves with these models. Therefore, although these cues seem to work differently for male and female respondents, I must stress that these results are nevertheless completely in line with the EP perspective. The same can be said regarding ad set 88 (including the child-friendliness cues of parental investment), where this time the inserted cues have a highly positive impact on the female likeability score, yet no (or even slightly negative) impact on the male scores.

The results for the ad sets in which combinations of cues to different dimensions of sexual attractiveness are inserted or enhanced, are summarized in Table 6. Notice that combinations of several cues do not necessarily lead to much higher ad preference scores than those obtained in the ad sets where a single cue was manipulated. On the contrary, some combinations seem to reduce the scores below the 50% level, as in ad set 125 where the cue manipulation is so pronounced that it is no longer realistic and it becomes obvious that the picture has been "photoshopped" by the advertising boys. Moreover, this likeability lowering seems to be especially the case when cues of sexual willingness or arousal are involved (as it is also the case in ad set 125), although, again (cf. ad set 94), males and females may diverge in their appreciation of those cues. Once more I will refer to the Madonna/Whore dichotomy. The combination of several cues makes the manipulation all the more pronounced and therefore noticeable. And as every woman knows, there is a fine line between make-up and clothing that makes you look sexier, and make-up and clothing that makes you look whorish. I would guess that in those cases where ad-likeability scores drop below the 50% level (for females or even for both sexes), the whorish impression prevails. This would mean that, although I've marked these scores in grey – thus indicating that they are contradicting EP predictions – these results are actually in line with the EP framework. Again, much more research is needed in order to fine-tune these aspects of cue management.

Finally, the results for the "reversed" cues are summarized in Table 7. These results confirm the often sex-specific nature of certain fitness cues as predicted by EP. For instance, adding male fitness cues of physical strength to a female model has devastating effects on the ad-likeability, as shown by the corresponding ad preference scores. However, one (ad set 87) remains puzzling: why do high-status cues such as jewelry substantially enhance female sexual attractiveness for both male and female respondents? More research is needed, although one might point here again to the higher internal consistency of the ad showing the model wearing jewelry, since her dress and looks also seem to position her as belonging to the upper social classes. If this is the case, it means that the higher likeability score is not so much related to the cue as such, but to the ad being more internally consistent and therefore "better made" (cf. our interpretation of ad set 128 in Table 4).

To end this paragraph, Table 8 summarizes our overall research findings.

Table 8 Overall research findings

Manipulation: Inserted or enhanced cue type	Results in line with EP	Contradicting EP	No significant impact
Non-sex-specific cues of sexual attractiveness	19	–	–
Cues of male sexual attractiveness	12	2	–
Cues of female sexual attractiveness	25	3	3
Combined cues	6	1	1
Reversed cues	3	1	–
Reliability check with no manipulations or with neutral cues	4	Because these had no impact on scores	
TOTAL	69	7	4

This global overview of my findings clearly shows the validity of the EP perspective as a guiding framework for cue management. Of the 80 ad sets I used in my experiment, only seven yielded results that contradict EP hypotheses, whereas 69 yielded results in support of EP hypotheses. Moreover, the four ad sets in which no manipulations were made or where neutral cues were manipulated did not yield any significant impact results. Therefore Miller seems to have had a point when he remarked that *only* fitness-related cues can succeed in drawing our attention and eliciting affective reactions.

6 Conclusion and Discussion

In this paper I started by arguing that – following the Elaboration Likelihood Model – one can distinguish between two forms or prototypes of advertising management: means-end-chain management and cue management. MEC management tries to persuade the consumer by providing relevant information (product or brand attribute information) to influence her/his attitudes towards the product or brand. Cue management tries to induce positive feelings by inserting or enhancing certain cues in the ad (such as music, humor, attractive people, babies, animals, etc.) and attempts to influence the attitudes of the target group by coupling these positive feelings (ad-likeability) to the advertised product or brand. This distinction between cue and MEC management can also be situated within the context of contemporary psychological theory and research revealing that there are two distinct brain systems at work in human information processing and decision making. Cue management relies on System 1 (S1, evolutionarily old, unconscious/preconscious, automatic, fast, and intuitive), whereas MEC management is more dependant on System 2 (S2, evolutionarily recent, conscious, controlled, slow, and reflective).

Although many research projects have investigated the effectiveness of specific cues such as music, humor, or the use of attractive people or celebrities in ads, no embracing theoretical framework for cue management has been suggested yet. I have argued here that EP might provide the advertising manager with such a framework. Indeed, on the one hand, EP investigates and describes the mental organs making up the human mind. Since these mental organs have to be understood as products of the Environment of Evolutionary Adaptedness (EEA), and therefore as evolutionarily old, largely unconscious or preconscious, and working fast and intuitively, the relevance of EP for revealing characteristics of S1 can hardly be overestimated. Moreover, EP also aims at identifying the specific cues that activate each of these mental organs, which again underscores the relevance of EP as a framework for cue management. With Miller (2009), we can call these cues "fitness cues". As Miller pointed out (Miller 2009:56): "Natural selection cannot favor animals' responding to any cues that do not identify an opportunity to promote their survival and reproduction". This means that, according to EP theory, fitness cues – and *only* fitness cues – will succeed in appealing to consumers and eliciting affective reactions. Cue managers aiming to increase advertising effectiveness through increased ad-likeability must therefore have a thorough knowledge of the mental organs of the consumer target group (e.g., males versus females) and the corresponding cues that will activate these mental organs. That is why I believe EP to be the only perspective on human nature capable of providing the cue manager with a sound theoretical foundation. As a framework for cue management, EP can then be used either for academic or managerial purposes.

In the second part of this chapter, I have presented the results of a large-scale experiment investigating the validity and potential fruitfulness of this framework. I created 80 ad sets, each consisting of a neutral ad and a manipulated ad version in which fitness cues were either inserted or enhanced. The results – with less than 10% of the ad sets contradicting EP hypotheses, and almost 90% of the research findings being in line with EP predictions – overwhelmingly confirmed the legitimacy of the EP-based cue management framework. Some manipulations even succeeded in creating a 90% (forced choice) preference for the manipulated ad, that is, the ad in which fitness cues were either inserted or enhanced. Moreover, the point I made following Miller (2009) – that *only* fitness cues can elicit an affective reaction and therefore increase advertising effectiveness – was equally confirmed by our findings. Indeed, none of the four ad sets in which I inserted no or neutral manipulations, led to significant deviations from the 50/50% response one expects by chance alone. Some of the results also proved the value of the EP perspective over more socio-cultural views on consumers and advertising. For instance, we currently live in Western societies in a culture where there is a high focus on fitness, sports, working out, being active, and having well-muscled bodies for both males and females (although more pronounced for males). From a socio-cultural perspective, one would therefore predict higher likeability scores for ads featuring well-muscled models, even if these models are female. Yet EP predicts that well-muscled bodies are only attractive as male cues to females and not as female cues to males. Ad set 97, in Table 7 (together with ad sets 91 and 140 in Table 4), clearly proves the better predictive power of the EP perspective over the more socio-cultural perspective on the nature of consumers.

However, many questions remain unresolved. How pronounced must cues be in order to be the most effective? I have noticed, for instance, that for some cues (e.g., full red lips, a blush on the cheeks, the showing of naked skin, etc.) there is only a tiny line between making the female model look more sexy (with a corresponding positive impact on ad-likeability) and making the model look whorish (with a corresponding negative impact on ad-likeability). Perhaps the failure of the neonatal traits I enhanced in some ad sets must equally be ascribed here to making the corresponding cues (e.g., enlarged eyes) too pronounced, causing faces to look unnatural. Also, with combinations of cues, the manipulations can become too obvious, leading to lowered ad-likeability scores, with consumers feeling betrayed by the all-too-obvious Photoshop work of the advertising boys. On the other hand, when cue manipulations are too subtle, they may go unnoticed and have no impact at all on ad-likeability.

Another point I want to stress is that some cues seem to work "better" than other cues, or are more effective for one sex (or target group) than the other. Since I only measured primary affective reactions through forced ad preference scores after a three-second exposure (and did not, for instance, conduct in-depth interviews or focus group discussions with my respondents regarding their ad preferences), I can only guess why this is the case. Although I have tried to make some educated guesses in my table comments, it is clear that much more research is needed here. Some cues even polarized the reactions of male versus female respondents, especially cues about sexual willingness. It must therefore be stressed that cues don't work in a vacuum, but are always interpreted in a specific context by a specific consumer. Depending on the context, cues may well be interpreted totally differently by different (groups of) respondents. At this point, I want to underscore the semiotic nature of cues. Indeed, all cues are also signs, that is, they are something that stands for something else. A 0.70 WHR stands for fertility, an expensive car or suit stands for high social status, a red blush on the cheeks may stand for health, but may also stand for sexual arousal or even plain embarrassment. And just as semioticians distinguish between natural and conventional signs, cues can be more of the natural or more of the conventional type. The WHR is an example of a natural cue, and may prove to be very stable across cultures. But cues about high social status (such as jewelry or an expensive suit) may be highly conventional and therefore only work in a specific cultural context or for specific target groups. This means that inserting or enhancing cues in ads can't be compared to adding salt to your potatoes or pepper to your soup. Rather it is more akin to high-end cuisine in which very specific ingredients are handled with extreme care and in precise amounts.

My research project must also be regarded as being substantially or even completely explorative. To my knowledge, this is the first project of its kind (especially in terms of scale and methodology), which leaves many questions unanswered. For instance, I only investigated cues to sexual attractiveness. Currently, EP – and especially the subfield of evolutionary aesthetics (for a good overview, see Voland and Grammer 2003) – is investigating many non-sexual cues such as music or landscape preferences, biophilia, art and design, and esthetic preferences in the world of artifacts. Many of the findings of EP in this field can of course also be used for cue management purposes inside or outside an advertising context (e.g., in product design and packaging). Even new fields within the marketing communication profession can profit from EP as a guiding framework. An area of growing interest such as sensory marketing, for instance, will probably be able to benefit from what EP has to say about our evolved esthetic smell, touch, or taste preferences.

Some remarks must also be made regarding the research methodology used in this experiment. Although I have tried to put some variation into the product classes for which I designed the ads, the question remains whether fitness cues perform equally well across all product classes and across different persuasion contexts (e.g., political campaigns). Also, my measure of advertising effectiveness (forced choice ad preference) must in future research be compared to more standard measures of ad-likeability, and to other measures of advertising effectiveness (such as brand-likeability, purchase intention, ad recognition, or ad recall).

Finally, and perhaps most importantly, there are those cues that were found to be in stark contradiction to standard EP theory (such as the high-status female cues turning out to be attractive to both male and female respondents in our experiment). Again, further research is needed here, but I think that EP can profit especially from the models and insights developed within the field of semiotics. This means that one has to investigate cues in their pragmatic sign dimensions, for instance, researching the iconic, indexical, or symbolic properties of cues, their natural or conventional nature, or the specific signifiers and signifieds that work in specific contexts. All too often, non-semioticians take signs, signification, and meaning making for granted. But if semiotics has made one thing clear, it is that the process of signification and meaning making – although a self-evident activity in which we are constantly engaged in throughout our everyday life – is far from being self-evident. Does the jewelry of the model in fact function as a cue to her high status, or is it a cue signifying her uniqueness, and would it therefore have functioned in the same manner if the model had been wearing a jeans jacket? As a semiotician, I am convinced that at this point semiotics has a lot to offer to EP, although this might mean that the current EP model, in which human beings are seen as information processors (comparable to computers), must be exchanged for a model in which humans are first and foremost seen as meaning processors.

Many of these questions are not easy to answer, but more research on the effectiveness of fitness cues in ads will surely lead us to more effective cue management practices. Ethical questions can arise, such as when cue management insights should be used in advertising to kids or in political advertising. But one can of course use these same insights for socially valued projects (e.g., I am currently investigating the usefulness of the cue management perspective within a social marketing and health communication context). Stories of irresistible buy buttons being manipulated by unscrupulous marketers have little to do with our current cue management model. Moreover, this kind of research can also lead to new insights into the workings of consumers' System 1 functioning – the importance of which can hardly be overestimated. Indeed, according to many dual processing theorists, S1 has to be seen as the default and dominant system of information processing, while S2 is a uniquely human process and as such is a recently acquired plug-in that does a great deal less than we generally assume. This is in line with Reber (1993), who argued for the "primacy of the implicit," proposing that consciousness was a late arrival in evolutionary terms, preceded by unconscious perceptual and cognitive functions by a considerable margin. He suggested that consciousness provided a unique executive function in human beings, but that this had led to an illusory belief in consciousness as the primary cognitive system. We hope that our cue management research projects will contribute to the unmasking of this illusion.

References

Ariely D (2009) Predictably irrational. The hidden forces that shape our decisions. Harper Collins, London
Bagozzi RP, Gürhan-Canli Z, Priester JR (2002) The social psychology of consumer behaviour. Open University Press, Buckingham
Batey M (2008) Brand meaning. Routledge, New York
Biel AL (1990) Love the ad, buy the product? Why liking the advertisement and preferring the brand aren't strange bedfellows after all. Admap 26:21–25 (September)
Bridgeman B (2003) Psychology and evolution: the origins of mind. Sage, Thousand Oaks
Brown G (1991) Monitoring advertising: big stable brands and ad effects. Fresh thoughts about why, perhaps, consistent promotion keeps them big. Admap 27:32–37 (May)
Brown SP, Stayman DM (1992) Antecedents and consequences of attitude toward the ad: a meta-analysis. J Consum Res 19:34–51 (June)
Buss DM (1999) Evolutionary psychology: the new science of the mind. Allyn & Bacon, Boston
Chaiken S (1980) Heuristic versus systematic processing and the use of source versus message cues in persuasion. J Pers Soc Psychol 39:752–766
Dröge C (1989) Shaping the route to attitude change: central versus peripheral processing through comparative versus noncomparative advertising. J Marketing Res 26:193–204 (May)
Evans D, Zarate O (1999) Introducing evolutionary psychology. Icon Books, Cambridge
Evans J, St BT, Over DE (1996) Rationality and reasoning. Psychology Press, Hove
Fine C (2006) A mind of its own. Icon Books, Cambridge
Frankish K, Evans JStBT (2009) The duality of mind: An historical perspective. In: Evans JStBT, Frankish K (eds) In two minds: dual processes and beyond. Oxford University Press, Oxford, pp 1–29
Gigerenzer G (2000) Adaptive thinking. Rationality in the real world. Oxford University Press, Oxford
Gigerenzer G (2007) Gut feelings. The intelligence of the unconscious. Viking Penguin, New York
Gigerenzer G, Todd PM, The ABC Research Group (1999) Simple heuristics that make us smart. Oxford University Press, New York
Gorn GJ (1982) The effects of music in advertising on choice behavior: a classical conditioning approach. J Marketing 46(1):94–101
Gutman J (1982) A means-end chain model based on consumer categorization processes. J Marketing 46(2):60–72
Haley RI, Baldinger AL (1991) The ARF copy research validity project. J Advertising Res 31:11–32 (April/May)
Hallinan JT (2009) Why we make mistakes. Broadway Books, New York
Hasson O (1994) Cheating signals. J Theor Biol 167:223–238
Jones JP (1990) Advertising: strong force or weak force? Two views an ocean apart. Int J Advertising 9:233–246 (July-September)
Krugman HE (1965) The impact of television advertising: learning without involvement. Public Opin Q 29:349–356 (Fall)
Krugman HE (1977) Memory without recall, exposure without perception. J Advertising Res 17:7–12 (August-September)
Lavidge RJ, Steiner GA (1961) A model for predictive measurements of advertising effectiveness. J Marking 25:59–62 (October)
LeDoux J (1998) The emotional brain. Orion Books, London
Lorenz K (1939) Vergleichende Verhaltensforschung. Zool Anz Suppl 12:69–102
Lunn P (2008) Basic instincts. Human nature and the new economics. Marshall Cavendish, London
Miller G (2009) Spent: Sex, evolution, and consumer behavior. Viking, New York
Mitchell AA, Olson JC (1981) Are product beliefs the only mediator of advertising effects on brand attitude? J Marketing Res 18:318–332 (August)

Montagu R (2006) Why choose this book? Dutton, New York
Myers DG (2002) Intuition. Its powers and perils. Yale University Press, New Haven/ London
Olson JC, Reynolds TJ (1983) Understanding consumer's cognitive structures: implications for marketing strategy. In: Percy L, Woodside AG (eds) Advertising and consumer psychology. Lexington Books, Lexington, pp 77–91
Petty RE, Cacioppo JT (1981) Attitudes and persuasion: classic and contemporary approaches. William C. Brown, Dubuque
Petty RE, Cacioppo JT (1986) Communication and persuasion: central and peripheral routes to attitude change. Springer, New York
Pieters R, Baumgartner H, Allen D (1995) A means-end chain approach to consumer goal structures. Int J Res Mark 12:227–244
Reber AS (1993) Implicit learning and tacit knowledge. Oxford University Press, Oxford
Saad G (2004) Applying evolutionary psychology in understanding the representation of women in advertisements. Psychol Market 21(8):593–612
Saad G (2007) The evolutionary bases of consumption. Lawrence Erlbaum, Mahwah
Shermer M (2008) The mind of the market. How biology and psychology shape our economic lives. Henry Holt and Company, New York
Shimp T (1981) Attitude toward the ad as a mediator of consumer brand choice. J Advertising 10:9–15 (Summer)
Stanovich KE (1999) Who is rational? Studies of individual differences in reasoning. Lawrence Erlbaum, Mahwah
Stanovich KE (2004) The robot's rebellion. Finding meaning in the age of Darwin. University of Chicago Press, Chicago
Strong EK (1925) Theories of selling. J Appl Psychol 9:75–86 (February)
Stuart EW, Shimp TA, Engel RW (1987) Classical conditioning of consumer attitudes: four experiments in an advertising context. J Consum Res 14:334–349 (December)
Sutherland S (2007) Irrationality. Pinter & Martin, London
Trivers RL (1972) Parental investment and sexual selection. In: Campbell B (ed) Sexual selection and the descent of man, 1871–1971. Aldine, Chicago, pp 136–179
Vakratsas D, Ambler T (1999) How advertising works: what do we really know? J Marketing 63 (1):26–43
Voland E, Grammer K (eds) (2003) Evolutionary aesthetics. Springer, Berlin
Zajonc RB (1980) Feeling and thinking: preferences need no inferences. Am Psychol 35:151–175 (February)
Zajonc RB (1984) On the primacy of affect. Am Psychol 39:117–123 (February)
Zajonc RB, Markus H (1982) Affective and cognitive factors in preferences. J Consum Res 9:123–131 (September)

"Evolutionary Store Atmospherics" – Designing with Evolution in Mind

Yannick Joye, Karolien Poels, and Kim Willems

Abstract Environmental psychology research shows that natural environments and natural habitat qualities are better able to positively influence human functioning (e.g., stress reduction) than most common urban environments. Such positive psychological states are often interpreted as remnants of our species' evolutionary history in natural environments. Nowadays a substantial part of the urban fabric is dedicated to commercial and business-related activities. Such environments however often lack those natural habitat qualities and elements, which have been found to promote positive psychological states. This chapter aims to demonstrate and illustrate the value of integrating such natural qualities into business-related environments, and specifically into retail environments. We coin this design strategy "Evolutionary Store Atmospherics" (ESA). The scope of this chapter is theoretical as well as practical. On the one hand, we provide an overview of the specific "ancestral" landscape elements and qualities that are found to have positive effects on human functioning. On the other hand, we discuss and illustrate how these key qualities can be integrated in store environments. Special attention is paid to situational factors that could interact with ESA design proposals, such as, for example, gender and type of shopping.

Y. Joye (✉)
Research Centre of Marketing and Consumer Science, University of Leuven, Naamsestraat 69 - box 3545, 3000 Leuven, Belgium
e-mail: yannick.joye@econ.kuleuven.be

K. Poels
Department of Communication Studies, University of Antwerp, Sint Jacobsstraat 2, 2000 Antwerpen, Belgium
e-mail: karolien.poels@ua.ac.be

K. Willems
Department of Business Economics, Hasselt University & Vrije Universiteit Brussel, Agoralaan – Building D, 3590 Diepenbeek, Belgium
e-mail: kim.willems@uhasselt.be

Keywords Store atmospherics · Prospect-refuge theory · Preference matrix · Evolved aesthetic preferences · Stress reduction · Attention restoration · Retailing · Evolutionary psychology

Introduction

Design is a matter of survival. In the cacophony of the High Street, you need to set yourself apart to survive

(Design Council 1997)

An important and recurring challenge for ancestral humans was finding a suitable habitat, that is, a good place for living. From an evolutionary psychology perspective, one would therefore expect that the human species will have evolved a set of cognitive mechanisms ("modules") that are specialized in processing information relevant to the habitability of a setting. Importantly, the notion "habitability" is multi-dimensional, in that there are numerous factors that make a setting into a potentially good place for living (e.g., presence of food resources). Research into the factors that contribute to the perceived habitability of an environment has been coined "habitat selection theory" (Heerwagen and Orians 1993).

It is no overstatement that ancestral living conditions and environments must have differed dramatically from our modern living environments. Ancestral humans did not roam the savanna in SUV's nor were there supermarkets and shopping malls where they could pick up the resources they needed. What cannot be doubted however is that our species has evolved in *natural* environments. On an evolutionary time scale, it only recently inhabits nonnatural urban settings and, as such, is it (largely) "divorced" from the natural world which it inhabited and on which it also depended for millennia. Undoubtedly, urban life conveys many advantages when compared to the living conditions in ancestral natural environments (e.g., relative abundance of food resources). Commercial and business-related environments play an important role in providing access to these advantages.

There is, however, a sense in which the "mismatch" between urban and ancestral (natural) environments can have negative consequences. Habitat selection theory claims that many of the evolved adaptations to natural features and conditions of ancestral habitats have taken on the form of preferential responses (Orians and Heerwagen 1992). Landscapes or settings containing physical characteristics that tap into these evolved preferences (e.g., cues of fresh water) will often be experienced as beneficial, evoke positive emotions, and trigger approaching behavior. Store environments, which is the type of business environment on which we will focus in this chapter, not only often lack the physical characteristics which can trigger such preferential responses, they are also places where stress, irritation, or cognitive strain regularly take place. In this chapter we argue that consciously bringing features or characteristics into store environments that tap into evolved habitat preferences can make such environments more pleasurable and can even dampen possible negative consequences that arise from the activity of shopping. For store-owners, this could imply a strategic benefit in terms of customer attitudes and behavior, e.g., prolonged stays and even increased purchase probabilities.

The chapter is structured as follows. In Sect. 1 we offer an extensive and critical review of research into evolved preferences for particular landscape-types, landscape configurations, and natural features/elements. In Sect. 2, we discuss why it could be beneficial to deploy such preferred characteristics and features in store environments. We coin this design strategy "Evolutionary Store Atmospherics" and we provide an extensive demonstration of the possible ways in which ESA can be practically integrated into store settings. In Sect. 3, we briefly discuss some implications and challenges related to ESA.

1 Evolved Affective Responses to Landscapes

1.1 Preferred Structural Landscape Features

Numerous environmental features could have communicated to our ancestors whether a certain environment was a suitable place for living, and whether it could provide, e.g., sufficient food resources and opportunities for protection. In the ensuing paragraphs, we will review research and models that propose that habitat quality already depends on the presence of certain *structural landscape features* (e.g., complexity) and briefly discuss how these have been linked to an evolutionary psychology framework.

1.1.1 Prospect-Refuge Theory

In the mid-1970s, geographer Jay Appleton developed *prospect-refuge theory*. This account states that particular aspects of the layout and structure of (natural) scenes influences the aesthetic perception and evaluation of landscapes (Appleton 1975, 1990). Specifically, according to prospect-refuge theory, humans' (positive) aesthetic responses to landscapes depend on whether the landscape offers the individual opportunities for both *prospect* and *refuge*, and on the relative absence of *hazards*. According to Appleton the preference for prospect and refuge is a hard-wired trait that has evolved to successfully negotiate an environment. "Prospect" refers to those landscape elements and configurations that enable the (human) individual to overview the environment in an unimpeded manner, allowing it, e.g., to anticipate possible predators and threats from out-group conspecifics or to look out for resource opportunities (e.g., a water hole). "Refuge" refers to places or landscape configurations where one can hide, rest, or find protection from meteorological conditions or predators.

There is little doubt that the preference for prospect and refuge – if hardwired – will have evolved in natural settings. Still, it is relevant to note that Appleton saw that prospect and refuge can also be effective in non-natural environments, that is, in *architecture* and *city planning* (Appleton 1990). Like in natural settings, prospect and refuge can be evoked by a number of scene organizations or configurations, and later in this chapter (Sect. 2.2.1) we readdress this issue and offer an overview of the different ways in which it can be integrated in retail environments. It should, however, be noted that to this day prospect-refuge theory has remained largely theoretical, and – although fairly often cited – research that has *directly* attempted to test the theory is quite limited. In particular, Stamps' (2006) review of articles citing Appleton's prospect refuge-theory shows that only a small percentage actually inquires about the viability of the specific claims made by the theory (e.g., Fischer and Shrout 2006).

1.1.2 Preference Matrix

From the 1980s onward, there has been a proliferation of empirical research in the field of environmental psychology, investigating which structural landscape qualities are preferred by human individuals. Perhaps the most influential explanatory model that has ensued is the "preference matrix", which has been advanced by Kaplan and Kaplan (1989). According to the Kaplans, humans are an information gathering species, and landscape configurations that facilitate the process of both negotiating and understanding the information conveyed by, and present in a landscape are preferred. In particular, the Kaplans contend that the aesthetic perception of a (natural) environment is influenced by the presence of the following four structural landscape features or "predictors".[1]

1. *Complexity*: this quality is defined as a measure for '... how much is "going on" in a particular scene, how much there is to look at' (Kaplan 1988: 48). A tropical forest often is highly complex, because it contains – on a limited spatial scale – many different (natural) elements, with different forms, textures, and colors. A desert, on the other hand, scores low on complexity because it does not contain many distinct objects/elements.
2. *Coherence*: this quality refers to the presence of visual features that contribute to the organization, understanding, and structuring of the scene, such as symmetries, repeating elements, or unifying textures. For example, an environment with trees is more coherent when those trees are grouped into separate clusters than when all the individual trees are scattered randomly over the landscape. Such grouping entails that the number of units of information is reduced and the scene becomes easier to grasp.

---

[1]Roger Ulrich has developed a similar model, coined the *psycho-evolutionary framework* (Ulrich, 1983, 1993). The "preferenda" that are part of this framework mostly overlap with the predictors of the Kaplans' model.

Fig. 1 Mystery evoked by a path curving out of sight

3. *Mystery*: this characteristic refers to landscape features or organizations where, from the perspective of the observer, a part of the scene is hidden or occluded, but more information can be acquired if the individual enters the scene more deeply. A clear example is a path curving out of sight. The fact that it is unclear where the path is leading to, can lead to curiosity and explorative behaviour (Fig. 1).
4. *Legibility*: this relates to the interpretation of spaces, and refers to the capacity to predict and maintain orientation in the landscape as one further explores it. For example, a conspicuous landscape element (e.g., a rock formation) that is visible from far away and from different locations in the landscape can serve as a point of orientation, and can thereby facilitate exploration and travel throughout the environment.[2]

According to the Kaplans, preferences for these structural landscape features are evolved adaptations: "... the nature of the [preferred] predictor variables and the nature of the preference response itself ... [tend] to support the existence of an evolved bias toward certain landscape configurations" (Kaplan 1992: 590). For example, when innately predisposed to prefer – say – mysterious landscape configurations, a human individual will probably have had higher survival changes than

---

[2]Bell et al. (2005: 45) note that the relation between the four predictors and preference remains somewhat ambiguous: "Although the relative importance of each element is not clear, coherence and complexity may require only moderate levels in order to facilitate information processing, whereas the more legibility and mystery in a scene, the better in terms of preference judgements".

an individual who remained aesthetically unaffected. The former will have been more inclined to further penetrate and explore the setting, and hence, he/she will thereby have had increased chances for finding new resources, shelter, and for opportunities to overview the landscape. Of course, there is the difficulty that mysterious settings can sometimes contain hidden dangers, so a tendency to explore them will only have been successful if it worked in tandem with evaluative mechanisms assessing the potential risk associated with entering a mysterious scene. However, as far as we know, such evolutionary claims have never been empirically tested.

1.2 Positive Effects of Unthreatening Nature on Affective and Cognitive Functioning

Habitat quality is not solely determined by structural landscape features, but also by the presence or absence of certain natural elements (e.g., animals, edible fruits). On a general level, a crucial difference between business and ancestral environments is that the former are natural, whereas the latter are mostly made up of (non-natural) manufactured objects and materials. In the following sections we will discuss research that contends that adaptive mechanisms have evolved for a number of evolutionarily relevant natural elements: specifically, vegetative elements, water-features and animals. In Sect. 2.2.2, we will then further point out which specific perceptual features are conspicuous to these elements, and how they can be deployed in retail design.

1.2.1 Vegetation

Within the field of environmental psychology a significant amount of research has been dedicated to the impact of unthreatening "naturalness" – or the lack thereof – on human emotional and cognitive functioning. In these contexts the concept "natural" is given a common sense interpretation, and applies to any scene containing predominantly natural objects and elements, as opposed to *artefactual* objects (e.g., buildings). Still, a review of this research literature learns that the type of natural element that is invariably present in the stimuli used in these experiments is vegetation (e.g., plants, trees, flowers).

A number of positive effects are associated with viewing natural/vegetated settings. It is found that such type of scenes are consistently (aesthetically) preferred over nonnatural, urban environments, or environments predominantly containing artefacts (for a review, see Ulrich 1993). A closely related finding is that such settings have so-called "restorative" effects on humans, both affectively and cognitively. The "affective" interpretation of restoration is clear from the fact that when individuals have experienced a stressful episode, exposure to vegetated scenery seems capable of undoing that stress better than nonnatural (urban) environments (e.g., Ulrich et al. 1991). "Cognitive" restoration has been demonstrated in experiments which show that contact with vegetation can restore an individual's capacity to concentrate, that is, to direct attention (Hartig et al. 1991; Hartig et al. 2003). As preferential and restorative responses toward natural scenes have been observed in both western and non-western populations they are sometimes believed to be a human universal (Ulrich 1993; but see Lewis 2005).

The evolutionary account states that quick, automatic affective responses toward vegetation are evolved adaptive traits (Ulrich 1993; Heerwagen and Orians 1993; Falk and Balling 2009; Hartmann and Apaolaza-Ibáñez 2009). Vegetative elements, like trees, could offer, say, protection against sun and rain, and when blooming they could bear flowers and sometimes also edible fruits (Orians and Heerwagen 1992; Heerwagen and Orians 1993; Ulrich 1993). Individuals with hardwired positive affective reactions toward such vegetative elements will have been more inclined to approach them, and hence, were probably more successful in obtaining resources than those individuals who remained emotionally unaffected. Restorative responses are claimed to be the result of the moderating effect of positive emotions (triggered by vegetative elements) on states of heightened arousal (Ulrich, 1993).

One problem with the evolutionary views underlying the environmental psychology experiments is that almost *any* kind of greenery leads to preferential reactions and restoration. *If* a hardwired aesthetic response to vegetative life would have evolved, then one would expect that such response would be more specific, that is, directed to features that indicate resource availability – not directed to greenery *in general*. In agreement with this assumption, some evolutionary psychologists have proposed that flowers are likely candidates for leading to positive affective reactions: they were a source of food, and they were a cue that fruits could be available in the near future (Orians and Heerwagen 1992; Heerwagen and Orians 1993).

A few empirical studies have been conducted to explore the aesthetic impact of flowers and they are consistent with the foregoing view. Todorova et al. (2004), for example, found that flowers are not only appreciated for their aesthetic value, but also for their positive influence on psychological wellbeing. Consistent with this, research by Yamane et al. (2004) shows that working with flowering plants has a more positive impact on emotions than their non-flowering counterparts. Haviland-Jones et al. (2005) found that receiving flowers induced positive moods in individuals and triggered genuine positive emotional expressions (determined by the frequency of non-fake smiles). A study by Park et al. (2004) examining the effects of exposure to vegetation on pain shows that female subjects have a higher pain tolerance, report less intense pain, and experience less pain distress when they watch flowering plants than when they are exposed to non-flowering plants.

1.2.2 Water Features

Failing to find drinking water, and thereby running the risk of becoming dehydrated, probably was a major source of selection throughout human and pre-human evolution (Coss 2003). In this regard Roger Ulrich contends that "[a] functional-evolutionary perspective ... implies that people should respond positively to natural settings having water ... The survival-related advantages would have included immediate availability of drinking water, ... attraction of animals that could be hunted, and in some locations (seacoast, estuary, salmon river) extremely high food productivity associated with fish, shellfish and crustaceans" (Ulrich 1993: 90). A piece of circumstantial evidence, supporting these evolutionary hypotheses, speaks from the fact that housing prices are oftentimes the highest when on a waterfront (cf., Luttik 2000).

Environmental psychology research also shows that the presence of water-features in (natural) landscapes is highly preferred by humans and has de-arousing properties. In an experiment probing the differential effects of urban versus natural scenes, Ulrich (1981) found that nature, and also water-features, positively influenced subjects' mood and feelings. Among others, it was found that the amplitude of alpha waves[3] was higher in individuals when they viewed vegetation and water-features than urban scenes, which suggests that subjects felt more wakefully relaxed in the former condition. The heart rate of subjects exposed to water or vegetation pictures was also higher than when they were watching urban environments, indicating that nature scenes are more successful in eliciting interest and attention. More recently, similar results have been obtained by Fredrickson and Levenson (1998). In this experiment, subjects were initially exposed to a fear-inducing film. After this, they watched different movies that were chosen to trigger different emotions in them (i.e., contentment, amusement, neutrality, sadness). A movie of ocean waves led to feelings of contentment, which in turn led to more rapid return to the baseline levels of cardiovascular activation when compared to the neutral movie. Although more research on this topic is needed, these few studies already suggest that exposure to water can have both relaxing and fascinating effects.

1.2.3 Animals

It cannot be doubted that failing to keep track of an ambushing predator could have had severe, if not life-threatening consequences for our human ancestors. An evolutionary psychology perspective would therefore expect that a number of hardwired cognitive "programs" will have evolved to solve predator- and prey-specific challenges. These adaptations could include mechanisms for the recognition, detection, and monitoring of animals (cf., New et al. 2007a), appropriate emotional responding to predator and prey (cf., Mineka and Öhman 2002), and information storing about animate categories (e.g., plants, animals) (cf., Atran 1995).

What might the *proper* (visual) input of these mechanisms be? Early humans evolved in a changing biotic environment and "fixed" mechanisms dedicated to

---

[3]This type of brain wave is associated with wakeful relaxation and is commonly measured by an Electroencephalograph (EEG).

specific animals would quickly have become maladaptive. To date only fixed templates have been observed for *perennial* threats, like snakes and spiders (e.g., Barrett 2005; Rakison and Derringer 2008). A plausible view is that the proper input of those specialist mechanisms handling predator and prey are probably a number of *constant* or *invariable* (perceptual) features that are characteristic to (interactions with) predator and prey, or to their behavior. Barrett (2005) has investigated this issue in-depth and proposes that such features could include – among others – specific movement cues or patterns (e.g., sneaking), morphological features (e.g., eyes), and contingency (i.e., the fact that an organism can suddenly react to a far-away occurrence, element or animal). In Sect. 2.2.2. we will illustrate how such features might be integrated in the design of store environments.

1.2.4 Savanna Hypothesis

Within the field of evolutionary environmental aesthetics it is often assumed that a substantial part of hominin and *Homo* evolution took place in East-African savannas. As a result, it is argued that (early) humans evolved a hardwired preference for landscapes that share (visual) qualities with savannas, or park-like landscapes (Ulrich 1983, 1993; Orians and Heerwagen 1992; Heerwagen and Orians 1993; Appleton 1975, 1990; Orians 1980, 2001). The implicit assumption is that some kind of phylogenetic "imprinting" of this ideal habitat has taken place in the human species (Ruso et al. 2003).[4]

One line of support for the savanna hypothesis is that aesthetic enhancements to artwork (e.g., landscape paintings) or landscapes (e.g., park designs) often entail an increase of features or configurations that are typical to savannas (e.g., openness) (Orians and Heerwagen 1992; Heerwagen and Orians 1993). Some empirical studies have also *directly* tested preference reactions toward different landscape types. For example, Balling and Falk (1982) showed that young children (aged 8) – as opposed to older individuals – prefer savannas over other biomes, despite the fact that the children are unacquainted with this type of environment. The researchers speculate that this could point to an innate preference for savannas (see Falk and Balling (2009) for a replication of the Balling and Falk (1982) study with non-western individuals).

Although the savanna hypothesis is frequently adopted as a given in the field of (evolutionary) environmental aesthetics, other experiments have failed to replicate Balling and Falk's (1982) initial results and consequently do not provide further support for an innate preferential bias toward savannas (cf., Han 2007; Lyons 1983; Hartmann and Apaolaza-Ibáñez 2009). Finally, it must be noted that the claim that savannas are the unique type of biome in which our species has evolved is still far

---

[4]This version of the savanna hypothesis should not be confused with Satoshi Kanazawa's savanna principle (Kanazawa 2004), or with Dennis and McCall's (2005) savannah hypothesis.

from settled (Potts 1998). *If* there would be a universal preference for savanna-type environments then the most probable explanation is that such settings contain an ideal "mix" of preferred structural landscape features and preferred natural contents, which were discussed in Sect. 1.1 and 1.2.

1.3 Commenting upon the Inborn Nature of Evolved Landscape Preferences

As can be surmised from our previous discussion, many hypotheses and speculations about evolved landscape preferences are based on environmental psychology research. Characteristic to this research is the interest in probing and charting aesthetic reactions and possible restorative effects, *not* in empirically testing the evolutionary claims to which they are often committed. Moreover, within the evolutionary psychology literature the main publications on the topic of evolved habitat preferences (Orians and Heerwagen 1992; Kaplan 1992) already date back to the 1990s, if not earlier (cf., Orians 1980), from the time when the first systematic academic treatments of the field of evolutionary psychology were made (Barkow et al. 1992).

This lack of academic interest does not necessarily imply that this research theme is mistaken or disproves all the proposed claims in the foregoing review. It points out that at this stage one must be cautious about making strong and definite claims that could otherwise be construed as "just so" stories about evolved responses to landscapes. In that regard we consider the cross-fertilization between research about designing business environments – that is, the store atmosphere – and landscape preferences as an opportunity to revitalize this research area. Furthermore, the fact that evolutionary explanations need further validation, does not necessarily imply that the design interventions to be proposed shortly will be less evidence-based or less effective.

What cannot be doubted, however, is that humans are highly adaptable, and as such can inhabit and exploit most environments, ranging from tropical rainforests to modern urban environments. In agreement with this, it seems most plausible to think that the "programs" assessing habitability do not "privilege" the *actual* natural contents or environments as input, but are directed towards the perceptual patterns, structures, and characteristics of (natural contents of) habitable landscapes. The upshot is that, according to this account, non-natural, artificial environments (e.g., interior, architectural and urban design) can be designed and transformed in such a way that they fall within the actual domain of these specialist programs, and thereby tap into these preferences. Note that this approach closely parallels that of "biophilic architecture" (Kellert 2005; Joye 2007; Kellert et al. 2008). This new architectural trend attempts to cause biophilic responses (Wilson 1984) by integrating nature and nature-like forms into architecture and design. In the following sections we will explain how such interventions can be realized in, and be effective for store environments.

2 Evolutionary Store Atmospherics

2.1 *Towards an Ultimate Understanding of Store Atmospherics*

More than three decades ago, Kotler (1973: 50) introduced the term *atmospherics* to denote "the effort to design buying environments to produce specific emotional effects in the buyer that enhance his purchase probability". He initiated a literature stream by which marketing researchers came to realize that if consumers are influenced by physical stimuli experienced at the point-of-sale, then, the creation of appealing atmospheres should be an important marketing strategy for retail environments (Turley and Milliman 2000). Current studies on store atmospherics have typically investigated the influence of a single environmental cue on shopping behavior, such as colour (Bellizzi et al. 1983), decorative style of the store (Ward and Eaton 1994), or in-store lighting (Areni and Kim 1993).

The impact of store atmospherics on consumer behavior has been predominantly studied from the perspective of Mehrabian and Russell's Stimulus–Organism–Response model (Mehrabian and Russell 1974). This framework models the process by which a store design intervention (i.e., stimulus) entails specific cognitive and affective processes in the consumer (i.e., the organism), which result in a behavioral response. One problem with the SOR model is that the "Organism" component has often remained a "black box". With evolutionary psychology, however, we now have an arsenal of tools that allow us to peek inside this box, enabling us to get better insight into the ultimate origins of consumer attitudes and behavior. Importantly, such insights can provide us with tactics to design store environments that are tuned to evolutionary predispositions, such as the evolved landscape preferences we discussed above. In this chapter we are mainly interested in this last issue. We define the strategy that brings evolved landscape preferences into store environments *"Evolutionary Store Atmospherics"* (ESA).

Although the act of shopping is an extremely recent phenomenon, some researchers have argued that it is similar to the hunting and gathering activities of early humans (Miller 2009; Dennis and McCall 2005). The nature of shopping also reflects situations or problems that were already relevant in ancestral environments. For example, we regularly shop for products that avoid or solve problems, make us attain status or prestige, or attract a mate. As such, it is reasonable to assume that the cues today's consumers use while scanning and exploring the shopping environment can, at least partly, reflect evolved processes related to hunting and gathering in ancestral environments. As we have discussed in previous sections, several landscape configurations have been proposed to influence and facilitate the process of resource gathering in ancestral surroundings. ESA predicts that by integrating such cues in modern shopping environments, the modern act of shopping can be facilitated and even be made more pleasant. The potential importance of such interventions is further underlined by the fact that the typical store environment nowadays frequently contains a cacophony of factors, both within the control of retailers (e.g., loud music) and beyond it (e.g., crowding), that can make the act of shopping into a stressful and cognitively taxing experience (d'Astous 2000; Fram and Ajami 1994).

2.2 Design Proposals Based on ESA

The potential significance and underlying evolutionary mechanisms of ESA interventions are only rarely acknowledged by those studying store atmospherics. One notable exception is the preliminary experiment by Buber et al. (2007), which shows that the presence of evolutionarily significant features in retail settings (e.g., plants, animals, water) has positive effects on consumer behaviour (e.g., a boost of sales). Although the value of ESA is largely based on our common evolutionary heritage and the fact that it appeals to preferences we all share with each other, it should also take into account *personal* (e.g., gender, age, personality) and *situational* (e.g., mood, type of purchase) differences. They are expected to moderate the strength and direction of the effects induced by ESA interventions. If the implementation is to result in a sustainable competitive advantage, retailers need to consider their target segment (e.g., male, utilitarian shoppers), and fine-tune the ESA implementation accordingly.

2.2.1 Preferred Structural Landscape Features in the Store Environment

In the earliest sections of this chapter we have discussed research that contends that humans display (evolved) preference reactions to some particular structural landscape features. In this respect it was pointed out that savanna-type environments seem to contain an ideal "synthesis" of those preferred features. Illustratively, Heerwagen (2003, unpaged) notes that '[s]avannah "mimics" are obvious in many of our modern built spaces including shopping malls, department stores ... Research on the design of retail settings shows how the manipulation of space and artifacts influences purchasing behaviors. Many of these manipulations – light, décor, sounds, food, flowers, smells, visual corridors – are consistent with the savannah hypothesis and other research on environmental preferences.' In the following sections we will reiterate the preferred landscape features (that appear to be characteristic to savannas) and illustrate how they can be applied to stores.

Prospect and Refuge

Architectural theoretician Grant Hildebrand (1999) employed Appleton's prospect-refuge theory to explain the aesthetic appeal of architectural work and has illustrated that feelings of prospect and refuge can be evoked by particular architectural organizations. Possible design strategies that refer to refuge are: using small spaces enclosed by thick walls, lowering ceilings, or reducing lighting intensity. In a store environment this could mean having separate, dimly lit spaces in which consumers can have a rest (e.g., lounge-like spaces where consumers can relax in a comfortable chair). Prospect can be evoked by creating spacious areas, raised ceilings, thin, transparent walls, wide and open views on surrounding spaces, building on an elevated site, or creating balconies. Note that prospect or refuge can be *augmented* in architectural design, which can lead to a dominance of either of these dimensions. For example, refuge areas seem particularly relevant for stores in which high-involvement decisions have to be made (e.g., a car, furniture) and in which the refuge area can create a private and relaxing environment in which consumers can elaborate their decisions.

Perhaps there is even a gender difference in preferences for prospect versus refuge. During the course of evolution men and women have faced partially different adaptive problems. For example women, compared to men, can procreate only a limited number of offspring and consequently invest more energy in their offspring (gestation, birth, lactation). Evolutionary psychology therefore predicts that the most pronounced sex differences will occur in those domains in which the sexes have faced different adaptive problems (Buss 1989; Symons 1979). Related to this, research suggests that compared to males, females have more affinity with refuges than with prospects (and vice versa for males) (Heerwagen and Orians 1993). These differences could be explained by a sexual division in foraging (i.e., men are hunters, women are gatherers) (Eals and Silverman 1994), combined with differences in mating strategies (i.e., due to a costly reproduction system women better apply restricted navigation) (Gaulin and Fitzgerald 1986, 1989). The ESA implication that follows from this is that – on average – ESA strategies based on refuge are probably more effective in shops with a predominantly female audience (e.g., beauty retailers), whereas ESA strategies based on prospect might better fit shops where males are the main customers (e.g., automotive showrooms).

Preference Matrix

In the first part of this chapter, we described the preference matrix by Kaplan and Kaplan (1989) which proposes that four structural landscape features positively influence the aesthetic perception of natural environments, namely complexity, mystery, coherence, and legibility. Below we describe how each of these features can be strategically implemented in stores to attract and appeal to customers.

Complexity refers to sufficient sensory stimulation. Applied to design factors in store environments, complexity can be interpreted as giving sufficient visual richness and variety to the consumer, that is, the store should contain enough interesting "material" for our senses. Complexity can be introduced in different ways: for example, by the sheer number of (decorative) elements in the store environment, the use of multiple colors in the store interior, the amount of products that are being displayed, or the amount of shelves and racks per square meter. As is clear from the preference matrix, complexity should not be randomly presented, but needs to be counterbalanced by *coherence*, which refers to visual features that contribute to structuring and comprehending the environment, for example, by consistently using specific recurring colors, motifs, or symbols to indicate areas where certain products can be found. Supermarkets often make use of floorings and color codes of displays to define coherent spaces of particular clusters of product-categories within the stores (e.g., "blue" for personal hygiene products).

It is important to note that the optimal degree of complexity and the optimal balance between complexity and coherence seem to depend on situational factors. In that sense, it would be very interesting to inquire about whether minimalistic store design is a suboptimal strategy, or, whether the use of different colors and variation in materials as a complexity-enhancing strategy is a better option. The answer could well depend on the type of purchase decision that has to be made. High-involvement products (e.g., cars, furniture) usually require a lot of deliberation, and store environments that are too complex might hinder this process, because added complexity requires more extensive cognitive processing. Especially within this high-involvement segment minimalistic stores have proven to be successful (e.g., designer stores). On the other hand, when purchasing low-involvement products (e.g., clothing, fast moving consumer goods) adding complexity to the store might make the shopping experience more enjoyable.

One could even add a situational "layer" to the previous one (i.e., level of involvement), based on gender. It is known that female shoppers put more effort and time into searching and comparing products in order to find the best value for money, whereas males tend to go straight for what they want in a fairly purposeful manner. This divergence in shopping behavior has been explained as reflecting an evolved affinity with either hunting and gathering activities, characteristic to males and females, respectively. In their version of the savannah hypothesis, Dennis and McCall (2005: 14) for example argue that "[...] gathering has been translated into comparison shopping, and hunting into earning money to support the family".

In terms of ESA implementation, the female shopping style could be accommodated by providing a fair amount of complexity in the store. Presenting many different offerings could meet up to the (female) desire to browse and compare multiple suitable products before finally deciding what to buy. A clothing retailer could strategically adapt his assortment to the male shopping style by, for example, coherently organizing it in terms of purpose (e.g., category of shirts, category of trousers, category of sweaters) and size. This could enhance shopping-efficiency, enabling male individuals to purposefully fulfill their buying objective. Likewise, off-shelf displays (e.g., dump bins with "leftovers") are often surrounded by female shoppers searching for a bargain (Sullivan and Adcock 2002), whereas male consumers are not that fond of finding what they need in a basket full of mixed products, or in a crowd of customers. The implication is that in "mixed" shopping environments the degree of complexity/variation of a certain store-section should be adapted to the target-public of that section.

Another preferred structural landscape feature is *mystery*, which refers to environmental configurations that promise that further information can be acquired when one further enters the scene. Mystery is known to be a significant predictor of preference and, hence, can play an important role in store-atmospherics.

Consider the frequent practice of shop-owners to place a great deal of the offerings that are sold in the shop's store-front. The assumption underlying this practice seems to be that fully displaying all offerings will motivate consumers to enter the store. However, the notion mystery points out that *insufficient* information can create curiosity, which can motivate customers to further explore the shopping environment. Store-owners might profit from only presenting smaller samples or hints about what one can expect to find inside the shop.

Quite probably, type of shopping will interact with mystery. In the case of utilitarian shopping, customers very often know what they want to buy and know where they can find the product, and too much mystery could hinder efficiency. Nevertheless, even in "functional" shopping environments (e.g., supermarkets) there is a role for aesthetic interventions, and adding a little bit of mystery (without compromising way-finding) can fulfill this aesthetic role. Mystery will perhaps be especially interesting for hedonic shopping contexts, where the uniqueness and exclusivity of products are further underlined by the fact that they are not directly visible, but require exploration and discovery. In hedonic shopping, the act of browsing in itself is pleasant and adding mystery to that activity can further enhance the pleasure and can create a sense of surprise.

Some claim that mystery can be conveyed by specific design elements: "When appearing around corners, attached to walls, and hung from ceilings, interesting objects, architectural details or motifs, graphics, video displays and artefacts can create a little mystery and surprise ..." (Hase and Heerwagen 2000: 30). A specific modality of mystery is called "enticement", which refers to the situation where an individual is in the dark, from where he/she can see a partially visible and enlightened scene (Hildebrand 1999). A clear example in a consumer environment is the situation where the most exclusive or premier products are brightly lit, whereas the surroundings only dimly lit.

Despite its appeal, too much mystery can make the layout of the store environment confusing and ambiguous, ultimately leading to challenges associated with orientation and way-finding. In this sense the last element from the preference matrix comes at play, namely *legibility*. This predictor refers mainly to the capacity to retain orientation inside an environment. Classic retail design scholars have already hinted to the importance of legibility. For example, McGoldrick (2002: 472) suggests that "unnecessary changes to product locations are all likely to give the impression of a chaotic or, worse, a conniving store". Furthermore, Titus and Everett (1995) note that a store layout needs to achieve "environmental legibility" to avoid causing anger and frustration among shoppers. The legibility of the shopping environment can be enhanced by integrating signalizations and distinctive markings, by offering views to the outside of the store, by making the building shape more regular (Evans and McCoy 1998) or by inserting a specific landmark into the setting.

An issue relevant to legibility is that men and women differ in how they find their way through a particular environment, and through shopping malls more specifically. A study by Chebat et al. (2008) shows that women prefer to use landmarks (e.g., other shops or central areas in a mall), rely more on social information (e.g., talking to other people), and more frequently make use of object properties such as shape and color. Men, on the other hand, use more spatial properties such as location and spatial relations. These findings are in line with evolutionary insights of women excelling in spatial memory and men having better spatial navigation abilities (Ecuyer-Dab and Robert 2004). However, it should also be noted that recent research indicates that when the navigational tasks involve specific contents a reversal of navigational skills can be observed (New et al. 2007a, 2007b). Specifically, females appear to more accurately remember where they have previously encountered food sources (i.e., vegetables) than men, which might reflect an evolved sex difference in foraging behavior.

2.2.2 Integrating Actual Nature in Store Design

There are many ways to integrate actual nature in store environments. For example, bringing vegetation (e.g., flowers, potted plants) inside a store can yield positive consumer emotions and potentially enhance social contact between customers and employees. Consistent with this, pioneering research within health psychology has shown that hospital patients have better health outcomes when placed in rooms with windows to natural settings than when in rooms overlooking built elements (Ulrich 1984). Also, when visiting someone in convalescence at a hospital or at home, people typically bring flowers or plants as gifts. Such findings can be translated into different store design strategies:

- Making outside nature visible from inside the store
- Potted plants and flowers in the retail environment
- Interior planting beds
- Greening the shopping streets
- Interior/exterior gardens
- Vines on the shop's exterior surface
- Roof gardens or green-roofs, and providing views to these
- Green or vegetated walls
- Natural materials, like wood or marble

Water can be integrated in stores in a number of ways: by a fountain, a small pond, waterfalls, interior/exterior water gardens, or kinetic water sculptures (Mador 2008). What is furthermore interesting is that a water-feature (e.g., a pond) allows one to elegantly and non-obtrusively integrate actual animals (i.e., fish) in the shopping environment. A possible difficulty with animals in store environments is that these could be experienced as a nuisance, or as being inappropriate for retail contexts. Moreover, certain customers will probably consider that animals are not meant to serve as decorative pieces for the fickle and frivolous enjoyment of mankind.

In a store context, the positive effects of views on greenery or water-features could either make customers less vulnerable for stressing factors (such as crowding) or dampen the stress that has already incurred. The relevance and value of such effects is clear from the fact that the number of shoppers entering a store in a negative mood comprises approximately 10% of the total shopping population (Maxwell and Kover 2003) and this segment tends to have an avoidance response towards stores (Eroglu and Machleit 1990). Many retail environments are furthermore laden with (sensory) stimuli and alternatives (Lipowski 1970). This can cognitively overload the shopper's limited processing capacity, and perhaps even further exacerbate negative feelings in shoppers. Although they may actually spend the same amount of money as consumers who are in a good mood (some basic human needs will always remain), negative mood shoppers could eventually spend less time shopping and are likely to be less satisfied overall (Babin and Darden 1996). Although retailers may not have direct control over consumers' pre-existing feelings when visiting a store, ESA interventions like integrating greenery might trigger more positively toned feelings in them and, as such, favor patronage and loyalty (Mano 1999; Joye et al. 2010).

Imitated Natural Contents in Store Design

Particularly relevant to ESA is that affective responses to natural landscapes can also be triggered by imitations (e.g., photos, videos) of actual nature (Joye 2007). The use of "imitated" nature increases the creative possibilities for store designers because there are many possible ways in which one particular natural element (e.g., a flower) can be imitated. Furthermore, it is sometimes undesirable (cf., hygienic reasons) or practically difficult to keep actual nature in the business environment (e.g., flowers are costly and wither). Therefore the majority of ESA design recommendations will concern imitated rather than actual natural contents.

Animal Life

Let us begin by relating some visual characteristics of animals to the design of retail environments (for a discussion about predator and prey characteristics, see Barrett 2005). A first observation is that biological entities – and animals specifically – have a specific way of moving about, which seems to be categorically different from the way manufactured objects move. Martin and Weisberg (2003) found that the observation of biological and mechanical movement activates distinct neural regions in the human brain, which also overlap with regions recognized as being specialized in processing (conceptual) information about animals and tools, respectively (Martin and Weisberg 2003). Biological movement is furthermore found to activate the amygdala, potentially reflecting the affective significance (e.g., fear) associated with processing biological features. These findings are consistent with the claim that there exist evolved domain-specific mechanisms for processing perceptual features about biological versus manufactured objects (cf., Camarazza and Shelton 1998).

In store environments design interventions can be created that meet up to the input conditions of these domain-specific mechanisms. For example, computers sometimes have screensavers displaying organically moving shapes. In a quite similar way, biological movement can be projected on walls or ceilings in stores, or it can be displayed on LCD or television screens, or even media walls. Research indicates that when such organic movement is slow or "heraclitean", it seems to have relaxing effects on the viewers (Katcher and Wilkins 1993). More arousing effects can probably be obtained by making the movement patterns more erratic: that is, with rapid and sudden changes in movement (Heerwagen and Gregory 2008). Notice that the application of either such slow or erratic movement in retail environments should preferably be situational, depending on the time consumers have available or their level of involvement. In that regard, it is relevant to note that a distinction can be made between utilitarian shopping or "shopping for work" and hedonic shopping or "shopping for fun" (Holbrook and Hirschmann 1982; Babin et al. 1994; Kaltcheva and Weitz 2006). Babin et al. (1994) found that utilitarian shoppers strive to complete shopping tasks in an efficient way, whereas hedonistic shoppers enjoy the act of shopping, and take their time to browse through the stores. In environments that profit from a quick turnaround, erratic movement could – just like uptempo music (Oaks 2000) – facilitate utilitarian customers to make faster use of the services offered (e.g., fastfood restaurant). (Care should however be taken that such movement is not a reason to avoid the setting in the first place). Slow organic movement better fits shopping in those hedonic environments where customers need sufficient time and a relaxed state of mind to make purchase decisions, such as an electronics or a furniture store.

Apart from biological movement, also the *shapes* characteristic to biological entities have a distinctly different affective tone compared to shapes more characteristic to manufactured objects. For example, research into the affective tone of different types of line configurations shows that organic and rounded shapes, which are characteristic to animals (cf., Levin et al. 2001), are preferred over sharp-angled shapes (Aiken 1998b; Bar and Neta 2006). fMRI studies furthermore indicate that downwardly pointing shapes (Larson et al. 2009) and sharp-angled objects (Bar and Neta 2007) activate brain regions that are involved in fear responses (i.e., the amygdala). It has been proposed that the lesser preference for sharp-angled objects is rooted in the fact that such shapes convey a sense of threat (Bar and Neta 2008). Coss (2003) even speculates that it is an evolved trait that must be related to the piercing characteristics of canines and horns, and to the thorny plants and seeds that are abundant in African savannas. Irrespective of whether this is a correct interpretation, it seems quite certain that curved forms and surfaces are more "affiliative" or inviting, whereas sharp forms predominantly lead to negatively valenced arousal and defensive responses.

The previous findings can be directly applied to different features of a store's atmosphere. For example, varying the amount of either curvilinearity or rectilinearity in fonts of product logos or of shopping displays can already convey a substantially different affective feeling. In agreement with this, research by Leder and Carbon (2005) indicates that subjects prefer car interiors with organic, rounded forms over more "straight" interiors. Figure 2 illustrates how soft, rounded surfaces have recently been integrated into retail environments. Note again, however,

Fig. 2 The romanticism women clothing store interior (by SAKO Architects), China (Courtesy SAKO Architects)

that – ideally – the application of this design feature should be situational. For example, the higher sense of arousal and excitement which sharp-angled shapes might evoke seems to be more compatible with a store selling the newest specs for youngsters hooked on skateboarding than with shopping centers' waiting corners that invite customers to relax. In the latter case, soft, organic forms that express a sense of calmness and serenity might be a better option.

According to Jay Appleton (1975) it was not only adaptive for our species to be sensitive to the prospect and refuge dimension of landscapes, but also to certain cues of *dangers* or *hazards*. Think for example of turbulent water, heights, predators, or signals of impending bad weather. Architecturally, the fascinating or arousing aspects of certain buildings could well derive from their hazardous or perilous character (Hildebrand 1999; Appleton 1990). In this regard, the fear of falling, associated with skyscrapers, could be one of the reasons for their appeal and arousing properties.[5]

In some circumstances it might be strategically relevant to include hints to such hazards in a store environment, especially when sensation-seekers are the target-audience. In that regard store atmosphere designers might get inspiration from (features about) animals that are known to elicit arousal and fearful reactions in humans, such as snakes, spiders, or scorpions. As contact with, for example, snakes was common during hominin evolution, it can be expected that affectively

---

[5]It must be noted that, historically, skyscrapers were not primarily constructed to appeal to this sense of hazards, but arose because of real estate realities, i.e., they were cheaper to build.

guided perceptual mechanisms have evolved to quickly recognize specific perceptual characteristics of these animals (Mineka and Öhman 2002; Coss 2003).

Predator animals or animal symbols are often present in product logos and commercials, and perhaps this can be interpreted as an intuitive recognition and application of their arousing and fascinating properties (Saad 2007). Probably one of the most famous examples of (unconsciously) integrating features about perennial threats in architecture can be found in the *Casa Battló* (Barcelona), designed by the Catalan architect Antoni Gaudí. The roof of the building consists of ceramic tiles and looks like the scaled-skin of a reptile. Quite similarly, skin patterns and prints of perennial threats could be integrated in certain designed features of store and commercial settings. In a retail context, skins or skin motifs of, say, snakes, leopards, tigers can be (and have been) applied to numerous products and design features, ranging from shoes, floor coverings, lighting designs, tiling designs, jewellery or as prints on furniture.

A morphological feature of animals, whose arousing effects have been more thoroughly inquired than skin patterns, are eyes or eye-like features/schemas. It is well-known that staring eyes can elicit fear in humans and other nonhuman species (Eibl-Eibesfeldt 1989; Aiken 1998a) because such patterns are associated with ambushing predators and aggressive conspecifics (Coss 2003: 115). Eyespots are exploited by certain organisms to ward off potential predators and sometimes they are even present in art, architecture, and design (Joye 2007). For example, some car brands seem to tap into these arousing effects by designing vehicles whose headlights are similar to frowning and threatening "eyes", which can give them a conspicuously aggressive look (Coss 2003; Joye 2007). Recent research by Aggarwal and McGill (2007) indeed confirms that car fronts are perceived as face-like and can express different types of emotions.

An intriguing finding, discussed in Coss (2003) and relevant for the theme of this paper, is that banners with eyespots significantly reduce shoplifting in stores. We already know from research that when subjects are exposed to eyespots during an economic game they behave more socially, i.e., they give more money to a second party (Haley and Fessler 2005). Although this is not really a "design" intervention, it would nevertheless be interesting to see how the insertion of eyespots in retail environments affects consumer behavior. One example of non-social behavior in clothing shops is that after fitting, customers frequently do not put the (unbought) clothing back from where they have taken it. Based on the previous research, a possible suggestion would be to introduce eye-like features in the changing rooms. The feeling of being watched will probably make customers more inclined to put the clothes back where they belong.

Vegetative Life

Imitations of vegetative elements can be incorporated in business environment in a number of ways (Joye 2007), for example with posters, pictures, photographs, or paintings of vegetated landscapes. In architecture, botanical motifs have been a perennial design element, especially in more traditional architectural styles or historical buildings, such as *Art Nouveau* and Classic architecture. In stores, plant-based motifs and ornaments can be integrated in floors, walls, ceiling, or stained glass. For example, the interior of the famous department store *Galleries Lafayette* in Paris is richly decorated with ornamental elements similar to, and reminiscent of vegetative elements. Of course, when using botanical decorations it is important to get a sense of what the audience of the store will be. Applying ornamental moldings of flowers can perhaps be a good idea for a classy jewelry store or premier clothing boutique, but it will be less convincing when introduced in a high-end sports store.

One important visual feature about natural structures (and vegetative elements in particular) is that they are characterized by a particular kind of geometry, coined "fractal geometry" (Mandelbrot 1982). A defining characteristic of a fractal is that it is self-similar, which means that the smaller details of the structure are more or less similar to the entire structure. In a tree, for example, the smaller branches, twigs, and even the individual leaves, are scaled-down versions of the entire tree, or structurally equivalent to it. Recent research seems to suggest that the positive responses triggered by natural/vegetated landscapes (as opposed to urban settings) are – for a part – due to their underlying fractal characteristics (Hagerhall et al. 2004; Joye 2007).

An innovative aspect of ESA would be to tap into the positive effects of interacting with nature by introducing fractals or fractal-like patterns in store environments. It is noteworthy that nature's fractal "language" is also used for creating attractive artificial or mathematical fractal patterns (Fig. 3) (as opposed to actual natural fractals). Such patterns could be inserted in store environments on wallpaper, on posters, or by playing so-called "fractal movies", which progressively zoom in on the finer details of the fractal. Fractal-like forms or organizations have been introduced in architectural design through floor-mosaics and ornamentation (Bonner 2003), floor and wall tiling (Mikiten et al. 2000), and stained glass (Joye 2007). In traditional architectural styles (e.g., Gothic architecture) building

Fig. 3 A mathematical fractal

Fig. 4 The fractal-like cupola of the *Galleries Lafayette*, Paris (Courtesy Wayne Boucher)

exteriors and facades often have fractal aspects because there is a "cascade of architectural detail" from the largest to the smallest scales (Bovill 1996). In retail environments, this continuous progression of detail on increasingly finer scales is very evident in the cupola of the *Galleries Lafayette* in Paris (Fig. 4). ESA proposes that integrating fractal-like structures into store environments can make the setting aesthetically fascinating for customers (and perhaps such designs will even have restorative effects).

3 Discussion and Future Research on ESA

Considering the high cost of retail design programs, and in some cases, their lack of commercial success, the need for a scientific approach to the design of retail environments is clear (McGoldrick 2002). The introduction of the notion ESA constitutes an attempt to fill in this void. Although ESA's benefits to customers seem clear from the previous discussion, retailers will probably wish to see how ESA affects their bottom line prior to investing in ESA. Although there are no exact numbers on this issue, there are some indications that carefully-planned ESA interventions can result in significant returns-on-investment. Consider Wolf's finding that the willingness-to-pay for certain goods is significantly higher in green shopping environments as opposed to retail settings without trees (see Joye et al. 2010). Of further relevance is that dampening negative consumer emotions in stores or creating positive affect are theoretically predicted to result in approach reactions towards the store (cf., the SOR-model, Sect. 2.1). Finally, it must be noted that not only customers, but also store employees could reap the benefits of properly designed store environments (Bitner 1992). For example, integrating (unthreatening) natural elements can offer a breather from stress and uplift moods, which in turn could translate into increased helpfulness and friendliness toward customers (Cohen and Spacapan 1978) and into more job satisfaction, which are obviously important components for retail service quality (Vazquez et al. 2001). Other possible effects which indirectly influence the bottom-line are: less stress-related health problems in employees; reduced costs associated with sick leaves (Bringslimark et al. 2007) and increased productivity (Lohr et al. 1996).

The evolutionary significance of specific atmospheric elements and their role in shaping consumer behavior and attitudes have hitherto remained largely unrecognized in the literature on atmospherics. Most of the ESA interventions we have proposed are therefore circumstantial, i.e., they are informed by empirical evidence from disciplines outside the field of consumer behavior. One of the future challenges is to directly test some of the actual proposals (e.g., are better decisions regarding high-involvement products indeed made within stores with a high refuge dimension?). When the effects would be robust across different cultures this could point to an underlying common heritage and thus further support the evolutionary assumptions underlying the ESA hypotheses. We have offered a substantial number of research possibilities and call for future studies to test the effects of ESA designs and the associated moderating factors in business settings.

Finally, some will perhaps note that ESA interventions are already frequently introduced in commercial and business related environments (albeit largely on intuitive grounds) (Fig. 5), so why should one be interested in the evolutionary psychology framework underlying it? Our answer is that better insight into the underlying (evolutionary) causes of consumer behavior and attitudes can have valuable practical ramifications, not anticipated by intuition. The insights we provide imply that conscious integrations of evolutionarily significant atmospheric elements (e.g., greenery) – as opposed to intuitive ones – should no longer be a shot in the dark, but can become theoretically informed. For example, an evolutionary-informed version of ESA is aware that the adaptive mechanisms handling, say, prey animals, do not necessarily favour the actual animal as input, but also certain key perceptual features. The upshot is that such an informed version can produce a much larger design vocabulary than an intuitive/uninformed account, which could become preoccupied with all too literal interpretations of natural elements in the store setting.

4 Conclusion

Dennett (1995) considered evolutionary theory as a "universal acid" that affects ideas/concepts in almost any field of (scientific) research. In agreement with this,

Fig. 5 The interior of the Mandarin Oriental Hotel in Barcelona seems to integrate different ESA interventions at once: fractal-like window screens, natural materials, vegetative elements and botanical motifs (Courtesy Mandarin Oriental Hotel Group)

evolutionary thinking is also beginning to penetrate research into the business sciences. In this paper we have discussed the fruitfulness of the cross-fertilization between research into evolved landscape preferences and the field of store atmospherics. We coined this new area of research "Evolutionary Store Atmospherics", which taps into evolved mechanisms specialized in scanning and processing the environment for habitability, resource opportunities, and threats (e.g., predators).

The approach adopted in this chapter was both theoretical and practical. On the one hand, we have discussed a substantial amount of theory and empirical research into human preferences for landscape features and characteristics. Although we were fairly critical to the evolutionary commitments that seem part and parcel to this field of research, we hope that future inquiries into ESA will invigorate interest to test these evolutionary assumptions. On the other hand, we have formulated a number of concrete design suggestions for ESA. If we have insights regarding the natural elements and structures that were present in ancestral environments, and if we know which kind of behavior these elements are able to activate, we can translate these elements into ESA proposals and make predictions about how consumers will react to them. However, it must be noted that we have only scratched the proverbial surface. The further elaboration of ESA and its concrete implementation are up to the actual store designers and marketers. Their creativity and strategic talent puts them in a unique position to choose the best fit according to the context of the shop and the type of experience which they wish their store environment to convey.

Acknowledgments Writing this paper was supported by the Research Program of the Scientific Research Foundation – Flanders (FWO), project G.0446.08. Many thanks to Tjerk van de Wetering of *BYTR* for his assistance with finding visual work illustrating ESA.

References

Aggarwal P, McGill AL (2007) Is that car smiling at me? Schema congruity as a basis for the evaluation of anthromorphized products. J Consum Res 34:468–479
Aiken NE (1998a) Human cardiovascular response to the eye spot threat stimulus. Evol Cogn 4:51–62
Aiken NE (1998b) The biological origins of art. Praeger, Westport
Appleton J (1975) The experience of landscape. Wiley, London
Appleton J (1990) The symbolism of habitat: an interpretation of landscape in the arts. University of Washington Press, Washington
Areni CS, Kim D (1993) The influence of background music on shopping behaviour: classical versus top-forty music in a wine store. In: McAlister L, Rothschild ML (eds) Advances in consumer research. Association for Consumer Research, Provo, pp 336–340
Atran S (1995) Causal constraints on categories and categorical constraints on biological reasoning across cultures. In: Sperber D, Premack D, Premack J (eds) Causal cognition. A multidisciplinary debate. Clarendon, Oxford, pp 205–233
Babin BJ, Darden WR (1996) Good and bad shopping vibes: spending and patronage satisfaction. J Bus Res 35:201–206
Babin BJ, Darden WR, Griffin M (1994) Work and/or fun: measuring hedonic and utilitarian shopping value. J Consum Res 20:644–656
Balling JD, Falk JH (1982) Development of visual preference for natural environments. Environ Behav 14:5–28
Bar M, Neta M (2006) Humans prefer curved visual objects. Psychol Sci 17:645–648
Bar M, Neta M (2007) Visual elements of subjective preference modulate amygdala activation. Neuropsychologia 45:2191–2200
Bar M, Neta M (2008) The proactive brain: using rudimentary information to make predictive judgments. J Consum Behav 7:319–330
Barkow JH, Cosmides L, Tooby J (1992) The adapted mind: evolutionary psychology and the generation of culture. Oxford University Press, New York
Barrett HC (2005) Adaptations to predators and prey. In: Buss DM (ed) The handbook of evolutionary psychology. Wiley, New York, pp 200–223
Bell PA, Greene TC, Fisher JD, Baum A (2005) Environmental psychology, 5th edn. Harcourt College Publishers, Fort Worth
Bellizzi JA, Crowley AE, Hasty RW (1983) The effects of colour in store design. J Retailing 59:21–45
Bitner MJ (1992) Servicescapes: the impact of psychical surroundings on customers and employees. J Marketing 56:57–70
Bonner J (2003) Three traditions of self-similarity in fourteenth and fifteenth century islamic geometric ornament. In: Sarhangi R, Sequin C (eds) ISAMA/Bridges 2003 conference proceedings Granada, Spain: University of Granada. www.bonner-design.com/downloads/Bonner-3017.pdf. Accessed July 5, 2009
Bovill C (1996) Fractal geometry in architecture and design. Birkhaüser, Basel
Bringslimark T, Hartig T, Patil G, Grindal G (2007) Psychological benefits of indoor plants in workplaces: putting experimental results into context. HortScience 42:581–587

Buber R, Ruso B, Gadner J, Atzwanger K, Gruber S (2007) Evolutionary store design. How water, plants, animals and sight protection affect consumer behaviour. In: Thyne M, Deans KR, Gnoth J (eds) Proceedings of the Australian and New Zealand Marketing Academy (ANZMAC) conference 2007 . University of Otago, Dunedin, pp 325–331

Buss DM (1989) Sex differences in human mate preferences: evolutionary hypotheses tested in 37 cultures. Behav Brain Sci 12:1–49

Camarazza A, Shelton JR (1998) Domain-specific knowledge systems in the brain: the animate-inanimate distinction. J Cogn Neurosci 10:1–34

Chebat J, Gélinas-Chebat C, Therrien K (2008) Gender-related wayfinding time of mall shoppers. J Bus Res 61:1076–1082

Cohen S, Spacapan S (1978) The aftereffects of stress: an attentional interpretation. Environ Psychol Nonver 3:43–57

Coss RG (2003) The Role of evolved perceptual biases in art and design. In: Voland E, Grammer K (eds) Evolutionary aesthetics. Springer, Berlin/Heidelberg, pp 69–130

d'Astous A (2000) Irritating aspects of the shopping environment. J Bus Res 49:149–156

Dennett DC (1995) Darwin's dangerous idea. Evolution and the meanings of life. Simon & Schutser, New York

Dennis C, McCall A (2005) The Savannah hypothesis of shopping. Bus Strat Rev 16:12–16

Design Council (1997) Design in Britain 1997–98. Design Council, London

Eals M, Silverman I (1994) The hunter-gatherer theory of spatial sex differences: proximate factors mediating the female advantage in recall of object arrays. Ethol Sociobiol 15:95–105

Ecuyer-Dab I, Robert M (2004) Have sex differences in spatial ability evolved from male competition for mating and female concern for survival? Cognition 91:221–257

Eibl-Eibesfeldt I (1989) Human ethology. Aldine de Gruyter, New York

Eroglu SA, Machleit KA (1990) An empirical examination of retail crowding: Antecedents and consequences. J Retailing 66:201–221

Evans GW, McCoy JM (1998) When buildings don't work: the role of architecture in human health. J Environ Psychol 18:85–94

Falk JH, Balling JD (2010) Evolutionary influence on human landscape preference. Environ Behav 42:479–493

Fischer MA, Shrout PE (2006) Children's liking of landscape paintings as a function of their perceptions of prospect, refuge, and hazard. Environ Behav 38:373–393

Fram E, Ajami R (1994) Globalization of markets and shopping stress: cross-country comparisons. Bus Horiz 37:17–23

Fredrickson BL, Levenson RW (1998) Positive emotions speed recovery from the cardiovascular sequelae of negative emotions. Cognition Emotion 12:191–220

Gaulin SJ, Fitzgerald RW (1986) Sex differences in spatial ability: an evolutionary hypothesis and test. Am Nat 127:74–88

Gaulin SJ, Fitzgerald RW (1989) Sexual selection for spatial-learning ability. Anim Behav 37:322–331

Hagerhall CM, Purcell T, Taylor R (2004) Fractal dimension of landscape silhouette outlines as a predictor of landscape preference. J Environ Psychol 24:247–255

Haley KJ, Fessler DMT (2005) Nobody's watching? Subtle cues affect generosity in an anonymous economic game. Evol Hum Behav 26:245–256

Han K-T (2007) Responses to six major terrestrial biomes in terms of scenic beauty, preference, and restorativeness. Environ Behav 39:529–556

Hartig T, Mang M, Evans GW (1991) Restorative effects of natural environment experience. Environ Behav 23:3–26

Hartig T, Evans GW, Jamner LD, Davis DS, Gärling T (2003) Tracking restoration in natural and urban field settings. J Environ Psychol 23:109–123

Hartmann P, Apaolaza-Ibáñez V (2010) Beyond Savanna: an evolutionary and environmental psychology approach to behavioral effects of nature scenery in green advertising. J Environ Psychol 30:119–128

Hase B, Heerwagen J (2000) Phylogenetic design: a new approach for workplace environments. J Qual Participation 23:27–31

Haviland-Jones J, Rosario HH, Wilson P, McGuire TR (2005) An environmental approach to positive emotion: flowers. Evol Psychol 3:104–132

Heerwagen JH (2003) Bio-inspired design: what can we learn from nature? http://biomimicry.typepad.com/bioinspire/files/BioInspire.1-01.15.03.pdf. Accessed 2 Feb 2010

Heerwagen JH, Gregory B (2008) Biophilia and sensory aesthetics. In: Kellert SR, Heerwagen JH, Mador ML (eds) Biophilic design. Wiley, Hoboken, pp 227–241

Heerwagen JH, Orians GH (1993) Humans, habitats, and aesthetics. In: Kellert SR, Wilson EO (eds) The biophilia hypothesis. Island Press, Washington, pp 138–172

Hildebrand G (1999) Origins of architectural pleasure. University of California Press, Berkeley

Holbrook MB, Hirschmann EC (1982) The experiential aspects of consumption: consumer fantasies, feelings, and fun. J Consum Res 9:132–140

Joye Y (2007) Architectural lessons from environmental psychology: the case of biophilic architecture. Rev Gen Psychol 11:305–328

Joye Y, Willems K, Brengman M, Wolf K (2010) The effects of urban retail greenery on consumer experience: reviewing the evidence from a restorative perspective. Urban For Urban Greening 9:57–64

Kaltcheva VD, Weitz BA (2006) When should a retailer create an exciting store environment? J Marketing 70:107–118

Kanazawa S (2004) The savanna principle. Manag decis econ 25:41–54

Kaplan S (1988) Perception and landscape: conceptions and misconceptions. In: Nasar J (ed) Environmental aesthetics: theory, research, and applications. Cambridge University Press, Cambridge, pp 45–55

Kaplan S (1992) Environmental preference in a knowledge seeking knowledge using organism. In: Barkow JH, Cosmides L, Tooby J (eds) The adaptive mind. Oxford University Press, New York, pp 535–552

Kaplan R, Kaplan S (1989) The experience of nature: a psychological perspective. Cambridge University Press, Cambridge

Katcher AH, Wilkins G (1993) Dialogue with animals: its nature and culture. In: Kellert SR, Wilson EO (eds) The biophilia hypothesis. Island Press, Washington D.C., pp 173–197

Kellert SR (2005) Building for life: designing & understanding the human-nature connection. Island Press, Washington, D.C

Kellert SR, Heerwagen J, Mador M (2008) Biophilic design: the theory, science, and bringing buildings to life. Wiley, New York

Kotler P (1973) Atmosphere as a marketing tool. J Retailing 49:48–64

Larson CL, Aronoff J, Sarinopoulos IC, Zhu DC (2009) Recognizing threat: a simple geometric shape activates neural circuitry for threat detection. J Cogn Neurosci 21:1523–1535

Leder H, Carbon CC (2005) Dimensions in appreciation of car interior design. Appl Cognitive Psychol 19:603–618

Levin DT, Takarae Y, Miner A, Keil FC (2001) Efficient visual search by category: specifying the features that mark the difference between artifacts and animals in preattentive vision. Percept Psychophys 63:676–697

Lewis J (2005) Challenges of interdisciplinarity for forest management and landscape perception research. In: Tress B, Tress G, Fry G, Opdam P (eds) From landscape research to landscape planning: aspects of integration, education, and application. Springer, Dordrecht, pp 83–94

Lipowski ZJ (1970) The conflict of Buridan's ass or some dilemmas of affluence: The theory of attractive stimulus overload. Am J Psychiatry 127:273–279

Lohr VI, Pearson-Mims CH, Goodwin GK (1996) Interior plants may improve worker productivity and reduce stress in a windowless environment. J Environ Hortic 14:97–100

Luttik J (2000) The value of trees, water and open space as reflected by house prices in the Netherlands. Landscape Urban Plan 48:161–167

Lyons E (1983) Demographic correlates of landscape preference. Environ Behav 15:487–511

Mador ML (2008) Water, biophilic design, and the built environment. In: Kellert SR, Heerwagen JH, Mador ML (eds) Biophilic design. Wiley, Hoboken, pp 43–57

Mandelbrot B (1982) The fractal geometry of nature. W.H. Freeman, San Francisco

Mano H (1999) The influence of pre-existing negative affect on store purchase intentions. J Retailing 75:149–172

Martin A, Weisberg J (2003) Neural foundations for understanding social and mechanical concepts. Cogn Neuropsychol 20:575–587

Maxwell S, Kover A (2003) Negative affect: the dark side of retailing. J Bus Res 56:553–559

McGoldrick PJ (2002) Retail marketing. McGraw-Hill, Berkshire

Mehrabian A, Russell JA (1974) An approach to environmental psychology. Massachusetts Institute of Technology, Cambridge

Mikiten T, Salingaros N, Yu H (2000) Pavements as embodiments of meaning for a fractal mind. Nexus Netw J 2:41–56

Miller G (2009) Spent: sex, evolution, and consumer behavior. Viking Adult, New York

Mineka S, Öhman A (2002) Phobias and preparedness: the selective, automatic, and encapsulated nature of fear. Biol Psychiatry 52:927–937

New J, Cosmides L, Tooby J (2007a) Category-Specific attention for animals reflects ancestral priorities, not expertise. Proc Natl Acad Sci USA 104:16598–16603

New J, Krasnow M, Truxaw D, Gaulin SJC (2007b) Spatial adaptations for plant foraging: women excel and calories count. Proc R Soc Ser B Biol Sci 274:2679–2684

Oaks S (2000) The influence of the musicscape within service environments. J Serv Mark 14:539–536

Orians GH (1980) Habitat selection: general theory and applications to human behaviour. In: Lockard JS (ed) The evolution of human social behaviour. Elsevier, New York, pp 49–66

Orians GH (2001) An evolutionary perspective on aesthetics. Bulletin of Psychology and the Arts, 2. http://www.apa.org/divisions/div10/ articles/orians.html. Accessed 5 July 2009

Orians GH, Heerwagen JH (1992) Evolved responses to landscapes. In: Barkow JH, Cosmides L, Tooby J (eds) *The adapted mind. Evolutionary psychology and the generation of culture.* Oxford University Press, New York, pp 555–574

Park S-H, Mattson RH, Kim E (2004) Pain tolerance effects of ornamental plants in a simulated hospital patient room. Acta Hortic 639:241–247

Potts RB (1998) Environmental hypotheses of hominin evolution. Yearb Phys Anthropol 41:93–136

Rakison DH, Derringer J (2008) Do infants possess an evolved spider-detection mechanism. Cognition 107:381–393

Ruso B, Renninger L, Atzwanger K (2003) Landscape perception as evolutionary foundation of aesthetics. In: Voland E, Grammer K (eds) Evolutionary aesthetics. Springer, Berlin, pp 279–294

Saad G (2007) The evolutionary bases of consumption. Lawrence Erlbaum, Mahwah

Stamps A (2006) Literature review of prospect and refuge theory: the first 214 references. http://ieq.home.att.net/LitReviewProspectAndRefuge.pdf. Accessed 2 Feb 2010

Sullivan M, Adcock D (2002) Retail marketing. Thomson, London

Symons D (1979) The evolution of human sexuality. Oxford University Press, New York

Titus PA, Everett PB (1995) The consumer retail search process: a conceptual model and research agenda. J Acad Market Sci 23:106–119

Todorova A, Asakawa S, Aikoh T (2004) Preferences for and attitudes towards street flowers and trees in Sapporo, Japan. Landscape urban plan 69:403–416

Turley LW, Milliman RE (2000) Atmospheric effects on shopping behavior: a review of the experimental evidence. J Bus Res 49:193–211

Ulrich RS (1981) Natural versus urban scenes – Some psychophysiological effects. Environ Behav 13:523–556

Ulrich RS (1983) Aesthetic and affective response to natural environment. In: Altman I, Wohlwill JF (eds) Human behavior and environment, vol 6. Plenum Press, New York, pp 85–125

Ulrich RS (1984) Views through a window may influence recovery from surgery. Science 224:420–421

Ulrich RS (1993) Biophilia, biophobia, and natural landscapes. In: Kellert SR, Wilson EO (eds) The biophilia hypothesis. Island Press, Washington, pp 73–137

Ulrich RS, Simons RF, Losito BD, Fiorito E, Miles MA, Zelson M (1991) Stress recovery during exposure to natural and urban environments. J Environ Psychol 11:201–230

Vazquez R, Rodriguez-Del Bosque I, Diaz AM, Ruiz AV (2001) Service quality in supermarket retailing: identifying critical service experiences. J Retailing Consum Serv 8:1–14

Ward JC, Eaton JP (1994) Service environments: the effect of quality and decorative style on emotions, expectations, and attributions. In: Acrol R, Mitchell A (eds) Enhancing knowledge development in marketing. American Marketing Association, Chicago, pp 333–334

Wilson EO (1984) Biophilia: the human bond with other species. Harvard University Press, Cambridge

Yamane K, Kawashima M, Fujishige N, Yoshida M (2004) Effects of interior horticultural activities with potted plants on human physiological and emotional status. In: Relf D, Kwack BH, Hicklenton P (eds) A proceedings of the XXVI international horticultural congress expanding roles for horticulture in improving human well-being and life quality. ISHS, Toronto/Leuven, pp 37–43

Rationality and Utility: Economics and Evolutionary Psychology

C. Monica Capra and Paul H. Rubin

Abstract Economics has always prided itself on having a unifying theoretical framework based on rational choice theory. However, data from controlled experiments, which often provide theory the best chance to work, refute many of the rationality assumptions that economists make. The evidence against rational choice, as traditionally defined, has forced economists to rethink their traditional models. However, despite the investment of many brilliant minds in the pursuit of better behavioral models of choice, behavioral economics has so far made little progress in providing an alternative paradigm that would be both parsimonious and accurate. In this chapter, we review the evidence against rational choice and the ways in which behavioral economists have responded. In addition, we put forward the idea that evolutionary psychology can give economics back its overriding paradigm. Evolutionary psychology can place structure on the utility function and provide content to rationality. By doing so, it can explain many of the behavioral anomalies that behavioral economists and psychologists have documented. If economists are willing to use the evolutionary psychology paradigm, then they can regain theoretical consistency of their discipline and have models that are better descriptors and predictors of behavior.

Keywords Economics · Rationality · Utility · Anomalies · Behavior · Experiments · Evolutionary psychology and economics

Introduction

In the last 30 years, experimental and behavioral economists have gathered vast amounts of data that suggest that human behavior systematically deviates from rational choice, narrowly defined as that prescribed by neoclassical economic

---

C.M. Capra (✉) and P.H. Rubin
Department of Economics, Emory University, 1602 Fishburne Drive 30322 Atlanta, GA, USA
e-mail: mcapra@emory.edu

choice theory. It is already possible to explain some of these deviations in terms of evolutionary psychology. In this article, we argue that economics would benefit from continuing to build bridges between economics and biological and psychological sciences. These bridges will enable us to establish Evolutionary Psychology as a unifying framework for explaining why such anomalies occur. In the first part of this chapter, we provide an overview of the arguments, and review evidence that have challenged the assumption of rationality in economics. We then discuss some of the ways in which economists have attempted to explain anomalous behaviors, and we present some of the challenges that these explanations face. In particular, current behavioral models do not derive from first principles. Many of current behavioral models are constructed with the purpose of fitting empirical observations. This means that there are likely to be as many models of behavior as there are behavioral anomalies. Many of the behavioral models fit data well, but mainly because they include many parameters that adjust to fit the data. In the third part of this chapter, we develop arguments for adopting evolutionary psychology as a workhorse for understanding behavior. In particular, evolutionary psychology can help us identify the nature of utility and choice. With respect to utility, we argue that it essentially represents the fitness evolutionary function. With respect to decision-making, we believe that the concept of ecological rationality – that is, the adaptation of decision processes to contex – is a promising step towards a theory of choice that is grounded on evolutionary principles. We believe that behavioral economics and economics in general would benefit from introducing a unifying paradigm that is alternative to rational choice and that is based on evolutionary psychology. We believe that this endeavor is both possible and that it would benefit not only economics, but also other sister disciplines.

1 The Rationality Critique

Critiques of the rationality postulate in economics trace back to the early 1900s when psychologists and some economists attacked the assumption that individual behavior was solely motivated by the urge to achieve maximum pleasure and minimum pain. To the early skeptics of rational choice, the reliance of economic theory on the hedonistic idea of utility maximization trivialized the fact that habit, instinct, evolution, and the environment influence choices. Thorstein Veblen (1909), for instance, believed that the hedonistic premise that all choice could be explained by the urge to achieve highest utility was too narrow to explain how people really behaved. Choice implied much more than pleasure and pain, it was a joint product of certain underlying psychological tendencies developed and given their shape and direction by the universe outside. "*[T]he facts of choice depend upon instincts interplaying with the great body of customs, current technology, and common-sense philosophy that have been handed down to them; above all by the kind of prowess held in most esteem*" (Veblen in Dickinson 1919).

Early twentieth century skeptics also acknowledged the notion that decisions involve costs. They argued that it is difficult, if not impossible, for a human being to always behave in a manner consistent with utility maximization. *"Decisions involve effort of attention, and this effort cannot be sustained beyond a few seconds at a time, nor repeated without limit"* (John Bates Clark 1918 p. 23). Indeed, Clark was referring to the contemporary idea that human rationality is a scarce resource, and as such, it is costly to always choose the optimum. Decisions imply costs of concentration, information acquisition, and analysis of available alternatives, thinking, deciding what to do, figuring out the best way to do it, and finally acting upon one's final decision. As Vernon Smith (1991) argues, many decisions that require complex calculations are too costly to follow compared to their value. Therefore, it makes sense to resort to habit or simple rules of thumb.

Despite the early criticisms, rational choice flourished and developed into a widely accepted postulate among economists. Most economists not only continued to regard instincts, habits, and decision costs as unimportant elements of choice, but they also stretched the assumption of perfect rationality to unrealistic extremes. Game theoretic models, for example, assume that super rational agents perfectly understand the model or game that the theorist is studying, probably with much difficulty. Here, an analyst might spend a year or two solving a difficult maximization problem and, then, automatically assume that the solution explains behavior of less persistent and less sophisticated game participants. Clearly, a problem with modeling economic behavior under such unrealistic assumptions is that the resulting predictions, although elegant, may have very little practical and empirical relevance.

Nevertheless, the ideas that individuals may not always optimize and that decision-making is a costly endeavor reemerged in the economic literature. In the 1950s research by psychologists such as Duncan Luce (1959) and economists such as Herbert Simon (1955, 1957) provided alternative ways of describing human behavior that better mirrors the way people actually behave. Simon, in particular, put forward the idea of bounded rationality. His basic idea was that almost all human behavior has a large rational component, but only in terms of the broader everyday sense of rationality, not the economists' more specific sense of maximization (Simon 1959, 1978). Rationality in economics is reflected entirely in the choices realized, whereas, according to Simon, human rationality is reflected in the *process* that involves a decision. Procedural rationality is the hallmark of "satisficing". As William Baumol (1979) puts it, *"... a person who is in a situation of having to find a needle in a haystack will quickly realize that there is little to be gained by looking further once the first good, usable needle has been found"*. Maximization requires a costly and careful process of comparison of all available alternatives. Satisficing involves comparing a candidate decision in terms of the acceptability of that decision. That is, the needle found in the haystack, even if it is not the best, may be usable enough to make one want to stop looking any further. Although Simon's ideas eventually earned him the Nobel Prize in Economics in 1978, many of his early contributions were all but ignored by mainstream economics.

Indeed, economists addressed some of these issues and attempted to salvage the model of rationality. For example, Armen Alchian (1950) followed by Milton Friedman (1953) argued that markets would select for maximizing behavior even if individuals did not seek or understand such behavior. In fact, in market interactions, all you need is a small percentage of agents who can exploit arbitrage opportunities to get rid of biased behaviors. This argument applied more to behavior of firms than of individuals. Garry Becker (1962) argued that many results of economics, such as the downward sloping demand curve, would follow even if individuals behaved irrationally. These arguments, especially those of Friedman, enabled economists to maintain the rationality assumption in the face of much contradictory evidence. Thus, although individuals may be irrational, they behave *as if* they were perfectly rational. A baseball player running to catch a ball does not really solve a system of differential equations to determine how fast to run, but he runs *as if* he did. The reluctance of early economists to abandon the rational framework is not surprising. Economists had been heavily influenced by physics, which aims at finding unified theories for understanding the physical world. Thus, economists differ from other social scientists in that we search for parsimonious models of economic choice that can be derived from first principles and that can be used to explain decisions in a wide variety of economic contexts. In other words, economists want a unified model of social behavior. This is in stark contrast to the way psychologists study choice; psychologists seem not particularly concerned with finding a unifying framework, but prefer to explain each phenomenon they face with a different theory.

In the 1970s through the early 1990s, the assumption of rationality was most strongly and successfully questioned through the important works of psychologists such as Amos Tversky and Daniel Kahneman.[1] Through a series of simple experimental tasks, these researchers were able to show large anomalies in judgment and decision-making including framing effects (which violates procedural and description invariance), the status quo bias and the endowment effect (which imply reference dependent utility and an asymmetry in how we treat gains and losses), and preference reversals (which challenges the stability of preferences) in both riskless choice and choice under risk. Faced with the overwhelming empirical evidence, economists could no longer ignore the evidence against rationality assumptions. In fact, there were some economists who became instrumental in emphasizing the importance of psychology in economics and finance. Richard Thaler (1985, 1981), in particular, pointed out that the models of saving and consumption that guide policy making do not test well against data.

Traditional models of inter-temporal choice rely on the assumption that people smooth consumption over their lifespan. However, consumption smoothing is rarely seen. Thaler showed that consumption is highly sensitive to income and that savings tend to increase when consumers are offered 401 K plans. This pattern of consumption and saving behaviors suggest that the marginal propensity to

---

[1] See Tversky and Kahneman (1974; 1991, and 1992) and Kahneman and Tversky (1979)

consume different types of wealth is not equal. In response to this and other evidence, Thaler proposed a model of mental accounts. The main premise of mental accounting is that people tend to label money for specific consumption or investment decisions. For example, people would use their salary moneys to buy food and other necessities, use gifts from parents or relatives to buy luxuries, but use bonuses to save. Richard Thaler (1999) suggested that people create mental accounts to facilitate comparisons between consumption goods, such as buying a computer or a new dress, and to exert self-control. That is, moneys labeled as "savings" (e.g., 401 K) are kept out of reach, but moneys labeled as "cash" can be used for consumption. When experiencing changes in income, for example, people correct their consumption accounts, but not necessarily their savings accounts, as they are usually "recorded" as different and independent from each other. Mental accounting, thus, violates the basic assumption that money is fungible, as investors behave as if its origin determined its use.

More recently, with the backing of a significant body of evidence that documented a systematic departure from the predictions of rational economic behavior[2] and the professional birth of a new generation of experimental economists, limitations on the rationality assumptions have become commonplace, as part of what is called "behavioral economics". For example, Kahneman shared the Nobel Prize in economics in 2002 (Tversky had died in 1996) and in 2004 Matthew Rabin, a scholar in behavioral economics, won the John Bates Clark medal, an important honor for young economists. Nowadays, virtually every issue of every important journal in economics has one or more articles reporting on non-rational behavior of some sort. Economics has now reached a point where non-rational behavior is, as common as, or possibly more common an assumption than rationality.

2 In Search for an Explanation

Throughout the debate regarding the inconsistency between theoretical predictions and behavioral observations, there has been little success in unifying the mounting evidence against perfect rationality into a consistent theory. There have been some attempts to meet the challenge. Kahneman and Tversky, for example, did propose "prospect theory" and "cumulative prospect theory" as a unifying set of hypotheses to explain anomalies in individual choice experiments. The main pillars of these are that individuals evaluate outcomes based on a reference point, and that people value gains differently from losses. In particular, the theory predicts loss aversion, which refers to the idea that losses feel worse (almost twice as bad) than equivalent gains feel good. A typical value function proposed by prospect theory treats gains and losses differently with respect to a reference point. It is concave over gains and is convex over losses, depicting diminishing sensitivity in both domains. This means

---

[2]See Conlisk (1996) for an extensive review of departures from rational predictions in games

that, with respect to a reference point, people are risk averse when they face uncertain positive outcomes, but risk seeking when they face uncertain negative outcomes. A gravely ill patient facing a choice between certain death versus a very small chance of a recovery through experimental therapy is likely to choose the later. In addition, to introducing a reference-point based value function, Tversky and Kahneman suggested that value drops faster in the loss domain than it rises in the gain domain. This later concept is called "loss aversion".

That losses feel much worse than equivalent gains feel good is not much of a surprise to anyone who has both lost and found money on the streets, or who has had papers accepted and rejected in a journal. Richard Thaler (1980) used Tversky and Kahnman's ideas to explain that endowments (such as owning a house) set an individual's reference point so that selling (e.g., selling the house) moves the individual in the direction of a loss and buying in the direction of a gain. So, the individual would "irrationally" ask more for an item she owes than she is willing to pay for it; this phenomenon was later named "the endowment effect". In addition, there is recent evidence that such a model can predict choices when the outcomes are non-monetary and negative, and when in "real-life" large stake games. Gregory Berns et al. (2007), for example, used painful electric shocks to induce negative non-monetary outcomes in a choice under risk task. They observed that the pattern of choices of the majority of the subjects could be explained by cumulative prospect theory. In a recent field study of the behavior of contestants in the popular TV show "Deal or No-Deal"[3] Thierry Post et al. (2008) find that contestants' decisions can be largely explained by a reference-dependent type of model, such as cumulative prospect theory. However, despite their descriptive appeal, these behavioral models do not derive from first principles, but rather represent methods of organizing observations. What these explanations lack is an account for why non-rational choice exists in the first place. What is the origin of observed "anomalous" behavior in individual choice tasks? What first principles can support reference points and loss aversion? These are questions that cumulative prospect theory does not address.

In games, the lack of a unifying paradigm for explaining anomalous behavior is even more evident. Traditional game theory assumes perfect rationality, rational expectations, and common knowledge of rationality. Not surprisingly, because of the stringent rationality assumptions, traditional game theory performs very poorly as a descriptive theory of choice. Persistent and systematic deviations from the rational prediction have been documented by innumerable experiments with different incentives, frames, and subject pools (see Conlisk 1996 and Camerer 2003). In general, it is not surprising that such disconnect between game theoretic predictions and behavior exists. Game theory is a branch of mathematics. As such, it is more

---

[3]*Deal or No Deal* is a game show broadcasted in the U.S. on NBC. It consists of a contestant selecting one briefcase of 26, each containing a cash value from $.01 to $1,000,000. Over the course of the game, the contestant eliminates the other cases in the game, periodically being presented with a "deal" from The Banker to take a cash amount to quit the game. Should the contestant refuse every deal, they win the value of the case selected at the start

concerned with the internal consistency of its theorems than with their practical relevance. It makes normative statements about how perfectly rational players would behave, but makes no statement about how real people would behave. Thus, it is not a descriptive theory of choice.

Perhaps because of its simplicity and applicability, the Ultimatum Game (Guth et al. 1982) represents a notorious example of what is wrong with game theoretic predictions. In an ultimatum game, a player makes an offer to another player of how to split an amount of money, say $10. The responder has the option to accept or reject the offer. If the offer is accepted, each gets the amount that the first player determined. If the offer is rejected, both players get nothing. The Nash equilibrium predicted by traditional game theory indicates that the first player will offer the minimum possible amount, and the second will accept it. However, this game has been played in innumerable countries including the Israel, Japan, US, and Yugoslavia (Roth et al. 1991) with different subject pools (see for example Harbaugh et al. 2000) and with both relatively small and relatively large stakes (Cameron 1999). Yet, the Nash equilibrium is virtually never observed.[4] In general, low offers tend to be rejected and first players, perhaps anticipating a rejection, tend to offer between 40% and 50% of the endowment (Camerer 2003).

Several explanations have been put forward to explain data of this game and other similar games; these include inequality aversion (Fehr and Schmidt 1999) and fairness preferences (Rabin 1993). These models have generated a large amount of studies that look at the effects of social preferences, such as envy and generosity on strategic decisions. However, just like prospect theory, these explanations are a way to organize behavioral data and do not derive from a unifying paradigm. Perhaps in an attempt to find a framework for understanding the role of social emotions on strategic choice, researchers have ventured into the area of neuroscience. Their initial motivation was to accumulate process data that would help us in understanding the mechanisms by which choices are made. With respect to the ultimatum game, brain imaging studies reveal that rejections are motivated by adverse physiologic reactions (visceral disgust) to low offers (Sanfey 2004). In other words, people seem to reject low offers in the Ultimatum game because low offers make them feel bad, and they need to take an action (rejection) to feel better, possibly to maintain homeostasis.[5] The idea that emotions play a role in rejecting offers in the Ultimatum Game has been further supported other behavioral experiments. For example, in a clever study, Dan Houser and Erte Xiao (2005) gave recipients a chance to vent their anger and pain from low offers. More specifically, they allowed recipients to write nasty messages to the first players before making a decision. Interestingly, the venting option significantly reduced rejection rates.

---

[4]High acceptance rates of low offers have been observed in underdeveloped, isolated communities and among very small children. Anthropologists argue that these choices reflect culture (see Camerer 2003 for a review of experiments done in small societies)

[5]According to (Damasio 1994), emotions are cognitive representations of body states that are part of a homeostatic mechanism by which the internal milieu is monitored and controlled, and by which this internal milieu influences behavior of the whole organism

The behavioral and neurobiological studies mentioned above, and others studies suggest that people's decisions are not uniquely motivated by a deliberate rational process; rather these are also influenced by emotions and instinct. This idea has gathered further support from mood studies (Capra 2004 and Capra et al. 2009) and hormonal studies (see Zak and Fakhar 2006). C. Monica Capra, for example, showed that subjects' decisions in games are affected by induced positive or negative affective states. Her results replicate observations in the psychological literature that show a long-lasting effect of background emotions or mood on helping behavior. In particular, C. Monica Capra found that positive mood tended to enhance generosity as measured by the amount a player offered in a Dictator game.[6] Similarly, Paul Zak and Alham Fakhar (2006) found that spraying oxytocin (the hormone responsible for regulating pro-social behavior) in subjects' noses make them more generous and trusting. Recent animal studies (Donaldson and Young 2008) also support the view that hormones are responsible for much of our pro-social behavior.

The challenge that these studies and other pose to social preferences is that they question their stability. As some authors have shown (Cherry et al. 2002), it is possible to generate both generous and spiteful behavior in the lab just by changing the decision environment, helping the subjects generate specific hormones, or helping them get into a specific mood. However, in general, it should not surprise us to see anomalous behavior in games. After all, in the lab, games cannot be defined as "*rule-governed strategic interactions*" (Gardner 1995). Laboratory games are rule governed *social* interactions; as such, unless the players have some psychiatric pathology, decisions ought to be affected by social emotions. The issue, then, is that we do not have a framework that can help us integrate emotions with strategic decision-making.

3 Evolutionary Psychology

Evolutionary psychology can contribute to our understanding of the origins and nature of utility and choice. The most basic economic paradigm of choice assumes that decision makers maximize an objective function subject to constraints. Evolutionary psychology can explain both the nature of the maximization (i.e., the decision making process) and also the nature of the objective function or utility function. In the next section, we discuss decision-making and utility from the point of view of evolutionary psychology. We argue that an evolutionary paradigm can explain the anomalies in decision making that have been widely documented by many behavioral and experimental economists.

---

[6]In a dictator game, one subject is given the task to split a given amount of money with another anonymous subject. The participant who receives the offer has no power to either accept or refuse the offer (as is the case in the ultimatum game)

Decision-Making

Consider first decision making. Generally speaking, economists assume that agents consider all possible alternatives, and choose the best available alternative. The satisficing literature mentioned above was the first body of analysis to criticize this assumption. Experimental evidence shows that individuals do not consider all possible set of options due to cognitive and motivational limitations. For example, Gad Saad and J. Edward Russo (1996) have demonstrated that individuals often use stopping decisions to arrive to a final choice. Although, satisficing implicitly recognized that human decisions such as choice under risk and decisions in games result from a physiological process, and is therefore subject to limitations in computational capacities and will, satisficing did not provide a unifying explanation for the origin and nature of such limitations.

More recently, evolutionary and cognitive psychologists (Cosmides and Tooby 1994) and (Gigerenzer and Goldstein 1996) have analyzed the decision making process from the perspective of evolutionary psychology. The thrust of this analysis is that the mind is not a general purpose computer ruled by the laws of pure logic. Rather, there are specialized modules in the brain aimed at solving particular problems that are evolutionarily relevant. The idea is that the brain, a physiological system, evolved from natural as well as sexual selection to solve problems that we faced in our evolutionary past. In addition, as all existing organic systems, our brains and their resulting decision strategies adapt to the environment. Thus, a new concept of decision making called "ecological rationality" replaces both satisfying and maximizing. Through the lens of evolutionary psychology, then, it is not surprising that choices in experimental setups seem irrational from a pure maximizing perspective. In experiments, seemingly irrational behavior may be explained in terms of evolved mechanisms. For example, in a series of studies (Peters 2007) showed that people do not naturally process probability information the way economists assume. Indeed, the ability to comprehend and transform probability numbers requires specialized training. Interestingly, over 50% of the subjects in his experiments (all college students, who are usually smart) were unable to fully comprehend relatively simple probability numbers. It is possible that the percentage may be much smaller among the general population, which is rather seldom targeted as a population of interest for these kinds of studies.[7] However, by providing probability information in terms of relative frequencies, it is possible to improve performance on judgment tasks, and reduce biases in decision making (Gigerenzer 2002). Pharmaceutical companies are well aware of the unnecessary anxiety that providing information in percentages can generate, so they opt for providing frequencies information. For example, "9 in 10 people did not experience any adverse effects" is preferred means of communicating that 90% of the people did not experience any adverse effects.

---

[7]See Joseph Henrich et al. (2009) for an interesting critique of the over-representation of Western and educated subjects in behavioral studies

In a recent paper Eileen Chou et al. (2009) found that the ability of subjects to make strategic decisions in a simple two-person guessing game depended on the way the game was presented. A two-person guessing game consists of two people guessing a number in a given range (e.g. 0 to 100); whoever guesses closer to a fraction, say 2/3, of the average wins a fixed prize. In this game, it is a dominant strategy to always guess a lower number as one is compensated for guessing below the average. Higher numbers are dominated by lower ones. When the game was presented in a familiar context – that is, with a description of what average means, and a graphical explanation of who wins the prize – subjects chose the dominant strategies. When the game was presented in an abstract context, utilizing language such as "if your number x is less than the average", very few subjects (mostly smart Caltech students) seemed to grasp the game. The gist of these studies is that our brain has neither evolved to understand mathematical constructions such as percentages, nor to decode abstract information.[8] As Paul Rubin argues, humans may simply not be good innate abstract thinkers (Rubin 2002). Related to this issue is the study of Leda Cosmides and John Tooby (1992). These authors investigated whether the evolved architecture of the human brain included specialization of reasoning for detecting cheaters in social contracts. Through a series of experiments they showed that participants, who do very poorly in identifying logical rules such as if P then Q, are remarkably accurate in identifying cheating in social exchanges such as "*if you help me, I help you*". Clearly, there is evolutionary advantage for identifying cheaters, which requires the ability to make logical inferences; however, that ability is constrained by the context in which it is called into action. More generally, the brain does better in dealing with other humans than with logical abstractions. This may be because the main force driving evolution of human intelligence was competitive pressure from other humans, not pressure from "nature".

The existence of loss aversion and other anomalies documented by Tversky and Kahneman can also be explained through the evolutionary lens (see McDermott et al 2008). For example, consider the exchange experiment of Jack Knetsch (1989), who endowed subjects with mugs and asked to exchange them for candy bars. He found that very few subjects (only 11%) exchanged their mugs. When a different group was endowed with candy bars and asked to exchange for mugs, again very few (10%) exchanged their candy bars for mugs. This seemingly irrational tendency of subjects in the experiment to value an item more when they own it, and therefore ask more for it than she is willing to pay for it, generating a gap between the willingness to accept (WTA) and the willingness to pay (WTP) for an item, was first conceptualized by (Thaler 1980). Interestingly, recent experimental studies with non-human primates suggest that anomalies in decision-making may have an evolutionary origin. Sarah Brosnan et al. (2007), for example, found

---

[8]Eileen Chou et al. (2009) interviewed subjects after the experiment and found that many of the subjects simply did not understand the structure of the simple game when the instructions utilized abstract language. This is remarkable, as their subjects were very intelligent Caltech students. Furthermore, subjects' understanding of the task was not responsive to the financial remuneration associated with performing well in the game

that chimpanzees favored items they just received more than items that could be acquired through exchange. They also found that this effect was stronger for food than for other objects, perhaps because of the historically greater risks associated with exchanging food versus keeping it. These results are relevant because they suggest a preference for the status quo among species other than humans. So, not only do humans favor the status quo, but chimpanzees are also inclined to forgo a likely gain in favor of what is safe and known. There were no standardized goods in the evolutionary environment, so exchange would have been subject to greater risks than is true today. Similarly, experimental economists have also replicated violations of expected utility theory in animal experiments. Like humans, Rats violate the independence axiom, suggesting that rats distort probabilities in ways possibly similar to the way humans distort them (see McDonald et al. 1991).

Other experiments with non-human primates and other animals also shed light into the evolutionary origins of inter-temporal discounting. In the 1960s Richard Herrnstein designed clever experiments that were later used to measure time discounting in humans and other less sophisticated animals. In his pigeon experiments, for example, Herrnstein (1961) presented the animals with two buttons, each of which led to varying rates of food reward. He observed that pigeons tended to peck (i.e., allocate time and effort) the button that yielded the greater food reward more often than the other button; however, they did so at a rate that was similar to the rate of reward, and in inverse proportion to their delays. This phenomenon is called the matching law. With respect to time discounting, the matching law suggests that the attractiveness of a reward increases exponentially, the closer one gets to its due date. That is, our psychological reward system is designed to assign high value to imminent rewards as compared to future ones. Thus, when we are asked to choose between say A: $100 in 25 days or B: $120 in 28 days, we clearly choose B. However, when we are asked to choose between C: $100 now or D: $120 in 3 days, our preferences reverse. This pattern of choices implies that our decisions are dynamic or time inconsistent and suggests that we are doomed to fail to comply with future plans. Indeed, dynamic inconsistent choices imply that we do not have self-control.

Richard Thaler's idea of mental accounting, which was explained earlier, may be an adaptive response to our inability to exert self-control. Having a mental account for savings only versus one for consumption only, may be a way to implement an internal commitment devise to stop us from consuming too much. Similarly, social emotions such as guilt and compassion may have evolved to pre-commit us to behave in a way contrary to our initial impulses and short-term self-interest in social contexts. Frank (1988), for example, suggests that the anger one feels when one is offered a low amount in the Ultimatum game commits us to reject the offer. This behavior is not selfish-rational in the short-run, but it may help us obtain higher benefits in the long-run, as building a reputation for getting angry at low offers would guarantee higher offers in the future. But, a more fundamental question is: why did we evolve to have no self-control? Larry Samuelson and Jeroen Swinkels (2006) explain that our lack of self-control is a consequence of our tendency to derive utility from intermediate actions rather than the evolutionary outcome. For example, we derive utility from sex, not from maximizing reproduction. The utility from sex may tempt us to engage in sexual activities even when it is irrational to do so (e.g., unprotected sex with a prostitute). Samuelson and Swinkels suggest that this is a result of us having an imperfect prior understanding of the *causal and statistical* structure of the world. For example, we do not know exactly what the changes are of reproduction when we meet a potential sexual partner. Indeed, many beautiful and young females are infertile, and there is no obvious way to infer that information.

Because our brains are not general-purpose machines, they make decisions that are situational rational. In recent papers, Gerd Gigerenzer and his collaborators (Gigerenzer et al. 2002), in particular, demonstrated that the decision mechanisms actually used by the human brain are often more efficient than more complex formal mechanisms. For example, the Recognition Heuristic exemplifies a cognitive adaptation where knowing less results in more accurate inferences than knowing more. A person using this heuristic would compare the relative frequency of two categories; if she recognizes one category, but not the other, she would conclude that the recognized category has a higher frequency. Thus, the individual exploits patterns of information in the environment to make inferences in a "fast and frugal" way. In their experiments, Daniel Goldstein and Gerd Gigerenzer, asked German and US students to guess the populations of German and American cities. Each group scored slightly higher on the foreign cities despite only recognizing a fraction of them. The experiment also demonstrated that having more information and knowing more is not necessarily better, as it may complicate the decision rule or heuristics employed in making an estimate. Their experiments demonstrated that, under some circumstances, less-is-better. Simple heuristics have been shown to be more accurate than complex procedures (Gigerenzer et al. 2008). The general idea of this way of looking at choice is that rationality must be interpreted in terms of the specific decision process one utilizes in a given environment, or the specific matching between the decision process and the environment in which it is utilized.

Finally, our evolutionary past may have also had an influence in determining our beliefs about social welfare. This idea has been put forward by Paul Rubin (2003) and called "Folk economics". The principles of folk economics include zero sum thinking about various aspects of the economy, such as trade. Under folk economics, the act of buying from other nations, communities, or tribes is seen as a loss. People, then, are not willing to support trade agreements that increase purchases from others. Folk economics also includes the belief in labor theory of value, and lack of understanding of incentives. All these principles can be shown to derive from the evolutionary environment. The idea is that during much of our evolutionary past, humans evolved in an environment which was essentially zero-sum. In such environment, there was little room for exchange, or any exchange implied a loss. There was little room for investment in human capital, and there was virtually no technological change. In teaching economics and in advocating policies, economists would do well to consider these evolutionary based arguments. Indeed, folk economics tells us that political economists face a difficult challenge in trying to get people to understand the mutual advantages derived from exchange, specialization, and incentives.

The Utility Function

Related to our understanding and modeling of rationality is the nature of the "utility function". Economists assume that people maximize a utility function, which has certain mathematical properties. However, economists have given themselves an out – the nature of this function (beyond the mathematical properties) is never specified. "Rationality" is then defined in terms of maximizing this function. Rationality is defined as certain properties of behavior which would result from consistent maximization of a function subject to (budget) constraints. For example, in most cases, a reduction in price will lead to an increase in consumption. (There may be exceptions, e.g., Veblen effects and Giffen goods, but the theory allows one to identify these exceptions as well). The experimental evidence discussed above consists of violations of some of the predictions of the theory of maximizing utility subject to constraints. Except for internal consistency requirements, however, utility functions are quite flexible and can be made to explain pretty much any preference. Such an approach is scientifically controversial, however, as the theory generates unfalsifiable hypotheses. Killing children, for example, would not violate any of the rationality assumptions. A preference for dead children can indeed be added to the utility functions. Similarly, elderly ladies who fill their houses with cats may be behaving consistently with respect to some utility function. But, common sense would suggest that there is a problem with this approach.

Economists take the preference or utility function as given and more or less arbitrary. In fact, the utility function of humans is essentially the fitness evolutionary function – that is, we get utility, or pleasure, from activities and consumption that would have caused our predecessors to successfully survive and reproduce. If we think about utility functions in these terms, then there are some implications, which can make the structure of the utility function more precise. For example, Paul Rubin and Chris Paul (1979) have explained the different risk preferences between young men and older men in evolutionary terms and utilizing life-history theory – this theory postulated that behaviors may be best understood in terms of effects of natural selection on the reproductive characteristics over the life cycle. In this context, young males who have no mates will not breed and leave any genes for the future unless they acquire sufficient resources to obtain a mate. Thus, a gamble that pays off will enable the individual to breed. A gamble that loses (perhaps resulting in death) will leave the person's genes no worse off than if the gamble had been refused. In this case, it pays to take bad gambles. On the other hand, once someone has offspring, then it pays to become risk averse and avoid even fair gambles – particularly in a Malthusian world where survival is at risk. Similarly, since successful males can have virtually unlimited numbers of offspring and successful females have much more limited fertility, we would expect males to be more risk seeking than females.[9] Experimental data[10] on gender differences in lottery choice tasks clearly show that women are more risk averse than men (for a comprehensive review of laboratory gender differences see Croson and Gneezy 2009). In addition to higher risk aversion, recent experiments show that women, even highly successful Harvard MBA females, are less likely than men to enter profitable tournaments (Niederle and Vesterlund 2007; Gneezy et al. 2003). These results suggest a higher competitive preference among males than females. Indeed, as explained above, the source of these intriguing results may lie in evolutionary forces that have shaped sex differences in risk-taking preferences. Other authors such as Gad Saad and Tripat Gill (2001) show that, in the context of the Ultimatum game, it is possible and fruitful to use evolutionary psychology as a framework to understand gender differences.

An important assumption that traditional economic theory makes about utility is that it is derived from the outcome of choice and is independent from the process of choice. Experimental evidence, however, hints to the possibility that utility is also derived from process. Consider the winner's curse (Kagel and Levin 1986; Lind and Plott 1991), which arises when subjects systematically overbid for an item whose value is uncertain and, therefore, lose money. Evidence suggests that, although most people are risk averse, as evidenced by their preference for safe bets, in an auction-type mechanism like the common value auction they act as if they were risk seeking. Interestingly, overbidding has also been documented in Private Value Auctions (Friedman 1992), which would imply risk aversion (Cox et al. 1988). So, why do people overbid in auctions? The answer seems to lie in the competitive nature of the auction mechanism. Winning the auction seems to be more important than making a profit. If we see utility as derived from the activities that caused us to survive and reproduce, signaling fitness by trying to out-bid others (be a winner or avoid being a loser) has value (Rubin 2003). Other "anomalous behaviors" such as competitive altruism, over-consumption, and conspicuous consumption may also be a result of sexual selection. The individual who is most altruistic among his peers can signal fitness – an unobservable characteristic valuable to the members of the opposite sex – by showing that he cannot only care for himself, but he also has the power and fitness to care for others. Similarly, over consumption and conspicuous consumption exist because they are signals for fitness (De Fraga 2009).

---

[9]See also Netzer (2009) for an evolutionary perspective on risk and time preferences

[10]We emphasize experimental data here because in the real world, many behavioral differences between men and women may be influenced by variables that are difficult to control for. The laboratory environment provides researchers with the ability to control the environment and more effectively isolate the variables of interest

4 Discussion

Economics has always prided itself on having a unifying theoretical framework based on rational choice theory. However, recently such a framework has come under scientific scrutiny. Data from controlled experiments, which usually provide theory the best chance to work, refute many of the rationality assumptions that economists make. If people do not behave rationally, then the theory of maximization subject to constraints loses its predictive power. The mounting evidence against rational choice as traditionally defined has forced economists to rethink their traditional models. However, despite the investment of many brilliant minds in the pursuit of better behavioral models of choice, behavioral economics has so far made at best very modest progress in providing an alternative paradigm that would be both parsimonious and accurate.

We believe that the discipline is lacking an adequate framework for thinking about thinking. We, humans, are part of a natural world ruled by physical and biological laws. Utility, which represents one of the most basic concepts in economics, can easily be conceived as representing fitness. Decision-making is the result of an interaction of our brains, a physiological system, and the decision environment. Adaptation is the main characteristic of all beings, humans included. Thus, the concept of ecological rationality may be more consistent with the natural world than rational choice. In this context, we can conceive two possible futures for our discipline. One would have evolutionary psychology at its heart, the other would not.

Evolutionary psychology can give economics back its overriding paradigm. One important feature of evolutionary psychology is that it can both place structure on the utility function and also provide content to rationality. By doing so, it can explain many of the behavioral anomalies that behavioral economists and psychologists have documented. If economists are willing to use the evolutionary psychology paradigm, then they can regain theoretical consistency of their discipline and have models that are better descriptors and predictors of behavior. Such an adoption would not be much of a departure.

The closeness of the theoretical structures can easily be seen in the context of evolutionary game theory, which was invented by biologists (Smith and Price 1973) and was developed jointly by biologists and economists. Even earlier, the link between Darwin and Malthus is well known. For example, it seems that Hayek understood quite well the relationship between economics and evolution (Rubin and Gick 2004). There is already a literature using evolutionary theory to discuss economic issues, often in the context of the evolution of utility functions (Rubin and Paul 1979; Frank 1988; Rogers 1994; Robson 2001; Somanathan and Rubin 2004; Witt 2008; Samuelson and Swinkels 2006).[11] In addition to the authors mentioned here, there are several other evolutionary-minded economists whose work, we believe, could be the foundation of evolutionary-based economic models.

---

[11] See also Arthur J. Robson's website for many other publications in this vein

For example, economists such as Geoffrey M. Hodgson and Thorbjørn Knudsen have written countless papers at the nexus of evolutionary theory and economics. Other influential economists who have incorporated evolutionary theory within their work include Larry Samuelson, Avner Ben-Ner, Louis Putterman, and Ted Bergstrom. It would be possible to build on this literature and extend the evolutionary analysis of economic behavior.

The theory of evolution is quite consistent with economic theory (Hirshleifer 1985). In economics, the maximand is utility; in evolution, fitness. But as indicated above, utility functions are essentially functions relating fitness and welfare. That is, we get satisfaction or utility from consumption of goods and services that would have caused our ancestors to improve their chances of survival and reproduction (Gigerenzer et al. 2002; Gigerenzer et al. 2001; Payne and Bettman 2001; Rubin 2002, 2003; Thaler 1985; Thaler 1992; Thaler and Benartzi 2004).[12] With respect to decision-making, there are recent successful attempts to explain anomalies using an evolutionary perspective (Haselton and Nettle 2006). In addition, the introduction of brain scanning technology into the economist's toolbox would improve our understanding of the mechanisms whereby people make choices. For example, there is evidence that valuation of a future reward is processed in lateral prefrontal and parietal areas of the brain, which suggests that evaluating the future engages the executive, more sophisticated, and more energy demanding systems in our brain (McClure et al. 2004). Present consumption, in contrast, tends to be processed in limbic-related structures. This suggests that the ability to form expectations from future rewards was possibly developed latter in our evolutionary past, and is developed later in life through a process of cognitive and personality development, and socialization.

What would happen if we do not adapt evolutionary psychology into economics? We believe that there is a good chance that economics will become a largely "atheoretical" discipline. Although economists will use powerful mathematical tools to analyze behavior, the basic paradigm will still be a set of ad hoc models, derived from observation but not from an overriding theory. For example, as mentioned above, cumulative prospect theory, which has been an important development in economics – possibly an important propellant to a Nobel Prize – is nonetheless a way of classifying observations, but has no deep theoretical foundations. The models of social preferences also fall prey to this problem. Economists recognize that humans can be altruistic, but there is no theoretical explanation for this behavior. Economists have explained altruism in terms of the "warm glow" or social emotions such as compassion that individuals obtain from altruistic behavior, but there is no deep theory of why people should feel positive emotions from sacrificing self-interest for others. Even with respect to modeling decision processes and learning, we have come up with a bouquet of models that fit the data well, but we still do not have a unified basis. The last two models trace decision process at the

---

[12]The literature also provides explicit discussions of the link between utility and fitness in the context of modern marketing (see Saad 2007; Miller 2009)

introspective level, and describe experimental data in one-shot games rather well. The gist of these models is that they assume that the decision-maker is rational, but that she believes others are not. However, there is a weakness in these models. These models ignore the ability of people to adjust their decision strategies to the environment. Indeed, it is possible to generate environments where people behave as if they were bounded rational, but others that are strategically identical where people behave perfectly rational and believe others are rational too (Cox and James 2010).

Unlike many other social scientists, economists have not been hostile to evolutionary reasoning. We have cited many articles that have appeared in important journals using evolutionary methods, and our citations are by no means comprehensive. Nonetheless, overall, it appears that this mode of thinking has had less of an effect on economics, and particularly on behavioral economics, than might be justified. We think there is much room for improvement, and we hope that economists will agree with us. In addition to providing a unified method for understanding behavior, there are other advantages from utilizing evolutionary psychology as our workhorse paradigm. For example, it may be possible to explain the degree to which culture influences innate behaviors. Economic theory can offer hypotheses that can be tested in experimental environments across different cultures. This may have already occurred, as anthropologists have started using economic models to understand culture (Henrich et al. 2001). We believe that collaboration between economists and evolutionary psychologists is fruitful in more than one way. It can build on the already existing collaboration between neuroscientists and economists, and it can serve to enrich all disciplines.

References

Alchian A (1950) Uncertainty, evolution, and economic theory. J Polit Econ 58(3):211–221
Baumol WJ (1979) On the contributions of Herbert A. Simon to economics. Scand J Econ 81(11):74–93
Becker GS (1962) Irrational behavior and economic theory. J Polit Econ 70(1):1–13
Berns G, Capra CM, Moore S, Noussair C (2007) A shocking experiment: new evidence on probability weighting and common ratio violations. Judgment Decis Mak 2(4):234–242
Brosnan SF, Jones OD, Lambeth SP, Mareno MC, Richardson AS, Schapir SJ (2007) Endowment effects in chimpanzees. Curr Biol 17:1704–1707
Camerer CF (2003) Behavioral game theory: experiments in strategic interaction. Princeton University Press, Princeton
Cameron LA (1999) Raising the stakes in the ultimatum game: experimental evidence from Indonesia. Econ Inq 37(1):47–59
Capra CM (2004) Mood-driven behavior in strategic interactions. Am Econ Rev 94(2):367–372
Capra C, Lanier KF, Meer S (2010) The Effects of Induced Mood on Bidding in Random nth-Price Auctions. Journal of Economic Behavior and Organization 75(2):223–234
Cherry TL, Frykblom P, Shogren JF (2002) Hardnose the dictator. Am Econ Rev 92(4):1218–1221
Chou E, McConnell M, Nagel R, Plott C (2009) The control of game form recognition in experiments: understanding dominant strategy failures in a simple two person guessing game. Exp Econ 12(2):159–179

Clark JM (1918) Economics and modern psychology. J Polit Econ 6(1):1–30
Conlisk J (1996) Why bounded rationality? J Econ Lit 34(2):669–700
Cosmides L, Tooby J (1992) Cognitive adaptations for social exchange. In: Barkow JH, Cosmides L, Tooby J, Barkow JH, Cosmides L, Tooby J (eds), The adapted mind: Evolutionary psychology and the generation of culture (pp. 163–228). New York, NY US: Oxford University Press
Cosmides L, Tooby J (1994) Better than rational: evolutionary psychology and the invisible hand. Am Econ Rev 84(2):327–332
Cox J, James D (2010) Arms or legs: isomorphic Dutch auctions and centipede games. Georgia State University Andrew Young School of Public Policy Working Paper http://excen.gsu.edu/workingpapers/GSU_EXCEN_WP_2010-01.pdf
Cox JC, Smith VL, Walker JM (1988) Theory and individual behavior of first-price auctions. J Risk Uncertainty 1(1):61–99
Croson R, Gneezy U (2009) Gender differences in preferences. J Econ Lit 47(2):448–474
Damasio AR (1994) Descartes error and the future of human life. Sci Am 271:144–144
De Fraja G (2009) The origin of utility: sexual selection and conspicuous consumption. J Econ Behav Organ 72(1):51–69
Dickinson ZC (1919) The relations of recent psychological developments to economic theory. Q J Econ 33(3):377–421
Donaldson Z, Young L (2008) Oxytocin, vasopressin, and the neurogenetics of sociality. Science 332(5903):900–904
Fehr E, Schmidt KM (1999) A theory of fairness, competition, and cooperation. Q J Econ 114(3):817–868
Frank RH (1988) Passions within reason: the strategic role of the emotions. Norton, New York
Friedman M (1953) The methodology of positive economics, essays in positive economics. University of Chicago Press, Chicago
Friedman D (1992) Theory and misbehavior of first-price auctions: comment. Am Econ Rev 82(5):1374–1378
Gardner R (1995) Games for business and economics. Wiley, New York
Gigerenzer G (2002) Calculated risks: how to know when numbers deceive you. Simon & Schuster, New York
Gigerenzer G, Goldstein DG (1996) Reasoning the fast and frugal way: models of bounded rationality. Int J Psychol 31:1315–1315
Gigerenzer G, Czerlinski J, Martignon L, Gilovich T, Griffin D, Kahneman D (2002) How good are fast and frugal heuristics? In: Shanteau J, Mellers B, Schum D (eds) Decision science and technology: reflections on the contributions of Ward Edwards. Kluwer, Norwell, pp 559–581
Gigerenzer G, Hoffrage U, Goldstein DG (2008) Fast and frugal heuristics are plausible models of cognition: reply to Dougherty, Franco-Watkins, and Thomas (2008). Psychol Rev 115:230–237
Gneezy U, Niederle M, Rustichini A (2003) Performance in competitive environments: gender differences. Q J Econ 118(3):1049–1074
Guth W, Schmittberger R, Schwarze B (1982) An experimental analysis of ultimatum bargaining. J Econ Behav Organ 3(4):367–388
Harbaugh WT, Krause K, Liday S (2000) Children's bargaining behavior. University of Oregon, Working paper. http://darkwing.uoregon.edu/~harbaugh/Papers/KidBargaining.pdf. Accessed 10 March 2010
Haselton MG, Nettle D (2006) The paranoid optimist: an integrative evolutionary model of cognitive biases. Pers Soc Psychol Rev 10:47–66
Henrich J (2009) In Search of Homo Economicus: Behavioral Experiments in 15 Small-Scale Societies. In: Hodgson GM (ed), Darwinism and Economics (pp. 110–115). Elgar Reference Collection. International Library of Critical Writings in Economics, vol. 233. Cheltenham, U.K. and Northampton, Mass.: Elgar
Henrich J et al (2001) In search of Homo Economicus: behavioral experiments in 15 small-scale societies. Am Econ Rev 91(2):73–78
Herrnstein RJ (1964) Aperiodicity as a factor in choice. Journal of the Experimental Analysis of Behavior 7(2):179–182

Hirshleifer J (1985) The expanding domain of economics. Am Econ Rev 75(6):53–68
Kagel JH, Levin D (1986) The winner's curse and public information in common value auctions. Am Econ Rev 76(5):894–920
Kahneman D, Tversky A (1979) Prospect theory – analysis of decision under risk. Econometrica 47:263–291
Knetsch JL (1989) The endowment effect and evidence of nonreversible indifference curves. Am Econ Rev 79(5):1277–1284
Lind B, Plott CR (1991) The winner's curse: experiments with buyers and with sellers. Am Econ Rev 81(1):335–346
Luce RD (1959) Individual choice behavior. Wiley, New York
McClure S, Laibson D, Lowenstein G, Cohen J (2004) Separate neural systems value immediate and delayed rewards. Science 306:503–507
McDermott R, Fowler JH, Smirnov O (2008) On the evolutionary origin of prospect theory preferences. J Polit 70(2):335–350
McDonald D, Kagel J, Battalio RC (1991) Animals' choices over uncertain outcomes: further experimental results. Econ J 103:1067–1084
Miller G (2009) Spent: sex, evolution, and consumer behavior. Viking, New York
Netzer N (2009) Evolution of time preferences and attitudes toward risk. Am Econ Rev 99(3):937–955
Niederle M, Vesterlund L (2007) Do women shy away from competition? Do men compete too much? Q J Econ 122(3):1067–1101
Payne JW, Bettman JR (2001) Preferential choice and adaptive strategy use. In: Gigerenzer G, Selten R (eds) Bounded rationality: the adaptive toolbox. MIT, Cambridge, pp 123–145
Peters G (2007) Uncertain judgments – eliciting experts' probabilities. J R Stat Soc Ser Stat Soc 170:1184–1185
Post T, van den Assem MJ, Baltussen G, Thaler RH (2008) Deal or No Deal? Decision making under risk in a large-payoff game show. Am Econ Rev 98(1):38–71
Rabin M (1993) Incorporating fairness into game theory and economics. Am Econ Rev 83(5):1281–1302
Robson AJ (2001) The biological basis of economic behavior. J Econ Lit 39(1):11–33
Rogers AR (1994) Evolution of time preference by natural selection. Am Econ Rev 84(3):460–481
Roth A, Prasnikar V, Okuno-Fujiwara M, Zamir S (1991) Bargaining and market behavior in Jerusalem, Ljubljana, Pittsburg, and Tokyo: an experimental study. Am Econ Rev 81:1068–1095
Rubin PH (2002) Darwinian politics: the evolutionary origin of freedom. Rutgers University Press, New Brunswick
Rubin PH (2003) Folk economics. Southern Econ J 70(1):157–171
Rubin PH, Gick E (2004) Hayek and modern evolutionary theory. In: Koppl RG (ed) Evolutionary psychology and economic theory, advances in Austrian economics. Elsevier, Madison, pp 79–100
Rubin PH, Paul CW (1979) An evolutionary model of taste for risk. Econ Inq 17:585–596
Saad G (2007) The evolutionary bases of consumption. Lawrence Erlbaum Associates, Mahwah
Saad G, Gill T (2001) Sex differences in the ultimatum game: an evolutionary psychology perspective. J Bioecon 3(2–3):171–193
Saad G, Russo JE (1996) Stopping criteria in sequential choice. Organ Behav Hum Dec 67(3):258–270
Samuelson L, Swinkels J (2006) Information, evolution and utility. Theor Econ 1:119–142
Sanfey AG (2004) Neural computations of decision utility. Trends Cogn Sci 8:519–521
Simon HA (1955) A behavioral model of rational choice. Q J Econ 64(1):99–118
Simon HA (1957) Models of Man. Wiley, New York
Simon HA (1959) Theories of decision-making in economics and behavioral sciences. Am Econ Rev 49(3):253–283

Simon HA (1978) Rationality as a process and as product of thought. Am Econ Rev 68(2):1–16, Papers and proceedings of the 90th annual meeting
Smith JM, Price GR (1973) Logic of animal conflict. Nature 246:15–18
Smith VL (1991) Rational Choice: The Contrast between Economics and Psychology. Journal of Political Economy 99(4):877–897
Somanathan E, Rubin PH (2004) The evolution of honesty. Journal Econ Behav Organ 54(1):1–17
Thaler R (1980) Toward a positive theory of consumer choice. J Econ Behav Organ 1:39–60
Thaler RH (1981) Some empirical evidence on dynamic inconsistency. Econo Lett 8:127–133
Thaler R (1985) Mental accounting and consumer choice. Market Sci 4(3):199–214
Thaler RH (1992) The winner's curse: paradoxes and anomalies of economic life. Free Press, New York
Thaler RH (2004) Mental Accounting Matters. In: Camerer CF, Loewenstein G, Rabin M (eds), Advances in behavioral economics (pp. 75–103). Roundtable Series in Behavioral Economics
Thaler RH, Benartzi S (2004) Save more tomorrow: using behavioral economics to increase employee saving. J Polit Econ 112(1):S164–S187
Tversky A, Kahneman D (1974) Judgment under uncertainty – heuristics and biases. Science 185:1124–1131
Tversky A, Kahneman D (1991) Loss aversion in riskless choice – a reference-dependent model. Q J Econ 106:1039–1061
Tversky A, Kahneman D (1992) Advances in prospect-theory – cumulative representation of uncertainty. J Risk Uncertainty 5:297–323
Witt U (2008) Recent developments in evolutionary economics. Edward Elgar, Cheltenham
Xiao E (2005) Emotion expression in human punishment behavior. Proc Natl Acad Sci USA 102(20):7398–7401
Zak PJ, Fakhar A (2006) Neuroactive hormones and interpersonal trust: international evidence. Econ Hum Biol 4:412–429

Media Compensation Theory: A Darwinian Perspective on Adaptation to Electronic Communication and Collaboration

Donald A. Hantula, Ned Kock, John P. D'Arcy, and Darleen M. DeRosa

Abstract This chapter proceeds from the paradox that virtual work, teams, and collaboration are generally successful, sometimes even outperforming face-to-face collaborative work efforts in spite of much theory that predicts the opposite. We review theories that have previously been used to explain behavior toward electronic communication media, highlighting a theoretical gap, which is partially filled with a new Darwinian perspective called media compensation theory. Eight theoretical principles are discussed – media naturalness, innate schema similarity, learned schema variety, evolutionary task relevance, compensatory adaptation, media humanness, cue removal, and speech imperative. Those principles are then used as a basis for a discussion of the impact that different media have on virtual collaboration, work and teams. Empirical evidence in connection with the theoretical framework is described. In particular, empirical studies of idea generation, problem solving, and business process redesign tasks are reviewed. The evidence reviewed provides empirical support for the theoretical framework proposed, and a future research agenda on virtual teams from a media naturalness perspective is proposed, especially in terms of temporal processes, adaptation, trust and cheater detection.

D.A. Hantula (✉)
Department of Psychology, Temple University, Weiss Hall (265-67), Philadelphia, PA 19122, USA
e-mail: hantula@temple.edu

N. Kock
Division of International Business and Technology Studies, Texas A&M International University, 5201 University Boulevard, Laredo, TX 78041, USA
e-mail: nedkock@tamiu.edu

J.P. D'Arcy
Department of Management, University of Notre Dame, 351 Mendoza College of Business, Notre Dame, IN 46556-5646, USA
e-mail: jdarcy1@nd.edu

D.M. DeRosa
OnPoint Consulting, 2 Fellsmere Farm Rd, Branford, CT 06405, USA
e-mail: dderosa@onpointconsultingllc.com

Keywords Human evolution · Electronic communication · Virtual teams · Virtual collaboration · Media compensation theory · Media naturalness · Mental schemas

1 Introduction

Technologically mediated interaction and work seems to represent the apex of achievement. Using modern information technology, people can break the boundaries of space and time, communicating and collaborating across countries and cultures. For people in most organizations, face-to-face meetings are no longer the norm and teamwork transcends the typical spatiotemporal constancy (Cascio 1999; Dubé and Robey 2009). However, this progress poses a paradox: how can a species that evolved in small groups using communication modalities constrained to minute areas be expected to work together successfully in an environment where spatial and temporal communication boundaries have been blurred by collaboration technologies? Answers to this question seem to focus more on the communication media (e.g., Workman et al. 2003), which is to be expected given the relative novelty of these technologies.

However, careful consideration of the organisms who use these technological media and their evolved characteristics leads to a better understanding of the interaction between people, technology, and communication. We contend that current electronic communication tools require substantial behavioral alterations from their users because humans have not been biologically designed to use those tools. Thus, in this chapter, we expand the theory of media naturalness (Kock 1998; Kock 2001a). We suggest a re-focus of research away from the technology and more towards the "ape that used e-mail" (Kock 2001b). While drawing on previous theoretical work on media naturalness, this paper advances a significantly expanded Darwinian perspective in virtual communication and teamwork. It does so by incorporating recent empirical evidence and conceptual developments into a new theory that focuses on adaptation to media, the *media compensation theory*. We first introduce and discuss the theory and its principles, then assess the theory's viability in light of the Evolutionary Advantage Test, and review research testing some of it principles. Following this theory development and review we outline some avenues for future research, focusing on the ways in which Media Compensation Theory challenges our current conceptualizations of two critical issues in technologically mediated communication and collaboration: behavioral adaptation and trust.

2 Media Compensation Theory: A New Darwinian Perspective

Media richness theory (Daft and Lengel 1984, 1986) has been the dominant theoretical perspective in organizational communication research. Media richness theory tends to be overly simplistic by focusing largely on the congruence between technological media and the type of task. Over a decade ago Dennis and Kinney (1993) and El-Shinmawy and Markus (1997) noted that media richness theory did not appear to handle preferences for "newer" media such as e-mail. Instant messaging, video chat and Internet 2.0 applications pose the same problems for the theory. Social theories offered as alternatives to media richness theory (cf. Fulk et al. 1990) are more imprecise because they tend to describe and explain in general terms, rather than predict, more complex communication behavior. Kock (2001b) noted that social theories offered as alternatives to media richness theory do not fully account for human behavior toward electronic communication technologies. Also, much of the research in these two types of theories focuses on either media adoption patterns or on participants' and managers' perceptions of outcomes, rather than on measuring the actual outcomes (e.g., quality and quantity) of technologically mediated work.

Most importantly, media richness and social theories do not incorporate any reference to biological and evolutionary explanations into a theoretical framework. Colarelli (1998, 2003) argued that ignoring evolution and evolved characteristics of humans is the chief reason why the results of psychological interventions in organizations rarely meet expectations. From a more positive perspective, recent research on foraging in e-commerce (DiClemente and Hantula 2003; Hantula et al. 2008; Rajala and Hantula 2000; Smith and Hantula 2003) and Internet information search (Pirolli 2007; Pirolli and Card 1999) has shown clearly that an evolutionary perspective on electronically mediated behavior brings innovative and valuable insights to understanding interaction with these new technologies.

To incorporate features of social and technological theories in an evolutionary perspective, Kock (1998, 2001a, b, 2002) proposed media naturalness theory, a framework that combines evolutionary theory with social and technological theories to account for behavior in electronic communication. From an evolutionary standpoint, synchronous face-to-face communication, using primarily auditory sounds and visual cues, has been the primary mode of communication in the evolutionary history of human beings. This observation leads to the almost unavoidable conclusion that the human biological communication apparatus must have been designed through evolution primarily for face-to-face interaction. The use of communication media that suppress certain face-to-face communication elements in order to solve problems created by modern society (e.g., instant-messaging allows for non-co-located communication, which is very useful today given the geographic distribution of families and organizations) is an exceedingly recent phenomenon in evolutionary terms. In fact, the first form of written communication, the proto-cuneiform language, appeared only approximately 5,000 years ago in the Sumerian culture (Nissen et al. 1993). That is, written communication has been around for less than 0.2% of our evolutionary cycle as hominids. Thus, it is reasonable to expect that humans would find face-to-face communication to be easier, less effortful, and more pleasant than electronic media in general, because the face-to-face medium is likely to be seen as the most "natural" for communication. And, when confronted

Table 1 The eight principles of media compensation theory

Principle	Explanation
Media naturalness	Media that integrate features of face-to-face interaction will be perceived as more natural and require less cognitive effort in communication.
Innate schema similarity	Humans evolved communication abilities in the Pleistocene era environment of evolutionary adaptation. There should be innate influences that are common to all individuals, regardless of their cultural and social backgrounds and certain fundamental language abilities and structures common to all members of the human species.
Learned schema diversity	Individuals learn and acquire communication schemas through interaction with the environment; individual differences are a result of learning.
Evolutionary task relevance	The functional similarity between a 'modern' and an 'ancient' task is directly correlated with both the degree to which evolved patterns of behavior will be evoked, and the level of perceived naturalness of the task.
Compensatory adaptation	Individuals using media that suppress elements of face-to-face communication do not accept the obstacles posed by unnatural media passively. Instead they compensate by changing their communicative behavior, often in an involuntarily manner.
Media humanness	Humans evolved as social creatures, and as such when in the presence of cues associated with another human being or social interaction, they will respond automatically in a social manner. People will behave in a social manner in the presence of human-like communication media.
Cue removal	Media that provide stimuli or cues but block people from sensing the information accompanying those cues will require more effort and adaptation than media that do not provide such cues at all.
Speech imperative	Costly adaptations are also more important for the underlying tasks they support than less costly adaptations. The ability of a medium to convey speech-related cues may be significantly more important than the medium's ability to convey information than are facial expressions and body language.

with media other than face-to-face, humans will compensate or adapt their behavior to the new media.

Early empirical investigations provided confirmation of some of media naturalness theory's principles, pointed to other facets of the theory that needed modification and also helped to identify additional principles. Building on this framework, we present *media compensation theory*, which emphasizes eight main principles as shown in Table 1 – *media naturalness, innate schema similarity, learned schema diversity, evolutionary task relevance, compensatory adaptation, media humanness, cue removal*, and *speech imperative*.

2.1 Media Naturalness

First, the *media naturalness principle* focuses on the degree of naturalness of a communication medium compared to traditional face-to-face communication, as well

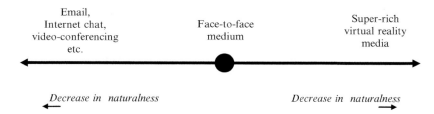

Fig. 1 The face-to-face medium is the most natural, located on a midpoint between lean and super-rich media

as the amount of effort necessary to use the communication medium. The media naturalness principle classifies face-to-face interaction at the midpoint of a one-dimensional scale where points further away from the midpoint, either richer or leaner, are viewed as less natural, thereby requiring an increase in effort as Fig. 1 illustrates. In this sense, media that integrate features of face-to-face interaction will be perceived as more natural and require less effort to be used in communication interactions. The reason underlying this assertion is that a brain designed primarily for face-to-face communication, which we postulate the human brain to be, is likely to require a greater level of effort (in the form of neural activity) to operate in a non-face-to-face communication context – that is, a context in which face-to-face communication elements are not present in the medium used for interaction. Put in a simplified way, the brain circuitry designed for face-to-face communication will not be used, requiring other circuits to be utilized in a non-face-to-face communication context. Those "other circuits" are most likely to be "learned" circuits; that is, neocortical circuits acquired through practice. As pointed out by Pinker and Bloom (1992), "learned" brain circuits are not nearly as effortlessly used as those that are "hardwired" (i.e., that owe much of their structure to genetic and/or epigenetic mechanisms).

There are seven key elements that typify natural face-to-face communication in organizational environments. First, individuals are co-located and can see and hear one another. Next, there is a high degree of synchronicity that allows individuals to quickly interact with each other. Third, individuals have the ability to observe and convey facial expressions. Fourth, individuals are able to observe and convey body language. Fifth, individuals can convey and listen to oral speech. Sixth, individuals are able to engage in mutual gaze; making and holding (or avoiding) eye contact, and seeing where other people are looking. Finally, individuals are able to use and sense subtle olfactory and tactile stimuli, such as pheromones or a light touch. Some communication media are designed to incorporate many of these seven elements that are found in natural interaction, while other media are designed in such a way that they prevent users from experiencing some of these elements (for example communicating by telephone prevents users from observing and conveying body language). According to the media naturalness principle, media that incorporate as much of these elements as the face-to-face medium should possess a high degree of naturalness. Compared to less natural media, such media should in turn require less effort, should be less ambiguous, and should lead to an increase in physiological arousal, from the perspective of the communication participants (Kock 2002).

Media richness theory classifies communication media on a linear continuum that ranges from low to high in amount of richness. This is problematic because some communication media may be labeled as "super-rich," or able to support the conveyance of significantly more stimuli than in face-to-face communication, such as immersive virtual environment technology (e.g., Bailenson et al. 2003). Therefore, according to Media Richness Theory these media would be conceptualized as being superior to face-to-face communication, at least in terms of their amount of richness, even though they would likely induce information overload and require greater effort from their users than the face-to-face medium (Kock 2004). Another example of "super-rich" medium would be one created by virtual reality tools that would enable one individual A to interact with two or more individuals B, C, D ... at the same time, without the individuals B, C, D ... being aware of each other's existence. This type of medium would enable individual A to receive substantially more stimuli than the face-to-face medium, where B, C, D ... would be unaware of each other and unable to divide up "air time" among themselves. Individual A would probably be overwhelmed by such stimuli overload. Decreases in satisfaction and other attitudinal variables as a function of a media's distance from face-to-face naturalness could reasonably be expected (e.g., Baltes et al. 2002). Communication media that are able to support the conveyance of significantly more stimuli than what is usually found in face-to-face communication, such as those enabled by certain group decision support systems, do not lead to increases in performance in group tasks (Dennis 1996), most likely because the additional stimuli cannot be processed and thus induces information overload (Kock 2000b). Similarly, providing too much information lowers consumer attitudes and decreases accuracy of their choices (Jacoby 1984) as well as degrading marketing decision making (Klausegger et al. 2007).

2.2 Innate Schema Similarity

Next, media compensation theory's *innate schema similarity principle* emphasizes that because humans evolved communication abilities in the Pleistocene era environment of evolutionary adaptation (Bowlby 1969), there should be innate influences that are common to all individuals, regardless of their cultural and social backgrounds. Certain fundamental language abilities and structures are held to be common to all members of the human species (Skinner 1957). Although a multitudinous array of languages have evolved throughout the world, it is generally agreed that a universal grammar (Bickerton 1990), as well as a universal set of body language and facial expressions (Bates and Cleese 2001; Cartwright 2000; Deacon 1998; Ekman 1993; McNeill 1998) exist within the human species.

While other characteristics of the species have evolved differently in certain subpopulations (largely structural features such as blood types, resistance/propensity to disease, skin pigmentation, facial types), given language's functional centrality in the species, there is no reason to expect that the fundamentals of language evolved separately for each subpopulation. Thus, individuals from different cultures should still possess, at a functional level, the same underlying biological mechanisms that influence face-to-face communication behavior, as well as behavior associated with the selective suppression of face-to-face communication elements, such as electronic communication behavior. That is, a certain percentage of behavioral variance should be explainable based on our common biological communication apparatus (such as the nearly universal common meanings of a smile and a laugh) while a certain percentage of that behavioral variance should be explainable based on cultural and social background (such as dialects)– as well as other elements, such as collaborative task complexity and geographic distribution of collaborators. The communication media employed do not change the function of communication or social behavior. New media may change the topography of communication, but the fundamental functions remain the same. Indeed, recent research on communication in massively-multiplayer online role – playing games finds that people obey the same social and communicative norms as in offline behavior (Yee et al. 2007).

2.3 *Learned Schema Diversity*

Media compensation theory's third principle, the *learned schema diversity principle*, points out that individuals learn and acquire communication schemas through interaction with the environment, and identifies the importance of individual differences as a result of learning. It has long been recognized that learning is an evolutionary – based selectionist process; the environment selects successful behaviors from many varied acts (Skinner 1981; Thorndike 1901). Indeed, it is this variation in behavior and selection by the environment that is at the core of individual adaptation. As a species, it is clear that human beings are very adaptive; however, there is ambiguity surrounding the temporal duration in which adaptation takes place (adjustment in behavior to environmental changes is often referred to as "adaptation" by behavioral researchers; neural researchers, e.g.., Japyassu and Caires (2008) sometimes use the term "behavioral plasticity"). Because of the vast variety of individual experiences, backgrounds, and environments, large individual differences with respect to the structure of communication would be expected; for example, individuals from the United States may introduce themselves on the telephone by saying "this is..." whereas an individual from another culture could say "here is..." Yet, the function of both utterances is the same.

In the case of virtual work and collaboration, learned schema diversity issues abound. While the technology allows instantaneous bridges across lands and oceans, it also brings together individuals with very different learned schemas. Individuals may have different cultural norms regarding electronic and face-to-face communication. Further, prior experience with different communications technologies will lead to different levels of learning and expertise with these technologies, making their use less effortful. For instance, individuals who have more experience using e-mail are more likely to report e-mail as being more natural than those who with less experience. Moreover, learned schemas partially subdue the role of innate schemas, although innate schemas are still present. In Jarvenpaa and Leidner's (1999) seminal study of global virtual teams, the learned schema of virtual team communication dominated expected cultural differences, as they summarized their findings (p. 811):

> Additionally, electronically facilitated communication may make cultural differences insalient: the lack of nonverbal cues eliminates evidence of cultural differences, such as different ways of dressing, gesticulating, and greeting. Likewise, the written media eliminates the effect of accents which would again reduce the saliency of differences in cultural background. In addition, because the asynchronous mode gives individuals more time to process messages and respond, there might be fewer language errors, particularly among nonnative speakers of the language being used by the group, which would in turn reduce the saliency of differences in cultural background.

2.4 Evolutionary Task Relevance

Media compensation theory's fourth principle, the *evolutionary task relevance principle*, puts forth the notion that the functional similarity between a 'modern' and an 'ancient' task is directly correlated with both the degree to which evolved patterns of behavior will be evoked, and the level of perceived naturalness of the task. This principle differs from the media naturalness principle in that while the media naturalness principle concerns the degree to which a *communication media* differs from face-to-face communication, the evolutionary task relevance principle concerns the degree to which a particular present-day *task* resembles a particular primordial task. For example, game hunting and food gathering (foraging) are basic tasks that have been accomplished recurrently in our evolutionary past. When faced with a functionally similar task, say purchasing goods online or finding information, it is expected that we would behave as foragers do, as research has confirmed (DiClemente and Hantula 2003; Hantula 2010; Hantula et al. 2008; Pirolli 2007; Pirolli and Card 1999; Rajala and Hantula 2000; Smith and Hantula 2003). This principle argues for the existence of a moderating effect associated with the degree of similarity between a given task and a corresponding "ancient" task. This comes from the assumption that in tasks that differ substantially from their corresponding "ancient" tasks, instinctive behavior is less likely to be similar to that associated with the corresponding "ancient" task, and the use of "hardwired" brain circuits less likely as well. Consider the task of cheating detection in social contracts – e.g., detection of lying about intentions to return a favor (Dunbar 1999). According to Cosmides and Tooby (1992), we have evolved "cheater detection" mechanisms, which from a media compensation perspective, would have occurred through face-to-face interactions. When social contracts are negotiated in an online environment, we would expect that the parties would be more skeptical and perceive others as less credible than in face-to-face negotiations, as Citera et al. (2005) have confirmed.

2.5 Compensatory Adaptation

Fifth, media compensation theory's *compensatory adaptation principle*, which is borrowed from Kock's (1998, 2001a) compensatory adaptation model, argues that individuals using media that suppress many of the elements of face-to-face communication (e.g., e-mail) do not accept passively the obstacles posed by the use of those unnatural media. Those individuals instead try to compensate for the obstacles posed by the unnatural media by changing their communication behavior, often in an involuntarily way. In the context of virtual work, this compensatory behavior such as exerting extra effort in virtual work tasks or reviewing and editing one's comments in a text-based medium may in turn lead teams to achieve task outcomes similar to, or even better than, those achieved by teams interacting face-to-face (DeRosa et al. 2007). The flip side is that teams communicating through unnatural electronic media usually take longer to achieve those outcomes than teams interacting face-to-face (Kock 2004; Pawlowicz 2003).

A general propensity and ability to compensate for obstacles posed appears to be common to all species; however for human beings this has been shown to be part of an important evolutionary strategy employed, which can be seen as a necessary precursor to our current species-wide problem-solving and tool-making abilities (Boaz and Almquist 1997). In essence, the communications technologies at hand are in themselves a compensatory adaptation to the temporally and spatially distributed configuration of business and other relationships, yet ironically these very compensatory adaptations then require additional compensatory adaptations by their users.

However, the "cost" of any compensatory adaptation may outweigh its benefits; in that case compensatory adaptation would not be observed. If there are situations in which there are severe constraints on compensatory adaptation, or where there is no motivation for compensatory adaptation, it would not be expected to occur For example, in a laboratory experiment involving groups of students performing a complex 5 min task employing two different media, face-to-face and video conferencing, there may be no observable compensatory adaptation – and thus a marked difference in the quality of the task outcomes generated by the groups in each media condition. The reason for that is that 5 min may not be enough for compensatory adaptation to "kick in" and have a significant influence on the outcomes. Also, even when a longer period of time is available, if there is no motivation for compensatory adaptation (e.g., a financial incentive tied to performance), there may be no observable compensatory adaptation either

2.6 Media Humanness

Sixth is media compensation theory's *media humanness principle*, which argues that because humans are evolved to be social creatures, when in the presence of cues associated with another human being or linked to social interactions, they will respond automatically in a social manner, as if they are in the presence of another human being (Walther 1992). This principle follows from the well-established phenomenon of social facilitation (Triplett 1898). Social facilitation is the strengthening of dominant or well-learned responses in the presence of other members of one's species. It is found in species ranging from insects, birds, and mammals (Guerin 1993), hence most likely is a fundamental evolved behavior, even in species not normally associated with strong social bonds (such as cockroaches). In the context of electronic communication, the extent to which any form of media take on human-like characteristics is the extent to which the media will be another "actor" in communication. Social facilitation occurs in the presence of interactive computers (Quintanar et al. 1982); for example an interactive interface evokes socially facilitated responding, such as better performance on quizzes from users.

Research in communications technologies proceeds from a tacit assumption that the media are socially neutral. But when interactive media are involved there is a chance that the media (even though inanimate) may enter into the communications process as another "person" or animate actor. Anthropomorphizing computer technology is rampant (Markas et al. 2000), but beyond the metaphor lurks a spandrel (Gould and Lewontin 1979) of social behavior directed toward non-social entities. ("Spandrel" is an architectural term describing the triangular space between two arches between two arches. Gould and Lewontin introduced the term into evolutionary parlance to describe exaptations, or features that were not initially adaptive, but rather occurred as fortuitous by-products of adaptation). People do more than simply speak of interactive technologies as animate actors (e.g., Prasad 1993); they often behave as if they were in the presence of another person. Indeed, even minimal sets of social cues such as using a name, self referencing, consistent personality – based phrasing of text (text that is consistent with a personality type such as dominant or submissive) and order of interaction are sufficient to induce people to behave as if the computer is another person (Nass et al. 1995). Further, natural sounding speech from a computer evokes attributions associated with humans (Nass and Steuer 1993) and computer personalities are "real" to users in the same way that human personalities are (Moon and Nass 1996; Nass and Moon 2000).

According to the media humanness principle, when computer interfaces used for communication incorporate elements that make them "look and feel" more human, they will also be perceived as more natural. For example, even though a computer interface may not actually allow two individuals to see each other's faces, it may generate facial representations locally (e.g., by using stored sequences of facial images) that will give those individuals the impression that they are seeing each other. MacDorman et al. (2009) found that people respond to computer generated photorealistic faces as if they are real faces. Increasing use of avatars may also make communication seem more natural; people choose avatars that are highly similar to themselves (Vasalou and Joinson 2009). Facial images and avatars will have an overall effect of reducing the perceived unnaturalness of the communication medium employed by individuals. On the other hand, the media humanness principle also predicts that the extent to which the media *itself* is perceived as a social actor will be the extent to which another sentient being effectively enters into the communication and work processes. That is, collaborators will instinctually attempt to develop social relationships as they accomplish a collaborative task, even though they may not consciously be aware of that (Walther 1996); even if the other "collaborator" is the computer interface.

2.7 Cue Removal

Seventh, the *cue removal principle* holds that media that provide stimuli (or cues) but block people from sensing the information accompanying those cues will require more effort and adaptation than media that do not provide such cues at all. Humans have adapted to expect that the visual presence of others will provide additional cues such as body language and smell, and also that a non face-to-face vocal presence (such as calling to one another across a field) will not provide any additional cues. If the stimuli associated with certain cues are present but the cues or information are absent, this would be perceived as an unnatural and more effortful mode of communication because we are actively suppressing the constant confusion over why certain cues that *should* be present are not.

The cue removal principle may be the primary reason for shortcomings of videoconferencing compared to face-to-face interaction (e.g., Crede and Sneizek 2003; O'Conaill et al. 1993; Spaulding et al. 2008). Although videoconferencing may be seen as a sufficiently rich media that includes both auditory and visual cues, even in the best of technological cases (full duplex, high resolution video) it is not as satisfactory as face-to-face communication, and sometimes is no different from audio-only communication (Daly-Jones et al. 1998), or as Sellen (1995) says "…adding a video channel doesn't much matter, and we might as well just settle for the telephone for remote conversations. (p. 440)." Despite its seeming richness, videoconferencing's blocking of expected cues makes it more effortful and less satisfactory and it is not a substitute for sharing the same physical space. By extension, although there seems to be an uncritical acceptance of adding video to online courses (e.g., Sprague et al. 2007), the cue removal principle would suggest that video may be an expensive and ineffective component. Indeed, adding a synchronous video channel to an online course does not improve learning, communication, or students' sense of community (Newman 2008).

2.8 Speech Imperative

Finally, the *speech imperative principle* is based on the observation that more costly adaptations are also more important for the underlying tasks they support (Zahavi and Zahavi 1997). This idea is an extension of Costly Signaling Theory. Smith and Bird (2000) propose that a costly signal is one that benefits others, is observed by others, is costly to the signaler in non-reciprocal ways, and is an 'honest' sign of the signaler's strength, ability or fitness. In the case of communication, oral speech evolved at a higher fitness cost than other traits associated with natural communication, where the cost is a survival handicap related to the morphology of the human vocal tract (Laitman 1993). The speech-related adaptations that our species evolved are among the most "costly" communication-related adaptations we have undergone in our evolutionary history. For example, an enlarged vocal tract with a larynx located low in the neck has been found to be a sine-qua-non condition for complex speech – i.e., the kind associated with most human languages (Laitman 1993; Lieberman 1998). Yet, those adaptations impose a serious handicap: among all primates; homo sapiens are by far the ones more likely to choke on ingested food morsels and particularly liquids (Boaz and Almquist 1997; Laitman 1993).

It does not seem likely that any adaptation in connection with the use of facial expressions or body language for communication imposes handicaps of the same magnitude. This notion suggests that the ability of a communication medium to convey speech-related cues may be significantly more important than the medium's ability to convey information than are facial expressions and body language. The speech imperative principle provides an explanation for the results of Valley et al. (1998), who compared face-to-face, telephone, and written communication in a bargaining experiment and found that telephone communication was not a midpoint between the other two conditions, but rather resembled face-to-face communication in terms of agreements and impasses. This principle perhaps provides an explanation for the otherwise puzzling findings of Sellen (1995), that adding video to high quality audio makes little difference to end users.

3 Media Compensation and the Evolutionary Advantage Test

A question arises: why is the face-to-face medium likely to be the most natural? Or, in other words, what evolutionary advantages human beings could have obtained from excelling in face-to-face communication? Evolutionary psychologists often try to explain certain psychological mechanisms, abilities, or preferences that seem to be inherent in the human species through what we refer to here as "the evolutionary advantage test" (Barkow et al. 1992). The test entails searching for the existence of assumed evolutionary advantages associated with those mechanisms, abilities, or preferences. The evolutionary advantages, if found, are seen as providing plausible reasons why the mechanisms, abilities, or preferences might have evolved. For example, if human beings in general seem to be particularly good at identifying cheating in social contracts (Cosmides and Tooby 1992), then there should be a good evolutionary reason for possessing this ability. From a genetic, or "selfish gene", evolutionary perspective (Dawkins 1990), this is equivalent to saying that the genes that make human beings particularly interested in and good at detecting cheating in social contracts (e.g., adultery) must have in the past improved the ability of the individuals with those genes to pass them on to the next generation, thus increasing the frequency of those genes in the genetic pool of the human species as a whole. On the other hand, it is important to note that also included in this argument is the recognition that any such abilities, attributes, or traits evolved and were selected in the environment of evolutionary adaptedness (EEA). The selection pressures that existed when a particular adaptation evolved are generally assumed to be in the Pleistocene era for humans (Bowlby 1969). Just because a particular feature is useful now, it does not mean that the feature was developed as something useful, or for its current use; such presently useful features may well be spandrels, or incidental by-products (Gould and Lewontin 1979).

Humans are not the only organisms that forage, hunt, or work in groups or teams (Hantula 2010; Trivers 1971, 1985), however from the writings of Aristotle on, it appears that the human species has been particularly defined by its social nature. Hence, cooperation, group and teamwork appear to have long histories in the human species, and as such it is not unreasonable to assume that during the long process of evolution, those individuals who were more adept at working in groups or teams had a survival advantage (Boehm 2004). It is also not unreasonable to assume that such group or team work co-evolved, or perhaps even accelerated the evolution of language and communication (Pinker and Bloom 1992). Watanabe and Smuts (2004) take this idea a step further and argue that communication and symbol manipulation both require and intensify capacity for social cooperation, which incidentally resulted in eventual incremental evolution of language. That is, language may be a spandrel of cooperation.

Over 99% of the period that goes from the emergence of the first hominids (the Australopithecines) up to this day, human beings have communicated face-to-face (Boaz and Almquist 1997; Kock 2001b; Lieberman 1991, 1998). It is reasonable to assume that the human biological communication apparatus has been designed by evolution to excel in face-to-face communication, particularly in regard to cooperative or shared work, and that the key principles of face-to-face communication elements mentioned before (co-location, synchronicity, the ability to observe and convey facial expressions, the ability to observe and convey body language, gaze, ability to sense subtle cues, and ability to convey and listen to speech) are thus likely to be used extensively for both expression and reception of communicative stimuli. Further, communication may have evolved after cooperative work evolved, so that communication may be a means of solving cooperative work problems posed by a changing environment.

4 Empirical Evidence in Connection with Media Compensation Theory

Media compensation theory evolved from media naturalness theory and is built on a synthesis of findings and concepts from a diverse array of fields, including anthropology, behavior analysis, evolutionary biology, information systems, organizational science, and psychology. As a new theory, media compensation theory does not enjoy a large volume of research. All of the theory's principles have not yet been tested, however some recent studies related to media compensation propositions and those that tested certain elements of the theory show promising results.

While not explicitly designed to test media compensation theory, Burke et al. (2001) found that over time, cohesion and satisfaction increased in computer supported workgroups regardless of media richness, perhaps reflecting adaptation predicted by media compensation theory (see also Burke et al. 1999). Similarly, although working from a different theoretical framework, Maznevski and Chudoba (2000) showed clear temporally based adaptation effects in virtual teams, and further echoing an evolutionary account of virtual team performance, they also reported a rhythmic pattern of effort in accordance with Gersick's (1988, 1991) punctuated equilibrium theory of group work. This model derived from the punctuated equilibria theory of evolution (Gould and Eldredge 1977) (which holds that evolution does not necessarily occur gradually, but rather occurs as a result of a major change in the environment that suddenly selects for and against certain characteristics – that is long periods of stability produce little evolutionary change, it is only when the equilibrium is disturbed that evolutionary changes occur).

Pawlowicz (2003) conducted an experimental test of some media compensation precepts with problem solving and idea generation groups. After three sessions of working on the tasks, attitudinal variables showed that people favored face-to-face communication as predicted by the media naturalness principle, although this difference declined over time. Idea quality did not differ across face to face or computer mediated groups, as predicted by the compensatory adaptation principle. In addition, all teams took less time to complete their work as the study went on, but computer-mediated teams did not require more time than the face-to-face teams by the end of the study, again reflecting compensatory adaptation. Finally, and perhaps most importantly, computer-mediated teams performed (based on proposal quality) as well as face-to-face teams by the second session. Similarly, Simon (2006) compared instant messaging (IM), videoconference, and face-to-face communication modes in idea generation, judgment, and intellective tasks. Consistent with media compensation predictions, task performance did not differ by communication media, but satisfaction with the media (measured in terms of effort) showed a linear decrease from face-to-face to videoconference to IM.

Kock and D'Arcy (2002) report a field experiment comparing virtual to face-to-face dyads in business process redesign tasks. Consistent with the compensatory adaptation principle, virtual dyad members spent more time preparing messages, but differences in quality of work did not occur between virtual and face-to-face dyads.

From a purely "mechanical" perspective, it is arguably more difficult for most individuals to type than it is to speak, which is a confounding effect that is not directly related to cognitive effort, in the sense employed by the media compensation theory. Kock (2005) controlled for that effect in a further analysis of the data in Kock and D'Arcy (2002), by looking into the effect of media naturalness on media "fluency" (media fluency is the number of words per minute that an individual can convey over different media, McQueen et al. 1999). Media fluency was significantly lower in the electronic communication condition than the face-to-face condition, declining far below what the "typing-versus-speaking effect" would allow one to expect.

5 Future Research on Media Compensation and Virtual Collaboration

Media compensation theory offers an intriguing alternative to current communication theories in the context of e-collaboration. First, the media naturalness principle explains the face valid claims of media richness theory and the compensatory adaptation principle explains the findings that attitudinal and preference measures generally favor face-to-face communication. Second, the learned schema diversity principle and the compensatory adaptation principle account for the temporal predictions of social theories such as adaptive structuration theory, channel expansion theory, and social information processing theory and can also allow for reconciliation between the seemingly disparate predictions of social and media richness theories. Third, the cue removal principle explains why videoconferencing is often less preferred to audio conference or even IM. Fourth, the media humanness principle explains the anthropomorphic nature of modern human-computer interaction. Finally, media compensation theory points to new directions in virtual work research. Although media compensation theory has great heuristic value, we focus on the methodological and theoretical issues that we see as the most fruitful and critical for future research, namely, behavioral adaptation and trust.

5.1 Adaptation

Organisms adapt. Species adapt through pressures that select for or against certain characteristics; individual members of a species adapt through pressures that select for or against particular behaviors. Because the key concept in media compensation theory is adaptation in terms of performance, shifts in research tactics are necessary.

The first necessary shift is that, because adaptation is change over time, longitudinal or repeated measures designs should become the norm in virtual communication, collaboration, and work research. "One shot" designs that measure process or outcome variables only once may not be able to capture the adaptive processes that are expected to occur. Indeed this proposition brings up the possibility that the adaptation processes predicted by media compensation theory may be part of by the type of punctuated equilibrium changes observed in group processes by Gersick (1991).

Second, while principled arguments can be made for studying intact, long-term work or collaborative teams in many areas of research, such an over reliance on intact experienced teams may obfuscate evidence of adaptation, because the teams and their members may have already adapted to the communication media under study. In testing media compensation theory, the use of intact teams or newly formed teams is a tactical decision based on the processes or outcome under study; intact teams neither are not automatically bestowed privileged status nor are newly formed teams assumed to be inferior.

Third, as Baltes et al. (2002) observed, the majority of the dependent variables used in computer mediated communication research are perceptual and attitudinal variables. These are neither right nor wrong variables to measure, but they may either reflect an implicit mapping of perceptual and attitudinal variables with performance; or they may be simply missing performance and outcome measures entirely. From a media compensation perspective, perceptual and attitudinal measures would be expected to diverge from performance measures, especially early on. Rather than rely on an assumed slight correlation between perceptual and performance measures, research in a media compensation framework explicitly considers perceptual and performance variables to be separate orthogonal constructs. Indeed, perceptual and attitudinal variables reflect emotional and evaluative reactions to the compensation and adaptation predicted by media compensation theory, while performance and outcome variables reflect the actual results of adaptation.

Fourth, current research in computer mediated communication uses face-to-face groups as a common control condition, and data are analyzed with respect to differences between face-to-face groups and those using some form of technological media (e.g., Baltes et al. 2002; Simon 2006). However, a media compensation perspective does not necessarily need or suggest face-to-face teams as a comparison or control condition; rather the theory focuses on the processes and behavior of those individuals communicating via electronic media. Indeed, from the perspective of media compensation, the similarities or differences between virtual and face-to-face teams are largely irrelevant. Future research from a media compensation perspective would echo the sentiments of Guzzo and Dickson (1996), who stated that because of the growth of electronic teams, " ...we therefore suggest that research on electronically mediated groups break free from the tradition of comparing those groups to face-to-face groups. Instead, future research should accept such groups on their own terms". (p. 323).

Future research should include stronger tests of media naturalness theory's compensatory adaptation principle by employing advanced research designs that control for the effects of form of message preparation (i.e., typing vs. speaking) on the level of cognitive effort exerted by participants. Extending the results of Kock (2005), research should move beyond explorations of simple mechanical effects to considerations of the evolved characteristics that may make certain media more or less effortful. Recent technological advances such as immersive virtual environment technology (Bailenson et al. 2003) provide a promising means for exploring media naturalness principle's classification of face-to-face interaction at the midpoint of a one-dimensional scale where points further away from the midpoint, either richer or leaner, are viewed as less natural, thereby requiring an increase in cognitive effort. Certainly, leaner media are common, but given that media richer than face-to-face communication is now available, this precept may be subject to empirical test.

Beyond theory testing, some worthy applications arise in terms of adaptation in the context of media compensation theory. The media humanness principle holds that as the media become more interactive and human-like, people will respond to it as if they are in the presence of another person. In virtual work, this may be the functional equivalent of adding another person to the team. Because a team by definition involves other people, further social facilitation effects are not expected due to the "human" technology, however a very "human" interface may contribute to social loafing (social loafing is the tendency for individuals to exert less effort when working as part of a group, Kraut 2003) by other team members, or may impede communication in other ways. By implication, efforts to make communications technologies and interfaces more human in an attempt to make users more effective may backfire.

The cue removal principle speaks directly to the seeming paradox of videoconferencing; a rich, real time media that has never gained widespread acceptance. Web cams still appear to function more as toys than as a work-related communications medium. According to this principle, the relative high cost of videoconferencing in terms of adaptation (compared to other media) would not be expected to be justified on the basis of effort or performance indicators. Further, there may not be more positive attitudinal results for videoconferencing, but given media compensation theory's emphasis on performance outcomes, these would be seen as secondary.

5.2 Trust

Even the most advanced information technologies only partially contribute to the success of virtual work (Lurey and Raisinghani 2001); the majority of successful performance is more likely due to interpersonal processes such as trust. The idea that trust is a necessary condition of virtual team performance appears to be an unquestioned assumption, but then again the role of trust in virtual team performance requires careful consideration (DeRosa et al. 2004). Kipnis (1996) stated that organizations employ technology as a means to exert greater control over employees (e.g., through greater supervision and surveillance). However, in the case of virtual teams this is ironic, because as the use of communication technologies and virtual teams increases, managers and team leaders will need to trust employees even more, especially so in virtual teams, where team members typically have greater levels of independence and autonomy in their work.

Trust is a final frontier for future research in virtual work and collaboration from a media compensation perspective. Virtual team members who never meet face-to-face, or who have very few meetings, may be less willing to trust other team members, as face-to-face contact is assumed to be important for reinforcing social similarity, shared values, and expectations in interpersonal trust. Nohria and Eccles (1992) suggested that face-to-face interaction is vital for the development and sustenance of trust, but Webster and Wong (2008) argue that requiring such face to face interaction may backfire in teams that will later work together in a virtual environment. Bargaining studies have shown that people using communications media other than face-to-face engage in more deception (e.g., Citera et al. 2005; Valley et al. 1998). From this perspective, virtual team members should find it most difficult to trust others when they are interacting through communication media that are most distinct from face-to-face communication.

Perhaps one distinction that should be made is between types of trust. Interpersonal trust is built on relationships and takes time to develop; if interpersonal trust were paramount in virtual team performance then it would be expected that virtual teams would not become effective quickly, or perhaps at all. However, Jarvenpaa and Leidner (1999) found that swift trust (depersonalized, action-based trust established around the tasks or work) established in early group communications was a distinguishing characteristic of successful virtual teams. Hence, it appears that a team member's task-oriented actions (which may be all the social input that one can provide in a virtual team) are adequate for trust to develop. Echoing the importance of task-based relations in virtual teamwork, Hertel et al. (2003) found that group member motivation and performance increased when individual contributions were instrumental to success. In terms of media compensation theory, swift trust and task-oriented motivation are further examples of compensatory adaptation

Media compensation theory calls into question the tacit assumption that interpersonal trust is a necessary condition for high performance in virtual teams. Instead, it may be expected that in accordance with the cue removal principle, seeking to develop interpersonal trust through technologically advanced communications media (that suppress many of the cues used for developing interpersonal trust) may interfere with team performance, or as Dubé and Robey (2009) state, mistrust is necessary to establish trust in virtual teams. Indirect evidence for this proposition comes from a longitudinal study of virtual teams by Aubert and Kelsey (2003) that found team performance to be independent of trust formation; instead higher levels of communication typified high performing teams. Similarly, Kirkman et al. (2002) conducted comprehensive interviews with team members, team leaders, general managers, and executives on 65 virtual teams at Sabre, Inc. and found that trust in virtual teams is based more on performance consistency than interpersonal issues. Again a task focus is at the forefront, which is seen as evidence of compensatory adaptation under media compensation theory. Behavior counts; interpersonal attitudes are secondary.

Further evidence regarding the reformulation of trust in virtual teams is the observation that it is increasingly common for employees to work together for transient periods of time in virtual teams; arguably these efforts have largely been successful. From a media compensation perspective, those individuals who have more experience working in virtual relationships will adapt to new teams and new members more quickly according to the learned schema diversity principle. It is also plausible that individuals who have learned to trust others when communicating through various media may experience less difficulty with interpersonal processes such as trust, which may account for the "swift trust" effect found in multinational virtual teams (Jarvenpaa and Leidner 1999). Natural media facilitate social perceptions (socio-emotional communication and positive socio-emotional climate) and perceived ability to evaluate others' deception and expertise (Kahai and Cooper 2003).

In addition, increased cultural diversity may be assumed to be an important factor in the formation of trust in virtual teams, as team member values may impact the formation of trust (Jones and George 1998), and increased levels of diversity may lead to more discomfort and lower levels of trust (Kipnis 1996). On the other hand, a strong task focus may lessen the importance of interpersonal trust in a virtual team context. Compensatory adaptation, along with the innate schema similarity principle suggests that an over-reliance or over-sensitivity to "cultural differences" among virtual team members may be unnecessary. Jarvenpaa and Leidner (1999) found no cultural differences in their global study of virtual work teams; perhaps these teams were too busy adapting to the media and to the task for any "cultural" variables to emerge. Although electronic communication media may suppress many diversity related cues, it may also let other diversity related cues become apparent. In these cases it would be naive to believe that the electronic media somehow obviates trust issues based on these cues, instead from a media compensation perspective it is argued that these cues are secondary to adaptation to the task.

In fact, the concept of 'trust' in virtual team work may have the issue confused. Work is the primary avenue of social exchange in virtual collaboration and virtual team work. As such, task accomplishment should be a primary motivator, and the important issue may not be trust as much as cheating and deception. Tooby and Cosmides (1992) argue that humans have evolved "cheater detection" modules, based on evidence from a social exchange conditional reasoning task; in their view cheater detection is a specialized design for social exchange. Other evolutionary psychologists argue cheater detection evolved in the context of face-to-face communication. For example,(Dunbar (1999), p. 206) states "... in establishing [trust] relationships... we appear to rely heavily on proximate cues of loyalty or honesty based mainly on facial expressions". From this viewpoint, a lack of face-to-face contact reduces nonverbal and social context cues that might be especially important for detecting deception and lying (Bavelas et al. 1990; Ekman 1993). From a media compensation theory perspective, it would be expected that humans would adapt to the virtual media and begin to identify and avoid working with cheaters over time, perhaps due to a combination of detecting violations of social exchange norms as posited by Tooby and Cosmides and by perceiving changes in language, such as alteration in levels of language dominance, already known to be a sign of deception in online communication (Zhou et al. 2004). Other adaptations may take the form of using emoticons and emotion – laden words and phrases to communicate earnestness, seeking out the same from others, and also by co-evolving subtle signals of honesty and lack thereof. Indeed, if the collective experience with telephone communication over the last 100 years is any indication, such adaptations will occur. A corollary to the compensatory adaptation principle would predict that younger people who have a history of interacting in chat rooms, instant messaging, text messaging and email would have more highly attuned cheater detection mechanisms in the virtual world than would their less experienced elders, which has implications for training and education for a virtual team based workplace (Hantula and Pawlowicz 2003). Further, given the vast array of virtual interaction platforms and sub communities that develop within them, the learned schema diversity principle would predict that the structural characteristics of signaling honesty and deception would be highly differentiated between these sub communities.

6 Conclusion

This chapter proceeded from two paradoxes: (1) Virtual communication, work, collaboration and teams are largely successful (sometimes even more so than face-to-face) despite much theory and conventional wisdom to the contrary; and, (2) The human species evolved in small groups using communications modalities in constrained areas, yet use electronic communication media to allow large groups to work together effectively across time and space. Media compensation theory provides a new Darwinian framework for resolving these seeming paradoxes and also for understanding and studying electronic communication and teamwork in organizations. The theory and its propositions subsume and refine older technical and social theories while it also explains the seemingly paradoxical findings of successful virtual teamwork, dissatisfaction with videoconferencing, drawbacks of too-human interfaces, and divergence between affective reactions, trust, and performance in virtual teams. Although advancements in technology are astounding, they still have to be used by the same humans who have not changed much in the many millennia. Perhaps we are strangers in a strange land, but if our brains are still those of Pleistocene-era hunter-gatherers as evolutionary psychologists argue, we have adapted well in the past, and show all signs that we will continue to do so in the future. No matter how complex the next new technology may seem, it is still the human that is the most complex, flexible, and adaptive part of the system.

References

Aubert BA, Kelsey BL (2003) Further understanding of trust and performance in virtual teams. Small Group Res 34:575–618
Bailenson JN, Blascovich J, Beall AC, Loomis JM (2003) Interpersonal distance in immersive virtual environments. Pers Soc Psychol Bull 29:819–833
Baltes BB, Dickson MW, Sherman MP, Bauer CC, LaGanke JS (2002) Computer-mediated communication and group decision-making: a meta-analysis. Organ Behav Hum Decis Process 87:156–179

Barkow JH, Cosmides L, Tooby J (eds) (1992) The adapted mind: evolutionary psychology and the generation of culture. Oxford University Press, New York

Bates B, Cleese J (2001) The human face. DK Publishing, New York

Bavelas JB, Black A, Chovil N, Mullett J (1990) Equivocal communication. Sage, Newbury Park

Bickerton D (1990) Language and species. University of Chicago Press, Chicago

Boaz NT, Almquist AJ (1997) Biological anthropology: a synthetic approach to human evolution. Prentice Hall, Upper Saddle River

Boehm C (2004) Large-game hunting and the evolution of human Sociality. In: Sussman RW, Chapman AR (eds) The origins and nature of sociality. Gruyter, Hawthorne, pp 270–287

Bowlby J (1969) Attachment and loss. Basic Books, New York

Burke K, Aytes K, Chidambaram L, Johnson JJ (1999) A study of partially distributed work groups: the impact of media, location, and time on perceptions and performance. Small Group Res 30(4):453–490

Burke K, Aytes K, Chidambaram L (2001) Media effects on the development of cohesion and process satisfaction in computer-supported workgroups: an analysis of results from two longitudinal studies. Inf Technol People 14:122–141

Cartwright J (2000) Evolution and human behavior: Darwinian perspectives on human nature. MIT Press, Cambridge

Cascio WF (1999) Virtual workplaces: implications for organizational behavior. In: Cooper CL, Rousseau DM (eds) Trends in organizational behavior: the virtual organization. Wiley, Chichester, pp 1–14

Chidambaram L, Jones B (1993) Impact of communication medium and computer support on group perceptions and performance: a comparison of face-to-face and dispersed meetings. MIS Q 17:465–488

Citera M, Beauregard R, Mitsuya T (2005) An experimental study of credibility in e-negotiations. Psychol Mark 22:163–179

Colarelli SM (1998) Psychological interventions in organizations: an evolutionary perspective. Am Psychol 53(9):1044–1056

Colarelli SM (2003) No best way: an evolutionary perspective on human resource management. Praeger, Greenwich

Cosmides L, Tooby J (1992) Cognitive adaptations for social exchange. In: Barkow J, Cosmides L, Tooby J (eds) The adapted mind: evolutionary psychology and the generation of culture. Oxford University Press, New York, pp 163–228

Crede M, Sneizek JA (2003) Group judgment processes and outcomes in video-conferencing versus face-to-face groups. Int J Hum Comput Stud 59:875–897

Daft RL, Lengel RH (1984) Information richness: a new approach to managerial behavior and organizational design. Res Organ Behav 6:191–233

Daft RL, Lengel RH (1986) Organizational information requirements, media richness, and structural design. Manage Sci 32(5):554–571

Daly-Jones O, Monk A, Watts L (1998) Some advantages of video conferencing over high-quality audio conferencing: fluency and awareness of attentional focus. Int J Hum Comput Stud 49:21–58

Dawkins R (1990) The selfish gene. Oxford University Press, Oxford

Deacon TW (1998) The symbolic species: the co-evolution of language and the brain. W.W. Norton, New York

Dennis AR (1996) Information exchange and use in group decision making: you can lead a group to information, but you can't make it think. MIS Q 20:433–455

Dennis AR, Kinney ST (1998) Testing media richness theory in the new media: the effects of cues, feedback, and task equivocality. Inf Syst Res 9:256–274

DeRosa D, Hantula D, Kock N, D'Arcy J (2004) Trust and leadership in virtual teamwork: a media naturalness perspective. Hum Resour Manage 43(2):219–232

DeRosa D, Smith C, Hantula D (2007) The medium matters: mining the long-promised merit of group interaction in creative idea generation tasks in a meta-analysis of the electronic group brainstorming literature. Comput Hum Behav 23(3):1549–1581

DiClemente DF, Hantula DA (2003) Optimal foraging online: increasing sensitivity to delay. Psychol Mark 20:785–809

Dubé L, Robey D (2009) Surviving the paradoxes of virtual teamwork. Inf Syst J 19:3–30

Dunbar R (1999) Culture, honesty and the Freerider problem. In: Dunbar R, Knight C, Power C (eds) The evolution of culture. Rutgers University Press, New Brunswick, pp 194–213

Ekman P (1993) Facial expression and emotion. Am Psychol 48:384–392

El-Shinnawy M, Markus ML (1997) The poverty of media richness theory: explaining people's choice of electronic mail vs. voice mail. Int J Hum Comput Stud 46:443–467

Fulk J, Schmitz J, Steinfield CW (1990) A social influence model of technology use. In: Fulk J, Steinfield C (eds) Organizations and communication technology. Sage, Newbury Park, pp 117–140

Gersick CJG (1988) Time and transition in work teams: toward a new model of group development. Acad Manage J 31:9–41

Gersick CJG (1991) Revolutionary change theories: a multilevel exploration of the punctuated equilibrium paradigm. Acad Manage Rev 16:10–36

Gould SJ, Eldredge N (1977) Punctuated equilibria: the tempo and mode of evolution reconsidered. Paleobiology 3:115–151

Gould SJ, Lewontin RC (1979) The spandrels of San Marco and the Panglossian paradigm: a critique of the adaptationist programme. Proc R Soc Lond B 205:581–598

Guerin B (1993) Social facilitation. Cambridge University Press, New York

Guzzo RA, Dickson MW (1996) Teams in organizations: recent research on performance and effectiveness. Annu Rev Psychol 47:307–338

Hantula D A (2010) The behavioral ecology of human foraging in an online environment: of omnivores, informavores and hunter-gatherers. In: Kock N (ed) Evolutionary psychology and information systems research: a new approach to studying the effects of modern technologies on human behavior. Springer, New York, pp 85–102

Hantula DA, Pawlowicz DM (2003) Education mirrors industry: on the not-so-surprising rise of the virtual classroom. In: Monolescu D, Schifter C, Greenwood L (eds) The distance education evolution. Idea Group Publishing, Hershey

Hantula D, Brockman D, Smith C (2008) Online shopping as foraging: the effects of increasing delays on purchasing and patch residence. IEEE Trans Prof Commun 51:147–154

Hertel G, Dieter C, Orlikowski B (2003) Motivation gains in computer-supported groups. J Appl Soc Psychol 33:2080–2805

Hollingshead AB (1996) Information suppression and status persistence in group decision making: the effects of communication media. Hum Comput Res 23(2):193–219

Jacoby J (1984) Perspectives on information overload. J Consum Res 10(4):432–435

Japyassu H, Caires R (2008) Hunting tactics in a cobweb spider (Araneae-theridiidae) and the evolution of behavioral plasticity. J Insect Behav 21(4):258–284

Jarvenpaa SL, Leidner DE (1999) Communication and trust in global virtual teams. Organ Sci 10(6):791–815

Jones GR, George JM (1998) The experience and evolution of trust: implications for cooperation and teamwork. Acad Manage Rev 23(3):531–546

Kahai SS, Cooper RB (2003) Exploring the core concepts of media richness theory: the impact of cue multiplicity and feedback immediacy on decision quality. J Manage Inf Syst 20: 263–299

Kipnis D (1996) Trust and technology. In: Kramer RM, Tyler TR (eds) Trust in organizations: Frontiers of theory and research. Sage, Thousand Oaks, pp 39–50

Kirkman B, Rosen B, Gibson C, Tesluk P, McPherson S (2002) Five challenges to virtual team success: lessons from Sabre, Inc. Acad Manage Exec 16:67–79

Klausegger C, Sinkovics R, Zou H (2007) Information overload: a cross-national investigation of influence factors and effects. Mark Intell Plann 25(7):691–718

Kock N (1998) Can communication medium limitations foster better group outcomes? An action research study. Inf Manage 34:295–305

Kock N (2001a) Compensatory adaptation to a lean medium: an action research investigation of electronic communication in process improvement groups. IEEE Trans Prof Commun 44:267–285

Kock N (2001b) The ape that used email: understanding e-communication behavior through evolution theory. Commun AIS 5:1–29

Kock N (2002) Evolution and media naturalness: a look at e-communication through a Darwinian theoretical lens. In: Applegate L, Galliers R, DeGross JL (eds) Proceedings of the 23rd international conference on information systems. The Association for Information Systems, Atlanta, pp 373–382

Kock N (2004) The psychobiological model: towards a new theory of computer-mediated communication based on Darwinian evolution. Organ Sci 15:327–348

Kock N (2005) Compensatory adaptation to media obstacles: an experimental study of process redesign dyads. Inf Resour Manage J 18:41–67

Kock N, D'Arcy J (2002) Resolving the e-collaboration paradox: the competing influences of media naturalness and compensatory adaptation. Inf Manage Consult 17:72–78

Kraut R (2003) Applying social psychological theory to the problems of group work. In: Carroll JM (ed) HCI models, theories and frameworks: toward a multidisciplinary science. Morgan Kaufman, New York, pp 325–356

Laitman J (1993) The anatomy of human speech. In: Ciochon RL, Fleagle JG (eds) The human evolution source book. Prentice Hall, Englewood Cliffs, pp 56–60

Leerberg T (2007) A spatial environment for design dialogue. In: MacGregor SP, Torres-Coronas T (eds) Higher creativity for virtual teams: developing platforms for co-creation. Information Science Reference/IGI Global, Hershey, pp 264–278

Lieberman P (1991) Uniquely human: the evolution of speech, thought, and selfless behavior. Harvard University Press, Cambridge

Lieberman P (1998) Eve spoke: human language and human evolution. W.W. Norton, New York

Lurey JS, Raisinghani MS (2001) An empirical study of the best practices in virtual teams. Inf Manage 38:523–544

MacDorman KF, Green RD, Ho C-C, Koch C (2009) Too real for comfort: uncanny responses to computer generated faces. Comput Hum Behav 25:695–710

Markas GM, Johnson RD, Palmer JW (2000) A theoretical model of differential social attributions toward computing technology: when the metaphor becomes the model. Int J Hum Comput Stud 52:719–750

Maznevski ML, Chudoba KM (2000) Bridging space over time: global virtual team dynamics and effectiveness. Organ Sci 11(5):473–492

McNeill D (1998) The face: a natural history. Little, Brown, Boston

McQueen RJ, Payner K, Kock N (1999) Contribution by participants in face-to-face business meetings: implications for collaborative technology. J Syst Inf Technol 3:15–33

Moon Y, Nass C (1996) How real are computer personalities? Psychological responses to personality types in human-computer interaction. Commun Res 23:651–674

Nass C, Moon Y (2000) Machines and mindlessness: social responses to computers. J Soc Issues 56:81–103

Nass C, Steuer J (1993) Voices, boxes, and sources of messages: computers and social actors. Hum Commun Res 19:504–527

Nass C, Moon Y, Fogg BJ, Reeves B, Dryer DC (1995) Can computer personalities be human personalities? Int J Hum Comput Stud 43:223–239

Newman J (2008) The effects of synchronous voice and video tools on acceptance of online communications by students in undergraduate technology courses. Unpublished Doctoral Dissertation, University of Nevada, Reno

Nissen HJ, Damerow P, Englund RK (1993) Archaic bookkeeping: early writing and techniques of economic administration in the ancient near east. University of Chicago Press, Chicago

Nohria N, Eccles RG (1992) Face-to-face: making networks organizations work. In: Nohria N, Eccles RG (eds) Networks and organizations: structure, form, and action. Harvard Business School Press, Boston, pp 288–308

O'Conaill B, Whittaker S, Wilbur S (1993) Conversations over video conferences: an evaluation of the spoken aspects of video-mediated communication. Hum Comput Interact 8:389–428

Pawlowicz D M (2003) Media naturalness and temporal adaptation in virtual team performance: a matter of time. Unpublished Doctoral Dissertation, Temple University, Philadelphia

Pinker S, Bloom P (1992) Natural language and natural selection. In: Barkow JH, Cosmides L, Tooby J (eds) The adapted mind: evolutionary psychology and the generation of culture. Oxford University Press, New York, pp 451–493

Pirolli P (2007) Information foraging theory: adaptive interaction with information. Oxford University Press, New York

Pirolli P, Card S (1999) Information foraging. Psychol Rev 4(106):643–675

Prasad P (1993) Symbolic processes in the implementation of technological change: a symbolic interactionist study of work computerization. Acad Manage J 36:1400–1429

Quintanar LR, Crowell CR, Pryor JB, Adamopoulos J (1982) Human-computer interaction: a preliminary social psychological analysis. Behav Res Meth Instrum 14(2):210–220

Rajala AK, Hantula DA (2000) Towards a behavioral ecology of consumption: delay-reduction effects on foraging in a simulated Internet mall. Managerial Decis Econ 21:145–158

Sellen AJ (1995) Remote conversations: the effects of mediating talk with technology. Hum Comput Interact 10:401–444

Simon A (2006) Computer-mediated communication: task performance and satisfaction. J Soc Psychol 146(3):349–379

Skinner BF (1957) Verbal behavior. Appleton, New York

Skinner BF (1981) Selection by consequences. Science 213:501–504

Smith E, Bird R (2000) Turtle hunting and tombstone opening: public generosity as costly signaling. Evol Hum Behav 21(4):245–261

Smith CL, Hantula DA (2003) Pricing effects on foraging in a simulated internet shopping mall. J Econ Psychol 24:653–674

Spaulding R, Davis K, Patterson J (2008) A comparison of telehealth and face-to-face presentation for school professionals supporting students with chronic illness. J Telemed Telecare 14(4):211–214

Sprague D, Maddux C, Ferdig R, Albion P (2007) Online education: issues and research questions. J Technol Teach Educ JTATE 15(2):157–166

Thorndike EL (1901) The human nature club: an introduction to the study of mental life, 2nd edn. Macmillan, New York

Tooby J, Cosmides L (1992) The psychological foundation of culture. In: Barkow JH, Cosmides L, Tooby J (eds) The adapted mind: evolutionary psychology and the generation of culture. Oxford University Press, New York, pp 19–136

Triplett N (1898) The dynamogenic factors in pacemaking and competition. Am J Psychol 9(4):507–533

Trivers RL (1971) The evolution of reciprocal altruism. Q Rev Biol 46:35–57

Trivers RL (1985) Social evolution. Benjamin Cummings, Menlo Park

Valley KL, Moag J, Bazerman MH (1998) 'A matter of trust': effects of communication on the efficiency and distribution of outcomes. J Econ Behav Organization 34:211–238

Vasalou A, Joinson A (2009) Me, myself and I: The role of interactional context on self-presentation through avatars. Comput Hum Behav 25(2):510–520

Walther JB (1992) Interpersonal effects in computer-mediated interaction: a relational perspective. Commun Res 19:52–90

Walther JB (1996) Computer-mediated communication: impersonal, interpersonal, and hyperpersonal interaction. Commun Res 23:3–43

Watanabe J, Smuts B (2004) Cooperation, commitment, and communication in the evolution of human sociality. In: Sussman RW, Chapman AR (eds) The origins and nature of sociality. Gruyter, Hawthorne, pp 288–309

Webster J, Wong W (2008) Comparing traditional and virtual group forms: identity, communication and trust in naturally occurring project teams. Int J Hum Resour Manage 19(1):41–62

Workman M, Kahnweiler W, Bommer W (2003) The effects of cognitive style and media richness on commitment to telework and virtual teams. J Vocat Behav 63:199–219

Yee N, Bailenson J, Urbanek M, Chang F, Merget D (2007) The unbearable likeness of being digital: the persistence of nonverbal social norms in online virtual environments. Cyberpsychol Behav 10(1):115–121

Zahavi A, Zahavi A (1997) The handicap principle: a missing piece of Darwin's Puzzle. Oxford University Press, Oxford

Zhou L, Burgoon JK, Zhang D, Nunamaker JF (2004) Language dominance in interpersonal deception in computer-mediated communication. Comput Hum Behav 20:381–402

Index

A
The ABC Research Group,
Actual nature, 304–310
Adaptation, 135–136, 138, 141, 143, 144, 154, 166, 168, 176, 266, 268, 339–358
  applications, 355
  behavioral plasticity, 345
  body language, 344, 349, 350
  by-products of, 348, 351
  as change over time, 353
  cost, 347, 355
  costly, 342, 350
  effort, 342, 349
  facial expressions, 342, 350
  handicap, 350
  individual, 345, 347
  to media, 340
  as performance, 347, 353, 354
  speech-related, 342, 350
  temporal duration, 345
Adaptive, 266–268, 270
Ad-likeability, 259, 261, 267–285
Ad preference, 274–276, 279–281, 284–285
Advertising, 18, 21, 23–25, 34, 271
  cues, 258, 264, 267, 274
  effectiveness, 257–285
  management, 258–259, 261, 263, 268, 274, 282
  processing, 258, 259, 261, 263, 264, 268
Affiliation, 19, 20, 22, 31, 33, 35
Africa, 174
Agricultural revolution, 174
Agriculture, 166
Alpha waves, 296
Al Qaeda, 173
Altruism, 20, 32–33, 97, 98, 103, 105, 237, 248
Amygdala, 305, 306

Animals, 294, 296–297, 300, 304–308, 311
  life, 305–308
  symbol, 308
Apple, 225–226, 242, 251
Appleton, J., 291, 292, 297, 300, 307
Architectural, 298, 300, 301, 303, 307–310
Architecture, 292, 298, 308–310
Art Nouveau, 308–309
Artwork, 297
ASA "the people make the place" model, 175
Atmospherics, 289–312
Attractiveness, 267–272, 275–277, 279–281, 284

B
Bankers, 112, 125
Beauty, 270
Behavior
  genetics, 169
  irrational, 322, 327
Behavioral plasticity, 168–169
Benefit-to-contribution ratio, 101, 104, 106, 111, 112, 118, 121, 126
Big Man model, 174
Biological movement, 305, 306
Biological sex, 135–159, 181
Biophilic architecture, 298
Bloomberg, 186
Bonuses, 125
Brain, 325, 327, 328, 330, 334
Brain systems, 258–259, 282
Brand-likeability, 261, 263, 274, 284–285
Buy button, 280, 285

C
Cardiovascular activation, 296
Carfronts, 308
Car interior design, 306

Casa Battló, 308
Central persuasive route, 258, 265
Central route, 259, 261, 262
Charity, 33
Charm, 267, 269–272
Cheater, 97, 103
　detection, 346–347, 357–358
Cheater-detection algorithms, 192, 193,
　　197–200, 203, 204, 206, 207,
　　209–211, 214, 215
Chimpanzees, 328–329
Choice
　inter-temporal, 322, 329
Classical conditioning, 260
Classic architecture, 308–309
Co-evolution, 167, 184
Cognitive leadership prototypes, 170, 173
Cognitive overload, 305
Coherence, 292, 293, 301–302
Collective action, 107
Compensation, 98, 100, 102, 104–105, 111,
　　112, 118, 121, 125
Compensatory adaptation, 342, 347, 352–354,
　　356–358
　benefits, 347
　cost, 347
　principle, 347, 352–354, 357–358
Competitive, 115, 119–122, 124
　altruism, 105, 106, 119, 120, 126, 127
Competitiveness, 115, 119–122
Complexity, 291–293, 301–302
Conditional cooperation, 104
Conflict, 167, 168, 170, 172, 179–180, 182, 183
Consequences (for free riding), 105, 107–109,
　　114, 117, 126
Conspicuous consumption, 3, 7, 49, 50, 226,
　　228, 248, 332
Consumer behavior, 258, 267, 268
Consumer skepticism, 227, 228
Contribution, 101–108, 110–112, 118,
　　119, 123, 125
Contributors, 100, 105, 108–111, 115, 118,
　　124, 127
Cooperation, 95–128, 167, 170, 174, 180, 182,
　　184
Coordination, 166–169, 171, 178, 182
Cost/benefit analysis, 176
Costly signaling theory, 350
Creativity, 20, 21, 25–27
Critiques
　rationality, 320–323
Cues, 227, 236–241, 244, 250, 257–285
　management, 257–285

removal, 342, 349
removal principle, 349, 353, 355, 356
Culture, 167, 170, 171, 173–176, 183, 185, 193,
　　194, 196, 198, 201–202, 205, 206, 215
Curvilinearity, 306

D

DAC. *See* Direction, acceptance and
　　commitment
"Deal or No-Deal", 324
Decisions
　time inconsistent, 329
Decorative style, 299
Descent of Man, 177
Detection, 109
Direct attention, 295
Direction, acceptance and commitment (DAC),
　　171
Division of labor, 170, 184
Dobzhansky, T., 2
Dominance, 73, 76, 83–85
　hierarchies, 168, 177
Dual-processing system, 258, 285

E

Ecological consciousness, 233, 237, 246, 248
Economic games, 182, 308
Economics
　behavioral, 319–320, 323–326, 333, 335
　Folk, 330–331
EEA. *See* Environment of evolutionary
　　adaptedness
EEG. *See* Electroencephalograph
Egalitarian, 169, 171, 173, 175, 184
Elaboration, 258–263, 265, 274
Elective affinity, 175
Electroencephalograph (EEG), 296
Emotions
　social, 322, 325, 326, 329, 334
Endowment effect, 322, 324, 325
Enron, 185
Enticement, 303
Entrepreneurship, 175
Environmental psychology, 292, 294–296, 298
Environment of evolutionary adaptedness
　　(EEA), 342, 344, 351
EP. *See* Evolutionary psychology
Equality, 115, 119–121, 122, 126
Equity, 107, 115, 119–122, 126, 127
　sensitivity, 113–115, 116, 126
　theory, 107, 112–115,117, 126
Erratic movement, 306
ESA. *See* Evolutionary Store Atmospherics

Evaluation, 354, 357
Evolution, 166, 168, 170, 172, 177, 179, 181, 183, 184, 186
Evolutionary advantage test, 340, 350–351
Evolutionary aesthetics, 284
Evolutionary psychology (EP), 258, 259, 264–268, 317–333
  applied across business disciplines, 5–6, 8
  applied across consumer-related phenomena, 5
  applied across product categories, 5
  Blank slate, 2
  and consilience, 6–7, 9
  domain-specificity, 2
  and generating new hypotheses, 7
  and interdisciplinarity, 7, 8
  Predecessor Darwinian disciplines, 2
  Standard Social Science Model, 2
Evolutionary Store Atmospherics (ESA), 289–312
Evolutionary task relevance principle, 342, 346
Executives, traits of, 73
Experiments, 319–320, 322–333, 335
Exploitation, 105–111
Eye, 109–110, 127
Eyespots, 308

F
Face, 172, 181
Face-to-face, 340–347, 351–357
  communication, 341–347, 349–353, 357–358
    seven key elements, 343
  differences between virtual teams and, 354
  interaction, 341–343, 346–347, 349, 356–358
  medium, 341–344, 350
  negotiations, 347
  teams, 347, 352, 354, 358
Fairness, 104–106, 112, 121, 124, 125
  preferences, 325
Family firms, 171
Feminine, 170, 172, 179–185
Fertility, 272, 277, 280, 284
Fitness, 166, 168, 174, 177, 267, 268, 283, 320, 331–334
  cues, 257–285
Flowers, 294, 295, 300, 304, 305, 309
fMRI. *See* Functional magnetic resonance imaging
Followership, 166–168, 170, 176–179, 183, 184, 186
  investment, 176, 180

Foraging, 341, 346, 351
  e-commerce, 341
  information search, 341
Formidability, 137–138, 143, 144, 147–156
Fractal geometry, 309
Framing effects, 322
Free rider, 95, 97, 102, 103, 105–112, 114, 116, 117–119, 126, 127
Free riding, 167
Frequency dependence, 115–118, 126
Frequency dependent selection, 169
Functional magnetic resonance imaging (fMRI), 306

G
Gallery Lafayette, 309, 310
Game
  Dictator, 326
  guessing, 328
  theory, 3, 177–178, 183, 324, 325, 333
  Ultimatum, 325, 326, 329, 332
Gathering
  lifestyle, 166
  technique, 179
Gaudí, A., 308
Gender, 179–181, 184
  differences, 301, 332
  schema theory, 156
The "gender gap" in compensation, 72–76
Generalized Darwinism, 3
Genetic replication, 167, 177
Glass ceiling, 72–76
Globalization, 184
Goodwin, F., 111
Google, 185, 186
Greenery. *See* Vegetation
Groups, 95–128
Group selection, 98, 99, 126

H
Habitat theory, 290
Hazards, 291, 307
Health, 269–272, 275, 277, 284, 285
Hedonic shopping, 303, 306
Heraclitean movement, 306
Herding behavior, 178
Heuristic, 172, 178, 260, 330
Hierarchical, 175, 184, 185
High involvement products, 302, 311
Hildebrand, G., 298
Hominids, 166, 173
  Homo sapiens, 1, 9, 166
  Homo businessicus, 9

Homo consumericus, 5
Homo corporaticus, x
Homogenization, 175
Hormones, 326
    cortisol, 4
    and the menstrual cycle, 7
    oxytocin, 7–8
    testosterone, 2, 7, 8, 172, 180, 184
Human capital, 186
Hunting, 99–101, 166
Hunting and gathering, 299, 302

I
IM. *See* Instant messaging
Imitated natural contents, 305–310
Individual-level, 95, 96–99, 102, 105, 107, 124–126, 128
Inequality aversion, 325
Information processing, 258, 264–266, 268, 280, 282, 285
Innate schema similarity, 342, 344–345, 357
    principle, 344, 358
Instant messaging (IM), 341, 352, 353, 357–358
In-store lighting, 299
Integrated Causal Model (ICM), 193, 194
Intelligence, 270
Interactive media, 348, 355
Intrasexual competition, 41–63

J
"just so" stories, 298

K
Kanazawa, S., 297
Kin care, 19, 21, 22, 28, 30, 33
Kin selection, 231
Kinship, 168

L
Language, 169
Leader categorization theory, 170
Leadership, 135–159, 165–186
    democratic, 166
    despotic, 166
    distributed, 174, 186
    emergence, 166, 167, 169–171, 173, 174, 176, 181, 183
    political, 166
    selection, 172
Leadership-followership, 168
Learned schema diversity principle, 345, 353, 356–358

Legibility, 293, 301, 303
Likeability, 268, 280, 281, 283
Logos, 306, 308
Loss aversion, 323, 324, 328
Luxury goods, 247, 248

M
Maladaptive, 268
Male Warrior *vs.* Female Peacekeeper Hypothesis (MWFP), 179–183, 185
Marketing, 299
    advertising, 227–229, 231, 232, 235, 240–242, 244, 246, 247, 249, 250
Market share repurchases, 235
Masculine, 170, 172, 173, 179–185
Mate choice, 178
Mate selection, 170
Mating, 19–22, 24–28, 31, 33–35, 267–271
McKinsey, 186
Means-end-chain, 258, 261–264, 282
Mechanical movement, 305
Media compensation, 339–358
    theory, 339–358
    virtual team work, 356–358
Media fluency, 353
Media humanness, 342
Media humanness principle, 348–349, 353, 355
Media naturalness, 340, 342–344, 353
Media naturalness principle, 342–343, 346, 352–355
Media naturalness theory, 341–342, 352, 354
Media richness, 352
Media richness theory, 340–341, 344, 353
Memetic theory, 3
Mental accounts, 323, 329
Mental organs, 258, 266–269, 282, 283
Mere exposure, 260
Minimalistic store design, 302
Mismatch
    leader prototypes, 173, 185
Mistrust, 356
Monarchs, 178
Monitoring, 110, 111, 116, 118, 191–219
Mood
    negative, 326
    positive, 326
Motivation, 17–35
Multilevel selection, 98, 126
Multinationals, 183
MWFP. *See* Male Warrior *vs.* Female Peacekeeper Hypothesis
Mystery, 293, 301–303

N

Naturalness
    environment, 290–292, 294–296, 298, 301, 304–312
Natural selection, 72, 83–84, 86–87, 266, 267, 278–279, 282
Nature *vs.* nurture, 2
Neocortex, 168
Neo-Darwinian, 166
Neonatal traits, 277, 283
Neoteny, 238, 245, 246
Nest fouling, 175
Neuroeconomics, 3–4
Neuromarketing, 3, 280
Non-human animals, 137–139, 155
n-person, 103

O

Occupational segregation
    blue-collar occupations, 79, 81, 82
    science and technology, 79–81
Organic shapes, 305–306
Organizational citizenship behavior, 235
Ornamentation, 309
Ostracization, 107–108, 111, 117
Outcomes
    non-monetary, 324

P

Paradigm
    evolutionary psychology, 320, 324–326, 333–335
    rational choice, 319–321, 330, 333
Parental investment, 267, 269, 280
Partner choice, 108, 111
Pastoralists, 174
Peace, 170–172, 180, 181, 183
Perception, 169, 172, 173, 176, 177
Peripheral persuasive route, 259, 265, 267
Peripheral route, 261, 268, 274
Personal and situational differences, 300
Persuasion, 23–25
Persuasive routes, 258, 259, 265
Pheromones, 169
Phylogenetic "imprinting", 297
Plateauing, 177
Pornography, 271
Positive assortation, 108, 111, 127
Predator, 291, 296, 297, 305, 307, 308, 312
Preference matrix, 292–294, 301–304
Preferenda, 292
Presidential election, 180
Prey, 296, 297, 305, 311

Primary affective reactions, 268, 274, 284
Primates, 168, 185, 328, 329
Pro-environmental behavior, 33
Prospect, 291, 301, 312
Prospect-refuge theory, 291–292
Prospect theory
    cumulative, 323, 324, 334
Prototype, 171–174, 182
Proximate *vs.* ultimate explanations, 2–3, 4, 9
Psycho-evolutionary framework, 291, 292, 311
Punctuated equilibrium theory, 352, 354
Punishment, 107–109, 127
Punitive sentiments, 197

R

Raiding and trading, 168
Rationality
    bounded, 177, 321, 335
    ecological, 320, 327, 333
    perfect, 321–325, 335
Receiver psychology, 225–252
Receiver skepticism. *See* Consumer skepticism
Reciprocal altruism, 95, 97, 98, 102–104, 114, 127, 201
Reciprocity, 102–104, 110, 112, 115, 116, 118, 126, 127
Rectilinearity, 306
Reference point, 323, 324
Refuge, 291, 300, 301, 311
Reproduction, 266, 267, 278–279, 282
Restorative effects, 294, 298, 310
Reward, 102, 104, 105, 106, 111, 112, 115, 118, 119, 123, 125
Risk, 20, 27–28, 322–324, 327, 329, 331, 332
Risk-taking, 184, 185

S

Satisficing, 321, 327
Savanna hypothesis, 297–298, 300, 302
Savannas, 297–298, 300, 306
Selection, 166–168, 170, 172–175
    group, 167
    natural, 167, 174
    pressure(s), 166, 167, 171
    sexual, 167, 174
    social, 174
Self-control, 323, 329
Self-protection, 19, 20, 22, 24, 28–30, 35
Self-similarity, 309
Semiotic, 280, 284, 285
Sensation seekers, 307

Sensory bias
  color, 238
  scent, 242–244
  sight, 238–242
  sound, 238–242
  taste, 242–244
  touch, 242–244
Sensory marketing, 284
Sex, 228, 240, 245, 269, 270, 272, 278–281, 284
Sex differences, 46–49, 61, 62, 97, 115, 120–124, 126, 127, 128
  cognitive abilities, 72, 76–82
  competitiveness, 73
  early development of, 87
  hours worked, 75
  job-attribute preferences, 82
  marriage and children, effects of, 74
  marriage and family, effects of, 76
  nonhuman animals, 137, 139
  nurturance, 73
  people-things dimension, 77, 80
  personality, 74, 76, 87
  productivity, 76
  reproductive variance, 83
  risk-taking, 77, 83, 84, 86, 87
  strength, 77, 82, 87
  vocational interest, 72, 76–82
  workplace deaths, 73, 75
Sex hormones, 180
  activational effects, 85–86
  estrogen, 180
  organizing effects, 84, 85
  testosterone, 2, 7, 8, 172, 180, 184
Sexual, 267, 277
  attractiveness, 269–272, 275–277, 279–281, 284
  selection, 83
Sharing, 115, 124–125, 128
Sharp-angled shapes, 306, 307
Signal
  of commitment, 234, 235, 239, 249
  costly, 227, 229–235, 237–239, 243, 247–248, 250
  design, 227–231, 238–244, 251
  dishonest, 227–230, 233–236, 238
  of fertility, 247, 248
  handicap, 231–235, 237, 239, 250
  honest, 229–231, 233, 235, 236, 238, 251
  index, 226, 239
  minimal cost, 230–231, 233–235, 239, 243
  of resource control, 231, 247, 248, 251
Signaling theory
  economic, 227, 228, 248
  signal reliability, 230–233, 239, 241, 251
Situations, Processes Qualities (SPQ), 172, 186
Skin patterns, 308
Small groups, 103–104, 110
Snakes, 297, 307–308
Social brain hypothesis, 168
Social comparison, 43, 44, 54, 62
Social construction, 137, 139, 155, 185
Social contract, 191–219
Social facilitation
  interactive computers, 348
Socialization, 136, 141, 156
Social loafing, 355
Social role theory, 156
Social species, 168, 177
  social mammals, 168
Spandrel, 348, 351
Speech imperative, 342, 350
Speech imperative principle, 350
SPQ. *See* Situations, Processes Qualities
SSSM. *See* Standard Social Science Model
Stained glass, 309
Standard Social Science Model (SSSM), 2, 72, 88, 193
Status, 19, 20, 22, 28, 29, 31, 33–35, 100, 101, 104–106, 120–125, 126, 128, 226, 231, 233, 237–239, 243, 247–249, 251, 270, 271, 276, 278–281, 284, 285
  quo, 329
  quo bias, 322
  syndrome, 4
Step-level public-goods game, 182
Stimulus-Organism-Response model, 299
Strength
  physical, 270–272, 276, 281
Stress, 290, 294–295, 299–300, 304, 311
Structural landscape features, 291–294, 298, 300–304
Summers, L., 88
Surplus resources, 115, 124–125, 128
Survival, 266, 267, 279, 282
Sutherland, S., 258
Symmetry, 227–228, 238, 269–270, 275

T

Teams, 101, 110, 111
Theory of media naturalness, 340–344, 346, 352–355
Tit-for-Tat, 183
Trust, 118, 127, 128, 355–356

cultural diversity, 357
interpersonal, 355–357
performance consistency, 356
swift, 356, 357
virtual team work, 356–358
virtual work, 345, 347, 353, 355–357
Twin registries, 4

U

Unconditional cooperation, 115–118
Uptempo music, 306
Utilitarian shopping, 303
Utility function, 326, 331–334

V

Vegetation, 294–296, 304, 308–310, 312
Vegetative elements. *See* Vegetation
Vegetative life. *See* Vegetation
Videoconference, 352
Videoconferencing, 349
Videoconferencing cost, 355
Virtual team

cultural differences, 346, 357
global, 346, 357
performance, 352, 355, 358
Virtual teamwork, 340, 356–358
Virtual work teams, 347, 355, 357

W

Waist-to-hip ratio (WHR), 271–273, 277, 278, 284
War, 170, 172, 173, 180, 181, 183
Wason selection task, 199, 202–209, 212–214
Water-feature, 294–296, 304
Wayfinding, 303
WHR. *See* Waist-to-hip ratio
Windfall, 115, 124–125, 128
Winner's curse, 332
Wisdom of crowds, 178

Y

Youthfulness, 272